GREEK TRAGEDY AND THE BRITISH THEATRE
1660–1914

Engraving by William S. Leney of Joseph George Holman in the role of
Hippolitus, in Edmund Smith's *Phædra and Hippolitus*

Greek Tragedy and the British Theatre 1660–1914

Edith Hall
and Fiona Macintosh

OXFORD
UNIVERSITY PRESS

OXFORD

UNIVERSITY PRESS

Great Clarendon Street, Oxford OX2 6DP

Oxford University Press is a department of the University of Oxford.
It furthers the University's objective of excellence in research, scholarship,
and education by publishing worldwide in

Oxford New York

Auckland Cape Town Dar es Salaam Hong Kong Karachi
Kuala Lumpur Madrid Melbourne Mexico City Nairobi
New Delhi Shanghai Taipei Toronto

With offices in

Argentina Austria Brazil Chile Czech Republic France Greece
Guatemala Hungary Italy Japan Poland Portugal Singapore
South Korea Switzerland Thailand Turkey Ukraine Vietnam

Oxford is a registered trade mark of Oxford University Press
in the UK and in certain other countries

Published in the United States
by Oxford University Press Inc., New York

British Library Cataloguing in Publication Data

Data available

Library of Congress Cataloging in Publication Data

Data available

Typeset by SPI Publisher Services, Pondicherry, India
Printed in Great Britain
on acid-free paper by
Biddles Ltd., King's Lynn, Norfolk

ISBN 0–19–815087–3 978–0–19–815087–9

3 5 7 9 10 8 6 4 2

For

Josh and Sam
Sarah and Georgie

Preface

Greek drama is being performed on both the commercial and amateur stages of Britain, as of the world, with greater frequency than at any point since classical antiquity. At times during the 1990s more plays by Euripides or Sophocles were available to the London theatre-goer than works by any other author, including Shakespeare. The reasons for the late twentieth-century revival of interest in the ancient Greeks and their theatre are connected, as we have argued in a previous volume, not only with theatrical and aesthetic trends but with the huge social and political shifts which marked the decades after the Second World War, especially the 1960s.[1] Yet the current fascination with Greek drama has an aetiology, a genealogy, which benefits from being traced further back into cultural history.

Attempts have been made by other scholars, with varying degrees of success, to document the performance history of Greek tragedy in some other countries.[2] We owe much to the pioneering work of Hellmut Flashar, whose *Inszenierung der Antike: das griechische Drama auf der Bühne der Neuzeit 1585–1990* was published in 1991. But Flashar's volume neglects Britain and the rest of Europe in favour of Germany, and is fundamentally different in that he is not very interested in the practice of adaptation, perhaps our most central concern. Our book begins slightly later than Flashar's study, tracing the antecedents of modern performances in Britain of Greek tragedy from 1660, when both the monarchy and live theatre were restored after the Interregnum, and it concludes on the eve of the First World War, by which time Greek tragedy in general and certain plays in particular (Sophocles' *Oedipus Tyrannus*, Euripides' *Medea* and *Trojan Women*) had secured permanent and hallowed places in the British performance repertoire. Our chronological boundaries

---

[1] See Hall, Macintosh, and Wrigley (2004).

[2] Some recent studies include Rogers (1986), Foley (1999–2000), and Hartigan (1995) on Greek tragedy on the North American stage, McDonald and Walton (2002) for views of Greek theatre in Ireland, Srebrny (1984) for Poland, and Wetmore (2002) for Africa.

have been chosen to demarcate precisely the period during which Greek tragedies were tentatively rediscovered and eventually came fully of age as playscripts for performance, and assumed roles in public theatre similar to those they fulfil today.

The book is authored by two enthusiastic theatregoers and has sprung from a conviction that the performance history of all 'classic' drama—Shakespeare or Racine as much as the Greek plays—is of academic interest in its own right, holding up a mirror to the shifting assumptions and contingent historical perspectives which have been brought to bear on these texts in their most public arenas of consumption. But performance history also constitutes time travel into a much more personal, individual arena of human history. It offers privileged access to the private imaginative worlds of the members of previous generations. Theatre critics have long been aware that there is something very special about the immanent presence of live performance in the memory. Far from being an ephemeral art, which happens, comes to an end, and vanishes without trace, a compelling theatrical experience can leave a much deeper impression on the memory even than the printed word or painted image.

Freud never recovered from the experience of watching Jean Mounet-Sully perform the role of Sophocles' Oedipus in the 1885–6 season at the Comédie-Française; Matthew Arnold was so overwhelmed by the lovely Helen Faucit's realization of the role of Sophocles' Antigone in 1845 that he designed his tragedy *Merope* along lines which he fervently hoped would make it suitable for performance by this superb tragic actress.[3] A couple of years earlier, in 1843, Søren Kierkegaard had published *Either/Or*, in which theatre provides no less than a paradigm of the aesthetic consciousness, a paradigm which has gone beyond notions of art to enter the sphere of the existential. Kierkegaard's ruminations lend philosophical legitimacy to the notions of the selectivity of memory, the aesthetic categories by which it prioritizes types of experience, and in particular the cognitive and emotional power of the experience of performed language and music (in his case, Mozartian opera). He believed that there is a difference in the experience of theatre between physical and mental time. For

---

[3] Ernest Jones (1953), 194. See Macintosh (forthcoming); and on Arnold below, pp. 330–1.

Kierkegaard, the immediacy of 'the Moment' of apprehension of a performance transcends time, for the images it leaves on the mind are uniquely powerful and indelible. The moment of performance ideally gains its emotive force from the 'immanent acceleration' in the representation as well as its sensual wholeness, grounded in the material instantiation of the characters and events. This moment is in one sense lost forever, but it can also be held in remarkable detail in the consciousness until death.[4] Ibsen was influenced by this argument when he makes the eponymous hero of his *Brand* (1885) observe at the end of Act IV that 'Only what is lost can be possessed for ever.'[5]

The other conviction underlying this book is less mystical and more pragmatic. One of the most dynamic areas of research now opening up within the fast evolving discipline of Classics investigates the 'bridges' between ancient and modern European culture. If Classics is to find a purpose and role in the third millennium, it needs to ask questions about its purpose and role in past centuries. 'Classics' needs to understand the history of Classics as practised and enjoyed both within and outside the confines of academic institutions and published scholarship. Chris Stray's brilliant *Classics Transformed* (1998), a study of the sometimes inspirational, usually elitist, and at times utterly disreputable history of classical education in Britain, has done much to illuminate the pedagogical dimension. Elizabeth Rawson, Philip Ayres, Norman Vance, Yopie Prins, Richard Jenkyns, Frank Turner, and others have also shown the way forward with excellent, sophisticated studies of the aristocratic and upper-middle-class British reception of ancient Greek and Roman political thought, philosophy, poetry, art, and architecture.[6] Our book is intended to tell part of the story of how a rather different British public imagined Greek antiquity. For amongst ancient literary genres Greek tragedy has exerted a particularly powerful influence on later cultural life. It has been a crucial medium though which people untrained in Greek or Latin could have access to classical mythology. Translated, adapted,

---

[4] See Kierkegaard (1987), 42, 68, 117–18, 239, 486–7, and the discussion of his theatrical aesthetics in Pattison (1992), 95–124.
[5] Translation taken from Ibsen (1972), 194.
[6] Other seminal contributions include Leppmann (1968), Gillespie (1988), Edwards (1996) and (1999), St. Clair (1998), Kurtz (2000), and Beard (2002).

interpreted, and *enacted*, it has also shaped our aesthetic sensibilities, our ethical categories, and our political thinking.

This project, along with the idea of a research centre with a more
international scope (an idea which eventually materialised as the
Archive of Performances of Greek and Roman Drama at Oxford
University), was conceived at about closing time on 27 July 1989,
when we were both tutors on a summer school for sixth-form
students run by the Joint Association of Classical Teachers. This
was shortly after the publication of Bruce R. Smith's *Ancient
Scripts and Modern Experience on the English Stage*, a study of
Greek and Latin plays in the Renaissance and Jacobean periods,
which shows that Greek tragedy has enjoyed a performed presence
in Britain for hundreds of years. The early performances mostly
featured in narrowly academic circles, but not entirely: George
Gascoigne and Francis Kinwelmershe's *Jocasta*, a descendant of
Euripides' *Phoenissae* through the Italian version of Lodovico
Dolce, was acted during the Christmas Revels at Gray's Inn in
the winter of 1566–7.[7]

Greek tragedy, for the Athenians of the fifth century BC an
exploration of their past, has had a long future. This book investigates a peculiarly formative period within that future, by focusing
on the two and a half centuries preceding the First World War.
Despite that 1566 *Jocasta*, by 1660 very few Greek tragedies had
actually been performed in Britain except in Latin and in pedagogical contexts.[8] But by 1789 the majority of the Sophoclean and
Euripidean plays had been rewritten (often radically) for performance in the English language. By the turn of the twentieth century
most of the plays had been acted in unadapted Greek and, on a few
exceptional occasions, in English. But it was the Edwardian stage
which finally saw the emergence of Greek tragedy in a form which
adumbrated the role it takes in the third-millennium theatre, its
uncut, authentic texts addressing the public's social and political
concerns in their own vernacular. By 1914 nearly all the thirty or so

---

[7] Gascoigne and Kinwelmershe (1566).
[8] See Boas (1914), Moore Smith (1923), Bruce R. Smith (1987), Cowling (1993).
There were occasional performances in English of plays deriving from Roman
comedy, for example the imitation of Plautus' *Amphitruo* published in London
anonymously in 1562–3 under the title *A New Enterlude for Chyldren to playe,
named Jack Jugeler, both wyttie, and very playsent Newly Imprentid*. See also Warner
(1595).

surviving tragedies—even obscure Aeschylean works—had been reappraised in Britain as performance texts, and the comedies of Aristophanes had begun to attract comparable attention, especially after Aristophanes' *Acharnians* was put to political use in a production at Oxford in February 1914, which satirized French, German, and British imperialist fantasies alike and explicitly proclaimed the play to be 'an unmistakable vindication of peace'.[9] Greek tragedy's obsession with the destructive effects of war, especially as lamented in Euripides' *Trojan Women* (see Fig. 0.1), was subsequently to speak louder than ever before to Britons—as to other Europeans and to North Americans—struggling to come to terms with the carnage of the First World War.[10]

Another war—the Greek War of Independence—occurred during the period covered by this book, and had enormous ramifications for its contents. The experience of watching ancient Greeks on stage in Britain could never be the same again after the 1821 uprising against the Ottoman Empire and the creation of the modern Greek nation. The presence of Greece is always in the background of our narrative, from the first Greek Orthodox Church, built in London shortly after the Restoration. Significant Greek individuals make appearances: John Nikolaïdis was a refugee from Turkish prosecution, as well as nephew of the Patriarch of Constantinople, when he was involved in an extraordinary production of *Oedipus Tyrannus* at Stanmore School in 1776 (see Ch. 8). The Phanariot Prince Alexandros Mavrokordatos, who taught Mary Shelley Greek in Pisa, was to play an important role in the British identification of Greek tragic conflict with the struggle against the Turcocracy in the 1820s when Percy Bysshe Shelley dedicated his *Hellas* to him, a visionary poem based on Aeschylus' *Persians* (see Ch. 10). We are painfully aware that much more could have been said on the relationship between the theatre

---

[9] In the programme, contained in a collection of papers related to Oxford University Dramatic Society 1884–1926, held in the Bodleian Library.

[10] For the *Trojan Women* and the First World War, see Macintosh (1997), 302–4. *The Times* of 13 Nov. 1918 published the 'hubris' chorus from *Oedipus Tyrannus* (873 ff.), in Gilbert Murray's translation, to illustrate the disastrous career of the Kaiser; on the 22nd it published Darius' speech from *Persians* (821 ff.): 'For the grain | Of overweening Pride, after full Flower | Beareth a sheaf of Doom, and garners in | A harvest of all tears'. For an intense expression of the war as a Greek tragedy see especially Osmaston (1928). Thanks to Clemence Schultze for pointing this out.

FIGURE 0.1   Sybil Thorndike as Hecuba and her daughter Anne Casson as Astyanax in a production of Gilbert Murray's translation of *The Trojan Women* at the Old Vic, London, *c.*1919.

history we have begun to excavate and the modern history of Greece and its people.

Over the years several people have asked us to describe our methodology. The word implies a greater degree of theoretical self-consciousness at the coalface of research than either of us possesses, but the simple answer would be that there are two fundamental questions underlying this book. The first is empirical: what exactly is the British performance history of Greek tragedy before 1914? Which plays were performed, where and when, by whom, in what types of adaptation and in whose translations? These apparently simple questions can be extremely difficult to answer, as is shown by the types of play used in an extraordinary pageant on British history performed mid-way through our period at Covent Garden on 12 February 1798. One scene was from *Edward the Black Prince* by William Shirley, a dramatist who is important in this book because his version of Sophocles' *Electra* had been proscribed three and a half decades earlier. Another scene drew on James Thomson's *Edward and Eleonora*, another once-censored play based on Euripides' *Alcestis*; a third scene was taken from William Mason's *Caractacus*, which transplanted the plot of Sophocles' *Oedipus at Colonus* to Roman Wales.[11] Plays that never made it to the stage, wholly un-Greek titles, historical contexts far from ancient Greece, and genres of theatre such as patriotic pageant, can therefore all conceal profound debts to Greek tragedy, and it is certain that we have failed to identify some important examples. Yet some answers to our basic question are laid out in Amanda Wrigley's Chronological Appendix, which we hope lends precision and order to such material as we discovered.

When we first naively asked each other this question fifteen years ago, we had no idea how much material there was to excavate, and we soon discovered that this was because no scholar had concentrated on most of it before. The subject-matter in which we are interested had simply disappeared, slipping down a vast chasm yawning between disciplines. We made great use of research tools and resources such as the index to the Lord Chamberlain's Collection of Plays, the holdings of the Theatre Museum at Covent

---

[11] For a detailed discussion see Gillian Russell (1995), 52–3. On the individual plays and authors see below, Chs. 4, 6, and 7.

Garden, the catalogues of the British and Bodleian libraries, the *Dictionary of National Biography* and its successor the *Oxford Dictionary of National Biography*, handlists of classical mythology in literature such as Douglas Bush's *Mythology and the Romantic Tradition in English Poetry* (1937), and Jane Davidson Reid's monumental *Oxford Guide to Classical Mythology in the Arts* (1993). We have consulted dozens of issues of eighteenth-, nineteenth-, and early twentieth-century journals, magazines, and newspapers, especially the *Illustrated London News*. But overwhelmingly our greatest debts are to theatre historians, especially the team responsible for the *Biographical Dictionary of Actors, Actresses, Musicians, Dancers, Managers and Other Stage Personnel in London, 1660–1800*, the meticulous researchers led by Charles Beecher Hogan who produced the superbly reliable eleven-volume *The London Stage* (1960–8), and, outstandingly, the work of the undisputed father of systematic theatre history, Allardyce Nicoll. We simply could not have written this book without his multi-volume *A History of English Drama 1660–1900*, on which he laboured for decades until its completion in 1959. But few twentieth-century theatre historians have known enough about Graeco-Roman myth even to recognize many literary archetypes in plays written by the more classically educated Georgians and Victorians.

Unfortunately the scholars who are indeed equipped to identify a Greek tragedian's influence—academic Classicists—have traditionally disliked studying anything involving translation *out* of the ancient languages, especially when it involves entertainment rather than scholarship. Even respectable specialists in the history of classical education have tended to lose their bearings when it comes to theatre history: M. L. Clarke's influential history of Greek Studies in Britain states that William Mason's two important tragedies 'on the Grecian model' in imitation of Euripides and Sophocles were never performed;[12] yet if he had known how to consult standard reference works in theatre history, he would have discovered that they were both huge hits in the commercial theatre of the later eighteenth century. Classicists have also only quite recently begun to take seriously what is usually called the 'reception' of Classical texts. Moreover, they usually take their cue as to the proper *content* of the study of the 'Reception of Classics' from

---

[12] M. L. Clarke (1945), 164.

departments of Comparative Literature, Modern Languages, and English Literature.[13] And these literary specialists have tended to regard the 'reception' of Greek tragedy rather narrowly, as denoting the study of its impact on major canonical thinkers (*Antigone* on Hegel, *Bacchae* on Nietzsche), on important authors such as Goethe (whose *Iphigenie auf Tauris* has long been accepted into the 'literary' as well as the theatrical canon), and on authors whose imitations of Greek tragedy were designed to be read rather than staged, such as Swinburne's *Erechtheus* and *Atalanta in Calydon*.

In departments of English literature, even after the seismic questioning of the canon which has characterized the last two decades, performance history is still not a central concern, and often perceived as being excessively bound up with what is even now sometimes dismissively called 'popular culture': although some of our authors (John Dryden and James Thomson, for example) are still considered important poets, several of the plays and performances discussed in this book, however popular and influential in their own day, would still be dismissed by some conservative literary historians as aesthetically insignificant ephemera. We have been sustained throughout by the prophetic voice of the incomparable Allardyce Nicoll. Much of our material was included in his own short selection of works requiring 'attention either intrinsically or historically' as being 'of prime importance for an understanding of the audiences of various periods and for an appreciation of dramatic development'. The authors, the significance of whose dramatic works he noted, and some of which we have subsequently discovered make great use of Greek tragedy, include Charles Davenant (notably his *Circe*); Thomas Rymer; Charles Gildon; John Dennis (especially his *Iphigenia*); Thomas Hull; William Mason (both his *Elfrida* and *Caractacus*); William Whitehead (his *Creusa*); and the Victorian playwrights E. L. Blanchard, Charles Mathews, and Henry Byron.[14]

The second part of our project has involved trying to make some preliminary interpretative sense of the factual performance history we have tried to assemble. Although the aesthetic dimension of art is of course never fully to be divorced from the political, it is

---

[13] Amongst 'comparativists' we have benefited greatly from Mueller (1980) and Steiner (1961), (1984); Burian (1997), Macintosh (1997), and Walton (1987) are earlier examples of reception study that engages with issues of performance.

[14] Nicoll (1925), 507–12.

undeniable that our personal temperaments and interests have produced an emphasis on the way that the performance reception of Greek tragedy throws light on and is in turn illuminated by social, legislative, and political changes. A fascination with transgressive sexuality (incest, adultery) marks the adaptations of Greek tragedy—Dryden's *Oedipus*, Joyner's *The Roman Empress*, and Davenant's *Circe*—staged between the Restoration and the new morality ushered in by the Glorious Revolution of 1688; the 1670s interest in mythical sexual deviants was part of a generalized theatrical articulation of the Restoration's libertarian reaction against the stringent moral legislation passed during the Interregnum, which had made incest and adultery capital offences. But it was equally a continuation of an earlier, pre-Civil War trope common in political discourse linking problems in the monarchy with sexual disorder. Anxieties about succession and the Jacobite threat are obsessively examined on the British stage between the Glorious Revolution and the 1750s, which explains in large measure the ways in which Greek tragedy was adapted. An outbreak of Medea plays in the mid-1850s is impossible to understand without acknowledging the importance of the 1857 Divorce Act.

Andrew Dalzel, a distinguished professor of Greek at Edinburgh from 1772 until 1806, proposed to his students 'that the Grecian spirit, which has always prevailed in England, tended greatly to counteract the encroachments of despotic power and to bring about that republican mixture in our constitution which has been the subject of so much admiration'.[15] It was thus to 'the Grecian spirit' of the English that, according to Dalzel, the credit needed to be given for no less an achievement than the Glorious Revolution. His words illuminate the particular status of Greek tragedy in the British psyche, apparent in the case of our authors. Almost all of them (and even some of our actors) are liberals and at least mildly progressive. Some are controversial, oppositional, or even republican.

The radical theatre critic William Hazlitt revealingly uses an image from a pagan Greek tragedy to describe how his father and other Dissenting ministers preached sermons in each other's churches, thus establishing a 'line of communication . . . by which the flame of civil and religious liberty is kept alive, and nourishes

---

[15] Dalzel (1821), i. 7.

its smouldering fire unquenchable, like the fires in the *Agamemnon* of Aeschylus, placed at different stations, that waited for ten long years to announce with their blazing pyramids the destruction of Troy'. In 1906, in 'The Author's Apology' to a selection of his dramatic criticism, George Bernard Shaw echoes both Hazlitt's sentiments and his image, when he robustly defends the importance of the theatre in a godless world:

Only the ablest critics believe that the theatre is really important: in my time none of them would claim for it, as I claimed for it, that it is as important as the Church was in the Middle Ages and much more important than the Church was in London in the years under review. A theatre to me is a place 'where two or three are gathered together.' The apostolic succession from Eschylus to myself is as serious and as continuously inspired as that younger institution, the apostolic succession of the Christian Church.[16]

In Henry Fielding's *Joseph Andrews* the Anglican Parson Adams is no Dissenter, but still the distinguishing mark of his incorruptibility and insistence on the pursuit of liberty and virtue is his attachment to the works of Aeschylus. More than one of our writers is an idealistic and pious clergyman—what Parson Adams might have become if he had fallen in with some friends in the theatre, as his real-life model, the Revd William Young, fell in with Henry Fielding and in 1742 even persuaded him to collaborate on a translation of Aristophanes' *Plutus*. Although there were a few Royalist responses to ancient Greek drama in the seventeenth century (see p. 40), the majority of our high-minded eighteenth-century authors, as well as the radical MP Thomas Talfourd in the 1830s, and, at the end of our era, George Warr and Gilbert Murray, really did come from progressive, politically radical and/or nonconformist backgrounds. The Victorians were correct when they saw the historical link between radical religious movements in Britain and a love of the ancient Greek language and literature.[17] We are convinced that our dramatists' often very creative, passionate, original, and committed uses of Greek tragedy put the lie to the commonly held stereotype of dry, stale, obsolete conservative neoclassical heroes

---

[16] Hazlitt (1917), 2; Shaw (1908), i, pp. xxii f.
[17] See e.g. Young (1862), 100.

keeping 'real', lively, contemporary humans from their rightful place in tragedy.[18]

Our interest in socio-political history has been one factor behind the broadly chronological arrangement of this book, especially since we are, as far as we know, the first to study this material systematically. After the handful of Restoration experiments with turning Greek texts into 'heroic tragedy', and with various untidy exceptions, we see our material as falling into four basic movements. Greek tragedy appears on the British stage as patriotic, emotive five-act variations on themes dear to Whig sensibilities between the late 1690s until the 1780s. After (largely) retreating from the Romantic stage it re-emerges as Victorian burlesque from the 1840s to 1870s, academic Greek plays in the late nineteenth century, and avant-garde Edwardian performances in the English language. The structure of the book reflects this conceptual shape.

However, some plays (for example, Sophocles' *Electra*), playwrights (Thomson), translators, directors (George Warr) and genres of performance (She-Tragedy, burlesque) have required whole individual chapters in order to explain their importance to the overall history. Our chapter headings have been selected because they seem to us to represent the more significant events, or shifts in taste and purpose, in the history of Greek tragedy in the British theatre; they have also been designed to avoid excessive reduplication of material covered elsewhere by ourselves, for example the impact of Greek tragedy on the drama of Ireland before the creation of the Republic, which has been analysed in Fiona Macintosh's *Dying Acts: Death in Ancient Greek and Modern Irish Tragic Drama*, or the reception of the figure of the ancient actor in English literature, the subject of a preliminary investigation by Edith Hall.[19] We have also avoided detailed discussion of topics already covered by other scholars, especially the early years of the Cambridge Greek play, Jane Harrison's 1887 performance as Alcestis, and the impact of the London premiere of Strauss's *Elektra*, which have been very well discussed by Pat Easterling, Mary Beard, and Simon Goldhill respectively.[20]

---

[18] Index s.v. John Dennis, James Thomson, James Shirley, William Mason, Samuel Parr, William Macready, Thomas Talfourd, and John Heraud.

[19] Macintosh (1994), Hall (2002*b*).

[20] Easterling (1999), Beard (2000), Goldhill (2002). See also Winterer (2001).

We are aware that many fascinating topics—for example, the practice of transvestism, the chorus, or historical costume and scenery in relation to archaeological discoveries—would have profited from a more thematic approach, but considerations of space precluded this. While finding Roger Fiske's *English Theatre Music in the Eighteenth Century* (1973, revised 1986) absolutely invaluable, as musical amateurs we have left embarrassingly untold the story of the musical contribution made by composers involved in staged versions of Greek tragedy (a list which includes such important names as Henry and Daniel Purcell, Handel, Arne, Mendelssohn, and Parry). We hope that the book as it stands will offer a useful starting-point for research into these areas by others. There are several other limitations to our study, or, rather, directions in which we are painfully conscious that the argument could have been more fully developed. Much of the book studies London stages, rather than those in the provinces and in the lively theatrical environment of Georgian and Victorian Dublin. Although the nature of theatre practice in the period under discussion, and the licensing system, mean that a London lens has not produced the degree of distortion that would result from its use if applied to the modern theatre world, it remains true that we have left undone much fruitful work on Greek tragedy outside the metropolis.

Moreover, we are aware that our narrative is sometimes too narrowly local when seen from a more international perspective. The book tells a story which involves British culture's constant revision of its idea of Greece, and this is especially apparent in the way that revivals of ancient Greek plays were influenced by literary models in other languages, or indeed manifestations of other types of revivalism (there remains considerable scope for investigating the cross-fertilization between the reception of Greek tragedy and theatrical settings involving ancient Persia and Egypt, Mogul India, Aztec or Inca Mesoamerica). The influence of French literary models, so pervasive at the Restoration, gave way during the eighteenth century to an equation of the ancient Greeks with ancient Britons; the Ottoman empire and its relationship with modern Greece was crucial in the first three decades of the nineteenth century, until a German adaptation of Sophocles' *Antigone* introduced Europe—and indeed the USA—to an innovative approach to the ancient theatre (see Ch. 12). By the second half of the nineteenth century, American and Australian star actresses, not to mention Scandinavian authors, assumed great importance for the British reading of Greek tragedy.

The history of the British stage is always inseparable from Continental culture, especially from the giants of the French stage and the Italian opera house. Although we have tried to identify any Continental precursors of our British plays, a task which has been made much easier by Jane Davidson Reid's indispensable work mentioned above, we are not experts on French or Italian literature, ballet or opera, any more than German romanticism or German classical philology, and the picture is therefore inevitably incomplete. Indeed, the history of classical scholarship—especially of editions, commentaries and textbooks on Greek tragedy—could also be much more closely tied to this performance history. Schoolboys and university students who used certain editions of particular plays were much more likely in later life to choose to adapt those they already knew;[21] many more scholarly books must have made a theatrical impact than those we have discussed, which include Thomas Stanley's edition of Aeschylus, André Dacier's of Aristotle's *Poetics*, and Charlotte Lennox's 1758 English translation of the *Greek Theatre of Father Brumoy*. Moreover, there still exists no comprehensive discussion of the history of translation of Greek tragedy into modern languages, which has presented us with a problem because the history of translation is very intricately tied up with performance history.[22] This is demonstrated above all by the impact made by the first entire English translation of Aeschylus, published by Robert Potter as late as 1777, or by the case of Sophocles' *Electra*, one of the first Greek tragedies to be made widely available in French and English, an availability which in large measure explains the length of the shadow which that archetypal play cast on the British stage (see Ch. 6).

When it comes to public exposure to Greek tragedy, our research has repeatedly brought us up against allied media in which this genre and performances of it played an important role. We regret in particular not being equipped systematically to investigate the

---

[21] For examples see below, pp. 279, 384.

[22] For some useful pointers see Gillespie (1988), (1992); Julie Stone Peters (2000), 316–17 n. 22.

visual arts and fiction.[23] We decided early on to devote ourselves to tragedy rather than attempt to provide adequate coverage of the performance reception of Aristophanes, which is equally important but very different in nature, since before the late nineteenth century material from his plays was almost always heavily disguised by English-language dramatists. There are also four particular types of subject-matter intimately related to the reception of Greek tragedy, which crop up in our analysis but require further attention. First, certain Shakespearean plays seem to have been conceptually paired with specific Greek heroes and plots (Hamlet and Orestes, ancient Thebes and Coriolanus, *Iphigenia in Tauris* and *The Tempest*). Secondly, certain biblical narratives were always traditionally compared both popularly and academically with specific Greek tragedies: Judas Iscariot with Oedipus, Jephthah's daughter with Iphigenia, the temple foundling Josiah with Euripides' Ion, or Job with Prometheus. Thirdly, ancient Greek and Roman history: from Nathaniel Lee onwards, the majority of our authors also wrote tragedies about subjects such as Sophonisba and Carthage, Alexander the Great, the Horatii, Cato, Brutus, Antony and Cleopatra, Nero and Agrippina, or the Emperor Constantine. Further light would undoubtedly be thrown on the performance history of Greek tragedy by relating it to ancient Mediterranean history in the theatre. The reception of, for example, Herodotus, Livy, Tacitus, Suetonius, and Julian the Apostate is deeply connected with the reception of Aeschylus, Sophocles, and Euripides.

We hope that our book will be read by Classicists as well as cultural historians, since we think that this experiment in excavating an aspect of the afterlife of the ancient Greek tragedians will help in the attempt to understand and appreciate their archetypal plays in the context of their original productions. The last few centuries have added dense layers of meaning to the texts of the Greek tragedians, through interpretation, criticism, translation and performance. We are convinced that if Classicists are to penetrate to the authentic meanings of Athenian tragedy in the historical contexts in which it was originally performed, it is essential that they raise to consciousness the ideas and interpretations that have subsequently attached themselves to these archetypal texts—

---

[23] On which see e.g. Kestner (1988), Jenkyns (1991), Easterling (1991). On theatrical portraiture in the 18th c. see Vince (1988), 63–8.

racist and orientalizing views of Aeschylus' barbarians, psychoanalytical readings of Sophocles' Theban royal family, patriarchal horror at Clytemnestra and Medea, or pro-Boer responses in 1905 to Euripides' incarcerated Trojan women.[24] Several chapters in this book argue that performance history has powerfully affected scholarly opinion of ancient texts.

Finally, in explaining why Greek tragedy should have proved so transhistorically useful and appealing, we have drawn inspiration from various intellectual quarters. They include Pierre Vidal-Naquet's historical relativism, which locates Greek tragedy's power to transcend history precisely in its susceptibility to radically different interpretations.[25] At times, especially when dealing with the portrayal of women, we have felt the importance of the Russian formalist Mikhail Bakhtin, and his notion that a measure of the greatness of literature is the degree to which it aboriginally holds 'prefigurative' meanings that can only be released by reassessments and revivals lying far away in what he calls 'great time' in the future.[26] Sometimes it has seemed that a more dialectical, Marxist-derived perspective can provide significant illumination by arguing with Jean-Pierre Vernant that important artworks actively condition the shapes taken by future artworks, whether the conditioning takes the form of emulation, modification, or rejection.[27] It has even been tempting to see Greek tragedy as actively conditioning not only later drama but the actual shapes taken by future society and its moral discourses, a position argued persuasively in relation to Shakespearean theatre history by Robert Weimann.[28] But beyond such high flights of theoretical fancy one returns time and again to the successive generations of ordinary British people who—often quite unintellectually—watched ancient Greek heroes and heroines perform great deeds in live theatres, and reacted with pleasure and excitement to the ancient texts, our own love of which originally inspired this book.

E.M.H.
F.M.

---

[24] See below e.g. pp. 114, 508–11.
[25] Vidal-Naquet (1988), 361–80. For a fuller discussion of various theoretical approaches to writing the history of Classical reception in performed arts, see Hall (2004a).
[26] Bakhtin (1986).
[27] See Vernant (1988).
[28] Weimann (1976), especially 46–56.

Acknowledgements

The research which lies behind this volume would not have been possible without the financial support, at different times and of different types, from University of Reading Research Fund, Goldsmiths' College, University of London, Somerville College, Oxford, Swarthmore College, Pennsylvania, the British Academy, the Leverhume Trust and the AHRB, to whom we are extremely grateful.

The fifteen years it has taken to research and write have seen us hold seven academic posts, endure eight household removals, and produce four children. The list of people who have helped us with the project over this period of time has therefore grown beyond control. We are particularly grateful to Pauline Adams, Chris Baldick, Mary Beard, Charles Benson, Richard Bevis, John Birkin, Clare Brant, Peter Brown, Marilyn Butler, Helen Carr, Paul Cartledge, Debbie Challis, Gill Cookson, Michael Diamond, Alan Downie, Pat Easterling, Helene Foley, Ewen Green, Dave Gowen, Lorna Hardwick, Tony Harrison, Isobel Hurst, Joanna Innes, Eva Jacobs, Margaret Kean, John Lumsden, Michael Lurje, Bill McCormack, Esther McGilvray, Norma Macmanaway, Jonathan Marcus, David Margolies, Peter Mason, Platon Mavromoustakos, Pantelis Michelakis, Fergus Millar, Paul Naiditch, Hilary O'Shea, Michelle Paull, Susanna Phillippo, Richard Poynder, Walter Puchner, Tessa Rajak, David Ricks, Kathleen Riley, Christopher Rowe, Michael Silk, Julia Sleeper, Fiona Stafford, John Stokes, Christopher Stray, Oliver Taplin, Colin Teevan, Theresa Urbainczyk, Jenny Wagstaffe, Andrew Wallace-Hadrill, Chris Weaver, Katharine Worth, David Wiles, and Amy Wygant. The contribution made at copy-editing stage by Leofranc Holford-Strevens, a true wit and polymath, was incalculable; we are more grateful to him than we can express for saving us from innumerable errors and infelicities of expression. It also gives us great pleasure that our magnificent index was provided by Brenda Hall. Finally, we remain indebted to Amanda Wrigley for all her extraordinary hard-work in compiling and checking the information in the Appendix. Her diligence and precision have been indispensable. Some of the chapters are revised versions of articles which have been published elsewhere; we are grateful to the editors of *Greece and Rome* with respect to Ch. 9 and parts of Ch. 14, and to the editors of *IJCT* with respect to Chs. 11 and 13. Some other passages draw on material published in *Cahiers du GITA*, *Classics Ireland*, and *Dialogos*, and we would also like to record our thanks to the editors of these journals.

Contents

List of Illustrations		xxvii
Notes on Nomenclature, Spelling, and Texts		xxxvii
1.	Regicide, Restoration, and the 'English' Oedipus	1
2.	Iphigenia and the Glorious Revolution	30
3.	Greek Tragedy as She-Tragedy	64
4.	James Thomson's Tragedies of Opposition	99
5.	Euripides' *Ion*, Coram's Foundlings, and Lord Hardwicke's Marriage Act	128
6.	Eighteenth-Century Electra	152
7.	Caractacus at Colonus	183
8.	Revolutionary Oedipuses	215
9.	Greek Tragedy in Late Georgian Reading	243
10.	Ruins and Rebels	264
11.	Talfourd's Ancient Greeks in the Theatre of Reform	282
12.	*Antigone* with Consequences	316
13.	The Ideology of Classical Burlesque	350
14.	Medea and Mid-Victorian Marriage Legislation	391
15.	Page versus Stage: Greek Tragedy, the Academy, and the Popular Theatre	430
16.	London's Greek Plays in the 1880s: George Warr and Social Philhellenism	462
17.	The Shavian Euripides and the Euripidean Shaw: Greek Tragedy and the New Drama	488
18.	Greek Tragedy and the Cosmopolitan Ideal	521
Chronological Appendix by Amanda Wrigley		555
Bibliography		591
Index		641

List of Illustrations

Frontispiece   Engraving by William S. Leney of Joseph George Holman in the role of Hippolitus, in Edmund Smith's *Phædra and Hippolitus*, reproduced from *British Theatre*, xxvi (1797) by courtesy of Durham University Library

0.1   Sybil Thorndike as Hecuba and her daughter Anne Casson as Astyanax in a production of Gilbert Murray's translation of *The Trojan Women* at the Old Vic, London, *c*.1919. Reproduced by courtesy of the APGRD   xii

1.1   William Hogarth, *Strolling Actresses Dressing in a Barn* (1738). Reproduced by courtesy of the British Museum   2

1.2   Burnet Reading, engraving of Thomas Sheridan in the title role of *Oedipus*, by Dryden and Lee. Reproduced from Bell's British Theatre, xv (1797), by courtesy of the Bodleian Library   4

1.3   Gerard van der Gucht, engraving after Hubert Gravelot depicting the suicide of Jocasta, reproduced from *The Dramatick Works of John Dryden* (1735), by courtesy of the British Library   19

2.1   Miss Chudleigh attends a masquerade in the character of Iphigenia (1749). Reproduced by courtesy of the British Museum   31

2.2   Louis du Guernier, frontispiece to Lewis Theobald's translation of *Oedipus, King of Thebes* (1715). Reproduced by courtesy of the Bodleian Library   47

2.3   Benjamin West, *Pylades and Orestes Brought as Victims before Iphigenia* (1766). Copyright Tate, London 2003   56

2.4   Frontispiece to Lewis Theobald's translation of Aristophanes' *Plutus: or, the World's Idol* (1715). Reproduced by courtesy of the Bodleian Library   57

2.5 Title-page and frontispiece, engraved by Isaac Taylor, to the 1771 London edition of Kane O'Hara's *Midas*. Reproduced by courtesy of the APGRD   58

3.1 J. Roberts, engraving of Miss Elizabeth Younge (later Mrs Pope) in the role of Hermione in Ambrose Philips's *The Distrest Mother* (published 1776). Reproduced by courtesy of the APGRD   68

3.2 J. Thornthwaite, engraving of William Farren in the role of Orestes in Ambrose Philips's *The Distrest Mother*, from *Bell's British Theatre*, vi (1797), reproduced by courtesy of the APGRD   69

3.3 James Heath, engraving of Hippolitus rescuing Phædra from a boar on the night of her wedding to Theseus, from the edition of Edmund Smith's *Phædra and Hippolitus* in *British Theatre*, xxvi (1797). Reproduced by courtesy of Durham University Library   73

3.4 J. Thornthwaite, engraving of Mrs Ann Barry in a revival of Edmund Smith's *Phædra and Hippolitus* (1777), for *Bell's British Theatre*, x. Reproduced by courtesy of the Bodleian Library   74

3.5 Frontispiece and title page from the earliest English translation of Sophocles' *Ajax*, published anonymously in 1714. The engraving, which depicts one of the altercations over Ajax's corpse, was designed and executed by Louis du Guernier. Reproduced by courtesy of the Bodleian Library   76

3.6 J. Thornthwaite, engraving of Mrs Hunter as Penelope in Nicholas Rowe's *Ulysses* (published 1778). Reproduced by courtesy of the APGRD   77

3.7 John Goldar, engraving of *Mrs Yates in the Character of Medea* (1777). Frontispiece to the *New English Theatre* Edition of Richard Glover's *Medea*. Photograph reproduced by courtesy of the Bodleian Library   81

3.8 George Romney, *Medea Contemplating the Murder of her Children*, chalk cartoon, *c.*1782.

Reproduced by courtesy of the Board of
Trustees of the National Museums (Walker
Art Gallery, Liverpool) 96

4.1 The monument to James Thomson in Westminster
Abbey. Copyright: Dean and Chapter of
Westminster 100

4.2 James Heath, frontispiece to James Thomson's
Edward and Eleonora, in the edition in *British
Theatre*, xxvi (1795). Reproduced by courtesy
of Durham University Library 119

4.3 William Blake, print entitled *Edward & Elenor*.
Published 1793. Reproduced by courtesy of
the British Museum 123

5.1 J. Thornthwaite, engraving of Miss Elizabeth
Younge (later Mrs Pope) in the character of
Creusa (1778), frontispiece to William Whitehead's
Creusa in *Bell's British Theatre*, xx. Reproduced
by courtesy of the Bodleian Library 131

5.2 Henry Brooke, engraving of Captain Thomas
Coram (1741) after a portrait by B. Nebot.
Reproduced by courtesy of the APGRD 136

5.3 Hannah Pritchard and David Garrick in *Creusa,
Queen of Athens* (Drury Lane, 1754), by George
Graham. Reproduced from the London edition
of 1797 by courtesy of the APGRD 145

6.1 Frontispiece, designed and engraved by Louis du
Guernier, to Lewis Theobald's translation of
Sophocles' *Electra* (1714). Reproduced by
courtesy of the Bodleian Library 156

6.2 Miss Elizabeth Younge (later Mrs Pope) in the
role of Zara in Congreve's *The Mourning Bride*.
Engraving published 1776, reproduced by
courtesy of the APGRD 158

6.3 The recognition scene in Congreve's *The
Mourning Bride*, engraving by Charles Grignion.
Reproduced from the 1753 edition of his *Works*,
vol. ii, by courtesy of the APGRD 160

6.4   Title-page and frontispiece depicting the dedicatee
      (Princess Elizabeth), in Christopher Wase's
      translation of Sophocles' *Electra* (1649).
      Reproduced by courtesy of the Bodleian Library   164

6.5   Title-page and frontispiece to Lewis Theobald's
      translation of Sophocles' *Electra* (1777), substituted
      in *Bell's British Theatre*, xvi for Thomas
      Francklin's translation of Voltaire's *Oreste*.
      The engraving, by J. Thornthwaite, depicts
      Mary Anne Yates in the role of Electra.
      Reproduced by courtesy of the Bodleian Library   176

6.6   Valentine Green, mezzotint after Benjamin
      West's lost painting *Ægistus, Raising the Veil,
      Discovers the Body of Clytemnestra: Francklin's
      Sophocles* (1780). Reproduced by courtesy of
      the British Museum   178

6.7   Sarah Siddons as Euphrasia in Arthur
      Murphy's *The Grecian Daughter, c.*1783.
      Engraving by J. Caldwell after a painting by
      W. Hamilton. Enthoven Collection, reproduced
      by courtesy of the Theatre Museum, London   181

7.1   Thomas Davidson, *Caractacus being Paraded
      Before the Emperor Claudius, AD 50* (1891).
      Reproduced by courtesy of the APGRD   185

7.2   Title-page and frontispiece by Burnet Reading,
      showing Thomas Caulfield in the role of
      Arviragus, to the 1796 *British Theatre* edition
      of William Mason's *Caractacus*. Reproduced by
      courtesy of the APGRD   186

7.3   George Romney, *Atossa's Dream*, chalk cartoon,
      1778–9, inspired by Robert Potter's 1777 translation
      of Aeschylus' *Persians*. Reproduced by courtesy of
      the Board of Trustees of the National Museums
      (Walker Art Gallery, Liverpool)   210

7.4   The monument to William Mason in Westminster
      Abbey, London, sculpted by J. Bacon (1799).
      The grieving woman probably depicts Melpomene,

the Muse of Tragedy. Copyright: the Dean and
Chapter of Westminster 212

8.1 *Lucifera's Procession. Fairy Queen*, engraving by
G. Humphrey, 12 May 1821, depicting Queen
Caroline as Lucifera in a coach drawn by her
supporters. Reproduced courtesy of the British
Museum 229

8.2 *The Como-cal Hobby*, engraving by G. Humphrey,
20 April 1821. Bartolomeo Pergami astride a
she-goat with the head of Queen Caroline.
Reproduced courtesy of the British Museum 232

9.1 An unidentified scene (possibly the opening of
Euripides' *Heracles*) from a performance of Greek
tragedy at Reading School. Reproduced from
'Oliver Oldfellow', *Our School* (1857) by
courtesy of the Bodleian Library 244

9.2 Mary Russell Mitford, *c*.1840. Reproduced by
courtesy of the APGRD 252

9.3 Dr Valpy prepares Benjamin Bockett for his
entrance as the distraught Phrygian messenger
in an 1821 performance of Euripides' *Orestes* at
Reading School. Reproduced from Oliver
Oldfellow, *Our School* (1857), by courtesy of
the Bodleian Library 260

10.1 Contemporary playbill for Peter Bayley's
Orestes in Argos at Covent Garden, 1825.
Reproduced by courtesy of the APGRD 276

10.2 Thomas Woolnoth, *Mr. C. Kemble as Orestes*,
frontispiece to *Dolby's British Theatre* edition
of Peter Bayley's *Orestes in Argos* (1825).
Reproduced by courtesy of the Bodleian
Library 278

10.3 The climax of Peter Bayley's *Orestes in Argos*,
from *Dolby's British Theatre* edition (1825).
Engraving by Henry White, reproduced by
courtesy of the Bodleian Library 279

11.1 Martha Macready, *Macready as Ion* (1836).
Reproduced from Martha Sarah Macready,
Dramatic Recollections (1839), by courtesy of
the Bodleian Library   283

11.2 Thomas Noon Talfourd by Daniel Maclise.
Reproduced from William Bates, *A Gallery
of Illustrious Literary Characters* (1873), by
courtesy of the APGRD   288

11.3 Ellen Tree as Clemanthe in the original
production of Talfourd's *Ion* at Covent Garden
(1836). Reproduced by courtesy of the APGRD   292

11.4 The Penshaw Monument, near Sunderland.
Photograph reproduced by courtesy of
Richard Poynder   307

11.5 Charlotte Cushman as Ion, Haymarket Theatre.
Reproduced from *ILN* 8, no. 199 (1846), by
courtesy of the Bodleian Library   312

11.6 Contemporary playbill for Talfourd's
Ion at Covent Garden (1836), after Helen
Faucit took over the role of Clemanthe from
Ellen Tree. Reproduced courtesy of the APGRD   313

12.1 *Punch* cartoon illustrating Antigone under arrest
by guards, in 'Antigone analysed', article
satirically reviewing the 'Mendelssohn *Antigone*'
at Covent Garden. Reproduced from *Punch*,
8 (18 January 1845), 43 by courtesy of the APGRD   323

12.2 *Punch* cartoon illustrating the chorus of the
'Mendelssohn *Antigone*', in 'Antigone analysed',
article satirically reviewing the Covent Garden
production. Reproduced from *Punch*, 8
(18 January 1845), 42 by courtesy of the APGRD   323

12.3 Antigone, arrested by guards, is brought
before Creon. Scene from *Antigone* at
Covent Garden, January 1845. Reproduced
from *ILN* 6, no. 142 (18 January 1845), 45
by courtesy of the Bodleian Library   325

12.4 Frederick Burton's portrait of Helen Faucit
in the role of Antigone (1845). Reproduced
by courtesy of the APGRD   329

12.5 *Punch* cartoon showing Sir Robert Peel
torn by the Maynooth controversy like 'the
heroes in the Greek tragedies, whose proceedings
were the subject of alternate abuse and praise
from the chorus' (1845). Reproduced from 'The
position of the Premier' in *Punch*, 8 (3 May
1845), 191 by courtesy of the APGRD   342

12.6 Tableau portraying Jason and Medea escaping
on the Argo. Conclusion of part 1 of Planché's
The Golden Fleece (Haymarket Theatre, March
1845). Reproduced from *ILN* 6, no. 152
(29 March 1845), 200 by courtesy of the
Bodleian Library   344

12.7 Scene from Planché's burlesque *The Birds of
Aristophanes*, Haymarket Theatre, April 1846.
Reproduced from *ILN* 8, no. 207 (18 April
1846), 253 by courtesy of the Bodleian Library   346

12.8 *The Triumph of Clytemnestra*, plate depicting
Becky Sharp dressed for a drawing-room charade
inspired by Aeschylus' *Agamemnon*. Reproduced
from William Thackeray, *Vanity Fair*, ii
(London, 1867) by courtesy of the APGRD   349

13.1 Scene from Robert Brough's burlesque *The
Siege of Troy*, Lyceum Theatre 1858–9.
Reproduced from *ILN* 34, no. 954 (8 January
1859) by courtesy of the Bodleian Library   352

13.2 Fanny Reeves in the title role of Robert
Reece's extravaganza *Prometheus; or the Man
on the Rock!* (New Royalty Theatre, London,
December 1865). Reproduced by courtesy of
the APGRD   360

13.3 Annie Bourke as Mercury in Robert Reece's
extravaganza *Prometheus; or the Man on the
Rock!* (New Royalty Theatre, London,

December 1865). Reproduced by courtesy of
the APGRD   368

13.4   A scene from the Brough brothers' extravaganza
The Sphinx (Haymarket Theatre, April 1849).
Reproduced from *ILN* 14, no. 366 (14 April
1849) by courtesy of the Bodleian Library   369

13.5   Domestic conflict in Henry Byron's burlesque
Orpheus and Eurydice (Strand Theatre,
January 1864). Reproduced from *ILN* 44,
no. 1239 (2 January 1864), 19 by courtesy of
the Bodleian Library   371

13.6   Landscape featuring the statue of Pan, in
Henry Byron's extravaganza *Pan; or, the Loves
of Echo and Narcissus*, New Adelphi Theatre,
London (April 1865). Reproduced from
ILN 46, no. 1313 (6 May 1865) by courtesy
of the Bodleian Library   380

14.1   Adelaide Ristori as Medea with her children,
in Ernest Legouvé's adaptation, *c.*1856.
Reproduced by courtesy of the APGRD   403

14.2   Adelaide Ristori as Medea striking an attitude,
in Ernest Legouvé's adaptation, *c.*1856.
Reproduced by courtesy of the APGRD   405

14.3   Frederick Robson as Medea, in Robert
Brough's *Medea; or, the Best of Mothers with
a Brute of a Husband, c.*1856. Reproduced by
courtesy of the Society for Theatre Research,
London   411

14.4   Isabel Bateman as Medea, Lyceum Theatre,
July 1872. Reproduced from *ILN* 61,
no. 1715 (20 July 1872), 61 by courtesy of
the Bodleian Library   426

14.5   Geneviève Ward, *c.*1875. Reproduced courtesy
of the APGRD   428

15.1   Playbill for a revival of Frank Talfourd's *Alcestis;
or, the Original Strong-Minded Woman* (July

1851) at the Royal Soho Theatre. Reproduced
by courtesy of the APGRD 437

15.2 Playbill for Henry Spicer's *Alcestis* at
St. James's Theatre, January 1855. Reproduced
by courtesy of the V&A Picture Library,
London 440

15.3 Drawing by Fleeming Jenkin illustrating
the correct draping of the ancient Greek female
peplos (1874). Reproduced from his essay 'On the
Antique Dress for women' (originally published
in the *Art Journal*, 1874), in *Papers Literary,
Scientific &c.* i (1887), by courtesy of the
APGRD 450

15.4 Final scene of the *Agamemnon* in Balliol Hall,
Oxford, 1880. Engraving reproduced from
The Graphic, no. 552 (26 June 1880), by
courtesy of the Bodleian Library 454

15.5 Scene from *Eumenides* from Frank Benson's
touring production of the *Oresteia* (1905).
Reproduced by courtesy of the APGRD 455

15.6 A performance of *Alcestis* at Queen's
College, Harley Street, London (1886).
Reproduced from *The Graphic* for
18 December 1886 by courtesy of the APGRD 458

15.7 'Classic Costume Revived at Oxford', *Punch*
cartoon accompanying article 'Very Original
Greek at Oxford', ostensibly a review of
Alcestis, starring Jane Ellen Harrison, at the
New Theatre, Oxford. Reproduced from
Punch, 92 (28 May 1887), 264 by courtesy
of the APGRD 460

16.1 Scene from John Todhunter's *Helena in Troas*,
performed in the 'Greek-style' theatre at
Hengler's Circus, designed by E. W. Godwin.
Reproduced from *The Graphic*, 5 June 1886,
by courtesy of the APGRD 464

16.2 Scene depicting Clytemnestra awakening
the Furies in George Warr's *The Story of*

Orestes, at the Prince's Hall, Piccadilly (1886),
reproduced courtesy of the APGRD 465

16.3 Fashion plate advertising 'Hellenic' couture
(1888). Reproduced by courtesy of the APGRD 481

17.1 'The Salvation Army on the Stage' at the Royal
Court Theatre in Shaw's *Major Barbara*, from *The
Sketch*, 13 December 1905. Reproduced by
courtesy of the V&A Picture Library 501

17.2 Edyth Olive as Medea, Savoy Theatre, 1907.
Photograph reproduced from *ILN* 131,
no. 3576 (2 November 1907), by courtesy
of the Bodleian Library 515

17.3 Banner of the Actresses' Franchise League,
c.1911. Photograph reproduced by courtesy
of the Museum of London 517

18.1 John Martin-Harvey as Oedipus in Max
Reinhardt's *Oedipus Rex*, Covent Garden,
January 1912. Reproduced by courtesy of
the APGRD 523

18.2 Edmund Dulac, *Lillah Borne by the Wings
of Love from the Wings of the Stage* (*c*.1921).
Reproduced courtesy of the APGRD 525

18.3 Jean Mounet-Sully as Oedipus in the
Comédie-Française production of *Œdipe Roi*.
Engraving by H. Bellery-Desfontaines,
reproduced by courtesy of the APGRD 527

18.4 Lillah McCarthy as Hecuba in *The Trojan
Women* at the Stadium, New York, in 1915.
Reproduced by courtesy of the APGRD 545

18.5 Frontispiece to *Maud Allan and Her Art*
([1911]). Reproduced by courtesy of APGRD 550

18.6 Portrait of Maud Allen in *Maud Allan and
Her Art* ([1911]). Reproduced courtesy of the
APGRD 552

Notes on Nomenclature, Spelling, and Texts

The spelling of proper names varies enormously between different translations and adaptations of ancient Greek dramas, even between those in the English language alone (Medea, Medeia, Medaea). Our policy has been to use the forms of the names as they appear in each author, adaptor, or translator during the discussion of that individual writer's work. But elsewhere, when discussing the plays in more general terms, we have adopted traditional spellings, largely in line with those used in the third edition of the Oxford Classical Dictionary. When referring to ancient Greek or Latin works in the original language, we have used the most recent edition published in the Oxford Classical Texts series.

Regicide, Restoration, and the 'English' Oedipus

'Tis the contrivance, the new turn, the new characters, which
alter the property and make it ours.

John Dryden, The Preface to Don Sebastian *(1690)*

Writing in the Preface to John Dryden and Nathaniel Lee's *Oedipus* in a collected edition of Dryden's works in 1808, Sir Walter Scott refers to a revival 'some thirty years ago', which had so offended the audience that the boxes had been emptied before the end of the third act.[1] That Dryden and Lee's play, first performed at the Dorset Garden Theatre in 1678, should have remained within the London repertoire some hundred years or more after its premiere (albeit now fading from it on grounds of taste), is of no small note. And in many ways this Restoration *Oedipus* is unique amongst the numerous late seventeenth- and early eighteenth-century tragedies based upon the ancient Greek plays in enjoying such a long production history.

In the eighteenth century, Dryden and Lee's *Oedipus* was revived in the provinces as well as the capital, and Hogarth's 'Strolling Actresses Dressing in a Barn' (1738) draws on at least one such provincial revival (Fig. 1.1).[2] Even as early as 1730, *Oedipus* is sufficiently familiar to a wide audience to allow Henry Fielding in the Preface to the second edition of his tragic burlesque

---

[1] W. Scott (1808), vi. 121.

[2] So Visser (1980), 107. Furthermore, the fact that Hogarth was interested in Dryden's theatrical works would lend credence to this. In 1732 he had engraved 'A performance of "The Indian Emperor"'; and he seems to have been particularly impressed by Gravelot van der Gucht's engravings in the 1735 edition of Dryden, especially the one illustrating Dryden's *Marriage à la Mode*, which was an important inspiration behind his own series of engravings under that title. Hogarth's familiarity with the 1735 edition makes it even more likely that van der Gucht's striking engraving of Jocasta's deathbed scene in the Dryden and Lee *Oedipus* (reproduced here as Fig. 1.3), with its attendant children, informed his 'Strolling Actresses Dressing in a Barn', which appeared three years later in 1738. See Uglow (1997), 374.

FIGURE 1.1   William Hogarth, *Strolling Actresses Dressing in a Barn* (1738).

Tom Thumb to assume not only a broad familiarity with its plot, but also details of the plot in performance that allow the play to serve as a byword for the wild histrionics of early eighteenth-century tragic acting:

> it is common in modern Tragedy for the Characters to drop, like the Citizens in the first scene of *Oedipus*, as soon as they come upon the stage.[3]

Indeed, the importance of Dryden and Lee's tragedy on account of its longevity cannot be overstated; and its performance history, like those of all great plays, provides a colourful (and often elaborately contrived) story in itself, involving not just deserted boxes but also a near-fatal encounter, when a real dagger was mistakenly issued by the prop man in a 1692 revival;[4] the first professional

---

[3] Fielding (1730) in Ioan Williams (1970), 4.
[4] Cited by Novak in Dryden (1984), 446 from Luttrell (1857), ii. 593. But see too Doran (1888), i. 349.

performance by a blind actor (when the recently blinded Michael Clancy appeared as Tiresias in 1744);[5] and most dramatically, in a revival in Dublin, we learn that it allegedly elicited such a powerful performance from Thomas Elrington's Oedipus that incipient madness was triggered in one of the orchestral players.[6]

Moreover, like all 'classic' plays, Dryden and Lee's tragedy attracted star performers to the leading role: Thomas Betterton, the most celebrated actor of the Restoration period, made Oedipus his role, earning widespread respect for his interpretation and at least one eulogy for his efforts in the part with Francis Manning's 'Mr Betterton, Acting Oedipus King of Thebes' (1701).[7] The eighteenth-century actor-manager Thomas Sheridan (father of the playwright Richard Brinsley Sheridan, and son of Dr Thomas Sheridan, the pioneer of revivals of Greek tragedy in ancient Greek in Ireland; see Ch. 9) himself took the part of Oedipus in a revival of Dryden and Lee's tragedy in 1755 (see Fig. 1.2); and towards the end of the eighteenth century, some time after the theatrical debacle referred to by Scott in his Preface, John Philip Kemble also appeared on at least one occasion in the part of Oedipus, and the frontispiece to a 1791 edition of the play commemorates that role.[8]

From the first night, it was hotly debated whether the Restoration *Oedipus* owed too much or too little to its Sophoclean source.[9] Gerard Langbaine, the staunchest critic of the widespread practice of plagiarism of the period, pointed out that Dryden and Lee had looted 'whole Scenes' from Sophocles, but he none the less conceded that their play was 'certainly one of the best Tragedies we have'.[10] Whilst the Preface to the printed edition of the play (1679) and the epilogue both spell out the multiplicity of sources (Sophoclean, Senecan, Shakespearean, and Cornelian), the prologue delivered in the theatre might well have led the unsuspecting spectators into believing that they were receiving Sophocles *au naturel*:

---

[5] Genest (1832), iv. 64–5.
[6] Reed (1812) iii. 93. The dating of this incident, however, is clearly wrong here: Reed gives 1760, although Elrington died in 1732. See further Summers (1932), 350.
[7] Novak in Dryden (1984), 447.
[8] The volume (London, 1791) appeared in the series *Bell's British Theatre*.
[9] Kewes (1998), 157–8.
[10] Langbaine (1691), 167.

FIGURE 1.2   Burnet Reading, engraving of Thomas Sheridan in the title role of *Oedipus*, by Dryden and Lee.

When Athens all the Græcian state did guide,
And Greece gave laws to all the world beside,
Then Sophocles with Socrates did sit . . .
Then, Oedipus, on crowded theatres,
Drew all admiring eyes and list'ning ears . . .
Now should it fail, (as heav'n avert our fear!)
Damn it in silence, lest the World should hear.
For were it known this poem did not please,
You might set up for perfect savages:
Your neighbours would not look on you as men,
But think the nation all turned Picts again.[11]

Whilst rejecting this Restoration *Oedipus* is somewhat deviously presented here as a rejection of Sophocles himself (with the attendant risk of appearing philistine to more sophisticated, neo-classically schooled, continental neighbours), Dryden and Lee's play was in reality very often perceived as the 'English' *Oedipus*—in marked contrast to the numerous French *Oedipus*es of the same period (notably Pierre Corneille's *Œdipe* of 1659, which was regularly revived within the repertoire of the Comédie-Française until its prominence was eventually usurped by Voltaire's *Œdipe* of 1718). But there is also a sense in which this 'English' *Oedipus* was to become in the long run indistinguishable from the Sophoclean original in the public imagination; and the prologue no doubt contributed to this confusion in important ways.

The influence of the Restoration *Oedipus* extended way beyond its one-hundred-year performance history, with Dryden and Lee's version shaping popular perceptions about Sophocles' own text and offending public taste well into the nineteenth and early twentieth centuries. In 1821, for example, we see Dryden and Lee's *Oedipus* staunchly praised over the Sophoclean version on account of its tragic ending, when Scott lauded Sophocles' *Oedipus at Colonus* for its 'lofty tone of poetry' yet expressed clear reservations about his handling of the myth. Scott insists that it is 'more natural' to the feelings of the modern reader ' . . . that the life of the hero, stained with unintentional incest and parricide, should be terminated, as in Dryden's play, upon the discovery of his complicated guilt and wretchedness'. But Scott's comments on the

---

[11] Dryden (1984), 118. For the wider European reception of the play at this time, see Lurje (2004).

modern tragedy turn out to be, in reality, no more than mere damnation with praise. For he continues:

the disagreeable nature of the plot [of Dryden and Lee's play] forms an objection now [in the early nineteenth century] to its success upon a British stage. Distress which turns upon the involutions of unnatural or incestuous passion, carries with it something too disgusting for the sympathy of a refined age.[12]

In this 'refined' Romantic age, the audience 'retreats with abhorrence even from a fiction turning upon such [incestuous] circumstances'.[13] And when Thomas Love Peacock tells Shelley in 1819 that his play *The Cenci* stands little chance of receiving a public performance owing to its handling of the themes of father–daughter incest and parricide, he invokes the increasing reluctance to stage Dryden and Lee's tragedy as precedent.[14]

The association of *Oedipus* with Shelley's controversial play was to become a major determinant in the Lord Chamberlain's refusal to license Sophocles' *Oedipus Tyrannus* for public performance on the professional stage in the late nineteenth and early twentieth centuries (see Ch. 18). The Lord Chamberlain's Examiner of Plays denied Sophocles' tragedy a licence 'on the ground that it was impossible to put on the stage in England a play dealing with incest.'[15] By way of explanation and justification, the Comptroller of the Lord Chamberlain's Office explained the ban:

There was a precedent for the action which the Lord Chamberlain took on this occasion in the refusal of successive Lord Chamberlains to license 'The Cenci'.[16]

Sophocles' play remained victim of the vagaries of the Lord Chamberlain's blue pencil until November 1910, but in many ways this was a ban on that non-Sophoclean *Oedipus* of Dryden and Lee, which loomed long and large in the British theatrical memory, and which placed a proud and defiant, and by no means wholly contrite incestuous parricide, centre stage.

However, it is not simply the play's afterlife that makes *Oedipus* worthy of close scrutiny at the beginning of this history. Dryden

---

[12] W. Scott (1808), vi. 121.   [13] Ibid.
[14] For details and comment, see Woodberry (1909), pp. xxxiii–xxxv.
[15] Letter from Douglas Dawson to Sir Edward Carson, 11 Nov. 1910. Lord Chamberlain's Plays' Correspondence File: *Oedipus Rex* 1910/814 (British Library).
[16] Ibid.

and Lee's play has received surprisingly little critical attention; and whilst the dominant focus of that criticism has fallen on its politics,[17] it is, above all, its representative status as a tragedy of the Restoration period, at a time of great innovation and restlessness in the theatre, that makes it so important. There were exciting changes attendant on the move to larger inside theatre spaces in Restoration London; and the development of new stage machinery was increasingly exploited to spectacular effect in the capacious theatres of Dorset Garden and Drury Lane from the 1670s. But if the scenic innovations opened up new realms of visual splendour, there was also considerable debate about the kinds of plays in which those effects should appear.

When the professional theatres opened after eighteen years of closure during the Civil War and Interregnum (1642–60), the returning Royalists brought with them various (essentially French) ideas about how plays should be written. Dryden and Lee's *Oedipus* provides a fascinating engagement with the heated theoretical discussion at this time, grafting elements from the modern English (especially Shakespearean) and French (principally Cornelian) traditions onto the ancient (essentially Greek, but partly Roman) paradigm. Furthermore, Dryden and Lee's play may also be considered representative in its reflection of recurrent political concerns and anxieties regarding the monarchy, which came to haunt the Stuart dynasty in the last decades of the seventeenth century almost as much as they had done in the years leading up to the Civil War. Sophocles' ancient tragedy with its themes of incest, tyranny, and regicide lent itself most effectively to comment upon the increasingly turbulent political events of the last three decades of the seventeenth century.

OEDIPUS IN ENGLAND

Before Dryden and Lee there had been very few English theatrical engagements with Sophocles' text. Although Dryden in his Preface refers to Corneille's version as the only modern adaptation, there had been a handful of earlier English *Oedipus*es. There were,

---

[17] e.g. Bevis (1988), 62–3; Hughes (1996), 261–2.

for example, at least two vernacular versions of Seneca's *Oedipus* in the sixteenth century, Alexander Neville's *Oedipus* of 1560 and another, anonymous translation;[18] and Neville's *Oedipus* may well have been staged (together with the *Hecuba*) at Trinity College, Cambridge in 1559–60. Although little is known about the production (except that it made a considerable drain on the college's finances), Neville's adaptation is of interest as an example of how an ancient tragedy could be readily rewritten in accordance with the conventions of the medieval mystery play, in which Oedipus' 'horrible crimes' could be fully atoned for with a chastened Oedipus at the end. The longstanding parallels between Oedipus and Judas, with the betrayer of Christ being guilty of parricide and incest and finally lamenting his sins, made Neville's reworking immediately comprehensible to a Renaissance audience.[19] But Neville's *Oedipus* is also of note because it was highly influential, not least in setting the trend for the Elizabethan and Jacobean fascination with and condemnation of incest.[20]

Cambridge was not alone in taking an interest in the character of Oedipus in the sixteenth century. William Gager, a Student of Christ Church, Oxford, wrote a Latin playlet entitled *Oedipus* around 1578. Gager was the leading neo-Latin dramatist of the day and Christ Church was one of the Oxford colleges most prominent in the promotion of drama in English and Latin. It is not clear whether Gager's 195-line playlet was intended for performance as it stands, or whether it is only a first attempt at a larger play.[21] But despite the brevity of the text, the main details of Oedipus' life are there and are placed within a broad context that includes the dispute between Polynices and Eteocles (sc. 3), recently made popular by its rendering in George Gascoigne and Francis Kinwelmershe's *Jocasta* of 1566–7. It seems that in the

---

[18] The anonymous translation can be found in the Bodleian: MS Rawlinson poet. 76 (Summary Cat. iii. 297, No. 14570). See further Bowers (1949), 141–2. Neville's translation was first published in 1563 under the title *The Lamentable Tragedy of Oedipus the Sonne of Laius Kyng of Thebes out of Seneca*; it was later heavily revised and incorporated into Thos. Newton (1581), where an editorial sleight of hand passed it off as identical with the 1560 text, making Neville into a child prodigy. For detailed comment, see McCabe (1993), 108–9.

[19] Bruce R. Smith (1988), 205–11. The definitive narration of Judas's life was that in Jacobus de Voragine (1993), i. 167–9 = (1998), i. 277–81, in his account of St Matthias (*Legenda aurea*, ch. 45). See Lurje (2004), 101–2 with n. 17.

[20] McCabe (1993), 109.

[21] Binns (1981), 1–8.

Renaissance the exemplarity of Oedipus is completely grasped
only through the full sweep of his life.

That the desire to see Oedipus' life diachronically is just as
strong in the early part of the seventeenth century is well illustrated by Thomas Evans's somewhat prurient version published in
1615. Evans's *Oedipus* is subtitled *Three Cantoes wherein is contained: 1) His unfortunate Infancy 2) His execrable Actions 3) His
Lamentable End*. The question of when and how Oedipus dies
(entailing as it does the neoclassical preoccupation with poetic
justice and the attendant concern with the edifying function of
tragedy) was to last throughout the seventeenth century in England, with Dryden and Lee's hero meeting his 'lamentable end',
albeit with spectacular defiance, in the final moments of their
play.[22]

We have already seen how Scott privileges the Dryden and Lee
plot over Sophocles' handling of the same material on the grounds
that poetic justice must be seen to be done; so here, in the Renaissance and Restoration periods, there is a clear need to resist the
open-endedness of both Sophocles' and Seneca's endings. The
highly influential French version of 1659 by Pierre Corneille,
with its vacillating protagonist, had followed ancient precedent in
making Oedipus blind himself rather than commit suicide. And in
the view of many English commentators and notably Dryden in his
Preface to his version, not only did the French Oedipus fail to
atone properly for his unintentional crimes against nature, he also
turned out to be not kingly enough.

Indeed it was its handling of the question of kingship that was to
make Sophocles' tragedy of particular interest to the Restoration.
Tudor dramatists had used incest as a metaphor for political corruption in general; and in the Elizabethan *Homilies* (as in the
ancient world and notably in *Phoenician Women*), clear connections
are drawn between civil war and incest in their common disregard
of kin.[23] In the aftermath of the Civil War, those earlier links (as we
will see) are felt even more acutely. In political debate sexual metaphors that recall the Sophoclean paradigm are prevalent: with
the king as head of the family of state, the regicide of Charles I

---

[22] Palmer (1911), 100; McCabe (1993), 111. Novak in Dryden (1984), 453–4
detects significant parallels between Evans's version and Dryden and Lee's *Oedipus*,
and infers that Lee must have read Evans's text.
[23] McCabe (1993), 120–1.

is deemed by royalists an act of parricide; and in republican discourse, monarchical rule is tainted with incest.[24] When the *Eikon Basilike* of 1649 proclaims that the king alone can beget authoritative laws, relegating Parliament to a mere consenting party, Milton rails:

And if it hath bin anciently interpreted the presaging signe of a future Tyrant, but to dream of copulation with his Mother, what can it be less then actual Tyranny to affirme waking, that the Parlament, which is his Mother, can neither conceive or bring forth any autoritative Act without his Masculine coition.[25]

When William Joyner's indirect engagement with Sophocles' tragedy, *The Roman Empress*, was performed by the King's Company at Lincoln's Inn Fields in the summer of 1670, many of these themes were employed in support of the monarchy during the increasingly unsettled political climate at the start of the second decade following the Restoration. *The Roman Empress* has a protagonist who appears to have been consciously drawn in marked opposition to Corneille's aberrant king. In the Preface, Joyner explains his choice of *Oedipus Tyrannus* as his primary source:

Having consider'd, that of all the Tragedies the old Oedipus, in the just estimation of the Antients and moderns carry'd the Crown; a Story as yet untoucht by any English Pen, I thought, though defective in my art, I could not be but very fortunate in this my subject.[26]

Yet unlike Dryden and Lee's tragedy some eight years later, Joyner's version is very far from being a faithful rendering of Sophocles' text. Joyner goes on to outline the reasons behind the numerous liberties he has taken with the Greek text in his creation of the supposedly first 'English' Oedipus. He makes a veiled allusion to the shortcomings of the Cornelian model as he proudly proclaims his protagonist, Valentius, a great Roman Emperor rather than a 'petty' Greek Prince; and in contrast to the French version (and cocking a clear snook at French neo-Aristotelian critics for whom poetry is more 'philosophical' than history), Joyner defends his departure from the ancient Greek source on the

---

[24] Boehrer (1992), 113–15.
[25] 'Eikonoklastes' (6 Oct. 1649), in Milton (1962), 467; and Boeher (1992), 113 for comment.
[26] Joyner (1671), sig. A2ʳ.

ground that his protagonist really existed (albeit with a different name—Valentius is clearly based on Constantius Chlorus, one of the last pagan emperors of the western Roman empire). But Valentius is nonetheless like Oedipus because he

incurs those very misfortunes, which with all imaginable care he shun'd; condemning his son [Constantine, who in reality went on to convert the entire western world to Christianity] without knowing him, and after death knowing him with all benefit: which makes him the best, and greatest of all Tragical subjects.[27]

Whilst Oedipus' blindness to the truth is indeed his hallmark, he is of course not alone in being afflicted with this condition in the Greek tragic corpus. Joyner's protagonist is closer in some ways to Theseus than Oedipus, with unintentional filicide rather than parricide being his crime. Indeed the play as a whole owes more than a passing debt to that other favourite ancient play of the sixteenth and seventeenth century, Euripides' *Hippolytus*,[28] and to other subsequent treatments of the Hippolytus–Phaedra myth by Seneca and Racine. Here Oedipal mother–son incest is replaced with the subjection of Valentius' son Florus to the unwanted (Phaedra-like) advances of the Emperor's second wife (unbeknown to him, his stepmother, and based on the historical empress Theodora). However, the true Roman empress in this play turns out to be not the rapacious stepmother, but the falsely accused and generally unimpeachable first wife (based on the Roman Catholic saint, Helena, the discoverer of the True Cross), who delivers the terrible news of her son's true identity to his father before killing herself. In Joyner's version, the final word is significantly given to his Jocasta figure after all.

Joyner's tragedy remains determinedly Sophoclean in its focus on the theme of parricide (threatened, presumed or actual) and on the metaphorical blindness of its protagonist. In the last few moments of the play, when Valentius realizes that he has not simply lost a trusted general but his own son as well with the death of Florus, the allusion to Sophocles' tragedy is made explicit

---

[27] Ibid., sig. A3ᵛ.

[28] McCabe (1993), *passim*. The play also draws on Euripides' *Medea* : as Joyner points out in the Preface, the Roman Empress escapes scot-free at the end like Medea; and in its representation of women as the victims of male oppression and especially in the lengthy speech bemoaning women's lot (Joyner (1671), 23–4), there are many echoes of Medea's 'Women of Corinth' speech.

with Valentius' complaint before killing himself in true Roman fashion: 'Are these my eyes thought worthy of the light?'[29] But it is, above all, in its concern with unwitting intergenerational chaos that *The Roman Empress* provides its most abiding point of reference with Sophocles' bleak ending in *Oedipus Tyrannus*. The focus on the breakdown in intra-familial relations that results from the civil war in Rome allows Joyner to make an implicit warning of any return to pre-Civil War schisms in England. As a convert to Roman Catholicism and alluding through his defence of Valentius to Constantius Chlorus and Constantine I and the dynastic struggle that determined whether the future of the world should be Christian or pagan, Joyner is offering his own contribution to the hagiographical tradition in early Church history. But more importantly in 1670, Joyner would appear to be underlining the fact that the glowing mythology surrounding the Restoration was beginning to tarnish. When he writes in the Preface that 'by advice of friends I have disguis'd the names',[30] we can only infer that overt references to early Church history are now deemed to signify Catholic allegiance; and that any public defence of Constantine's lineage could be construed as explicit support for Charles II's Catholic brother, James, Duke of York. If Valentius is shown to have been sufficiently duped into believing his own son guilty of treason (an event that could have denied the world Christianity), so now in 1670 similar accusations of treachery could be ominously about to deny England the continuity and stability promised by the Restoration.

If Joyner's tragedy invokes Oedipus in support of the monarchy, Milton's allusions to the myth in *Samson Agonistes* (also published in 1671)[31] could be said to serve broadly republican ends. Here through the character of Samson we engage with the second part of Oedipus' life and with Sophocles' *Oedipus at Colonus* in particular. In the 'Epistle' to the play, Milton invites comparison with the Greek tragedians, referring primarily to formal rather than thematic concerns. Indeed, Milton's use of a permanently onstage and participating chorus makes his debt to the Greek example obvious. But his statement of debt is not simply about aesthetic preference; his deployment of a Greek-inspired interrogatory chorus in *Samson Agonistes* is in many ways a reflection of his unfailing

---

[29] Joyner (1671), 66.   [30] Ibid., sig. A2^r.

[31] According to a number of critics, Joyner had read *Samson Agonistes* in MS. See Sauer (2002), 88–110. Thanks to Margaret Kean for this reference.

republican sentiments and his rejection of Royalist neo-classical strictures.

Formal and thematic parallels can be made with Aeschylus' *Prometheus Bound*, but the comparison with *Oedipus at Colonus* is the most sustained. Samson's embittered blindness and devastating revenge on the Philistines recall not only Milton's own personal response to his straitened circumstances, but also allude to the blinded Oedipus, whose fatal curse on his sons will ultimately wreak havoc on all the Thebans, who had formerly rejected him and now cynically require his body. In this respect, the physically mutilated and enchained Samson shares with the elderly, stateless Oedipus the ability to draw for one last time upon the suprahuman energies that propelled him into greatness in the first place. Like Oedipus, he too has pre-sentiments of this resurgence of strength: 'I begin to feel | Some rousing motions in me, which dispose | To something extraordinary my thoughts';[32] and we infer that Samson also departs this world in the knowledge that his death will reward those he loves and exact a devastating revenge upon his enemies.

Milton's verse drama was not designed for performance, even though recent stagings have shown just how intensely performable it is;[33] and the power of the play derives in no small measure from its being deliberately cast in contradistinction to the 'heroic' plays and to the performance conditions of the Restoration theatre. From the messenger speech at the end of the play, we learn that the site of Samson's revenge was 'a spacious theatre'.[34] In the 'intermission'[35] during the games, when Samson is seemingly seeking respite after the physical exertion demanded of him by the crowd, he leans on the pillars that support the roof of the theatre and proclaims:

> Hitherto, lords, what your commands imposed
> I have performed, as reason was, obeying,
> Not without wonder or delight beheld.
> Now, of my own accord such other trial
> I mean to show you of my strength, yet greater
> As with amaze shall strike all who behold.[36]

---

[32] Milton (1997), 390, ll. 1382–3.
[33] e.g. the Northern Broadsides' production in autumn 1998.
[34] Milton (1997), 408, l. 1605.   [35] Ibid. 409, l. 1629.
[36] Ibid. 409–10, ll. 1640–6.

With these words (which clearly allude to that other great moment
of self-revelation and revenge at the beginning of *Odyssey* 22), the
messenger tells us that Samson bowed and tugged down the pillars
forcing the entire theatre roof to come crashing down over the
heads of 'Lords, ladies, captains, counsellors, or priests'[37] and
over Samson himself. With more than a touch of republican fervour, perhaps, Milton's messenger adds that only those 'vulgar'[38]
members of the audience, who could not afford the privileged seats
with a roof over their head, managed to escape the widespread
destruction.

   In marked contrast to the 'heroic drama' being performed at the
Lincoln's Inn theatre, in which the aristocratic hero typically
engages in chivalric acts in order to win the love of a princess,
Milton's protagonist is deemed too filthy for even the giant Har-
apha to challenge to a fight.[39] In the same year as the publication of
Samson Agonistes, the Duke's Company moved to the Dorset
Garden Theatre, ushering in a new era of spectacular theatre.
Indeed, the theatre of the 1670s as a whole is marked by a significant increase in the use of sophisticated stage machinery, and the
extensive use of stage spectacle may well be considered the defin-
ing feature of English tragedy by the end of the decade.[40] In
returning to Greek tragic form in *Samson Agonistes*, Milton was
deliberately eschewing current aesthetic tastes; and in setting the
revenge of his decidedly 'non-heroic' hero in a theatre, we see how
(as was the case in France) aesthetic and political preferences were
inextricably linked at the time.

RESTORATION OEDIPUSES: ANCIENT OR MODERN?

That Milton's engagement with Greek tragedy and with the Oedipus myth in particular had considerable influence on Dryden's
own choice of subject-matter some years later is evidenced by the
considerable change detectable in Dryden's theoretical stance
during the course of the 1670s. Milton had included Aristotle's
definition of tragedy in ch. 6 of the *Poetics* as 'an imitation of an
action that is serious, of some magnitude and complete in itself' as

---

[37] Milton (1997), 410, l. 1653.   [38] Ibid., l. 1659.
[39] Ibid. 382, l. 1107.   [40] Cannan (1994), 250.

the epigraph to *Samson Agonistes*. It was inevitable that the playwrights of the Restoration should turn to Aristotle for guidance in how to write their plays. Dryden himself had already given the most spirited account of the theoretical debate in England with his dramatic dialogue *An Essay of Dramatic Poesie* in 1668—reprinted in 1684 and 1693 at the height of the 'Battle of the Books'[41]—in which the Aristotelian position advocated by Crites is hotly contested by the advocates of other (French and English) positions within the debate. What, however, was different with *Samson Agonistes*, is that Aristotle and the ancients were now being presented without the mediation of the French theorists.

The Royalists who arrived in Court from the Continent in 1660 were well versed in French neo-Aristotelian theory, especially the theoretical discussions of La Mesnardière in *La Poëtique* (Paris, 1640) and more recently of the abbé d'Aubignac in *Pratique du théâtre* (Paris, 1657).[42] It was French theory, rather than the dramatic practice of either Corneille or Racine, that was to have the greatest impact on English theatre in the last part of the century. In many ways the French commentators on Aristotle continued in their master's vein, advocating both a deep reverence for ancient dramatic form and devising a strict set of prescriptions (the so-called three 'Unities') to which the modern playwright was supposed to adhere. The row attendant on Corneille's tragicomic *Le Cid* in 1637, which had led to the codification of the neo-Aristotelian rules, showed exactly how aesthetic and political strictures were inseparable in France. And in some ways, the adoption and rejection of French neoclassical theory at this time was closely bound up with responses to monarchical authority as it was enshrined in the autocratic court of Louis XIV. What Milton's *Samson Agonistes* was showing Dryden and his contemporaries in 1671 was that generic purity in practice need not involve a blind adherence to French neoclassicism; it demanded, moreover, outright rejection of that theory and a return to the Greek example itself.

That Dryden should have responded favourably to Milton's example was not surprising given his deep respect for both

---

[41] For a lucid account of the theoretical debate during this period, see Levine (1999).

[42] D'Aubignac's treatise was not translated into English, however, until 1684, when it was canonized for the English theatre under the title *The Whole Art of the Stage*.

Milton's work and his erudition (Dryden had already thought of adapting *Paradise Lost* for the stage, which, though never performed, was published in 1677). Dryden's *An Essay of Dramatic Poesie* is in many ways a robust defence of the English theatrical tradition against the claims of French dramatic practice, with Lisideius, the advocate of French neo-classical rules and unities, losing out to the wit and verve of the advocate of English disorder and vitality, Neander. But Dryden's *Essay* is not merely a defence of the native tradition; it also, in line with French theoretical debate, offers, through the persuasive figure of Eugenius, a robust defence of the primacy of the ancient models as the best guides at the outset of composition.

If Milton's example was a major reason for Dryden to move beyond his tentative espousal of Neander's (English vernacular) position within the theoretical debate, there was another important influence in 1674 with the publication of Thomas Rymer's English translation of the theoretical treatise by the Jesuit Père Rapin entitled *Reflections on Aristotle's Treatise of Poesie with Reflections on the Whole of the Ancient and Modern Poets and the Faults Noted*.[43] Although Dryden was very much an implicit (if not explicit) opponent of Rymer (especially in politics),[44] he was definitely influenced by his interpretations of Rapin. Rymer's Preface to his translation (published later in 1677 as *The Tragedies of the Last Age*) explained the moral and formal superiority of the ancient models, even going so far as to advocate the adoption of an ancient chorus, which with the exception of the late plays of Racine, had barely been seen on the modern stage.

Dryden may not have accepted all Rymer's precepts (the chorus, for one, was an ancient practice, whose general abandonment in the modern world he felt sure was a mark of progress rather than decline),[45] but he did take heed of much of what both Rymer and Rapin said in defence of the ancient paradigms. From 1674 onwards Dryden could be said to move far closer to his fictional character, Eugenius (the advocate of ancient practice as the model, which could, on occasions, be surpassed by certain modern

---

[43] Rapin's *Les Réflexions sur la poëtique* was first published in Paris, also in 1674.
[44] Levine (1991), 79–86; Silk (2001), 173–80.
[45] See too Dryden's 53 points of comment appended to his copy of Rymer's edition and published (1677) as 'Heads of an Answer to Rymer': Dryden (1970), 143–9.

practices and a certain few practitioners). In the Preface to his reworking of Shakespeare's *Antony and Cleopatra, All for Love, or the World Well Lost* (1678), Dryden explains:

> ... I have endeavoured in this play to follow the practice of the Ancients, who, as Mr Rymer has judiciously observ'd, are and ought to be our Masters.[46]

Although Dryden goes on to express a preference for Shakespeare over Sophocles because of his 'larger compass', in his own reworking of Shakespeare here, he has clearly pared down the original in accordance with Aristotelian dictates of plot. If Rymer's mission had been to purge English drama and return it to the classical *exempla* in order to bring about its rebirth, then Dryden now with his next play, written together with Nathaniel Lee,[47] was poised to do just that.

When *Oedipus* was first performed at the Dorset Garden Theatre in 1678, with its busy subplot and large crowd scenes (recalling *Julius Caesar* and *Coriolanus*), it would on first appearance seem far more Shakespearean than Greek. With Samuel Sandford, who was well known to Restoration audiences as a chillingly convincing Richard III, now in the part of the villainous Creon conspiring his way to the throne, and with the troubled Oedipus sleepwalking as if he were another Macbeth, the debts to Shakespeare were legion and explicit. But if it was the Shakespearean 'larger compass' that attracted Dryden on the level of plot in general, this was because it afforded his play visual splendours that the ancient drama had eschewed.

Dryden and Lee's *Oedipus* was in many ways the epitome of the tragedies of spectacle against which Milton had cast his verse drama, *Samson Agonistes*. At Dorset Garden—as at the new Drury Lane theatre which opened in 1674—there were three separate performance spaces. The first and most routinely used was the forestage in front of the proscenium arch, which served as the site of the rollicking Restoration comedies. With the select members of the audience now seated in the onstage boxes situated to the sides of the forestage, this intimate performance space was in

---

[46] Dryden (1984), 18.
[47] On the question of joint authorship, see Kewes (1998), 154–62. It is generally accepted (following Dryden's own claim) that Acts I and III are his, as was the overall design, and that Lee is responsible for Acts II, IV, and V.

many ways a vestige of the medieval theatre, and reminiscent of the Renaissance performance spaces in college dining-halls, in which the enactment of the play was primarily a rhetorical event.[48] Here in Dryden and Lee's tragedy the scenes of intrigue and deception that fuel the subplot take place upon the forestage.

New in the Restoration theatre were the two additional stage spaces behind the proscenium—the scenic stage and beyond that the vista stage—both of which were used for the many scenes of spectacle in the play. The scenic stage, for example, was used in the opening scene depicting the plague (that was to cause much mirth to Fielding in 1730), during which '*Dead bodies appear at a distance in the Streets; some faintly go over the Stage, others drop*',[49] and when Creon's lackeys conspiratorially occupy the forestage and comment on the action beyond the proscenium arch (I. i). But in the final scene of Jacobean carnage, after the lovers from the subplot (together with the chief Machiavel, Creon) have been slaughtered one after the other, the scenic stage can be seen to serve a function akin to the opening of the doors of the ancient Greek *skēnē*, when the *ekkyklēma* is rolled out to reveal a tableau within. With the arrival of the messenger (Haemon in this case) and Tiresias to report the terrible off-stage (Medea-like) killing by Jocasta of her two sons, the scenic stage is drawn back to reveal '*Jocasta held by her Women, and stabb'd in many places of her bosom, her hair dishevel'd, her Children slain upon the Bed*'[50] (see Fig. 1.3). This tableau (which alludes very strongly to the stock Restoration rape scene),[51] with its reference to 'dishevel'd' hair, disordered clothing, and the phallic dagger, graphically re-enacts the consummation of the incestuous union that is merely implicit in the Sophoclean messenger speech of Jocasta's suicide.

If the Restoration scenic stage could function like the *ekkyklēma*, the third performance space, the vista stage had a function analogous to the ancient Greek theatre's *theologeion*/roof space. As with the *theologeion*, the vista stage in the *Oedipus* is reserved for the numerous supernatural events in the play. When the apparitional figures of Oedipus and Jocasta appear in the sky during the portentous storm in Act II, and when the ghost of Laius and the other ghosts loom out from the distance in Acts III and V, their

---

[48] Bruce R. Smith (1988), esp. 51 ff.   [49] Dryden (1984), 120.
[50] Ibid. 211.   [51] Marsden (2000), 181–9.

FIGURE 1.3 Gerard van der Gucht, engraving after Hubert Gravelot depicting the suicide of Jocasta.

other-worldly status is highlighted by their symbolic position at the back of the stage. When Oedipus makes his final suicidal leap from the western tower, he may well have plunged from a high point on the vista stage,[52] making of his departure from this world a kind of apotheosis akin to the Sophoclean protagonist's hallowed exit in *Oedipus at Colonus*.

Indeed Oedipus' final defiant words, refusing to acknowledge any guilt, would imply at least some kind of supernatural strength:

> May all the Gods too from their Battlements,
> Behold, and wonder at a Mortal's daring;
> And, when I knock the Goal of dreadful death,
> Shout and applaud me with a clap of Thunder.
> Once more, thus wing'd by horrid Fate, I come
> Swift as a falling Meteor; lo, I flye,
> And thus go downwards, to the darker Sky.
> [*Thunder. He flings himself from the Window: The Thebans gather about his Body.*][53]

In Oedipus' last words we detect more than a note of Senecan bombast, and in a very immediate sense Seneca is Dryden and Lee's main source here. But we can also discern more than a passing nod at that other defiant Oedipus of the same decade, Milton's Samson, who had earlier challenged his all-too mortal, aristocratic, onlookers with similarly histrionic disdain:

> Now of my own accord such other trial
> I mean to show you of my strength, yet greater
> As with amaze shall strike all who behold.[54]

With the invitation from both these English Oedipuses for their onlookers to 'behold' the marvel they are about to witness, and with Dryden and Lee's protagonist plunging to his death to the accompaniment of a thunder clap strongly evocative of the Miltonic theatre roof collapsing 'with burst of thunder', Dryden's appropriation of Milton is unequivocal.

Whilst it is not surprising that Dryden, now Poet Laureate, is silent in the Preface about his debt to his former republican colleague, his silence about Shakespeare is perhaps somewhat curious. However, by the following year in the Preface to his

---

[52] Bruce R. Smith (1988), 256–7.   [53] Dryden (1984), 213.
[54] Milton (1997), 410, ll. 1643–45.

re-working of Shakespeare's *Troilus and Cressida*, Dryden is advocating the primacy of the ancient over the modern models; and it is
clearly his engagement with the Sophoclean material that has led
him to that conclusion.

In the Preface to *Troilus and Cressida* (1679), Dryden includes a
section entitled 'The Grounds of Criticism in Tragedy' in which
he answers the question 'how far we ought to imitate Shakespeare
and Fletcher in their plots' with the following recommendation:

... we ought to follow them so far only, as they have Copi'd the
excellencies of those who invented and brought to perfection Dramatic
Poetry.[55]

Dryden's main models now, it seems, even as he reworks a Shakespearean play, are the Greek ones. The shortcomings he detects in
Shakespeare's *Troilus and Cressida* are remedied here by turning to
Euripides' *Iphigenia in Aulis*, whose quarrel between Agamemnon
and Menelaus (317–542) provides Dryden with a model for the
final lengthy scene between Troilus and Hector in Act V. But
the model to which Dryden most regularly defers in this Preface
is the neo-Aristotelian paradigm and the source of his previous
play, Sophocles' *Oedipus Tyrannus*. When Dryden speaks of character, it is clearly Oedipus to whom he is referring when he explains the need for

such a man, who has so much more in him of Virtue than of Vice, that he
may be left amiable to the Audience, which otherwise cannot have any
concernment for his sufferings; and 'tis on this one character that the pity
and terror must be principally, if not wholly founded.[56]

And he goes on to explain his preference for an essentially modern
hero-centred tragedy with reference to his own version of the
Sophoclean paradigm:

If Creon had been the chief character in *Oedipus*, there had neither been
terror nor compassion mov'd; but only detestation of the man and joy for
his punishment; if Adrastus and Eurydice had been made more appealing
characters, then the pity had been divided, and lessen'd on the part of
Oedipus: but making Oedipus the best and bravest person, and even
Jocasta but an underpart to him; his virtues and the punishment of his
fatall crime, drew both the pity, and the terror to himself.[57]

---

[55] Dryden (1984), 233.   [56] Ibid. 236.   [57] Ibid. 237.

In his Preface to the *Oedipus*, the only 'modern' source to which Dryden had referred was Corneille's *Œdipe*, with reference to its vacillating king who is upstaged by the 'greater hero' Theseus and against whom (like Joyner's before him) Dryden and Lee's protagonist is deliberately cast.[58] And if he had been silent about his very obvious debt to Shakespeare here, that is only because in 1678 Dryden is determined to make public his newly revised, pro-classical stance. *Oedipus* is Dryden's attempt to reconcile the conflicts debated within his *Essay of Dramatic Poesie* (1668), and to reproduce the 'best' aspects of all his sources, both ancient and modern.

The debt to Sophocles, by contrast, is both considerable and acknowledged in the Preface. We have already seen how the Prologue could have led the unsuspecting spectator to infer that they were going to witness Sophocles pure and simple. In some places that is indeed what they get: the Sophoclean prologue (1–150), for example, is included almost verbatim, despite being relegated to the second part of Act I; Sophocles' pivotal scene between Oedipus and Jocasta (697–862), when the question of regicide is linked to the fear of incest and parricide, is also adopted here in Act II following Oedipus' dream; and finally the recognition scene (IV. 1), with the Corinthian messenger and the shepherd, reads much like a close translation of the Sophoclean original.

We have already seen that in some circles the play was criticized for being too dependent on its principal Greek source and perilously close to being an act of pure plagiarism.[59] To the modern audience, however, such accusations might well appear to have missed the obvious point that Dryden is no less dependent on the Senecan *Oedipus*. This is the case especially in regard to the ubiquity of both the fear and reality of incest, and the perception of an implacable fate as inextricably linked and controlling forces in the play. Fate is felt externally through both the supernatural events—the storms, the prodigies in the sky—and (as in Sophocles) through the coincidences in the plot (and so at the end of Act I, when Jocasta walks in immediately after Oedipus' curse, she unwittingly wishes it upon both him and herself). But fate also makes itself known internally through the incest motif, which (as in Seneca) becomes the governing force in the play.

<hr/>

[58] Dryden (1984), 115–16.   [59] Kewes (1998), 157–8.

Here in Dryden and Lee, we get the sense that Oedipus and Jocasta are driven to incest; that Oedipus, propelled to Thebes to escape the workings of the oracle that prophesy incest with his mother, is none the less governed by the oracle's ordinance, which is never far from his consciousness nor indeed from the consciousness of the other characters in the play. At the very beginning, we are reminded of Oedipus' striking resemblance to Laius.[60] As in Corneille, this Oedipus fears the match between Creon and Eurydice on grounds that uncle and niece 'are too near . . . 'tis offence to kind'; and in his excessive response: 'Nature would abhor | To be forced back again upon herself | And like a whirlpool, swallow her own streams', he confesses '. . . I know not why, it shakes me, | When I but think on incest.'[61]

In Act II, before retiring to bed, Oedipus alone confesses to an 'unusual chillness' in his sexual encounters with his wife:

> An unknown hand still check'd my forward joy,
> Dash'd me with blushes . . .
> That ev'n the Act became a violation.[62]

Oedipus then sleepwalks, with dagger in one hand and taper in the other, clearly witnessing the events that are soon to be played out in the waking hours, and he later confesses to Jocasta that he dreamt of her as his mother. Here, as with the tableau scene in Act V when Jocasta appears having stabbed herself and her children as if she herself had been violated, what is implicit in Sophocles is once again magnified for the Restoration audience. But it is in the penultimate scene of the play (as in Seneca) when the blinded Oedipus meets up with his mother/wife that the incestuous nature of their relationship comes most obtrusively to the fore. Oedipus pronounces:

> O, in my heart I feel the pangs of Nature;
> It works with kindness o're: Give me way;
> I feel a melting here, a tenderness,
> Too mighty for the anger of the Gods!
> Direct me to thy knees: yet, oh forbear,
> Lest the dead Embers should revive.[63]

---

[60] Dryden (1984), 123, ll. 61 ff.   [61] Ibid. 140, ll. 546 ff.
[62] Ibid. 150, ll. 292–5.   [63] Ibid. 204, ll. 206–11.

This is an Oedipus for whom nature's compulsions are too strong to resist. Dryden and Lee's Jocasta, as in Seneca, proclaims their innocence and blames fate, declaring passionately 'For you are still my husband'.[64] Oedipus wishes to believe her espousal of nature over conventional taboo, and promises to

> ... steal into thy Arms,
> Renew endearments, think 'em no pollutions,
> But chaste as Spirits joys: gently I'll come,
> Thus weeping blind, like dewy Night, upon thee,
> And fold thee softly in my Arms to slumber.[65]

But immediately Laius' ghost appears from beneath in the vista stage to prohibit this ultimate violation of taboo. Seneca's *Oedipus* in the final scene becomes a tragedy about a guilty incestuous parricide; here in Dryden and Lee's version, the final scene proffers a meditation on the prohibition of incest altogether.

OEDIPUS AND POLITICS

During the Commonwealth incest was made a criminal offence for the first time and punishable by death under the Act of Parliament for May 1650.[66] Hitherto and following the Restoration (and until 1908; see Ch. 18) the offence was not punishable by the civil courts, only the ecclesiastical courts, which rarely exercised their jurisdiction in this or any other matter owing to the aggressive stance of the common-law courts. The 1650 legislation collapsed in 1660 because it was in no sense a reflection of public opinion on the subject, which considered the prohibition to be a repressive measure both fundamentally unenforceable and at odds with emotional and sexual reality.[67] For this reason alone, Dryden and Lee's play was a bold espousal of Restoration values, as well as providing a strong dose of titillating and risqué sensationalism for the libertine courtiers within the audience.

It was not simply the examples of Corneille and Milton that would have attracted Dryden to the myth of Oedipus in the late 1670s; nor indeed could the neo-Aristotelian privileging of Sophocles' tragedy alone have provided him with his source. It was, more

---

[64] Dryden (1984), l. 220,   [65] Ibid., ll. 221–5.
[66] Firth and Rait (1911), 387. For comment, see McCabe (1993), 265 ff.
[67] McCabe (1993), 265.

generally, the crisis over the question of succession in the late 1670s—better known as the Exclusion crisis, when Parliament sought to bar the Catholic James, Duke of York, from succeeding his brother to the throne—that made an ancient myth dealing with regicide and restoration so pertinent.

As early as the mid-1660s there had been widespread dissatisfaction (even amongst his supporters) with the king's extravagance and promiscuity, and the Plague of 1665 and Fire of 1666 were readily construed as divine retribution for royal transgressions (both domestic and international in his unpopular war against the Dutch). From 1670 onwards, there is a notable shift, with the plays of the period no longer celebrating the Restoration but offering varying degrees of criticism of the monarchy;[68] and in the late 1670s, Exclusion is construed as another crisis of restoration, or by some, a form of regicide itself.[69]

Beaumont and Fletcher's tragicomedy *A King and No King* (1611) is regularly revived at this time.[70] With its plot concerning the miraculous restoration of the 'legitimate' heir and its (albeit averted) incestuous union between king and queen, it bore a striking resemblance to Sophocles' tragedy. Dryden himself praises it for having 'The best of... designs, the most approaching to antiquity...' and he identifies their probable source as 'the story of Oedipus';[71] but his interest in the parallels had more to do with the political resonances shared by both plays. Whilst the regular revivals of the Jacobean tragicomedy were frequently mounted with a view to promoting the continuity of the Restoration, wider resonances were generated when the title was adopted as a 'political catchword' to describe the crisis in the monarchy in general: in 1662, for example, the committed royalist Sir Roger L'Estrange had observed: 'We are now upon the very Crisis, of King or no King'; and in 1681 the Exclusionist lawyer Sir Francis Winnington similarly alludes in parliamentary debate to the Jacobean play in relation to the possible accession of the Duke of York: 'if he be King and have no power to govern, he is King and no King.'[72]

Dryden had already modelled his protagonist Almanzor in *The Conquest of Granada* (Part I 1670, Part II 1672) on Beaumont and

---

[68] Hughes (1996), 79.   [69] Susan J. Owen (2000), 158.
[70] Maguire (1992), 56–8.   [71] Dryden (1984), 233.
[72] Both these statements are cited by Maguire (2000), 99.

Fletcher's hero (who was in turn, according to Dryden, modelled
on Alexander the Great) in order to enhance what is Dryden's
evident tribute to James, Duke of York.[73] With Dryden and
Lee's *Oedipus*, the parallels with the Jacobean tragicomedy were
even stronger. Here much play is made by Creon and his co-
conspirators of the fact that Oedipus is 'King and no King'.
Creon's lackey Diocles rouses his rabble thus:

> While Lajus has a lawful Successor,
> Your first Oath still must bind: Eurydice
> Is Heir to Lajus; let her marry Creon.
> Offended Heav'n will never be appeas'd,
> While Oedipus pollutes the Throne of Lajus,
> A stranger to his Blood.[74]

As the 'King' who is 'no King', the *tyrannos*/outsider who comes
from without and who has not inherited the throne by birthright,
Oedipus of course turns out to be 'King' after all, the Greek
basileus, the ruler who has inherited the throne by birthright. For
Dryden the authority of the king (even of a deeply flawed king) is
paramount and vital to avert the bloodshed of civil war. The
Oedipus myth, and its associations with the Jacobean tragicomedy,
turn out to be an especially potent weapon in the royalist armoury.

However, although Dryden and Lee's *Oedipus* may well promote the royalist cause, like many plays of the late 1670s, it offers
royalism with a strong dose of scepticism.[75] With Oedipus as
protagonist, the play may well offer a model of kingship. But this
Oedipus remains (albeit unintentionally) a deeply flawed king: he
is, of course, 'King' but too much like the old 'King' in relation to
his queen. If Charles II saw himself reflected in the Greek hero, he
would have been fully aware that this was a heavily qualified
measure of praise. Indeed, Oedipus may well be moderate and
dignified in victory at the beginning of the play, but he is perceived
by the mounting opposition to be aloof and out of touch with his
people.[76] As we would expect from a royalist play of the period, the
Greek chorus is replaced by the intermittent heckling crowd for
whom the occasional interjection alone is permitted (Acts I and
II), and for Oedipus they are merely the 'wild herd'.[77]

---

[73] Maguire (2000), 98. Dryden cites Alexander as Beaumont and Fletcher's
model in the Preface to *Troilus and Cressida*: Dryden (1984), 233.
[74] Dryden (1984), 131, ll. 292–79.   [75] Susan J. Owen (2000), 164.
[76] Dryden (1984), 129, ll. 222 ff.   [77] Ibid. 149, l. 253.

In this highly political play, with the recent memory of plague to highlight the topicality of the opening scene, and regicide and the prospect of descent once more into civil war now being discussed on the stage, the parallels with contemporary figures are not hard to find. Behind Laius clearly lurks Charles I, and behind Oedipus we have allusions to both Charles II and to Cromwell himself; but the clearest parallels are between Creon and the Earl of Shaftesbury, who regularly supplied the stock villain of royalist tragedy of the period,[78] and who would shortly instigate the Monmouth Rebellion (1685) in a bid to remove Charles II and replace him with his illegitimate son, the Earl of Monmouth, in order to preserve Protestant succession.

Following the bloodbath of retribution that floods the subplot in the final act, and after the tableau of the dead children and the suicides of Jocasta and Oedipus, Haemon is left together with Tiresias, who first reassures, then warns the Thebans/English audience confronted with Oedipus' corpse:

> The dreadful sight will daunt the drooping Thebans,
> Whom Heav'n decrees to raise with Peace and Glory.
> Yet, by these terrible Examples warn'd,
> The sacred Fury thus Alarms the World.
> Let none, tho' ne're so Vertuous, great and High,
> Be judg'd entirely blest before they Dye.[79]

Left with the clerical authority of Tiresias and the political and military skills of Haemon (here Captain of the Guard and no member of the royal family), there is none the less no indication to the audience as to what monarchical 'authority' will fill the vacuum now the king is dead. With all Oedipus' legitimate heirs killed by Jocasta, the polluted dynasty is no more; and it may well be that the faction surrounding the illegitimate Earl of Monmouth would have found some covert support for their cause here too. Lee was a notorious anti-Catholic and no doubt his sympathies would have been squarely behind the rumours of the fictitious Popish plot spread by Titus Oates. Just as the conflicting viewpoints within the theoretical debate are never resolved outright within *An Essay of Dramatic Poesie*, so here in the final scene of the play (maybe fuelled in some ways by the dual perspectives arising from the two authors) the conflicting political positions are not so much reconciled by the deaths as left in a state of suggestive tension.

---

[78] Susan J. Owen (2000), 163.   [79] Dryden (1984), 213, ll. 465–70.

The survival of Dryden and Lee's *Oedipus* well into the eighteenth century was in no small measure due to the representative status (traceable from at least the Renaissance) of Sophocles' *Oedipus Tyrannus* as the paradigmatic tragedy (see Chs. 8 and 10–11). The publication in Paris in 1692 of André Dacier's commentary on the *Poetics* reaffirmed its supremacy for the next half century in both France and England. In the same year as his commentary, Dacier produced a translation of both the *Oedipus Tyrannus* and Sophocles' *Electra* as a companion piece to his study of Aristotle. In the Preface to his translations, Dacier declared that now his readers had heard the rules in the commentary, he was now offering them examples of how to write plays for the modern playhouse with his translations. And when Dacier's edition of the *Poetics* was translated into English in 1705, its impact was no less considerable, and it led to a flurry of vernacular translations of the *Electra* (see Ch. 6). If this was not the case in relation to *Oedipus Tyrannus*, this was due in large measure to the fact that the 'English' *Oedipus*, with which this chapter began, was already widely known in Britain. Its status as representative 'English' tragedy, moreover, was not only acknowledged by critics, it was also truly celebrated through its regular revivals in the repertoire.

In 1692, the same year in which Dacier's commentary first appeared in France, a London production of Dryden and Lee's play benefited from the addition of incidental music by Henry Purcell for the Senecan incantation scene. Both Dryden and Purcell, who collaborated on a number of plays at the turn of the century, believed music and poetry to be sister arts; and whilst Dryden maintained that the music should always be subordinate to the word, his collaboration with Purcell in the *Oedipus* meant that his play became an even more 'authentic' attempt to revive ancient Greek tragedy for a modern audience. Indeed, not only did the music for the incantation scene prove sufficiently popular to act as the source of the famous song 'Music for a while',[80] it was also used in two early eighteenth-century musical versions of the Oedipus myth.[81]

---

[80] Thompson (1995), 41.

[81] Both J. E. Galliard's *Oedipus Masque* (premiere *c*.1722 at Lincoln's Inn Fields) and Thomas Arne's opera *Oedipus King of Thebes* (premiere 19 Nov. 1740 at the Theatre Royal) used Dryden and Lee's version as libretti. See *Grove 7*, ix. 453, ii. 42 respectively.

If the musical additions enhanced the play's popularity well into the eighteenth century, it was, above all, its sympathetic portrayal of a flawed but defiant leader which made the play sufficiently open-ended to survive the ever-changing political circumstances that were to unfold beyond the Restoration. And if the Renaissance versions had resisted the open-endedness of the Sophoclean and Senecan versions in their preoccupation with the question of poetic justice, it could be said that it is ultimately the failure of the Dryden and Lee version (despite Oedipus' suicide) to live up to this particular neo-classical dictat that led to its longevity. For in some senses, Dryden and Lee's *Oedipus* presented a 'King' and 'no King' according to one's perspective: for the Tories, the play enacted the restoration of the legitimate heir; for the Whigs, it provided a timely reminder of the need for constitutional monarchy; and for those with republican sentiments (as was to be the case in France during the second part of the eighteenth century), the character of Oedipus here in Dryden and Lee's version could be construed as either the dangerous tyrant (of part one of the play) or the Miltonic model of liberationary defiance that emerges in the Senecan final speech.

2

Iphigenia and the Glorious Revolution

POPULAR IPHIGENIA

In 1749 the notorious Elizabeth Chudleigh, a maid of honour at the court of the Princess of Wales, appeared at a masquerade almost bare-breasted in the role of Iphigenia. 'So naked was she', wrote Lady Mary Wortley Montagu, 'that the high priest might easily inspect the entrails of the victim'; Horace Walpole thought she might just as well have appeared, entirely unclothed, as Andromeda.[1] Although the apparel of Greek and Roman goddesses and heroines was common currency at masked balls,[2] this particular costume exceeded all conventional bounds of decency; several semi-pornographic prints of Miss Chudleigh's exploit entered circulation (see Fig. 2.1).

The Victorians openly acknowledged that Greek tragic roles offered potential for allowing seductive glimpses of skin to appear through antique drapery. Some of them also enjoyed the erotic art of *poses plastiques*, or *tableaux vivants*, static spectacles in which minimally clad models assumed postures reminiscent of classical sculptures. But the relationship between 'classical' costumes and performance arts designed to elicit an erotic reaction extends back into the eighteenth century: the classical attitudes favoured by Emma, Lady Hamilton, who posed for George Romney, had included Calypso, Medea, and 'a Bacchante'.[3] The most famous dancer of the earlier part of the century, Marie Sallé, had stunned the Covent Garden audience in 1734 by appearing as the statue in *Pygmalion* wearing only a diaphanous shift.[4] Although her

[1] Montagu (1763), iii. 158; Walpole (1937), ii. 153. See also Castle (1995), 88–91.
[2] See Ribeiro (1984).
[3] On Hamilton's classical attitudes see Ittershagen (1993) and Kidson (2002), 33–4. Emma Hamilton was probably the model for Romney's chalk cartoon of Medea, reproduced below as Fig. 3.8. On the development of *tableaux vivants* and *poses plastiques* from the 18th-c. 'attitude', see Altick (1978), 345–9, Holmström (1967), and George Taylor (1989), 47.
[4] Beaumont (1934), 20–3.

FIGURE 2.1   Miss Chudleigh attends a masquerade in the character of Iphigenia (1749).

professed intention was to free her limbs from the restricting conventional ballet costume, the effect was exciting. As a result Handel, who had joined forces with John Rich at Covent Garden,

interpolated ballet divertissements into all his subsequent productions that season, including *Oreste*, a *pasticcio* opera derived from
Euripides' *Iphigenia among the Taurians* (hereafter *IT*).[5]

Although the Victorians displaced Iphigenia from the centre of
the Greek tragic stage,[6] she maintained her profile during the
eighteenth century; 'Farewell my child', a popular duet, was published in 1745 with instructions that it was to be sung by a man and
a woman as Agamemnon and Iphigenia respectively.[7] Iphigenia
was prepared for sacrifice in Abel Boyer's *Achilles*, performed at
Lincoln's Inn Fields in 1699–1700 and revived at Covent Garden
by Thomas Hull and Mrs Barry, under the title *Iphigenia*, as late as
1778. The heroine's name was popular currency: when word came
the following year that Captain William Douglas had discovered a
new Hawaiian island, the ship in the headlines was *HMS Iphigenia*. What was so exciting about this heroine seems to have been the
threat of cold steel to young female flesh, for the sensational
sacrifice of a lovely maiden was a favourite theme in popular
spectacles. Such displays were an indignity Iphigenia shared with
Jephthah's daughter, the biblical virgin sacrificed by her father,
with whom Iphigenia had often been paired ever since the Renaissance.[8] *Jephthah's Rash Vow; or, The Virgin Sacrific'd* was performed in a booth erected on the bowling green in Southwark
during a fair in September 1750, and the same story was a standard
eighteenth-century theme at Bartholomew Fair.[9] Similarly, *The
Sacrifice of Iphigenia*, to Dr Arne's music, was billed as an 'entertainment' in Clerkenwell in 1750. The cast consisted of Agamemnon, Calchas, Iphigenia, First Priest, and the goddess Diana.[10]
A ballet of the same name, with music by James Hook, was performed at Richmond Theatre in 1766.[11]

---

[5] Keates (1992), 181–2.

[6] There were of course occasional exceptions: Helen Faucit starred in an
adaptation of *IA* in Dublin in 1846 (see Ch. 12); Madame Rachel acted Racine's
Iphigénie (along with his *Phèdre*) at St James's Theatre several times between 1846
and 1853 (see Cole (1859), ii. 268–9); in 1894 *IT* was selected to be the Cambridge
Greek play.

[7] Highfill et al. xvi. 322.

[8] Thus the only English academic play in Greek to have survived from the 16th
c. is John Christopherson's elegant Ἰεφθάε, which was inspired by and modelled in
detail on one of the scenes in *IA*, as he explained in a letter to the Bishop of Durham.
See the detailed discussion in Boas (1914), 43–59.

[9] See *LS* iv/1. 205; Rosenfeld (1960) 15, 94.

[10] *LS* iv/1. 191.

[11] Nicoll (1952–9), iii. 342. Only the overture was published.

The immediate precursor of these sensational Iphigenias was the more serious heroine who had walked all the major London stages more than any other Greek tragic figure in the first seventy-five years covered by this book (1660–1734). This was partly a result of the attention paid to both Iphigenia plays in Aristotle's *Poetics*, and by Dryden to *Iphigenia in Aulis* (hereafter *IA*) in his 1679 *Troilus and Cressida* (see above, Ch. 1). Moreover, in comparison with most of Euripides' plays, *IA* was already familiar.[12] After being translated into Latin by Erasmus (1506), it was the first Greek tragedy to be translated into English, by Lady Jane Lumley (1558);[13] the play's fame in England had later been sealed by the instant success with which the first performance of Racine's *Iphigénie en Aulide* had met at Versailles in 1674.

HUGUENOT IPHIGENIA

It is difficult to overestimate Racine's influence on the British stage in this period. The English-language theatre of the eighteenth century both loved and hated the plays of Corneille, Racine, and subsequently Voltaire; dramatists writing in English suffered from a tension between artistic admiration for French cultural achievements and literary models (exhibited in their proud acknowledgements of French sources in prologues and prefaces),[14] and a profound anti-French prejudice of a political and ideological nature. The tension was neatly expressed at the end of an English adaptation of a Molière comedy in 1691, when the Anglo-French conflict in Ireland was raging: 'were it in my Power, I would advance | French *wit in* England, English *arms* in France'.[15] English dramatists could even achieve the feat of turning plays originally written in French into anti-French propaganda (see below); John Dennis is aware that the theatre is a good place for nurturing a sense of collective identity defined in opposition to a common foe. The English will feel more English if the theatre fosters

---

[12] See the detailed study of Gliksohn (1985).

[13] See the recent edition by Purkiss (1998).

[14] Lynch (1953), 218–19.

[15] Caryl (1691), 68. For the importance of Francophobia as a unifying factor in the creation of an English and subsequently a British identity, see in general Colley (1992) 17, 24–5, 33–5.

anti-French sentiment. 'The Stage is useful to Government, by having an influence over those who are govern'd, in relation to the common enemy.'[16]

Racine's plays had been adapted for performance in London occasionally before Boyer's *Achilles*, the first attempt to imitate Racine's *Iphigénie* in England.[17] One much-cited example is John Crowne's lugubrious *Andromache* (1675). But Boyer's play throws more light on the bifurcated British perception of French neoclassical tragedy: Boyer was an expatriate Frenchman noted for the fervour with which he hated France and with which he had embraced life in William and Mary's London. He enthusiastically claims Racine's play as his source in the 'Preface'; in the advertisement to the 1714 edition of his play, Boyer describes *Iphigénie* as Racine's 'Master-Piece', which he had himself but 'translated into English, with considerable Additions'.[18]

Boyer is the first of several Huguenots and individuals of Huguenot descent to be encountered in the course of this book: David Garrick's Huguenot grandfather had fled to London in 1685 after the revocation of the Edict of Nantes.[19] Huguenots were famed for their skills in crafts and design as well as their prominence in printing and publishing: the refugee Luc du Guernier, after collaborating on a series of works commemorating the Duke of Marlborough's victories, engraved most of the frontispieces to Greek tragedy published in Britain during this period, several of which are reproduced here (see Fig. 2.2) and in other chapters. Huguenots were in touch with the ideological requirements of the London stage partly because of their loyalty to the Hanoverian succession: the disproportionate number of Huguenot volunteers in the English armies fighting the Stuarts and the French in the early eighteenth century has only recently been acknowledged.[20] But the Huguenot refugees in London also had privileged access to the French language and its literature, along with contacts in France, which meant

---

[16] Dennis (1698), 58.

[17] Racine's tragedy was occasionally performed, in French, at the Haymarket, e.g. on 23 Jan. 1722 (though his authorship is not stated), coincidentally on the same night as Terence's *Eunuchus* was performed at Westminster School (*LS* ii/2. 660).

[18] Boyer (1714), 'Advertisement'.

[19] In the 19th c. the connection between the Huguenot heritage and the British theatre would be represented by James Robinson Planché, John Heraud, and E. L. Blanchard.

[20] See e.g. Gwynn (2001), 102–3, 184–90.

that they constituted a living bridge *of a politically safe nature* between the works of the French theatre and the English-speaking public. Moreover, the two greatest Classical scholars at the beginning of the seventeenth century had been Joseph Scaliger and Isaac Casaubon, both Protestant refugees (one in Holland and one in England), whose erudition engendered enormous respect for the Huguenot study of Greek Classics. The brilliant French scholars of Greek drama, Anne and André Dacier, had both been born and raised in humanist Protestantism, although they had publicly renounced it. It is therefore hardly surprising that the first man to bring Euripides' *IA* to the English stage, via Racine, was a Huguenot refugee. Abel Boyer led a circle of Huguenot intellectuals based in Marylebone, where he earned his living by translating French texts into English. He had made his name with his *Compleat French Master*, which ran into twenty-three editions after its publication in 1694. He was also author of the French–English *Royal Dictionary* (which was to remain standard for a century), and, revealingly, panegyrical histories of the reigns of William and Anne.[21]

Boyer's version of *Iphigénie* reveals a French Protestant, intensely loyal to the Hanoverian dynasty, rewriting Racine in a manner calculated to accommodate it to English taste after the Glorious Revolution. Anti-French prejudice is always apparent in the discussion of Racine from Dryden to Hazlitt and Macaulay, who dismissed *Iphigénie* by saying that it put the 'sentiments and phrases of Versailles' in the Camp of Aulis.[22] But Boyer used idiomatic English, heightened the action and spectacle, added racy stage directions, and broke up the longer speeches. He thus did a good job of taking the Versailles out of Aulis altogether. His play was made even less austere and more in tune with the indigenous British tradition of spectacular theatre when it was plagiarized by Charles Johnson under the title *The Victim*, in a version performed at Drury Lane in 1714 and occasionally revived at Covent Garden as late as 1778.[23]

---

[21] Boyer has attracted a great deal of attention from Huguenot historians: see Gwynn (2001), 107, with bibliography in n. 20, and pl. 21.

[22] Quoted in Eccles (1922), 26.

[23] On the 1714 plagiarism see Boyer (1714); on the 1778 revival see *LS* v/1. 156 (23 March at Covent Garden).

There were, however, more numerous English-language adaptations of Euripides' other play about the same heroine, the 'tragicomedy' *IT*. The list includes Charles Davenant's *Circe* (1676–7, but revived in 1682, 1689, 1690, 1701, 1704, 1706, and occasionally thereafter), John Dennis's *Iphigenia* (which competed for the public's attention with Boyer's *Achilles* at the turn of the century), and Lewis Theobald's 1731 *Orestes*; it also includes Handel's *Oreste* (1734), performed in Italian. The subterranean influence of *IT* on the British stage is also apparent in tragedies such as Charles Gildon's *Phaeton* (see Ch. 3). That the interest in *IT* was international is shown by the dozen or so Italian, French, and German operas and ballets (and occasional plays) emerging between 1678 and 1750.[24] But the British versions were enacted against a quite different historical background of fast-changing revolutionary politics.

ROYALIST IPHIGENIA

The adaptability of Euripidean tragicomedy to diverse ideological agendas is exemplified by the different English-language versions of *IT* of the Restoration and the first few decades after the Glorious Revolution. The earliest English-language version of *IT*, which antedates the arrival of William of Orange in England by more than a decade, can actually be read as a legitimation of authoritarian monarchy. The drama was called *Circe* because it imported the famous Odyssean enchantress into the tragic plot by marrying her to Thoas, Euripides' Taurian King. *Circe* was written by the 19-year-old Charles Davenant, the son of William Davenant, a leading cavalier dramatist who had been patronized by Henrietta Maria and ended up in the Tower of London during the Interregnum. He also spent four years in France between 1645 and 1650, and married a young French widow, Henriette-Marie Du Tremblay, in 1655 (she soon gave birth to Charles). Thereafter William began to test the boundaries of the Puritans' proscription on theatre, introducing the word *opera* into the English language in order to avoid the offensive terms *theatre* and *play*, and claiming that his entertainments (performed, for example, at his home in Rutland House in 1656) comprised 'Declamations and Musick; after the manner of

[24] See Gliksohn (1985), 229–30.

the Ancients'. He went to France to join the soon-to-be-crowned Charles II in March 1660, and was rewarded upon the Restoration by receiving, along with Thomas Killigrew, one of the two patents allowing him to manage a new theatrical company, the Duke's at Dorset Gardens.[25]

William Davenant was renowned for innovations in scenic effects, for the training of actresses, and for heroic dramas with a royalist bias. One of his most popular productions was a version of *The Tempest* (1667), on which he collaborated with John Dryden, and which probably informed his son Charles's choice of classical archetype in *Circe*.[26] For of all Shakespearean plays *The Tempest* bears the strongest similarity to *IT*, with which it shares its generic hybridity, farflung exotic setting, encounter with ethnic and cultural difference, and exploration of the colonial experience.

William Davenant died in 1668, when his son Charles was 12 years old, leaving 'Lady Mary' (as his formidable French widow was known) to run his playhouse industry. She was involved in the building of the new Dorset Garden Theatre, and encouraged her eldest son to follow in his father's footsteps.[27] His *Circe* was performed there on 12 May 1677, with Mr and Mrs Betterton as Orestes and Iphigenia. Dryden wrote the prologue. This reworked Greek tragedy is dominated by the themes of love and horror; it is in rhyming couplets and occasionally, when the emotional temperature rises, even rhyming triplets. It is described in its first published edition of 1677, as in all subsequent editions, as a 'tragedy', although in two 'metatheatrical' passages the terminology suggests its spectacular qualities: Thoas' uncouth populace is desperate to watch the executions of Pylades and Orestes, as if they were in 'but a Pageant Tragedie', later described as a 'Tragick Pomp' (20, 29).[28]

The description 'Pageant Tragedy' illuminates the nature of this species of theatre, which fuses song (notably a long scene in Act IV, scene ii featuring a chorus of Bacchanals) with a plot and verse form typical of Restoration heroic tragedy, and then adds tableaux

---

[25] See Harbage (1935), 102, 120–39.
[26] See Dryden and Davenant (1670); Harbage (1935), 259–67; Summers (1934), 228–9.
[27] Harbage (1935), 161.
[28] This and all further references to Davenant's *Circe* are to the original edition of 1677.

and processions characteristic of the masque. Indeed, *Circe* seems
to pay homage to William Davenant's work by harking back nos-
talgically to the court masques favoured by Charles I and his
French queen: it includes ascending and descending divinities
(Pluto, Iris, Cupid), personifications of non-concrete ideas
(Sleep, Dreams), and spectacles almost unrelated to the plot,
such as Orpheus 'discovered' playing his lute on Mount Parnassus.[29] The music was popular, especially after John Bannister's
original score was replaced in the early 1680s with songs by Henry
Purcell.[30] It is, indeed, not at all unlike the 'operatic' works from
the pen of the teenage dramatist's more famous father, which in
addition to *The Tempest* included a musical version of *Macbeth*
complete with flying witches. Yet recently it has been argued that
the strong love interest in *Circe* is a new development and paralleled, rather, in the amorous complexities of Dryden's *Aureng-
Zebe* (1675), Otway's *Don Carlos* (1676), and Durfey's *The Siege
of Memphis* (1676).[31] Nor is *Circe* dissimilar to Dryden's *The
Indian Queen* (1664) in its portrayal of a complicated pattern of
requited and unrequited love, leading to disaster. *Circe* offers a
'love heptagon' out of which only Pylades and Iphigenia survive:
Thoas and his jealous wife Circe are both killed by Orestes; Ithacus
(Circe's son by Ulysses) dies from a battle wound, motivating
Osmida (Thoas' daughter by a previous marriage) to commit suicide; Orestes stabs himself.

The exotic setting is half-heartedly associated with the Ottoman
empire, through the name of Thoas' daughter, Osmida. The equation of the Turks with the barbarian opponents of Greeks to be
found in ancient tragedy was facilitated by the growing awareness,
in the later part of the seventeenth century, of the continued
existence of the Greek nation, an awareness fostered by Milton's
interest in the state of affairs there and by the cultural prominence
of the Greek visitors to England, who were sponsored by Charles
II himself.[32] Yet *Circe* reveals little evidence of the awareness of

---

[29] Rosenfeld (1981) 42; Summers (1934), 232–3, 247. When the Very Revd
Rowland Davies went with two friends to watch a production of *Circe* in the very
year of the Glorious Revolution (13 Aug. 1689), he described its 'extraordinary'
scenes in his diary. See Rowland Davies (1856), 24.

[30] *LS* i. 332.

[31] Cannan (1994).

[32] Spencer (1954), 110–26.

Britain's colonial destiny which permeates the two later versions of *IT* by Dennis and Theobald. This was probably a good thing, since this royalist tragedy was performed on important state occasions before the ambassadors both of Morocco (at Dorset Gardens) and of Bantam in Java.[33]

When the Greeks kidnap Osmida they threaten her with similar brutality as they had themselves expected at the hands of the Taurians. The most pleasant male character transcends the cultural divide: he is the mixed race Ithacus, born of a barbarian enchantress to the Greek hero Ulysses. Indeed, one of the most arresting features of *Circe* is its almost complete absence of interest in the interface between Greek and Scythian, relative to the jingoistic tenor of Dennis and Theobald's later versions of the *IT*: Orestes in Dennis becomes a culture hero educating a barbarous fantasy colony in civilized values and the ideology of liberty before accepting colonial rule, installing a Deputy Governor, and returning home, booty in hand, to his free and advanced metropolis. Only twenty-three years earlier, in Davenant's account, the central interest had been not Liberty but the way that erotic passion threatens the possession of absolute power. Davenant's Orestes, far from being a culture hero, had been just one of several psychologically tortured lovers whose corpses littered the stage at the end.

Davenant's Thoas is a weak, vacillating king, embarrassingly afraid of his own people. He is aware that a marriage between his stepson Ithacus and his daughter Osmida is desired by the Taurians, 'And their Rebellious fury threatens all' (3). Thoas dislikes the practice of human sacrifice, but not enough to use his royal prerogative to abolish it. He must tolerate even rebarbative practices if they are beloved by his restive populace: 'I'm forc'd by Custom, that unwritten Law, | By which the People keep even Kings in awe' (17). The idea of the 'lazy Monarch' who brings destruction on himself and his country is recurrent. Pylades argues that the gods mete out justice appropriately: 'Think not the Gods, like lazy Monarchs, give | To their bold Subjects their Prerogative' (12). Circe is scornful of old men and 'lazy Monarchs' who fail to act decisively against suspected traitors (27). Indeed, Circe is the most articulate political theorist in the play, an advocate of

[33] *LS* i. 304, 309.

autocratic pragmatism. She cautions Thoas that he will need her help to face an invasion by a foreign army, for his 'Coward States-men do all danger shun, | And from the Empire's Helm in tempests run' (37). The Taurian Senate 'protracts' its councils, and con-strains on his royal power to initiate policy: Circe argues that they have become 'advising Tyrants' to whom he, the King, is humili-atingly forced to bow (38).

Circe, the first known version of a Greek tragedy to be per-formed in Restoration England, is rare because there are so few examples of pre-Victorian British readings of Greek drama wholly unaffected by Whig ideals. Davenant is a residual representative of the Cavalier Classicists who had briefly tried to appropriate Greek drama to the cause of the Stuart dynasty: they included Christo-pher Wase, the author of a dissident *Electra* in 1649 (see Ch. 6), Henry Burnell, the anti-Commonwealth translator of Aristopha-nes' *Plutus* in 1659, and Thomas Stanley, who translated Aris-tophanes' *Clouds* (1655) and edited Aeschylus (1663, see Ch. 4). But after *Circe* the still youthful Davenant never attempted to write for the theatre again, instead becoming Inspector of Plays under James II. Subsequent to the Glorious Revolution he relin-quished all loyalty to his ancestral politics, entering parliament, inveighing against France, and faithfully serving Queen Anne. As her Inspector-General of Export and Imports he became respected for his expertise on trade and economics, using his excellent Greek in order to read Xenophon's *Ways and Means* rather than Euripi-dean tragedy.[34]

There is one other way in which Davenant's boyish, exuberant, monarchist *Circe* bears witness to the challenges facing the re-searcher into Greek tragedy's performance reception. The play has never featured in discussions of the *Nachleben* of *IT*, despite its status in that cultural narrative. Many experts have been un-aware that *Circe* uses the *IT* at all, because it has fallen between disciplinary stools.[35] Classicists have been uninterested in per-formance reception, and scholars of literature in modern languages often do not recognize classical archetypes unless the title gives them a clear indication of the source material. Why should anyone

[34] See Whitworth (1771), i, pp. v–vii; Harbage (1935), 162.
[35] Both Gliksohn's excellent diachronic study and Robert Heitner's much-cited article on the *IT* in the 18th c., for example, are unaware of it, urging the influence, rather, of Minato's opera of a year later, *Tempio di Diana in Taurica* (1678).

suspect a Euripidean 'Iphigenia' play of underlying an 'Odyssean' title like *Circe*? Musicologists have begun to pay *Circe* attention as an important work in formal terms, for it adumbrates the evolution of distinctively British theatrical performances, adorned with songs, popular in the eighteenth century. But some critics' lack of engagement with literary history have led them to see it as 'a wholly original composition' with no obvious precursor.[36] There are, however, at least three known works which might have inspired the half-French Davenant, whose father had nurtured such close links with the Continental theatre that he had revisited France after the Restoration in order to update his ideas about scenic effects. Giovanni Rucellai's seminal Renaissance *Oreste*, although it may not have been performed before 1726, had adapted *IT* as early as 1525; Coqueteau de La Clairière's *Pylade et Oreste*, now lost, had been performed by Molière's company, en route to Rouen, in 1659; and in 1666 Joost van den Vondel had published a translation of *IT* into Dutch.[37]

GREEK TRAGEDY AFTER THE GLORIOUS REVOLUTION

Within little more than a decade of *Circe* Charles II was dead, James II had fled, and his son-in-law William III had stepped onto the English sand dunes of Torbay. When he and Mary accepted the Bill of Rights in 1689, the Revolution seemed Glorious indeed. But the new order of things felt fragile, and the theatre in the early eighteenth century became explicitly political. The playhouses sometimes became physical battlegrounds as audiences perceived political subtexts everywhere. They turned the first night of Addison's rousing *Cato* (1713) into a fray, both Whig and Tory claiming the Roman Republican patriot for their own. The politicization of the theatre was most exactly described by the (con-

---

[36] Cannan (1994), 231.

[37] Rucellai's play was certainly performed at the Collegio Clementino during the Roman carnival (where plays were traditionally performed before the cardinals). The subtitle of the 1726 edition reads 'tragedia . . . rappresentata nel Collegio Clementino nelle vacanze del Carnovale dell'anno 1726.' On the Molière production see Gliksohn (1985), 70. The important story of the Dutch reception of Greek tragedy at this time remains largely untold. Michel Le Clerc and Jacques de Coras's *Iphigénie* (first performed Paris in 1675, a year before Davenant and published in 1678), is a version of *IA*.

sciously apolitical) Lewis Theobald (subsequently author of *Orestes*) in *The Censor* for 25 May 1717:

Party and Private Sentiments...wrest an innocent Author to their own Construction, and form to themselves an Idea of Faction from Passages...a War of *Whig* and *Tory* is carried on by way of *Clap* and *Hiss* upon the meaning of a single Sentence, that, unless prophetically, could never have any Relation to Modern Occurrences.

But this type of atmosphere had already prevailed at the time of Dennis's *Iphigenia*, when the Restoration heroic drama was being replaced by 'a drama of Whig self-fulfilment, which signally simplifies both the national and parliamentary perception of the King and his policies'.[38]

The debate preceding the 1701 Act of Settlement, which provided for the Hanoverian succession in the teeth of French opposition, had a lasting impact on the theatre, especially on the fictional worlds created in tragedy. Paradoxically, tragedy was in closer touch than the superficial realism of comedy with the currents of political thought.[39] By taking as its ostensible subject the affairs of noblemen in remote times and exotic places, tragedy's 'self-bounded' world offered imagined contexts in which practical solutions to real problems could be safely explored. A famous example is the dramatic legitimation of the constitutional principles used to justify the Glorious Revolution in Nicholas Rowe's *Tamerlane* (1701). Loftis has shown how plays such as this set the tone of British tragedy for decades, with their 'seemingly endless series of variations on Lockean political ideas'.[40] By the time George I ascended the throne in 1714, dramatists were ransacking history for acts of defiance against tyranny which could be adorned with declamations in support of Whig ideals: ancient Egypt in Edward Young's *Busiris* (1719), ancient Ireland in William Phillips's *Hibernia Freed* (1722), early England in Ambrose Philips's *The Briton* (1722), ancient Spain in Philip Frode's *The Fall of Saguntum* (1727), and classical Athens in Samuel Madden's *Themistocles* (1729). Indeed, the first Prime Minister Walpole's desire to censor the theatre in the 1730s, under George II, reflected the effectiveness of theatre as political propaganda (see Ch. 4).

[38] Hughes (1996), 452.   [39] Loftis (1963), 5.   [40] Ibid. 34.

Ancient myth offered fertile ground for those hunting for exemplary mythical problems of succession, in particular tyrants ousted, like James II, by their sons-in-law. The zeal with which William, Anne, and the first two Georges were acclaimed as legitimate monarchs fails to obscure the anxieties about the dynastic problem, which, along with its constitutional and ecclesiastical implications, failed to go away until after the second Jacobite invasion of 1745. The security of the Protestant succession was felt to be under permanent threat from the exiled Catholic Stuarts, who might at any time attempt to reimpose an absolutist monarchy. In Greek myth the Argive Danaus (succeeded by his daughter Hypermnestra and son-in-law Lynceus) offered a prototype for James II. Robert Owen's tragedy, *Hypermnestra, or, Love in Tears* (1703), is typical of several works on this theme during this period.[41] Owen's tragedy tells how the tyrant Danaus was expelled by the virtuous new king, Lynceus. Danaus' penitent final words ask the audience to 'Behold the just effect of Pow'r abus'd!', and point out that he must now imitate James II and 'wander thro' the world a Royal Beggar'.[42] Sturmy's *Love and Duty: or, The Distres't Bride* (1722) reworked the same myth to identical political effect.[43] Edmund Smith even redesigned Euripides' *Hippolytus* so as to make Hippolytus and his bride Ismena, both outsiders in Crete, candidates for the throne superior to the indigenous but despotic royal family; at the end this 'heav'nly pair', prototypes of William and Mary, leave the 'Continent' of Crete in order to preside over a peaceful freedom-loving empire in mainland Greece.[44]

The Theban Polynices, who attacked his own country with a foreign army, was a useful model for both the Old and the Young Pretenders. The first British attempt since 1566 to stage a play derived from Euripides' *Phoenician Women*, the archetypal civil war tragedy, was conceived in the aftermath of the 1715 Jacobite

---

[41] So great was the influence of Aristotle's *Poetics* that dramatists were inspired to write plays going under the titles of ancient tragedies to be found in that treatise, even though they were lost to posterity. In this case the lost model was Aristotle's discussion of Theodectes' lost *Lynceus* in the *Poetics* (1455^b29). See Gildon (1718), 241. On the impact of the debate around the Act of Settlement on literature in general, see Downie (1994).

[42] Robert Owen (1703), 68.

[43] Sturmy (1722), 53–6. *Love and Duty* opened on 22 Jan. 1722, and ran for six nights. See *LS* ii/2. 659–61.

[44] Edmund Smith (1796), 91.

invasion. Jane Robe's *The Fatal Legacy* (Lincoln's Inn Fields, 1723) blatantly adapts both Racine's *La Thébaïde* and Euripides' *Phoenician Women* in order to support the anti-Jacobite cause. Polynices is a despotic pretender, and in the Epilogue a resurrected Jocasta tells her audience that the 'State-Affairs' of the present day have 'tally'd pretty well' with those of ancient Greece:

> You see, they'd Men their Country would undo,
> Rebellions, Plotters and Pretenders too.

Ancient Thebes has become ancient Britain, the Theban civil war the Jacobite uprising, and Euripides' message been identified as a warning against traitors and pretenders.[45]

JOHN LOCKE AMONG THE TAURIANS

Most successful playwrights of this era publicly espoused anti-Jacobite sentiments, even if they did not go as far as the fanatical John Dennis, whose first play, performed at Drury Lane in 1697, was a propagandist comedy entitled *A Plot and No Plot, or, Jacobite Cruelty*. Dennis argued at about the same date that drama helped to keep people 'from frequenting Jacobite Conventicles, and contributing to our non-swearing Parsons...for as long as the enemies of the State are diverted by publick Spectacles', they will not have time to listen to seditious preachers.[46] Dennis thus actually perceived theatre as an important rival to the allure of Jacobite politics and religion. Two decades later he was still beating the same drum in a rabidly anti-Jacobite Shakespearean adaptation, *Coriolanus, The Invader of his Country* (Drury Lane, 1720).

This may seem absurdly extreme, but the dark days of Charles II's movement into absolutism in the early 1680s were still a recent memory. Many members of the theatrical audiences had witnessed the dreadful persecution of religious dissenters, the expulsion of legitimately elected sheriffs, and the rigged treason trials and executions of influential Whigs. Most of them will have been overjoyed when James II was expelled, and will have shared the passionate allegiance to William III which Dennis so loudly

---

[45] After its premiere on 23 Apr. 1723, however, Robe's crude allegory ran for only two more nights (*LS* ii/2. 720).
[46] Dennis (1698), 66–7.

expressed in his panegyric, *The Monument: A Poem Sacred to the Immortal Memory of the Best and Greatest of Kings*:[47]

> Renown'd Restorer of Lost Freedom, hail!
> Great Patron of the Christian World, all hail!
> At thy approach fierce Arbitrary Power,
> And bloody Superstition disappear.

John Dennis's adaptation of *IT* is not only the earliest but by far the most blatant of all the British Whig appropriations of Greek tragedy (a category that can subsequently be traced to the 1770s and briefly reappeared in the 1830s). For Dennis was not only a fanatical patriot and political zealot; he was also a keen disciple of Dryden,[48] student of Locke, and a versatile man of letters, although he was no great versifier and perhaps deserved his unkind treatment in Pope's *Dunciad* and Swift's *Miscellanies* (1727).

In common with many of the authors in this book, Dennis, the son of a London saddler, came from lowly origins. But he inherited a fortune from a wealthier uncle. His origin and his acquired status as a Man of Property explain his espousal of radical Whig ideas. When his *Iphigenia* was performed at Lincoln's Inn Fields in the winter of 1699 to 1700, the action was concluded by the Genius of England, who drew a parallel between ancient Greek and modern British heroism:

> With silent awe, my Britons, then attend,
> View the great action of a Grecian friend...
> From Grecian fire let English hearts take flame
> And grow deserving of that noble name.
> For not the boundless Main which I controul
> Can so delight my Eyes, or charm my soul,
> As I am pleas'd with my brave Sons I see
> Worthy of Godlike Liberty and me.[49]

The 'great action' consisted of two ancient Greek males, Orestes and Pilades, asserting the superiority of Greek maritime skills, mercantile culture, religion, politics, intellect, valour, and sensibility over those of the introverted, superstitious Scythians of the

---

[47] Dennis (1702), 34.

[48] On Dennis's correspondence with Dryden, see especially Levine (1999), 89–91.

[49] This and all subsequent references to Dennis's *Iphigenia* refer to the text in Dennis (1700).

Black Sea. Beneath the title Dennis inscribes famous words from Cicero's *De Amicitia* (24) in which he praises the man who helps his friend in time of peril, a sentiment which shows that Dennis was less interested in the spinsterly Iphigenia than in the idealized masculinity and mutual loyalty of 'Pilades' and Orestes.

This friendship seems to have had a resonance for the eighteenth-century British middle class, illustrated by the American émigré Benjamin West's dignified painting of 1766 (see Fig. 2.3). West, whom we shall meet again in the chapter on Sophocles' *Electra* (Ch. 6), was the foremost history painter in England in the 1760s, and President of the Royal Academy. He was inspired by Gilbert West's fine translation of *IT*, published originally in his 1749 collection *Odes of Pindar, with Several Other Pieces in Prose and Verse*. This was one of the very few translations of any Euripidean tragedy to have appeared in English by this date. The artist chose the most famous scene from *IT*, and paired its neo-Stoic moral—that male friendship may entail the Ultimate Sacrifice—with that of his Roman History painting, exhibited alongside it, *The Continence of Scipio*. Six decades previously John Dennis had already carved out this terrain by using the same myth to explore some of the most important ideological configurations of the new bourgeois British culture of enlightened, free, male citizens, running a farflung colonial network of global businesses.

Dennis's play offers variations on themes associated with John Locke, the 'idol' of the Whig settlement of 1689. In Locke's *Two Treatises of Government* (1689), especially the second, were found the fundamental concepts of the new dominant British ideology: 'liberty', 'rights', constitutionalism, revolution, public spirit, private property, natural law, social contract, and consent. Locke had himself used Greek myth in his allusion to Ulysses' defiance of Polyphemus' right to govern in the section on 'dissolution of government' in the second *Treatise*.[50]

A recent collection of source materials on the reception of Locke's ideas assembles works published between 1690 and 1704 in defence of the Glorious Revolution. Amongst speeches, sermons, pamphlets and essays, only one drama has been included, and that is a 1704 tragedy by none other than John Dennis, *Liberty Asserted*.[51] Its Canadian setting and Indian characters provide a

---

[50] Locke ('1690'), 228 = (1993), 231.   [51] Goldie (1999).

FIGURE 2.2 Louis du Guernier, frontispiece to Lewis Theobald's translation of *Oedipus, King of Thebes* (1715).

primitivist locale in which to assert the governmental principle of liberty in opposition to (French) tyranny. In *Appius and Virginia* (1709) Dennis was to choose Rome to argue that a Whig perspective is of universal merit. But it had been in the Tauric (i.e. Crimean) peninsular, that Dennis had first experimented with this type of tragedy. Pilades' reproof of the Scythian queen in Act IV of *Iphigenia* is typical of the Lockean rhetoric marking every scene: 'against Nature's Laws we are your Victims, | Against the Right of Nations we're your Captives'. He argues that it is legitimate to use any available means to secure 'fair Liberty. | Which we were born for, and for which we'll die' (34). This is a poetic expression of Locke's account of the legitimate resistance to tyranny, composed in the 1680s in the face of Charles II's repressions.

Inspired by Racine's *Phèdre*, Dennis had flirted with the idea of adapting Euripides' *Hippolytus*, but his attention was drawn to *IT* by Lagrange-Chancel's *Oreste et Pilade*, performed in Paris in 1697. This French play must have been attractive to Dennis, because its one remarkable feature, and the one which most distinguishes it from the providential piety of Rucellai's seminal Renaissance reading of *IT*,[52] is the extent to which the action has been humanized: the *dea ex machina* and most references to divine intervention have been replaced by a plot close to Euripides but far less dependent upon supernatural causation. Dennis's play also shows a 'modern' intolerance of supernatural paraphernalia. This is striking when contrasted with the divine and supernatural beings who thronged Davenant's earlier 'pageant tragedy': demonic spirits, Pluto, Furies, Iris, 'Syrens', nymphs, airborne dragons, Cupid, Morpheus, Phobetor, personifications of pleasant dreams and nightmares, and the ghost of Clytemnestra.

In contrast, Dennis's *Iphigenia* is a humane, serious but optimistic, drama concerned with social anthropology, in particular the stages of political evolution. His barbarous Scythians, forced by custom to sacrifice strangers, learn from their Grecian visitors to transcend their primitive superstitions and learn the ways of the Enlightenment gentleman. The play accords with Dennis's pamphlet polemics against Catholicism and priestcraft, in which he denounces priestly pride as the mainstay of all tyrannies,

---

[52] On which see Di Maria (1996), especially n. 24.

declares the essence of religion to be the humanistic virtues of charity and fellowship, and pronounces pagan Greece to have achieved greater virtue than any Christian society.[53] His upbeat *Iphigenia* is a proto-imperial fantasy in which even savages can abandon superstition and behave like their Grecian/British overlords, thus implicating themselves in the burgeoning colonial ideals of the early eighteenth century. The Greeks are gallant and virtuous: even Agamemnon is exonerated—he did not sacrifice his daughter but smuggled her off to safety in exile in a merchant vessel. Dennis's Whig agenda becomes especially clear if his lively reading of *IT* is compared with the drearily apolitical Hellenism of the two French models he used, which included Quinault's *Phaëton* in addition to Lagrange-Chancel's *Oreste et Pilade*.

Dennis's concept of the educable savage contrasts with the Thoas of every other version of this period performed in England. In Euripides Thoas finally obeys both the will of both the Greeks and of Athena, and survives on his Pontic throne. In both Davenant's *Circe* and Handel's *Oreste*, he dies.[54] But Dennis omits Thoas altogether in favour of a Scythian queen, a beautiful, silly, and superstitious woman, who yet learns to emulate British virtues through the redemptive power of love. She is taught a series of Lockean lessons on contracts, consent, and the subordinate role of religion in diplomacy and politics. She then releases all her Grecian captives and *voluntarily hands over* colonial rule of the Taurian Empire to Orestes. For good measure she throws in his right to select his own bride, for, like a progressive Whig, she has learnt that marriage needs to be grounded in love (see below, Ch. 5):

> Thy souls surpassing greatness I admire!
> Which Heaven that form'd it sure design'd for Empire;
> Accept of mine, thy wiser nobler Sway
> Will polish these *Barbarians* into Men.
> Thine are the vast extended plains of Tauris.
> My self, my Subjects, Men and Women, all
> Shall govern'd be by thy unbounded Sway. (53–4)

It would not be possible to find a clearer example of Greek tragedy adapted to justify Whig principles and the early eighteenth-century expansion of the British empire.

---

[53] Hughes (1996), 442.   [54] On Handel's piece see below, p. 62.

WHIG IPHIGENIA

Whig adaptations of Greek tragedy also absorbed languages derived from British political traditions going further back than Locke, especially Ancient Constitutionalism, which had anticipated Whig historiography's emphases on history, law, and precedent. An idealistic variant was seventeenth-century Classical Republicanism,[55] which had stressed the *freedom* and moral virtue believed to have been enjoyed under some of the ancient constitutions in Greek and Roman history. The quest for classical models of free nation-states was articulated in two non-dramatic poems by authors who subsequently attempted to adapt Greek tragedy for the London stage. James Thomson's *Agamemnon* was preceded by his didactic poem *Liberty* (published between 1734 and 1736), which traces Liberty back to classical Greece, like the serial temples in the 'moral gardens' at Stowe, built from 1711 onwards by 'the greatest Whig in the army', Marlborough's general Richard Temple;[56] Richard Glover's *Medea* was a later work than his famous epic *Leonidas* (1734), which idealizes ancient Greece (especially the Spartans who fell at Thermopylae under Leonidas, their 'Patriot King'), while covertly assaulting Robert Walpole and the King, accused of being no Patriot at all.[57]

In the theatre, indeed, where a Whig perspective was dominant, Athens was offered as an object of emulation several decades before it became an approved ideal amongst politicians or political theorists. The discovery of classical Athens as a legitimate model for mainstream thought is often traced to the ancient historian George Grote in the first half of the nineteenth century.[58] But in 1774 Dorning Rasbotham's tragedy *Codrus* portrayed a mythical war between Sparta and Athens (the source for which was probably Pausanias, *Description of Greece*, 1. 19. 6), and explicitly urged the superiority of the Athenian 'republic' (this term, rather than

---

[55] Fink (1945).   [56] On Stowe see above all Dickinson (1977).
[57] Stern (1940), 119, 124.
[58] Jenkyns (1980), 14–15 argues that it was only in the Victorian era that Periclean Athens had become respectable in mainstream circles, even though it is possible to find enthusiasm for Athenian democracy amongst radicals at the end of the 18th c. Turner (1981), 11, acknowledges that the political parallel between ancient democracy and modern democracy had been established in English writing 'by 1790'. The Athenian democracy was also praised by Bulwer: see Bulwer (2004), and the discussion of Grote and Bulwer in the introduction to Bridges, Hall, and Rhodes (forthcoming).

'democracy', was the one usually deployed at this time). The play's Advertisement describes it as containing 'sentiments which will not be displeasing in a land which prides itself on being a peculiar residence of Freedom' and as an attempt 'at a display of PATRI-OTIC VIRTUE'.[59] Three decades previously James Ralph, a theatrical commentator and advocate of the Athenian 'Republic', had expressed his admiration of the political fervour of the earlier Athenian plays;[60] as early as the turn of the eighteenth century John Dennis had offered the relationship between Athens and her tragic theatre as an ideal. Britons needed to be inspired by the theatre to defend their Liberty against the tyrannical French (Lord Marlborough was about to wage war against them under Queen Anne); they should remember that the Athenians had been able to become the scourge of Asia and the 'Terror of the great King' (of Persia) because their tragic poets 'animated their Armies and fir'd the souls of those brave men, who conquer'd at once and dy'd for their country'.[61]

Yet the most important feature of Dennis's *Iphigenia* is his attempt to marry generic questions to those of contemporary politics. Performed just before the Act of Settlement (1701), which instituted the Hanoverian succession, Dennis recasts his model as a celebration of British spiritual values under threat from continental counter-reformation Catholicism. Greekness symbolizes English valour, while the barbarous Taurians initially represent Continental (and especially French) despotism. But Dennis suggests that the country about to be called Britain (the Act of Union was passed in 1707) requires a new, humane, sophisticated form of theatre all of its own. He turns to Greek tragedy for inspiration at the historical point when dramatists were searching for new, distinctively British forms in which to affirm the identity of their post-revolutionary and newly expanded nation-state. British theorists at this time wrestled with the question of which elements of Neoclassicism—the Aristotelian 'Rules', for example—were to be

---

[59] Rasbotham (1774), p. v. Rasbotham (High Sheriff of Lancashire in 1769), was an amateurish playwright, but did get his politically charged *Codrus* performed in Manchester in 1777 and again in 1778, with actors of the distinction of Kemble and Siddons (see *ODNB* xlvi. 46). The Prologue draws parallels between the ancient Athenian struggle for freedom and the contemporary plight of Greece, ruled by 'the turband tyrant'.

[60] Ralph (1743), 16.

[61] Dennis (1698), 59, citing the Athenian successes at Salamis and Marathon.

rejected as reactionary Continental restrictions on creativity, and which needed to be reformulated as what have (often confusingly) been labelled 'Augustan' aesthetic principles.

Critics of the Whig literature of this era used to dismiss it as complacent and closed off, suffering from a 'fallacy of premature teleology' which misleadingly suggested that the triumph of Liberty in 1689 meant that British history had achieved its ultimate purpose.[62] But recently it has been countered that the Whig project was interrogative and restless, incorporating a vigorous quest for new literary forms, including forms of tragedy, inseparable from the exploratory affirmation of the new political and ideological formations. There was a conviction that only liberty could create inspiration, but also that the Britons' national achievements in the political and social spheres had, at least so far, outstripped their achievements in the arts. Longinus' *On Sublimity*, much studied in Britain after its translation into French in 1674 by Boileau, concludes that sublime art can only flourish under conditions of political liberty (*On the Sublime*, ch. 44). Dennis himself, nicknamed 'Sir Longinus' by his contemporaries,[63] appealed to this Longinian notion of the relationship between freedom and inspiration in *The Grounds of Criticism in Poetry* (1704). After the Earl of Shaftesbury's discussion in his influential *Characteristicks* (1711), it was to surface in the work of almost every man of letters in the eighteenth century. Above all it encouraged Whig writers to attempt to make art for their new Britain truly great.

The inseparability of their aesthetic and their political projects is illustrated by Dennis's account, in the preface to *The Monument* (see above), of the conceptual contiguity of political and poetic freedom. He had decided to abandon rhyme and write in blank verse because he it would give him 'more Liberty', and would allow him 'to shew the Harmony of our Mother Tongue...above that of our Neighbours the French' (pp. ix–x, xiii). The question was not only one of rhyme versus blank verse, or the desirability of the Aristotelian 'Rules' identified with the most reactionary Neoclassicism of the French academy, or even of the preferability of private, domestic stories over heroic tales of siege and conquest

---

[62] See the subtle analysis of this kind of criticism in the preface to Meehan (1986).
[63] Bosker (1930), 27.

(see Ch. 3): the debate was inflamed by the arrival in Britain, at the end of the seventeenth century, of Continental opera.

The opera craze was deplored by scholars and Whig dramatists alike. When Oxford's first Professor of Poetry, Joseph Trapp, delivered his lectures on poetry between 1708 and 1718, he fulminated against Continental opera, 'introduc'd among us from foreign Parts, by the mercenary Traffic of Eunuchs and Courtezans'. The problem with opera, besides its castrato singers and sexually profligate female performers, was the 'monstrous' idea that 'the whole Drama should be Sing-Song'. Trapp upbraids his fellow citizens: 'Broken and unnerv'd *Britains*! Into what shameful Effeminacy are we sunk?'[64]

Trapp was responding to the same situation that had made John Dennis so anxious to distinguish his own serious English-language drama from the fashionable all-sung imported opera of Italy and France. The Prologue to *Iphigenia* opposes opera and tragedy by linking them with the self-definition of the Englishman. The Tragick Muse has left 'the enslav'd Italian' and 'servile Gallia', hoping that in England, where Liberty flourishes, she can once more 'inspire Athenian flights, | And once more tow'r to Sophoclean heights'. But she finds England in love with foreign opera. The Genius of England, in turn, laments that even male audiences are now 'Dissolv'd and dying by an Eunuch's Song'; he urges them to prefer the 'wholesome' and 'severe' tragedy by Dennis.[65] Britishness, manliness, and political liberty are thus symbolized by spoken tragedy; Mediterranean effeminacy and slavishness, on the other hand, are represented by the singing eunuchs and spectacle of the opera house.

Yet the cheerful tone of Dennis's drama confused everyone, even though contemporary taste tolerated wholesale alterations to the plots of Shakespearean tragedy, and dramatic theorists had recently been discussing the constitution and legitimacy of tragicomedy.[66] Charles Gildon, whose own experiments with adapting Euripides were gloomier (see Ch. 3), was unsure whether *Iphigenia*

---

[64] These lectures were delivered in Latin, and are quoted from the English translation published later: Trapp (1742), 240–2. On the history of the arrival of Italian opera in London see especially Nalbach (1972), and *Grove* 7, xv. 114–16, bibliography 129–30.

[65] Dennis (1700), 'Prologue'.

[66] See Maguire (2000).

was a tragedy.[67] Dennis adopts precisely the *lieto fine* that was a staple convention of the opera so irritating to Whigs, by making even happier the 'happy ending' to be found in Euripides (and which Davenant had replaced with the huge body count of his heroic climax). In Dennis nobody important dies, the Greeks escape victorious, love triumphs, and the Scythians are better off than before they were colonized. This is similar in overall thrust to the version of *IA* invariably used in the eighteenth century, in which Iphigenia escapes sacrifice, to general rejoicing. Here, perhaps, lies a clue to the persistent appeal of the Iphigenia plays in the theatre after the Glorious Revolution: both of them enacted human sacrifice joyfully averted. They offered performed affirmations of the possibility not only of surviving trauma but also of emerging from it triumphantly. This plot-shape resonated at a deep psychological level with the experience of the British after the trauma of the seventeenth century and the glorious new dawn of 1689.

COMIC IPHIGENIA

The jolly dimension of *IT* is clearest in Lewis Theobald's *Orestes*, first performed at Lincoln's Inn Fields on 3 April 1731, with Quin as Thoas, Ryan as Orestes, and Mrs Buchanan as Iphigenia. It is described in its published edition as a 'dramatic opera', but it was performed in English. Although it features several choral songs, one solo aria by Pallas, and incidental music accompanied by dancers including Marie Sallé, its long spoken episodes make it seem more dramatic than operatic.[68] In one sense it belongs to the genre of light entertainment on themes from myth exemplified by Elkanah Settle's wildly successful 1707 extravaganza (which Settle himself described as a 'tragicomedy'), *The Siege of Troy*.[69] Theobald himself had made money with spectacular reworkings of classical myths, especially his Ovidian *Apollo and Daphne* and *Rape of Proserpine* at Lincoln's Inn Fields in 1726 and 1727 respectively.[70] This type of entertainment persisted even during decades when Greek tragedy was absent from the stage: there was a show performed at Sadler's Wells between April and July

---

[67] Gildon (1702), 37.   [68] Richard Foster Jones (1919), 151.
[69] Settle (1708).   [70] Rosenfeld (1981), 16–18, 32, 51–2.

1792, for example, to the delight of the Duke of Clarence, which was based on the fourth book of the *Aeneid* and entitled *Queen Dido, or the Trojan Ramblers*. It was complemented by the harlequinade *Medea's Kettle* (not based on the tragedy), which included a scene in which the sorceress aroused witches who ranged 'abroad in the shape of animals'.[71]

Orestes, however, was rather more than a classical spectacular. Theobald was an accomplished Greek scholar. In addition to his important translations of Sophocles (see Chs. 6 and 8; Fig. 2.2), he published translations of Aristophanes' *Clouds* and *Plutus* in 1715 (fig. 2.4). He also worked for years on a translation of Aeschylus which remained unpublished and has disappeared.[72] The unique status of Theobald's *Orestes* as an eighteenth-century comic burlesque of a specific Greek tragedy results from its author's engagement with both the contemporary theatre (he was not only an inveterate playgoer, but a significant dramatic critic) and with Greek theatrical texts in the original. The burlesque element is a sign of Theobald's times, for this genre was largely created in Britain during the first half of the eighteenth century.[73] Parodying elevated classical texts came easily to English-language authors; a large proportion of the texts listed in Richmond Bond's register of British burlesque poems published between 1700 and 1750 are responses to Greek or Latin epics.[74] It was also commonplace to defend burlesque by pointing to the ancient Athenians' taste for parody, as exhibited, for example, in Aristophanes.[75] But Greek tragedy was still too unfamiliar a form to generate a tradition of burlesque at this stage, which makes Theobald's humorous experiment all the more exceptional.

[71] British Library, *Collections Relating to Sadler's Wells*, ii: *1787–1795*, nos. 102, 105, 109.

[72] *Orestes*, most unusually, shows knowledge of Aeschylus' *Eumenides*, above all in the dialogue between Orestes and Clytemnestra's ghost in Act II; like Aeschylus' spectre at the Delphic oracle, Theobald's ghost of Clytemnestra arises and talks of how she, her Furies, 'and my wound' shall persecute her son, a clear reminiscence of *Eumenides* 103. Although Clytmenestra's ghost had also appeared in *Circe*, the verbal reminiscences of Aeschylus are clearer in the Theobald version. Theobald's *Persian Princess* (performed 1708, published 1715) also has echoes of Aeschylus' *Persians*. His personal collection of books contained the editions of Aeschylus by both Turnebus and Stephanus: see Corbett (1744), 6, 12.

[73] Bond (1932), p. ix. On the importance of Theobald's dramatic criticism in the *Censor*, see Charles Harold Gray (1931), 53–4.

[74] Bond (1932), 237–453.

[75] Ibid. 52.

FIGURE 2.3 Benjamin West, *Pylades and Orestes Brought as Victims before Iphigenia* (1766).

This is interesting given the direction in which British adaptation of Greek tragedy was to move in the early Victorian era, when comic, musical burlesques of *Antigone* or *Medea* were to become staples of the popular theatre (see Chs. 12–14). Like Theobald's *Orestes*, which is saturated with the texts of Shakespeare which he had edited, the Victorian burlesques were to specialize in combining Shakespearean and Greek tragic elements.[76] There was an intermediate phase in the second half of the eighteenth century, when parodic musical entertainments on mythical themes were popularized through the classical 'burlettas' of the Irish playwright Kane O'Hara. These had juxtaposed demotic Irish jigs with elevated arias from operas, and mocked conventional reverence for

---

[76] Theobald's monumental critical edition of Shakespeare was first published in 1733 in seven volumes. For an evaluation of his methods and achievement as a scholar and editor, see Richard Foster Jones (1919).

FIGURE 2.4   Frontispiece to Lewis Theobald's translation of Aristophanes' *Plutus: or, the World's Idol* (1715).

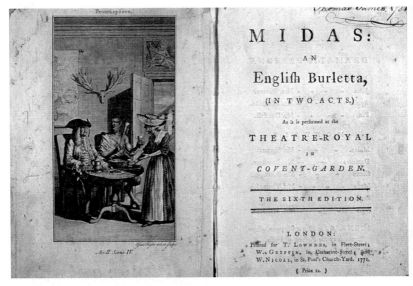

MIDAS:

AN

Engliſh Burletta,

(IN TWO ACTS.)

As it is performed at the

THEATRE-ROYAL

IN

COVENT-GARDEN.

THE SIXTH EDITION.

LONDON:

Printed for T. LOWNDES, in Fleet-Street;
W. GRIFFIN, in Catharine-Street; and
W. NICOLL, in St. Paul's Church-Yard. 1771.

(Price 1s.)

FIGURE 2.5   Title-page and frontispiece, engraved by Isaac Taylor, to the 1771 London edition of Kane O'Hara's *Midas*.

the Greeks and Romans. O'Hara's *Midas*, first performed in London in 1764, updated the myth of Midas and the ass's ears (see Fig. 2.5), and *The Golden Pippin* (Covent Garden, 1773) burlesqued the story of Paris and Oenone. Contemporary reviewers objected that O'Hara's 'gods and goddesses frequently speak the language of a Wapping landlady'.[77] Theobald's *Orestes* anticipates these burlettas, but it remains the only eighteenth-century English burlesque of Greek tragedy.

Theobald had collaborated on John Rich's revival of Davenant's *Circe* at Lincoln's Inn Fields in April 1719, and this must have inspired his own *Orestes*, a decade and a half later.[78] Despite playing simultaneously with Fielding's Drury Lane hit *The Tragedy of Tragedies* (which parodies an earlier work by Theobald, *The Persian Princess*), large audiences came to see *Orestes*, and it enjoyed the favour of the Prince of Wales.[79] Yet Theobald disliked

---

[77] *The Westminster Magazine* no. 1, February 1773, p. 165, quoted in the discussion of the tone of O'Hara's burlettas by Maxwell (1963), 135.

[78] Richard Foster Jones (1919), 151.

[79] Woods (1949), 419–24.

politics, and at the time of *Orestes* was distancing himself from the Whig 'patriot opposition' to the unpopular Prime Minister Robert Walpole, a group which clustered around the Prince; *Orestes* is actually dedicated to Walpole, in thanks for a recent favour. But despite its avowedly apolitical (and arguably Tory) author, if *Orestes* is compared with *Circe*, it exemplifies the penetration of Whig ideology into British thought.

When Thoas confronts Orestes and Pylades, Pylades answers him by telling him to stick to 'lording it over' his own people, and stop trying

> to stretch Controul o'er those,
> Who are not subject to your Scepter's Sway.
> Kings, who impose Commands that are unjust
> Forfeit that name to wear the Brand of Tyrants. (10)[80]

Yet radical politics are a subject of mirth in this reading of *IT*. The third act of *Orestes* has one deeply Aristophanic sequence, where the Greek sailors discuss setting up a new colonial state in Scythia. This send-up of a constitutional debate, which draws on ideas in both *Birds* and *Assemblywomen*, is comically larded with the language of earlier English revolutions than the Glorious one of 1689: 'We are to be a Commonwealth, and every Man shall have an equal Vote' says the first sailor (42), commended by his third colleague, who turns out to be a Leveller: 'Ay, ay, all upon a Level. I'll suffer no Man to be greater than my self'.

The chief importance of this play, however, is generic. Theobald's prologue discusses the relationship of this work to Davenant's *Circe*, a tragedy which used rhyming couplets 'your Fathers' Ears to charm'. In place of rhyme, Theobald says his version offers song, dance, and 'the Painter's Art', for *Orestes* was scenically beautiful. The musical numbers, which owe much to Davenant's play, included a song-and-dance in honour of Mithra in Thoas' palace at the end of Act I, and a lamplit song to 'Harsh Musick' by the three Furies pursuing Orestes in Act II. Act III boasts a song by Pallas, descending in a chariot of Clouds, an epiphany of Circe in a dragon-drawn chariot, and an erotic number in her bower as she tries to seduce Orestes. In this Act three magicians sing an

---

[80] This and all subsequent references to Theobald's *Orestes* are to the text in Theobald (1731).

invocation to Hecate, drawing on *Macbeth*. The climax is the rescue of the statue of Pallas, followed by the fight between the Scythians and the Greeks, led by Thoas and Orestes respectively. This was displayed by clever machinery as 'A Wheeling Fight seen thro' the Wood'.

Some of the best moments are provided by the 'Shakespearean' diversion of working-class Greek mariners, whose comic banter in prose imitates *The Tempest*'s sailors. Yet Theobald regarded *Orestes* as less trivial than much indigenous theatrical entertainment, typified (allegedly) by Fielding's *The Tragedy of Tragedies*. The prologue to *Orestes*, curiously written by Fielding, argues that there is a place for a form of English drama that *Orestes* exemplifies. The quest seems to be for an elegant yet cheerful theatre which avoided coarseness and could offer an alternative to the Italian opera house on the one hand and to uproarious satire on the other: Mrs Younger (who played Hermione) asked the audience,

> Once in an Age, at least, your Smiles dispense
> To English Sounds, and Tragedy that's Sense.
> These are Variety to you, who come
> From the Italian Opera, and Tom Thumb. (77)

Like Dennis before him, Theobald thus turned to the 'hybrid' tragicomedy of Euripides' *IT* when trying to develop a new form of theatre. Yet ultimately his proto-burlesque, however expertly written, remains a reworking of Davenant's meaty 'pageant tragedy', minus Davenant's fatalities. The ideological flexibility of Euripidean tragicomedy is better demonstrated by comparing the adaptations of Davenant and Dennis, which show that within twenty-three years the same text could be used to defend the ideology of royal prerogative or to dismantle it and replace it with a passionate defence of the British businessman's right to rule the global waves.

THE INVESTIGATION OF IPHIGENIA

This chapter has taken the versions of Euripides' Iphigenia plays performed between the Restoration and the early 1730s as a case study in the British performance of Greek tragedy at this time. After the Glorious Revolution, and for the first few decades of the eighteenth century, the appeal of both plays was related to their affirmation of escape from suffering into a brave new world, a positive message which resonated in the early years of the Whig settlement. *IT* had other attractions, especially the scope it offered for exploring issues related to an expanding empire and its mercantile culture. But the most important result has been the revelation of the transparent methods by which Greek tragedy was adapted in order to fit the ideological imperatives of the time. This was in a period during which the emergence of journalism, through the media of the political pamphlet, the periodical essay and above all the newspaper, produced an informed London middle class, fascinated by public affairs, and expecting to see them discussed in serious theatre. The generic and ideological elasticity of *IT*, the sole example of Euripidean tragicomedy to be revived in this period (*Ion* was not discovered in Britain until 1754, while *Helen* and *Electra* scarcely featured at all), produced exceptionally heterogeneous theatrical reactions. In Davenant, Dennis, and Theobald, the play inspired an extreme monarchist, an extreme Whig, and a lapsed Tory; they respectively wrote a rhymed heroic tragedy, a redemptive adventure story in blank verse, and a musical burlesque with comic dialogue.

From this perspective, the variegated story of Euripides' Iphigenia is atypical of the experience of Greek tragedy on the eighteenth-century British stage, but in other ways it exemplifies certain general features of the reception of Greek tragedy in this era. Investigating the experience of the Iphigenia plays has shown that there is a relationship between the theatrical revival of ancient Greece and several other modish types of setting and revivalism (Roman, Turkish, ancient Egypt and Persia, North American Indian). Adapting a Greek tragedy for performance, as opposed to merely translating it, seems to have been seen as a rite of passage for aspiring men of letters. Those who did it only once include Davenant, Boyer, Dennis, and Theobald: others whom we shall meet in subsequent chapters include Charles Johnson, Richard West, Edmund Smith, and William Whitehead. This can not be explained solely by the limited success with which some (though by no means all) of these experiments in Greek tragedy met in the commercial theatre. It is as significant that their versions are sites for *practical* experimentation with dramatic form and aesthetics, signposted in the prefaces and prologues, and related to their more *theoretical* meditations, published in treatise and pamphlet. Dennis and Theobald, for example, both wrote extensively on the nature and function of drama. This Augustan and early Hanoverian phenomenon—the 'initiatory' Greek tragedy—must partly have been a response to the Dryden–Lee *Oedipus*, seen in relation to Dryden's theoretical discussions of tragic form, translation, and adaptation (see Ch. 1).

Three years after Theobald's *Orestes*, the first of many operas based on *IT* was performed in London, with Madame Sallé (again) as one of the dancers: the work was Handel's *Oreste*.[81] Handel used an anonymous libretto adapted from Giangualberto Barlocci's *L'Oreste*, which had been written for Benedetto Michaeli's opera of that name (first produced in Rome in 1723), and its monochrome politics have little to say about the British scene: Thoas is both wicked tyrant and sexual predator, but he is killed when the Greeks restore liberty to his rebellious people. Handel's text diminished even further the political impact of Barlocci's play by cutting some recitative discussing Thoas' tyranny in the first act.[82] Handel's *Oreste* heralds the fate of *IT* for the next century and a half, during which it was rediscovered as an elevated text for serious adaptation in opera, in particular Tommaso Traetta's *Iphigenia in Tauride* (1763, first performed in London at Mrs Blaire's private house in London in 1789), and subsequently Gluck's *Iphigénie en Tauride* (of which the first performance in England took place at the King's Theatre in 1790). The same destiny awaited the Aulic Iphigenia. Despite the occasional revival of revised versions of Boyer's play, the continuing presence of the sacrificed maiden at masquerades and fairground spectacles, and by the 1790s in Italian opera (Cherubini) and French ballet (Noverre),[83] from quite early in the century onwards she was not prominent as a serious tragic heroine. What had made Iphigenia so appealing during the political and aesthetic upheavals of the late seventeenth and early eighteenth centuries was her generic versatility. But it was not many years into the eighteenth century before a new type of tragic

---

[81] In 2000 Handel's *Oreste* was given its first revival in England for over two and a half centuries, during the English Bach Festival, in the Linbury Studio Theatre at Covent Garden.

[82] See Hicks (2000), 10.

[83] Noverre's *Iphiginia* [sic] *in Auliede* [sic] (King's Theatre, 23 Apr. 1793 and repeatedly thereafter) was very magnificent indeed: see *LS* v/3. 1540.

heroine, modelled on much less flexible lines, was to oust almost all others from the patent theatres. The eighteenth century developed an insatiable appetite for distressed mothers facing moral quandaries. The time had come for Euripides' virginal Iphigenia to give way to his suffering matrons—Phaedra, Alcestis, Andromache, Hecuba, Creusa, and Medea. It is to these distressed mothers that the next chapter turns.

3

Greek Tragedy as She-Tragedy

'THE WRONGS OF WEEPING BEAUTY'

Towards the beginning of Beryl Bainbridge's novel *According to Queeney* (2001), the hypochondriacal Dr Johnson suffers a terrible turn. Unshaven, distracted, convinced he is on the threshold of death or madness, he locks himself in his bedroom. He will not unbolt the door until the well-meaning Revd John Delap, paying a chance visit, is persuaded to go to him. Dr Johnson gabbles wildly; Delap declaims the Lord's Prayer. In a crisis witnessed by Johnson's servants and newly arrived visitors, the Thrales, Johnson falls to his knees and wrestles with the good clergyman. Delap flees from the house, his white stockings falling round his ankles. It is an emotional—indeed hysterical—scene, full of pain and terror, passions in the delineation of which the real Delap, a keen tragedian, saw himself as a specialist.[1]

It is not clear from Bainbridge's novel whether she had sensed the comic potential of this clergyman from studying his fascination with the more sensational scenes in Euripides. For two of Delap's plays were emotional adaptations of Greek tragedy, and his choice of subject matter illustrates the eighteenth century's prodigious attraction to virgins facing sacrifice. The appeal of the sacrifice of Iphigenia at all levels of public entertainment was illustrated in the previous chapter; this one begins with the other two Euripidean virgins who palpitated on the altar, Polyxena and Macaria. Delap scored only a modest success with *Hecuba* (1761), and blamed Mrs Pritchard for identifying herself so much with the Trojan queen's role that she had suffered fits and 'spoilt his *Hecuba* by sobbing so much'.[2] But he was not to be deterred from his Euripidean project, and in the prologue to his turgid adaptation of *Heraclidae*, which

---

[1] Bainbridge (2001), 16–20.
[2] See Highfill et al. (1979–93), xii. 185. The anecdote was related by Thomas Gray to William Mason (see Ch. 7).

he confusingly titled *The Royal Suppliants*, he promised 'to make soft bosoms sigh' again.[3]

The play enjoyed a prologue by Hester Thrale (Queeney's mother and Dr Johnson's muse), who recorded in her diary after the first night that the performance 'swims delightfully';[4] it subsequently enjoyed a fairly long run, and found its way to the provinces, including the Theatre Royal in Bath.[5] The opening reflects the Euripidean original—Heracles' family is gathered at an altar on Athenian territory, taking refuge from 'Eurystheus' impious rage'. Yet Delap's primary focus is the sacrifice of Macaria, a theme which is stretched all the way from Act II, when Macaria is told of the oracle demanding either her life or her mother's, to the final act, when she reappears, rescued, to a reunion with her mother and betrothal to her beloved, Prince Acamas of Athens.

This tale of mother–child devotion entails demanding roles for two actresses. Miss Elizabeth Farren was ravishing as Macaria and Mrs Ann Crawford (the incomparable Ann Barry, who had taken her new husband's surname) was regal as her mother Deianira, imported from Pausanias, *Description of Greece* 1. 32. 5 rather than Sophocles' *Trachiniae*. Macaria is all 'lovely tears'; Acamas responds to her 'filial sighs, | The wrongs of weeping beauty, that might move | The world to arms'. The audience watches her mysterious calm in Act II, her terror as she prepares to die in Act III ('whence are these | Loud throbs? Why rush my spirits through my breast?'), her advance across the stage in Act IV, 'drest like a Victim, attended by Priests', culminating in her apparent last words 'My full heart must not—oh, it cannot speak | This tumult of emotion.' Act V offers a titillating description of her walk to the altar, her 'bosom bare' and her head 'uplifted for the stroke'. The role written for Deianira is no less emotive: she laments her dead husband, says farewell to her son Hyllus as he goes into battle, and gushes throughout her scenes with her daughter, culminating in a physical fight as they vie for the privilege of being slaughtered. Like Hecuba in Euripides' *Hecuba*, Deianira refuses to release her beloved child: 'thus entwined, | We'll die together in each other's arms, | Mother and daughter.' Greek tragedy has been refashioned

---

[3] Delap (1781). Euripides' *Helen* more remotely informs a third Delap drama, *The Captives* (1786).
[4] See Balderston (1942), i. 484–5; Knapp (1961), 12, 13.
[5] *LS* v/1. 409–23; Hare (1977), 77.

as a concatenation of pathetic 'situations' exploiting maternal pain and persecuted loveliness.[6]

Delap's *The Royal Suppliants* is the last and most sensational example of a minor but persistent genre in the 1700s—the ancient Greek tragedy transformed into a 'She-Tragedy', the label bestowed early in the century on a type of drama focused on a woman in pain. The majority of Greek tragedies adapted for the eighteenth-century British stage were by Euripides, and most of them were dominated by a suffering heroine. This trend began eight decades before Delap's *The Royal Suppliants* with Charles Gildon's adaptations of *Medea* as *Phaeton* (1698), and *Alcestis* as *Love's Victim* (1701). In addition to Delap's plays and those involving Iphigenia discussed in the previous chapter, the subsequent Euripidean She-Tragedies included Edmund Smith's *Phaedra and Hippolitus* (1707), Jane Robe's *The Fatal Legacy* (1723, an anti-Jacobite play, also discussed in Ch. 2, related to Euripides' *Phoenician Women*), Richard West's *Hecuba* (1726), Charles Johnson's *The Tragedy of Medæa* (1730), James Thomson's 1739 *Edward and Eleonora* (based on *Alcestis*, see Ch. 4), William Whitehead's 1754 *Creusa* (based on *Ion*, see Ch. 5), and above all Richard Glover's *Medea* (1767). The feminized, emotional adaptation of Euripides, more than any other phenomenon discussed in this book, casts doubt on the long-standing academic assumption that between the Restoration and the late eighteenth century it was Roman models, rather than Greek, which dominated manifestations of English classicism.[7]

DISTRES'T MOTHERS IN THE RESTORATION

This is not to say that the influence of Seneca was not still palpable. A significant forerunner of the female-focused adaptation of Greek tragedy was *The Destruction of Troy* (1678) by John Bankes (or Banks), which drew heavily on Seneca's *Troades*. Ostensibly in the longstanding tradition of the male-dominated 'siege-and-conquest' heroic play (e.g. Dryden's *Conquest of Granada*, which appeared in two parts in 1670 and 1672 respectively), this tragedy

---

[6] Delap (1781), 14, 26, 44–5, 69–73.

[7] See e.g. the absence of Greek tragedy from James Johnson (1972), and note also the underlying assumption that the Victorians rejected the longstanding primacy of Roman influence, in Frank Turner (1989).

nevertheless focuses more closely than the Latin play on the psychological effects of the siege on Cassandra, an erotic Helen, a tragic Deianira, and a tender Andromache. Moreover, it challenges the heroic play's perspective on empire and violence by seeing them from a female perspective which casts them as male cruelty: Achilles urges his men, 'Against the Women shut your Eyes, and Ears, | Be deaf to their loud Cries, and blind to all their Tears'.[8] In the same year the *Oedipus* of Dryden and Lee, of which Seneca is one source, had significantly increased the role of Jocasta to extend from her appearance at the end of the first act until her sensational expiry near the close of the fifth (see Ch. 1).[9] In accordance with Restoration tragedy's fondness for presenting the traumatized female body as spectacle, the impact of her death-scene can be surmised from the stage direction (V. i), '*Scene draws, and discovers Jocasta held by her Women, and stabb'd in many places of her bosom, her hair dishevel'd, her Children slain upon the Bed*' (see Fig. 1.3).[10] Jocasta's maternal love for her children is stressed by the addition to the plot of her crazed infanticide, and her conjugal love for Oedipus is upgraded to a passionate attachment.

Dryden and Lee, of course, drew on a French tradition of adaptation in which Senecan tragedy had been important. And despite one or two Restoration experiments with updating Senecan plays, notably John Crowne's *Thyestes* (1681), the Senecan influence on English-language tragedy at this time was usually mediated through French dramas, above all those of Racine. The sources of his masterpiece *Andromaque* (1667), an account of Andromache's experiences as captive in Epirus after the fall of Troy, include several passages from Seneca as well as Euripides' *Andromache*. More formative than either, however, is Aeneas' account of his encounter with the heroine in *Aeneid* III. The crucial point is that the success of *Andromaque* drew English authors' attention to Euripides' lovelorn and maternal heroines, and eventually inspired one of the most durable of all eighteenth-century English-language She-Tragedies, Ambrose Philips's *The Distrest Mother* (1712, see Figs. 3.1 and 3.2).

---

[8] Bankes (1679), 50. On Bankes's plays as the forerunners of 'She-Tragedy' see Waith (1971), 267–9.

[9] Ashby (1927), 8–9 and n.1.

[10] See Howe (1992), 39–43.

FIGURE 3.1　J. Roberts, engraving of Miss Elizabeth Younge (later Mrs Pope) in the role of Hermione in Ambrose Philips's *The Distrest Mother* (published 1776).

FIGURE 3.2　J. Thornthwaite, engraving of William Farren in the role of Orestes in Ambrose Philips's *The Distrest Mother* (published 1797).

A new perception that the heroines of the original Greek tragedies might be more important than Seneca's underlies the critical practice of the influential theorist Thomas Rymer, who in the same

year as Dryden and Lee's *Oedipus* compares Senecan tragedy with
its Greek prototypes. Inspired by the success of Racine's *Phèdre* in
France the year before (1677), he dwells on the figure of Phaedra.
His sensitive discussion of Euripides' portrayal of this heroine
commends her modesty, her virtue in not naming Hippolytus to
the nurse, and especially her restraint in not 'solliciting her Son
face to face'. Rymer is impressed by Phaedra's first scene in Euripides, because her derangement is a believable result of her
physical state:

And now for three days had she neither eat nor slept . . . No wonder then if
she talks very madly, she is in an hundred minds all at once, she tries all
places and postures, and is always unesie . . . Here is a *Scene* of *Madness*,
but not of *Bedlam*-madness, here is *Nature* but not the *obscenities*, not the
blindsides of Nature.

Euripides, says Rymer, is superior to Seneca in probability, in
occasioning 'pitty', and in ethical example. He also argues that
women would 'pitty' Euripides' Phaedra more, because they know
no woman resembling Seneca's heroine, 'Nor can they allow her
more compassion than to a Bitch or *Polecat*'.[11] Here Rymer is
laying the theoretical groundwork for the British theatrical debut
of Greek tragic heroines, impersonated by famous actresses for an
audience with an influential female component, and designed to
elicit emotional identification and sympathy.

THE INVENTION OF SHE-TRAGEDY

Rymer's preoccupations prefigure the changes shortly to take place
in the content and emotional impact of tragedy. In the 1690s the
London stage underwent a transformation, culminating in Jeremy
Collier's polemic against the raucous and often near-obscene content of Restoration drama, *A Short View of the Immorality and
Profaneness of the English Stage* (London, 1698). The rising generation of theatre-goers preferred a more domestic and pathetic
drama; causes for this shift in taste have been sought in the monarchy's declining interest in the theatre under Mary and Anne, the
greater decorousness and familial culture of the aristocratic court
circles, and the middle class's increasing access to the theatre.[12]

---

[11] Rymer (1678), 79–98.   [12] See Ballaster (1996), 279–80.

English-speaking dramatic authors were consciously looking
around for stories about suffering (but fundamentally decent)
women at exactly the same time as Euripides, quite suddenly,
become more accessible to them. In 1694 there was published in
Cambridge the first complete edition of Euripides by an Englishman, Joshua Barnes; his *Euripidis quae extant omnia* is an intelligent piece of scholarship and a spectacularly beautiful volume.
Within seven years of his edition the London stage witnessed the
two earliest heroine-dominated tragedies based on Greek models,
which were also the first ever English-language adaptations of
Euripides' *Medea* and *Alcestis*. The author was the feminist and
deist Charles Gildon. His *Phaeton* owes details to Quinault's *Phaëton* and Euripides' *IT*, but most of its speeches and situations to
Euripides' *Medea*, in particular in its emotive use of children.[13]
The author commended Frances Mary Knight for her striking
delivery of demanding 'rants' in the role of the Medea-figure
Althea, especially after her two small sons have been torn to pieces
off stage.[14] In Gildon's *Love's Victim, or the Queen of Wales* of
three years later, the heroine, Queen Guinoenda, is persuaded to
drink poison in order to save the life of her husband (who boasts
the name Rhesus, the title of a play attributed—although probably
wrongly—to Euripides), but only expires after a long death scene
featuring the loving couple and their children. The dominant
model is *Alcestis*, although in his Preface Gildon says that he
also used 'incidents' and 'sentiments' from Euripides' *Helen* and
Andromache.[15]

The rediscovery of Euripides' own mothers, combined with the
outstanding success of Racine's *Phèdre* (1677), inevitably produced an interest in Euripides' *Hippolytus*. Edmund Smith's *Phædra and Hippolitus* of 1707 has often, quite wrongly, been
dismissed as a pale imitation of the French adaptation. It is actually
quite different—far more Euripidean, far less Senecan, and with a
much more tender heroine; she fell passionately in love with Hippolitus when he manfully rescued her from an attack by a wild boar

[13] See Rothstein (1967), 153. On Gildon's religious radicalism, and progressive
views on gender and even race, see Hughes (1996), 442–3.

[14] See John Harold Wilson (1958), 55–6.

[15] See Robert D. Hume (1976), 451. *Love's Victim* premiered on an unknown
date in the spring of 1701. Betterton played Rhesus to Mrs Bracegirdle's Guinoenda. See *LS* ii/1. 10.

(see Fig. 3.3), and has developed a chaste and affectionate friendship with him, but never acts on her desire until she believes she is
a widow. Her loving nature is further demonstrated in her tenderness towards her own baby son by Theseus. As the epilogue puts it,
the topic of the play is love. Its author is

> An Oxford man, extremely read in Greek,
> Who from Eu-ripides makes Phædra speak;
> And comes to town to let us know
> How women lov'd two thousand years ago.

The play premiered at what was then known as The Queen's
Theatre (after Queen Anne's death the King's Theatre) on 21
April 1707, with a stellar cast including Betterton as Theseus and
Booth as Hippolitus, in addition to the incomparable Elizabeth
Barry. It ran for several nights. But, more importantly, it was not
only held in high critical esteem throughout the century (see
Fig. 3.4), but actually revived until as late as 1785, including
exciting performances by Mrs Boheme in 1723, Mrs Porter in
1726–7, and in three separate seasons in the 1750s by Hannah
Pritchard at Drury Lane.[16]

The trend towards plots based on a nuclear family including
young children had made *Medea*, *Alcestis*, and *Hippolytus* attractive. It went in tandem with the innovative delicacy of feeling
which, in his *Iphigenia* (1699–1700), John Dennis ascribes to his
Greek model. In his Preface he says that when the *Iphigeneia in
Tauris* was first performed, 'the Athenians, who were certainly the
most ingenious, and most delicate people that ever were in the
world, were not only charm'd, but ravish'd with it'. The language
of 'ingenuity', 'delicacy', and 'charm' signals the new aesthetics of
tragedy, replacing heroic drama's associated concepts of terror and
awe. This is apparent in the virtue of the young females. Iphigenia
misses Greece, and 'the sweet society of Ladys' whose souls were
'with ev'ry Grace and Virtue fraught'; she thus incarnates the taste
for 'virtue in distress' which was to condition the fiction and drama
of the entire eighteenth century.[17]

---

[16] It was also performed at the Theatre Royal, Bath, in 1754: see Hare (1977), 7.
An operatic version, with music by the Irish organist and composer Thomas
Roseingrave, was produced at Smock Alley, Dublin on 6 Mar. 1753: see Nicoll
(1952–9), iii. 339. For the esteem in which the play was held in the second half of the
18th c. see Charles Harold Gray (1931), 126–7.

[17] Dennis (1700), 2–4.

FIGURE 3.3   James Heath, engraving of Hippolitus rescuing Phædra from a boar on the night of her wedding to Theseus (published 1797).

FIGURE 3.4 J. Thornthwaite, engraving of Mrs Ann Barry in a revival of Edmund Smith's *Phædra and Hippolitus* (1777).

The symbolic figure of the distressed maiden expressed the complex relationship between the belief that humans were fundamentally benevolent, and the realization that the world was often inimical to the achievement of happiness: as has been argued in relation to eighteenth-century fiction, the 'sentimental tribute of a tear exacted at the spectacle of virtue in distress was an acknowledgement at once of man's inherent goodness and of the impossibility of his ever being able to demonstrate his goodness effectively'.[18] Iphigenia has survived a rape attempt and a shipwreck, undergoes numerous harrowing emotional vicissitudes, and spends much of the play in chains, awaiting sacrifice.

The increasing availability of French and English translations of Greek tragedy during the early eighteenth century, especially the translation of Sophocles' *Electra* by André Dacier (1693, see Ch. 6), was an important factor in the invention of 'She-Tragedy'. It was perhaps inspired by the distinction made in Aristophanes' *Women at the Thesmophoria* between a tragic plot with a man at the centre of the action (*andreion drama*) and one revolving around a woman (*gunaikeion drama, Thesm.* 151–5). The term 'She-Tragedy' seems to have been coined in the first few years of the eighteenth century by the dramatist Nicholas Rowe; it is to be found, for example, in the telling context of the epilogue to his 'pathetic' tragedy *Jane Shore* (1714), featuring a distressed heroine from English history. Rowe profoundly influenced the eighteenth-century stage, including its response to Greek tragedy, but the reverse influence, Greek tragedy's impact on Rowe, has been underestimated. A fine classical scholar, he wrote an important translation of Lucan's *Pharsalia*. But he also studied Greek drama closely, and almost certainly collaborated with Lewis Theobald on a translation of Sophocles' *Ajax* published anonymously (Fig. 3.5).[19]

Rowe had begun to depart from heroic themes in *The Ambitious Stepmother* (1700), when he first announced that he was seeking to elicit pity and tears. By the time he wrote the prologue to *The Fair Penitent* (1703), he was formulating his aim as the substitution of 'A melancholy tale of private woes' for the now obsolete material of heroic tragedy, which he describes as 'The Fate of Kings and

---

[18] Brissenden (1974), 29.
[19] Anon. (1714*b*). On the question of its authorship see Ingram (1965).

FIGURE 3.5   Frontispiece (designed and engraved by Louis du Guernier, showing one of the altercations over Ajax' corpse) and title page from the earliest English translation of Sophocles' *Ajax* (1714).

Empires'.[20] Rowe used one Greek heroine, Penelope, when experimentally developing the 'She-Tragedy' (see Fig. 3.6). In *Ulysses* (Drury Lane 1705), the prologue promises that the hero's wife is a model of dutiful wifehood:

> To Night, in Honour of the marry'd Life,
> Our Author treats you with a Virtuous Wife;
> A Lady, who for Twenty years, withstood
> The pressing Instances of Flesh and Blood.

But Penelope is also confronted with the kind of feminine moral conflict which enthralled Rowe's audience. She must choose between sacrificing her son, thus betraying her duty as a mother, and

[20] Burns (1974), 68, 77–8.

FIGURE 3.6   J. Thornthwaite, engraving of Mrs Hunter as Penelope in
Nicholas Rowe's *Ulysses* (published 1778).

yielding to the suitor Eurymachus, thus betraying her husband. Rowe prolongs the pathetic scene in Act III in which she explores this feminine dilemma.[21] Rowe did not himself attempt to modernize a Greek tragedy for the stage, but his work so conditioned the theatrical climate that it helped to determine which particular Greek tragedies would appeal to eighteenth-century dramatists looking for heroines; the majority were to choose Euripides.[22]

A THEATRE FOR THE LADIES

The feminization of drama at this time is partly a result of the number of women now attending the theatre. The diverse audience in the Restoration playhouse included the wives of Members of Parliament, craftsmen, and merchants, numerous female aristocrats and servants, as well as the notorious orange-sellers.[23] Dryden's prologue to Davenant's amorous *Circe* (1677) presents the youthful author as a young man looking for love from women: it argues that 'The Sex that best does pleasure understand', will be tolerant of this inexperienced young playwright, because 'There's such a stock of love within his Veins. | These Arguments the Women may persuade.'[24] The audiences of the late seventeenth and eighteenth centuries, though increasingly middle-class, were to retain a sizeable female contingent whose reaction to a play might determine whether it succeeded or failed. Moreover, playwrights often dedicated their works to female patrons, who exerted an influence on the types of play that were produced.[25] Bankes dedicated *The Destruction of Troy* to Lady Katherine Ross, implying that his choice of subject-matter was connected with the sex of his patron: 'the history of Heroick Women shall henceforth own you to be the *Greatest* and *Noblest* Pattern of 'em all'. Boyer dedicates his *Achilles* to 'The Beautiful and Ingenious Diana', pointing out the coincidence of the dedicatee's name with that of the tragedy's goddess. He comforts himself for the play's lack of

---

[21] Burns (1974), 138–40.

[22] The exceptions were James Thomson's *Agamemnon*, which comes close to making a She-Tragedy out of Aeschylus' and Seneca's prototypes, and Thomas Francklin's version of Voltaire's *Oreste*, itself based on Sophocles' *Electra*. See below, Chs. 4 and 6.

[23] David Roberts (1989), 94.

[24] Davenant (1677), 'Prologue'.

[25] See David Roberts (1989), 95–126.

success by remembering that it had 'pleas'd the fairest Part of the Town, I mean the Ladies'.

The most important agent in the 'feminine' transformation of tragedy was, however, the female actor. The increasing cult of individual star performers of both sexes is apparent from Boyer's observation in 1702 that 'Formerly *Poets* made *Players*, but nowadays 'tis generally the *Player* that makes the *Poet*', yet the popularity of actresses meant that the female roles created by the dramatists were of relatively greater importance.[26] The 'type-casting' of the most famous actresses such as Mrs Bracegirdle (Gildon's Guinoenda) and Elizabeth Barry shaped the way in which many tragedies were written.[27] Drama's increased interest in heterosexual love was also a result of women's arrival on the Restoration stage, when theatregoers like Samuel Pepys could appreciate their sexual allure, even when the play was tedious.[28] Dennis, who defended the stage against the moral criticisms of Collier, conceded that the theatre's profound sexual charge encouraged womanizing, but argued that this offered protection against the 'unnatural sin' of homosexual love. Dennis also described the two greatest innovations of the Restoration stage as 'Scenes and Women; which added probability to the Dramatick Actions and made everything look more naturally'.[29]

The reputation of the actresses of the period interacted radically with the public's perception of the roles they played. The premiere of *The Distres't Mother*, a play about female rivalry, was notoriously jeopardized by a riot protesting against Mrs Oldfield's realization of the character of Andromache; the claque had been organized by Oldfield's vindictive rival Mrs Rogers, because she felt the role was rightfully hers. Some of these colourful women acted several 'Greek tragic' roles. Elizabeth Barry played both the Scythian Queen in Dennis's *Iphigenia,* and Phædra in Smith's *Phædra and Hippolitus.* In two successive years Mary Betterton played Iphigenia in Davenant's *Circe* and Jocasta in the Dryden–Lee *Oedipus.*[30] After her magnificent performance as Gildon's

---

[26] See Gay (1967 [1711]), 18 with John Harold Wilson (1958), 19–20, 55, 88.

[27] Rothstein (1967), 141–4.

[28] See Payne (1995).

[29] Dennis (1698), 26; id., 'The Causes of the Decay and Defects of Dramatick Poetry', in Dennis (1939–43), i. 275–99 at 277–8.

[30] On Mrs Rogers and Mrs Oldfield see *LS* ii/1. 271–2; on Mary Betterton see Gilder (1931), 151–60.

Medea-based Althea, Mrs Knight created the role of Clytemnestra in Boyer's *Achilles*, a Greek tragic queen to whom she returned in Johnson's *Iphigenia* in 1714. The role of the actresses, including the specialists in Greek heroines, later became even more important. The famous Mrs Porter attempted both West's Hecuba and Johnson's Medæa, but it was her Clytemnestra in Thomson's *Agamemnon* (1738) of which her audience 'expressed the highest approbation by loud and reiterated applause.'[31] Mrs Porter was particularly commended for the emotional effects she produced both in her 'spirited Propriety in all Characters of Rage', and also 'when Grief and Tenderness possessed her', when 'she subsided into the most affecting Softness'.[32]

By the middle of the century, when Mrs Porter was followed as the dominant exponent of Greek tragic heroines by Mrs Pritchard (Whitehead's *Creusa*, Delap's *Hecuba*), David Garrick, the actor-manager of Drury Lane, was taking acting to new heights of sophistication. Actors' skills were assessed according to their representation of emotions, categorized by Samuel Foote as 'the Passions of Desire, such as Pleasure, Pain, Love, Hatred &c. and the irascible ones, namely, Courage, Anger, Despair &c.'[33] Emphasis was laid on moments of emotional *change*: 'The transition from one Passion to another, by the Suddenness of the Contrast, throws a stronger Light on the Execution of the Actor.'[34] Any actress playing Creusa had to represent remarkable emotional transitions in her struggle between tenderness towards Ilyssus-Ion and anger against Xuthus, assisted by stage directions such as 'She turns away disordered', and by Ilyssus' description, 'now, now she softens, | I can see it in her eyes'.[35] In Act III of Glover's *Medea*, an even clearer example, Mrs Yates represented a transition from tearful dialogue with her child into a furious rant. Here her Colchian attendant gave a running commentary on her emotional vicissitudes: 'Heart-breaking sorrow now succeeds to rage.'[36] Again, in the 'banishment' scene she underwent a transition from terrifying anger with Creon to pitiful lamentation, culminating in a fainting fit when the stage directions instructed her to be supported by her women (Fig. 3.7).

---

[31] Thomas Davies (1784), iii. 467–9.   [32] Victor (1761), ii. 56–8.
[33] Foote (1747), 10. See also George Taylor (1972); Barnett (1987).
[34] Foote (1747), 18.   [35] Whitehead (1778), 36–7.   [36] Glover (1777), 27.

FIGURE 3.7 John Goldar, engraving of *Mrs Yates in the Character of Medea* (1777).

Unsurprisingly, Mrs Yates was concerned about excessive exertion when scheduled to act Medea and another tragic heroine on two successive nights.[37] By mid-century audiences were deeply absorbed in tragic scenes, in response to the emotional investment of the star actors. A German commentator on the British theatre contrasted the low attention-levels in France and Italy, and reported that in England, conversely, when Mrs Bellamy became so overcome in playing Jocasta in the Dryden–Lee *Oedipus* as to lose consciousness, the audience left the theatre distraught.[38] When Ann Barry acted the 'Alcestis' role in Thomson's *Edward and Eleonora* in the same year, the *Morning Chronicle* commented with approval that 'the audience . . . confessed their sensibility, and wept applause.'[39] The cult of tears in the theatre, although more easily documentable in French audiences than British, nevertheless held sway in London theatres throughout the eighteenth century.[40]

Actresses had a counterpart in female dramatists. One anonymous woman produced *The Unnatural Mother*, which has echoes of Euripides' *Medea*, at Lincoln's Inn Fields in 1697: the oriental Callapia poisons her husband and kills her son, before announcing in Act V that 'Ceres will send her winged Dragons for me, and bear me through the air'. She threatens the apparition of her murdered husband with a visit to a friend: 'I'le send thee to *Medea* to be new boil'd, and when thou art young again I will be fond of thee'.[41] *The Fatal Legacy* of Jane Robe, another 'She-Author', was performed at Lincoln's Inn Fields in 1723 after being puffed by no less a writer than Alexander Pope.[42] This adaptation of Racine's *La Thébaïde* (1664), itself based on Euripides' *Phoenician Women*, offered strong roles for both Mrs Boheme as the disturbed mother Jocasta and Mrs Bullock as the victimized Antigona. The audience was encouraged to consider the differences between Robe's play and its Euripidean archetype by the publication of a companion piece. Its author admires the ending of Euripides' *Phoenician Women* (i.e. from the death of Menoeceus), which he calls 'the most tragical of all'.[43]

---

[37] Oulton (1796), ii. 204–9.   [38] Cited in Kelly (1936), 54–5.
[39] Cited in Clifford (1947), 119.   [40] See Vincent-Buffault (1991), 54–76.
[41] 'A Young Lady' (1698), 49, 52.
[42] For the term 'She-Author' see Gildon (1702), 27. For Pope's (incognito) promotion of *The Fatal Legacy* see Charles Harold Gray (1931), 60.
[43] Anon. (1723).

Robe's ending differed from both Euripides and Racine in em-
phasizing romantic love and the psychological trauma of Jocasta.
In particular, it highlighted the fatal outcome of the love of Phocias
(Euripides' Haemon) for Antigona. In both Euripides and Racine
Jocasta kills herself off stage, but in Robe she enters 'Raving and
Bloody', raves, stabs herself again because her blood 'seems loth to
leave my canker'd veins', raves again, and finally dies. Moreover,
Mrs Boheme, minutes earlier impersonating a bloody corpse, was
resurrected to deliver the epilogue.

Robe's production had precedents amongst the plays by other
female authors in having a French model and ancient subject-
matter (Katherine Philips's *Horace* (1671) was translated from
Corneille), and the formulaic nature of its title (cf. Catherine
Trotter's *The Fatal Friendship* of 1698). But generally women
authors, even as caricatured in drama,[44] did not favour Greek
tragic models, perhaps because they were excluded from education
in the Greek language.

SOFT PITY'S PRIEST

Euripides was seen as the Greek tragedian best at delineating
different emotional states—what the Restoration audience would
have described as 'the several passions'. The prologue to Gildon's
Phaeton proclaims that '*Euripides* to Night adorns our Stage, |
For Tragic Passions fam'd in every Age.' In the preface, Gildon
enumerated the 'tragic passions' he adopted from Euripides,
and which he felt marked out this tragedian as superior to Sophocles:

I have closely follow'd the Divine *Euripides*, in the *grief, despair, rage,
dissimulation*, and *resentment* of *Althea*; as I have in her several Passions in
the fourth Act...All just Critics have agreed in preferring *Euripides* to
Sophocles himself, in his lively draught of the Passions.

Yet by the turn of the century, discussions of tragedy begin to be
concerned less with its 'lively draught' of extreme passion, and
more with the intensity of the *com*passion it arouses in the spectator. In 1701 Dennis opines,

---

[44] See Fidelis Morgan (1981); Ballaster (1996), 273–83. On learned ladies as both
authors and as characters in the dramas of this period, see Gagen (1954), 32–54.

I am no further pleas'd by any Tragedy, than as it excites passions in me...the greater the Resemblance between him who suffers, and him who commiserates, the stronger will the Apprehension, and consequently, the Compassion, be.[45]

A few years later Johnson described the ideal spectators as those who enjoy

the Distress of a well wrought scene, who...behold the Conduct of our Passions on the Stage, and with a generous Sympathy feel alternate Joy and Pain, when Virtue either conquers, or is contending with adverse Fate.[46]

Johnson's formula is symptomatic of the early eighteenth-century development of what has been called an 'affective theory of emulation'. This entailed the audience not only identifying with the distress of virtuous characters, but consequently modifying their own behaviour.[47]

  This notion of tragedy belongs to a contemporary debate about the relations between passion, reason, and sympathy, most famously instanced in David Hume's *A Treatise of Human Nature* (1739–40). By 1728 Frances Hutcheson had argued in *An Essay on the Nature and Conduct of the Passions and Affections* (1728) that sympathy makes people aware of the need to discipline their passions: it restrains and educates their influence.[48] As the prologue of West's *Hecuba* put it, the audience should feel free to shed tears at the play, because,

Pity's the generous Feeling of the Soul,
And ought less gentle Passions to controul.[49]

The audience, it is implied, could learn how to control their own passions by feeling pity for the characters in the tragedy. Indeed, throughout the eighteenth century, the movement for reform of theatre assumed that it was an instrument for moral education. Tracts argued that the stage was an effective medium for training the sentiments in a similar way to sermons, because of its psychological immediacy.[50]

---

[45] Dennis (1939–43), i. 128.
[46] Charles Johnson (1710), 'Dedication'. See Zimbardo (1986), 216–17.
[47] Zimbardo (1986), 206.   [48] See Mullan (1988), 18–19, 31.
[49] Richard West (1726), 'Prologue'.   [50] Discussed in Winton (1974).

Sympathy was seen as the element in human nature which both made society possible and offered the hope of a *good* society. This optimistic conception informed the emergent bourgeois ideal of the 'greatest happiness for the greatest number', a phrase invented in the eighteenth century.[51] The importance of 'sympathy' further illuminates Euripides' popularity, for the discourse around him stresses his pre-eminence at producing pity and tears. Boyer was inspired to stage a play about Iphigenia by the effectiveness with which this heroine 'drew tears' in the French theatre.[52] It has often been claimed that Elizabeth Barrett was heralding a new, tender, Victorian appreciation of Euripides when in *Wine of Cyprus* (1844) she praised 'Euripides, the human, | With his droppings of warm tears'. But by then this was an absolutely conventional British view: exactly a hundred years earlier Joseph Warton had entitled Euripides, 'soft Pity's priest, | Who melts in useful woes the bleeding breast'.[53] Delap's *Hecuba* was typically described in its Prologue as a 'modern ancient piece' designed to imitate a 'Grecian Bard' who 'Wakenen'd each soft emotion of the Breast | And call'd forth Tears, that would not be Supprest'.[54]

Yet often the eighteenth-century dramatists needed to help Euripides to call forth those insuppressible tears. One strategy was to identify the 'situations' in his tragedies with affective possibilities, and to subject them to prolongation and repetition, the two distinctive techniques of English sentimental drama defined by Arthur Sherbo in a seminal study.[55] Certain scenes in Euripides, for example Medea's parting from her children, Hecuba's from Polyxena, or Creusa's recognition of her son Ion, were instantly arresting to eighteenth-century sensibility, and in the plays under discussion are always extended and sometimes repeated later in the play. Another way of improving upon Euripidean pathos was to guide the audience's reactions towards 'humane' sympathy. In Johnson's *Medæa* Creusa, the heroine's rival, says that her 'reflecting Soul | Will feel the Sufferings of poor *Medæa*' (I. ii); in Delap's

---

[51] Brissenden (1974), 31–4.
[52] Abel Boyer (1700), 'Preface'.
[53] Joseph Warton, 'Ode to Mr West on his Translation of Pindar', st. 5 (1744), in Chalmers (1810), xviii. 169.
[54] Delap (1762), 'Prologue'.
[55] Sherbo (1957), especially ch. 3, 32–71.

Hecuba a Greek pities Hecuba after Deianira has been led off to her death, because,

> nature in my heart
> A spark hath lighted of humanity
> That shines for every mortal in distress.[56]

The prevalent ideology perceived human beings as good, or at least as having the capacity to act benevolently rather than malevolently if given the chance. Expressions of this conviction are so pervasive that it has been called both an eighteenth-century collective 'fantasy' and 'the propaganda of benevolence and tender feeling'.[57] The 'drama of sensibility' which dominated this period was confident in the goodness of average human nature; at its most extreme this confidence was expressed in Rousseau's conceptualization of virtue itself as a vehement and voluptuous passion.[58] Eighteenth-century tragedy often articulates its understanding of virtue through giving its female protagonists such 'interiorized' speeches in reaction to their distress: like Euripides' own Medea and Phaedra, they explore the conflicts raging in their minds, between virtue and passion or counterpoised familial loyalties; Smith's Phædra certainly exhibits a more complex and protracted internal battle than Racine's Phèdre.[59]

The plays also stress the virtue, delicacy of feeling, and 'humanity' of the *dramatis personae*. In Johnson's *Medæa* Ægeus announces that 'The love of Virtue | Now fires my Soul, uplifting it to Heaven' (III. i), and that his heart is swollen by 'Humanity, the pride of doing good'. In this play the word 'virtue' occurs no fewer than twenty-eight times (a record subsequently broken by Thomson's *Agamemnon*).[60] The discussion of Glover's *Medea* below will

---

[56] Delap (1762), 38.
[57] See the discussion of 'sentimentalism' in Brissenden (1974), 27–9.
[58] Bernbaum (1958), 2; Babbitt (1919), 132.
[59] See the admiration expressed by 'Mr. Oldisworth', the author of Smith's biographical notice, prefixed to his collected *Works*, for the way in which this poverty-stricken near-orphan had not only improved the Phaedra of Euripides and Seneca, but surpassed her characterization in Racine (Edmund Smith (1719), 'A character of the Author', n.p.) The author of this notice also writes that Smith was interested enough in She-Tragedy to draw up detailed plans for a play about Jane Shore. The frontispiece engraving to the *Works*, the work of Charles du Puis, portrays an altercation in the play, probably at the moment of the return of Theseus to the court.
[60] Ashby (1927), 171–2.

reveal the extent to which a plot could be altered in order to excise or ameliorate the (usually feminine) crimes found in the Greek texts. Smith's Phædra is also exculpated to an unprecedented degree. Smith so surgically enhances his heroine that she is guilty of almost nothing except a temporary loss of temper. He makes two momentous changes in her behaviour. First, she does absolutely nothing about her love for Hippolitus until she believes that she is a widow and free to remarry; secondly, far from accusing Hippolitus of rape, she defends him to Theseus and assumes all responsibility for the situation which has developed. This Phædra is entirely a victim of male evil: Smith has added to the plot a corrupt Minister of State named Lycon, who manipulates her and lies to her in his ambition to destroy Hippolitus and secure the throne for himself.[61]

Other examples include Creusa in Whitehead's *Creusa*, who, rather than exposing her baby son, entrusted him to the safekeeping of her nurse. This surgical enhancement of the plot was necessary on account of the 'natural antipathy, which the more refined system of cultivated society, in the present æra of mankind, will inevitably raise against' Euripides' authentic heroine, because 'the Mother of an Infant, exposed by her own hand, could [not] be . . . tolerated on a modern theatre of enlightened Europeans'.[62] Even more radically, in Delap's *Hecuba* the plot is engineered so that the delicate queen, whose 'weak brain' is afflicted,[63] does nothing immoral whatsoever. Instead of blinding Polymestor and having his children slaughtered, she concludes the play, raving, between her own children's corpses.

When the eighteenth-century playwrights adapted Greek tragedy, therefore, they intrusively emphasized the virtue of the characters, regarded as necessary to the eliciting of sympathy. The earlier plays tended to reward virtue, punish turpitude, and draw an explicit moral. This tendency is shared with much of the polite literature of the time and is indigenous: the authors influenced by a French adaptation of Greek tragedy did not find the moralizing habit in them. Boyer's *Achilles* replaces both the Euripidean and Racinean endings with Calchas helpfully drawing a

---

[61] This and all subsequent references to Smith's *Phædra and Hippolitus* refer to the text in Edmund Smith (1796).

[62] Jodrell (1781), i. 247, 230–1.

[63] Delap (1962), 35.

moral inference for posterity: the gods 'are just, and ever recompense, | True piety, and spotless Innocence.'[64] A similarly unprecedented moral is drawn by Smith's Hippolitus (for whom see the engraving reproduced as frontispiece to this volume), who (unlike Racine's) does not die. He is rewarded for his resistance to his amorous stepmother and fidelity to his fiancée by surviving the end of the play, upon which he opines that 'the righteous gods' always protect 'Goodness' and 'unguarded Virtue'.[65] This tendency towards disposing the fortunes of characters according to 'poetical justice' was later superseded by a luxuriant pleasure in the contemplation of unalloyed sorrows: neither Creusa nor Medæa, both portrayed as innocent victims of circumstance, survives the end of Johnson's *The Tragedy of Medæa* (1730). Part of the reason for this transformation lay in the dramatists' awareness of ancient Greek tragedy, which the dramatist Richard Steele argued was superior to modern tragedy precisely because it eschewed 'poetical justice' in favour of a sterner contemplation of unmitigated distress:

the wise Athenians in their theatrical performances laid before the eyes of the people the greatest affliction which could befall human life, and insensibly polished their tempers by such representations.[66]

SENTIMENT AND SOCIETY

Between the late 1730s and the 1760s tragedy became increasingly mawkish and sentimental, as highly actable poetic tragedies were produced with an unabashed interest in the emotional frailty of a traumatized mother, wife, sister, or daughter.[67] It is this type of mid-century 'sentimental' tragedy which prompted a paternal writer of 'Conduct' Literature to advise his daughters to avoid comedy as 'offensive to delicacy', but to attend tragedy enthusiastically, for its 'sorrows will soften and ennoble your hearts'.[68] Smith's *Phædra and Hippolitus*, along with Rowe's She-Tragedies, was revived,[69] but the repertory was dominated by new plays; the

---

[64] See Ashby (1927), 170–1.

[65] On this important English interpretation of the Phaedra myth (which John Dennis also once planned to dramatize), see Eccles (1922), 9–10.

[66] *Tatler* no. 82; see Bernbaum (1958), 111.

[67] Lynch (1953), 21, 38.

[68] Gregory (1774), cited in Vivien Jones (1990).

[69] See Lynch (1953), 38.

outstanding 'Greek' examples are Whitehead's *Creusa*, and Glover's *Medea*. The word 'sentimental' made its first appearance in
any dramatic context in the prologue to Whitehead's *The Roman
Father* (Drury Lane 1749),[70] for Greek and Roman settings were
voguish, just as society ladies had themselves painted in classical
disguise as Hebe, or in classical drapery, performing a pagan
sacrifice.[71] The female interest in Greek tragedy in the eighteenth
century can be no better illustrated than by Lady Sarah Bunbury,
who modelled for Reynolds's famous *Lady Sarah Bunbury Sacrificing to the Graces* (1765) only a couple of years after performing
the role of Whitehead's ill-starred mother in private performances
of *Creusa* (see Ch. 5).

The theatre's fusion of fashionable Graeco-Roman contexts
with suffering heroines also finds a parallel in contemporary classical-subject painting. Gavin Hamilton's *Andromache Mourning
the Death of Hector* (commissioned 1759) and *The Death of Lucretia* (1767) both focus on female heroism, but are also 'sentimental'
in the sense that feeling is their subject.[72] This artistic view of the
role of the imagination in creating sympathy must be associated
with the philosophy of Adam Smith, who in *Theory of Moral
Sentiments* (1759) argued that while 'pity' signifies fellow-feeling
with another's *sorrows*, 'sympathy' can denote 'our fellow-
feeling with any passion whatever'.[73] The audiences of the time
came to feel *everything*—Lucretia's patriotic fervour and outrage,
Medea's love and anger—along with their antique heroines.

The popularity of the Euripidean heroine is consonant with the
preference in sentimental tragedy for the central figure to be a
suffering female. Women in love, tormented mothers, and victimized virgins were central vehicles for the eighteenth century's
exploration of its contradictory ideology of gender. This encompassed simultaneously the ideal of passive female asexuality, a
superficially contradictory conviction that women were more vulnerable to love, an increasing cult of conjugal passion, and a
veritable sanctification of motherhood. The ideals expressed in

[70] See Sherbo (1957), 2.
[71] See Perry (1994), 21 on Reynolds's *Lady Sarah Bunbury Sacrificing to the
Graces* (1765) and *Mrs. Masters as Hebe* (1785), 21. On Greek and Roman revivalism
in general see Sambrook (1993), 195–209.
[72] See MacMillan (1994), 88.
[73] Heilbroner (1986), 108.

the popular genre of 'conduct literature' aimed at unmarried women equated 'natural' femininity with asexual virtue. Yet other texts offer explanations for women's potentially rampant sexuality. 'Love, and the Effects of it, is the darling and predominant Passion of the Sex', as a treatise on marital infidelity opined in 1739.[74] Female sexuality was thus simultaneously constructed as both natural and unnatural, 'its potentially anarchic power contained by reducing it to the socially sanctioned duty of motherhood'.[75]

Charlotte Lennox, who put several Greek plays into English while translating Pierre Brumoy's *Le Théâtre des Grecs* of 1730, is far more famous for her novels about traumatized women, including *Euphemia, Henriette,* and *The Female Quixote.* The relationship between the eighteenth-century heroines of fiction and of Greek tragedy also worked in the other direction, for by the time of the last significant eighteenth-century adaptation of Greek tragedy, Delap's *The Royal Suppliants* (1781), Greek tragic heroines had been transformed into the theatrical equivalents of Samuel Richardson's Pamela and Clarissa. Delap's Macaria is an exemplar of affected and persecuted feminine sensibility, in whom 'virtue is articulated in the capacity to feel and display sentiments, the capacity called "sensibility"'. The instrument of sensibility is 'a massively sensitized, feminine body; its vocabulary is that of gestures and palpitations, sighs and tears.'[76] This notion of the tragic heroine also finds a parallel in medical writings, where women possess a 'sensibility' based in physiology. Sensibility could easily veer into excess or out of control, and, in both Richardson's novels and theatrical texts, female delirium and suicidal despair figure large. These states are played out in swoons and sighs; like the subjects of medical treatises, fictional and dramatic heroines suffer from emotional turns articulated in a common vocabulary of nervous disorders, marked by the voguish lexical items 'sympathy', 'delicacy', and 'passion'.[77]

The eighteenth-century Greek tragic heroines swoon, rave, or announce impending suicide with exhausting frequency. Glover's Medea, in her spectacular first delirium, reenacts her spells over the dragon guarding the golden fleece, fantasizes that she is cling-

---

[74] 'Philogamus' (1739), quoted from Vivien Jones (1990), 77.
[75] Ibid. 57–8.   [76] Mullan (1988), 61.   [77] Ibid. 216–19, 230.

ing to a desert cliff with her infants, and receives a visitation from a personified figure of Revenge. After her children's death she raves again, passes out, revives, sees the blood on her hand, gradually regains her senses, and becomes suicidal—a scene both typically eighteenth-century, and clearly dependent on Heracles' 'recovery' in Euripides' *Heracles* and Agaue's in his *Bacchae*.

This specifically eighteenth-century construction of femininity thought it found a reflection of itself in Euripidean tragedy's complex female protagonists. Yet certain features of the women in the ancient Greek texts repelled eighteenth-century sensibility, in particular their frankness about erotic love. Gildon, whose tragedies had drawn on several Euripidean wives, argued that the modesty appropriate to unmarried women must inhibit playwrights. He commends the Greek tragedians for their treatment of love 'as Euripides in his *Alcestis* and *Helen*, but then it is between Man and Wife'. But it is not consistent 'with that Character of Modesty, which is essential to the Sex, to fly out into those Transports and Fondnesses' before matrimony.[78] Dennis, similarly, describes the difficulty posed by Sophocles' Antigone, because 'the thing that lay most heavy upon her Heart was that she was to go to Hell with her Maiden-head'. Dennis says that the Athenians had a worse view of women, and ascribed to them a more dominant 'Passion'. If a 'maid' had expressed Antigone's view in Dennis's day, it 'would have appear'd a frailty particular and surprizing'.[79]

Euripidean tragedy, then, appealed to the eighteenth-century dramatists because of its passionate heroines and pathetic 'situations'. But his tragedies then had to be shaped to fit contemporary ideals of pre-marital modesty, conjugal affection, and sanctified motherhood. His heroines were conceptualized in terms of a specifically eighteenth-century vocabulary of sensibility. Tragedy was certainly designed to provide the large female sector in the audience with positive paradigms of womanhood. Yet it is important to remember that tragedy's consumers included men. It has recently been argued that the eighteenth century's dominant ideal of femininity, with its emphasis on feeling and morality, was one of the

[78] Gildon (1718), i. 200.
[79] John Dennis, *The Impartial Critick* (1693), in Springarn (1909), iii. 148–97 at 150.

most powerful factors in establishing a *general* middle-class identity. It has plausibly been urged that the emergence of female-
dominated sentimental literature really demonstrates 'an evolution
of a particular ideological construction of a new class identity,
displaced into a discussion of female virtue'.[80] Even the rising
cult of motherhood was related to the expansionist ideology of an
upwardly mobile middle class.[81] An examination of the most important 'Grecian' She-Tragedy will clarify the way in which Euripidean heroines were contorted to suit this audience and its
ideological requirements.

CASE-STUDY: THE EXCULPATION OF MEDEA

Euripides' deliberately infanticidal Medea presented a nearly impossible challenge to eighteenth-century sentiment. One critic
specified her crime as one of the most deplorable in drama, committed by 'such monsters that degrade the whole human system'.[82]
A revealing account of the problem is expressed in Gildon's preface to *Phaeton*. He explains that while his play owes 'a great many
of its Beauties to the *Immortal EURIPIDES*', he was compelled to
alter the heroine's character,

> in consideration of the different Temper and Sentiment of our several
> Audience. First I was Apprehensive, that *Medea*, as *Euripides* represents
> her, wou'd shock *us*. When we hear of . . . the murdering of her own
> Children, contrary to all the Dictates of *Humanity* and *Mother-hood*, we
> shou'd have been too impatient for her Punishment, to have expected the
> *happy Event* of her barbarous Revenge; nay, perhaps, not have allow'd the
> Character within the Compass of Nature.[83]

Gildon therefore exculpated his heroine by transferring the child-
killing to the hands of the local people, causing their bereaved
mother to go mad and commit suicide.

Johnson's *The Tragedy of Medæa* (1730) is influenced by Corneille's *Médée*, but depends closely on Euripides. His preface
articulates his aim: since *Medea* 'had never, that I have heard,

---

[80] See Ballaster (1996), 280 and n. 28.
[81] Vivien Jones (1990), 11, 59.
[82] He also cites the murder of Clytemnestra by Orestes in Sophocles on the
ground that it is encouraged by Electra, who is female: Hiffernan (1770), book 2, 57.
[83] Gildon (1698).

been in *English*, I have ventur'd it on our Stage, and in some Places alter'd the Œconomy from the original'.[84] Those alterations self-consciously improved the morality of the characters. Even Creon abdicates in shame at the wrongs he has done Medæa. More startling still is Johnson's decision not to have the children killed *at all*. Medæa sends them to safety in Athens before stabbing herself out of despair at the grief she has caused her beloved Jason.[85]

Yet Johnson's play was still an outstanding failure. The author blamed the orchestrated interruptions of 'Criticks . . . not only in feeble Hisses, but in Hootings, horse Laughs, squalings, Catcalls, and other mechanical and judicious vociferations'. This was despite 'Mrs Porter's wonderful Performance, and the glorious Spirit, with which she rose in her Action'.[86] The cause of the play's failure, despite the ethical improvements, was its fidelity to the original, resulting in a sombre tone and lack of love scenes (although Aegæus is motivated by attraction to Medæa rather than infertility). It faithfully replicates many speeches and situations— Medea's plotting of her revenge, her confrontations with Jason, her encounter with Aegæus, the ode in praise of Athens, Medea's tears over the children, and the messenger speech. Johnson is aware that his play failed on account of its 'severe Morality': he regretfully notes that the strongest disapproval was expressed in the passages lifted directly from Euripides.

Although there were popular lowbrow entertainments on the Medea theme during the eighteenth century, such as the masque *Jason and Medæa* performed at the New Wells Theatre in Goodman's Fields in August 1747, there was only one successful attempt by a serious British dramatist. Richard Glover's *Medea* succeeded precisely because of the reciprocal love interest (Jason still loves his wife) and pathetic deaths of the children. But since it was ideologically impossible to present a mother killing her children in cold blood, Glover exonerates Medea by allowing her to kill her children under the influence of madness. His heroine would probably have been acquitted of murder in the eighteenth century, which engaged in a heated discussion of whether 'temporary phrenzy' absolved child-killing mothers of guilt; in reality such cases (where the deaths were usually perinatal) frequently

---

[84] Charles Johnson (1731), p. viii.   [85] Ibid. 62, 66–7.   [86] Ibid., pp. i–ii.

revolved around the issue of intent, and the courts admitted evidence about state of mind.[87] The word 'phrenzy' is used of Medea's madness in Glover's play.

The audience must have gathered excitedly to see this tragedy, on which Glover was reputed to have expended meticulous care.[88] This famous patriot had already used antiquity in a popular play (*Boadicea*, Drury Lane, 1753) and a well-known epic (*Leonidas*, 1737). Some regarded *Leonidas* as superior to *Paradise Lost*, although in time it was forgotten save as a forerunner of romantic Hellenism.[89] Moreover, since the death of Mrs Cibber in 1766, Glover's leading actress Mrs Yates had become the unchallenged queen of tragedy in England. She did not disappoint: she 'melted every audience that has seen her inimitable Medea',[90] and the production inspired revivals into the 1790s by several actresses, perhaps including Mrs Siddons.[91] *Medea* encouraged Mrs Yates to choose another Greek tragic heroine for her benefit performance at Covent Garden (1769) in Francklin's *Orestes*, a play she subsequently revived at Drury Lane as *Electra* (see Ch. 6). She also flirted with Glover's sequel to *Medea*, an elaborate *Jason*, which was, however, rejected by the managers of both theatres, who objected to 'the grandeur of the scenery, and the expense required to bring it forward'.[92]

In *Medea* Mrs Yates was required to look dazzlingly beautiful, her eye surpassing 'that refulgent star, | Which first adorns the evening' (Act I). Moreover, Medea is exceedingly intelligent, having a 'soaring mind' and 'the sublimest knowledge'. But Medea's supernatural wisdom cannot save her from the destructive power of love. The prologue promised that Glover had reworked 'Medea's mournful strain' so as to prove that 'Where

---

[87] Mark Jackson (1996), 40, 120–3, 142–3.
[88] See Doddington (1809), 192.
[89] See e.g. Stern (1940), 123–6.
[90] Thomas Davies (1780), i. 132.
[91] It was revived by Mrs Yates at Drury Lane in 1775, 1776, and 1779, and by Mrs Pope (formerly Miss Younge) at Covent Garden in March 1792: see *LS* iv/3. 1533, 1877, 1959; v/1. 30, 243; v/2. 1440. Although Mrs Siddons is not otherwise known to have played Medea, the cast list for an edition published in 1790 suggests that she had appeared in the role at Drury Lane, and an engraving held at Yale (Yale D.H.3.12, 011) portrays her as Medea, wearing a leopard-skin sash and a striped shawl.
[92] Glover (1799), 'Preface', 3

love and fury, grief and madness' are joined, they 'O'erturn the structure' even 'of a godlike mind'.[93]

In common with all the actresses who attempted the heroines of Greek tragedy, Mrs Yates had to deliver complex rhetoric marked by heavy anaphora, the self-dramatizing use of the third person in soliloquy, and especially the cataloguing of emotions, often in asyndeton. Above all Mrs Yates had to express Medea's *struggle* between emotion and virtue; in Act I she bewails

> That anguish, want, despair, contempt and shame
> Are heap'd together by the hands of fate,
> Whelm'd in one mass of ruin on my head,
> And dash my struggling virtue to the ground.[94]

Medea's moral struggle is engendered by conjugal love. Even her Senecan sorcery scene in Act IV (with a transvestite Hecate played by Mr Bransby) emphasizes her grief for her loss of Jason. Her maternal love also remains fundamentally unchallenged. Although she stabs her children to death, it is 'madness' that 'mingled smiles with horror' (see the frightening expression on her face in Fig. 3.8, George Romney's picture of Medea contemplating her children, a scene specifically inspired by Glover's play).[95] Her last entrance was admired, 'when, still raving and distracted, she comes upon the stage, her hands dripping with the blood of her children', for, as one critic expressed it, 'her words and appearance perfectly harrow up the soul'.[96] Like Whitehead's Creusa, Glover's Medea becomes suicidal when she finds out what has really happened, but she is saved by divine intervention. The tragedy ends with her departing into exile in the dragon-drawn chariot of her 'Bright forefather'. But this is only after a touching dialogue with the husband she still adores. Glover's Medea, although a sorceress, remains a model eighteenth-century matron. Her virtues as wife and mother, astonishingly, emerge intact.

---

[93] Glover (1777), 12, 3.

[94] Ibid. 12.

[95] See Pressly (1979), 121–2; and Kidson (2002), 128, who also notes that the translator Robert Potter had sat for Romney in 1778, and indeed had corresponded with him about possible ideas for Jason and Medea subjects.

[96] Robert Anderson, 'The Life of Glover', in Anderson (1795), 467–82, 471.

FIGURE 3.8   George Romney, *Medea Contemplating the Murder of her Children*, chalk cartoon, *c*.1782.

EURIPIDES IMPROV'D

Euripidean tragedies presented a paradox to the eighteenth century. Their gallery of memorable female protagonists, emphasis on mothers and virgins, use of children, representation of emotion, tear-jerking situations, and interiorized monologues, guaranteed that they were much more attractive to this era than has previously been realized. Yet these heroines were profoundly unsuited to contemporary notions of femininity and sentiment. Instead of romantic love, the tragedians found in Euripides visceral sexual politics. Instead of eroticism expressed in the coded language of sensibility, they found plays without love interest and Medea talking about her insulted marriage-bed. In particular, they wanted idealized maternal love, and instead found in Phaedra a stepmother with adulterous and quasi-incestuous urges, in Medea a cold-blooded maternal infanticide, in Hecuba a grandmother who kills her enemy's sons, and in Creusa a wife who had sex before marriage, abandoned her child, plots his death, and survives the end of the play.

Thus the eighteenth-century audience could only cope with Euripides' heroines after subjecting them to the extensive plastic surgery required to make them fit its social imperatives. There was no shame attached to this project: contemporary critics frequently *praised* the strategies the playwrights devised for 'correcting' the ethical or affective material they found in their ancient archetypes. In the preface to the second edition of his Iphigenia play, Boyer said that the neo-classical adapter of Euripides was 'The One Improving what the other Writ'.[97]

This demonstration of the tension between the attractiveness of the Greek tragic heroines to the eighteenth century, and the problems they presented, can be concluded by musing on the ignominious fate of the only commercial attempt to stage a Greek tragedy in translation rather than adaptation, West's *Hecuba* (Drury Lane, 1726). West recalled that he had thought that Euripides' *Hecuba* would prove 'an elegant Entertainment for a polite Assembly'. Contemptuous of the emotional tragedies then popular, he writes, 'I vainly imagin'd some Regulation of our Stage might not unsuccessfully be attempted, under the Authority of so great a Master as Euripides'.[98] West's only significant alteration was to replace the Euripidean prologue, delivered by the ghost of Polydorus, with a scene in which the same information is presented by Polymestor. Otherwise the order and content of the translated scenes replicate the Greek model, adding no love interest, presenting the blinding of Polymestor and the murder of his children without sentiment or amelioration, and even retaining most of the choral material, expressed through the mouth of Iphis, Hecuba's servant. The

---

[97] Boyer (1714), 'To the Plagiary of Mr Boyer's Iphigenia'.

[98] Richard West (1726), pp. iii–iv. *Hecuba* continued to attract the attention of learned gentlemen, who wistfully fantasized about reviving Greek tragedy unadapted. The Revd T. Morell, the author of a libretto for Handel, wrote a faithful translation of *Hecuba*, in the preface to which he too reveals his view that 'were some of these ancient plays judiciously translated, and the Choric-songs reduced to a proper Measure, and masterly set and perform'd, a more engaging and rational Entertainment could not be desired by the most polite audience.' Morell (1749), 'Preface'. On yet another plan to perform *Hecuba* see below, p. 195.

remarkably faithful blank-verse translation certainly merits the account in the Epilogue, which claims of the author that,

> Instead of the prevailing, powerful Arts,
> By which, perhaps his Play might move your Hearts,
> He boasts, that from Eu-ri-pi-des 'tis writ!

But this epilogue was never heard. 'A Rout of Vandals in the Galleries intimidated the young Actresses, disturb'd the Audience, and prevented all Attention'.[99]

A critic who claims to have attended rehearsals published a pamphlet in which he explicitly *complains* that West's *Hecuba* was 'not only a close Translation, but a very bare one too'. Predictably, the critic concedes the power of the 'situation' where Hecuba is parted from the Polyxena of Mrs Cibber (later Cassandra in Thomson's *Agamemnon*), which he finds 'greatly moving, and truly tragical'. But he cites as an example of extreme tedium the faithfully translated stichomythia between Agamemnon and Hecuba, and the plethora of Hecuba's lamentations prompts him wittily to suggest that the play be renamed *The Distres't Grandmother*, in imitation of Philips's hugely successful *The Distres't Mother*.

Most revealing of all are the critic's half-serious suggestions for the rewriting of the play to make it accord with contemporary taste. In Euripides' tragedy there is no love interest and the death of Polyxena is not seen by the audience. The critic proposes correcting these defects by staging the exciting 'situation' of Polyxena's sacrifice, and making Pyrrhus (and by implication the audience) actually see her pull down her robe. Pyrrhus' soul should then 'have been wholly captivated with the Virgin's Charms'. As a result, 'violently agitated by the Passions combating against each other', he would have delayed the Sacrifice.[100] An erotic response to virtue in *visible*, half-naked distress is thus an absolute requirement for the 'improver' of Euripides. West had been tempting fate in refusing to recognize the painful truth articulated by his critic:

there is not one Drama of Antiquity, that in a meer Translation, would not suffer Persecution on the present Stage.[101]

---

[99] Richard West (1726), p. iv.   [100] Anon. (1726), 5, 7, 9, 11, 13–16.
[101] Ibid. 12.

4

James Thomson's Tragedies of Opposition

INTRODUCTION

In a quiet corner of Westminster Abbey, above Charlotte Brontë's memorial, the sculpted image of James Thomson still leans on a pedestal decorated with rural figures symbolizing his most famous poem, *The Seasons* (see Fig. 4.1). This delicate cycle, with its innovative experiments in the description of nature, informed critical debates of the Romantic period and is now regarded as an important forerunner of Romantic aesthetics and sensibility.[1] It impressed the critic Lessing, influenced the poets Coleridge and Wordsworth and the painter Turner, and, translated into German, provided the libretto for Haydn's secular oratorio *Die Jahreszeiten* (1801). But Thomson left other, more controversial legacies, especially through his dramas, represented on his monument by an austere tragic mask beside the Greek cithara. Not only did this lowland Scot in 1740 pen the masque *Alfred*, whose oppositionist patriotism is encapsulated in the chorus 'Rule Britannia', but with his *Edward and Eleonora*, another story from earlier English history, this time grafted onto Euripides' *Alcestis*, he became only the second dramatist to have a play banned under the provisions of the 1737 Licensing Act.

Thomson is significant in the story of Greek tragedy's relationship to the British stage for two other reasons. He was the first poet to stage a consciously 'oppositional' Greek tragedy attacking the ruling power of his day, the government of the first Prime Minister, Robert Walpole. For Thomson's proscribed *Edward and Eleonora* was actually his second attempt at adapting Greek tragedy for the contemporary stage: his equally political *Agamemnon* of 1738 had just escaped the censor. Since *Agamemnon* draws on both Aeschylus and Seneca, a further accolade therefore deserved by Thomson is that he was the first dramatist to attempt

---

[1] See Strachan (2000).

FIGURE 4.1 The monument to James Thomson in Westminster Abbey.

to domesticate Aeschylus to the British stage. Dryden and Lee chose Sophocles, Gildon, Dennis, and Smith preferred Euripides, but before 1738 Aeschylus had made no overt impact on drama in the English language. While his obscure plays may, via Latin translations, have affected English Renaissance drama in subterranean ways,[2] it is not until after 1663 that Aeschylus begins to make his presence felt, and that is for a specific reason: the publication of Thomas Stanley's edition.

Stanley offered his readership a text, commentary, and an easy Latin translation. This finally allowed men with a moderate education access to this most recalcitrant of Greek tragedians. The late-seventeenth-century theatrical taste for imperial settings and elevated diction occasionally seems to have echoed scenes at least from *Persians*, for example the ghost scene in John Crowne's *Darius, King of Persia* (1688), which, however, is set at the time of Alexander the Great and has nothing to do with Aeschylus' Darius; clearer Aeschylean influence is apparent in the admonitory ghost of Herod and the crowd of lamenting Jews in his earlier siege-and-conquest play *The Destruction of Jerusalem by Titus Vespasian* (1677). But generally Aeschylus' works were felt to be bizarre, and alien: Thomas Rymer's plan to relocate *Persians* to the court of Spain at the time of the defeat of the Spanish Armada is purposely comical.[3] Aeschylean drama was inimical to the taste for female-dominated pathetic plays ushered in by the new sensibilities of the 1690s (see Ch. 3), but the political stance of Stanley, Aeschylus' first English editor, must also have deterred the Whig-dominated theatre. Stanley was an ardent and unrepentant Royalist, first admitted to the degree of Master of Arts at Oxford in March 1641/2, coincidentally in company with the young Prince Charles. He had spent much of the Civil War in France, and on his return went into a literary retirement until the Restoration, producing amongst other things the first English translation of Aristophanes, amounting to about two-thirds of *Clouds*. He took the pledge alongside Dryden in 1660; he presented his Aeschylus to the King. On 2 July 1663 Charles II endorsed it from Whitehall as 'much tending to the advancement of learning', and rewarded his 'Trusty and Well-Beloved' servant with a twenty-one year privilege.[4]

---

[2] See Ewbank (forthcoming).   [3] Rymer (1693), 11–17.

[4] Stanley (1663), 'Preface'; on Stanley's politics, see Crump (1962), pp. xii–xxxiv. His blank-verse translation of *Clouds*, issued as part of a biography of Socrates, is included in his 1655 *A History of Philosophy*. See Langbaine (1691) and Hines (1966), 9–40.

GREEK TRAGEDY AND THE BRITISH CENSOR

Thomson's politics could not have been more different from those of Stanley. Besides *The Seasons* and his dramas, his most important work is his Whig epic *Liberty* (1735–6, the text of which he is reading on his monument). This is a massive poetic disquisition on the history of Liberty from ancient Greece via Rome and Anglo-Saxon freedoms to eighteenth-century Britain, inspired by watching Voltaire's Brutus declaim on liberty to a French audience on a visit to Paris in 1730, followed by a visit to the ruins of Rome.[5] An advocate of the British Union (his family were committed Scottish Whigs) and opponent of Walpole, Thomson designed his *Agamemnon* to be a manifesto of Whig ideals. It is strong political meat, as was his *Edward and Eleonora*. One reason why Thomson turned to Greek tragedy was that he and other opposition writers were beginning to look to classical Athens for the model of a state-subsidized theatre which educated its citizen audience,[6] exactly the type of model of which Edward Bulwer and Thomas Talfourd were to dream a century later (see Ch. 11).

Thomson's mentor Aaron Hill shared his dream of a reformed stage which could break the power of the profit-driven managers, but without putting their theatres under any neo-puritan or (worst of all) governmental restrictions.[7] Hill, who had travelled in the Near East, was an expert on the Ottoman Empire, and regretted 'the present Condition of Subverted *Greece*, that Ancient *Theatre* of *Power* and *Learning*, and *Nurse* of the most Illustrious *Propagators* of *Wisdom* and *Morality*'.[8] He encouraged Thomson to idealize the Athenian stage, where emotion, '*moving* Enthusiasm', was joined to moral edification; young people, directed by the state-funded *poets*, grew 'to love liberty, and hate tyranny, and acquired a propensity to arms and eloquence'.[9] Thomson agreed, and wrote to Hill in terms which adumbrate much more recent debates about

---

[5] Stern (1940), 119.

[6] By late 1736, when Thomson began to plan a new tragedy, he was inspired by the visit to England in 1735–6 of the Marchese Francesco Scipione Maffei, author of a three-volume collection of early Italian tragedies which Thomson owned (*Teatro Italiano*, Verona, 1723–5), and advocate of the establishment of a national theatre in Italy.

[7] Sambrook (1991), 139.

[8] Hill (1709).

[9] Hill (1731), pp. xii f.

the desirability of state subsidy for the theatrical arts, arguing that putting 'such an important public Diversion, the School which forms the Manners of the Age' into the hands of profit-driven private individuals inevitably leads to art designed to please 'the most profligate, tasteless, and ignorant of Mankind!'[10]

The idea of a socially responsible drama had already informed Thomson's first tragedy *Sophonisba*, a patriotic tale based on ancient Carthaginian history, which has recently been rehabilitated by scholars as an excellent stage play.[11] But it also affected Thomson's less familiar attempts to rewrite *Agamemnon* and subsequently *Alcestis* for the Georgian stage, a decision which brought him into conflict with Walpole. From our current standpoint it may be astonishing to discover that audiences in the past were ever prevented from seeing versions of Greek tragedy in Britain. But even a brief look into the annals of the Lord Chamberlain's Office will reveal how Greek tragedy in adaptation and translation has fallen foul of the censor on a number of occasions subsequent to Thomson, including the proscription of William Shirley's *Electra* (see Ch. 6). In the early stages, in which Thomson plays a leading role, the objections to the plays were broadly political; but by the middle of the nineteenth century, there was a marked shift in taste and the grounds for refusing a licence were largely moral. As late as 1910 audiences were unable to watch a professional production of *Oedipus Tyrannus* because, in the words of a leading actor-manager of the day, it might 'prove injurious' and 'lead to a great number of plays being written...appealing to a vitiated public taste solely in the cause of indecency'[12] (see further Ch. 18).

The Licensing Act of 1737 provided the basis for the law surrounding theatrical censorship that survived, substantially unchanged, until the 1968 Theatre Act when the British stage was finally freed from the clutches of the censor.[13] Under the Act of 24 June 1737, the Lord Chamberlain was granted the power to refuse a licence to any play acted 'for hire, gain, or reward'

---

[10] Letter of 23 Aug. 1735, in McKillop (1957), 98.

[11] See e.g. Hammond (2000), with further bibliography.

[12] Sir John Hare, Member of the Advisory Board on Stage Plays, in a letter to the Lord Chamberlain, November 1910. Lord Chamberlain's Plays' Correspondence File: *Oedipus Rex* 1910/814 (British Library).

[13] On stage censorship in Britain generally, see Fowell and Palmer (1913), Findlater (1967), and Johnston (1990). On the 1737 Act see Vince (1988), 14–15, 25–6.

anywhere in Great Britain 'as often as he shall think fit'. All theatres were 'under the immediate Directions of a Court Officer'. The main thrust of the legislation was political, having been drawn up by Walpole in order to curb political attacks on him in the theatre, especially the satires of Henry Fielding that were playing to packed houses at the Little Theatre in the Haymarket: they included *Historical Register for the Year 1736* in March 1737, and *Eurydice Hiss'd* (whose katabatic theme drew on Aristophanes' *Frogs*) in April. The immediate effect—besides driving Fielding into attacking Walpole through translations of Aristophanes instead of directly from the stage[14]—was to reduce to two the number of London theatres and thus to cut the number of new plays acted each season. The survivors were the old patented houses Covent Garden and Drury Lane, plus the King's Opera House, which did not perform new stage plays.

THOMSON'S OPPOSITIONAL AGAMEMNON

By the mid-1730s, under George II, Britain was riven with the conflict between the Whig ministry, run by the Prime Minister Robert Walpole, and the so-called 'Country', or 'Patriot' opposition, whose ranks included (besides Thomson), Jonathan Swift, John Gay, Alexander Pope, George Lillo, and Richard Glover (the author of the most important English-language *Medea* of the eighteenth century, discussed in Ch. 3). Early in 1737 Frederick, Prince of Wales, went officially into opposition, lending the anti-Walpole elements a new focus (he is represented by the young patriot Orestes in Thomson's *Agamemnon*). Their view was that Walpole was exploiting George II's frequent absences, and Queen Caroline's dependence upon his chief ministers, in order to undermine fundamental British liberties.[15] They presented themselves as the true 'patriots' in a land which had sold its soul to a corrupt tyrant. They opposed Walpole's peace policies, and his arrogance towards the merchant classes, by advocating energetic military campaigns and commercial ventures: it is in this bellicose context

[14] See pp. 57 and 86 of Fielding and Young's translation of *Plutus* (1742), with Hines (1966), 158–231.

[15] See Speck (1983), 14–35. Gerrard (1994) p. vii, writes that 'Politics and poetry were more closely intertwined in this period than they were (arguably) ever to be again.'

that Thomson's 'Rule, Britannia' in *Alfred*, produced for Frederick in 1740, needs to be understood.

His *Agamemnon* has ties with contemporary plays on themes from ancient history, such as Samuel Madden's oppositional *Themistocles, the Lover of his Country* (1729), and plays on episodes from the Roman republic such as William Bond's *The Tuscan Treaty; or, Tarquin's Overthrow* (Covent Garden 1733) and William Duncombe's *Junius Brutus* (Drury Lane 1734). These were thinly veiled defences of the constitutional principles of the Glorious Revolution against their perceived betrayal. They certainly helped to create the atmosphere which eventually precipitated the Licensing Act. Such was the climate of hostility to the King and Walpole amongst most prominent literary men that even John Gay's *Achilles* (Covent Garden 1733), a light-hearted burlesque of a classical myth, was read politically.[16]

By the time Thomson was writing *Agamemnon* the mood was mutinous. The King was absent from May 1736 and did not return until January 1737, an absence during which it was felt that Walpole's hold on power had become uncontrollable. Thomson's hatred of Walpole was increased even before the Licensing Act, in April 1737, when the government introduced a Bill of Pains and Penalties to punish the people of Edinburgh on account of the Porteous riot there the previous September.[17] However enthusiastic a supporter of the British Union, no Scot educated at Edinburgh University can have enjoyed watching Walpole's authoritarian treatment of that city. By September 1737 the rift between Frederick and the King became incendiary, with the Prince of Wales, his wife Augusta, and their newborn daughter expelled from St. James's Palace. There was fear that the Licensing Act would lead to wholesale censorship of the press, and in January 1738 (on the 14th of which month *Agamemnon* was submitted to the Lord Chamberlain's Examiner of Plays), the publisher Andrew Millar reprinted Milton's *Areopagitica*, with a new preface by Thomson. Probably out of concern for the safe passage of *Agamemnon* through the licensing office, Thomson decided to remain anonymous, writing simply as 'another hand'. But his preface thundered in defence of 'the best human Rights', and the 'Use of our noblest Faculties'. As in *Liberty*, Greek and Saxon

---

[16] Loftis (1963), 111.   [17] Boyer (1737), 360–2, 400–4.

freedoms are paired, for freedom of thought was treasured by ancient Greeks and by Alfred the Great. Thomson warns every 'True Briton' against being deceived by those who argued for control of publishing.

Yet all that was censored of *Agamemnon* were the last six lines of a prologue written by another opposition playwright, Thomson's Scottish friend David Mallet. This did contain a contentious reference to the Licensing Act.[18] The play opened at Drury Lane on 6 April, with Pope honouring his friend by attending, and Thomson himself, sweating profusely in the upper gallery, reciting the speeches along with the actors. Despite the difficulties attending upon any brand new play so late in the season, it ran for nine nights (a satisfactory performance in the eighteenth century), and made a comfortable profit. The last two acts were, however, not successful, and Thomson rewrote them mid-way during the run, excising a whole sub-plot, inspired by Sophocles' *Antigone*, involving a love affair between Hemon (a son of Egisthus) and Electra.[19] The first edition of this revised version, printed in three thousand copies and one hundred royal copies, was sold out almost immediately, leading to a second edition of fifteen hundred ordinary copies being printed three days later.[20]

Loftis has argued that the play escaped censorship because Walpole was deliberately slow to use his new prerogative and chose not to ban any play for two years, until incensed by Henry Brooke's *Gustavus Vasa* (1739), an allegory set in an only nominally identified Sweden.[21] It was more surprising when in March of the same year a second play fell foul of the new censorship, James Thomson's *Edward and Eleonora*. Perhaps Walpole was taking belated

---

[18] An allusion to the British stage 'unbias'd yet by party rage', and pleas for the audience to supply 'our last best licence', were both to be omitted from the stage production.

[19] Kern (1966) compared in detail the manuscript version of *Agamemnon* in the Larpent collection with the first printed edition, and is able to chart extensive early revisions. The play was notoriously catcalled and hissed on its first night, especially the last two acts, as Benjamin Victor, present on the first night, later recalled: Victor (1776), iii. 27–8.

[20] Grant (1951), 186. For details of 18th-c. editions, see Feather (1988), 94. The majority appear to have been of 1,000 to 1,500 copies, so that Thomson's first edition of 3,000 was well above average. The popularity of his play must have been assisted by the applause with which the most obviously anti-Walpole speeches were greeted in the theatre: see Thomas Davies (1780), ii. 32.

[21] Loftis (1963), 151.

vengeance for the political implications of Thomson's earlier
Agamemnon, implications which he may simply have not seen, or
to which he did not want to call attention. But it is more likely that
Agamemnon's failure to get itself banned resulted from the death of
Queen Caroline on 20 November 1737, early in the winter preceding its production. She had been Walpole's *de facto* working partner, represented in the play by Clytemnestra. This may have
removed its sting, but it may also have made any criticism of
Caroline look tasteless and redundant. Despite the recent rumours
about her relationship with Walpole, Caroline had remained
popular well into her middle age. She bore her husband eight
children, tolerated his affairs, and never lost his affection. Her
only real mistake was to have left her son Frederick behind in
Hanover at the age of seven, an abandonment for which he never
forgave her. It is tempting to ask whether Thomson modified his
Clytemnestra, whose final delineation is unusually virtuous, after
Caroline died.

Perhaps the picture of Agamemnon (played by James Quin, the
deep-voiced star actor of the 1730s) was far enough removed from
the 'patriots'' caricature of George II to deter Walpole from intervening. Indeed, an intensification of the parallels between George
and Agamemnon was actually the change which Aaron Hill urged
Thomson to make in the last two acts of the play.[22] For the real
dramatic conflict is between Agamemnon and Egisthus, and this
rupture did not square with the picture Thomson's public had of
the relationship between their King and his Prime Minister. The
first encounter between Agamemnon and Egisthus (II. iii) establishes their differences. Egisthus indulges in nauseating flattery;
Agamemnon, the patriot king, lectures Egisthus on the rule of law
versus corruption (II. iii). Yet although the play was not seen as an
overwhelming indictment of Agamemnon-George, it does not
wholly excuse him, either. The sage Melisander thinks that although Agamemnon's crimes are more of omission than commission, absentee monarchs with poor choices of regent are asking for
trouble (III. i):

> I think that *Agamemnon*
> Deserves some touch of blame. To put the power,

---

[22] Hill (1754), ii. 49. See further Hammond (2000), 19–20. On Hill's relationship
with Thomson see Sambrook (1991), 38–44.

> The power of blessing or oppressing *millions*,
> Of doing or great good or equal mischief,
> Even into doubtful hands, is worse than careless.

But nobody lays any other political charge against Agamemnon, which is more than can be said for Walpole-Egisthus, one of

> those dust-licking, reptile, close
> Insinuating, speckled, smooth court-serpents,
> That make it so unsafe, chiefly for kings,
> To walk this weedy world.

The language is so close to the opposition's criticisms of Walpole's circle as to be indistinguishable. So is the loyal Arcas' description of what has happened in Agamemnon's ten-year absence: the state swarms with villains. Egisthus has bought off the citizens with luxury (III. ii), 'He taught them wants, beyond their private means: | And strait, in bounty's pleasing chains involv'd, | They grew his slaves.'

Thomson's tragedy, which first established the Clytemnestra––Aegisthus–Agamemnon story as a stageable theme for the eighteenth century internationally, was originally called *The Death of Agamemnon* (it is so titled in the Larpent manuscript). This is only significant because Clytemnestra is excluded from the planning and execution of the murder. The play is fundamentally not about her but about conflict between men. The sole vice of the returning king, Agamemnon, has been physical absence; towards Cassandra, who reminds him of Electra, he has only fatherly feelings (IV. ii, a detail culled from the mythographer Hyginus). Egisthus is an irredeemable opportunist, a corrupt palace official, exclusively responsible for organizing his cousin's death. There is a political triangle, but it is not Clytemnestra who completes it. The third important political individual is a male type of ideal civic responsibility, a heroic, freethinking (Athenian) sage, Melisander (played by no less an actor than Theophilus Cibber), who has developed his innate wisdom into enlightened politics after an encounter with Nature on a deserted Aegean island. Clytemnestra's only role is to have become the weak link in the Argive political chain: it is only by seducing her that Egisthus could destroy the previous settlement between citizens and king. This settlement closely resembles that made by the Glorious Revolution, and its importance is only understood by the proto-Whig Melisander.

AGAMEMNON AND ITS SOURCES

A letter from Bishop Rundle to Mrs Sandys of December 1736 reports that subsequent to his freedom-loving Sophonisba, Thomson was bringing 'another untoward Heroine on the stage . . . His present story is the death of AGAMEMNON. An adultress who murthers her husband, is but an odd example to be presented before, and admonish the beauties of *Great Britain*.'[23] But Thomson's Clytemnestra is no murderess, and her alienation from Egisthus is so intense that she scarcely even qualifies as an adulteress. Thomson's Clytemnestra is broadly based on her Senecan prototype (she an emotionally vulnerable and erotically interesting figure), but is more innocent and virtuous than in any other version of *Agamemnon* ever written; not only is she a model mother and forgiving wife, but she absolutely refuses to condone the murder of her husband, and declines into near-insanity because of psychological pressure.

This is the Clytemnestra beloved of the eighteenth century, a woman of little moral autonomy, caught between competing loyalties, and beset by a tendency to swoon. As the play opens she is quivering with anxiety because the beacon signal was seen some nights ago, and Agamemnon will return any minute. Through a summary of the plot of *Iphigenia in Aulis* supplied by her own old (Senecan) nurse (I. i), the audience learns how the afflicted queen suffered the loss of her daughter, and was abandoned by her husband to a 'soothing lover's power', the attentions of a skilful and charming swain. But the most important piece of information is that Clytemnestra resisted his advances for years. For at the heart of Thomson's conception of the Agamemnon story lies Nestor's version in the third book of the *Odyssey* where Agamemnon leaves Clytemnestra under the supervision of a bard, and does not renounce her wifely loyalty until Aegisthus disposes of this guardian of her morals. 'Melisander' in Thomson is a sage from Athens (IV. v), the birthplace of what progressive people in the eighteenth century already regarded as the first true republic (a viewpoint which had permeated the Greek section of Thomson's epic *Liberty*). The nurse says of Aegisthus,

[23] See McKillop (1958), 108–9.

> yet could he not,
> With all his arts, his love, submission, charms,
> O'ercome the struggling purpose of your soul;
> Till *Melisander*, to a desart isle,
> He banish'd from your ear (I. i).

Clytemnestra's unstable feminine psyche was meant to be supervised by this sage, 'Whom every science, every muse adorn'd, | While the good honest heart enrich'd them all' (I. i). She stresses that she would never have departed from the road of virtue, whatever the pressure, had Melisander been present to protect her (I. i).

Melisander's genius for political theory was perfected while he communed with Nature when confined on a Cycladic isle. When in *Agamemnon* Talthybius arrives to report the storm, he tells Clytemnestra that Agamemnon's ship put in at one of the Cyclades, hailed by 'A miserable figure... | Horrid and wild, with famine worn away', who called upon the passing ship plaintively 'in *Greek*', begging it 'To bear him thence, from savage solitude' (I. vii). The eighteenth-century reader will have thought at once of the castaway Achaemenides in the third book of the *Aeneid* as well as the adventures of Robinson Crusoe, the hero of the subtly political, utopian novel by Thomson's fellow Whig Daniel Defoe, published in 1719 and an instant success; but this part of the play is also informed by Sophocles' *Philoctetes*, from which is derived much of Melisander's poetry: his descriptions, during his lyrical scene with his old friend Arcas, of his mossy cave, his quests for food, his hunting snares, and his lonely meals (II. i). Thomson may have acquired a text of the first English translation of *Philoctetes*, written and published in 1725 by Thomas Sheridan to accompany a Greek-language performance by boys at his School in Dublin (see Ch. 9).

Indeed, Thomson has used a variety of sources. Aeschylus' terrifying Clytemnestra may have been avoided, but Aeschylean poetry is certainly present: there are several indisputable signs of the Greek *Agamemnon*, for example in the watchman's description of the beacon relay (I. ii), and in a large proportion of Cassandra's lines, especially her lines about the song of the nightingale (IV. iii), the ghosts of Thyestes' children, and the offstage murder of Agamemnon, 'the Lion' and 'the Victim Bull'.[24] The delivery

---

[24] For a detailed illustration of the similarities between the Cassandra scenes of Aeschylus and Thomson see Ingram (1966), 150–5.

of this poetry was much enhanced by the vocal talents of the actress Susannah Maria Cibber, aged 24, an excellent oratorio singer (she was Thomas Arne's sister as well as Theophilus Cibber's wife). Cassandra's poetry certainly struck its audience as 'well calculated to fill the audience with alarm, astonishment, and suspense, at an awful event, obscurely hinted at in very strong imagery'.[25] This is important because rare: there are very few traces of Aeschylean influence on the eighteenth-century stage in Britain, at least until after the appearance of the first complete English translation, by Robert Potter, in 1777.[26]

Aeschylus was simply too forbidding to most contemporary authors. His Greek was far too difficult—in Fielding's *Joseph Andrews* (1742) Parson Adams's taste for Aeschylus is a sign of eccentricity[27]—and his dramas lacked the distressed heroines required by the early Georgian theatre. The only developed character in all of Aeschylus who must have seemed promising was Clytemnestra, since she is a woman with interesting maternal and erotic feelings, and it is no accident, therefore, that the only Aeschylean tragedy which was adapted for the eighteenth-century British stage was 'her' play, *Agamemnon*. The adapter, Thomson, was fluent in Latin, and certainly used Thomas Stanley's 1663 edition, with its Latin crib. But Thomson's education prepared him unusually well to understand Aeschylus' Greek itself; his friends later recalled his 'learned' talk on the subject of Greek tragedy.[28]

He had studied at Jedburgh Grammar School in the Scottish lowlands, where pupils were required to speak exclusively in Latin during school hours. He studied Virgil, Horace, Ovid, Terence, Sallust, Lucan, and the works of the Scottish Latin scholar George

---

[25] See Warton in Pope (1797), iv. 10 n.

[26] This was despite the persistent and eventually unrealized rumours in the second and third decades of the century that Lewis Theobald, a translator of both Sophocles and Aristophanes, was working on Aeschylus. There are documentable echoes of *Eumenides* in Theobald's light-hearted spectacular *Orestes* of 1731. *Prometheus Bound* was the one Aeschylean play to have been published in English translation before 1777 (see Morell (1773)), and the only one besides *Agamemnon* which can be associated with a performance; an anonymous pantomime entitled *Prometheus* was performed at Covent Garden on 26 Dec. 1775, two years after Morell's translation appeared. See Nicoll (1952–9), 340.

[27] On the Revd William Young, the impecunious curate of Gillingham befriended by Fielding and on whom he based his Aeschylus-loving Parson Adams, see Dudden (1952), i. 157–9, 357–63, and 398–400.

[28] Warton in Pope (1797), iv. 10 n.

Buchanan, whose *Tragoediae* as well as his *Psalms* and *Historia Scotorum* were on the curriculum.[29] He must have been involved in productions of plays in Latin, which were important in border grammar schools; he also certainly studied arithmetic and Greek. At the University of Edinburgh he entered Professor William Scott's Greek class, in which he spent two whole years, and probably attended Charles Mackie's class on Greek and Roman antiquities. He was swept away with the enthusiasm of the Scottish Enlightenment for Newtonian philosophy and science, and was member of an 'Athenian Society' which published poetry.

The major source of his *Agamemnon*, despite the unusual Aeschylean input, is certainly Seneca: examples are the first dialogue with the nurse, Clytemnestra's scenes with Egisthus (in the first of which she cites the Senecan motive of pride in her descent from Jove, I. iv), her castigation of the malign affect of 'debasing, thoughtless, blind blind love', fear, and shame (I. iv), and the fantasy of flight into exile (I. iv). From Seneca Thomson has also absorbed the chorus of Trojan captives attendant upon Cassandra, their lament for Troy (IV. iii), and above all the cynical manner in which his Egisthus plays on Clytemnestra's emotions.[30] This is a challenge, however, because Thomson's Clytemnestra is so ashamed of herself, and so in love with Agamemnon, that she fears she will not be able even to meet his gaze (I. iv: 'How shall I bear an injur'd husband's eye? | The fiercest foe bears not a look so dreadful | As does the man we wrong'). Egisthus uses both wheedling and emotional violence, often in quick succession; on one occasion he rebukes her for weeping when he has just deliberately distressed her with a description of Iphigenia's death-throes (I. iv).

THOMSON'S TRAGIC FAMILY

In the final interview between these former lovers, their relationship descends into open conflict. Clytemnestra refuses to countenance the murder of Agamemnon. If Egisthus does not drop his murderous plan, she will expose him and commit suicide (v. i). Egisthus tries hard to dissuade her, but, ultimately, it does not matter, since he has already arranged the killings of both Agamemnon, who will

---

[29] Mary Jane W. Scott (1988), 24–5.
[30] See Seneca, *Agamemnon*, 162, 131–8, 123, 589–658.

be assassinated in the bath, and of Cassandra (V. i). Clytemnestra goes into psychological meltdown, incapable of intervention to stop the imminent murders, and expressing a death-wish for all four of them—Agamemnon, Cassandra, herself and Egisthus. When the back-scene opens at the beginning of V. vi, Egisthus stands crowing over the corpse, Electra throws herself upon it, and Clytemnestra enters, half-crazed, and drops into a dead faint after accusing Egisthus of destroying her 'happy family', her virtue and her honour (V. viii).

For Thomson's Clytemnestra is an unimpeachable mother. She has kept Orestes close, adores Electra, and is tortured by the thought that her besmirched sexual reputation might adversely affect her 'poor blameless children' (I. i). She would like also to have been a loving spouse: the reunion between Agamemnon and Clytemnestra could not be more different from the tense formality of Aeschylus. It begins with a passionate embrace, Agamemnon charging on to the stage demanding to know 'Where is my life! my love! my *Clytemnestra*! | O let me press thee to my fluttering soul' (II. ii). She tearfully reproaches him with Iphigenia's death and his prolonged absence; the whole encounter is entirely Thomson's, and suggests why Lessing admired his warm emotionalism (see below).

The impact of this virtuous Clytemnestra must have been enhanced by its performance, by an actress famous for both the passionate conviction of her delivery and her own respectable private life, Mary Anne Porter. Horace Walpole, far from being offended by the parallels between Egisthus and his father Robert, was so impressed by Porter's performance as Clytemnestra that he bored his friends and wrote an essay on the subject (which, unfortunately, has been lost).[31] She had previously attempted two Euripidean heroines, both Richard West's Hecuba and Charles Johnson's Medæa, but it was her Clytemnestra in Thomson's *Agamemnon* of which her audience most approved.[32] Mrs Porter was thought to be a plain but particularly intelligent actress, with an excellent ear for poetry. She was commended for her 'spirited Propriety' even when delineating rage, and also for her portrayal of grief, when 'she subsided into the most affecting Softness'.[33]

---

[31] Sambrook (1991), 177. See also Ketton-Cremer (1940), 50–1.
[32] Thomas Davies (1784), iii. 467–9.   [33] Victor (1761), ii. 56–8.

For what Porter's acting helped Thomson achieve was the transformation of an ancient tragedy into an excellent example of the popular eighteenth-century British genre of pathetic drama, dominated by a suffering, virtuous heroine, which, as we have seen in the previous chapter, went under the title 'She-Tragedy'. His tender Clytemnestra is engaged in a constant struggle with her desire to be virtuous, with her conscience, and with emotional vulnerability. She is a woman of whom audiences sharing an eighteenth-century notion of ideal, submissive femininity could approve. A perceptive theatrical critic later in the century actually praised Thomson for diminishing the Aeschylean Clytemnestra's personal authority: 'the author has varied from the idea of Aeschylus; and, I think with great propriety . . . gives some shades of tenderness to this princess, and makes her yield with reluctance to the persuasions of Aegisthus'.[34]

The degree of Thomson's distance from Aeschylus, despite his knowledge of the Greek play, emerges not only in his whitewashing of Clytemnestra but in the concomitant redemption of Agamemnon. Thomson gives him the best speech in defence of the sacrifice of Iphigenia he has ever been given (II. ii), and the reason for this is the Whig neo-Stoic ideology of private sacrifice for the public good (Cato was the Whigs' favourite hero, a predilection confirmed for ever by Addison's *Cato* of 1713). The world cannot be sustained by 'indulging private inclinations, | The selfish passions'. Even if Thomson's audience was not persuaded that 'The public good, the good of others' must take precedence if you are a leader, whatever the personal cost, Agamemnon must have struck them as genuinely convinced of this principle, and as a man who had given political ideals a great deal of responsible thought. The other notes he sounds would have also sounded at least plausible in 1738: he was doing the constitutional will of the people who had ordained him, 'By common voice, the general of the *Greeks*'. The military operations have been against a land of unquestionably enemy status, 'faithless *Asia*'; most telling of all, how could he pull rank and refuse but one life 'to those generous thousands . . . | . . . stood all | Prepar'd to die?' Taking into account the good Whig principles of 'honour, duty, glory, public good' he actually had no choice at all; he could not but put his duties as

'The *Greek*, the chief, the patriot, and the king' above his rights as a father. He says that Clytemnestra could not have continued to love him if he had proved so selfish and dishonourable, and, for a few minutes at least, it is possible to believe him.

Agamemnon has never been so convincing, and the persuasive force is heightened by his uxorial tenderness. This is an Agamemnon as Patriot King (popular Whig political terminology in Thomson's time),[35] entirely reconfigured to fit the eighteenth-century British model of ideal male sensibility. He and Clytemnestra are both inherently virtuous human beings, on whose capacity for beneficent action have been placed intolerable strains. At the heart of the play Clytemnestra relents towards him, just before the arrival of Electra and Orestes (II. iii), and parents and children together engage in a group embrace and an effusive affirmation of mutual regard. The Argive royal family, astonishingly, is rewritten as the new bourgeois ideal nuclear family of the mid-eighteenth century, destroyed by the malign ambition of an interloping politician.

EDWARD AND ELEONORA AND EURIPIDES' *ALCESTIS*

Thomson's *Agamemnon* ensured that its ancient Greek mythical figures became, if only briefly, popular currency in London culture. It was this play that gave Walpole the nickname 'Egisthus' in Pope's opposition satire of later the same year, *One Thousand Seven Hundred and Thirty Eight, a Dialogue, Something Like Horace* (i. 51). The tragedy's elevated, heroic subject-matter had almost instantly been seen to have comic potential; a mock prologue to *Agamemnon* published in *The Literary Courier of Grub Street* on 27 April, only two days after the last performance and the original publication of Thomson's text, compares Clytemnestra with Catherine Hayes (a notorious murderess who had been hanged at Tyburn in 1726), Egisthus with Francis Charteris (a versatile villain and a convicted rapist), Melisander with Robinson Crusoe, and Cassandra with the apocryphal prophetess Mother Shipton.[36]

Perhaps it was this type of mockery that made Thomson, when next adapting Greek tragedy, consciously write a play less heroically vulnerable to comic deflation, and more emotionally affecting.

[35] See Hugh Cunningham (1989).   [36] See Sambrook (1991), 185–6.

Edward and Eleonora is not only set in the English (rather than ancient Greek) past, but is by far the most emotive and sentimental of Thomson's dramas. The prologue actually invites the audience to weep in response: 'If these best Passions prompt the pleasing Woe | Indulge it Freely—Nature bids it flow.' Thomson carefully provides not one but two appealing roles for women: Eleonora was to be played by Christiana Horton, admired as Shakespeare's Cordelia and Rowe's Jane Shore; the role for Daraxa was assigned to Anne Hallam, a famous Lady Macbeth. The slimline play is consciously modelled on the Greek pattern, for it contains only three other characters, and at only about 1,500 lines is relatively short.

The subject-matter is partially derived, along with the context, from a story about the last crusade. At the siege of Jaffa in 1272, Prince Edward (later Edward I) was injured by a poisoned blade and was only saved because his wife Eleonora sucked the poison from the wound, thus jeopardizing her own life. Thomson's sources probably included Sir Richard Baker's *Chronicle of the Kings of England* (1643) and the fourth volume of Rapin de Thoyras's *History of England* (1724–31), but Thomson has filled out their narratives with the idea that the self-sacrificing wife becomes mortally ill, before having her life restored by an exotic hero. This idea is taken from Euripides' *Alcestis*. Alcestis is restored to her husband Admetus after Heracles vanquishes Death; Eleonora is cured by the humane Sultan Selim of Jaffa, temporarily disguised as a dervish.

Alcestis had lurked behind the scenes rather than taking centre stage before the eighteenth century in Britain, appearing in handbooks or poetry as a symbol of constancy, devotion, and (frequently false) hope in her good fortune to have defied the bounds of mortality. It is this restored Alcestis who had been famously recalled by Milton in Sonnet 23 (*c*.1658), written upon the death of his wife:

> Methought I saw my late espousèd Saint
> Brought to me like *Alcestis* from the grave,
> Whom *Joves* great son to her glad Husband gave,
> Rescue'd from death by force though pale and faint.[37]

---

[37] Milton (1952–5), ii. 156–7.

In his treatise *Of Education* (1644), Milton had previously cited Euripides' *Alcestis* as the ideal play for study by young boys (see Chs. 8–9); and the pedagogical value of the drama seems to have been acknowledged from at least the 1540s, when there is evidence to suggest that the pupils of Westminster performed it in the Latin version of George Buchanan.[38] It should also be remembered that in the original sketches for *Paradise Lost*, which Milton had considered designing as a tragedy, Death was intended to be a stage character as he is in the opening scene of *Alcestis*.[39]

However, the final scene of Shakespeare's *The Winter's Tale* (1609) is probably the nearest we can get today to gauging the presence of Alcestis on the English Renaissance stage. The parallels between this late Shakespearean play and the Euripidean drama of death and rebirth have long been detected on account of both their broadly similar mood and content. Shakespeare's Leontes is the far-from-perfect husband, who, like Admetus, only becomes chastened after the death of his model wife; and, like Admetus, the reformed widower is rewarded in the final moments of the play by the 'return' of his wife, in silent, statuesque form. With the increasing evidence that Greek tragedy was more widely known in Shakespeare's day, especially through Latin translations like Buchanan's, than has hitherto been allowed,[40] it becomes necessary to acknowledge the possibility of some direct Euripidean influence on Shakespeare's last scene.

Alcestis also lies behind the plot of Charles Gildon's *Love's Victim* (Lincoln's Inn Fields, 1701), in which Queen Guinoenda is persuaded to drink poison in order to save the life of her husband, and enacts a long death scene with her husband, and their children (see above, Ch. 3).[41] This inaugurated the eighteenth-century performance history of *Alcestis* in Britain, when the selfless wife makes several appearances on stage, but either heavily disguised or in the opera house.[42] In 1718 Gildon also singled out Euripides' *Alcestis*

---

[38] Bruce R. Smith (1988), 201.

[39] See Jodrell (1789), 318–20, who also argues that Euripides' figure of Death, Thanatos, probably informed William Alabaster's *Roxana*, acted at Trinity College, Cambridge in 1632.

[40] Schleiner (1990), Kerrigan (1996), Ewbank (forthcoming).

[41] Cf. Robert D. Hume (1976), 451.

[42] It is surprising that in his book about *Alcestis*, published in 1789, the Euripidean scholar Paul Jodrell, who is normally well versed in the performance reception of Greek tragedy (see below on Whitehead's *Creusa*), does not include

(together with *Helen*) for its treatment of conjugal love;[43] his interest in the play is no doubt inextricably linked with the popularity of
Lully's operatic version, *Alceste, ou le triomphe d'Alcide* of 1674,
with its libretto by Philippe Quinault. Gildon had previously engaged with Greek tragedy through the mediation of Quinault, most
notably in his tragedy *Phaeton* (1698), which, as was seen in Ch. 3,
draws on both Quinault's *Phaéton* and Euripides' *Medea*.

Handel turned to the myth of Alcestis at least twice in his career.
He composed music in 1750 for the (now lost) masque by the
novelist Tobias Smollett, but had previously enjoyed immediate
success with his full opera *Admeto, re di Tessaglia* when it was
performed at the King's Theatre in 1727. It may well have been
Handel's feisty operatic Alcestis, who returns to test Admetus'
fidelity, that inspired James Thomson to write the first full English
adaptation of the Greek tragedy; certainly on his arrival in London
in 1725 he had become completely stage-struck.[44]

Thomson's play draws heavily on Euripides, even though this is
not immediately obvious because of the Crusade setting. The
medieval tale is fleshed out, however, with details and (very
often) verbatim translations from Euripides' play concerning Alcestis' similarly altruistic act to save her own husband's life. In Act
III, for example, the Arab princess, Daraxa, gives an account of
Eleonora's death taken from Euripides' *Alcestis* (152 ff.):

> When this pride of women,
> This best of wives, which in his radiant course,
> The sun beholds, when first she, sickening felt
> Th' imperious summons of approaching fate,
> All rob'd in spotless white she sought her Altars;
> And, prostrate there, for her departing soul ...

Later in Act III, when Eleonora lies dying on her couch (see
Fig. 4.2), the scene is closely modelled on *Alcestis* 244 ff.; in

Thomson's *Edward and Eleonora* among the numerous adaptations (mostly French
and Italian) discussed in his lengthy 'Final Essay' devoted to this play's afterlife
(312–65). He does, however, include some interesting observations on the difficulties presented by the resurrection motif ('a heathen fiction', p. 365) to the 18th-c.
British mind, which was at once devout and profoundly rationalizing.

[43] See above, Ch. 3, p. 91.
[44] Sambrook (1991), 28. In 2000, the English Bach Festival mounted the premiere staging of Handel's *Alceste* in the Linbury Studio, Covent Garden, drawing
on various sources in an attempt to reconstruct Smollett's lost masque.

FIGURE 4.2   James Heath, frontispiece to James Thomson's *Edward and Eleonora* (1795).

Act V, when the Arabian prince (who is both Death and Heracles here), protesting his innocence, calls in a witness who turns out to be Eleonora, the model is *Alcestis* 1006 ff.

UNDER THE BLUE PENCIL

Thomson's play, however, had to wait until 1775 for its first production. The Lord Chamberlain's office had no problem with decoding this particular political allegory; by transposing the Alcestis myth to a moment in British history, Thomson had arguably given himself rather *less* freedom to articulate contemporary political dissatisfaction than if he had exploited the distance afforded by adopting the ancient myth *tout court*. In February 1739 Thomson's *Edward and Eleonora* was in rehearsal at Covent Garden, and a transcript was sent to the Stage Licenser, who took until 27 March, two days before the play was due to open, to forbid its performance. This was only a fortnight after *Gustavus Vasa* was proscribed, and the timing seems to have been designed to be 'admonitory and vindictive'.[45]

Samuel Johnson, writing some forty years later, had difficulty understanding the censor's objections,[46] but the parallels between Edward (the Admetus figure) and Thomson's patron, Frederick Prince of Wales, are obvious. Thomson was eulogizing the Prince and thereby advancing the cause of the Opposition once again. At the beginning of the play, Edward is urged by Gloster to abandon war in the Holy Land and to return to affairs of state at home, where his aged father has fallen prey to evil counsellors (Act I). Towards the end of the play (after the death of Eleonora) comes the news of the death of the King, and Edward is roused into taking revenge. Once the Sultan has rescued Eleonora from death with a miraculous cure, Edward is set to return to England, realizing that is was misplaced zeal that led him to go to war against the Sultan in the first place.

While the parallels with *Alcestis* serve to dignify the Princess of Wales, Augusta of Saxe-Gotha (to whom the first printed edition is dedicated), it is the deviations from Euripides' play, above all, that serve to ennoble the Prince. In Thomson's version, Edward (unlike Admetus) does not endorse his wife's self-sacrifice at any

---

[45] See Sambrook (1991), 194.   [46] Samuel Johnson (1794), iv. 242.

point, but actively seeks to oppose it once he discovers the identity of the willing substitute. The most notable deviation, however, is the absence of a confrontation between father and son, which would have mirrored contemporary events rather too sharply. Of course, topography precludes any such encounter in Thomson's version, but by suppressing this scene in particular—where Admetus' moral duplicity is exposed no less than the opportunism of his father—Thomson guarantees that Prince Edward's conduct remains unimpeachable. A few marks on the censored manuscript indicate which lines offended the Licenser, including Archdeacon Theald's assurance in Act IV, Scene ii that he was promoted without any form of corruption, and Edward's denunciation in Act IV, Scene viii of his father's 'servile Vermin' at court, his 'Corrupt, corrupting Ministers and Favourites'.[47] But there are several other passages about ministerial greed and corruption that must have been equally inflammatory. The scandal surrounding the banning of the play increased its sales: 4,500 copies were printed, and Thomson made a handsome profit. His political message must have been enhanced by the explicit parallel drawn in the dedication between the virtues of the Princess of Wales and those of Eleonora, and by the 'Saxon' type of the lettering of the date on which the play was prohibited, suggestive of the ancient Saxon liberties that the Licensing Act had put in jeopardy.[48]

EDWARD AND ELEONORA REVIVED

The play was admired throughout the middle of the eighteenth century, and in 1772 John Wesley wrote in his famous *Journal* that not only are the sentiments just and noble, but that the diction is 'strong, smooth and elegant, and the plot conducted with the utmost art and wrought off in a most surprising manner. It is quite his masterpiece, and I really think might vie with any modern performance of the kind.'[49] Sure enough, in March 1775 at the Theatre Royal, Covent Garden, Thomson's play was finally enjoyed by London audiences (albeit with slight changes from the 1739 edition on account of the indisposition of the celebrated actor and rival of David Garrick, Spranger Barry, who had been

---

[47] Sambrook (1991), 195.   [48] Ibid. (1991), 196.
[49] Wesley (1906), iii. 488.

intended for the part of the Sultan). The actor-manager Thomas Hull mounted a production of *Edward and Eleonora* at the suggestion of Barry's wife Ann, one of the most distinguished actresses of her day, who went on to play Eleonora in Hull's production. Hull himself took the part of Gloster; and in the Preface to the printed edition of the 1775 production of the play, Hull is circumspect about the earlier problems with the censor, although he makes it clear that Thomson's work ought to be more widely known than it is. However, against the background of the early stages of the American War of Independence, Hull is able to vindicate the radical playwright in his prologue to the play that he delivered in his theatre:

> 'Tis your own Thomson—he whose lib'ral Mind
> Breath'd love to all the friends of Human Kind![50]

Hull, in the part of Gloster, denounces religion and racial bigotry (Act I, p. 3); and after the death of Eleonora, he urges the young king to assume his regal responsibilities, which include guarding the arts and securing the sacred rights of industry and freedom (Act IV, p. 43). In 1775 at Covent Garden, these sentiments would have met with an attentive, if not wholly sympathetic, audience with an increasingly liberal outlook (on which see Ch. 6).

The aesthetic climate of the period both accommodated and even promoted sentiment of the kind generated in the first part of Euripides' play; and the fulsome praise for the production in *The Morning Chronicle* on 20 March 1775 is no doubt due in large measure to that coincidence of mood. The production, the reviewer averred, had been received

with that best test of excellence, where the tender passions are attempted to be excited—gushing tears. The audience, which was more brilliant and more numerous than ever yet seen in this theatre, confessed their sensibility, and wept applause.

But it was, above all, the fact that in the newly liberal climate of 1775, the voices of tolerance and reason could prevail; and the final words of wisdom in the play are significantly spoken by the formerly demonized 'other', Sultan Selim:

[50] Thomson (1775), 1.

Let holy rage, let persecution cease,
Let the head argue, but the heart be peace.
Let all mankind in love of what is right,
In virtue and humanity unite. (Act V, p. 59)

The resurrection of this eighteenth-century Alcestis affords not
just marital but political unity as well; and Thomson's play not
surprisingly remained in the repertoire until at least the end of the
century. A picture by Angelica Kauffman (who later painted the
dying Alcestis) of the scene in which Eleonora sucks the venom
from her husband was exhibited at the Royal Academy in 1776, the
year after the play's 1775 revival; and William Blake engraved a
more elaborate picture of the scene in 1793, which is not only
extremely theatrical but also suggestive of the ancient roots of the
fable (see Fig. 4.3).[51] In 1796 at Drury Lane the leading tragedi-

FIGURE 4.3   William Blake, print entitled *Edward & Elenor*, 1793.

[51] For Kauffman's oil painting and the popularity of the prints of it, see Roworth
(1992), 62, 164–6, with figs. 43 and 140; for her *Death of Alcestis* see p. 189. The
striking Blake engraving is also reproduced as fig. 6 in Essick (1983), with discussion
on pp. 14–17.

enne Sarah Siddons took the part of Eleonora in a production with her brother John Kemble. On this occasion, however, the arrival of the children in the farewell speech was greeted with mirth rather than empathy.[52] Whilst the political sentiments of this adaptation still remained urgent, the affective scene of farewell now seemed cloyingly sentimental at a time when the age of sensibility had finally run its course.

THOMSON'S INFLUENCE

Thomson's dramas were aesthetically prefigurative. His *Agamemnon* helped draw the precursors of the English Romantic poets' attention to the poetry of its Aeschylean original, quoted, for example, in the epigraph to Thomas Gray's *Ode to Adversity*, a poem deeply imbued with Greek tragic imagery (composed 1742, published 1753).[53] *Edward and Eleonora,* on the other hand, adumbrated the literary watershed that coincided with the fall of Walpole three years later, in 1742. Thereafter progressive and critical poets adopted a new agenda which rejected obvious allegory and the type of satire identified with Pope in favour of a romantic engagement with the explicitly British, and often very distant British, past. This type of engagement was, in the second half of the century, to come to fruition in the plays of William Mason (see Ch. 7).

But Thomson's impact is rather more international than this, even extending to North America.[54] *Agamemnon* was certainly admired on the Continent. It influenced Alfieri, whose twin verse tragedies *Agamennone* and *Oreste* were popular in Britain after they appeared in English translation in 1815. Alfieri was desperate to build up an Italian theatrical literature to rival those in English and French, spent much time in London, and also wrote a *Sophonisba* (the title of Thomson's most famous play).[55] Thomson's *Agamemnon,* unusually for an English-language tragedy in the eighteenth

---

[52] *LS* v/3. 1907. The play was also performed outside London, for example on 21 Nov. 1788 at the Assembly Rooms in Snargate, Dover. See Rosenfeld (1978), 137.

[53] On Gray's use of *Agamemnon* see further Gleckner (1997), 44–5 and 145. He sees it as marking a stage in Gray's intense relationship with his beloved (and recently deceased) Richard West. In their intense correspondence ancient Greek quotations had been significant.

[54] Hilbert H. Campbell (1976), 104.

[55] See Alfieri (1810), ii. 33–8, and Edith Hall (forthcoming *a*).

century, was also translated into French and performed in Paris in 1780;[56] Thomson's other works attracted interest in France around the time of the Revolution,[57] and this revival of *Agamemnon* may lie behind Citizen Louis Jean Népomucène Lemercier's attraction to the political potential of the story. His *Agamemnon* shows the influence of Seneca (Aegisthus is much troubled by the ghost of Thyestes, I. i), but also of Thomson, for example in the handling of the sacrifice of Iphigenia (I. iii). Lemercier's adaptation was performed on 5 floréal year V (24 April 1797) at the Théâtre de la République, then considered the finest theatre in Paris. It had been formed in 1792 after the Comédie-Française was split by political differences and the actors sympathetic to the Revolution, including Citizen Talma, joined actors from the Variétés Amusantes to form the new theatre of the new republic. *Agamemnon* is a five-act verse tragedy, in which Clitemnestre (Françoise Vestris) owes much to Thomson's conception; she is a devoted mother, fearful that Agamemnon, with his filicidal record, may sacrifice Orestes (I. iii). Yet she is vain and silly (not unlike popular stereotypes of Marie-Antoinette), swooning her way throughout an ideologically charged vision of the assassination of the corrupt head of a decadent dynasty, fast becoming obsolete.

But Thomson's greatest impact was in Germany. The influential critic and playwright Gotthold Ephraim Lessing was an admirer, bestowing praise on Thomson's powers of expression, his innovative brilliance in the description of landscape, and for his painterly qualities, especially in *The Seasons*.[58] Lessing, whose seminal essay *Laocoon* (1766) explored the differences between poetry and visual art, had become interested in Thomson because of their shared fascination with ancient statuary: Thomson himself owned a collection of drawings of what were believed to be Greek sculptures, and, in Part Four of *Liberty*, he had included set-piece descriptions of eight of them—not only the Laocoon but others including the Farnese Hercules, the Vatican Meleager, the Dying Gladiator, the Apollo Belvedere, and the Farnese Flora. The sculptural parallels in Thomson's *Seasons* reveal the extent of his

---

[56] See Thomson (1780) and Wartelle (1978), 24.

[57] Barrell and Guest (2000), 231–2.

[58] Lessing (1968), iv. 205, 218, v. 97, 227, 235. This poetic cycle, repeatedly reprinted both in and after James Thomson's lifetime, was first translated into German in 1758.

fascination with the sentimental possibilities of expressing emotional agitation through classical form,[59] a fascination which finds an analogy in his *theatrical* synthesis of classical literary form with eighteenth-century emotional warmth and sensibility. This combination led to his tragedies being translated into German no fewer than three times in the mid-eighteenth century; Lessing was so impressed by *Agamemnon* that he began to translate it himself, as he also translated Robert Shiels's *Life of Thomson* for a German readership.[60]

In Lessing's *Laocoon*, widely regarded as the foundation text of modern aesthetics, a passage in Thomson's *Agamemnon* is singled out. It is one of the sage Melisander's speeches describing his confinement on an Aegean island, beginning 'Cast in the wildst of Cyclad Isles'; Lessing provides the speech both in English and in the German verse translation of Johann David Michaëlis (1750). What Lessing admires in Thomson is not only his 'classical' poetic art, but the proto-Romantic manner in which Melisander's communion with the beauties of Nature is connected with his spiritual and moral growth.[61] Through *Laocoon* Thomson thus entered the canon of poets universally recognized as forerunners of Romanticism. But Lessing also saw Thomson's dramatic works as part of an important breakthrough which had taken place in British socially sensitive drama in the 1730s (he pairs his plays on more than one occasion with Lillo's 1731 Drury Lane 'domestic tragedy' *The London Merchant, or The History of George Barnwell*). In 1756 Lessing wrote a flattering introduction to a German prose translation of Thomson's tragedies, admiring his knowledge of the human heart as well as his magical art, and comparing him with Corneille in his brilliance in updating Greek tragedy.[62] Lessing argued that Thomson took tragedy beyond the rule-bound form prescribed by antiquity and into new realms of feeling. Through Lessing, Thomson's *Agamemnon* made a lasting impression on German dramatic thought, and must have contributed to the interest in Thomson's own Aeschylean archetype which in due

---

[59] Sambrook (1991), 1144.

[60] See James (1750), (1756), and (1771); Lessing (1968), iii. 734, 732; Shiels (1753).

[61] Lessing (1968), v. 35–6.

[62] Lessing, 'Vorrede' to Thomson (1756), 3–4, reprinted in Lessing (1968), iii. 699–705.

course produced Wilhelm von Humboldt's 1816 translation. This in turn lies behind the operas of Wagner.[63] Such is the impact that an intelligent stage adaptation can have on the reception of an ancient tragedy.

[63] For Wagner's use of Humboldt's translation, see the discussion of Wagner's study of Aeschylus in Ewans (forthcoming).

5

Euripides' *Ion*, Coram's Foundlings, and Lord Hardwicke's Marriage Act

INTRODUCTION

Foundling heroes are perennially fascinating. From the Akkadian myth of Sargon, discovered in a basket on the river Euphrates,[1] through Moses and Nimrod to Cyrus, Romulus and Remus, the Japanese hero Hiruko, the Indian Karna of the *Mahabharata*— almost every ancient mythical system features an abandoned baby at its centre. The twentieth century produced Clark Kent, Superman, whose birth narrative was invented in 1939;[2] the twenty-first has already created the touching story of David, the robot foundling in search of parental love, in Steven Spielberg's movie *AI* (*Artificial Intelligence*, 2001). Foundling tales were already a staple of the ancient theatre, appearing in numerous (now lost) Euripidean tragedies, and in many of Menander's Hellenistic New Comedies. But, besides Oedipus, the only Greek tragic foundling to have survived exposure to the intervening centuries is Euripides' Ion. This chapter tells the story of the English-language recovery of this charming hero, and offers explanations for the particular date at which he was rediscovered.

It is Saturday, 20 April 1754. An excited London audience has gathered at Drury Lane to watch the premiere of a new play by the fashionable author William Whitehead. Based on Euripides' *Ion*, it has been retitled *Creusa, Queen of Athens*. It stars David Garrick, the incomparable actor-manager. This will be his only significant role in a play based on a Greek tragedy, despite his interest in that genre.[3]

---

[1] For the myth of Sargon and its texts see Brian Lewis (1980).

[2] See Bridwell (1971), 20–1, Redford (1967), Gaster (1969), 224–6. Brian Lewis (1980), 149–95, lists 72 different examples of foundling heroes, from the 13th c. BC until the 20th c. AD. On the ubiquity of this type of myth see also Binder (1964) and Huys (1995), 377–94.

[3] See further below, Ch. 7. Garrick was fascinated by ancient costumes, and reputed to have a large personal collection. See Price (1975), 57.

His co-star is the animated Hannah Pritchard, now established as his leading lady.[4] Their glamorous partnership in Shakespearean tragedy, especially *Macbeth*, is already legendary; John Zoffany and Henry Fuseli will paint famous pictures of them in the leading roles of this Shakespearean classic.[5] Whitehead has already made his name, in 1750, with a tragedy on an antique theme; *The Roman Father* was an adaptation from Corneille's *Horace*, in which Garrick had played the Roman republican patriot of the title to Mary Anne Yates' swooning Horatia.[6]

Hannah Pritchard has also already distinguished herself as the female lead in a revival of Smith's *Phaedra and Hippolitus* (1751–2) and in Richard Glover's patriotic *Boadicia* (Drury Lane 1753).[7] But *Creusa*, the new 'Grecian' production, promises more than one beautiful woman. Also performing, in breeches, are the legendary legs of Miss Maria Macklin, a 21-year-old expert transvestite, who plays the Delphic foundling.[8] Macklin, the daughter of the famous actor Charles Macklin, was born like Whitehead's young hero into a marriage of ambiguous validity; but her piety and refinement suited her casting as the self-possessed young priest at Delphi.[9]

Although not a smash hit, *Creusa* proved popular, especially with women in the audience: Whitehead was no political radical, but the emotional tenor of his dramas was perceived to be sympathetic, and progressive. His updated and modish Greek tragedy ran into May, was revived at Drury Lane in 1755, and was

---

[4] Hiffernan (1770), 98.

[5] See Vaughan (1979), pls. 1 and 6. Fuseli's powerful picture of Mrs Pritchard as Lady Macbeth is regarded as one of his masterpieces. For details see also Vaughan's cover and Fuseli (1975), 58–9.

[6] Lynch (1953), 187, notes that Whitehead considerably altered his French model in order to bring *The Roman Father* 'as near as possible to the form of Greek tragedy'. *The Roman Father* was a huge hit, one of the seven most popular tragedies of the mid-18th c., enjoying seven seasons at Drury Lane and four at Covent Garden by 1777.

[7] The same was not so true of her performance in Samuel Johnson's *Irene*, a tragic story of Sultan Mahomet II's love for the freedom-loving Grecian heroine set against the backdrop of the fall of Constantinople to the Turks; this had failed at Drury Lane in 1749, when Johnson had unfairly blamed Pritchard for the debacle. On Johnson's play and its sources see Spencer (1954), 250–6.

[8] As a critic wrote in *The Gray's Inn Journal* for 16 Feb. 1754, 'I do not remember to have seen any Actress wear the breeches with so good a grace.' See Highfill et al. (1973–93), x. 34.

[9] Macklin's ambitious father put her on the stage at a tender age; as a child her repertoire had included the little Duke of York in *Richard III*, and Tom Thumb (another foundling) in *The Tragedy of Tragedies*.

performed there twice in each of the years 1757, 1758, and 1759; this was in an era when a run of only nine nights meant a tragedy was accounted a success.[10] The play was a staple of private theatricals for years after its premiere; Lady Sarah Lennox starred in it at Holland House, where as Henry Fox's sister-in-law she was staying, on 20 April 1762.[11] The role of Creusa was one of those in which actresses liked to pose for publicity purposes (see Fig. 5.1). *Creusa* was much admired in its day for the economy of its plot construction and adherence to the Unities; it certainly helped Whitehead beat his friend William Mason to the poet laureateship three years after its premiere, in 1757, when Thomas Gray (a better poet than either of them) declined the appointment.[12]

THE RECOVERY OF *ION*

Many of the adaptations of Greek tragedy that appeared on the British stage in the late seventeenth and eighteenth centuries were inspired by an earlier Italian or French version. The Continental adapters usually selected ancient Greek texts which had been praised by Aristotle (*Oedipus, Iphigeneia in Tauris*), retold by Ovid (*Agamemnon*), dramatized by Seneca (*Medea, Phoenissae*), or translated into Renaissance Latin (*Alcestis, Hecuba, Iphigenia in Aulis*). But not one of these criteria applies to Whitehead's *Creusa*, before which the performance history of Euripides' *Ion* had been slight. Although Sophocles wrote both a lost *Ion* and a lost *Creusa*, and Euripides' play itself was certainly performed in later antiquity (Demetrius, *On Style* 195), nobody besides the Roman republican tragedian Accius and the ancient writers of pantomime libretti produced a version of the story after the fifth century BC.[13] Moreover, both Accius' tragedy and those libretti

---

[10] *LS* iv/1. 421–7, 471, 479; iv/ii. 595–6, 641, 643, 711; Lynch (1953), 11, 25.

[11] Rosenfeld (1978), 124; Tillyard (1995), 153, 160. Less than two months later Sarah Lennox became Lady Sarah Bunbury, under which name she was to model for Reynolds'a famous painting *Lady Sarah Bunbury Sacrificing to the Graces* (1765), discussed above, Ch. 3, p. 89.

[12] For praise of *Creusa*'s construction see e.g. Anderson (1795), xi. 895. The award of the laureateship may have had something to do with Whitehead's connection, through the Earl of Jersey (whose son he had tutored), to the then Prince of Wales. Whitehead's tenure was undistinguished, but he was held to have succeeded in avoiding 'fawning' in his odes for either George II or George III. See Broadus (1921), 135–7.

[13] See Simon (1990), 702–5.

FIGURE 5.1 J. Thornthwaite, engraving of Miss Elizabeth Younge (later Mrs Pope) in the character of Creusa (1778).

are lost, which meant that no Latin version of the story was bequeathed to later Europe.

Even after the Renaissance rediscovery of Euripides there are few signs of any theatrical interest in this tragicomedy. No known Italian operas had appeared on the theme, in France no Corneille, Racine, or Voltaire attempted to adapt it for the stage, and in his influential edition of Aristotle's *Poetics*, published in 1692, Dacier actually asserted that the subject of *Ion* could not succeed on the modern stage.[14] Perhaps Whitehead had noted the rare praise bestowed in 1718 by Charles Gildon, who had read more Euripides than most Englishmen, on the recognition scene of *Ion*.[15] Whitehead could also have heard of the one obscure French opera on the theme, by Louis Lacoste (1712, see below),[16] but this is not likely. A late eighteenth-century classical scholar called Paul Jodrell, a Fellow of Hertford College, Oxford whose *Illustrations of Euripides on the Ion and the Bacchae* (1781) reveals a keen awareness of performance history and of Whitehead's play, shows no evidence even of knowing of the existence of Lacoste's *Creüse*.

Jodrell was surely correct, however, in suggesting that Whitehead was influenced by Racine's *Athalie*, whose young hero Joas bears 'a strong resemblance to the royal Foundling of Athens. Both are Princes of the last surviving branch of the most illustrious royal families.'[17] Racine's tragedy is based on the story of Athaliah and Josiah, narrated in 2 Kings 11 and 2 Chronicles 22–3, which also inspired an opera by Apostolo Zeno and Metastasio's *Gioas, Rè di Giuda* (1735).[18]

Racine's Josiah play, *Athalie*, first performed in 1691, was the first of his tragedies to use a biblical story. It was written for performance at the girls' boarding school of Saint-Cyr, and the role of the child Joas (Josiah), although out of line with contemporary stage practice, was suited to this context.[19] Racine had read (and even written a marginal comment on) a text of Euripides'

---

[14] Dacier (1692), 222.   [15] Gildon (1718), i. 257.

[16] Lacoste (1712).   [17] Jodrell (1781), i. 245.

[18] Ibid. 246. In an example of cross-fertilization between biblical and Greek tragic narratives, Metastasio had probably imitated Euripides' *Ion* by introducing the figure of Sebia, the mother of the young prince, and writing an 'interesting scene' for the mother and the child before they are made known to one another.

[19] France (1966), 24, 163. The story of Joas had been used in at least one French school play previously; for bibliography see ibid. 15 n. 2.

Ion.[20] *Athalie* is also the only Racinian tragedy to use a chorus, and it is infused with the thought and tone of Greek tragedy.[21] The temple setting in the quarters of the resident high priest at Jerusalem, and the innocence of the foundling boy-priest, are both informed by Euripides' Delphic drama. One scene in particular imitates *Ion*: when Athalie encounters the boy Joas, and is affected by his responses to her interrogation (Act II, Scene vii), Racine comes close to repeating whole lines from Creusa's first scene with Ion.[22] The psychological tension in Racine's brilliant drama, however, centres on the foundling, the priest, and the queen. Whitehead, although superficially adhering more closely to the Greek model, actually departs further away from it by introducing a love story as the central focus.

As an educated man looking for plays to adapt for Drury Lane, it is virtually impossible that Whitehead did not know *Athalie*, even if he did not know it had actually been performed in London (in French), in 1735 (Haymarket).[23] As we have seen in Chs. 2 and 3, other plays by Racine had already been adapted to the English stage in the earlier 1700s. Moreover, Smith's *Phaedra and Hippolitus* had been revived very recently indeed (see above). But there is actually little correspondence between Racine's *Athalie* and Whitehead's *Creusa* besides the basic 'situation' of the temple foundling.

There is even less correspondence between the first English *Ion* and Lacoste's spectacular opera *Creüse l'Athénienne* (1712), which involves a sensational scene in which the Pythia performs a prophecy (II. iv). There is a conspicuous difference between Whitehead's freedom-conscious Whig British vision of the plot and Lacoste's French monarch-centred conservatism. Lacoste has altered Euripides so that Creüse thinks for most of the opera that her son is her brother. The most important thing about the Greek play for Lacoste was its interest in authenticating a royal 'divine' bloodline and in defusing anxieties about royal succession. The monarchical political environment in which he was writing makes Lacoste keep no fewer than *three* generations of the royal family

---

[20] Knight (1950), 425.

[21] See France (1966), 35, 38–9, and his note to *Athalie* Act II, Scene vii; on similarities with the *Oresteia* and other Greek tragedies see E. E. Williams (1937) and especially Mueller (1980), 182–93.

[22] For a detailed comparison see Knight (1950), 386–92.

[23] *LS* iii/1. 480 (Wednesday, 16 Apr. 1735).

alive—Creüse's father Erectée is reassured at the end not by Athena but by Apollo the Sun God, loyal allusion to the Roi Soleil and divine father of the new heir apparent himself, that only true Athenian and divine blood runs in Idas' (the renamed Ion's) veins. The royal family's untainted succession is therefore guaranteed. Nor will there even, apparently, be any embarrassing intervening period in which government is assumed by Creüse and her foreign husband. Erectée will be succeeded directly by his grandson, a mixture of his daughter's blood and that of the God of the Sun. What a difference, therefore, between this version and the *Creusa* of Whitehead, who was a near-agnostic. His ancient Athens is a constitutional, popular monarchy, from whose bloodline Apollo is ousted altogether. The substitute offered by the English eighteenth-century imagination for Euripides' divine rapist of a father is a virtuous, ardent, lower-class, and emphatically human lover.

DELPHI AS FOUNDLING HOSPITAL

Whitehead had personal reasons for an attraction to *Ion*, since the love of his life was his widowed mother and yet he regarded himself as suffering from the disadvantages of an orphan. He had lost his father (a Cambridge baker) at an early age, and was only enabled to study at Winchester and from 1735 at Clare Hall (now Clare College), Cambridge, because he was granted a scholarship open to 'orphans' of tradesmen of the town. But this gentle, fatherless outsider, on a scholarship to Winchester, had fallen in love with the ancient theatre when he acted a female role in Terence's *Andria* and Marcia in Addison's *Cato*. He had also learnt sufficient Greek to read it with ease.[24] Interestingly, Whitehead also attempted to adapt the other famous ancient 'foundling' play, Sophocles' *Oedipus Tyrannus* (see Ch. 8); the text, unfinished on his death, was completed by his friend William Mason, whose own experiments with turning Greek tragedy into topical theatre are discussed in Ch. 7.[25]

Whitehead was led to *Ion* by contemporary cultural taste. In 1751 Richard Dalton had begun to publish a series of engravings of Greek antiquities, the first impression most Britons had received

---

[24] See Mason (1788*a*), 6, and cf. *DNB* xxi. 106.
[25] For a description of the Whitehead–Mason version of *Oedipus*, and a comparison with the plays on that theme by Corneille and Dryden and Lee, see Mason (1788*a*), 123 and n.

of Greek temples and monuments.[26] But it was more important that the earlier and middle part of the eighteenth century saw an explosion of foundling literature. Notable examples include both Henry Fielding's classic novels, *Joseph Andrews* (1742), which features not one but two foundling tales,[27] and *The History of Tom Jones, A Foundling* (1749). Fielding himself much admired Edward Moore's affecting comedy *The Foundling* (1748, but running into numerous editions), in which the lovely orphan Fidelia provides an affirmation of the possibility of such a child exhibiting virtue and common sense. Moore's play became perhaps the most famous dramatic treatment of the theme of unknown parentage so beloved by all the 'sentimentalist' playwrights working during the fifty years between Richard Steele's *The Conscious Lovers* (1722) and Richard Cumberland's *The West Indian* (1771).

For the literary foundling, however voguish, was nevertheless an expression of a shocking social reality. There was a sudden population increase in the early eighteenth century; the inhabitants of Birmingham, for example, multiplied sevenfold between 1658 and 1725. The reasons were complicated, but they included better food supplies and less censorious attitudes towards sexual activity. Since the responsibility for supporting illegitimate and abandoned children fell on parishes, many of them faced sudden financial crisis. A parliamentary Act of 1733 had sought to protect parishes against such financial pressure, but the issue would not go away. Thomas Coram, a retired sea-captain (see Fig. 5.2), was appalled by the dozens of newborn babies abandoned on London dunghills. He worked for seventeen years with philanthropic aristocrats, especially women, to get his vision of a Foundling Hospital brought into existence by Act of Parliament in 1740; the Blooms-bury Fields site was completed in 1747.[28] No fewer than six hundred children were being raised there by the time that White-head's *Creusa* was performed in 1754. The enterprise proved so oversubscribed that by the 1750s additional branches were opened in Shrewsbury, Aylesbury, Barnet, and Chester.

Whitehead's *Creusa* implicitly supports the notion that a properly loved and nurtured child can thrive in the absence of its natural family. This was a new enough idea in the eighteenth

---

[26] See Spencer (1954), 159–60.   [27] See Dudden (1952), i. 352.
[28] See Nichols and Wray (1935), 2–4.

FIGURE 5.2 Henry Brooke, engraving of Captain Thomas Coram (1741) after a portrait by B. Nebot.

century, and of course the fundamental premise of the brand-new Foundling Hospital. Opponents argued that the hospital's existence encouraged fornication in young females, their seduction by males, and parents of illegitimate children to neglect their responsibilities.[29] Its supporters, on the other hand, insisted that abandoned children needed nurture and that women should not be punished throughout their lives for indiscretion or 'loving impulses' in their youth; a hospital was regarded as necessary 'to prevent the Destruction of illegitimate infants, and to preserve from Forfeiture the Lives of many wretched Mothers whom a strong Sense of Shame might otherwise precipitate into capital Offences'.[30] Whitehead examines Euripides' Creusa and her child from exactly the perspective held by liberal eighteenth-century supporters of Coram's vision. The play never judges Creusa for her teenage pregnancy, shows how the exposure of her baby was almost inevitable, and demonstrates that the care given her baby, as a foundling raised in the adoptive community run by responsible officials at the Delphic oracle, had produced a well-balanced, intelligent, and healthy youth.

In the seventeenth and eighteenth centuries foundling hospitals had been established in Spain and France, but far from being state-supported cultural centres, they operated as religious hostels associated with Catholic convents.[31] The Foundling Hospital in Britain was a much more prominent and secular response to child abandonment, an emblem of civic philanthropy. It swiftly became a tourist attraction, visited by large numbers, especially Londoners. As a consequence there had never been a better time for foundlings in the British arts. Handel raised money for the hospital by performing in the chapel, and he also donated an organ; popular painters such as Hayman, Hogarth, Gainsborough, and Reynolds all worked to beautify and support the institution. The Foundling Hospital itself provided the venue for both concerts and displays of paintings; many of them depicted notable biblical foundlings such as Josiah and Moses, for example Francis Hayman's *The Finding of*

---

[29] See e.g. Anon. (1760), 9, 13–19, and 27: the hospital 'does not only *kindle* ... Carnalities but *inflames* them, pushing the before timid, *hesitating* youth now *fearlessly* on, first to Fornication, afterwards to Adultery, to Incest,—and, in that way, to what not?'

[30] Massie (1759), 1.

[31] See Pullan (1989).

the Infant Moses in the Bulrushes (1746).[32] The search was seriously on for literary and mythical archetypes of the children in care. It was therefore only a matter of time before someone discovered the most appealing ancient Greek story of a hero discovered in a basket, dramatized in the upbeat and charming *Ion* of Euripides.

In Whitehead's *Creusa*, Ion (known for most of the play by his adoptive name Ilyssus) had been discovered in an osier basket lined with leaves eighteen years previously 'in the temple's portal...A sleeping infant' (13).[33] The play engages with the contemporary debate about the nature of the foundling child and the impact of nurture by surrogate parents. More traditional thinkers believed that adoptive parents could never offer their children sufficient love; they were opposed by advocates of the 'modern' position, that proper education and role models could not only be a substitute for biological parenting, but actually produce a super-child. (This was the precursor of the Romantic notion that bastards, conceived in the heat of sexual passion, were more able than legitimate offspring of wedlock.)[34] The play reflects the mid-century view of the children at the Foundling Hospital as objects in a social experiment as much as recipients of charity. One pamphleteer pointed out in 1761 that, since the hospital had only been open for two decades, few of the foundlings had yet reached 20 years of age, and so nobody could be sure into what kind of adults they would develop.[35] At the time of Whitehead's *Creusa* most of the children at the hospital were not even yet 13.

The play therefore asks whether a foundling can be brought up virtuous; the answer is slightly ambiguous. Ilyssus affirms to Creusa that he has received a 'gen'rous education' partly because the Delphic oracle has proved to be an efficient Foundling Hospital (14):

---

[32] The collection is housed at the Foundling Museum in Brunswick Square, London, which was opened to the public in 2004. On the close involvement of the hospital with high culture in the 1740s and 1750s see Nichols and Wray (1935), 249–53; McClure (1981), 61–75.

[33] This and subsequent references to Whitehead's *Creusa* refer to the Bell's British Theatre text in Whitehead (1778).

[34] Pullan (1989), 8, 17.

[35] Anon. (1761), 38–9.

> The good priests
> And pious priestess, who with care sustain'd
> My helpless infancy, left not my youth
> Without instruction.

But he is equally emphatic that the priests' influence was out-weighed by the ethical, spiritual, and physical education which the sage Aletes had bestowed on him—and Aletes is, of course, the youth's own biological father (and knows it). The words Ion uses to describe the difference between the training given him by the other priests and that he received from Aletes signify the degree of 'energy' and 'conviction'—terms which echo the type of contemporary arguments used by those who believed that children should be raised by their natural parents.

The destiny of most boys brought up at the Foundling hospitals was to enter military or naval service. Ion has been trained by Aletes in wielding shield and javelin (15). Yet here Whitehead is thinking less of the upbringing of foundlings than of the 1745 Jacobite rebellion and the exigencies of his plot: Ion has briefly to be a plausible enough Young Pretender for Creusa, as a Briton disguised as a democratic Athenian, to plan to kill him. Even more important is an image of ideal masculinity. Ion's training at his incognito father's hands has been designed to inculcate into him some identifiably eighteenth-century male virtues (15): although he has been advised to 'adore high Heaven', his religion has a distinctly secular character—he must strive to 'venerate on earth Heaven's image, Truth'. He must also 'feel for others' woes' and bear his own with 'manly resignation'. Aletes has been an ideal father figure to emulate—and yet Aletes, as the play reveals, once had a love affair with a girl of higher status, married her clandestinely, and impregnated her. The play as a whole argues with some emotional force that virtue is not incompatible with clandestine love nor with love children: clandestine lovers, even cross-class lovers, should be allowed to become publicly recognized spouses and co-parents.

CREUSA'S CLANDESTINE MARRIAGE

In his *Creusa* the near-agnostic Whitehead dispenses with Apollo altogether. For an irresponsible divine father to Ion he substitutes a socially responsible mortal. Indeed, Whitehead's biggest problem in choosing to adapt Euripides' *Ion* for Drury Lane was that there was no role for David Garrick, who was too old even to consider playing the youthful hero. Garrick needed a powerful role for a mature male, offering emotional range and big scenes with the leading lady. So Whitehead invented Aletes, 'a Grecian sage', who is actually Nicander, Creusa's long-lost lover, and father of her exposed baby son. This massive piece of surgery is defended in Whitehead's advertisement to the first published edition as justified because the subject of the play is 'so ancient, so slightly mentioned by historians, and so fabulously treated by Euripides in his Tragedy of *Ion*'.[36]

But the most important contemporary issue which Whitehead's reading of Euripides' tragedy allows it to explore is the importance of love between spouses and the legality of clandestine marriage. There had just been a seismic shift in the marriage law, the so-called Marriage Act, masterminded by the Lord Chancellor, Philip Yorke, first Earl of Hardwicke. It was passed in 1753 but only brought into effect in 1754, the year of the premiere of *Creusa*. The Act was designed to create desperately needed clarity in the marital status of Britons. It is now regarded by social and legal historians as the most important piece of matrimonial legislation ever passed in Britain, with the sole exception of the 1857 Divorce Act, discussed below in Ch. 14. Lord Hardwicke, quite simply, laid the foundations for our modern notion of legally recognized marriage. Part of his reasoning was that it would help reduce the foundling problem by deterring women from conceiving children without the name of a father already inscribed in the parish register.[37]

Before Lord Hardwicke's Act there had been several ways of getting married. These ranged from simply being recognized by your community as a cohabiting couple, through 'contract marriages' made merely by verbal or written contract (or even by the exchange of tokens), to marriages by easily forged and mislaid special licences, and clandestine marriages with a hired parson (which required cash but no inscription in a register). It was difficult to prove the validity of a marriage, and virtually impossible to disprove it. Lawyers and clergy sometimes still insisted that legal matrimony could consist of habit, repute, cohabitation,

---

[36] Whitehead (1754).　　　[37] Mark Jackson (1996), 4.

and consent, however informally given. This had produced social and legal chaos.

But from 1754 onwards all marriages were at last to be made null and void unless preceded by banns or an official licence, carried out in a church or chapel by a regular clergyman in prescribed daylight hours, and recorded in the parish register with signatures of the bride, groom, two witnesses, and the officiating clergyman. Lord Hardwicke's Act also outlawed juvenile clandestine marriages by nullifying all marriages made by people under the age of majority (21) without their parents' consent. This was partly to prevent teenage elopements (like that of Whitehead's Creusa and Nicander) and the clandestine emotional pressure put upon very young women by avaricious or lascivious men. Yet it was also intended to endorse free choice of partner for all adults over 21. Moreover, although this measure seems as though it were designed to strengthen patriarchal authority, in fact what Lawrence Stone calls 'the ideology of affective individualism' was becoming so dominant that the Act served to encourage love marriages even for younger lovers, since now only the most extreme parents could bring themselves to invoke a *legal* right and to refuse consent. Fathers who would not let their daughters marry for love were made much more conspicuous by Lord Hardwicke's Act and as a result were increasingly vilified in public ideology.[38]

The social tensions which had produced this landmark legislation also dictated that the rival merits of marriages based on love and expediency, and the legitimacy of clandestine unions, were two of the hottest issues in mid-eighteenth century British drama, literature, and art. Whitehead's *Creusa* is one of several plays on the theme. They also included his own *The Roman Father* (1750), in which Horatia commits suicide after the death of the Curiatius brother she calls her 'husband', an enemy of Rome and of her family; although her father has forbidden the union, she implies that she was secretly wed.[39] Another important example was a Drury Lane play by Garrick himself, in collaboration with George Colman, actually entitled *The Clandestine Marriage* (1766).[40] This play had in turn been inspired by Hogarth's series of engravings

---

[38] Stone (1995), 58.   [39] Whitehead (1777), 41.

[40] Recently republished in an edition by Chevalier (1995). In 1994 Nigel Hawthorne directed and starred as Lord Ogleby in a revival of *The Clandestine Marriage* at the Queen's Theatre in London.

Marriage à-la-Mode (1745), and especially by John Shebbeare's satirical novel, *The Marriage Act* (1754, the same year as *Creusa*). Shebbeare had directly responded to Lord Hardwicke's legislation by attacking parents who contracted loveless marriages for their children in order to make money.[41]

Although in Whitehead's play Creusa feels no passion for her husband Xuthus, it is clear from the outset that he is her lawful wedded husband, the 'partner of her bed' (8), with whom her 'hands were join'd' fifteen years ago (9). But it is equally clear that she once was in love with a commoner, Nicander, whom she should have been allowed to marry. Contemporary ideology was beginning to see the prevention of a love match as an action open to moral criticism. Thus when Creusa's father King Erectheus (now deceased) had banished her lover, it was seen as his life's only 'unkind act' (10). The relationship between the ill-starred pair was certainly an emotionally committed one—Creusa commemorates Nicander with 'annual rites to parted love', and her 'heart is buried with Nicander' (11).

Whitehead deliberately develops the issue of the huge status gap between Creusa and Nicander. Nicander was 'Athenian born, but not of royal blood' (10). Creusa's present husband Xuthus, however, himself of a royal line, is suspicious of love relationships between people of different social classes. In reaction to Creusa's hostility towards him when she imagines Ilyssus (Ion) to be his son by another woman, he says that while he had hoped that Creusa and he might have enjoyed at least a peaceful marriage, he knew that she had never loved him because she loved a mere commoner (42):

> Thy tend'rer thoughts,
> The wife's best ornament, I knew were buried
> In a plebeian grave.

As their quarrel gets more acrimonious, Xuthus' characterization of Nicander reduces him to an even lower status, contrasting his own regal 'scepter'd arm' with Creusa's supposedly dead lover, who had been but an 'infamous slave' (43). Yet the opposite point of view had already been most articulately expressed by Aletes to

---

[41] Chevalier (1995), 23. In time, as memory of the Act receded, new editions of the novel were published under the title *Matrimony*.

Ion when the youth feared that an ignominious birth would harm his prospects at Athens (22):

> Thy birth!
> Did I not teach thee early to despise
> A casual good? Thou art thyself, Ilyssus,
> Inform me, youth, would'st thou be what thou art,
> This fair, thus brave, thus sensibly alive
> To glory's finest feel, or give up all,
> To be descended from a line of Kings,
> The tenth perhaps from Jove?[42]

Whitehead's own humble background may well be one explanation for the play's insistence on the unimportance of social hierarchy.

There is no hint at first that Nicander and Creusa had actually been married—which is of crucial importance to Creusa's respectability in the eyes of the audience and, more importantly, to Ilyssus/Ion's eligibility for the Athenian throne. This revelation is saved for the climax of the second act. Creusa is grappling with the notion that the youth who has so impressed her—who reminds her of Nicander, and who she has briefly hoped is her long-lost son—must be killed in order to preserve Athens from being ruled by a foreign interloper. She swears both her male attendant Phorbas and her female servant Lycea to secrecy, and then divulges the astounding news that she once had a baby son. Almost immediately, to alleviate the shock, she reassures them that the baby was not illegitimate (32).

> ...yes,
> I had a son; but witness every God
> Whose genial power presides o'er nuptial leagues,
> Nicander was my wedded lord.

The news that a clandestine or contract marriage had taken place is of the utmost importance since it had produced a legitimate baby who should be heir to the Athenian throne. Phorbas declares that if he had known Creusa and Nicander were married, and that in the baby they had produced a 'dear pledge' of their 'unspotted

---

[42] These scathing sentiments were originally followed with more in similar vein in Whitehead's text—there follow lines about all the greatest human heroes and philanthropists stemming from unknown families—but Garrick omitted them in performance, clearly feeling that his audience could only take so much preaching on the subject of the unimportance of high birth.

loves', he would have raised a pan-Athenian rebellion in Nicander's cause (32–3) rather than letting him be banished. From this point on in the play Nicander is referred to as Creusa's 'lord' or 'wedded lord' (66), not as her 'lover'. Yet Whitehead does not exonerate Nicander *completely* through the strategy of making sure that he and Creusa were married. When he finally has his scene with Creusa he admits that he 'wrong'd' her by marrying her secretly when she was still so young (53)—thus implicitly vindicating every detail of Lord Hardwicke's legislation.

It is not until the climactic closing scene of the fourth act that the star-crossed lovers and parents of the young hero are finally brought alone together (see Fig. 5.3). The audience's long-awaited encounter between the golden partnership of the London stage, Garrick and Pritchard, finally begins, and it is all the more tantalizing on account of its whiff of transgression—Creusa, after all, is also 'married to', and indeed has sexual relations with, another living man. Only a few lines into the encounter Aletes declares that he is actually Nicander, causing Creusa to pass out in a dead faint. This allows her long-lost husband to initiate an embrace which, if she had been conscious, might have been almost too shocking to be enacted (54):

> —Yes, yes, Creusa, thy Nicander lives,
> And he will catch at least this dear embrace,
> Though now thou art another's.

Creusa regains consciousness, and in a passionate outpouring of emotion gazes upon her long-lost beloved's appearance: 'My lord, my life, my husband!' In the ensuing dialogue she learns that her baby son lives, and that he was called 'Ion' by her old nurse, who gave him to Nicander (55). At this point Creusa remembers, with despair, that she has recently arranged to have the youth poisoned. But Ion's story is completely upstaged by the passionate reunion of his clandestinely married parents. The play is an overwhelming affirmation of the importance of love in marriage, even if that love crosses social boundaries, and of Lord Hardwicke's Marriage Act.

Creusa's father Erectheus was entirely responsible for the marriage of state convenience between Creusa and Xuthus, and this marriage descends into vicious squabbling as soon as there is the slightest conflict of interests. That love matches are preferable is further underscored by the fact that the separated lovers Creusa

FIGURE 5.3   Hannah Pritchard and David Garrick in *Creusa, Queen of Athens* (Drury Lane, 1754), by George Graham.

and Nicander have, independently of each other, evolved into altruistic parents. Both of them die in the final act, Creusa swallowing the poison destined for Ion in order to protect him, and Nicander receiving a mortal wound when he saves Ion from the mistaken patriotic zeal of Phorbas. The play closes with a poignant double *anagnōrisis* or recognition scene, as Ion discovers both his parents before they die, one after another, in his embrace. He is then left alone, now truly orphaned, but poised to ascend the imperial Athenian throne.

Poor Creusa, in Whitehead's play, has been a complete victim of her society's inadequate marriage law. The terror which leads her to attempt murder is a result of the fear that Xuthus had some previous secret marriage whose legitimacy can be proved. She believes that 'Ilyssus' has been raised secretly at Delphi to be foisted on the Athenian throne, and is (36–7)

> perhaps the son
> Of Xuthus' self, plac'd here at first, to hide
> The guilt and shame of some dishonest mother,
> Though now applied to more pernicious ends.

In order to understand Creusa's anxiety it is crucial to understand her position under English law before Lord Hardwicke's legislation. The potential problem facing Creusa is there was some kind of clandestine or contractual marriage between Xuthus and the boy's mother, antedating her own marriage to Xuthus. This would cancel her own marriage, make her relationship with Xuthus technically adulterous, and render illegitimate any children she might *ever* bear to him. Before 1753, even longstanding marriages with numerous offspring were vulnerable to sudden claims from pre-existing 'husbands' and (more commonly) 'wives', claims which could prove catastrophic to relationships, succession, and the inheritance of property.[43]

In Whitehead's version Creusa commits suicide because she has to face her own status as bigamist, a status which brings with it such deep sexual shame that she cannot live with herself. As Whitehead's advocate Jodrell bluntly put it, 'How could the Lady, in the singular predicament of beholding two living husbands at once, be suffered on the stage without dying to save

---

[43] See the fascinating case studies in Stone (1992) and (1993).

her decorum?'[44] After she has drunk the lethal poison, Nicander protests that she might have found a way to live 'with honour' (63). How, she responds, could he possibly think through her situation without perceiving that 'death was my only refuge? |—Am I not Xuthus' wife, and what art thou?' In her torment, she tells him, she 'Saw Xuthus, thee, Ilyssus, Athens bleed | In one conspicuous carnage'. Creusa's unintentional bigamy jeopardizes not only her family members but even more importantly the Athenian state itself.

ATHENS AND ANTICLERICALISM

Although what is now most striking about Whitehead's *Creusa* is its noble foundling and its ringing endorsement of love as the basis for marriage, what most contemporary critics noticed and indeed praised was its religious (or irreligious) dimension. Some aspects of the religious practices in Greek tragedy have always posed a challenge not only to Enlightenment opponents of religion but also to Christians; perhaps the most strenuous attempt to reconcile the robust Whig Christianity of the early eighteenth century with Greek tragic metaphysics was made by the devout Anglican churchman George Adams, in the Preface to his first full translation of all seven Sophoclean tragedies in 1729. But the particular form of rational, pragmatic, and worldly Anglicanism espoused by many in Whitehead's circle found the religion they encountered in Greek tragedy at best silly and at worst repugnant. The most execrable play of all was thought to be *Bacchae*, which simply could not be performed, 'because the Religion of Modern Europe revolts against the extravagant idea of so incredible a story, which was entirely supported on the basis of Pagan Theology'.[45] *Ion*, with its amoral Apollo and semi-divine hero, was not at all attractive to the eighteenth-century audience for which Whitehead was writing: as the same critic who so disliked *Bacchae* put it, 'The most superficial reader of the romantick fables of Pagan antiquity must often have been shocked with those terrestrial crimes, which credulous men have imputed to their visionary gods'.[46] Thomas Francklin, a classicist who wrote for the commercial stage, observed in his 1758 translation of Sophocles that the greatest

---

[44] Jodrell (1781), i. 1247.   [45] Ibid. ii. 564.   [46] Ibid. i. 1.

advantage of modern tragedy over the ancient is its 'judicious descent from the adventures of demi-gods, kings and heroes, into the humbler walk of private life, which is much more interesting to the generality of mankind.'[47] Whitehead prided himself on the reduction of the 'fabulous' element he found in his Euripidean model, and indeed the erasure of Apollo from both action and theodicy, the removal of all that was 'miraculous and improbable' was a stratagem much admired by his contemporaries.[48] Of all eighteenth-century readings of Greek tragedy, Whitehead's *Creusa* is the most secular and humane. His transformation of perhaps the most numinously devout of all Euripides' plays into a sentimental domestic tragedy entails a bleak and wholly un-Greek picture of ancient religion, but Whitehead certainly does not even implicitly advocate the alternative of Christianity. Indeed, some of the play's earlier critics, in reaction to its pro-nounced secular tenor, even went so far as to deem it 'anticlerical'.

Creusa is certainly anti-*Catholic*. The over-religious foreigner Xuthus, who is so respectful of centres of fraudulent priestcraft beyond the borders of Athens, becomes, in the imagination of Phorbas and Creusa, a kind of Jacobite. He and his supposed son are seen as foreign 'pretenders' to the Athenian throne, 'These vile usurpers on the rights of Athens' (46). In the early 1750s, in the wake of the Jacobite invasion of 1745, the British public was still suffering from one of its periodic waves of heightened anti-Popery. *Creusa* is particularly critical of priests whose power depended upon the superstitious practices rife in Catholic countries—veneration of relics, belief in miracles, pilgrimages to saintly shrines.[49]

Phorbas, the loyal Athenian patriot, regards Xuthus as 'perhaps too pious' (11), and it is this excessive religiosity which, it is implied, sends Xuthus to the Delphic shrine to address the god. For Phorbas, who often sounds like a somewhat lapsed Anglican Whig, 'the gods of Athens would suffice' (12). It is through the character of Phorbas, indeed, that Athens and even its democracy have become identified, however loosely, with eighteenth-century Britain. Fearing that Creusa will not oppose a takeover by the

---

[47] Francklin (1758), i. 57 n.   [48] Mason (1788*a*), 73–4.
[49] Haydon (1993), 3–6. On the strong British Whig tradition of hostility to clerical interference in politics, see Stromberg (1954), 132–3.

foreign Xuthus, Phorbas laments the imminent demise of 'liberties' in his own free country (45). His reflections on religion and politics—which are to him inseparable—render him, indeed, rather more interestingly drawn than Euripides' fanatical *paidagōgos*. For example, he is deeply suspicious of

> that piety which brings us
> To search for kings at Delphi. Might not Athens
> Have chosen her own monarch? Her brave youth,
> Her bearded sages,—are they not the flower
> And pride of Greece? (19)

Here he is, in effect, suggesting that the Athenian people *select* (though perhaps not actually *elect*) their own monarch—a proposal informed by the memory of the Glorious Revolution, when the English themselves 'selected' their king, the charter myth of the eighteenth-century constitutional monarchy. Above all the play shows how deeply problems of succession can blight hereditary kingships.

Whitehead had a potential problem in identifying Delphi as a prototype of the Foundling Hospital, since it was important to the British that it was a state foundation, not run, like the orphan hostels in France and Portugal, by suspect Catholic priests prone to inculcating superstition in their young charges.[50] Whitehead's clever way out of this impasse is to present the Delphic Oracle as a total fraud, which was an allegation he could have found in any one of several ancient sources, notably the *Exhortation to the Greeks* written by the early Christian writer Clement of Alexandria, or Origen's *Against Celsus*. But Whitehead's rationalizing account of the oracle is modified by making its fraudulence serve altruistic purposes, rather than malevolent ones, at least under its present administrator. This particular view of the Delphic oracle's activities is likely to have been inspired, rather, by the several articulate pagan defences of its philanthropy and the benefits its wise advice has been able to confer on both individuals and whole communities. Whitehead could have found these expressed by Quintus in Cicero's *On Divination*, or in a more intense form by Celsus, whose views can be inferred from his opponent Origen.[51]

---

[50] Anon. (1761), 42.
[51] For an accessible account of the ancient opponents and defenders of the Delphic Oracle, see Lipsey (2001), 197–227.

The fraudulent nature of the oracles in Whitehead's Enlightenment Delphi is already signalled rather prejudicially in the play's
jocular prologue (p. iv):

> Our scene to-night is Greece.
> And, by the magic of the poet's rod,
> This stage the temple of the Delphic god!
> Where kings, and chiefs, and sages came of old,
> Like modern fools, to have their fortunes told.

The epilogue, moreover, which was delivered by Miss Haughton,
the actress who had played the Pythia herself, includes the admis-
sion that she disavows 'the whole deceit, | And fairly own my
science all a cheat'. But it is the action as the plot develops that
really shows how difficult it was for an enlightened eighteenth-
century author like Whitehead to do *anything* with a pagan oracu-
lar shrine but reveal it as a fraud, which could be either life-
threatening or, in well-meaning hands, potentially beneficial.

Aletes himself invents all the oracles delivered at Delphi, and
gives them to the Pythia to deliver in a plausibly inspired manner.
Aletes uses the reputation of the oracle, combined with his 'experience in the ways of men', in order to give visitors to the oracle
'secret kind advice'. As the Pythia says to him, he must exert
himself on Athens' behalf (23):

> Now, good Aletes, if thy pregnant mind,
> Deep judging of events, has ever fram'd
> Such artful truths as won believing man
> To think them born of Heav'n, and made thy name
> Renown'd in Greece, Oh now exert thy power!

His response is to give her, on stage, a written copy of the oracle
which will, by the end of the play, put Ion on the Athenian throne.
The Pythia is to declare that the Athenians are to 'Bestow th'
imperial wreath' on 'the young unknown, | Who tends my
shrine' (25).

THE FUTURE OF *ION*

In his exploration of the idea that the Delphic oracle was fraudulent Whitehead has much in common with William Golding, a
much later writer in the English language. In his posthumous
novel *The Double Tongue* (1995), narrated by a trainee Pythian

priestess, the oracles at Delphi are presented as pure invention. Euripides' *Ion* features in the novel, and Golding could have been drawn to the play via any one of several avenues, for ever since Whitehead had brought the attention of the English-speaking world to him, Ion has resurfaced with some frequency on its stages. The dashing castrato Venazio Rauzzini, resident of Bath and toyboy of the Burney sisters, staged his popular *Creusa in Delfo* in London at the King's Theatre in 1783, an opera with 'entirely new' music, but partly modelled on Lacoste's French version.[52] In the 1830s *Ion* produced Thomas Talfourd's radical republican adaptation at Covent Garden (see Ch. 11). It was chosen for performance as the Cambridge Greek Play in 1890, less than a decade after the institution was inaugurated, probably in order to coincide with the publication of a new edition of the play by Arthur Verrall, a controversial Cambridge don.[53]

In the preface that Verrall supplied to the text of the play published to accompany the Cambridge production, he described the recognition scene and resolution of the play as a 'melodramatic contrivance', but it was a contrivance bound to create interest:[54] either the performance or his edition, or both, in turn almost certainly suggested the famous 'handbag' scene in Oscar Wilde's *The Importance of Being Earnest*. *Ion* also underlies T. S. Eliot's *The Confidential Clerk* (first performed at the Edinburgh Festival in 1953, almost exactly two centuries after the first performance of Whitehead's *Creusa*), in which the literary genealogy of Colby Simpkins, who loves music and birds, plays delicately on the Greek archetype.[55] Since the 1990s the ancient Greek tragedy has itself enjoyed regular performances on the professional stages of both Europe and North America.[56] But it is most unlikely that this obscure tragicomedy would have been rediscovered on the British stage until considerably later were it not for the reality of life for foundlings in early and mid–eighteenth century London.

---

[52] See Rauzzini (1783); Highfill et al. (1973–93), xii. 260–1.
[53] Verrall (1890*a*).   [54] Verrall (1890*b*), p. viii.
[55] See Hinchcliffe (1985), 52, 172–5.
[56] See Padel (1996); Hall (2004*b*), 2.

6

Eighteenth-Century Electra

Peggy Ashcroft, Fiona Shaw, Zoe Wanamaker—some of the most powerful actresses to perform on British stages during the second half of the twentieth century were drawn to play Sophocles' Electra.[1] In this chapter some of their stellar eighteenth-century fore-bears—Anne Bracegridle, Claire Clairon, Mary Ann Yates, Ann Barry, Sarah Siddons—will appear performing the same Sopho-clean heroine or roles fundamentally informed by her. Although Euripides' *Electra* is one of the few Greek tragedies scarcely to register in performance history during the period covered by this book, Sophocles' version has always been prominent (it was the only Greek tragedy on the syllabus of Magdalen College, Oxford, in 1800),[2] and has exerted a profound influence on both dramatic theory and performance practice. Subsequent chapters will discuss its appearances in nearly every type of adaptation to be found in the nineteenth and early twentieth centuries—late Georgian Covent Garden tragedy, spectacular early Victorian burlesque, academic Greek play in the 1880s, and avant-garde psychosexual opera, imported from the Continent, in Edwardian London. Yet this chapter will argue that those adaptations cannot be understood without recovering the *Electra* of the eighteenth century; and although it was only itself staged in a translation of Voltaire's *Oreste*, its status as exemplary tragedy meant that it exerted great aesthetic and political influence on the cross-fertilizing practices of criticism, translation, performance and the visual arts.

EXEMPLARY ELECTRA

According to the eminent French neoclassical theorist Hippolyte-Jules Pilet de La Mesnardière in *La Poëtique* (1640), Sophocles' *Electra* is the finest of all extant Greek tragedies. The reasons

---

[1] See further Hall (1999*a*).   [2] Hurdis (*c*.1800), 2; see Clarke (1945), 34.

behind de la Mesnardière's privileging of *Electra* may come as some surprise to modern audiences and interpreters of the play: for him, its superiority lies in its exemplary reversal (*peripeteia*), during which the wrongdoers, Clytemnestra and Aegisthus, are punished most appropriately and most severely at the very moment when they most exult in their crime.[3] Although this crudely providential reading of Greek tragedy does not last much beyond the neoclassical period, the privileging of Sophocles' *Electra* extends throughout the eighteenth century. Sophocles' tragedy was central not only to theoretical studies of drama of the period but to theatre practitioners as well. Electra's force can be felt in the most unexpected quarters, in some of the most popular tragedies of the century, and in terms of both its form and content. The 'subterranean' *Electras* discussed here include William Congreve's *The Mourning Bride* and Arthur Murphy's *The Grecian Daughter*, which between them remained mainstays of the London repertoire for around 150 years. Christian Biet has shown the extent to which Sophocles' *Oedipus Tyrannus* may well be considered France's eighteenth-century Greek tragedy;[4] and there is a strong case to be made for speaking of the *Electra* of Sophocles as the most influential Greek tragedy in Britain during the same period.

It is, of course, by no means fortuitous that these two plays—*Oedipus Tyrannus* and *Electra*—should be conjoined at this time. It is not only the modern psychoanalytical theory of Freud and Jung that has recognized the inherent similarities and clear oppositions between the myths (in their respective treatments of the departure/return story pattern; the overprivileging/underprivileging of mother–son relations, and so on). In the neoclassical period that twinning was a consistent and systematic one, which was formally sealed in 1692 with the publication of the first French vernacular translation of and commentary on Aristotle's *Poetics* by André Dacier. In his commentary Dacier echoes the praise of the *Electra* on formal grounds heard some fifty years earlier in La Mesnardière's work (although now for Dacier it is less the reversal that is of especial note than the recognition). But he also aligns it with what had become, from at least the Renaissance, the paradigmatic tragedy, Sophocles' *Oedipus Tyrannus*. Moreover in 1692, the same year as his commentary on the *Poetics*, Dacier produced his

---

[3] La Mesnardière (1640). [4] Biet (1994).

translation of both the *Oedipus Tyrannus* and *Electra*, a work conceived as a companion piece to his study of Aristotle. In the preface to the translation he declares to his reader: you have heard the 'rules', now you can study the examples. These two plays are for him the supreme examples: *Oedipus* is the best; and although Electra is deemed the 'inferior' play, it contains scenes of exquisite beauty and has, in Dacier's view, the best of all recognitions.

So in 1692 France's first vernacular translation of *Electra* naturalizes it as the most instructive of all Greek tragedies. The impact of Dacier's edition and his translations was immediately felt in France with versions of both the *Oedipus* and *Electra* appearing on the stage in rapid succession (notable French *Electra*s at this time include the 1702 *Électre* of Longepierre, and the 1708 version of Crébillon). Its impact was no less significant in Britain, at a time when French theory (rather than practice) enjoyed immediate and wide-ranging influence.

Although Thomas Stanley's edition of Aeschylus (1663) had been followed in 1668 by an unnamed and mediocre edition of Sophocles at Cambridge in 1668, this was completely superseded by Thomas Johnson's superior *Ajax* and *Electra* in 1705, *Antigone* and *Trachiniae* in 1708, and the third instalment in 1746.[5] These editions, combined with the translation of Dacier's edition of the *Poetics* into English in 1705, ensured that *Electra* would meet a widespread British audience. In an era when hardly any Greek tragedies were available in English, Dacier's work inspired not one but two quite different English translations of *Electra*, both of which appeared in 1714. One, which was anonymous, was dedicated to Lord Halifax. It is in simple prose, and the translator claims to 'have aim'd at following the *Greek* original the nearest I can; at leaving no Word unexpress'd.'[6] In comparison, Lewis Theobald's poetic version is impressive. After Chrysothemis' first exit the chorus reflect (Soph. *El.* 473–83),

> Or my prophetick Soul mistakes,
> Or I in hope from Reason err;
> Or vengeance swift advances makes,
> Upon the Conscience-haunted Murtherer.

[5] See Ingram (1966), 18–20; Clarke (1945), 59–60.
[6] Anon. (1714*a*), p. iv. See e.g. the translation of *El.* 1058–62, 'Why behold we those very wise Birds above, taking care of their Parents who have begot and bred them up, and why don't we do the same?' (39).

Daughter she comes; she comes away
With Pow'r and Justice in Array;
I'm strong in hope, the boding Dream,
The Herald of her aweful Terrors came.
The King's Resentments shall not cease,
Nor shall he bury Wrongs but in redress.[7]

Theobald's version, decorated with a powerful engraving illustration of Aegisthus' discovery of Clytemnestra's corpse, engraved by the Huguenot refugee Louis du Guernier (Fig. 6.1), was the most-read *Electra* in England for fifty years. It was much admired by Richard Porson.[8] But it never saw the stage, despite a misunderstanding to the contrary (see below).

Yet the impact of Dacier's two books had been felt much earlier in English-language dramatic theory than in actual translation. Immediately after their publication in 1692 there appears in English writers a presumed familiarity with Sophocles' play: only a year later, in 1693, John Dennis discusses the absurdity of the chorus—the way it undermines the neoclassical requisite of *vraisemblance*—with reference to *Electra*. How, Dennis asks, can 'the discovery that Orestes makes of himself and his design, to Electra, in the fourth Act of that Tragedy . . . [be done] in the presence of the Chorus; so that he entrusts a Secret, upon which his Empire and Life depends, in the hands of Sixteen Women'?[9] And Nicholas Rowe, a few years later in his 1709 edition of Shakespeare, similarly presumes intimate acquaintance with *Electra* when he compares it unfavourably with *Hamlet*. Picking up on Dacier's own expressed concerns about the morality of the matricide and especially Electra's onstage exhortation of Orestes' crime, Rowe attributes to Shakespeare a contrasting 'wonderful art and justness of judgement that [enables] the poet [to] restrain . . . him from doing violence to his mother'.[10]

SUBTERRANEAN ELECTRA

In his edition Dacier seems to be laying down the gauntlet to modern practitioners and some, it appears, rose to his challenge. It is in his commentary on ch. 10 of the *Poetics* that he holds up

---

[7] Theobald (1714).   [8] Buchanan-Jones (1966), 424 n. 1.
[9] Dennis (1693), dialogue V, 46.   [10] Rowe (1709), Preface.

FIGURE 6.1   Frontispiece, designed and engraved by Louis du Guernier, to Lewis Theobald's translation of Sophocles' *Electra* (1714).

Oedipus and *Electra* as the best models for *peripeteia* and recognition (praising *Electra* for its double recognition, first by Orestes of Electra and then Electra of Orestes). Dacier goes on to note that modern playwrights tend mistakenly to avoid recognition—either, he infers, because it is not inherent in their chosen subject-matter or because they find it difficult to effect. But recognitions, he adds, have 'wonderful effects on stage' (as Sophocles' *Electra* shows us): 'Mr Corneille was convinced of this, when he said the remembrance is the greatest ornament of Tragedies, but it is certain, that it hath its inconveniences.'[11] In both *Electra* and *IT*, however, the recognition scene is masterfully executed because it provides a means and not (we presume, as in the classic comic denouement) the end.

Five years later in 1697, we find Dacier's challenge being taken up by the leading comic playwright of the time, William Congreve, in his only tragedy, *The Mourning Bride*, which was extremely successful and revived consistently for several decades (see Fig. 6.2). Surprising as it may seem to find Electra transformed into a bride, albeit a perpetually mourning one, and Orestes no longer the brother/son but the husband, there is none the less a sense in which it seems as if Congreve had not just been reading Dacier's commentary, but had now chosen in his play to act on these neo-Aristotelian precepts. For not only does *The Mourning Bride* include a recognition scene that is closely modelled on the *Electra* (Congreve, who read widely in the classics in the original, was well placed to write one),[12] but it also follows Dacier and his neoclassical contemporaries in favouring a tragicomic ending, in which poetic justice is seen to be done to the full.

When Dacier comments on the ending of Sophocles' play, he detects no ambiguity at all: Orestes is shown to be the divine agent *par excellence*, an instrument of the gods sent to punish the terrible crime of Aegisthus and Clytemnestra (and although Dacier does not spell it out explicitly, for late seventeenth-century sensibilities, that terrible crime is of course that all too recent actuality in England, the crime of regicide). Here at the end of *The Mourning Bride*, the Orestes figure Alphonso—disguised during most of the play as the Moor Osmyn—announces that he has killed Almeria's

---

[11] Dacier (1705), 160–1 = (1692), 148–9.   [12] Thomas Davies (1784), ii. 348.

Act I.   THE MOURNING BRIDE.   *Scene 6.*

MISS YOUNGE in the Character of ZARA.

—— But when I feel
These Bonds, I look with loathing on myself.

FIGURE 6.2   Miss Elizabeth Younge (later Mrs Pope) in the role of Zara in Congreve's *The Mourning Bride* (1776).

father.[13] And Congreve's Orestes killed his father-in-law 'where he design'd my Death'—a clear allusion to Orestes' injunction to Aegisthus to enter the palace to meet his death at the same place in which Agamemnon had met his at Aegisthus' hands. It was, moreover, these last few words of Sophocles' tragedy that made a deep impression on Dacier: with Orestes' words, Sophocles had been able, Dacier maintains, to redeem the atrocity of the matricide and transform Orestes into a divine agent. And here in Congreve's play the crime of the Orestes-figure is fully mitigated: he has not been guilty of regicide himself (the King is killed by one of his henchmen through mistaken identity). Congreve has written a moral tragedy of which neoclassical theorists could thoroughly approve.

But it is the recognition itself that needs scrutiny in the light of Dacier's comments. Congreve's recognition scene was much admired by Samuel Johnson later in the century;[14] but that Johnson was not alone in his admiration is testified by the engraving of this scene serving as the frontispiece to the 1753 edition of the *Complete Works* (Fig. 6.3). It should be pointed out that although Sophocles' example lies behind Congreve's scene, there are numerous departures from it. First there is no Chrysothemis (and consequently no offstage tomb; here as in *Choephoroe* Orestes/Osmyn appears ghost-like from behind the tomb); there is also no 'false' messenger speech and no urn (there is no need here because Almeria believes her husband is already dead); and also there are no tokens to effect the recognition (because the separation of husband and wife has not been that long). Above all, there is no dramatic irony since the audience has no reason before this scene to suspect that Osmyn is in fact the long-lost husband. But the Sophoclean model lies behind the psychological realism of the scene—especially in the length of playing time required to convince the princess that her husband is not dead after all, but is indeed there in reality looming from the tomb of his recently deceased father.

As Osmyn emerges from behind the tomb, he too marvels at the miracle of discovering the image of his own long-lost wife floating before his eyes:

---

[13] Here—again in accordance with Dacier, whose misgivings concerning the matricide were, as we have already seen, widely felt at this time—Alphonso is the Fortinbras figure rather than Hamlet, returning to liberate his wife and his people, not to confront the misalliance of his mother.

[14] Samuel Johnson (1794), iii. 55–6, maintains that it includes the 'most poetical paragraph' in all English poetry.

F I G U R E 6.3   The recognition scene in Congreve's *The Mourning Bride*,
engraving by Charles Grignion (1753).

Amazement and illusion!
Rivet and nail me where I stand, ye Pow'rs, [Coming Forward]
That motionless I may be still deceiv'd.
Let me not stir, not breathe, lest I dissolve
That tender, lovely Form of painted Art,
So like Almeria. Ha! it sinks, it falls;
I'll catch it ere it goes, and grasp her Shade.
'Tis life! 'tis warm! 'tis she! 'tis she herself;
Nor dead, not shade, but breathing and alive!
It is Almeria, 'tis, it is my Wife! (II. vi)

Then comes the moment captured on the engraving, when Leonora (the *confidente*/choral substitute) and Heli (the Pylades figure
also now realizing for the first time that this is his long-lost companion) come to assist both ailing lovers. Osmyn too is stunned but
comes round swiftly to realize that this miraculous reunion is
indeed for real; Almeria's recovery, by contrast, is more protracted
and she now mistakes him for her tyrannical father. But after
reassurances, she begins the process of slow recognition: first by
way of assent, then mild rejection. She tells Osmyn, who is confused by her unrelenting gaze:

I know not [why]; 'tis to see thy face, I think—
It is too much! too much to bear and live!
To see him thus again is such profusion
Of joy, of bliss—I cannot bear—I must
Be mad—I cannot be transported thus. (II. vii)

The recognition scene proper continues for some eighty lines
further, during which time psychological realism is never undermined by any overt theatrical convention. Whilst Dacier had felt
that the exchange after the recognition in *Electra* was too long for
modern audiences, here in *The Mourning Bride* Congreve intro-
duces the two *confidents* Heli and Leonora to provide variety at this
point. Congreve would appear to be saying to his mentor: here is
my recognition, and I have sought solutions to the shortcomings
you yourself have highlighted in Sophocles' text.

It seems, moreover, as if Congreve's attention to Dacier continued right to the end of the play. We have already noted how the
ending to *The Mourning Bride* offers more than a passing nod to
Electra on moral and lexical grounds. Congreve also appears to be

attempting to address other misgivings Dacier has concerning the *Electra* recognition scene. For Dacier the inferiority of *Electra* in comparison to *Oedipus* stems from its failure to combine the *peripeteia* and *anagnōrisis*. Here in the ghoulish confusion of the final moments of Congreve's play, Almeria again believes her husband dead. Kneeling down to kiss him for the last time, she reels in horror when she finds only a headless corpse. When she comes round from her swoon, we witness the second (albeit truncated) recognition as she finds her dead husband alive. This time, however, the recognition is coincident with the *peripeteia* as she discovers, that with the death of her tyrannical father, there is no longer any barrier to her marriage.

The Mourning Bride was a runaway success, especially remembered for the performance of Anne Bracegirdle, Congreve's mistress, in the role of Almeria; in the first instance the returns were so good that it managed to save Betterton's company at the Theatre Royal, Drury Lane.[15] But it is very far from offering any point-for-point parallels with Sophocles' play. Indeed, other sources have been identified for it—Dryden's *Indian Queen* (1663–4) and his *Indian Emperor* (1665) as well as Racine's *Bajazet*.[16] And in accordance with the spirit of the time, Congreve not surprisingly fought off various mild accusations of plagiarism. This was a time (as Paulina Kewes has ably shown in her recent study)[17] when there was a very fine line between literary piracy and legitimate appropriation: creative reworkings of other sources provided the staple for the London stage. But none of these other possible sources detracts from Congreve's demonstrably close reading of Dacier, which reminds us that reception histories of ancient plays cannot afford to restrict themselves to revivals of the originals alone.

POLITICAL ELECTRA

More ancient even than *Electra*'s status as aesthetic exemplar is its role as political manifesto, a role which can be traced back to Julius Caesar's funeral games, when lines from a Roman adaptation by Atilius were sung in order, 'to rouse pity and indignation at his

---

[15] Bevis (1988), 298.   [16] See Wheatley (1956), 78.   [17] Kewes (1998).

death' (Suetonius, *Divus Julius* 1. 84. 2). And politics were the major thrust of John Pikeryng's Elizabethan *Horestes* (the first English revenge tragedy, performed by 1567), an exploration of the relation of the Elizabethan English crown to Scotland.[18] But although Sophocles' *Electra* had begun to make some impression upon the imagination of English-speaking lands after the circulation of the 1548 Latin translation of *Ajax, Antigone*, and *Electra* by the Dutchman Georgius Rotaller,[19] Pikerying's play drew on medieval versions of the tale of Orestes and had excluded Electra altogether. The English-language performance history of Sophocles' tragedy really begins in the hall of Christ Church, Oxford, where Thomas Goffe's *The Tragedie of Orestes* was performed between 1609 and 1619.[20] It is a free composition in the vernacular, influenced by the plays popular on the public stages of London. It is a bloodthirsty revenge tragedy, boasting the on-stage murder of Agamemnon and a disgusting climax which makes the imminent Puritans' Ordinance of September 1642, forbidding the acting of all stage plays, seem positively desirable.

The prologue to *The Tragedie of Orestes* names Euripides as the source. But, besides Euripides' *Orestes*, Goffe draw on Seneca's *Agamemnon* and *Thyestes*, Shakespeare's *Hamlet*, and Sophocles' *Electra*. *Electra* is evident in the false account of Orestes' death (II. v), the despair of Electra in response to it, Clytemnestra's cooler reaction, the (albeit highly truncated) recognition scene (IV. v), and in the notion that Clytemnestra and Ægystus have a child, which occurs only in the Sophoclean version of the story. Its implicit politics are illuminated by the fact that Goffe also wrote a drama, *The Careless Shepherdess*, performed in the Caroline court under the auspices of the French Queen of England, Henrietta Maria.[21] Her theatricals were indissoluble in the Puritan mind from the ceremonial display of her Roman Catholic religion. Goffe's anarchic play on the Orestes theme, requiring young men to impersonate females, would also have infuriated the Puritans, and it was they who were attacked in the earliest known English

---

[18] Pikerying (1567), reprinted in Axton (1982), 94–136. The author was probably Sir John Puckering, Lord Keeper under Elizabeth I.
[19] Rotaller (1550); see Sheppard (1927), 128.
[20] Goffe (1633); see *ODNB* xxii. 635–6, Hiscock (1946), 64, 174; Ewbank (forthcoming).
[21] Veevers (1989), 50.

translation of any play by Sophocles, Christopher Wase's royalist *Electra* of 1649, published in direct response to the execution of Charles I on 30 January of that year.

Wase addressed the translation to the Princess Elizabeth (Fig. 6.4), Charles's second daughter, a prisoner of the Parliamentarians since the Civil War had begun in her seventh year. She was now imprisoned in Carisbrooke Castle on the Isle of Wight. Wase's royalist sympathies lost him his fellowship of King's College, Cambridge. In the dedication to *Electra* he inveighs against censorship and the Puritans' closure of the theatres:

Playes are the Mirrours wherein Mens actions are reflected to their own view. Which, perhaps, is the true cause, that some, privy to the Uglinesse of their own guilt, have issued out Warrants, for the breaking of all those Looking-glasses.

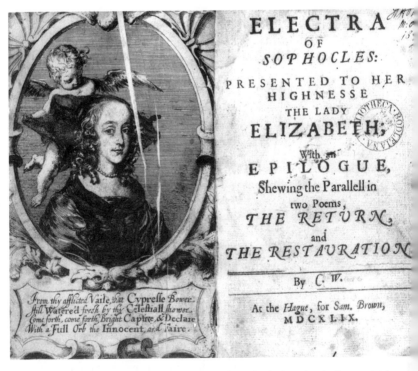

FIGURE 6.4   Title-page and frontispiece depicting the dedicatee (Princess Elizabeth), in Christopher Wase's translation of Sophocles' *Electra* (1649).

The volume contains four further dedications by sympathizers. The first reassures Elizabeth that 'Foreign Princes' crowd to support her, and that she will one day become a mother to Kings who will avenge her father. The writer of the next, anonymous dedication draws an explicit parallel between Sophocles' Aegisthus and Cromwell, saying that the book makes Cromwell's followers in London fear that their '*Egist*' will fall. The current situation is thus conceived as a real-life reenactment of Sophocles' tragedy, except that its vengeful ending has not yet been performed.

The translation itself is in English so robust that Wase must stand accused of insensitivity towards his dedicatee. He has slightly adapted the language used to describe the actual murder of Agamemnon in order to bring home the parallel with Charles I. The chorus remember the blow struck in the chamber,

> Where with the broad steel-faced Cleaver
> The Royall Temples they dissever,
> Treason was the Privy-Counsellor.[22]

Later the same action is couched yet more savagely, describing the 'Poll-ax Razor-edg'd' which decapitated the 'Sovereigne', and even adding a pictorial diagram of a hatchet! Wase repeatedly underlines the parallel with the contemporary situation. Orestes' last words ring out like a defiant speech from the Civil War:

> 'Twere fit this Martiall law did still prevail
> That who so durst transgress the statutes pale,
> Might streight be kild, for villains soon would fail.[23]

Wase lived to publish a Latin poem celebrating the Restoration of his Orestes, Charles II, in 1660, when the theatres were reopened.[24] But poor Elizabeth, unlike Electra, did not survive. She died, at the age of 14, on 8 September of the following year (1650).

Sophocles' *Electra*, through Wase, was thus associated with suspect politics. Those politics may have become correct again under Charles II, but after 1688 any play about the restoration of a rightful king might smack of Jacobitism, and this is probably why no attempts were made to stage an actual adaptation until the

---

[22] Wase (1649), 8.

[23] Ibid. 57. On these lines see Dacier below, and Holford-Strevens (1999), 219–20 n. 1.

[24] *ODNB* lvii. 527–8.

middle of the eighteenth century. It is certainly less than surprising that the first known attempt to stage an English version of *Electra*, the archetypal regicide tragedy, ran into trouble. In 1762 an adaptation of Sophocles' *Electra* by the merchant and playwright William Shirley was refused a licence altogether. Shirley published his play in 1765, prefixing an address 'To the Reader'. He claims that he began to write it in 1744, but had laid it aside on receiving first tidings of the Jacobite rebellion in 1745, 'from an apprehension that the subject, which he had casually chosen, might be considered as invidious and offensive'. Garrick of Drury Lane had much later turned the play down, but in 1762 Mr Beard, the manager of Covent Garden, had commissioned from Shirley a theatrical compliment on the birth of George III's first son, to consist of the tragedy and a masque, *The Birth of Hercules*. The plays went into rehearsal at the end of November, and copies were sent to the Lord Chamberlain to procure the necessary licences. The masque was approved, but the tragedy received a notice of refusal, writes Shirley, 'to the very great surprise of all persons who had ever seen it'. He protested to the Lord Chamberlain that the play 'was no other than the ELECTRA of SOPHOCLES, adapted to the English stage' and that no 'malignant intention' could be imputed to him.[25]

Shirley claims that his play might have been taken for a pro-Jacobite text in 1745, when the only candidate for an analogue of Orestes was the Young Pretender. Some scholars have assumed that it was the association of *Electra* with the Stuarts (underpinning Wase's translation) which led to the censorship of the play in 1762.[26] But Shirley, far from being a Jacobite, was an ardent Whig. His earlier plays, for example *Edward the Black Prince* (1750), had demonstrated his profoundly Whig view of English history.[27] In the late 1750s he had published two trenchant periodicals, *The Herald, or Patriot-Proclaimer*, and *The Citizen*; in 1759 he had published an attack on the legal system in Portugal in which he

---

[25] Shirley (1765), 'To the Reader'.   [26] Conolly (1976), 73–4.

[27] A scene from *Edward the Black Prince*, which dramatized Edward's victory over the King of France at the battle of Poitiers, was performed as part of an extraordinary patriotic pageant on British history at Covent Garden on 12 Feb. 1798. For a detailed discussion see Russell (1995), 52–3. Among the other scenes enacted were two interpretations of history which are discussed elsewhere in the present book because they depend heavily on Greek tragedies: James Thomson's *Edward and Eleonora* and William Mason's *Caractacus* (see Chs. 4 and 7).

detailed abuses of power under the Stuart kings of England, and condemned the 'evil-disposed' James II. Against him the Britons, 'in defence of their Liberty...honourably took up arms, and gloriously secured their own rights, and those of their posterities, by the resolute expulsion of him and his male-issue'.[28] Moreover, Shirley seems to have been obsessively opposed to censorship; in this pamphlet he cites Charles II's persecution of the possessor of a manuscript; in a satirical poem published in 1762 he fulminated against all those who 'dare in chains to bind | The bold productions of the Poet's mind', and lamented that

> In vain, alas! deceiv'd BRITANNIA boasts,
> That heav'n-born freedom guards her chalky coasts.[29]

It was in the same year that Shirley rewrote *Electra* as a denunciation of the then Prime Minister, John Stuart, third Earl of Bute, and his influence over the Royal Family.

George III had come to the throne in 1760; encouraged by Lord Bute, he began an onslaught on the old Corps of the Whig party. The Prime Minister Pitt, 'the Great Commoner' who had appealed to a popular constituency beyond the landed and parliamentary classes, resigned in October 1761, followed by Newcastle in May 1762. Bute became Prime Minister. His tenure of office was one of the most turbulent periods in British political history. The King's quarrel with the Whig leadership created a charged political atmosphere which galvanized rich and poor alike, and was expressed in political theatre which developed allusive techniques of commentary.[30]

By June 1762 John Wilkes, champion of individual liberties, had begun his attacks on Bute in the weekly periodical *The North Briton*. This term for 'Scotsman' was almost as old as the Union, but in 1762 it would have been taken as referring specifically to Bute. Wilkes was particularly supported by the members of the merchant classes, like William Shirley.[31] The temperature rose exponentially, until Wilkes was finally arrested in 1763. At the

---

[28] Shirley (1759), 69. For his periodical journalism see Charles Harold Gray (1931), 144–5.

[29] Shirley (1759), 8–9; (1762), 32–3.

[30] For example, Samuel Foote's *Mayor of Garret*, which attacked Bute. See Brewer (1979–80), 16–21. I am grateful to Jo Innes for bibliographical suggestions and other invaluable advice on the political climate of 1762.

[31] Brewer (1979–80), 15.

time when Shirley's *Electra* was put into rehearsal, and refused a licence, Bute had just been mobbed with such ferocity at the opening of parliament (5 November 1762) that he was lucky to escape with his life.[32]

Whig propaganda presented Bute as totally unaccountable, thereby threatening the balance of the constitution. It also targeted his friendship with George III's mother Augusta. Hundreds of cartoons attacked the alleged sexual liaison almost as soon as George III had ascended the throne, purveying the image of a petticoat government under Scottish influence.[33] Bute was labelled 'the Thane', the bestower of posts and pensions to hordes of hungry Scots. His family name made it more plausible to depict him as a Francophile Jacobite and the enemy of Liberty and Magna Carta. He was compared with Macbeth, with Rizzio (the murdered lover of Mary Queen of Scots), and with Sejanus. The Princess Dowager was portrayed as the Queen in *Hamlet*, directing Bute to pour poison into her sleeping son's ear, or as Isabella, Queen of Edward II, who had murdered her husband and ruled with her lover.[34] Shirley was trying to add Aegisthus and Clytemnestra to this list. The arrival of the new baby son to the King in 1762 had supplied an analogue for Orestes, since Hanoverian Kings were traditionally opposed by their disaffected sons.

Although many of the famous Sophoclean scenes—Electra's argument with her mother, the messenger speech, the laments over the urn, the recognition—are taken from Sophocles, Shirley's adaptation charges the ancient story with contemporary political meaning. Ægysthus' terrible tyranny is underscored throughout; the 'griev'd people of two kingdoms' suffer under his scourge.[35] Ægysthus is himself from Mycenae but wants to take over Argos, which in 1762 is a transparent expression of Englishmen's fears of a tidal wave of Scots taking over high office in England. Orestes' revenge is framed as a struggle for 'liberty' against 'oppression' and the tyrant's 'ambition'. The relationship of Ægysthus to Clytemnestra is presented as that of an upstart underling to a queen whose favour he has won with 'feign'd observance and obsequious vows', and whom he now tyrannically dominates.[36]

---

[32] Coats (1975), 30.   [33] George (1959), 122–3 and pl. 33; Coats (1975), 30.
[34] George (1959), 119–21, 127.   [35] Shirley (1765), 2.   [36] Ibid. 23.

The chief hope of the fallen Whigs was that the now ageing Duke of Newcastle would lead his cohorts back: as 'the Old Corps man *par excellence*,' he tried to form a coalition of Whig groups to oppose the Crown and Bute.[37] Shirley's play stresses that under Agamemnon Argos was a happy country. In the climactic third act, Orestes meets a 'band of loyal and intrepid nobles' of advancing years. He assures them that he will respect the old compact between King and people: 'The thrones of kings, | . . . are only firm | While fix'd on public use and approbation'. He pledges to restore all his nobles to 'The full possession of your natal rights, | Those rights which none but tyrants e'er invade'.[38] But Shirley's most striking alteration is to make the people responsible for dethroning Ægysthus. The rioting populaces of both Mycenae and Argos take over the palace, under the leadership of the ageing nobles and Melisander (the equivalent of Sophocles' *paidagōgos*), and arrest the tyrant. Melisander tells Orestes (v. ix),

> The government and city
> Are in our hands. So total a revolt
> Was wonderful!—and worthy of the people
> O'er whom immortal Agamemnon reign'd.[39]

Shirley's *Electra* thus dramatizes a return to the fondly remembered compact between the deceased King George II (i.e. Agamemnon) and his people. Shirley carefully avoids making any figure in the Argive royal family tree correspond directly to George III. The hope—and threat—expressed through the play was that the new baby Prince of Wales would one day join forces with the populace and displaced Whig leaders, to depose the tyrannical usurper Bute. Shirley may be telling a lie when he claims in his address 'To the "Reader" that the published play has not been altered except 'by meer touches of the language'. But even in its published version, it is manifestly a vitriolic Whig attack on Bute's regime.

However, Bute was not without his defenders. Indeed, when the Irish playwright Arthur Murphy made the first of his two engagements with Sophocles' tragedy in his play *Alzuma*, he wrote with the express purpose of opposing Shirley's strident anti-Bute reading. Murphy was well versed in Greek and Latin, having received a

---

[37] Brewer (1976), 62, 13.   [38] Shirley (1765), 53–4.   [39] Ibid. 97.

fine classical education in France at the Jesuit College of Saint-Omer; and during the later years of his life, he was to devote much of his time to classical translation.[40] He may well have been aware of the deliberate reworking of Sophocles' *Electra* in *The Mourning Bride*, when he took the part of Osmyn in a Drury Lane revival for Garrick's company in 1755; but it was undoubtedly Shirley's proscribed *Electra* that led him back to the Sophoclean model again in 1762. Murphy had previously attacked Shirley in *The Examiner*; and at the time of the play's composition, he was involved in a pro-Bute political periodical, which was started in opposition to *The North Briton*, entitled *The Auditor*.

Murphy's *Alzuma*, set in Peru, is a damning critique of Spanish imperialism at a time when Bute's government had only recently (January 1762) declared war on Spain. On account of his education at Saint-Omer, Murphy shared with Bute the ambivalent status of 'Celtic' outsider; and in this play, which exposes Spanish tyranny as a threat to British liberties, he is demonstrating that Bute, whatever his enemies might say, was a sound British patriot. The Orestes figure, about to meet his death at the hands of the Spanish tyrant, cries out in a clear plea to the would-be British liberators to 'kindle fierce war'; those who hail from a 'happier state', the 'foes of tyranny',

> . . . Who found their laws
> On the broad base of reason and of nature;
> Oh! May that happy state, if such there be,
> With bolder prow triumphant o'er the deep
> Pursue you hither with avenging thunder,
> In your own harbours wrap your ships in fire,
> And bow ye down to seek detested gold
> For other uses! Be that curse upon ye![41]

Although its ending draws heavily on Voltaire's *Alzire*, and although the horror at the accidental matricide is clearly echoing Voltaire's *Oreste*, Murphy himself instructs his readers in the Preface to 'look into the plays of Sophocles and Euripides' for the true source for his play.[42]

---

[40] See e.g. his four-volume Tacitus of 1793. For an account of Murphy's life based on his own autobiographical notes, see Jesse Foot (1811).

[41] Murphy (1773), 41.

[42] Ibid. 4.

Here Alzuma (the absent Orestes-figure in Chile) is eagerly awaited as the liberator of 'Prostrate Peru [so that she] may lift her head again'.[43] The Clytemnestra-figure, Orazia, is the queen of the last Inca kingdom, the colonial subject who has been seduced by both the religion and the sexual power of the Spanish tyrant, Pizarro; whilst her daughter, Orellana, vows never to compromise with her country's enemies. When Alzuma arrives in disguise as a slave leader, he proclaims himself 'One born in freedom! | One, who while yet he lives, like freedom's son | Will dare to think'.[44] Arrested for gross insubordination, Alzuma declares to his friend Ozmar/Pylades that it is intolerable to witness 'a nation bleeding round us, | Yet fetter'd thus in chains'.[45] With the arrival of Orellana, having daringly secured a warrant for the slaves' release, Murphy teasingly offers and then denies his audience the recognition scene proper. Orellana inquires generally of her long-lost brother and Alzuma is reduced to tears; but the Pylades-figure urges caution and restraint upon his friend because Orellana's identity is not yet known to them. However, the subsequent scene, set inside the Temple of the Sun, provides the audience with a close paralleling of the Sophoclean recognition. Orellana, accompanied by a chorus of the daughters of the sun, invokes the Sun God in her prayers to save her brother, whilst he watches together with his friend in the wings. When she urges the strangers to take a braid of coloured cloths to her brother as token, Alzuma can contain himself no longer, confirming his identity with a scar from a tiger's fang on his chest.

With its ending urging reconciliation between different religious and ethnic groups,[46] *Alzuma* may well be said to be providing a bold counter to the anti-Jacobite prejudice fuelling the opposition to Bute. Garrick clearly understood this when he turned it down for performance on the ground that 'A certain political society would damn any production known to come from the pen of the present writer'.[47] *Alzuma* was not in fact performed until 1773, some ten years after its composition (and a year after Murphy's, as we shall see, much more successful *Electra*-inspired *The Grecian Daughter*), when its indictment of Spanish imperialism was no

---

[43] Ibid. 13.   [44] Ibid. 20.   [45] Ibid. 24.
[46] Murphy was to take a stand against the Gordon riots in 1780.
[47] Murphy (1773), 4.

longer urgently topical. The changing political circumstances of
the 1770s—with Bute out of office, and the Seven Years War long
over—was undoubtedly one of the reasons why it failed to hold the
public imagination when it was eventually performed at Covent
Garden in 1773.

In *Alzuma*, Murphy grants considerable prominence to the
recognition scene between brother and sister, following the Sophoclean scene even more closely than Congreve's earlier aesthetic
experiment. He even offers a second recognition of sorts, when
the Clytemnestra figure narrowly avoids the crime of infanticide
through recognizing her son by a scar received in childhood.
Alzuma is an exciting play and a fascinating refashioning of the
tragedy. But *Electra* was no longer primarily of aesthetic interest to
eighteenth-century audiences: it was politics that prompted
Alzuma; and changing political circumstances were to engender
new versions of Sophocles' play.

ELECTRA VISUALIZED

This politicized clash of unperformed Electras in the early 1760s is
probably in part a response to the two new English translations that
had appeared in 1759. Pierre Brumoy's *Le Théâtre des Grecs* was
published in an English translation by Charlotte Lennox with the
assistance of the Earl of Cork and Orrery. Brumoy again reaffirmed
the centrality of *Electra* within the extant corpus of Greek drama,
since, as was the case with Dacier, his theorizing was immediately
followed by translations of both *Oedipus* and *Electra*.

The previous year had seen the appearance of the first complete
English verse translation of Sophocles. Although George Adams's
two-volume prose translation of all seven plays had appeared in
1729 (thus underlining the primacy of Sophocles, because this was
half a century before most of Euripides or Aeschylus was made
available in English), it never circulated widely. But in 1759 Theobald's admired poetic translations of *Oedipus* and *Electra* were
finally superseded by those of Thomas Francklin. A product of
Westminster and Trinity, Francklin became professor of Greek at
Cambridge in 1750, when Jeremiah Markland—a much better
scholar—refused to stand for the position.[48] Francklin was not a

---

[48] Clarke (1945), 29–30.

distinguished Hellenist, but these were the days when Lord Chesterfield could write to his son in 1748 recommending that he pursue a Greek professorship, since 'It is a very pretty sinecure, and requires very little knowledge (much less than, I hope, you have already) of that language.'[49]

Yet Francklin was a versatile eighteenth-century gentleman with a high profile in the cultural and theatrical life of London. He resigned his professorship in 1759 and transferred himself to the literary circles of the capital. He was a friend of Johnson and Reynolds, preached famously at St Paul's, and became the first chaplain of the Royal Academy. His translations of Voltaire, Cicero, and Lucian were, in their day, respected.[50] He produced two successful theatrical works, *The Earl of Warwick* and *Matilda*, in which the heroines, Margaret and Matilda respectively, are torn between conflicting duties like the Antigone 'of Francklin's obvious model'.[51]

Francklin's Sophocles remained standard well into the nineteenth century. It is aimed at a readership including women, whose responses Francklin guides: 'The ladies may observe the modesty of Tecmessa's behaviour; she answers [Ajax] only with a sigh.' There is even a long note discussing whether it is seemly for Chrysothemis, as a virgin princess, to walk fast.[52] Just as the recognition scene was regularly privileged and prized by the engravings that accompanied the printed editions to the eighteenth-century Electra plays, so Francklin also demands that his readers *visualize* the theatrical action, capping his praise of the last scene of *Electra* with the following admonition:

Let the English reader conceive those inimitable actors, Quin, Garrick, and Cibber in the part of Aegisthus, Orestes, and Electra, and from them form to himself some idea of the effect which such a catastrophe would have on a British audience.[53]

Although he had persuaded David Garrick to subscribe to the edition, Francklin unsurprisingly failed to persuade him to stage Sophocles unadapted. But he did arrange performances of his version of Voltaire's *Oreste*, a tragedy based on *Electra* which had

---

[49] Dobrée (1932), iii. 1084, no. 1518.   [50] See Lynch (1953), 180–3.
[51] Ibid. 186.   [52] Francklin (1758), i. 24, 26 n.; see also 127–8 n., 148 n.
[53] Ibid. 193–4 n.

been successfully staged in France in 1750, with Mlle Clairon in the leading role, which she had revived with spectacular success in 1761. In London the starring role went to Mary Ann Yates, recently applauded for her performance in Richard Glover's *Medea* at Drury Lane (1767).

Francklin's *Orestes* was not a hit when it appeared at Covent Garden on 13 March 1769, and yet critics admired Yates's performance. A spectator wrote that

for tone, and justness of elocution, for uninterrupted attention, for everything that was nervous, various, elegant, and true, in attitude and action, I never saw her equal but Garrick.[54]

In 1774 she tried to win the hearts of the Drury Lane theatre with the same tragedy, renamed *Electra*. The new Prologue and Epilogue by Garrick were 'greatly receiv'd with great applause', and the excellent set by Philippe de Loutherburg comprised 'perspective scenery of Argos, the Palace of Aegisthus, and the Tomb of Agamemnon', with costumes deemed both 'elegant and characteristic'.[55]

The 1714 English translations of *Electra* had each offered excellent visual illustrations of one of the tragedy's canonical scenes: the urn scene in the anonymous version, and the revelation of Clytemnestra's corpse in Theobald's (see Fig. 6.1). Sixty years later Loutherburg's emphasis on the visual recreation of ancient Greece is significant, because scene design was beginning to respond to the publication of Greek monuments, in particular the first volume of James Stuart and Nicholas Revett's *The Antiquities of Athens* (1762). At the beginning of the eighteenth century scenery had not been individuated historically or geographically. But Garrick's engagement of Loutherburg at last put topographical scenery before the British public.[56] The admired costume which Mrs Yates wore to play Electra also strove for authenticity. It daringly dispensed with the pannier, thus revealing the exact natural contours of her body, and substituted an unadorned black drape; her hair, although piled high, was partly left to fall over her shoulders.

---

[54] Quoted in Highfill et al. (1973–93), xvi. 328. For less enthusiastic contemporary reactions to Yates's Electra, see *LS* iv/3. 1390–1.

[55] *Westminster Magazine* (Oct. 1774), quoted ibid. 1841. When Dr Samuel Parr staged *Oedipus Tyrannus* and *Trachiniae* in 1776, he was lent costumes by Garrick, perhaps those designed for the Drury Lane *Electra* of 1774. See Ch. 8.

[56] Rosenfeld (1981), 33.

Mlle Clairon had introduced this very costume in the same role in Paris in her drive to introduce a more naturalistic style to the tragic performances at the Comédie-Française.[57] The novel visual appeal of the revamped tragedy in London ensured it greater success, but it was still held to suffer from an excess of declamation.

Four years after Mrs Yates's second attempt to breathe life into Francklin's version of Voltaire, the multi-volume series Bell's British Theatre published an *Electra*. The title-page claims that the play had been acted at Drury Lane, and the engraving depicts Mrs Yates as Electra, above a quotation from Francklin's text (Fig. 6.5). But the published text is, instead, Theobald's translation of Sophocles. This has thoroughly confused historians of the British theatre,[58] and the reason is a mystery. It may have been a simple clerical error, or it may demonstrate the flexible approach of the eighteenth-century mind towards translation: both Theobald and Francklin's plays were notionally versions of Sophocles' *Electra*. But Francklin was probably trying to imply that the *Electra* which had met a lukewarm response was not by him but by his deceased rival. Francklin had long attacked Theobald's translations (as had Pope) in order to maximize the market for his own: while still Professor at Cambridge he had concluded his poem *Translation* with an appeal to the 'Genius of Greece' to inspire him with Sophocles' fire, and

> From hands profane defend his much lov'd name;
> From cruel Tibbald wrest his mangled fame (209–10).

Francklin here appended a scornful note, declaring that 'Tibbald translated two or three plays of Sophocles, and threaten'd the public with more.'[59]

Francklin's tragedy of 1769/1774 brought Electra into the cultural limelight. We have already heard of Murphy's *Alzuma* (1763, but performed 1773) and *The Grecian Daughter* (1772); in May 1775 Francklin's *Electra* also prompted Simonin Vallouis, a French dancer, to star with his wife in a 'Grand Tragic Ballet'

---

[57] Pentzell (1967), 109–10; see Jacobs (1989), 249 n. 8; Marmontel's *Mémoires* in Barrière (1846–81), v. 198. There is a contemporary picture of Clairon in the role of Electra reproduced in Sayer (1772).

[58] See e.g. Bevis (1988), 133, 268.

[59] Francklin (1754), 13 and n. 'Tibbald' was the correct way of pronouncing the name.

FIGURE 6.5　Frontispiece (engraving by J. Thornthwaite of Mary Anne Yates in the role of Electra) and title-page to Lewis Theobald's translation of Sophocles' *Electra* (1777).

Oreste et Électre at the King's Theatre. Although its plot is not certain, there was a role for Clytemnestra.[60] Francklin's *Electra* also had reverberations in the visual arts. The 1769 production inspired a beautiful miniature by Samuel Cotes, which circulated on fashionable prints from an engraving,[61] and in the 1770s Sophocles' tragedy became a popular theme in painting.

Francklin had taken the prudent step of dedicating his translation of Sophocles to the then Prince of Wales, and was rewarded by

---

[60]　Ivor Guest (1972), 148; see also the article 'Simonin Vallouis' in Highfill et al. (1973–93), xv. 102–3.

[61]　The engraving, by P. Dawe, is reproduced in Highfill et al. (1973–93), xvi. 335. The miniature is reproduced in Foskett (1972), pl. 62. See the discussion in Jacobs (1989).

being made the first chaplain of the Royal Academy and its Professor of Ancient History. One of the founding members was Benjamin West, an American, who was inspired by Francklin's translation of *Electra* to paint a picture entitled 'Ægistus, raising the veil, discovers the body of Clytemnestra. Francklin's Sophocles' (see Fig. 6.6). When exhibited in the Academy in 1780, it provoked an admiring reaction.[62] It was with pictures such as this and his illustration of a scene from *IT* (see Ch. 2) that West established himself as the most advanced proponent in England of the neoclassical style, which used antiquity to provide illustrations of 'modes of behaviour that were to inspire devotion to ideals of self-sacrifice for the sake of justice, honor, duty, and country'.[63]

West may have selected this particular scene because Francklin, his fellow Academician, was by now working on his translation of Lucian. Perhaps he drew West's attention to a passage in *The House* (§23) where Lucian's narrator describes scenes painted in a hall. One is a 'righteous deed, for which the painter derived his model, I suppose, from Euripides or Sophocles' (although the scene fits only Sophocles' *Electra*). Lucian's narrator describes this 'righteous deed' thus:

The two youthful comrades Pylades of Phocis and Orestes (supposed to be dead) have secretly entered the palace and are slaying Aegisthus. Clytemnestra is already slain and is stretched on a bed half-naked, and the whole household is stunned by the deed—some are shouting, apparently, and others casting about for a way of escape.

West's picture was perhaps an attempt to recreate the painting in this ancient *ekphrasis*. He was not the only artist drawn to *Electra*. Fuseli, who moved in the same circle, had in 1776 drawn a sketch portraying the same scene as West, the actual revelation of Clytemnestra's corpse to Aegisthus.[64] But Angelica Kauffman, one of the two female founding members of the Academy, had by 1786 painted a picture which, like West's, explicitly labelled itself as

---

[62] See von Erffa and Staley (1986), 260. The painting is now lost, but an excellent mezzotint copy by Valentine Green, associate engraver of the Royal Academy, has been preserved. See Whitman (1902), 4, 159.

[63] Von Erffa and Staley (1986), 41–2.

[64] *Orestes und Pylades führen Ägisth vor den von Elektra enthüllten Leichnam der Klytämnestra*, in Schiff (1973), i. 2, 87, no. 392. The picture is now in Dijon. Thanks to Catherine Steel for help on this.

FIGURE 6.6   Valentine Green, mezzotint after Benjamin West's lost painting *Ægistus, Raising the Veil, Discovers the Body of Clytemnestra: Francklin's Sophocles* (1780).

inspired by Francklin's Sophocles: in her case, however, the scene depicted Electra and Chrysothemis.[65]

ELECTRA COMES CENTRE STAGE

Kauffman's choice of topic—a scene of female colloquy containing no men—represents an important shift in response to the play. For it was only when *women* began to study the play in earnest that the character of Electra and her conflicts with her mother and sister began to strike chords of recognition, dislodging from centre stage the recognition of a man by his sister, a wife's corpse by her husband, or the politicized battle between Orestes and Aegisthus.

[65] See Roworth (1992), 186; Manners and Williamson (1924), 224.

Moreover, with a few significant exceptions, the characters of all three women had previously been sweetened and made secondary to the men's struggle over the throne.

As we have already heard (p. 155), Dacier had concerns about the morality of the matricide and especially about the onstage exhortations delivered by Electra; and Rowe had commended the comparative restraint of Hamlet in this regard. Pierre Brumoy had been so perturbed by the sentiments expressed by Electra and her mother in their bitter confrontation that he departed significantly from the Greek in what is otherwise a faithful translation.[66] Electra's harshness and unbecoming behaviour—of which she is herself painfully aware (see 221–2, 307–8, 616–17)—repelled most eighteenth-century gentlemen. Paul Hiffernan was outraged in 1770 by the murder of Clytemnestra in Sophocles. It is one of the theatrical crimes by 'such monsters that degrade the whole human system', because it is encouraged by a woman.[67] Electra's character seemed too masculine: Coleridge invoked it to support his view that 'the Greeks, except perhaps for Homer, seem to have had no way of making their women interesting, but by unsexing them'.[68] Even Shirley had turned Clytemnestra into a victim of her lover's ambition, and toned down Electra's vindictiveness, replacing it with a devotion to the liberation of her fatherland; Francklin had shaped both Clytemnestra and Electra to fit eighteenth-century notions of ideal femininity: their difficult confrontation is muted, and his Electra regrets the murder.

We now are disappointed by the pusillanimity of these writers' reactions to Sophocles' magnificent women. There were, however, three brave exceptions. In 1714 Theobald had seen the importance which Sophocles attached to Electra, rather than her brother Orestes. Theobald argues from a perspective informed by the conventions of early eighteenth-century 'She-Tragedy' that the play's power lies in the multiple emotions Electra expresses:

. . . she is equally Wonderful, in her strong and implacable Resentments against her Father's Murtherers; in her Impatience for Orestes to come

---

[66] 'This whole scene, between the mother and daughter, is so much in the Greek manners, that no art is capable of rendering it exactly, and yet agreeable to us. I was apprehensive that a too close translation would rob it of all its beauty'. Brumoy translated by Lennox (1759), i. 119 n.

[67] Hiffernan (1770), 57.

[68] Raysor (1936), 37.

and revenge him; in her excessive Sorrows for her Brother's supposed Disaster; in her Transports, when she comes to know he is living; and in her Zeal, for the performance of his Revenge.[69]

Shelley agreed, for Electra stands behind the bitter, vengeful, dishevelled Beatrice of his tragedy *The Cenci*, written in 1819.[70] Earlier, in Arthur Murphy's most famous and successful tragedy, *The Grecian Daughter*, we find an Electra figure who comes straight out of Kauffman's circle. Murphy's play opened at Drury Lane in 1772, with Mrs Barry in the leading role of Euphrasia, but it was to remain prominent in the repertoire for over seven decades, with that famous Electra, Mary Ann Yates, taking the part in 1782. It was, however, really Sarah Siddons, Joshua Reynolds's 'Tragic Muse', who became associated in the popular imagination with Euphrasia (see Fig. 6.7), and this Electra, more than any other in the eighteenth century, seems to accept the full implications of her Sophoclean role.

In marked contrast to neoclassical theorists and adapters, who broaden the personalized vengeance of Orestes to include the dispossessed and the disaffected mob and consequently marginalize the role of Electra, Murphy's second reworking of Sophocles' tragedy makes Electra the focus of the play. In *The Grecian Daughter*, she is deprived of a brother altogether (as with Congreve's *Mourning Bride*, the returning avenger is her husband, who in this case has departed with her young child); with the Agamemnon-figure breathing his last (rather than already dead) incarcerated in his dead wife's tomb and starved by order of the usurping tyrant, revenge can be Euphrasia/Electra's alone. Moreover, Murphy's heroine does not simply seek to perpetuate her father's memory, she actually manages to preserve his life in an extraordinary off-stage scene in which she suckles the dying man—a sensational detail Murphy had found in Valerius Maximus' *Facta et Dicta Memorabilia* (5. 4. 1), illustrating filial piety.[71]

In the final scene of the play, when the rebel forces are nearing victory, and Dionysius (the Aegisthus-figure) threatens the life of her father on stage, Euphrasia stabs the tyrant in the heart before proclaiming to the guards,

---

[69] Theobald (1714), 69, 70. [70] See further Hall (1999a), 289–90.

[71] For a depiction of this scene see Rubens's painting 'Simon and Pero (Roman Charity)' (1625), in the Rijksmuseum, Amsterdam. It was a popular subject for Italian and Dutch painters between the 16th and the 18th cc.

FIGURE 6.7 Sarah Siddons as Euphrasia in Arthur Murphy's *The Grecian Daughter*, *c*.1783. Engraving by J. Caldwell after a painting by W. Hamilton.

> Kneel to your rightful king! The blow for freedom
> Gives you the rights of men. And oh! my father,
> My ever honour'd sire, it gives thee life.[72]

To her, as saviour of her father and liberator of her people, the dying king bequeaths his throne and his dominions: and as a paradigm of filial piety, Euphrasia is celebrated by all to the end of the play:

> ...stretch the ray
> Of filial piety to times unborn,
> That men may hear her unexampled virtue,
> And learn to emulate the Grecian daughter.[73]

We have come a long way from the swooning heroine of Congreve's *Mourning Bride*, and we are now on the edge of the territory of the 'masculine' woman of Mary Wollstonecraft's circle, territory into which the Sophoclean Electra herself was hardly allowed until women began to respond to her play in earnest. Elizabeth Barrett compared the emotional response of France to the corpse of Napoleon with Electra's emotions on receiving Orestes' ashes; elsewhere she likened her depression before a reunion with her lover to Electra's 'sepulchral urn'.[74] Beyond Barrett, the line of important women writers to have appreciated appreciate Sophocles' *Electra* includes George Eliot, who even quotes the Greek in ch. 13 of *Janet's Repentance*,[75] and above all Virginia Woolf in her seminal essay 'On Not Knowing Greek', in which this tragedy is made the foundation of Woolf's case.[76] But even here the literary theory is once again related, as has been shown to be the case repeatedly throughout this chapter, to the history of drama in performance. Woolf learnt her Greek partly from Janet Case, an outstanding Classical student who had taken the title role in the first-ever British production of the authentic Sophoclean play, by an all-female cast at Girton College, Cambridge, in 1883 (see further below, Ch. 16). Exemplary Electra, Subterranean Electra, Political Electra, and Visualized Electra—to these manifestations of Sophocles' archetypal heroine, whose shadow was cast so long over the eighteenth-century British stage, the late nineteenth century was to add yet another significant mutation—Electra the herald of feminism.

---

[72] Murphy (1772), v. iii.   [73] Ibid.
[74] 'Crowned and Buried', stanzas 19–20; *Sonnets from the Portuguese*, stanza 5, in Barrett Browning (1994), 255, 219.
[75] See Jenkyns (1980), 114.   [76] Woolf (1925), 41, 43–4.

7

Caractacus at Colonus

Bring then to Britain's plain that choral throng;
Display thy buskin'd pomp, the golden lyre;
Give her historic forms the soul of song
And mingle Attic art with Shakespeare's fire.
(Richard Hurd, 'Ode' prefixed to Caractacus*)*[1]

THE CRISIS OF COLONIAL CONFIDENCE

After the astonishing successes of the Seven Years War (1756–63), during which the British conquered Canada, drove the French out of West Africa, took Havana from the Spanish, and asserted the supremacy of the British navy over all its European rivals, the euphoria of acquired empire evaporated with speed. One anxiety was that the British empire was now supported by oppressive military might. The parallel with the militaristic Roman empire, which had grown out of the Roman republic so admired by the earlier eighteenth-century aristocracy, began to seem pressing; it was rendered unavoidable by Edward Gibbon's *The History of the Decline and Fall of the Roman Empire* (1776–88), the idea for which was conceived as early as 1763. As Linda Colley has argued in *Britons*, the spoils of unprecedented victory were unsettling partly because they challenged the long-standing mythology of Britain as the land of liberty founded on Protestantism and commerce.[2] By April 1775, this mythology was to be subjected, moreover, to its greatest challenge since the Glorious Revolution: the gunshots heard at Lexington announced that the Thirteen Colonies in North America were saying an unambiguous 'no' to dictation from London.

A few months after British imperial self-confidence was left reeling from the shock of the American Declaration of Independence in July 1776, a tragedy on the theme of colonial

---

[1] Mason (1811), i. 104–5.   [2] Colley (1989); (1992), 103.

rule opened at Covent Garden (6 December). It continued to be performed until May, and was revived the following season. The author was the Revd William Mason, a progressive Yorkshire clergyman who, like many decent Anglicans, opposed war with the Protestant republicans in America; the play was *Caractacus*, a rousing tale of ancient British resistance to the Roman army. That it was interpreted politically, at least by those who favoured American independence, is clear from the recitation, during a Shropshire Whig meeting held to protest against the war, of 'Additional lines to *Caractacus*'. Although probably not by Mason himself, the new lines urged liberty for the colonies.[3] In this version Caractacus was equated with the American rebels, and the Roman army with the British military. The identification was made easier because support for American independence was strong in the 'Celtic' fringes of Britain, including North Wales.

Caractacus was significant in British drama's relationship with Classics. It stages a conflation of Tacitus' description of Caractacus (or rather Caratacus), the indomitable Briton captured during the reign of Claudius (*Annals* 12. 33–7), whose courage at Rome was to inspire several subsequent British artworks (see Fig. 7.1), with the same historian's account of the last stand of the druids of Mona (Anglesey) against Suetonius Paulinus (*Annals* 14. 29–30). Mason's tragedy was the most innovative theatrical manifestation of Roman history since Addison's *Cato* (1713). But it is with Greek tragedy that *Caractacus* bears its most profound relationship. This is not only inherent in its content (the plot is modelled on Sophocles' *Oedipus at Colonus*), but in its form. 'Written on the model of the ancient Greek tragedy' (see Fig. 7.2), *Caractacus* represented the Covent Garden debut of one of the most outlandish features, to eighteenth-century taste, of Sophocles' authentic dramas: the singing, dancing, involved, and interactive tragic chorus.

This chapter argues that the aesthetic experiment Mason conducted in *Caractacus* was a crucial intervention in the eighteenth-century debate about the tragic chorus, particularly because his choice of identity for the chorus (druids and bards) demonstrates the extent to which Hellenic and ancient British revivalism were conflated. But it also argues that the case of Mason demonstrates the impossibility of separating the aesthetic from the political:

---

[3] See the *Gentleman's Magazine* 46 (1776), 427; Draper (1924), 177–8.

FIGURE 7.1 Thomas Davidson, *Caractacus being Paraded Before the Emperor Claudius, AD 50* (1891).

Mason's druids, by singing of ancient Celtic resistance to Roman tyranny in the ancient Greek plural lyric voice, are a dramatic analogue of Collins's Druidic temple of freedom in the British woodland, allegorically also representing the renewal of English poetry (*Ode to Liberty*, 1746):

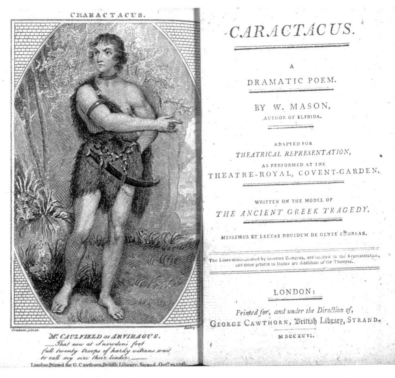

FIGURE 7.2 Frontispiece (by Burnet Reading, showing Thomas Caulfield in the role of Arviragus) and title-page to William Mason's *Caractacus* (1796).

> In Gothic pride it seems to rise,
> Yet Græcia's graceful orders join
> Majestic through the mixed design.

Making connections between ancient Britons and ancient Greeks seemed appropriate at a time of British opposition to Rome's descendants in the 'ancient regimes' of Europe. *Caractacus* encouraged identification with the Greeks (especially by the more radical, pro-American members of the audience) and the drawing of parallels between the culture of Athens, where tragedies were performed, and that of early Britain. This was a new vision of Greece, informed by poetics and politics, which adumbrates both the romantic Hellenism of Shelley (on which see Ch. 8), and the association of Gaelic and Greek culture by Irish poets and dramatists, especially Yeats, in the late nineteenth and early twentieth centuries.[4]

CARACTACUS IN ANGLESEY

The climax of Mason's *Caractacus* entails the desperate last battle between the Roman army and those ancient Britons who chose to defy it. Even in defeat, the moral victory is won by the colonized rather than their masters. The Roman general Aulus Didius arrives at Mona, in pursuit of the British King Caractacus, who, with his daughter Evelina, has sought refuge at the druids' grove. There are complications involving the treachery of other Britons, but the central story is simple. Caractacus' son Arviragus arrives, leads an army out against the Romans, temporarily routs them, but is wounded and later dies. Caractacus makes a last heroic stand in battle, but is captured. The play concludes as he and Evelina are led off as captives to Rome.

The figures of the father and daughter are modelled on the Sophoclean Oedipus and his loyal daughter Antigone. Just as Antigone and the infirm Oedipus arrive at the grove at Colonus, the aged Caractacus enters on his daughter Evelina's arm. Like Oedipus in *OC* he engages in tender dialogue with this daughter, but is estranged from his son. That Oedipus was on Mason's mind in this scene is underlined by Caractacus' remark that this desertion by his son 'was parricide'. Evelina, however, fears that her brother is dead, and in imitation of Antigone in more than one Greek tragedy laments that she can never prepare his body for burial.[5] Other features derived from *OC* include the father's hostile reception of his son, the reunion of brother and sister, and especially the struggle in Caractacus' breast. He oscillates between anger and a troubled questioning of his relationship with the gods. Yet this gives way to a tranquil understanding of his destiny (like Oedipus, he hears a mystical 'thundering voice' calling him to

---

[4] On the fusion of Grecian and Gothic in 18th-c. poets, see Sambrook (1993), 209–11. On the Irish literary revival and the Greek Classics see above all Macintosh (1994), especially 4–18.

[5] Mason (1796), 21–3, 24. All quotations from *Caractacus*, first published in 1759, are taken from this edition.

death). This is coupled with a prophetic foreknowledge of his people's future.[6]

Arviragus is at first modelled on Oedipus' estranged son Polynices, but later he turns into Theseus. He leads the Britons into battle against the invading army at the pass beyond the grove, just as Theseus and his Athenians take on Creon's Thebans in the Sophoclean archetype. Another influence is Euripides' *Heraclidae*, which supplies Caractacus' rejuvenation and charge into battle, based on Euripides' elderly Iolaus. It is a surprise to find this obscure tragedy influencing the British stage in the eighteenth century, until it is remembered that Mason's curate, John Delap, was working on a version of the same play, *The Royal Suppliants*, staged at Drury Lane in 1781 (see above, Ch. 3).[7]

Caractacus quaintly evokes the druids' sacred grove, inspired by the grove of the Erinyes in *OC*. Aulus Didius is warned that the sanctuary is inviolable. The olive trees of Colonus are replaced by oaks, but the altar, the dark stream, the detailed sacrifices, and the 'wide circus | Skirted with unhewn stone' recall details of the Attic sanctuary in the Sophoclean play. The hero of *OC* is described as descending stairs to a subterranean chamber: in *Caractacus* there is adjoined to the grove a 'deep cavern', where rites are enacted: access to it consists of 'a thousand rugged steps of moss-hewn rock'.[8]

Audiences were enticed into the theatre by the scenery painter Nicholas Dall's depiction of Mona. The stage was set with 'mighty piles of magic-planted rock', where 'at times of holiest festival | The Druid leads his train', and the play's rituals blatantly conflate the British druids with ancient Greek choruses. The druids enter with a circular dance in the 'sacred space' of the grove on Mona. Later, they perform rites to the sound of the harp: the chorus leader Mador sings antiphonally to them, 'Rustling vestments brush the ground, | Round, and round, and round they go'. The druids share the grove with bards, who play 'immortal strains' on

---

[6] Ibid. 59–60, 81.

[7] Delap (1781). On Delap and Mason see Gosse (1884), ii. 309; iii. 128. They may have known about Jean-François Marmontel's tragedy *Les Héraclides* of 1752. Delap's *The Captives* (Drury Lane 1786), whose plot is distantly related to another then obscure Euripidean play, *Helen*, has an ancient Scottish setting, and a prologue delivered by a Caledonian bard, who claimed that the author had been inspired by 'all the Grecian stage'.

[8] Mason (1796), 13, 11, 50.

their harps: 'In visible shapes dance they a magic round | To the high minstrelsy'. The choral odes are sometimes sung by the druids, sometimes by bards, and evince diverse metrical patterns, antiphony, solo and *kommos*, refrain, and dyadic or triadic systems with strophe, antistrophe and epode.[9]

Moreover, *Caractacus* is an impressive stage play. The druids are awesome and fascinating, the main characters are firmly drawn, the action suspenseful, and there are moments of genuine pathos. It raises sophisticated questions about empire, liberty, and religious tolerance. It leaves magnificently unresolved the tension between the early British and Roman ways of life. Caractacus embodies a form of superior spirituality, and an admirable independence.[10] But his druids, the 'primitives' in his *Caractacus*, also practise torture and human sacrifice. The Roman conquest is both a brutal act of imperialism, and a necessary prelude to modern civilization. This tension, partly derived from the ambiguous presentation of Rome's imperial mission in Virgil's *Aeneid*, is exemplified in Caractacus' speech to the Roman prisoners of war. They are to be made human sacrifices, which Caractacus deems an honour:

> You are not slaves. Barbarians tho' you call us,
> We know the native rights man claims from man,
> And therefore never shall we gall your necks
> With chains, or drag you at our scythed cars
> In arrogance of triumph. Nor 'til taught
> By Rome (what Britain sure should scorn to learn)
> Her avarice, will we barter ye for gold.[11]

Yet Aulus Didius is no two-dimensional villain. He refrains from desecrating the grove, because Roman 'laws give licence to all faiths'. He is convinced that Romans fight 'Not to enslave, but humanize the world'.[12] The ethical complexity of *Caractacus* caused it to be appropriated by individuals across the political

[9] Ibid. 12, 18–21, 29, 13.

[10] It is relevant that Mason (who, like William Wilberforce after him, was educated at Hull Grammar School) was one of the first Englishmen to agitate against slavery; as Rector of Aston in Yorkshire he delivered a sermon at York demanding the abolition of the African slave trade, making the daring point that black people had been responsible for the culture of ancient Egypt. See Mason (1788*b*), 17 n.

[11] Mason (1796), 84.

[12] Ibid. 93–4.

spectrum, and it still makes exciting reading. As late as 1962 one of the few scholars to study *Caractacus* in depth is surprised to find himself concluding that it was undoubtedly 'the most outstanding heroic drama of the eighteenth century'.[13]

The play's depth is partly a result of the tension which had developed in Mason's own views, which were by no means unrepresentative of those held by the British middle class, between *Caractacus*' first publication in 1759 and the text performed at its 1776 Covent Garden debut. By 1776 it had become harder not to connect Mason's Roman Empire with British rule in North America, but this was not the spirit in which some of the more jingoistic members of the audience will have received it, and it was certainly not the spirit in which it had been conceived in the less complicated—even triumphant—political atmosphere of the 1750s. Although by the mid-1770s Mason supported the cause of the American rebels, and had become extremely critical of British conduct abroad, he had also originally intended *Caractacus* 'to fight the cause of liberty and Britain',[14] by encouraging the popular patriotic identification of ancient and contemporary Britons. The druids had never come to terms with Rome, and their defiant intransigence had spoken loud to earlier poets including Pope, whose work was adored by Mason, and who once planned a *Brutus*, complete with choruses, portraying the conflict between Rome and the British druids. Other poets whose patriotic fervour was inspired by the druids included Michael Drayton and Thomas Warton.[15] But it was Mason who put Caractacus firmly on the British patriotic map alongside the more familiar Boadicea, inspiring many others to do the same: a poem by the Revd Sneyd Davies, for example, begged Caractacus and the druids to rouse their countrymen against 'tinsel France'.[16]

THE LEARNED RECTOR OF ASTON

Mason was known for his absolute hatred of the Tories.[17] He had previously written another tragedy on the Greek model, *Elfrida*,

---

[13] See A. L. Owen (1962), 147.   [14] Mason (1811), ii. 10.

[15] Discussed in A. L. Owen (1962), 140–1. On Pope's projected *Brutus*, see Pope (1797), i. 158.

[16] See Pennant (1781), 422–4; Snyder (1923), 127.

[17] John Mitford (1853), p. xii n.

which had echoes of *Philoctetes, Trachiniae, Hippolytus*, and *Phoe-nissae*. Set during the reign of King Edgar in tenth-century Here-fordshire, this tale of piety and doomed conjugal love included a chorus of Anglo-Saxon maidens, whose pious odes owe much to Mason's interest in church music.[18] Yet Mason was outraged when the stage version turned the phrase 'godlike youth' into 'royal youth'. Mason complained to Horace Walpole that 'royal' was an epithet 'which I fancy will be approved no where but at St. James's, for it carries the *ius divinum*.'[19] There is, moreover, a mildly anti-monarchical tone to *Elfrida* going beyond the references to invasive Scottish savages so suggestive of the 1745 Jacobite invasion. The play's villain is the rapacious King Edgar, who operates *droit de seigneur*, and there is criticism of the corrupting pageantry and vice of royal courts. But Mason would later be terrified by the French revolution, and his political stance—a deeply Christian moral sense inherited from his father (also a clergyman)—is best understood in terms of his charitable principles and his philanthropy, especially his agitation against slavery, his campaign for the reform of the York lunatic asylum,[20] and his undoubted courage in allowing his name to be placed in the front of the Yorkshire Petition of 1780, which demanded far-reaching political reforms in part as a guaran-tee against oppressive taxation.[21]

Mason's radicalism stemmed from 'a scholastic admiration of the antique republics'.[22] Walpole, however, preferred to see his sympathies with republicanism as 'old fashioned Gothic relics'.[23]

---

[18] See his *Essays on Church Music*, where he argues that words and melody must be connected, in Mason (1811), iii. 287, 408. Interest in dramatic form also led Mason to experiment with a tragedy on the alternative 'Old English' model: *Argentile and Curan* opens with a chorus, but they thereafter disappear. Like a Shakespearean heroine, Editha adopts male disguise, and the blank verse of the leading characters alternates with semi-comic scenes in prose for the lower-class individuals. Mason also wrote an unperformed lyrical tragedy, *Sappho*. It incorpor-ates translations of Sappho's fragments (cast in an acceptably heterosexual mode), which were to be sung to music composed by Felice de Giardini, famous for sensuous violin music (Mason (1811), ii. 207–318, 319–61). Mason also completed Whitehead's tragic *Oedipus*, which seems to have had no chorus (see below, Ch. 8). Giardini wrote music for one of the revivals of Mason's *Elfrida*: see Highfill et al. (1973–93), vi. 167.

[19] John Mitford (1851), i. 45.

[20] Mason (1772).

[21] John Cannon (1972), 75–6.

[22] Hartley Coleridge (1836), 403.

[23] Letter of July 1782 to Mason, in John Mitford (1851), ii. 313.

But in this period Graeco-Roman and 'Gothic' political revivalism were not so very different. Whigs believed that early British culture, until the Norman invasions, had enjoyed democratic assemblies like those of classical Athens. An expression of this view was to be found in the defence speech delivered by Joseph Gerrald, a republican campaigner for universal suffrage, convicted of sedition in 1794. He had acted the role of the ostracized monarch Oedipus at Stanmore School two decades previously (see the next chapter), and had apparently allowed its political subtext to go to his head. Gerrald mentions ancient Greek democracies with approval, but also claims that he wishes to see the restoration of the Anglo-Saxon *myclegemot*, a legislative body consisting of representatives chosen by *all* the people.[24]

GREEKS AND EARLY BRITONS

The success of *Caractacus* was partly a result of the mid-eighteenth-century craze for druids, complemented by an interest in musical traditions believed to be inherited from the ancient Celtic bards. Just as Homeric scholars in the 1930s were enthralled to discover the epic singing of the Muslim *guslar*s of Serbia, so Mason's friend Thomas Gray was affected by a blind Welsh harper called John Parry; he wrote to Mason in 1757, while he was working on *Caractacus*, that Parry's 'ravishing blind harmony, such tunes of a thousand years old . . . have set all this learned body a-dancing'. Gray was inspired by Parry to complete his visionary poem *The Bard* (1757), on the theme of Edward I's alleged extermination of the Welsh bards.[25] Another friend of Mason who combined Greek and druidical interests, William Whitehead (see Ch. 5), produced a version of old Welsh verses, *The Battle of Argoed Llwfain*, scored for harp, harpsichord, violin, or flute; this trend culminated in a popular scoring of Welsh songs supposedly derived from ancient bards.[26]

---

[24] Gerrald (1794), 188–9.
[25] Gosse (1884), ii. 312. The poem is published in Starr and Hendrickson (1966), 18–24.
[26] Edward Jones (1784). Edward Lhuyd had published his *Archaeologia Brtannica* in 1707; Edward Williams, alias Iolo Morganwg, would hold his first pseudo-Druidic Gorsedd in 1792.

The fascination with Celtic music was inseparable from interest in the music of ancient Greece. Eighteenth-century admirers of Greek tragedy fantasized about Greek melody; Collins wrote a (lost) 'Ode on the Music of the Grecian Theatre', and in 'The Passions, An Ode for Music', called upon Music to arise from her Athenian bower and confirm her ancient reputation.[27] Parallels were drawn between ancient British and ancient Greek singing: Whitehead's *Verses to the People of England* (1758) equated ancient British bards with Tyrtaeus, the Spartan composer of war songs. When *The Scots Magazine* celebrated the building of the new Edinburgh theatre in 1773, the poem there published imagined the hills of Scotia anciently resounding to Gaelic epic and pastoral while the poets of Greece were alive.[28]

The most important factor in the fusion of classical and ancient British revivalism was the stir caused by James Macpherson's 'translations' of old Gaelic poetry in the 1760s, culminating in *The Works of Ossian, Son of Fingal* in 1765. The debate over the authenticity of these works, which began almost as soon as they appeared, long obscured their importance as a cultural phenomenon. But an excellent book by Fiona Stafford has reinstated Macpherson as a seminal influence on the Romantic poets and British cultural life in general.[29] At the time of the appearance of Ossian's works, the parallels between them and Homeric epic were laboriously studied, for example in an anonymous treatise published in London in 1762, *Occasional Thoughts on the Study and Character of Classical Authors with Some Incidental Comparisons of Homer and Ossian*. The parallels were underscored by the learned gentlemen who translated Macpherson into Greek verse, and by poets like Thomas Mercer, in whose *Elysium*, in imitation of *Aeneid* VI, the authorial voice encounters the shades of both Ossian and Homer.[30]

MUSICAL THEATRE

Mason's drama would probably never have been staged were it not for the Ossian phenomenon. By 1763 arrangements of Ossian were

---

[27] William Collins (1765), 81–7. See Stern (1940), 144–6. [28] Anon. (1773).
[29] Stafford (1988). [30] Mercer (1774).

being produced in Edinburgh,[31] and *Oithóna, a Dramatic Poem,
Taken from the Prose Translation of the Celebrated Ossian*, was
performed as an opera to music by F. H. Barthelemon at the
Theatre Royal, Haymarket in 1768. A modern authority on eighteenth-century theatre music is surprised that the Ossian libretto
imitates Greek tragedy in dividing the choruses into strophe, an-
tistrophe, and epode,[32] but the librettist was either copying Mason
or similarly connecting early British singing with the ancient
Greek chorus.

Caractacus, which had already been performed in Dublin, was in
1769 experimentally recited during a single 'Attic evening's entertainment' at the Haymarket.[33] But in 1772 George Colman, the
manager of Covent Garden, decided to stage Mason's plays. He
began by altering the more sentimental *Elfrida* and commissioned
a score from Thomas Arne. The heroine was to be played by the
stunning redhead Elizabeth Hartley, and Athelwold by William
Smith. Either Attic art or Shakespeare's fire went to the heads of
these stage lovers, who later eloped.

Mason, who had not been consulted, was apprehensive. He
complained to Colman, who wittily threatened him with a chorus
of Grecian washerwomen (the identity of the chorus of Euripides'
Hippolytus). Mason, who was not without a sense of humour
himself, wrote to Horace Walpole that any success would be due
to the novelty of 'such a strange sight as twenty British virgins'.[34]
In fact the success may have been owed as much to the performance of the chorus leader 'Albina', the outstanding oratorio singer
Isabella Mattocks. In 1773 Walpole nevertheless reported that 'the
virgins were so inarticulate that I should have understood them as
well if they had sung choruses of Sophocles'. But he insisted that
the play was 'very affecting and does admirably for the stage';
Garrick of Drury Lane was envious because the King had already
been to see the play twice.[35]

Mason had been an undergraduate at St. John's College, Cambridge, and was made a fellow of Pembroke Hall in 1749. Learned
gentlemen from that university were particularly delighted by
Elfrida, because it seemed to represent a revival of superior

---

[31] David Erskine Baker (1763).   [32] Fiske (1986), 315.
[33] *LS* v/1. 42; *LS* iv/3. 1383.
[34] Letter of 1 Dec. 1772 to Walpole, in John Mitford (1851), i. 45.
[35] Letter of Walpole to Mason, 19 Nov. 1773, in Mitford (1851), i. 100–1.

drama, and even to imply that the world was now ready for a commercial staging of a Greek tragedy. In February 1773 someone signing himself 'Cantab.' suggested in the *Gentleman's Magazine* that the 'English Roscius', David Garrick, should attempt the *Oedipus Tyrannus* at Drury Lane:

As the tragedy of Elfrida, written (after the Greek manner) by that most excellent poet Mr Mason, has met with such singular applause at Covent Garden Theatre, I cannot help lamenting that our English Roscius has never had a play of Sophocles (translated into English blank verse) represented at Drury Lane. The plays in general, are the finest ever written; and the *Oedipus Tyrannus* is, in my opinion, the properest to be represented at present, both for the grandeur of the choruses and the magnificence of the scenery.[36]

Unsurprisingly this fantasy was not fulfilled, although Garrick (who died in 1779) was reputed to have wanted late in his life to stage Euripides' *Hecuba* in the as yet unpublished translation of Robert Potter (on whom see further below), and procured expensive costumes. The plan was abandoned because of the cost of the accompanying Greek chorus. Garrick was certainly interested in 'Greek' tragic costumes, for he donated some to the production of *Oedipus Tyrannus* at Stanmore School in 1775.[37] But instead of an authentic Drury Lane *Oedipus* or *Hecuba*, the admirers of Mason's ancient model were to be compensated by the production of *Caractacus*. Although not quite so popular with the general public as *Elfrida*, according to Garrick it was much frequented by 'men of taste and classical men'.[38] Elizabeth Hartley once more starred as the heroine.

Mason disliked Arne's music, but it helped these tragedies to succeed commercially. It is most unfortunate that no score of *Caractacus* now exists, since it was said by Samuel Arnold to contain 'some of the brightest and most vigorous emanations of our English *Amphion*'.[39] Rumours about its excellence—and indeed the survival of a score—were still circulating in musical journals at the end of the nineteenth century,[40] and may even have given Elgar

---

[36] Quoted in *LS* iv/3. 1691.
[37] Letter from Daniel Watson to John Carr, 2 Apr. 1788, in John Nichols (1817–18), i. 431. See further Stoker (1993), 286.
[38] Letter to Hannah More in Meakin (1911), 99.
[39] Quoted in Highfill et al. (1973–93), i. 114.
[40] See Draper (1924), 15.

the idea for his own *Caractacus*. Arne prefixed to this score an essay describing his use of sounds and rhythms corresponding to the ideas expressed in the drama. To recreate the music of the druids, he used clarinets, the serpent, liberal harp sequences, and marches accompanied by trombone. The music has been praised for innovative attempts at local colour, especially in the overture, which has been described as 'a singular attempt at programme music'.[41]

THE ANCIENT MODEL

Before Mason, Greek tragedy's relationship with the British commercial stage in the eighteenth century had consisted of adapted content rather than adopted form. It was a remarkable achievement to realize the form of Greek tragedy in a manner acceptable to his era. His plays are, however, not the first British works to incorporate elements similar to the Greek tragic chorus. Choirs of angels sang in medieval miracle plays; choruses were performed as interludes between the acts of early vernacular tragedies such as *Gorboduc* and *Jocasta*; Shakespeare had used a chorus of sorts to open the first two acts of *Romeo and Juliet*, and passages in blank verse are delivered by a character named Chorus at the beginning of each of the acts of *Henry V*.[42] In early seventeenth-century closet tragedy it was not only Milton's *Samson Agonistes* (studied by Mason[43]) that experimented with using a chorus. Usually the chorus in the closet was confined to the ends of acts, but sometimes it interacted with characters, as the chorus of Egyptians converse with the messenger in Samuel Daniel's *The Tragedie of Cleopatra* (1594, rev. 164). A chorus even occasionally appeared in performed tragedies, for example Ben Jonson's *Catiline* (1611). But after the separation of music from serious spoken drama, which

---

[41] For further details see the appendix on Arne's music to Mason's plays in Draper (1924), 331–3.

[42] For a survey of the chorus in earlier British drama see E. Griffin (1959), 1–48. Schiller's experimental use of choruses in *Die Braut von Messina* (first performed 1803) and his prefatory essay 'Über den Gebrauch des Chors in der Tragödie', are discussed in Brunkhorst (1999). This essay compares German, French and British attitudes, including reactions to Mason's plays, but Brunkhorst is seemingly not aware that Mason's dramas were successfully performed.

[43] See Mason, 'Letters concerning the following Drama', prefixed to *Elfrida* (1752), p. v.

occurred with the introduction of Continental opera to London at the end of the seventeenth century, choruses in English-language tragedy became rare. Where they did appear, their function was confined to plausible songs in staged rituals (for example, the invocation of Laius' ghost in Dryden and Lee's *Oedipus*, hymns in the temple in Dennis's *Iphigenia*, or the lament for Troy in Thomson's *Agamemnon*). Hostility to the choral convention amongst theatrical people was so strong that Gray thought that if *Elfrida* were to be staged it would have to lose its choruses;[44] and eighteenth-century academic attempts to stage ancient Greek tragedy minimized or dispensed with the chorus altogether, including the productions of Sophocles in Greek at Stanmore School.[45]

Moreover, Mason was using the chorus in a manner distinct from anything that had gone before. His choruses participate fully in the continuous action, affecting the decisions of the central actors and engaging in dialogue with them. Mason thus came closer to actually staging a Greek tragic model than any other playwright before the nineteenth century. Modern music critics argue that if the choral convention of Greek tragedy emerges elsewhere in the eighteenth century, it is in Handel's oratorios, especially *Hercules*, advertised as 'a musical drama' (1745); its libretto used both the pseudo-Senecan *Oedipus Oetaeus* and Sophocles' *Trachiniae* and gives an essential function to the chorus.[46]

Mason's achievement in popularizing the tragic chorus is further underlined by remembering how recently it has been accepted in the theatres of the modern world. Late nineteenth-century novelists, especially Eliot and Hardy, may have been influenced by the chorus, but nineteenth-century British performances of Greek tragedy almost always reduced or removed altogether the problematic chorus (a singular exception was the *Antigone* staged at Covent Garden, to music by Mendelssohn, in 1845; see below, Chs. 12 and 18). Even today comedy can be derived from the popular notion of a squadron of sages intrusively intoning Universal Truths and apostrophizing peculiar divinities, most recently in Woody Allen's film *Mighty Aphrodite* (1995). The landmark production in theatrical realization of the chorus is usually regarded as Karolos Koun's famous *Persians* in the mid-1960s, which used

---

[44] Gosse (1884), ii. 212.   [45] Field (1828), i. 78.
[46] Keates (1992), 128, 256–8.

collective dance formations and moved the chorus away from the
periphery to the centre of the ritualized tragic action.[47] Even
classical scholars have only relatively recently succeeded in turning
'perceptions of the chorus from an encumbrance into a core
strength of Greek tragedy', by exploring both its collective perspective and its unique capacity for survival.[48]

THE CONTROVERSIAL CHORUS

Despite the rejection of the tragic chorus in theatrical practice, a
theoretical debate about its validity marks English dramatic criticism from Dryden onwards.[49] It was fuelled at the end of the
seventeenth century by Dacier's French editions of Aristotle's
Poetics and of Sophocles, which had ardently defended the
chorus.[50] For a century countless essays propounded arguments
for and against the chorus.[51] Its supporters were usually clergy-
men, while its detractors were practising dramatists. It was
Mason's achievement to bring these two opposing viewpoints—
however temporarily—together, and the reason why *Caractacus*
could achieve this was, quite simply, druidical revivalism.

For it was inherently plausible that druids would sing in a sacred
druidical setting, and the most important objection to the chorus
had always been its improbability. Its presence was almost always
found inherently ridiculous by sensible theatre professionals. Supporters of the chorus could find few good counter-arguments:
James Beattie, the professor of Moral Philosophy at Aberdeen,
resorted to the desperate measure of asserting that important personages in ancient 'reality' always had trains of attendants, of
whom the chorus was a 'probable' reflection.[52] The probability
argument was connected with one about theatrical authenticity:
sensible critics saw that reviving the chorus alone was inconsistent.
If authentic reconstruction of ancient theatrical practice were the
goal, other ancient conventions would have to be revived, includ-

[47] On the late 20th-c. rediscovery of the chorus see further Fischer-Lichte (2004).
[48] See especially Taplin's remarks on the revival of the chorus by a 20th-c.
playwright, Tony Harrison, in Taplin (1997), 172–3. For Edwardian experiments
see below, Ch. 18.
[49] See E. Griffin (1959), 59–63.
[50] Dacier (1692); (1693).
[51] For an overview of the academic controversy about the chorus, see Green
(1934), 219–25.
[52] Beattie (1776), 12.

ing pipe or lyre accompaniment,[53] or even the much-derided mask.[54] Such discussions usually centred on the 'rules' of neoclassical theory. Francophile neoclassicists maintained that the unitary choral identity facilitated the obligatory 'unities' of time and place, which they believed to have been prescribed by Aristotle. But opponents of the 'tyranny' of the unities argued that dropping the chorus liberated modern playwrights to travel in their plots through space and history, thus making far more types of story candidates for representation.[55]

More burning was the issue of the chorus's role in ensuring the morality of tragedy, a central plank in Dacier's defence of the chorus. A high-minded English advocate of the chorus translated Sophocles' *Electra* and urged a revival of dramas like those of the Athenians, which served 'as so many Publick Lessons, or Sermons, to instruct the People in Religion and good Manners'. If modern playwrights were to produce morally edifying drama, there would be need to re-establish 'the Use of their Chorus; whereby an occasion is given to instil, by the Charms of Musick, into the Minds of the Hearers those Sentiments of Virtue and Goodness'.[56]

Yet, as objectors pointed out, the chorus did not always set a virtuous example. In *Hippolytus* Phaedra said things in front of the chorus 'improper to be heard by a number of women', and the chorus immorally kept quiet when Hippolytus was arraigned by his father. In *Medea* the chorus are effectively turned into accomplices of murder.[57] Others argued that moral comments from the chorus were useless if the morality did not suffuse the entire piece.[58] Even the ancient playwrights were not immune from immorality: had not Aeschylus been indicted for impiety?[59] Furthermore, a moralizing chorus might actually conceal morally dangerous material: one paranoid critic implies that Hellenizing features such as the chorus serve to 'decorate vice in fascinating colours, and turn the sober sentiments of virtue into ridicule'.[60]

By the time of the publication of *Elfrida* in 1752, this often sterile debate was adopting from France the more exciting issue of the chorus's class profile. Corneille and Dacier had objected to

---

[53] Colman (1783), p. xxv. [54] See Pye (1792), 533.
[55] e.g. Cooke (1775), 90. [56] Anon. (1714*a*), pp. i–iii.
[57] Cooke (1775), 100–1. [58] Pye (1792), 232; Colman (1783), p. xxiv.
[59] Pye (1792), 234.
[60] 'The British Theatre', *London Magazine*, 40 (May 1771), 262–5, at p. 264.

the lack of loyalty—even treasonable insubordination—which the chorus in Euripides' *Medea* shows towards their king by taking Medea's side.[61] Brumoy's *Le Théâtre des Grecs* (1730), read widely in Britain, sees the political culture of democratic Athens as explaining the chorus: they are a reflection of the Athenian spectators, who were 'accustomed to be involved in public affairs' and therefore had 'a quite different taste from the French spectators, who meddle not with anything in their own happy and tranquil monarchy' (see Ch. 8).[62]

In England, on the other hand, Ralph suggests that the chorus was a result of the *decline* of Athenian freedom, added as an ornament after Pericles established the theoric fund, to mask the decreasing political freedom of the playwrights.[63] Richard Hurd was one of the few to see the political complexity of the relationship between democratic Athens and her tragic choruses. The chorus can only speak the *truth* if it consists 'of citizens, whether of a republic, or the milder and more equal roialties'. Yet Hurd sees that a good playwright can use the chorus even of a play set in a tyranny to imply political truths. His subtle reading of *Antigone* points out the chorus's reluctance to protest against Creon's edict, and the way they 'obsequiously go along with him in the projects of his cruelty'. Yet Sophocles, he argues, was still using the chorus in a morally effective way. He is deliberately showing how men become incapable of moral protest under despotism. Sophocles 'hath surely represented, in the most striking colours, the pernicious character, which a chorus, under such circumstances, would naturally sustain'.[64]

Mason's plays gave all these issues a new focus. He courted this reaction by prefixing five explanatory letters to *Elfrida* in 1752, claiming that his aim had been 'to pursue the ancient method so far as it is probable a Greek Poet, were he alive, would now do'. The advantages of the chorus were that it made the playwright concentrate on the unities, that it was a resource for 'Picturesque Description, sublime allegory, and . . . *Pure Poetry*', and that it added pomp and metrical variety. It guided the moral sentiments of the specta-

---

[61] See the discussion in Hurd (1749),79–80.
[62] Cited from Lennox's translation, in Lennox (1759), vol. i, p. cix.
[63] Ralph (1743), 16.   [64] Hurd (1749), 76–7.

tors and helped, like an internal audience in a painting, to heighten pathos.[65]

The first reaction to Mason's revival of the chorus was an encomium written and published anonymously by Nevile Thomas, a schoolmaster. Mason's chorus is not annexed to the action, 'but rises naturally out of the subject'; its moral purity is so outstanding that even Plato would let Mr Mason into his *Republic*; the ornamental diction has excelled the ancient Greek tragedians themselves.[66] A less unctuous note was struck by the hilarious letter sent to *The Covent-Garden Journal* by an 'inmate of Bedlam' calling himself 'Tragicomicus' (probably Henry Fielding), complaining that someone has thrown *Elfrida* into his cell. The main objection of 'Tragicomicus' recycles the 'probability' argument: who wants a chorus, he asks, to tell Desdemona to pick up her handkerchief? But this fictional madman makes the more original point that no competent dramatist needs a chorus to announce entrances, instead of making his audience *work* in order to discover the identity of the characters.[67]

After the publication of *Caractacus* in 1759, there was a flurry of further responses, both admiring and critical.[68] 1761 saw a theatrical pastiche by Richard Bentley (son of the famous scholar), *The Wishes; or Harliquin's Mouth Opened*.[69] Bentley was intrigued by the chorus's policy of non-interventionist commentary even on violence. *The Wishes* contains a play-within-a-play entitled *Gunpowder Treason* by Mr Distress. Guy Faux, the tragic hero, insanely informs the chorus that he is about to enter the vaults, which contain a magazine of gunpowder, and blow up the Houses of Parliament. The chorus fail either to prevent disaster or leave the vicinity, instead delivering a lengthy ode later paraphrased from memory by Scott:

> O unhappy madman,
> Or rather unhappy we,
> The victims of the madman's fury
> Or thrice, thrice unhappy
> The friends of the madman,

---

[65] Mason (1752), pp. ix–xii.   [66] Anon. (1752), 9, 15, 19, 21, 25.
[67] *The Covent-Garden Journal*, no. 62 (16 Sept. 1752), in Jensen (1915), ii. 93–5.
[68] Collected in E. Griffin (1959), 100–6.
[69] *The Wishes* does not seem to have been published. There is a copy in the Larpent Collection (British Library microfiche 199, F 253/85).

> Who did not secure him and restrain him
> From the perpetration of such deeds of frenzy!
> Or three and four times hapless
> The keeper of the magazine,
> Who forgot the keys in the door![70]

Yet Guy Faux remains determined. When asked why the chorus does not summon a constable, and carry the villain before a justice of the peace, the dramatist Mr Distress answers 'Poh, poh, that would be *natural*'—far too *probable* a reaction for any chorus. Although it was enjoyed in private performances,[71] Bentley's play was not a success when it appeared at Drury Lane, because its target was a convention of Greek tragedy still totally unfamiliar to the play-going public. But opponents of slavish imitation of the ancients continued to quote *The Wishes*—perhaps the funniest parody of the Greek chorus ever written—for decades.[72]

WHEN DRUID MET GREEK

The problem with the chorus has always been the emphasis given by northern European culture to the individual. The paucity of living collective dance traditions has made it difficult to understand the communal ritual function of this plural lyric presence. Mason's tragedies were written at a time when comparative anthropology was beginning to affect the understanding of drama. Hurd made intelligent comparisons between Peruvian theatre and the Roman *Praetexta* and *Togata*, and also between Chinese tragedy and Sophocles' *Electra*.[73] John Brown drew parallels with the Iroquois in North America. He argued that a form of drama similar to Greek tragedy is practised by all primitive tribes: a Chief sings some great action of a god or hero, and 'the surrounding Choir answer him at Intervals, by Shouts of Sympathy or concurrent Approbation'.[74]

Yet British men of letters discovered the primitives who caused the revival of the ancient chorus in their own back yard. In the

---

[70] Walter Scott (1870), 225.
[71] For example, at Brandenburgh House in 1761. See Rosenfeld (1978), 59.
[72] See 'The British Theatre' (*The London Magazine*, 40 (May 1771), 262–5); Walter Scott (1870).
[73] Hurd (1751), 89–90, 162–7.
[74] John Brown (1763), 41–2.

mid-eighteenth century huge enthusiasm (a phenomenon often known by the blanket term 'Celtic revival') was aroused for all the inhabitants of pre-Norman Britain: the tribes encountered by the Romans, the Welsh, the Cornish, the Gaels, the Irish, the Celts, the Norsemen, and the Anglo-Saxons. Most popular were the early British bards and druids. The ancient texts ransacked for druidical lore were Caesar, Tacitus, Pliny the Elder, Lucan, Pomponius Mela, Diogenes Laertius, Ammianus Marcellinus and Cassius Dio.[75]

One of the greatest druidical experts, William Stukeley, advised the dowager Princess of Wales on the 'Celtic' remains discovered by men digging in Kew gardens. In 1763 he dedicated a book to her as 'Veleda, archdruidess of Kew'. Veleda was believed to be the name of an important ancient female mystic.[76] Mason was also convinced that there had been female druids, which illuminates the odd status of the chorus in *Elfrida*, experts in druidical song. The messenger in *Caractacus* reports that, prior to the battle,

> through our ranks
> Our sacred sisters rush'd in sable robes,
> With hair dishevel'd and funereal brands,
> Hurl'd round with menacing fury.[77]

Mason's notes to the play point to a passage in Tacitus which he has lifted almost unaltered.[78] Tacitus says that women were involved in defending Mona against the Romans (*Annals* 14. 30):

On the beach stood the adverse army, a serried mass of arms and men, with women flitting between the ranks (*intercursantibus feminis*). In the style of Furies, in robes of deathly black and with dishevelled hair, they brandished their torches; while a circle of druids, lifted their hands to heaven, showering imprecations . . .

It is scarcely surprising that this colourful passage enthralled enthusiasts for ancient Britain.

Their interest was not entirely new. Jacobean dramas engaging with the Roman invasions, such as Beaumont and Fletcher's

---

[75] See A. L. Owen (1962) and Snyder (1923). The translation of *Caesar's Commentaries* by William Duncan (London, 1753) had helped to make druids accessible.

[76] Stukeley (1763b), 'Dedication'.

[77] Mason (1796), 84–5.

[78] Ibid. 101.

Bonduca (1614), had displayed some druidical elements.[79] Yet the
seventeenth-century conceptualization of early Britain had drawn
little distinction between Roman and indigenous culture. Inigo
Jones had created scenery for masques set in Arthurian England,
for example *Albion's Triumph*, but had visualized the British past
in Roman terms.[80] In 1620 he told James I that Stonehenge was
Roman: it was clearly based on four intersecting equilateral tri-
angles, which was exactly the diagram deduced by Palladio from
the Roman Vitruvius' account of the theatre.[81]

  But at the beginning of the eighteenth century the prehistoric
circles of standing circles at Stonehenge and elsewhere began to be
interpreted, rather, as *pre-Roman* druidic relics. Once this crucial
separation of early Briton and Roman occurred, stone circles
became associated, rather, with the Greeks. The Greeks were
suddenly felt to have a greater affinity than the technocrats of
Rome with indigenous British culture. An important publication
in popularizing the new 'Hellenic' view of the druids was Henry
Rowlands's *Mona Antiqua Restaurata* (1723). Rowlands believed
that ancient Welsh was the oldest language in the world and that
the culture of its speakers had numerous parallels in both Hebrew
and early Greek society. The ancient Greek philosophers, including Pythagoras, had imitated and adopted the mystical lore of the
druids. Rowlands and his followers detailed features shared by
Greek and Druidical religion, for example mountain worship and
snake symbolism, discovered at the Avebury circle.[82]

SOPHOCLES AND STONEHENGE

Rowlands argued that the ancient Britons, like the Greeks, had
cultivated groves for the worship of their gods, and that Anglesey
was a special place of worship. He was inspired by a passage in
Diodorus about the Hyperboreans (2. 47):[83]

In the regions beyond the land of the Celts there lies in the ocean an island
no smaller than Sicily. This island . . . is situated in the North and is
inhabited by the Hyperboreans . . . Apollo is honoured among them

---

[79] Snyder (1923), 3.   [80] Peacock (1995), 69, 321.
[81] Jones's idea was later developed and published, in 1655, by his pupil John
Webb. See Summerson (1966), 71–2.
[82] A. L. Owen (1962), 124.
[83] Rowlands (1723), 76.

above all other gods; and the inhabitants are looked upon as priests of Apollo . . . since daily they praise the god in song and honour him exceedingly. And there is also on this island both a magnificent sacred precinct of Apollo and a notable temple . . . which is spherical in shape.[84]

This passage was to thrill admirers of the druids: Calypso's island of Ogygia was one candidate for the island beyond the Celts, making Calypso a druidess.[85] But Diodorus goes on to tell the story of the Hyperborean mystic Abaris, who travelled to Delos, where great performances on the cithara and choral dances were instituted. These celebrated Apollo and the revolution of the stars in the heavens. The Abaris story produced the exciting identification of Diodorus' northern island with either Britain or Anglesey.

Rowlands argued that Abaris (whose name in ancient Welsh obviously meant 'son of Rees', *ap Rhys*) took the Druidic ritual of circular choral singing, accompanied by the harp, from Britain to Greece.[86] Thence it was a small inferential leap to identify a round floor found to the eastern end of the druidic monument at Trevwry on Anglesey (probably the place now known as Tref Alaw) as an ancient theatre, a view supported by the discovery of ancient 'operas' and plays on religious themes in the old Cornish language.[87] By 1740 Stukeley was arguing that the old Welsh name for the druidical temple at Stonehenge, *choir gaur*, should be etymologized as *chorus gigantum* ('The Giants' Dance'), or, preferably, as *chorus magnus* ('The Great Choir').[88] Stukeley reports ancient explanations of the names of stone circles, such as 'the company dancing' and 'the band of musick', and notes traditions that stone circles were composed of petrified choruses. He argued that the Avebury stone circle could have held 'an immense number of people at their panegyres and public festivals', and would have 'form'd a most noble amphitheater'.[89] The connection between stone circles and the Greek chorus had become irresistible.

Cranky theories about the ancient chorus abounded. Some asserted that the Greeks inherited their dance movements from the ancient Egyptians, and that the gesturing of the Greek chorus was 'a significant *Hieroglyphical* expression'.[90] Another view held

---

[84] Translated by Oldfather (1935), ii. 37–41. [85] Stukeley (1763*a*), 15.
[86] Rowlands (1723), 76. See A. L. Owen (1962), 81.
[87] Rowlands (1723), 61, 68, 76, 89 and pl. IV, 342.
[88] Stukeley (1740), 8. [89] Stukeley (1743), 25, 83.
[90] Ralph (1731), 92–3.

that the chorus could be illuminated by the Epicurean notion that Chaos ruled creation with its warring atoms, 'before this world was tun'd by the MUSICK of the spheres into a regular DANCE'.[91] More specifically, it was held that Greek choruses had 'imitated in their evolutions the supposed motion of the heavenly bodies'.[92] This idea was derived from antique scholars, including scholiasts on Euripides and Pindar, and was believed to stem from a treatise by Ptolemy, the Alexandrian astronomer of the second century A D. The strophic structure of ancient choral lyric—'turn' and 'counter-turn'—reflected the dancers' movements. They revolved in alternately opposing directions in imitation of the sun, moon, planets and constellations of the zodiac.[93] Although sensible men like Brown protested that a more likely aim had been the prevention of giddiness,[94] this idea gained popular currency.

It was given new weight by the astronomical activities which the ancient Druids were believed to have performed at Stonehenge. This theory had been suggested earlier, but was most concisely expressed in the title of Dr John Smith's influential dissertation (Salisbury, 1771): *Choir Gaur; The Grand Orrery of the Ancient Druids, Commonly Called Stonehenge, on Salisbury Plain, Astronomically Explained, and Mathematically Proved to be a Temple Erected in the Earliest Ages for Observing the Movements of the Heavenly Bodies*. This notion was warmly received by Mason, whose coryphaeus Modred, the Chief Druid in *Caractacus*, swears an oath before the final battle:

> By the bright circle of the golden sun;
> By the brief courses of the errant moon;
> By the dread potency of every star
> That studs the mystic zodiac's burning girth.[95]

Mason had extracted such ideas from the numerous books he had consumed about the ancient Britons, their religion, and their monuments. These researches are evident in the notes he appended to *Caractacus*, which document the play's ethnography, and in his correspondence with Gray.

---

[91] Ibid. 114.   [92] Pye (1792), 231 n. 6.

[93] e.g. *Etymologicum Magnum* s.v. προσόδιον. The ancient sources are collected by Crusius (1888), 10–11. Thanks to Ian Rutherford for help on this.

[94] John Brown (1763), 114.

[95] Mason (1796), 74.

In these letters Gray urges Mason to lessen the 'Greek' tone of the druidical lore, and make it more distinctively 'Celtic'. Mason's divinity Andraste, for example, has 'too Greek an air'.[96] Andraste is linked with the theory that the heavenly bodies are involved in the chorus's singing. In the last ode, a dirge for Arviragus, Mador orders his chorus to play their harps:

> Ring out ye mortal strings!
> Answer, thou heav'nly harp instinct with spirit all,
> That o'er ANDRASTE'S throne self-warbling swings.
> There, where ten thousand spheres, in measur'd chime
> Roll their majestic melodies along.[97]

The chorus respond, in their final lines,

> ANDRASTE'S heav'nly harp shall deign
> To mingle with our mortal strain,
> And Heav'n and Earth unite, in chorus high
> While Freedom wafts her champion to the sky.[98]

Gray assumed that Andraste was a synthesis of the Greek personifications Ananke and Adrasteia. Mason, however, had found her in Cassius Dio's account of Boudica's uprising (62. 6), and she stayed in the play. His blatant Hellenization is evident, however, in the musical detail. There is no evidence that this British war-goddess was ever honoured by a tragic chorus or named in the dirges of hero cult, let alone visualized, like the Greek god Apollo, as strumming a harp.

THE POLITICS OF THE CHORAL REVIVAL

The language in which Mason's revival of the chorus was discussed was politicized. Mason's plays had politically motivated detractors, and the debate was not a simple matter of personal stance on colonial policy or on America. In 1782, for example, Bentley's *The Wishes* was revived in Ireland, and a London revival was cancelled at the last minute. Mason wrote to Walpole in great relief, acknowledging the excellence of Bentley's parody of his 'poor Greek chorus'. But the focus in the revised version had been changed, according to Walpole, into a bitter Tory libel on the Whig opposition: Bentley was a committed Tory.

[96] Letter of September 1757, in John Mitford (1853), 106.
[97] Mason (1796), 92.   [98] Ibid.

An attack on Mason's classicism was made by the frustrated dramatist Percival Stockdale, in his *An Inquiry into the Nature and Genuine Laws of Poetry*, published in London in 1778, when Mason's plays had held the London stage consistently for five years. In his view Mason has been deceived into a high opinion of his poetical talents, 'by the temporary power of the press to give dignity to trifles; by the miserable arts of theatrical managers to procure popularity for a tinsel play;—and by the crowds that frequent our theatres.' Stockdale cannot understand why the 'fascination of Greek and Latin is yet unbroken', leading to a situation in which 'the old, impertinent chorus is obtruded on our stage by some little scholastic poets'.[99] He inconsistently objects both to the learned classicism of Mason's plays, and to their popular appeal amongst the uneducated theatre-goers. This confusion marks the ideological complexity underlying Mason's synthesis of Hellenic and Celtic revivalism.

Greek tragedy at this time was a contested property. Its neoclassical manifestations were associated with élite and backward-looking social forces, especially with the theatre of the French Ancien Régime. Yet the new Greek revivalism, connected with the 'discovery' of the early Britons, had a progressive face. Greek tragedy was increasingly appealing to truly radical intellectuals in Britain, a trend brought to its consummation by Shelley (see Ch. 8). The reaction to Mason's plays is thus implicated in what can be seen as the struggle between conservative neoclassicism and proto-romantic Hellenism. His plays became a bone of contention between classical purists and supporters of innovation in the theatre, groups who, in the political sphere, were sometimes identified with conservatives and radicals respectively.

Robert Lloyd, for example, was a classicist, a libertine, and a friend of the radical John Wilkes. His politics—though not his morals—did not differ much from Mason's own. Yet Lloyd felt that his political views were inseparable from his hatred for neoclassical plays, which he regarded as inherently conservative. In a poem published after his death in prison he criticizes 'those who breathe the classic vein', poets 'Delighted with the pomp of rules | The specious pedantry of Schools'. He singled out Mason's dressing of a fable 'in ancient-modern taste',

[99] Stockdale (1778), 117, 179.

> While Chorus marks the servile mode
> With fine reflection, in an ode,
> Present you with a perfect piece,
> Formed on the model of Old Greece.

The term 'servile', often used by the critics of the 'slavery' of neoclassicism and its 'tyranny' of rules, reveals their conviction that attempts to revive the ancient theatre were conservative.[100] Mason was confusing because the progressive ideology of his plays seemed at odds with the perceived conservatism of their form. The plays pleased both conservative philologists and popular audiences, but they were also attacked from both sides of the political fence.

THE CONSEQUENCES OF *CARACTACUS*

The vogue for Mason's plays had consequences more important than the plays themselves. They created an environment at last receptive to the little understood Aeschylus. Although Thomas Morell had included an English translation of *Prometheus Bound* in his edition of 1773, the other plays were not available in the vernacular until the first complete English translation appeared in 1777, at the height of the craze for Mason's tragedies, to create profound implications for English Romanticism.[101] A reason for Aeschylus' inaccessibility had always been the length and opacity of his choruses. But the translator, a kindly Norfolk clergyman named Robert Potter, who had previously paraphrased Aeschylus' *Eumenides* in a political context when describing the miseries of the workhouse, now reassured his readers that the Aeschylean chorus is 'always grave, sententious, sublime, and ardent in the cause of liberty, virtue, and religion'.[102]

Potter's translations were rightly admired; it was discussing Aeschylus with Potter, who sat for him in 1778, that inspired the painter George Romney to produce a series of chalk 'cartoons' of the more striking scenes (see Fig. 7.3). The Greekless Horace

---

[100] 'Shakespeare: An Epistle to Mr Garrick', in Kenrick (1774), i. 80–1. Lord Kames wrote that to revive the chorus would be 'to revive the Grecian slavery' of the unities: Kames (1763), iii. 314. See Green (1934), 224.

[101] *Elfrida* made money steadily between 1772 and 1775, and was revived until 1792. *Caractacus* held the stage for two and a half seasons. Both plays were performed in the provinces, for example at York and Bath. See Draper (1924), 90; Hare (1977), 237, 235. J. J. le Franc de Pompignan's French translation of Aeschylus had been published in 1770.

[102] Potter (1775), 55; (1777), p. xii.

Walpole was one of many delighted with *Prometheus*, although confiding to Mason that he did not 'approve of a mad cow for first woman'.[103] The playwright Richard Cumberland was bowled over by the choruses of *Agamemnon*. But Cumberland was reading them as lyric poetry, and remained a critic of the chorus as theatrical convention. Cumberland laments that 'to have a genius like this of Æschylus encumbered with a chorus, is as if a mill-stone was tied round the pinions of an eagle'.[104]

The impact of Mason's plays on the contemporary understanding of Greek tragedy cannot be overestimated. It may be comical

FIGURE 7.3 George Romney, *Atossa's Dream*, chalk cartoon illustrating Aeschylus' *Persians* (1778–9).

[103] Letter of Walpole to Mason in 1778, in Mitford (1851), i. 328–9.
[104] See Richard Cumberland's essays from *The Observer*, reprinted in Chalmers (1807), 172–3, 176, 178. On the contemporary reception of Potter's Aeschylus see especially Stoker (1993).

today to find Potter asserting that Mason's tragedies 'united the powers of the three illustrious Grecians . . . with the tenderness of Euripides in *Elfrida*, with the force of Æschylus and the correctness and harmony of Sophocles in *Caractacus*'.[105] But Mason's plays impressed the literary consciousness of their day. John Cooper wrote an influential volume of criticism before either of Mason's plays was even performed, which judges all of Seneca's tragic output of less worth than *Elfrida*, and compares Mason's work favourably with Sophocles' *Philoctetes* and *Oedipus at Colonus*.[106] Gray regarded the last ode of Mason's second play on the 'Grecian model' as one of the best things he had ever read.[107] During the later years of his life Mason was regarded as 'England's greatest living poet'. The perceived emotional power of his tragedies is reflected in the figure of the weeping tragic muse, Melpomene, who adorns his Westminster Abbey monument (Fig. 7.4). Mason is placed on a pedestal with Shakespeare, Milton, Dyer, Akenside and Cowper by a gentleman who declares that his classical productions 'would have done honour to Athens in her most refined period.'[108] They appealed to women as much as to men: Anna Seward knew much of Mason's 'exquisite Grecian dramas' off by heart, and declared their author one of the greatest poets of all time.[109] Both Byron and Wordsworth show traces of Mason, and his type of Hellenism lay behind the self-styled 'Greek school' of minor romantic poets. These included Frank Sayers, who in 1790 published two tragedies using 'the Greek form' with choruses of bards or druids, and Robert Southey, who remembered watching Mrs Siddons in the role of Elfrida in Bath.[110]

Mason's plays inspired visual artists even before they were performed: Angelica Kauffman painted a scene from *Elfrida*, and John Flaxman's attention must have been drawn to *Caractacus*' Greek tragic archetype before he painted his lost *Œdipus and*

---

[105] Potter (1777), p. xxiv.   [106] John Gilbert Cooper (1755), 103.

[107] Gosse (1884), iii. 47.

[108] Hartley Coleridge (1836), 462; Drake (1798), 27, 463.

[109] Seward (1811), iv. 363–4.

[110] See Hartley Coleridge (1836), 433; Sayers (1830) includes *Moina* and *Starno*, two of his 'Dramatic sketches of northern mythology'. Sayers, who also translated Euripides' *Cyclops* and a chorus from Aristophanes' *Thesmophoriazusae*, argues that the Greek form of drama affords in its chorus 'the most favourable opportunity for the display of mythological imagery' (p. 25). On Southey see Haller (1917), 73, 77, 80–5. Mrs Siddons played Elfrida in April 1785: see Thomas Campbell (1834), ii. 67.

FIGURE 7.4 The monument to William Mason in Westminster Abbey, London, sculpted by J. Bacon (1799). The grieving woman probably depicts Melpomene, the Muse of Tragedy.

Antigone in 1770. The plays were translated into both ancient Greek and Latin, making the reputation of at least one 'Grecian' at Oxford.[111] They influenced the Teutonic revival in Germany through Klopstock's *Die Hermannschlacht* (1769), a celebration of the ancient Germanic hero Arminius, and were also translated into French and Italian.[112] There was a vogue for Mason's poetry in America in the early nineteenth century: besides an American edition, published at Baltimore in 1804, an article in *The Monthly Review* of July 1808 declares that Mason was one of the writers who had best 'served the language'. As late as 1834 a literary critic could declare Gray, Mason, and Collins the three best writers of odes in the English tongue.[113]

Mason's contribution to the Celtic revival was enormous, since many people learnt everything they knew about the Druids from *Caractacus*. The play inspired the foundation of a Grand Lodge of the Order of Druids at a tavern in central London, followed in 1789 by a 'Caractacan Society'.[114] Mason was a freemason, and *Caractacus* may also have spoken to that (at that time) enlightened organization. Moreover, the druidical chorus remained popular. John Fisher's *Masque of the Druids*, complete with a Greek-style chorus, was a long-running success at Covent Garden. James Boaden's chorus of bards in *Cambro-Britons* enjoyed a run in 1798 at the Theatre Royal, Haymarket: Act III, Scene v, set on Snowdon, dramatizes Gray's *The Bard*. Edward I has invaded Wales, and, as a stage direction insists,

with a hideous yell, the Bards rush to the verge of the cliffs, and with haggard forms, seen only by the glare of the torches they carry, like furies pour out their execrations upon his head, in a full chorus to the harp only.[115]

Two years later William Sotheby published his *Cambrian Hero, or Llewelyn the Great*, which has a chorus of four druids, and as late as

---

[111] Glasse (1781). On the visual arts see Gray's letter of October 1760 in John Mitford (1853), 224; on Kauffman's picture, see Roworth (1992), 166, 186 and, for an engraving possibly related to Mason's *Caractacus*, 181; on Flaxman, see Constable (1927), 6.

[112] On Klopstock see Draper (1924), 9; see also Mathias (1823).

[113] See the Revd J. S. Buckminster, quoted in Draper (1924), 10 n. 45; Anon. (1834), 553.

[114] Snyder (1923), 238, 165, 157, 161.

[115] See Snyder (1923), 11; Boaden (1798).

1808 a balletic version of *Caractacus* was performed at Drury
Lane. It opens on Mona with a chorus of harp-strumming bards,
and concludes with another bardic chorus singing defiantly in the
Roman forum.[116] All these choruses ultimately derive, via Mason,
from Greek tragedy.

Mason's *Caractacus* remains confusing. It was enjoyed by
learned philologists and by the least educated theatregoers. Its
neoclassicism was felt to be formally conservative, but it was
simultaneously progressive in the challenge it presented to uncritical jingoism, and its suggestion that the democratic culture,
music, and religion of ancient Britain were analogous with those
of the Greeks. It appealed both to simplistic British patriots and to
the most ardent critics of the British monarchy and its policies in
America, including a republican who will become significant in the
next chapter, the orientalist William Jones: it was certainly
Mason's play that in 1775 inspired this radical young Welshman
to gaze across Conway Bay, and confide in his companions that the
view thrilled him because it encompassed 'the isle of Angelsea, the
ancient Mona, where my ancestors presided over a free but unciv-
ilized people'.[117]

---

[116] Anon. (1808), 10, 12, 26.   [117] Quoted in Garland Cannon (1970), i. 199.

8

Revolutionary Oedipuses

> And just when they seem engaged in revolutionising themselves
> and things, in creating something that has never yet existed,
> precisely in such periods of revolutionary crisis they anxiously
> conjure up the spirits of the past to their service and borrow from
> them names, battle-cries and costumes in order to present the
> new scene of world history in this time-honoured disguise and
> this borrowed language.
>
> (Karl Marx, 'The Eighteenth Brumaire of Louis Bonaparte'
> *Collected Works*, xi. 103–4.)

In his account of the life of his friend William Whitehead, the poet
and playwright William Mason refers to an incomplete version of
Oedipus Tyrannus that he found amongst Whitehead's papers after
his death. Mason explains that although he himself went on to
finish his friend's play, 'I am, however, sufficiently convinced,
that the time for this, or any other tragedy founded on classical
story, to appear, is by no means the latter end of the eighteenth
century'.[1]

There was considerable misgiving about the 'English' *Oedipus* of
Dryden and Lee towards the end of the eighteenth century. Walter
Scott's reference to a production some time in the 1770s, during
which the boxes were emptied by the end of the third act, is an
important illustration of a radical change in taste.[2] The reason,
Scott implies, was the moral indignation felt by the members of the
audience at the prominence granted to the incest motif in this
'English' version of Sophocles' play (see Ch. 1). And the fact that
Garrick had turned down a suggestion in 1754 to mount a production of Beaumont and Fletcher's *A King and No King* on account
of its handling of incest might well lend credence to Scott's claim.[3]

---

[1] Whitehead (1788), 123 n.
[2] According to A. W. Ward (1875), 516 n. 4, Scott is referring to a production
*c.*1778.
[3] Lynch (1953), 345 n. 25 cites Thomas Davies (1784), ii. 41–9.

Indeed there is much evidence to demonstrate that the moral reservations about the Oedipus story were to persist in varying degrees throughout the next century, and were to cloud judgement of the Sophoclean version well into the first decade of the twentieth century (see Ch. 18).

Although Mason is by no means specific about his conviction that 'the latter end of the eighteenth century' is not 'the time for this, or any other tragedy founded on classical story, to appear', one might safely infer that changing public taste lurks somewhere behind his reservations concerning the popularity of Sophocles' tragedy. Mason's recent success with *Caractacus* in 1776 would lead us to believe that he was not denying the validity of classical subjects *per se* (see Ch. 7). But the prevalence of classical models in France at this time, as they were increasingly invoked in support of the revolutionary cause, may well have led Mason to have exercised some caution in 1788. And whilst the French revolutionaries were to make very extensive use of Roman republican symbols to promote their cause, Sophocles' *Oedipus Tyrannus* was regularly used in the latter part of the eighteenth century in France in order to explore the burning issues surrounding the competing republican and monarchical ideologies.[4]

Oedipus Tyrannus was the most frequently adapted and translated classical play in France from 1614 to 1818, during which time approximately thirty adaptations and six translations were published.[5] Yet if this was the most favoured Greek tragedy in eighteenth-century France, that other seminal Aristotelian text discussed by André Dacier in 1692, Sophocles' *Electra*, may be considered the most favoured ancient play of the period in Britain (see Ch. 6). But what is not usually acknowledged is the extent to which scholars and writers in Britain were also engaged with *Oedipus Tyrannus* in the latter part of the eighteenth century. As the 'English' version of Dryden and Lee began to fall from favour on moral grounds, the French revolutionary associations of Sophocles' tragedy were being keenly felt in Britain. Mason's misgivings about airing his completion of Whitehead's *Oedipus*, then, must be assessed against the background of changing social and political

---

[4] Biet (1994), identifies six versions of Sophocles' *Oedipus Tyrannus* written in France between 1784 and 1818.
[5] Ibid.

contexts in France and Britain, which were now promoting radical rereadings of Sophocles' paradigmatic tragedy.

This chapter charts the late eighteenth-century refiguring of the Sophoclean protagonist, who is now subject to increasing critical scrutiny. Oedipus had been adopted as a figure of the Enlightenment as early as 1718, when Voltaire challenged Dacier in claiming that the fifth-century Oedipus' curiosity was the only admirable quality he possessed.[6] Now that the limits of Enlightenment thinking were increasingly felt against the background of political turmoil, it was perhaps inevitable that Oedipus' trajectory from apparent knowledge to a realization of actual ignorance should become paradigmatic. Moreover, if Dryden and Lee's Oedipus had been drawn in response to the 'ignoble' figure of Corneille's play, now the Restoration 'noble' Oedipus was being toppled in favour of an Oedipus who was to demonstrate traits implicit in the ambivalence of the *tyrannos* of the title; for *Oedipus Tyrannos* points to both Oedipus' status as 'outsider' (rather than hereditary monarch) but also serves as a reminder of the 'tyrannical' conduct that such rulers often displayed. In France, the revolutionary versions of Oedipus at this time grant new prominence to an interrogatory chorus, whose function is primarily to scrutinize the behaviour of the *tyrannos*.[7] We have already heard of Mason's own contribution to the late eighteenth-century discovery of the formal functions of the Greek chorus in Britain (see Ch. 7); and with the second wave of British Romantic Hellenism, and especially through Shelley's own engagement with the Oedipus myth, we shall see just how radically the subversive potential of an interrogatory chorus was adopted in Britain in the early part of the nineteenth century.

THE 'GREEK' OEDIPUS IN BRITAIN

The eighteenth-century reception of Oedipus in Britain is as much about the prevalence and then decline in popularity of the 'English' *Oedipus* of Dryden and Lee as it is about the rediscovery of Sophocles' play. When André Dacier's enormously influential translation

---

[6] 'Troisième Lettre, contenant la critique de l'Œdipe de Sophocle': Voltaire (1719), 103.

[7] Biet (1994), esp. 124.

and commentary on the *Poetics*, to which were appended transla-
tions of *Oedipus Tyrannus* and *Electra,* was published in 1692,
it also generated interest in the two plays in Britain (on *Electra* see
Ch. 6). It may well have been Dacier's commentary that inspired
'Mr. Low's Scholars' to mount two performances in ancient
Greek of Sophocles' *Oedipus* on 1 and 4 April 1714 in Mile End
Green, London.[8]

More importantly, for our purposes here, however, was the
extent to which Dacier's commentary on the play was to provide a
counter to the perceptions of Oedipus derived from the Dryden and
Lee version. According to Dacier, Oedipus' rashness and blindness, not the crimes of parricide and incest, are the causes of his
misfortune. Dacier's guilty Oedipus was in large measure a response to Corneille's reading of Sophocles; and Corneille's
ultimately 'redeemed' Oedipus, whom Dryden had found weak
and vacillating and who was regularly appearing on the stage at
the Comédie-Française, could not have been more different (see
Ch. 1). If Dryden and Lee had sought to improve upon Corneille's
protagonist, when the first English translation of Sophocles' tragedy appeared in 1715 the reader found a protagonist cast in the
Dacier 'flawed' mould absolutely. The translator, Lewis Theobald,
fully acknowledges his debts to Dacier's commentary in the notes.
Explaining Oedipus' conduct in the scene with Tiresias, he adds:

The prophet at first refused to do it [i.e. tell the truth], but provok'd at last
by the severe language of Oedipus, he accuses him of the murder of Laius.[9]

However, in Theobald's translation, we have not only an Oedipus
with flaws; we also find a Tiresias who provides a robust defence
of his immunity from the overweening pride of an insouciant
monarch:

> What though you awe the Crowd with Regal Pow'r,
> I have a right of speech, as uncontroul'd,
> And large, as any boasted Lord of Empire!
> I serve not thee, but am Apollo's Priest
> Nor e'er shall court the patronage of Creon.[10]

With Creon, moreover, Theobald's Oedipus is reminded that his
powers of regency are by no means unlimited:

[8] *LS* ii/1. 319; see Ch. 9, p. 246.   [9] Theobald (1715*d*), 73.
[10] Ibid., ll. 231–5.

> *Oedipus*:   Still I've a monarch's right to rule thy Fate.
> *Creon*:   No lawless Right ov'r me, a Prince, as thou art.[11]

That Theobald's translation is a magnification of Dacier's reading cannot be overemphasized; and it is instructive to compare the markedly less strident prose translation of George Adams, which appeared in 1729, where Tiresias' declaration of independence from the king is far less robust:

> Though you are King, it is but just that I answer you with the same Freedom which you use in speaking to me. I am not your Subject, but Apollo's, neither will I employ Creon to protect me.[12]

Compare too the bitter exchange between Oedipus and Creon, in which Adams's Oedipus is far less overbearing than Theobald's imperious monarch:

> *Oedipus*:   But you are a wicked Man.
> *Creon*:   But what if these are the Dictates of Blind passion?
> *Oedipus*:   Yes even then I may use my Power.
> *Creon*:   No, unless you use it lawfully.[13]

A slightly more intemperate Oedipus is found some years later in Thomas Francklin's translation of 1758. Francklin's text appeared the year before Charlotte Lennox's translation of Père Brumoy's *Théâtre des Grecs* (Paris, 1730), and demonstrates some of the historical awareness of Greek drama that informs Brumoy's Preface. In a note, for example, on the interchange between Creon and Oedipus, he notes Dacier's unease with Creon's 'republican sentiment' and adds: ' . . . were an Englishman to comment on this passage, he would perhaps be of a direct contrary opinion, and prefer the sentiment of Sophocles to that of the French critic'.[14]

However, the language of the translation is broadly domestic, and even acts of sedition are devoid of contemporary resonance:

> *Oedipus*:   Audacious Traitor, thinkst thou to escape
>   The hand of vengeance?
> *Tiresias*:   Yes, I fear thee not;
>   For truth is stronger than a tyrant's arm.[15]

Elsewhere Francklin praises the superiority of modern over ancient tragedy with reference to its 'judicious descent from the

---

[11] Ibid., ll. 133–6.   [12] Adams (1729), i. 189.   [13] Ibid. 200.
[14] Francklin (1758), ii. 221.   [15] Ibid. 203.

advantages of demi-gods, kings and heroes, into the humbler walk
of private life, which is more interesting to the generality of mankind.'[16] And there is a sense in which Francklin in his translation
of *Oedipus Tyrannus* has taken Sophocles' tragedy of state 'into the
humbler walk of private life.' When Francklin's Oedipus is with
Creon, for example, the protagonist sounds less the haughty autocrat than the exhausted patriarch whose insubordinate dependants
have worn him down:

> *Oedipus*: A king must be obey'd.
> *Creon*: Not if his orders are unjust.
> *Oedipus*: O Thebes!
> O Citizens!
> *Creon*: I too can call on Thebes,
> She is my country.[17]

Brumoy in his commentary, even more than Francklin in his,
was at pains to emphasize the very different political circumstances
in which Greek tragedy had been developed. As early as 1674,
René Rapin had noted the modern French preference for gallantry
and sentiment in comparison with what he considers the ancient
Greek delight in the humiliation of kings.[18] Although Brumoy was
not the only modern commentator to highlight the challenges to
kingship that were contained within many of the ancient Greek
tragedies, he was nonetheless the first to go so far as to imply that
Greek tragedy provided, for its fifth-century-BC audiences, an
object lesson in the evils of kingship.[19]

Francklin in his translation of 1759 may well have been reflecting in his portrait of Tiresias the anti-clericalism he shared with
Voltaire, whose *Oreste* he was to translate for the English stage in
1769 (see Ch. 6). But as someone who was to become an ardent
friend of the future George III, Francklin would have bridled at
the possibility of allowing his Oedipus to serve as the target for any
anti-royalist sentiments.

It is, perhaps, by no means fortuitous that Francklin's translation of *Oedipus Tyrannus*, which was broadly unaffected by any
French 'proto-republican' readings of Sophocles' tragedy, went on
to be reprinted in a collected volume of Francklin's translations of
Sophocles that appeared in 1788. But no less surprising, perhaps,

---

[16] Francklin (1758), i. 57 n.   [17] Ibid. ii. 221–2.
[18] Rapin (1674), ch. XX, 182.   [19] See Brumoy in Lennox (1759), vol. i, p. cix.

was the appearance that year of a second collection of *The Traged-ies of Sophocles* translated by Robert Potter.

Potter explains in the Preface, written on 18 February 1788, how he had delayed publication of his own translations of Sophocles because of the existence of Dr Francklin's work. A request, how-ever, from an 'illustrious' person had persuaded him to publish his own translations. Potter had already been responsible for introdu-cing Greekless readers to Aeschylus, with his collected volume of 1777 (see Ch. 7), in which he identified, amongst other things, a concern for liberty, virtue, and religion in the Aeschylean choruses.[20] Here in his 1788 volume of Sophocles, Potter explains that Oedipus is not impious at all; his excesses, he avers, are all explicable. In Potter's reading, Oedipus' faults are not personal, because the Sophoclean tragedy is simply a tragedy of fate. With this metaphysical reading of the play, Potter's *Oedipus King of Thebes* is very far from Francklin's domestic tragedy. In the Pref-ace, he compares Aeschylus to an impregnable castle on a rock; Euripides to a Gothic temple with dim light effusing through the window; and Sophocles to an imperial palace with perfect sym-metry. And in his translation, Oedipus 'Sovreign of Thebes, Im-perial Oedipus',[21] is a conscientious king, who defers to his people when under pressure: 'I know thee wise and good', he tells the chorus when they urge moderation during his altercation with Creon, 'why then persist | Thus to depress me, and to damp my heart?'[22] Potter's chorus is no cowering body, but reply to their dignified sovereign with confidence and authority: 'Let me repeat what I before declared. | Know then, O king...'.[23]

In part, Potter is responding to the earlier critical readings of Oedipus proffered by Dacier and Theobald, just as Francklin (less explicitly) may well have been. But Potter (urged by his 'illustri-ous' friend) was also no doubt seeking to redress other, less ortho-dox, French readings that were in ready circulation in Britain in the 1780s. Whether the decision to bring out a new edition of Francklin's collection that year was due to commercial and/or personal pressures (Francklin was clearly not devoid of personal ambition; see Ch. 6), is hard to determine. But given the timing of both these collections, it is perhaps not difficult to infer that their

---

[20] Potter (1777), p. ix.   [21] Potter (1788), 1.
[22] Ibid. 37.   [23] Ibid.

appearance was designed in no small measure to counter the other startlingly different engagements with Sophocles' tragedy that had begun to emerge in Britain in the previous decade.

DR PARR AND HIS PUPILS

In 1779 the poet and orientalist Thomas Maurice of University College, Oxford published a volume of *Poems and Miscellaneous Pieces with a free translation of the Oedipus Tyrannus of Sophocles*. In the foreword to the volume as a whole, Maurice proclaimed that the purpose of tragedy is to 'expose to public detestation those vices, to which the distinguished rank of the offender . . . may have given a long and secure dominion over the human mind.'[24] This is Greek tragedy cast in the Brumoy mould: a public exposé of aristocratic venality, which social divisions have for too long occluded from public scrutiny.

The Preface to the translation is generally recognized as the work of Samuel Johnson rather than Maurice himself.[25] But it is none the less of note, for it offers in many ways a reading of Sophocles' play as it is mediated through Maurice. When Johnson comes to discuss the character of Oedipus, he comments that the protagonist's conduct is

by no means as irreproachable as some have contended . . . His character, even as a king, is not free from the imputation of imprudence, and our opinion of his piety is greatly invalidated by his contemptuous treatment of the wise, the benevolent, the sacred Tiresias.[26]

Although the observations here may well partly recall the earlier readings of Dacier and Theobald, when Johnson continues his explication of Oedipus' conduct, we enter markedly different terrain:

By making him [Oedipus] criminal in a small degree, and miserable in a very great one, by investing him with some excellent qualities, and some imperfections, he [Sophocles] at once inclines us to pity and to condemn. His obstinacy darkens the lustre of his other virtues; it aggravates his impiety, and almost justifies his sufferings.[27]

---

[24] Maurice (1779), sig. A2^r.
[25] See Greene (1984), p. xxiv; and the Preface is reprinted here, 588–90. All citations in this chapter, however, are taken instead from Maurice (1779).
[26] Maurice (1779), 150.
[27] Ibid. 151.

When Maurice's 'criminal' Oedipus confronts Creon with his brother-in-law's alleged treachery, we could just as easily be listening to the words of Creon himself in confrontation with Sophocles' eponymous heroine in the *Antigone*:

> Oedipus: Thou traitor!
> Creon: But thou hast not prov'd me such.
> Oedipus: Absolute is a king, and his commands
>   Must be obey'd.
> Creon: If founded on injustice,
>   They ought to be resisted unto death.
> Oedipus: Thebes, hearst thou this?
> Creon: Yes, hears and triumphs too.
>   I am her son; she taught my infant soul
>   The glorious precept.[28]

Johnson makes it clear in the preface that this is a 'free' translation, 'not fettered by . . . [the] text, [but] guided by it'. It was, moreover, 'professedly written on very different principles' from Dr Francklin's, 'by whose excellent performance he [Maurice] has been animated and instructed'. Maurice's own text, he insists wryly, catches instead 'at the capricious taste of the day'.[29]

Indeed, when we turn to the translation, we are especially struck by Maurice's reflection of the 'capricious taste' of the next few years. In the encounter between Tiresias and Oedipus, for example, as the blind priest clings to the principle of truth in a tyrant's world, he articulates a viewpoint that is to become increasingly prominent in political discourse in the early 1790s:

> Oedipus: Miscreant, and hop'st thou for this daring insult
>   To go unscourged?
> Tiresias: Tyrant, I scorn thy threats;
>   Truth is my fortress, and, against thy power,
>   Girds me, as with a coat of adamant.[30]

Here in the bitter exchange between Crown and accused, we witness a debate that was to come centre stage during the treason trials of the period.[31] In his *Enquiry Concerning Political Justice* (1793), William Godwin confidently proclaims:

---

[28] Ibid. 189.   [29] Ibid. 151–2.   [30] Ibid. 174.
[31] On which generally, see Goodwin (1979).

...sound reasoning and truth, when adequately communicated, must always be victorious over error: sound reasoning and truth are capable of being so communicated. Truth is omnipotent.[32]

As Maurice's Tiresias continues to conduct his defence against the Crown, he seems more than aware of the validity of Godwin's principle:

> *Oedipus*:   Shall thy tongue spit forth its dark abuse
>   Against thy sovereign?
> *Tiresias*:   I regard thee not,
>   While truth remains my shield.[33]

Maurice's emboldened Tiresias, armed with Truth, knows that he will overcome royal excess because in reality he is not inferior to his adversary:

> *Tiresias*:   What, though a mighty empire wait thy nod,
>   A monarch is but man, and I, as man
>   Am not inferior to the proudest prince.[34]

One such 'Tiresias' at the centre of the treason trials of the 1790s was the West Indian radical of Irish descent, Joseph Gerrald. In Scotland in 1792, Gerrald was one of two members of the London Corresponding Society who were arrested in Edinburgh, together with the secretary of the Society of the Friends of the People, and charged with sedition. When Gerrald appeared in court in March 1794, he refused to answer the charges but took the opportunity to continue to advocate political reform. He was sentenced to fourteen years' transportation to Australia, where he met a tragic and premature death.[35] In the same year in England, the assistant counsel for the defence, Felix Vaughan defended Thomas Hardy, secretary of the London Corresponding Society, against the charge of treason. Debate about 'Truth' was central to all the treason trials of the early 1790s, just as it rings out loudly in the show trial of Tiresias in Maurice's version some thirteen years earlier. The conjunction of these names and circumstances is not without significance, for all three men, Maurice, Gerrald, and Vaughan were pupils of the charismatic headmaster, Dr Samuel Parr, dubbed 'the Whig Dr Johnson', during his time at Stanmore School.[36]

---

[32] Godwin (1793), Bk. I, ch. 5, p. 140.   [33] Maurice (1779), 175.
[34] Ibid. 177.   [35] For an account of Gerrald's life, see *ODNB* xxi. 958–9.
[36] Derry (1966).

We do not know for sure what Parr's views on Sophocles' tragedy were, but we can safely infer that Maurice's version would not have come about without Parr's tutelage.[37] In his preface, Maurice makes it clear that his translation dates from some years previously; and it is no coincidence that *Oedipus Tyrannus* was staged by Parr's pupils in Greek at his school in Stanmore in 1776. Indeed, included in Maurice's collection, is the prologue written (but not used) for the school's production of the *Trachiniae* in Greek. Some of the costumes had been procured from Garrick, who was a great supporter of amateur dramatics and who had been prevailed upon through the intermediary services of Langton Bennet;[38] others were designed by Parr himself from his researches, and were made by his wife. The accents of the pupils were perfected with the aid of the nephew of the Patriarch of Constantinople, John Nikolaïdes, whose assistance had been secured by the mediation of Parr's close friend, the political radical and founder of comparative philology, the orientalist William Jones.

Although Garrick himself was not able to be present at the performance, many eminent scholars were members of the audience at this rare production of a play in Greek.[39] Amongst those present was George Henry Glasse, who went on some years later to translate both Mason's *Caractacus* into Greek verse, and (with Parr's assistance) Milton's *Samson Agonistes*.[40] Glasse may well have been disappointed at Parr's decision to omit the choruses, which were the focus of much critical attention during this period and were later in the year to be seen on stage in the production of *Caractacus* at Covent Garden in December (see Ch. 7). The omission of the chorus at Stanmore, moreover, was somewhat surprising since Parr himself was known to be very interested in choric metre and 'had also been seen plucking at the strings of a cello and to this accompaniment lustily chanting choruses from

---

[37] Maurice (1822), n.p. makes this debt explicit, when he dedicates his second edition to Parr: 'My preceptor in youth and my firm friend in more advanced life. This free translation . . . commenced under his auspices and [is] sanctioned by his approbation.'

[38] Ibid. 27; Motter (1944), 63–75.

[39] There is, perhaps, some suggestion in Butler (1896), i. 28 that the *Medea* was performed in Greek at Rugby a little later in 1798. Thanks to Paul Naiditch for this reference.

[40] Derry (1966), 27 n.

Aeschylus'.[41] But although Parr believed passionately in the value of performance, the plays were for him 'the most difficult [yet] honorable of school business'.[42]

If the chorus was too difficult to get right in performance, enactment of the episodes of Greek tragedy was clearly a highly effective way of executing this 'most difficult and honorable of school business.' One other important way in which Parr chose to enliven the arduous task was to teach the plays with reference to other modern imitations; and so, according to Maurice, with 'the *Oedipus Tyrannus*, all the pathetic ejaculations of Milton, relative to his blindness, were adduced to increase the interest, from *Paradise Lost* and *Samson Agonistes*.' And Parr was allegedly so affecting and effective with his range of references, that he would regularly reduce his pupils to tears, '... and, I believe, none who heard them ever after forgot them.'[43]

Whilst it might seem from this anecdotal evidence that Parr's pupils were being urged to sympathize with rather than scrutinize the actions of Sophocles' protagonist, it must be emphasized that the focus on a chastened Oedipus was not in any way incompatible with the revolutionary readings. In Marie-Joseph Chénier's *Œdipe-Roi*, for example (written around 1811 but published posthumously in 1818), Oedipus is transformed from tyrannical king of the *ancien régime* to a man at war with the tyrannical side of his nature by the end of the play. And it may well be that Parr was offering a similar reading with his Miltonic parallels, which proved unforgettable and which reduced his pupils to tears.

One pupil who never forgot his learning at the feet of Parr was Gerrald, who, having suffered terrible privation following a sentence of fourteen years' transportation and now on his deathbed, pronounced: 'I shall die the pupil of Samuel Parr.'[44] Gerrald had appeared in the part of Oedipus some twenty years earlier at Stanmore School 'with an unfaltering eloquence and moving pathos that excited general admiration.'[45] As a barrister in America, he would have made use of that aptitude for 'unfaltering eloquence'; but it was as a political radical on his return to Britain and at his trial in Scotland, in particular, that he was to combine

---

[41] Derry (1966), 27.   [42] Parr, cit. ibid. 26.
[43] Maurice, cit. Johnstone (1828), i. 212.
[44] Letter to William Phillips, 16 May 1795, cit. ibid. 455.
[45] Derry (1966), 27.

'unfaltering eloquence and moving pathos', which was once more to earn him 'general admiration'.[46] William Godwin was one who was especially affected as friend and ally of Gerrald; and he was so moved by his friend's fate after having visited him in prison that he rewrote the conclusion of his own Oedipal novel *Caleb Williams* (1794), because its pessimism was too evocative of Gerrald's own end.[47] The parallels in the novel with Sophocles' tragedy are many: distemper/plague, real and social, pervades the novel; Caleb is guilty of unintentional 'parricide' in his search to discover the 'truth' about Falkland; and towards the end he is temporarily rewarded with the 'prize' of a mother-figure to whom he is strongly physically attracted, an episode that heralds the denouement. It is by no means fortuitous that Godwin had read Voltaire's *Œdipe* and Horace Walpole's play dealing with mother–son incest, *The Mysterious Mother* (1768) during the novel's composition.[48]

Whilst Parr's sympathy for the victims of repressive policies remained unerring, and although he had danced round the 'Tree of Liberty' following the fall of the Bastille, he nonetheless stopped short of endorsing what he saw as 'the cruel execution of the unhappy prince' in France.[49] Moreover, he had urged caution on his one-time wayward pupil, Gerrald (whom he had reluctantly expelled from Stanmore for some 'extreme' indiscretion);[50] and he may well have detected a strong dose of Oedipus' impetuosity in his former pupil's makeup as Gerrald now once again declined to heed his beloved master's advice and to flee before his trial. That Gerrald remained a favourite to the end is testified by Parr's strong (albeit vain) efforts on Gerrald's behalf, the financial support he offered him personally (which Gerrald failed to receive),[51] and by his commitment to the education of Gerrald's son following his father's death.

Indeed, Parr was surrogate father to a generation of radicals who came into prominence during the 1790s. As young boys, they had been amongst the forty pupils of Harrow School who had followed

---

[46] Gerrald's reputation was long-lived for in 1832 his name was included with the 'Scottish martyrs' on the banners in the streets of Edinburgh (ibid. 158).

[47] Hindle (1988), pp. xxvii f.

[48] Ibid., p. xxxvi.

[49] Cit. Derry (1966), 27.

[50] So Johnstone (1828), i. 453–4.

[51] See letter to Mr Windham, 8 May 1795 cit. ibid. 451.

Parr to Stanmore in 1771, in the wake of what has been called the 'Parr rebellion', when his pro-Wilkes sympathies had failed to secure him the headmastership of Harrow.[52] Parr was to remain a champion of liberty way beyond his years as assistant master at Harrow, during his time as Headmaster of Stanmore (which folded in 1777 owing to a falling roll), Colchester, and later Norwich Grammar School. In 1793 Parr's endorsement of Godwin's *Enquiry concerning Political Justice* (advocating revolution without violence), which was conveyed to Godwin through the mediation of Gerrald, was most welcome to the author. When the two men met the following year through their shared anxieties over Gerrald's fate at his forthcoming trial, it was clear that as a liberal churchman Parr was likely to prove a problem to a visionary rationalist like Godwin. Parr, moreover, found Godwin's doctrine of universal benevolence, which privileged the public good over all natural human affections, untenable. Some years later on 15 April 1800, Parr delivered his famous Spital Sermon in which he set out, in very broad terms, his objections to Godwin's *Enquiry*. Godwin's reply the following year registers more than a degree of disappointment at having to respond to criticism from someone with 'generosity of . . . sentiments and . . . warmth of . . . temper'; for just as Gerrald had felt the need of Parr's blessing until the end, so many radicals in some Oedipal sense also needed the endorsement of their Whig father figure.[53]

PARR'S LEGACY

In his *Life of Shelley*, Thomas Jefferson Hogg speculates on a meeting between Parr, the Whig divine, and Shelley, the atheist and rebel.[54] If the tensions between the 1790s radicals and Parr were palpable and required indulgence on all sides, now Hogg in 1858 more than acknowledged the clash of generations, which would have precluded any fruitful interchange. Whilst those divisions may have been acute on a personal level, Parr's legacy is none the less still evident in the philhellenism of Shelley and his generation. Even if Parr's imprint is not felt in an immediate and obvious sense, the mediating influence of his pupils, and most

---

[52] Derry (1966), 15.   [53] Ibid. 160–1. See further Godwin (1801), 20.
[54] Thomas Jefferson Hogg (1906), 429–30.

definitely that of Maurice, can be gauged in Shelley's engagements with Greek tragic form.

Parr's own broader influence on the second generation of British Romantics was long and persistent and can be felt most keenly in 1820–1, when the paths of both Parr and Shelley intersect with the publication of Shelley's version of Sophocles' *Oedipus Tyrannus*. In May of 1821, during the crisis with Queen Caroline, a satirical cartoon entitled 'Lucifera's Procession' based on a scene from Spenser's *Faerie Queene* (I. iv. 12–51) was published (see Fig. 8.1).[55] It depicts the carriage of Queen Caroline on the road signposted to Ruin, being drawn by six 'sage Counsellors' riding on various animals. With Alderman Wood (Lord Mayor of London) having fallen from his ass, Samuel Parr finds himself riding on a pig at the head of a procession of the reforming Whigs, who rallied round the Queen during her public confrontation with her

FIGURE 8.1 *Lucifera's Procession. Fairy Queen*, engraving by G. Humphrey, 12 May 1821, depicting Queen Caroline as Lucifera in a coach drawn by her supporters.

[55] George (1952), x, no. 14182.

estranged husband, George IV. Parr, labelled 'loathsome Gluttony', is followed by Lord Grey on a goat, Henry Brougham on a wolf, Sir Francis Burdett on a lion, and finally Barnes of *The Times* astride a camel. This caricature was designed to trivialize the sizeable support in the country for the Queen in her opposition to George IV, who had acceded to the throne in January 1820 following the death of his father, George III.

George IV had tried to dissolve his marriage on grounds of adultery in order to prevent Caroline from becoming queen. Since the alleged adultery had occurred abroad in Italy, she could not be accused in a British court; instead her trial had been conducted in the House of Lords. The marriage of Caroline of Brunswick and Prince George had never been a happy one: he had famously rejected her at first sight; and after some time in Blackheath, she had moved to Italy, from where she had returned in June 1820 in order to take up her right to the throne.[56] The reason why Parr and other radicals supported Caroline was that the King, a notorious philanderer, had set about a campaign of vilification designed to prevent her from receiving her official title as monarch. What rankled with both the radicals and the general public was that George had sought to accuse his wife of an alleged adulterous relationship with an Italian count (depicted in 'Lucifera's Procession' as Satan, the whip-wielding driver of the coach), when the King himself was the most inveterate serial adulterer that the Hanoverians had yet been able to produce.

When Caroline landed on the English coast in June 1820, she was fêted all the way to London. The radicals seized the opportunity to capitalize on this growing opposition to the King, and Parr was prominent on her side from the summer of 1820 onwards, when he spent some months as her first chaplain and a most trusted adviser. It was only ill health that caused him to leave London just before the opening of her trial on 17 August. However, his association with the trial remained strong: a witness for the defence William Gell, who had served the Queen for some time in Italy, was another former pupil of Parr's; and Parr had assisted Brougham with his closing speech for the defence, with its parallels between Caroline and Octavia, the equally ill-fated wife of Nero.[57]

---

[56] For a sympathetic account of Queen Caroline, see Fraser (1996).
[57] Derry (1966), 322.

If Parr is being vilified as a bloated glutton by the royalist camp in the cartoon, the irony was, of course, that the label was far better fitted to George himself. Parr's erysipelas—an inflammatory disease which causes an especially heightened red face—made the porcine parallel (and the allusion to the emblematic figure of Gluttony in Spenser's poem) cruelly apt. But the decision to have Parr mounted upon a pig, book in hand, had just as much to do with his political affiliations as it did with any physical attributes, or with any allegedly shared appetitive proclivities. It was, of course, Edmund Burke in his anti-revolutionary *Reflections on the French Revolution* (1790), who had made the connection between the mob in France and the 'swinish multitude' explicit. Very soon the term became a by-word for both the populace and the radicals who acted on their behalf.[58] Now in the cartoon of May 1821, Parr is shown to be ludicrously in league with the porcine populace in his defence of the Queen.

The image of Caroline's six 'Sage Counsellors' astride various animals is echoed in a caricature of April 1821, depicting her alleged Italian lover Bartolomeo Pergami astride a she-goat with the head of Caroline herself (see Fig. 8.2).[59] An earlier painting by Carloni entitled 'The Public Entry of the Queen into Jerusalem' portraying the Queen on an ass, was exhibited in London and pilloried throughout 1821.[60] Similar caricatures undoubtedly lie behind the final scene of Shelley's slightly earlier radical reworking of these events, *Oedipus Tyrannus; or, Swellfoot the Tyrant* (1820). In the final scene of Shelley's play, Iona Taurina (Caroline) puts on '*boots and spurs, and a hunting cap, buckishly cocked on one side, and tucking up her hair, she leaps nimbly on ... [the] back*' of the newly emerged Ionian Minotaur, who proudly proclaims:

> I am the Ionian Minotaur, the mightiest
> Of all Europa's taurine progeny—
> I am the old traditional man-bull;
> And from my ancestors having been Ionian,
> I am called Ion, which, by interpretation,
> Is John; in plain Theban, that is to say,
> My name's John Bull ...[61]

---

[58] Michael Simpson (1998), 247.   [59] George (1952), x, no. 14171.
[60] Ibid., p. xxiv.   [61] Shelley (1970), 409, ii. ii. 103–9.

FIGURE 8.2 *The Como-cal Hobby*, engraving by G. Humphrey, 20 April 1821. Bartolomeo Pergami astride a she-goat with the head of Queen Caroline.

But Shelley's Minotaur is not the rakish Italian count of contemporary caricatures; as Ion, the Minotaur here is, of course, the foundling who discovers he is true ruler of Britain.[62] As John

---

[62] Shelley (1970), 409, ll. 117–19.

Bull, moreover, the Minotaur is the restored spirit of the oppressed working classes of England; and the play ends with the Queen, mounted upon the Minotaur, leading her 'loyal pigs' in the hunt against the King and his 'ugly badgers', 'stinking foxes', 'devouring otters, | These hares, these wolves, these any thing but men.'[63]

Shelley's play was begun in August 1820, some time after the beginning of Caroline's trial for alleged adultery in the House of Lords. It was published in September (when the trial was still going on) by the radical publisher James Johnson, but was withdrawn on threat of prosecution after only seven copies had been sold.[64] Following Caroline's acquittal in November, there was widespread celebration in the streets of London for three days and three nights. Although the following year on 19 July, the people were to show little concern when Caroline was locked out from Westminster Abbey during the coronation (a traumatic event from which she never recovered, and which led ultimately to her death nineteen days later), when Shelley was writing his play, the prospect of an end to Hanoverian rule and even the emergence of a British republic were far from utopian ideals.[65]

Although Shelley's play was not intended for immediate performance, its status as 'closet' drama does not in any sense deny its potential for performance. As with many of his plays, its plot 'can be read to recommend a direct political materialization of [the text's] imperatives.'[66] His *Oedipus Tyrannus*, moreover, displays both an acute awareness of the Greek play in its original performative context as well as broadly similar preoccupations to those found in recent French refigurations of Sophocles' tragedy. As the subtitle *Swellfoot the Tyrant* shows, Shelley was very much in tune with the ambiguities inherent in the *tyrannos* of the Greek title; and, as we shall find, he is more than interested in the role of an interrogatory, participating chorus.

We have already heard of Mason's aesthetic experiments at the end of the eighteenth century with the Greek chorus (see Ch. 7).

---

[63] Cf. Ch. 11 on Talfourd's *Ion* (1836), which is heavily indebted to Shelley and to Sophocles' *Oedipus Tyrannus*.

[64] Webb (1977), 88.

[65] For similar conclusions from different perspectives, see Paul Foot (1980) and Fraser (1996).

[66] Michael Simpson (1998), 2.

But it was perhaps Parr's pupil Thomas Maurice in particular who provided Shelley with a model for his politicized choruses. In Maurice's play, *The Fall of the Mogul, A Tragedy, Founded on an Interesting Portion of Indian History, and Attempted Partly on the Greek Model* (1806), his main source is the study *Nadir Shah* (1773),[67] by Parr's life-long friend William Jones. The 'Greek Model' to which Maurice refers in the title is above all Aeschylus' *Persians*, the tragedy that lies behind Shelley's *Hellas* (see Ch. 9). But there are echoes of the Oedipal archetype too in the fall of the tyrant and in the struggle between the true-born son and heir versus the interloper.

Maurice's use of the *Persians*, however, is not the only point of comparison with Shelley's play. Maurice's use of two highly op-positional and politically critical and subversive choruses is a device adopted by Shelley as well in his version of Sophocles *Oedipus Tyrannus*. The main chorus of Brahmin priests in *The Fall of the Mogul* decry their brutal subjection under the Mogul Empire at the outset:

> Full thirty centuries have seen the race,
> Who boast from Brahma their sublime descent,
> Beneath a foreign despot's iron scourge
> Bend their reluctant neck.[68]

The play closes with this same Brahmin chorus threatening Nadir with eventual revenge when 'A thousand furies shall thy bosom wring',[69] bringing about the Fall of the Mogul Empire and the liberation of the Hindu people of India. By identifying the Greek chorus with contemporary eastern groups (Hindus and in the case of the second chorus Zoroastrians) oppressed by Islam, Maurice is not only transferring the philological model of Indo-European linguistic genealogy (invented by Jones) to fit a wider notion of shared culture and ideals; he is also showing how the form of the Greek chorus can be fairly transferred to different groups as a poetic vehicle for dissent, and especially politically radical descent.

Shelley had already translated Euripides' *Cyclops* in 1819, and had very recently published his sequel to Aeschylus' *Prometheus Bound*; these both lie behind his treatment of *Oedipus Tyrannus*, which he began in the summer of 1820. It is undoubtedly the play's

---

[67] Maurice (1806), p. x. On Jones, see Franklin (1995), pp. xv–xxx.
[68] Maurice (1806), 30.   [69] Ibid. 126.

deliberate generic hybridity that has led to much critical confusion.[70] Shelley's witty subversion of the Romantic cult of the discovery of an ancient (forged) text (see Ch. 7), is exploited from the outset with the title page proclaiming his play a 'Tragedy . . . Translated from the original Doric.' The play begins as a parodic reworking of *Oedipus Tyrannus*, with the state of Thebes afflicted by famine (although here the overbloated tyrant and his court are miraculously untouched by the famine). Similarly recognizable is the subsequent scene between Mammon (Tiresias) and Purganax (Creon/the Foreign Secretary, Lord Castlereagh, whose name is alluded to in 'purg-anax'/'castle-reagh'), during which the oracle (also the epigraph to the play) is sounded loudly: 'Boeotia, choose reform or civil war! | When through thy streets, instead of hare with dogs, | A Consort Queen shall hunt a King with hogs, | Riding on the Ionian Minotaur'.[71]

With this first mention of the troublesome Queen, we enter into other non-Sophoclean territory, with Queen Iona Taurina recalling Aeschylus' persecuted Io in *Prometheus Bound*, chased throughout Europe by a Leech, a Gadfly, and a Rat, who have spied upon her every move. And with the appearance of the Gadfly, we have a witty parody of Io's pitiful monody in *Prometheus Bound* (561–88):

> Hum! hum! hum!
> From the lakes of the Alps, and the cold grey scalps
> Of the mountains, I come
> Hum! hum! hum!
> From Morocco and Fez, and the high palaces
> Of golden Byzantium;
> From the temples divine of old Palestine,
> From Athens and Rome,
> With a ha! and a hum!
> I come! I come![72]

Although the 'Advertisement' to the play very soon makes any earlier claims to seriousness transparently comic, it is the emergence of an animal chorus of supplicating pigs that has led critics to

---

[70] For Highet (1949), 421, it is Shelley's 'greatest failure'—a view regularly shared. See too *TLS* review 3rd October 2003, p. 12, of Shelley (2003), by Richard Cronin: 'few will regret' its absence from the new edition.

[71] Shelley (1970), 389.

[72] Ibid. 396, I. i. 220–9.

find parallels with Aristophanes.[73] But it may well be with the satyr-play that the closest parallel can be found. For Shelley's adaptation shares with the ancient Greek satyr-play the themes of discovery and transformation: its porcine chorus members (rather than its hopelessly corrupt and bloated protagonist) discover their own true identity as descendants of the Minotaur; and once nourished, they are metamorphosed into bulls. When the pigs become bulls, their association with Dionysus (as with the ancient satyrs) may well become deliberate.

However, it is perhaps with the centrality of the chorus to Shelley's design that the affinity with the satyr-play is felt most acutely. For although the chorus of pigs are at first marginalized— they appear as straggly suppliants around the steps and altar of the Temple of Famine in the first scene completely unnoticed by Swellfoot the Tyrant—they increasingly begin to find a voice for themselves, both because and in spite of their abject state. Above all, like Maurice's Brahmin priests in *The Fall of the Mogul*, they have access to a collective memory of another, better world in which they had a different role:

> I have heard your Laureate sing
> That pity was a royal thing;
> Under your mighty ancestors, we pigs
> Were bless'd as nightingales on myrtle sprigs,
> Or grass-hoppers that live on noon-day dew,
> And sung, old annals tell, as sweetly too,
> But now our styes are fallen in, we catch
> The murrain and the mange, the scab and itch;
> Sometimes your royal dogs tear down our thatch,
> And then we seek the shelter of a ditch;
> Hog-wash or grains, or ruta baga, none
> Has yet been ours since your reign begun.[74]

As the 'swinish multitude', they agitate and confront Swellfoot directly in this opening scene; here it is not through the mediation of the [Sophoclean] priest:

> You ought to give us hog-wash and clean straw,
> And styes well thatched; besides it is the law![75]

---

[73] So Highet (1949), 421; Wallace (1997), 75; Michael Simpson (1998), 248.
[74] Shelley (1970), 391, I. i. 37–48.   [75] Ibid. 392, I. i. 65–7.

But as with the Peterloo massacre the previous summer, cry for reform meets only with repression; and Swellfoot resounds:

> This is sedition, and rank blasphemy!
> Ho! there, my guards![76]

ushering in the royal butchers to slaughter the subversives.

Towards the end of the next scene between Mammon, Purganax, and the spies, the chorus is heard offstage:

> Ugh, ugh, ugh!
> Hail! Iona the divine,
> We will no longer be swine,
> But bulls with horns and dewlaps.[77]

Once Swellfoot has arrived, we hear that offstage there is '*A loud tumult, and cries of "Iona for ever!—No Swellfoot!"*';[78] and a few minutes later, the offstage chorus chant loudly: 'Long live Iona! Down with Swellfoot!'[79]

In Act II in the Public Stye (the House of Commons), the Pigs are heard heckling in the background 'She is innocent! most innocent!';[80] and then later in the scene, we are told: '*A great confusion is heard of the Pigs out of Doors, which communicates itself to those within. During the first Strophe, the doors of the Stye are staved in, and a number of exceedingly lean Pigs and Sows and Boars rush in.*'[81] Now with the two semichoruses centre stage, Semichorus II have sufficiently grown in stature and voice to demand that their voice be heard:

> I vote Swellfoot and Iona
> Try the magic test together;
> Whenever royal spouses bicker
> Both should try the magic liquor.[82]

The two semichoruses unite once the arrival of the Queen is imminent, and express their solidarity with her. And now, as is the case in the *Prometheus Unbound*, Shelley's united chorus can display a newfound confidence. Here they are even able to make prophetic pronouncements, once they realize that the 'magic test'

---

[76] Ibid., ll. 67–8. [77] Ibid. 397, I. i. 272–4. [78] Ibid. 398, I. i. 292.

[79] Ibid. 399, I. i. 324. [80] Ibid. 401, II. i. 3. [81] Ibid. 403, II. i.

[82] Ibid. 404, II. i. 127–30.

is in fact a 'truth test', which will plainly reveal to all the hypocrisy surrounding the trial:

> The oracle is now about to be
> Fulfilled by circumvolving destiny ... [83]

In the penultimate scene of the play, we see precisely how destiny is 'circumvolved', when Iona snatches the Green Bag containing the 'truth test' from Purganax's hand and pours its contents over the King and his court, *'who are instantly changed into a number of filthy and ugly animals'*.[84] If the 'swinish multitude' has already undergone its inner transformation with the prospect of liberty in the previous scene, here in the final moments of the play, we witness their literal transformation: those *'who eat the loaves are turned into Bulls'*.[85]

The final chorus is made up of Iona and the swine/bulls, and it may well be that Shelley is registering some reservations about the unlikely alliance between the populace and the jilted Queen. The Minotaur would seem to be implying at least the short-term pragmatism of such an alliance, when he turns to Iona and issues his invitation:

> And if your Majesty will deign to mount me,
> At least till you have hunted down your game,
> I will not throw you.[86]

The final strophe of the exodus, moreover, would seem to fly in the face of the prayer for restraint made by Liberty in the previous scene. In marked contrast to Liberty's plea to Famine to 'lead them not upon the paths of blood', the chorus together with Iona sing in pursuit of their quarry to an opening rhythm that is strikingly evocative of the chorus of that most popular French revolutionary song, *Ça ira!*

> Tallyho! tallyho!
> Through pond, ditch, and slough,
> Wind them, and find them,
> Like the Devil behind them,
> Tallyho! tallyho![87]

---

[83] Shelley (1970), 405, II. i. 151–2.   [84] Ibid. 408, II. i.
[85] Ibid. 409, II. i.   [86] Ibid., ll. 113–15.   [87] Ibid., ll. 134–8.

Even if such an alliance is an uneasy and precarious one, it would at least serve the purpose of ridding everyone of the common enemy. In his spoof advertisement to the play, Shelley had already claimed that the only 'liberty [that] has been taken with the translation of this remarkable piece of antiquity' is 'the suppressing of a seditious and blasphemous Chorus of the Pigs and Bulls at the last act';[88] and this teasing remark clearly demands of his audience to imagine such a suppressed and subversive coda to his play.

In his political pamphlet, 'A Philosophical View of Reform', Shelley refers to the effectiveness of 'large bodies and various denominations of the people';[89] and as with his chorus in *Hellas* and *Prometheus Unbound*, the chorus of Shelley's closet drama concerning Oedipus may be said to serve as the dramatic correlative to such efficacy at a time when such assertions were subject to severe censure.[90]

Shelley's adoption here of a Greek chorus for overtly political, rather than simply aesthetic, purposes builds on Maurice's work and forges major development in the British reception of Greek tragedy. Whether Shelley had any knowledge of the French revolutionary reworkings of Sophocles' tragedy—one thinks particularly of Chénier's subversive *Œdipe-Roi*, which had only very recently been published in 1818—it is clear that his version needs to be placed alongside its French counterparts. Like these French plays, Shelley's version contains a tyrannical king of the *ancien régime*. However, when we witness Swellfoot and his court being deliberately challenged by a chorus with overtly republican sentiments, we realize that Shelley's handling of a Greek chorus turns out to be even more brazen than the efforts of the revolutionary playwrights across the channel.

CONCLUSION

It has been claimed that 'As the extreme expression of social defiance, incest was a serviceable symbol for the Romantics, who took seriously their obligation as rebels and social critics.'[91] It may well be that the increasing middlebrow moral indignation about

---

[88] Ibid. 390.   [89] Shelley (1920), 86.
[90] Cf. Michael Simpson (1998), 410–11.
[91] Miyoshi (1969), 11, cit. Hindle (1998), p. xxxvi.

the Dryden and Lee *Oedipus* paradoxically inspired the younger generation of Romantic writers to turn to Sophocles' play in search of 'the extreme expression of social defiance'. George Steiner has eloquently discussed the Romantic fascination with brother–sister incest with reference to the *Antigone*.[92] But the political connotations that linked incest to the *ancien régime* were of long standing and also contributed to the importance attached to Sophocles' play in the eyes of the revolutionaries. Allegations had been made at Marie-Antoinette's trial in October 1793 about her alleged incest with her son by the presiding judge, M.-J.-A. Herman. These, however, were based far more on the perception of the links between political and sexual disorder within the royal family than they were on actual fact.[93]

Whilst 'revolutionary Oedipuses' were not the only versions of Sophocles' play available at this time, their imprint was hard to resist. Even the 1790 utilitarian prose translation by George Somers Clark, *Oedipus, King of Thebes* shows just how much other radical readings had filtered through to all levels. Somers Clark advocates the presence of a chorus throughout the play on the grounds that it is more 'naturally' and 'rationally' used than modern shifts in scene. He correctly describes the Chorus of Elders as 'principal citizens of Thebes', but later in Act II, Scene i says '*Oedipus, Chorus, the people assembled*'.[94] Somers Clark's Oedipus may well be less strident than some of his contemporaries, but he none the less works within a strict constitutional monarchy and he is not without blemish.[95]

However, in 1821 and just over a year after the suppression of Shelley's *Oedipus Tyrannus*, we once again find the return of an unblemished Oedipus on the London stage. On 1 November, *Oedipus: A Musical Drama in 3 Acts* was performed at the Royal West London Theatre. The author of the play was John Savill Faucit, although (as Faucit himself was quick to stress) his task was more one of speedy compilation, selection, and adaptation (with abundant use of anachronism) than of authorship. He had ten days in which to put together his version of *Oedipus*, which he had made at the request of Mr J. Amherst, the proprietor of the

---

[92] Steiner (1984).   [93] See Décembre-Alonnier (1975), ii. 365.

[94] George Somers Clark (1790), 13 and n.

[95] Ibid. 23, citing Francklin's criticism of his treatment of Tiresias.

Royal West London Theatre. The play is dedicated to Amherst, whom Faucit praises for his boldness in taking the risk of both personal criticism and considerable financial expense in attempting to mount a revival of a Greek play.[96]

His debts to Dryden and Lee, Corneille, and Maurice are clearly stated on the title page to the published edition of his text. Although his debt to Maurice is slight—at the very beginning of the play, his High Priest's recitative is a rearrangement of Maurice's parodos set to the music of a Mr Mueller—the production did prompt an indignant Maurice to produce a second edition of his text a few months later.[97] But the greatest debt owed by Faucit is to Dryden and Lee (and through them indirectly to Corneille), whose text he substantially relies on, often verbatim, but most often truncates. In this sense, Faucit's play provided a much less unwieldy version for an audience less tolerant of elaborate subplots and Senecan bombast. This is a 'modern' Oedipus, reflecting the growing interest in an (albeit limited) singing and dancing chorus (this occurs only once although the play is significantly dubbed 'A Musical Drama'); and with its Gothic details and its handling of recent past (rather than current) events, it resembles the popular historical tragedies of the day.[98]

In Faucit's version the confrontation between Tiresias and Oedipus, which had proved so powerful a focus of interest in eighteenth-century versions of the play and which is a major source of anti-clerical vehemence in his main source, is absent. Faucit has chosen to avoid any scene which shows Oedipus in any critical light; instead this Oedipus is the conscientious and valiant head of state, who is beset by a treacherous brother-in-law intent on fomenting dissent. Faucit has gone much further than Dryden and Lee in his rehabilitation of Sophocles' protagonist: following his realization of the truth about his marriage to Jocasta, Oedipus is revealed on a neoclassical terrace in the palace gardens, lounging (Orestes-like) upon a Grecian couch in a fit of madness. In clear allusion to the former King George III, we witness the priests' efforts to restore him to sanity. Oedipus then delivers his last Senecan speech from Dryden and Lee (see Ch. 1), before

[96] Faucit (1821), Preface. For a contemporary review see Talfourd (1821).

[97] Maurice (1822). See the Advertisement by Maurice (n.p.), where he refers to the 'very unwarrantable liberty having been taken, unknown to me' with his text.

[98] George Taylor (2000).

dashing to the tower to attempt suicide. Here in Faucit, however, Oedipus is unsuccessful in his attempt and has somewhat ignobly to suffer the restraints of his courtiers. But in the final moments of the play he redeems himself when he rushes to protect Eurydice from Creon, whom he stabs fatally just before dying himself at the hands of his adversary. His last wish is that Adrastus and Eurydice should remain together, and the final scene consists of a solemn tableau of the dead king.

What is significant here in Faucit's version is that the 'English' Oedipus has been restored to the stage after some time of absence. But, in accordance with modern taste, there is no reunion between the incestuous couple after their realization of the truth of their marriage. If the final scenes recall recent history with the madness of George III, the last scene's omissions are in clear deference to the strictures on taste, which from the late eighteenth century at least had made the Dryden and Lee version impossible to perform. This is no longer *Oedipus* the tragedy of state; it is once more *Oedipus* the family drama.[99] Like the projected image of the deeply religious family man George III, the strength of which had acted as the central stabilizing force of the counterrevolutionary movement in the 1790s in Britain, this Oedipus is the king who demands pity rather than censure. Here then, in Faucit's version of 1821, we have an Oedipus on the public stage who whilst seemingly in opposition to the protagonist of the proscribed closet version of Shelley, is at the very least a veiled exhortation to George IV to emulate his father in familial matters. Whilst Shelley sought to exploit the constitutional crisis of 1820 in order to revive the republican ideals of the 1790s radicals, Faucit resorts to 1790s iconography in order to restore the myth of the monarchy as the mirror of the family; and in so doing, of course, Faucit is setting Sophocles' tragedy upon a path which is eventually to provide the quintessentially 'modern' reading of the play as a metaphor for family dynamics.

---

[99] Six months previously, on 11 May 1821, Faucit's wife (with whom he had had six children, including the actress Helen Faucit, see Ch. 12) made an unsuccessful attempt to have their marriage annulled on the alleged grounds that she had married Faucit under the legal age and without her parents' consent. The reason for her action was, not surprisingly, her lover, with whom she subsequently went to live. See Carlisle (2000), 10–11. Faucit's *Oedipus* is, perhaps, a family affair in a personal sense too.

9

Greek Tragedy in Late Georgian Reading

ORESTES IN BERKSHIRE

The residents of the Berkshire town of Reading might in 1821 have been tempted by the advertisement in their local newspaper for forthcoming attractions at the neighbourhood's commercial theatre. Should their taste encompass Graeco-Roman themes, they might have wanted to see 'Monsieur DECOUR, the renowned FRENCH HERCULES!! Who will perform... FEATS AND EVOLUTIONS...'. If they preferred oriental stunts, they would choose 'The Chinese JUGGLERS from the Court of Pekin!!' Such exhibitions are typical of the entertainments enjoyed during the late Georgian era in any fast industrializing provincial town. But what is surprising is that the same newspaper offers a review of a production in the town hall of Euripides' then little-known tragedy *Orestes*.

It had been acted in full costume by the pupils of Reading School (see Fig. 9.1). According to the reviewer (the local writer Mary Russell Mitford), it had impressed its audience:

The correct and vivid representation of one of the Greek Tragedies is all the more interesting, because, from the days of Euripides until now, there have been no works of genius produced... A deep repose is shed over the grandeurs and mournful beauties of the spectacle. What a triumph... not in our opinion only, but in that of some of the most distinguished Greek scholars who were present... The enunciation of the sweetest of languages was in every instance so correct and clear, that the young performers seemed to be speaking their native tongue.[1]

This *Orestes* is particularly surprising, because it is often assumed that the practice of performing ancient Greek plays in Britain began in earnest in around 1880. Yet educational performances of ancient drama in the British Isles have a much longer history, at least when it comes to plays in Latin. Enactment had been initiated

---

[1] Mary Russell Mitford (1821).

FIGURE 9.1   An unidentified scene (possibly the opening of Euripides' *Heracles*) from a performance of Greek tragedy at Reading School (1857).

as a pedagogical method by humanists on the Continent in the fifteenth century, whence it had spread to England. University performances of ancient drama reached their first zenith in the sixteenth century: staples were Latin comedies such as Plautus' *Menaechmi* and Terence's *Adelphi*. Seneca's tragic *Troades* also enjoyed an occasional performance; so, indeed, did Aristophanes' more 'moral' comedies *Peace* and *Wealth*, in the original Greek. But Greek tragedies were a rarity. There is not much evidence for Greek tragic drama being performed during the Renaissance on the English side of the Channel in either Greek or in English: even the Latin translations of Euripides, popular on the Continent, were little performed in England.[2]

The Puritan closure of the theatres in the seventeenth century had an impact even on school theatricals. Recitation was one thing, and performance quite another. The theatrical writer Westland Marston reports that as late as around 1830, his own father (a Dissenting minister) had praised his son's declamation of Sophocles' *Electra* at a school event in Grimsby, while opposing any performances involving costume and scenery.[3] Richard Valpy,

---

[2] See Boas (1914), 11–17. There may have been an *Antigone* in Greek at St. John's College, Cambridge, in the early 1580s: see Bruce R. Smith (1988), 216.

[3] Marston (1888), i. 3–4.

the headmaster of Reading School responsible for that singular *Orestes*, needed to defend the propriety of acting plays at his school at all by claiming that theatricals had brought nothing but benefits to his Scholars.[4] Valpy was not alone: the previous chapter discussed the two Greek plays put on by Samuel Parr at Stanmore School in 1775 and 1776.

Parr justified his thespian experiments with Sophocles by invoking the authority of a pedagogical recommendation made by John Milton. In his treatise *Of Education*, addressed to Michael Hartlib, Milton had advised that young men, once they had studied politics, law and theology, would be ready for the *recitation* of the ancient historians, epic poems, and Attic tragedies

of stateliest and most regal argument, with all the famous political orations... which, if they were not only read, but some of them got by memory, and solemnly pronounced with the right accent and grace, as might be taught, would endue them with the spirit and vigour of Demosthenes or Cicero, Euripides or Sophocles.[5]

But Parr's immediate inspiration for a costumed performance was a conversation with William Jones about a Greek play put on earlier in the century in Ireland. The organizer had been the schoolmaster Thomas Sheridan, at his school in Capel Street, Dublin, before his move in 1735 to the Mastership of the Free School at Cavan. Sheridan was the distinctly apolitical scion of an old Irish Jacobite family, father of the actor Thomas Sheridan, and grandfather of the dramatist Richard Brinsley Sheridan (himself, as it happens, a devoted pupil of Dr Parr). Thomas Sheridan senior had social connections with the theatre, and was from 1713 the intimate friend of Jonathan Swift. His most senior class used to perform plays publicly before leaving for university. They were accustomed to acting in Shakespearean plays, for example *Julius Caesar* in 1718 and in 1732,[6] and also Latin comedies. There was a Plautus in 1719, and Terence's *Adelphi* in 1727, to which the prologue was delivered by a 'Scholar, riding on an Ass'.[7] But there were also at least three Greek plays.

---

[4] Valpy (1804), pp. vii f.   [5] Milton (1963), 89–110, at 105.

[6] On the latter date it was acted by the boys, rather excitingly, 'at Madame Violante's Booth' (Robert Hogan (1994), 187). Madame Violante ran a troupe of Dublin child actors, one of whom went on to become the stellar Peg Woffington.

[7] Ibid. 170.

In 1720 Sheridan's senior pupils acted Euripides' *Hippolytus* in Greek, with an English prologue, in front of dignitaries including Archbishop King, the Lord Lieutenant and probably Swift.[8] *Oedipus Tyrannus* followed on 10 December 1723 at the King's Inn's Hall. *Philoctetes* seems to have been performed next, in 1724 or 1725, since one of Sheridan's few substantial literary productions was a 1725 translation of *Philoctetes*, intended for the Lord Lieutenant's wife (and perhaps other women in the audience). The all-male cast of this tragedy might well have recommended itself to the master of a boys' school. There was certainly at least one more Greek play, performed just before the Christmas of 1728, but the surviving prologue gives no clue as to which author or play was chosen that year.[9]

Even Thomas Sheridan's *Hippolytus*, despite claims to the contrary, was not the earliest post-Restoration performance of Greek tragedy in Ireland or Britain: as we have already seen in Ch. 8, on Thursday, 1 and Saturday, 3 Apr. 1714, 'Mr. Low's Scholars' had performed *Oedipus Tyrannus* in ancient Greek at Mile End Green in East London. Little seems to be known of this production, although the director must have been Solomon Lowe, the celebrated Hammersmith schoolmaster, grammarian and expert on mnemonics, whose work on Greek composition and grammar was published in 1719.[10] Yet the Mile End, Dublin, and Stanmore experiments were not on such an ambitious a scale as Reading School's triennial tradition of performing plays, by both Sophocles and Euripides, between 1806 and 1827.

THE HEADMASTER

The plays were the brainchild of Reading School's domineering headmaster, Dr Richard Valpy—a Whiggish gentleman of terrifying stature, famous for his flogging expertise (one of his nicknames was 'Dr Wackerbach'), to which his daughters were as vulnerable as his sons and pupils. He also had a zeal for the British navy which amounted to an obsession. The plays were performed in aid of naval

---

[8] Robert Hogan (1994), 36–7, 108–11.

[9] See the prologues reproduced ibid. 131–2, 178–9; Sheridan (1725).

[10] *LS* ii/1. 319; Lowe (1719). Lowe also published several works on Latin grammar.

charities: an *Amphitryo* in 1797 raised £130 for the widows and orphans resulting from Lord Duncan's victory over the Dutch fleet.[11] Valpy's naval enthusiasm also led him to insist on the dancing of a hornpipe at the end of all his plays. One reviewer wrote,

> We could have dispensed with the hornpipe . . . Dr. Valpy may well afford to break custom which his good taste must reject. His learning and talent do not require such adventitious aid.[12]

Despite or perhaps because of his eccentric style, Valpy turned the school's fortunes round, transforming it into one of the most respected of its kind. His name was known to almost every British boy of the middle and upper classes in the nineteenth century, for he wrote some of the standard textbooks of the day, all of which ran into numerous editions. They included *The Elements of the Latin Language* (1782), *The Elements of Greek Grammar* (1805), and a famous *Delectus sententiarum Graecorum* (1815).

The open-mindedness of his approach to education probably resulted from his background on the cusp between English and French culture: he was a Channel Islander, born into a wealthy Jersey family in 1754, and educated until he was fifteen at Valogues in Normandy (thereafter at schools in Southampton and Guildford, and Pembroke College, Oxford). There had long been a tradition of amateur theatricals in Jersey, and in the second half of the eighteenth century this little island received regular visits by both French and English companies.[13] Reading School retained an interest in the Channel Islands, deriving many of its pupils from them throughout Valpy's career.[14] Valpy, moreover, was impressed by French scholarship, advocating Pierre Brumoy's *Le Théâtre des Grecs* to the Reading intelligentsia.[15] He had visited Paris in 1788, and written about his nights at the Comédie-Française and the Théâtre Italien.[16] As a youth he had been obsessed with the commercial theatre and had attempted to meet the great Garrick. His own adaptation of Shakespeare's *King John*

---

[11] Fines (1967), 17.

[12] This cutting is said (ibid.) to be in W. C. Eppstein's collection of cuttings relating to Reading School (1794–1808), held in Reading Public Library. It is not there now.

[13] Raoul Lemprière (1981).

[14] Fines (1967), 11.

[15] Mary Russell Mitford (1854*a*), i, p. xvii.

[16] Valpy (1814).

had actually been performed at Covent Garden in 1803.[17] Abraham John Valpy, the second of the headmaster's numerous sons, was a printer who loved the Classics, and edited the *Classical Journal* from 1810 until 1829;[18] but he was also responsible for *The New British Theatre*, which published serious contemporary dramas such as John Peter Roberdeau's *Thermopylae* (see below, p. 266 n. 7), in an attempt to persuade London theatre managers to raise the moral tone of their theatres.

Some have said that the plays performed under Elizabeth I at Winchester were the inspiration behind Valpy's Greek plays.[19] His contemporaries, however, believed that he had consciously set out to compete with the ancient institution of the Latin comedy, performed at Westminster School. A comic account of Reading School written by a former pupil (see below) portrays Dr Valpy as choosing a Greek play on the ground that its language would trump Latin by virtue of its greater antiquity:[20]

If... the W---r youths are able to do justice to the pure Latinity of the Roman poet, why should not my boys equally shine in reproducing upon the stage the Greek tragic Muse? I have it!' exclaimed the excited man; 'we will act a Greek play... and the world of letters shall shortly see that the youth of the Royal grammar-school of... can 'fret their brief hour upon the stage' in a more ancient language than that of Rome.

Yet the source of Valpy's idea of a Greek play was almost certainly contact with Samuel Parr, with whom he was a correspondent. Valpy can scarcely have failed to hear about the two Stanmore productions of Sophocles, especially since Parr 'often expressed a wish that his example had been followed in other seminaries':[21] it is significant that Valpy, like Parr, chose the *Oedipus Tyrannus* for his first attempt at a Greek tragic production (in 1806: see below).

Ever since Richard Valpy had been appointed by Reading Council to head Reading School in 1781, he had encouraged the thespian talents of his 'Scholars'. His theatrical aspirations were facilitated by the school's favoured status as recipient of a Triennial Visitation

---

[17] *DNB* xx. 85–6.
[18] See further Clarke (1945), 85–6, 93; he is even better known for reprinting the Delphin Classics with new indexes and notes by various hands. See *ODNB* lvi. 67.
[19] Naxton (1986), 53. On the Winchester College plays in the 16th c. see Motter (1929), 28–35, and Cowling (1993).
[20] Bockett (1857), 73.
[21] Field (1828), i. 80.

by dignitaries from Oxford University, an occasion which offered an excellent context for performances. The august Visitors were encouraged to fulfil their duty by emoluments arising out of an endowment made in 1640 by Reading's most famous son, Archbishop William Laud.[22] The Oxford Visitors who, Laud had decreed, should in perpetuity visit Reading School included the Vice-Chancellor, one of the Proctors, and the heads of several houses, notably St John's, All Souls, and Magdalen.[23]

Valpy appreciated the value of the school's link with Oxford, and enhanced the ceremonial aspect of the Visitations. English-language dramas had previously been performed at the school, since there is testimony to a *Cato* in 1731 (presumably Joseph Addison's famous tragedy of 1713).[24] Before 1790 Valpy encouraged the boys to perform puppet shows and poetic recitations to audiences known to have consisted of between 300 and 400.[25] But he soon began to organize English-language and Latin theatricals: the performances between 1790 and 1801 consisted of Shakespeare (*Hamlet*, *King Lear*, *King John*, and *The Merchant of Venice*), alternating with Plautus.[26] The Latin plays at Reading were remembered by a Mary Sherwood, a pupil at the girls' school run in the old Reading Abbey by Madame and Monsieur St. Quentin; it speaks volumes for Dr Valpy's liberal views on both the theatre and women that he regularly took all his Scholars to watch the French plays acted by the girls. Sherwood's cousin Thomas had been in a Valpy production of Plautus' *Aulularia* (1791), and had looked very fine 'as a young lady', with golden grasshoppers in his hair.[27]

It was for the Triennial Visitation of 1806 that Valpy attempted his first Greek play, an innovation which was immeasurably to enhance the reputation of the school. Some of the Old Redingensians maintained 'a sort of club' which met at one of the town's principal inns; in triennial years they used to stay for days—even weeks—to help with rehearsals for the Greek play.[28] This became a

[22] Trevor-Roper (1988), 402.
[23] Mary Russell Mitford (1854*a*), i, p. xv; Newdick (n.d. *b*), 13; Bockett (1857), 72; prologue to *Hecuba*, *Reading Mercury* no. 5564, 29 Oct. 1827, p. 4 col. 3.
[24] Carlisle (1818), i. 37–8. See Ch. 2.
[25] Fines (1967), 15.
[26] Valpy (1826), p. vii.
[27] Sherwood (1910), 82–5, 130–3, 145.
[28] Mary Russell Mitford (1835), i. 313.

fashionable highlight of the Reading calendar; one account vividly lists the notable local politicians, doctors, and lawyers who were to be seen in the front row.[29] The Reading aldermen, complete with their furred gowns, were expected to attend *ex officio*.[30] The Triennial Visitation was traditionally concluded by a large banquet, provided by the Mayor: in 1827 it was described as a 'most sumptuous banquet at the Town-hall, at which turtle, venison, and every delicacy in season, with wine and fruits' were served to the Reverend Visitors, the worthies of the borough, and 'upwards of a hundred gentlemen'.[31]

THE PERFORMANCES

The first Reading Greek tragedy was Sophocles' *Oedipus Tyrannus*, performed in 1806; a booklet was published to accompany the production which contained an adaptation of the 1759 English translation by Thomas Francklin. The cast list reveals that Valpy involved even his own smallest children: one little son played Jocasta's attendant and another Teiresias' child guide.[32] Although the translation omits the choral odes, there was certainly a chorus of Thebans to be seen, since the eye-witness who wrote the review for the local newspaper attests to their 'majestic' gestures (this, incidentally, is probably the earliest surviving detailed description of the performance of an authentic Greek tragic text in Britain or in Ireland):[33]

The scene opens with a slow and dignified advance, while gentle and most plaintive sounds of music, from behind, interest the feelings of every spectator, which are progressively heightened, till the palace of Oedipus is discovered on one side, on the other a temple . . . some Thebans appear with boughs in their hands waving in majestic movements.

Of particular interest is the reference to that 'plaintive' music from backstage. Although nothing further is known about the music as early as 1806, one individual who remembered the Greek plays was

---

[29] John J. Cooper (1923), 82.
[30] Mary Russell Mitford (1835), i. 312–13; (1854a), i, p. xv.
[31] Anon. (1827).   [32] Francklin (1806).
[33] Anon. (1806). Mary Russell Mitford (1854a), vol. i, p. xv was later to claim that she had written all the reviews for the *Reading Mercury*, and she certainly composed all those from 1818 onwards. But it is unlikely that she wrote the earliest review in 1806.

William Darter, a Reading flautist who had been enlisted in the 1820s into the orchestra which accompanied the performances.

Darter recalls that in around 1819 the Amateur Musical Society had been established in the town under the direction of one Monsieur Venua. The Society had about 150 members, who regularly performed in the Town Hall, thus naturally suggesting themselves as accompanists to any plays enacted there. Darter recalls that 'the orchestra consisted of all the local professors of music of any standing, as also of some amateurs', and lists the instruments as first and second violins, violas, cellos, double basses, flutes and French horns.[34] This was quite a large symphonic ensemble. The implication seems to be that in the 1820s, at least, the music was chosen or composed by Monsieur Venua.

The ground is firmer when it comes to the venue, described in elegant detail in a slightly fictionalized account of the Reading Greek plays in the novel *Belford Regis* by Mary Russell Mitford (see Fig. 9.2). She was the friend of Dr Valpy who usually reviewed his plays in the local press, and her description corresponds with information drawn from factual sources. The plays were put on in a large, elongated school-room which at that time communicated at one end with the school-house (then in the civic heart of Reading), and at the other opened 'into the entrance to the Town-hall, under which it was built.' These buildings no longer exist, but it is clear that the town hall and the school were architecturally difficult to distinguish. At the school-house end of the hall was the stage, 'excellently fitted up with scenery and properties, and all the modern accessories of the drama'. There was a proscenium arch, 'just the right size, just a proper frame for the fine tragic pictures it so often represented,'[35] with a curtain that was raised at the beginning of performances.[36] Mitford's review of the 1821 *Orestes* suggests that the scenery was quite sophisticated, that torchlight was used imaginatively, and that characters *ex machina* had access to stage doors and some kind of device in which they could be elevated:[37]

Nothing could be more beautiful than the scene at Agamemnon's tomb—the sepulchre among the woods—the Choral women hanging tenderly over it . . . Orestes, holding the sword over the trembling Hermione . . . the

---

[34] Darter (1888), 111–14, 125.   [35] Mary Russell Mitford (1835), i. 310.
[36] Bockett (1857), 77.   [37] Mary Russell Mitford (1821).

FIGURE 9.2   Mary Russell Mitford, *c*.1840.

torches casting a broad glare over the scene . . . and then the radient [*sic*] vision of Apollo, at whose beck the scene opened, and discovered the bay, with Helen in a cloud, which the god also entered and began to ascend.

   Valpy must have been affected by the death in 1808 of Richard Porson, the Regius Professor of Greek at Cambridge and titan of Euripidean textual criticism, because his own former star pupil Peter Paul Dobree (a Guernsey boy) was one of Porson's intimates and later held the same chair at Cambridge. In any event, it was in 1809 that Valpy began his long career as a director of Euripides (he was later to direct a recital of parts of *Medea* and a performance of

Hecuba, both of which had been famously edited by Porson). His choice of *Alcestis* was however perhaps informed, like Samuel Parr's *Trachinians*, by Milton's *Of Education*. For in that treatise Milton specifies *Trachiniae* and *Alcestis* as representative of 'those tragedies . . . that treat of household matters' deemed suitable for study even by fairly young pupils.[38] The Reading Greek play was now becoming fashionable. Tickets of admission for the second and third nights of *Alcestis* were in so much demand that many hopefuls had to be refused, and 'during these representations' the town of Reading 'had a great influx of company, which proved so good an harvest to the inns,' that beds were only 'with difficulty obtained'.[39] And well they might: after the last performance,

a Ball was given by the Members of the School Meeting to the ladies and gentlemen in the town and neighbourhood, who had attended the Plays, and contributed to the charitable object. The company was brilliant and numerous.

Indeed, on this occasion the Reading Greek play's significance was seen as lying as much in its status as high point in the Berkshire civic and social calendar as in the niceties of the production itself: moreover, local memories of the Valpeian play seem to have been an important factor in the initial experiments at Bradfield School, which is very near Reading, over fifty years later.[40] Yet Mr Currie's 1809 *Alcestis* was outstandingly 'grand and mournful', Mr Fell's style of speaking the role of Admetus was 'animated' (the review suggests that this was not entirely appropriate!), that Hercules was dressed in a real lionskin, and that there was beautifully painted scenery.

Three years later there was an 'entertainment', which may have consisted of enactments or recitations of passages from Sophocles' *Antigone*; in 1815 it is certain that the 'entertainment' comprised recitations from Homer and Euripides' *Medea*.[41] But in 1818 Valpy decided once again on a full-scale, costumed production of a tragedy, and chose one which has rarely been performed anywhere until the late twentieth century, Euripides' *Heracles*. It is almost certain that Valpy's interest in this play was aroused by the

[38] Milton (1963), 104.   [39] Anon. (1809).
[40] Lewis Campbell (1891), 319, 321 n. 1.
[41] See Anon. (1812); Mitford (1854*a*), vol. i, p. xvii, who recalls a Reading Greek play featuring Antigone, which is more likely to have been Sophocles' *Antigone* than Aeschylus' *Septem*, Sophocles' *OC*, or Euripides' *Phoenissae*; Anon. (1815).

innovative 1794 *Tragoediarum Delectus* edited by Gilbert Wakefield, the two volumes of which attempted to encourage the educational study of plays which had previously not figured large on
school syllabuses. These included *Heracles*, *Orestes*, and *Ion* (the
last of which was to have a major impact on Valpy's pupil Thomas
Talfourd, Ch. 11).[42] When it comes to *Heracles*, Mitford's review
attempts something approximating to literary criticism: the reader
of the local newspaper is informed that the simple plot 'contains
much striking situation, much of the fitness for representation,
which distinguishes Euripides from his great rival, and much of
the tender pathos, for which he is so justly celebrated'.[43] It was
thus being discovered, by staged enactment, that Euripides' ancient reputation for working so well in the theatre was fully justified. The review commends the acting of Mr Butler as Iris ('so
beautiful and inexorable'), and especially the manner in which
Mr Harington as Heracles recovered from his 'trance' and represented 'the agony which seized him at the sight of the dead bodies'.

Encouraged by the success of *Heracles*, in 1821 Valpy chose
another play popularized amongst schoolteachers by Wakefield's
Delectus, the *Orestes* with which this chapter began: it proved a
triumph, and a repeat performance was exhibited by popular
demand.[44] *Orestes* has a large cast, and Valpy may have been
pushed to find amongst his pupils sufficient numbers who could
handle the demands of the ancient Greek: at any rate, no fewer
than three roles, all with major speeches (Menelaus, Orestes, and
the Argive messenger), were taken by the three brothers Palairet.
The chorus consisted of three 'Argive ladies', although the lyric
sections of this long play were somewhat cut. The published
English translation, which in this year seems to have been enacted
as a supplement to the three Greek-language performances, is
divided in the manner of a neo-classical tragedy into five acts.[45]

---

[42] Wakefield (1794). This edition did not, however, become widely known outside scholarly circles, nor even much used in schools, perhaps because Wakefield
held controversial religious and political views, and indeed was imprisoned for
seditious libel in 1798. His reputation as a polemicist may illuminate Byron's choice
of *Heracles* as the play studied by an earnest bluestocking' in *Don Juan*, published in
1821; he alleges that she had translated *Heracles*: 'That prodigy | Miss Araminta
Smith | Who at sixteen translated *Hercules Furens* | Into as furious English' (11. 52).

[43] Mary Russell Mitford (1818).

[44] Fines (1967), 16.

[45] Valpy (1821); Darter (1888), 113.

In 1824 Valpy's choice alighted once again on *Alcestis*. This performance made a strong visual impact, especially Mr Frederick Bulley's painting-like beauty in the title role: when his veil was drawn at the end, 'the fixed composure of his features on which death seemed to have imprinted a calm and holy beauty, would have been a study for a Painter.' Dr Valpy was not always willing to make his Scholars impersonate ancient Greeks with blatantly deficient morals, and the outrageously selfish Pheres was excised from the play as a bad moral example, while little master Spankie's rendition of the role of Alcestis' son Eumelus was accomplished 'with the most captivating artlessness. It was very pleasant to hear so young a boy lisping Greek.'[46]

The last play was the *Hecuba* of 1827, twinned with *King Lear*. Mitford thought its star was 'Mr. Maul' as Hecuba, who 'had all the hurried and agitated vehemence of a woman's revenge, the manner in which he rushed on the scene, holding in his hand the bloody dagger, will not soon be forgotten.'[47] Yet this morally bleak play was carefully cut. Just as he had omitted Admetus' selfish father Pheres from the 1824 *Alcestis*, from *Hecuba* he deleted Polymestor's prophecies concerning the miserable fates of Agamemnon and Hecuba.[48] This turned the play into a much simpler morality tale.

By this time the Reading Greek play was perceived as something much more important than a 'dramatic curiosity', or so insisted Thomas Talfourd, a former pupil by then working in London as theatre correspondent for the *New Monthly Magazine* (and later to become MP for Reading). He even persuaded the editor of this national organ to publish a review of the Reading *Hecuba*, alongside his review of no less a theatrical event than Edmund Kean performing in one of his most lauded roles as Shylock at Covent Garden. In his letter to the editor, Talfourd writes that the *Hecuba* had been 'a very singular and beautiful exhibition'. In his review he records that the youth who played Polyxena performed on a par with professional actors; Talfourd emphasizes that the event had attracted 'many persons distinguished by classical and poetic tastes'.[49] This was not the first time that the Reading Greek play

---

[46] Mary Russell Mitford (1824).   [47] Mary Russell Mitford (1827).
[48] See Mary Russell Mitford (1824); Potter (1827).
[49] Thomas Noon Talfourd (1827–52), 21.

had been noticed by the press beyond Reading, for the London *Star* had reported the performances of both 1818 and 1821.[50]

THE WOMAN WRITER RESPONDS

The most revealing picture of the Reading Greek play emerges from the various writings of the literary lady, Mary Russell Mitford, who wrote the reviews for the local newspaper. Mitford was to become a friend of Elizabeth Barrett Browning; she was much involved with both drama and periodical literature ranging from more serious publications to the *Lady's Magazine*. Mitford's own works were informed by the Greek plays she watched in her town hall; a sequence of her own tragedy *Julian*, performed in London in 1823, was suggested to her by the opening of the Reading *Orestes* of 1821.[51] She made most of her living from writing serialized fiction; this was greatly admired at the time and has recently been enjoying a renaissance in departments of English literature. Mitford lived in or near Reading from 1802, when she was fifteen. In her fictionalized account of Reading life, *Belford Regis*, she creates a whole chapter out of an idealized and sentimental account of the Valpy productions, translated to 'Belford School'.[52] The tone is more humorous than that of her reviews, but the underlying sense of reverential awe for the good Doctor and for ancient Greek literature is identical.

Yet Mitford, like many female intellectuals throughout the nineteenth century,[53] had an ambivalent attitude towards the study of Greek. Although during that century more women began to learn Greek than ever before, there were still very few in her generation who had access to this most elite of languages, the jealously guarded badge of the well-educated gentleman. Mitford loved the emotional power and humanity she perceived in Greek tragedy, and yet she despised the narrow philology of contemporary scholars. In her youth one of the most formidable editors of Greek tragic texts had been Richard Porson, whom she had observed at close quarters since his step-daughter was one of her closest

---

[50] *DNB* xx. 86.   [51] Mary Russell Mitford (1854*a*), i, p. xxvi.
[52] 'The Greek Plays', in Mary Russell Mitford (1835), i. 294–318. For a recent reassessment of Mitford's work in the context of the other women writers on close terms with the Romantic poets, see Wordsworth (1997).
[53] Jenkyns (1980), 63–5.

childhood friends. She had been convinced that the great scholar 'cared little for the pathos' of Euripides 'or the vivid bits of truth and nature'. No, 'what he delighted in was his own new readings'.[54] An unappealing scholar whom Mitford modelled on Porson is to be found editing Euripides' *Troades* in her novel *Atherton* (1854).

This ambivalence towards Greek studies often leads Mitford to deprecating the female intellect in a heavy-handed manner designed to imply the opposite. She writes in *Belford Regis*,

I must hasten to record, so far as an unlettered woman may achieve that presumptuous task, the triumphs of Sophocles and Euripides on the boards of Belford School.[55]

In the 'Introduction' to her own dramas, she remarks with some sarcasm on the paradox of her own role as newspaper reviewer of the Greek plays, a role on which Valpy had apparently insisted: 'For myself, as ignorant of Latin or Greek as the smuggest alderman or slimmest damsel present, I had my own share in the pageant.'[56] This remark reveals the social function of the Reading Greek plays as drawing cultural boundaries, through the ancient language, along the lines of class, education, and sex. On the one hand stood Valpy's Scholars and the Oxford Visitors they were trying to impress, and on the other the womenfolk and local Reading citizens who constituted much of the audience. In private, moreover, Mitford's idealization of the Valpy plays is revealed as only one side of the story. When writing informally to a female friend, she assumes the rhetorical posture of one denigrating the much-lauded 1821 *Orestes* as terribly dull:

I never yawned half so much in my life. The language is beautiful...but even that won't do for four hours, and it lasted little less. Everything that evening crept, crawled, 'trailed its slow length along'. The last time I was in that hall was at the election. O what a difference...! The action [sc. in an election] is so much more interesting, the characters so much better developed and the speeches not half so long.[57]

---

[54] Mary Russell Mitford (1872), ii. 213.

[55] Mary Russell Mitford (1835), ii. 308. See also p. 315, on the effect of the tragedies: 'Even the most unlettered lady was sensible to that antique grace and pathos.'

[56] Mary Russell Mitford (1854*a*), i, p. xv.

[57] Mary Russell Mitford (1872), i. 116–17, to Mrs Hofland.

It is impossible to be sure whether the encomiastic style of her newspaper reviews and other publications, or the humour of her private correspondence, more truly reflects Mitford's experience of sitting through the Reading plays. Yet she certainly realized that *performing* a tragedy might cast a different light on (what we should call) issues of gender. She was particularly struck by the way that the sheer size of Hecuba's role undercuts the expressions of misogynist sentiment in the play: 'Woman-hater though Euripides were ... yet in this tragedy he has paid a substantial compliment to the sex, by resting the whole of his interest on the female characters.'[58] Indeed, she was lost in admiration for the young Mr Maul in his realization of the role of Hecuba, for he

overcame the difficulties of the double disguise of age and sex, in a manner which would have done credit to the most experienced artist. We do not allude merely to the graceful and lady-like deportment ... which stood him (really we had almost written *her*) in so much stead ... that which appeared to us so striking was, that his very passions were feminine.[59]

Mitford is also particularly sensitive to the boys' impersonation of females (especially Alcestis, Antigone, and Electra), and in lighter vein describes the trials of theatrical transvestism: when performing female roles the actors' 'coarse red paws' had to be whitened with cold cream and chicken skin gloves, and they were even put into stays![60]

It is indeed remarkable that Valpy was so attracted to plays with strong female roles such as *Alcestis, Orestes,* and *Hecuba.* Mitford states that he refused to countenance a female-free production: the Doctor's boys, she says, were so famous for their women that she could never

prevail upon him to get up that masterpiece, 'Philoctetes', where pity and fear are moved almost as strongly as in 'Lear', not on account of the obvious objection of the physical suffering, but because there is no lady in the play.[61]

[58] Mary Russell Mitford (1827).   [59] Ibid.
[60] Mary Russell Mitford (1872), i. 116–17; (1835), i. 314–15.
[61] Mary Russell Mitford (1854a), i, p. xvi.

THE OLD BOYS REMEMBER

A rather different picture of the Reading Greek play emerges from the humorous memoir of Reading School by a former pupil named B. B. Bockett, who had gone on to become an ordained minister in the Church of England. Bockett assumed the pseudonym 'Oliver Oldfellow', invented new names for the principal characters, and three decades after the last Reading Greek play published *Our School; or, Scraps and Scrapes in Schoolboy Life*, a title which perhaps suggests a deliberate evocation of Mitford's *Our Village*.

Bockett had been chosen to play the role of the Phrygian slave in the *Orestes* of 1821 (this is confirmed by the programme), and his description of the preparations suggests a much more light-hearted operation than some of the other sources imply. Yet the tone may be a result of the anecdotal genre in which he is writing, or of the natural perspective of a 14-year-old boy. Bockett describes how Valpy's daughter had organized the wardrobe 'of our Grecian habiliments'; he particularly recalls the humiliation of being instructed by this frightening woman to try on his costume, an oriental 'splendour of spangles and bright glazed calico'.

The role of the Phrygian slave in *Orestes* requires the actor to run onto the stage in distraught panic. Bockett claims that Dr Valpy favoured a primitive form of 'method acting', and recalls that his own 'abject terror and crouching humility' had been highly commended (see Fig. 9.3). He claims that he only achieved such emotional authenticity because Dr Valpy (the renowned flogger going in Bockett's memoir under the name of 'Duodecimus', i.e. 'Twelve of the Best'), used deliberately to hit him before his stage entrance:

With stealthy, cat-like tread did Duodecimus the crafty glide behind those scenes, and approaching the said Oliver at the *happy* moment, most unceremoniously did he deal him such a cuff or blow, as to draw forth *veritable* tears from the eyes of the now *really frightened* and agitated slave. Moreover, the same irresistible hand that dealt the blow proceeded, at the same moment, to hurry on to the stage the sufferer, who, thanks to that clever experiment whereby fact was substituted for fiction, did for once succeed in 'bringing down the house'.

Bockett records with pride that his performance earned him an invitation to the Reading Corporation banquet. He drank until he

FIGURE 9.3   Dr Valpy prepares Benjamin Bockett for his entrance as the distraught Phrygian messenger in an 1821 performance of Euripides' *Orestes* at Reading School (1857).

passed out and had to be carried home from the feast, leaving his hat behind.[62]

But a more significant literary legacy of the Reading School play was sitting beside Bockett at that feast, in the person of Thomas Talfourd, whose own tragedy *Ion* captivated Covent Garden in 1836, as will be seen in Ch. 11. After Valpy's death Talfourd prefixed a valedictory notice to the latest edition of *Ion*, singling out as his greatest pedagogical virtue his transmission to his pupils of love for Greek tragedies, 'those remains of antique beauty'. Valpy 'awakened within me', says Talfourd, 'the sense of classical grace', which was consolidated by 'the exquisite representations of Greek tragedy' which 'made its images vital'.[63]

---

[62] Bockett (1857), 81.   [63] Thomas Talfourd (1844), 3–4, 260.

VITAL IMAGES

The 'vital images' provided by the Reading plays were remarkable in the context of theatre history, because in the first two decades of the nineteenth century serious drama had retreated from the public stages of Britain almost altogether. Valpy was perfectly aware of this, and saw himself as in some sense challenging the dearth of important drama in the commercial theatre. The Epilogue to the 1809 *Alcestis* not only refers to James Thomson's adaptation of the tragedy, *Edward and Eleonora* (see Ch. 4), and to one of Mrs Siddons's nicknames ('The Tragic Muse', after the famous painting of her in that role by Joshua Reynolds), but includes a condemnation of current practices in London theatres:[64]

> The Tragic Muse has left her Shakespeare's isle,
> And Comedy no longer deals her smile.
> Were Garrick now the London boards to try,
> His silver accents would in utterance die.

Indeed, their early drive for authenticity, which actually anticipated by several years the same developments on the commercial stage, made the Reading plays noteworthy. Mitford's 1821 review of *Orestes* contrasts the Westminster Latin play, which adopted the 'dress and manner of the latest English fashion', with the historical accuracy of the Reading Greek play. This was performed

amidst scenery correct yet splendid, and in costume every fold of which has been studied, with extreme care, and copied with the most exquisite taste from the noblest of antique statues.[65]

It may be no coincidence that the Elgin marbles had arrived in London in 1806, the year of the first Reading Greek play, and caused a considerable stir. Details of the Reading productions confirm that they aimed at visual authenticity: in the 1824 *Alcestis* not only was Apollo 'unearthly', but 'the zone, tunic and pallium were faithfully displayed'.[66] In *Heracles* the costume 'was exact even in the minutest details. Iris had her rainbow, Lyssa her snakes, and Theseus his Athenian grasshoppers.'[67] Those grasshoppers, inspired by Thucydides' account of old-fashioned hair accessories in Athens (1. 6), were symptoms of a literal archaeologism which,

---

[64] Valpy (1826), 173. See Macintosh (2001).
[65] Mary Russell Mitford (1821).   [66] Mary Russell Mitford (1824).
[67] Mary Russell Mitford (1818).

as will be noted in the next chapter, was only just beginning to penetrate the commercial theatre.[68]

The quest for authenticity extended beyond the visual dimension of the tragedies. Dr Parr's two Sophoclean productions at Stanmore school had omitted all the tragic choruses, but at Reading some choruses were certainly performed, at least in the later plays. In the 1827 *Hecuba* the chorus consisted of three boys, who alternated with each other in delivering individual strophes as solos, apparently in order to share the burden of learning these difficult sequences of ancient Greek.[69] Care was taken over pronunciation; in the 1821 *Orestes*, at any rate, the actors distinguished clearly between the Attic and Doric dialects of the iambic and lyric metres, and, to the ruination of the metre, inauthentically restored final vowels throughout.[70]

Yet the most important function of the Reading Greek plays was to make those involved sense the beauty of ancient literature and art: the costumes and scenery may have been modelled on Greek originals, but the writers of the reviews already speak like pre-Raphaelites of the sculptural or painterly beauty of the dramatic representations themselves (see Ch. 16). Another sentiment expressed by those who wrote about the plays is an apprehension that enactment of drama uniquely revealed a 'common humanity' shared by the ancient Greeks and themselves. In an era when a Classical education often meant torture by birchings and grammatical exercises, some lucky Reading pupils, including Dobree and Thomas Talfourd (who was virtually dyslexic and could not cope with grammar), discovered what it was like to be *inspired* by their cultural ancestors in Greece.

Decades later, witnesses of the Cambridge Greek plays were to speak of the *life* which performance breathed into these sepulchral texts. In an important article Pat Easterling has shown how reviewers spoke of the 'vivifying influence' of these performances, and the way they offered 'contact with actual life' as it was lived in ancient Greece.[71] This sense was enhanced by the entirely incorrect belief held by some that the Cambridge plays were the first performances of Greek dramas since antiquity. Yet the perception that enactment offers access to the 'universal' concerns of the

---

[68] See Pentzell (1967), 221–2.   [69] Valpy (1827).
[70] Mary Russell Mitford (1821).   [71] Easterling (1999).

human soul, a profound spiritual communion with the ancients, was anticipated by reactions to the Reading plays. It is best expressed in Mary Russell Mitford's eulogy of that singular 1821 *Orestes*:

It was, indeed, delightful that these touches of pathos ... were again awakening the same electrical sympathy, as of old—again swaying the heart of a large audience as a single bosom, and proving the human soul to be unaltered thro' all the long fluctuations of fortune.[72]

[72] Mary Russell Mitford (1821).

10

Ruins and Rebels

THE GREEK UPRISING

Far away from the British stage, the Greek-speaking world in 1821 embarked upon eight painful years of revolutionary upheaval. Years of planning were put into action by Alexandros Ypsilantis in Odessa, the ancient city on the Black Sea which Catherine the Great had refounded and populated with the prosperous merchant caste of Greeks known as Phanariots. After announcing in early March that the War of Independence had commenced, he invaded Ottoman Moldavia. In the Peloponnese, Bishop Germanos of Patras hoisted the Greek flag and began the mainland uprising. Part of the text of Ypsilantis' call to arms read as follows:

Brave and valiant Greeks, let us remember the ancient freedom of Greece, the battles of Marathon and Thermopylae; let us fight on the tombs of our ancestors who fell for the sake of our freedom. The blood of our tyrants is dear . . . above all to the shades of Miltiades, Themistocles, Leonidas, and the three hundred who massacred so many times their number of the innumerable army of the barbarous Persians—the hour is come to destroy their successors, more barbarous and more detestable![1]

The struggles of the Greeks against the Achaemenid Persians nearly two and a half thousand years before were thus adopted as the charter myth of the new Hellas, and its warriors roused with echoes of the exhortation with which the Greeks, according to tradition, had been inspired prior to the battle of Salamis, an exhortation which Aeschylus had quoted in his *Persians* (402–5): 'O children of the Hellenes, come on, liberate your fatherland, liberate your children, your wives, your ancestral gods and the shrines of your ancestors!' These stirring words were already one inspiration behind the song of the revolutionary balladeer Rhigas, 'Rise, children of the Hellenes', and the French revolutionary

---

[1] See Tsigakou (1981) and Robert and Françoise Etienne (1992), 85–8.

anthem *Le Marseillaise*, 'Allons enfants de la Patrie | Le jour de gloire est arrivé'.[2]

Aeschylus' *Persians* holds a distinguished place in the post-antique performance history of Greek tragedy, since it was actually the first known play to receive a Renaissance enactment, one which had made an early equation between Achaemenid Persia and the Ottoman Empire. In 1571 a western naval alliance, essentially Spanish, Papal, and Venetian, led by Don John of Austria, had defeated the Ottoman fleet at the Battle of Lepanto. In order to celebrate the victory *Persians* was performed, perhaps in Italian translation, in the private house of a member of the Venetian nobility who ruled the island of Zante (Zakynthos). The dissemination of the text of Aeschylus' play to these western Greek islands was facilitated by the channels of communication linking Greek intellectuals and Italian centres of scholarship.[3] Michael Sophianos of Chios, for example, translated Aristotle, collaborated on the seminal 1552 edition of the tragedies of Aeschylus published by Francesco Robortello in Venice, and became a professor of Greek at Padua.

A French *Les Perses*, inspired by Aeschylus, was in the early nineteenth century dedicated to Alexandros Morouzis, Phanariot Prince of the Danubian principality of Moldavia, and may have been produced at his court in Jassy.[4] And although *Persians* was probably not performed in Britain before 1907,[5] in stark contrast with its rediscovery for patriotic purposes in France in 1862 and

---

[2] On Rhigas' song see Woodhouse (1969), 60; on the importance of Salamis and the Persian wars in the French revolution, and of another Greek source (Tyrtaeus) in *Le Marseillaise*, Vidal-Naquet (1995), 95, 101. *Persians* was very attractive to late-18th-c. republicans: William Jones, for example, had written a play 'on the model of a Greek tragedy', with 'a chorus of Persian sages', called *Sohrab*. See Teignmouth (1804), 529. For a fascinating discussion of the part played by the Salamis narrative in the origins of political theory both ancient and modern, see Euben (1986). The same Aeschylean speech was quoted by Metaxas on the 'Day of the No', 28 Oct. 1940, when he roused the Greek people to resist Mussolini's ultimatum. For studies of the cultural impact of *Persians* see Hall (1996), 1–6 and Hall (forthcoming).

[3] On the Zante *Persians* see Protopapa-Mpoumpoulidou (1958), 9–11; Valsa (1960), 164; Knös (1962), 303, 654; on Greek intellectuals at the universities and publishing houses of Venice and Padua, Geanakopoulos (1976), 63–6.

[4] Knös (1962), 656.

[5] This was an avant-garde realization of a prose translation by B. J. Ryan, performed at the Literary Theatre Society at Terry's Theatre, with Lewis Casson in the role of Darius' ghost. See *ILN* 130, no. 3546 (6 Apr. 1907), 518 col. 3.

Greece in 1889,[6] it had long been influential. Two strands are apparent in its British reception. The first is a generally conservative, patriotic tendency, which led at different times to the battle of Salamis being connected with various famous British naval victories. These included the defeat of the Spanish Armada, in an idea for a play set in the court of Spain which Thomas Rymer outlined in some detail in his treatise *A Short View of Tragedy* (1693), and naval encounters in the Opium Wars, in an anonymous burlesque of *Persians* entitled *The Chinaid*, published in 1843. This strand, however, is best exemplified by the anonymous poem *The Battle of the Nile: A Dramatic Poem on the Model of the Greek Tragedy* (1799), which imitated *Persians* while celebrating Nelson's famous victory over Napoleon Bonaparte in the Battle of the Nile.[7] The other, far more radical strand in the British reception of *Persians* was developed by Thomas Maurice in *The Fall of the Mogul* (1806), a tragedy 'attempted partly on the Grecian model', which borrows from the Sophoclean model of Maurice's earlier *Oedipus* (on which see Ch. 8), but also from Aeschylus' *Persians*. The latter is especially apparent in the battle narrative and the laments of its mutinous choruses of Brahmin and Zoroastrian priests, who predict that the persecution their religions have suffered will become worse under their newest Islamic ruler, Nadir Shah, before the subject Hindu and Parsee peoples shall one day be liberated from imperial oppression.

The transhistorical vision of Maurice's choruses, as well as the aspirational politics, Islamic principal characters, and eastern palace setting of his play, directly anticipate those of Shelley's *Hellas*, a slightly later adaptation of *Persians* published in 1822 and dedicated to the Phanariot Prince Alexandros Mavrokordatos; as a refugee from the Turcocracy in Pisa, he had recently been instructing Mary Shelley in ancient Greek. Shelley's Preface twins the Aeschylean Greek tragic vision of the struggle for

---

[6] The students of Rhetoric at an Orléans seminary performed *Persians* in an anonymous translation in honour of the memory of Joan of Arc on 7 May 1862. See Egger (1862). On the Athenian production see Wartelle (1978), 135–6.

[7] See also Sotheby's similar celebration of the Battle of the Nile (1799), which by means of verbal echoes of *Persians* (e.g. the 'awful order' of the British fleet, p. 4) implicitly equates Napoleon with Xerxes. John Peter Roberdeau's *Thermopylae; or, the Repulsed Invasion* (published 1814) drew on Richard Glover's 18th-c. epic *Leonidas* and was actually enacted by recruits at Gosport Naval Academy in April 1805.

freedom with the 1821 uprising. Shelley writes that 'the Persae of Æschylus afforded me the first model of my conception, although the decision of the glorious contest now waging in Greece being yet suspended forbids a catastrophe parallel to the return of Xerxes and the desolation of the Persians'.[8] He therefore replaced the Aeschylean lament for the dead of Salamis with his captive Greek chorus's visionary account of the utopian future which the liberation of Greece might offer the whole world. In was in the Preface to this drama that Shelley made his famous declaration, 'We are all Greeks ... our laws, our literature, our religion, our arts have their roots in Greece', and added that 'a new race has arisen throughout Europe, nursed in the abhorrence of the opinions which are its chains, and she will continue to produce fresh generations to accomplish that destiny which tyrants dread and foresee.'[9]

GREEK RUINS

However much they may have supported the idea of pan-European revolution, the phlegmatic residents of London in the early 1820s were less likely to risk their lives in support of Hellas and global liberty than their contemporaries on the European mainland. Despite the public prominence of the philhellene Lord Byron, and the exploits of Captain Hastings on the Hydriote ship *Themistocles*, only twelve known British volunteers went to Greece, in comparison with 260 Germans and 71 Frenchmen.[10] The Londoners who stayed at home were, however, able for the first time in decades to see adaptations of Greek tragedy on the commercial stage; besides Faucit's 1821 *Oedipus* at the Royal West London Theatre (discussed in Ch. 8), the offerings included Edward Fitzball's *Antigone* and Peter Bayley's *Orestes*, based on Sophocles' *Electra*.

Although it can be no coincidence that Greek tragedy was rediscovered on the stage at almost exactly the same moment as the outbreak of the War of Independence, the political equation of the ancient Greek struggles for freedom with the contemporary Greek uprising was not in an *unmediated* sense the cause of the

---

[8] Shelley (1965), iii. 7. On Mavorkordatos see Dakin (1972), 81–2.

[9] Shelley (1965), iii. 9.

[10] Puchner (1996), 86 n. 5. On the puzzling paucity of Britons who actually went to Greece at this time see also Woodhouse (1969), 7–8. On Hastings see Howarth (1976), 46–7.

experiments with ancient tragedy. They were, rather, a response to
the popularity of other types of spectacular drama set against back-
drops portraying the ruins of classical Greece. It was plays enacting
the Greek struggle with the Turks, rather than the struggle itself,
that stimulated the interest in representing the exploits of Greek
heroes, performed in landscapes littered with ancient pillars. This
interest, as we shall see in the next section, inevitably led authors
and theatre managers in the direction of Greek tragedy.

Yet theatrical interest in classical archaeology, especially in relation to Shakespearean plays set in the ancient world, had been
developing for more than two decades by the time of the Greek
uprising. As was noted in Ch. 6 in reference to Loutherburg's
designs for Garrick, archaeological discoveries were having a
mild effect on the theatre by the second half of the eighteenth
century. But this process was fundamentally a phenomenon of
the early nineteenth century. It was long customary amongst literary historians to condemn the theatre of this period, but recently
there has been fuller appreciation of the important technological
and scenic developments at this time. They laid the groundwork
for the modern theatre, and it is hard to overestimate the role of
ancient archaeology and art in this process.

The Kemble siblings (John, Charles, and to a lesser extent
Sarah) were, at least in Britain, the founding parents of 'archaeological theatre'. In 1794 John Kemble erected a much enlarged
theatre at Drury Lane, and began reproducing architectural features in unprecedentedly faithful detail. This date coincided with
the publication of the third volume of James Stuart's *The Antiquities of Athens*, which, for the first time, offered to its hungry
readership a precise delineation of the Doric style in architecture.[11]
Antiquarian exactitude was established at least as an ideal by 1799,
when a mythological pantomime at Sadler's Wells, the *Oracle of
Delphi*, included representations of the temple at Delphi, the
palace and gardens of Omphale, and the grottoes of Bacchus.[12]
More significantly, when Kemble opened the new Covent Garden
Theatre on 18 September 1809, it was partly modelled on the
Parthenon. Robert Smirke's auditorium boasted an imposing
flight of marble steps leading to a Doric screen.[13]

[11] See further Spencer (1954), 195–6.   [12] Rosenfeld (1981), 35–8.
[13] Rosenfeld (1972–3), 69; a contemporary engraving is reproduced in Ackermann et al. (1809), ii. 263.

Smirke was criticized for using such an imposing architectural style for what was basically a place of entertainment (at that date, indeed, predominantly light entertainment), but he himself believed that a dignified theatrical building might in itself improve public taste and therefore the type of repertoire performed.[14] Smirke's Grand Front was decorated with relief sculptures which included depictions of Greek figures representing Comedy (Aristophanes, Menander, and Thalia), and, for Tragedy, Aeschylus with the trial scene from his *Eumenides*. Kemble's inaugural address traced the history of the stage back to Aeschylus and especially Sophocles, under whom 'builders and decorators came', alluding to the ancient tradition that Sophocles had introduced painted sets to the theatre, while betraying the fact that his own late Georgian interest in ancient drama was primarily scenographic.[15]

John Kemble's scenery for the 1811 *Coriolanus*, which combined Doric and Corinthian orders, set new standards in antiquarian set design.[16] This heightened interest in representing Mediterranean antiquity was stimulated by the influence of specific archaeological discoveries and of publications containing illustrations of ruins and reconstructions of them. A new drop was painted at the Adelphi in 1815, in which a triumphal palace arch 'in exquisite style' and adorned with statues was directly copied from a Doric masterpiece discovered at Albano; in the same year in *Timon of Athens* at Drury Lane, there was spectacular new scenery including a view of Athens based on a picture in the book Lord Byron's fellow traveller John Hobhouse had published on his return: *Travels in Albania and Other Provinces of Turkey in 1809 & 1810*.[17] By the early 1820s, the fashion for classical sets for Shakespeare, in conjunction with the international situation, became crucial in determining the choice of subject-matter dramatized in the theatres.

---

[14] Denvir (1984), 48.
[15] Aristotle, *Poetics* 4, 1449^{a}18–19. See the *Courier* for 19 Sept. 1809, in the collection 'Covent Garden: Newspaper Cuttings' in the Bodleian Library; Wyndham (1906), i. 331.
[16] Rosenfeld (1972–3), 68.
[17] Rosenfeld (1981), 174, 150. On Hobhouse's journey see Woodhouse (1969), 15–16.

STAGING THE WAR OF INDEPENDENCE

In 1809, the year the new Covent Garden theatre opened, Sydney Owenson (the future Lady Morgan) published her then notorious novel *Woman: or, Ida of Athens*. From the perspective of theatre history its importance lies in its fusion of idealized classical Greek ruins, memories of the fall of Constantinople—prominent when Ida dresses for a masquerade as Irene, the famous Greek heroine of that era[18]—and a nearly contemporary setting against the background of Ottoman rule. It also contrasts the wonders of the ancient theatre with the trivial drama, so despised by Sir Robert Smirke, dominating the theatrical repertoire of Georgian London. When in the novel an Englishman visits Athens, the Archon's lovely daughter Ida proudly shows off to him the 'theatre of Bacchus'; but when she is taken to London art galleries and a modern farce, she is dismayed. Having 'acquired her judgment in the school of Phidias, amidst the ruins of the Parthenon', she is bored by 'the over-strained sentiment of what is termed genteel comedy'.[19]

The London stage's rediscovery of the Greek tragedies born in Ida's 'theatre of Bacchus' is inexplicable except in the context of its bullish reaction to the Graeco-Turkish conflict. The most conspicuous feature of the 1820s British theatre was a crop of 'War of Independence' dramas, especially at the Coburg Theatre. By November 1821 the Coburg audience was watching C. E. Walker's 'entirely new grand Melo-Drama' *The Greeks and the Turks; or, the Intrepidity of Jemmy, Jerry, and a British Tar*. The star of this spectacle, set in Thessaloniki harbour but boasting pillared antique colonnades, was Fan Fireproof, a British grandmother. She proved 'ardent in the cause of Greece and universal Liberty', while a British hornpipe dancer was awarded the role of 'connecting the Greek revolution with the liberal feelings of the British people'.[20] The most important example of this type of Coburg play was *Lazaria the Greek; or the Archon's Daughter*, another 'Greek

---

[18] Owenson (1809), iv. 206. On Irene in the 18-c. theatre, see above, Ch. 5 n. 7.
[19] Owenson (1809), i. 85; iv. 188.
[20] Mikoniatis (1979), 333. The hornpipe dancing throws interesting light on Dr Valpy's apparently eccentric taste for combining hornpipes with Greek tragedy (p. 247).

Melo-Drama' performed in 1823, when serious fund-raising was
under way, under the august aegis of the London Greek Committee itself. The hero (despite the feminine subtitle) was a male slave
named Demetrius Lazaria. Beneath the heading *Greek Cause* the
playbill included the following notice:

> The great struggle in which the Greek Nation is engaged has occupied the
> attention of every friend of humanity, and every heart imbued with honour
> and sensibility echoes these words, GREECE is fighting for LIBERTY!
> All mankind declare the numerous deeds of COURAGE and VALOUR
> achieved by this Brave People, deserve to be recorded in letters of GOLD,
> and worthy to be handed down to posterity as worthy [of] their great
> Ancestors. The Manager of the ROYAL COBURG THEATRE ... has
> rendered his Stage the vehicle for exciting public interest, in their behalf,
> by the production of a SPLENDID GREEK MELODRAMA under the
> IMMEDIATE PATRONAGE of the Noblemen and Gentlemen forming
> the Greek Committee.[21]

One month later the offering was J. Dobbs's *Petraki Germano; or,
Almanzar the Traitor*, an account of the Bishop of Patras's leadership of the 1821 Peloponnesian uprising, but including scenes of
far greater antiquity—the ruins of ancient Laconia, including the
'Senate House' and the amphitheatre.[22] The play was intended to
celebrate the Peloponnesians' attempt to 'rekindle the Sacred
Flame of Liberty. Sparta may take honour to herself of having
preserved even to this day, among her Offspring, some few Men
who possess all the heroic Spirit of their Fathers.'[23]

These remarkable pieces instigated a trend which also produced
The Revolt of the Greeks; or, the Maid of Athens (Drury Lane,
1824, including a view of the Acropolis), the spectacular *The
Siege of Missolonghi; or, the Massacre of the Greeks* (Astley's, July
1826), H. M. Milner's musical drama *Britons at Navarino* (Coburg
Theatre, 1827), an extravaganza entitled *The Mufti's Tomb; or,
The Turkish Misers* (Astley's 1828), and *The Suliote; or, The
Greek Family* (1829), which offered its Drury Lane audience a

---

[21] British Library Playbill, dated 24 Nov. 1823. One of the earliest members of
the London Greek Committee has been encountered in an earlier chapter,
Dr Samuel Parr. See Woodhouse (1969), 73.
[22] Mikoniatis (1979), 336.
[23] Ibid.

romantically dilapidated ancient temple.[24] Such plays were also popular in the British provinces.[25]

From the perspective of the current book the most striking aspect of these plays, besides their depictions of classical architecture, is that their freedom-loving heroes are sometimes given ancient Greek names, even names taken from Greek tragedy. In *Ali Pacha; or, the Signet Ring* (Covent Garden 1822), a Suliot chief improbably named Zenocles triumphed over the bloodthirsty Turkish despot of Epirus, after admonishing his men to 'show the expecting world that Greece is not extinct, and give some future Homer themes for a mightier Iliad'.[26] The hero of J. Smith's tragedy *Creon the Patriot*, performed in Norwich in 1825, may have derived his name from Greek tragedy, but he was a contemporary klephtic revolutionary.[27] The War of Independence meant that ancient Greek 'liberty' and modern Greek 'liberation' had become inseparable in the popular imagination.

BRITISH READINGS OF GREEK TRAGEDY IN THE 1820S

The theatrical reverberations of the Greek Revolution extended to a renewed interest in dramas concerned with the entire history of the Greeks. Plays set at the time of the fall of Constantinople in 1453 now found performance (e.g. Joanna Baillie's *Constantine Palaiologos*, staged in Dublin in 1825), along with a few dramas on themes from ancient Greek history, and—for the first time since the eighteenth century—a handful of adapted Greek tragedies. Western Europe began to unearth this genre after Sophocles' *Philoctetes*—a profound statement of the pain of exile from the fatherland—had been staged in 1818 by the Phanariot community at Odessa.[28] While on the Continent the works of Voltaire and

---

[24] See Droulia (1974), no. 1732. In this category should probably also be placed the anonymous musical *Lord Byron in Athens; or, the Corsair's Isle* (Sadler's Wells, June 1832).

[25] An 1825 scenery catalogue for the Theatre Royal, Birmingham, includes two columns and a 'fire piece' for Walker's *The Revolt of the Greeks*. See John E. Cunningham (1950), 153.

[26] Act I, Scene iii. See further Mikoniatis (1979), 334–6.

[27] [J. Smith] (1827); see Nicoll (1952–9), iv. 623.

[28] See the article reproduced in Spathes (1986), 145–98, and Topouzes (1992), 166–7.

Alfieri were rediscovered,[29] all three British performed adaptations of Greek tragedy were at least notionally new. Their ultimate sources were all Sophoclean (in contrast with the predominant Euripides of the eighteenth century), and they all dramatized struggles against tyrants, perceived to be a broadly topical theme. It was as if the possibility of a free, autonomous Greece in the political sphere finally liberated the imaginations of the men of the theatre, allowing them to weld the ancient plays to the archaeological realities of the Mediterranean. And it is in this context that the experiments in the 1820s with ancient Greek theatre need to be read.

A spate of tragedies owing form and content to ancient Greek drama was published in Britain in the early 1820s,[30] and given the contemporary theatre's addiction to classical ruins, this trend would inevitably find enacted expression sooner or later. By June 1821 *Dirce; or, the Fatal Urn* (a distant relative of Metastasio's opera *Demofoonte*) was attracting large audiences at Drury Lane through the exertions (in breeches) of Madame Vestris (on whom see below, Chs. 12–14), playing the young hero Cerinthus. *Dirce* was informed by Greek tragedy (Apollo demands that a maiden be offered for sacrifice), but its importance lay in its scenery. The interior of Apollo's temple was 'correct in character, beautiful in design, and finished in execution'.[31] *Dirce* was also the first all-sung English opera, and the note struck by one reviewer is fascinating because it betrays the intertwining of generic and aesthetic questions with immediately topical affairs. Objecting to the operatic indignities to which the composer (Charles Horn) subjected his ancient Greeks, the reviewer (Thomas Talfourd, a former pupil at Reading School) complains:

---

[29] Puchner (1996), 101.

[30] See e.g. R.C. Dallas, *Adrastus: A Tragedy* (London, 1823), William Boscawen Bell, *The Queen of Argos: A Tragedy in Five Acts* (London, 1823), and David Lyndsay's *The Nereid's Love* in *Dramas of the Ancient World* (Edinburgh, 1822), dedicated to 'the Manes of Eschylus'. The Constantinopolitan Gregorios Palaeologus' important modern Greek prose tragedy *The Death of Demosthenes* survives, indeed, only in the English translation in which it was published in Cambridge in 1824. See Droulia (1974), no. 516.

[31] *The Drama; or, Theatrical Pocket Magazine*, 1 (1821), 95. A playbill for *Dirce* at the Coburg Theatre on 16 July 1821 said that it boasted striking scenery (cit. Rosenfeld (1981), 132).

...to reduce the God-like Greeks to ballad-mongers—to melt that heroism which is a possession to the world for ever into quavers—is neither just
nor wise ... A first-rate singer, or a woman dressed in male attire, may be a
fit representative of a Persian Satrap ... but will scarcely be worthy to
represent that race who fought at Thermopylae and Marathon.[32]

Only a few months later, at the Royal West London Theatre, the
audience was promised classical Greek heroes delivering suitably
solemn speeches (alongside musical interludes), in the remarkable
adapted tragedy discussed in Ch. 8, John Savill Faucit's version of
the '*Œdipus Tyrannus* of Sophocles ... being its first appearance
these 2440 years'.[33]

Yet even the West London *Oedipus* was not the first of the 1821
Greek tragedies, for Edward Fitzball's *Antigone*, starring one Mrs
Clifford, was first produced in Norwich Theatre Royal in the
spring of that year, with the subtitle *The Theban Sister*.[34] Fitzball
was then the owner of a Norwich printing shop. A five-act tragedy
in blank verse, his *Antigone* is archaizing in style (at least in
comparison with other types of stage play written in the 1820s),
replete with archaic diction ('thou wast' and 'war's stern panoply').
It draws on both Sophocles' *Antigone* and Euripides' *Phoenician
Women*, but raises the romance between Antigone and Haemon to
prominence, thus portraying Creon as the enemy of Love as well as
Liberty. The action takes place over two days, and moves through
various settings, from Polynices' camp outside Thebes, to Antigone's apartment, the 'Interior of a magnificent Theban temple', a
civic scene within the gates of Thebes, a mountainside, and a
cavern containing a statue of Oedipus. By Act III, Scene iv the
audience is watching the ramparts of Thebes from the outside,
with Eteocles shouting at Polynices from the battlements, and the
fourth act reveals a state apartment and a Theban street scene. The
climax returns to the cavern, in which Antigone and Polynices and
Eteocles die, before thunder sounds and the curtain falls on
Creon's despair.

By 1824 Fitzball had been engaged as salaried author at the
Surrey Theatre in London, where his Norwich *Antigone* was 'got
up with great splendour, and played many nights'.[35] Charles

---

[32] *New Monthly Magazine and Literary Journal*, 3 (1821), 330.
[33] *The Drama*, 2 (1821), 99–100.
[34] Larpent 2206. See Fitzball (1859), i. 58 and n.   [35] Ibid. 139.

Tomkins, engaged at the Surrey as principal scene-painter under Thomas Dibdin, in 1824 also provided scenery for three other pieces by Fitzball, including one of the contemporary plethora of nautical melodramas. His designs made the theatre popular; the temples, civic scenes, state apartments and statues for *Antigone* were pronounced grand, original and 'calculated to raise' the Surrey management 'to the highest pinnacle of their profession'.[36]

The third and last Greek tragic adaptation was Peter Bayley's *Orestes in Argos*, based on Sophocles' *Electra*, which played at Covent Garden in 1825, with John Kemble's much younger brother Charles in the role of Orestes (Fig. 10.1). Bayley's play was symptomatic of the Europe-wide revival of interest in the tyrant-slaying theme of Sophocles' *Electra* in the wake of the 1821 uprising. Bayley may have been prompted by reports of the tragic *Oreste* by Jean-Marie Janin, performed at the Théâtre Français in Paris in June 1821.[37] Alexandre Soumet, who was also involved in entertainments more directly related to the Greek war (such as the libretto for Rossini's 1826 *Le Siège de Corinthe*), wrote a *Clytemnestre*, first performed at the Paris Odéon on 7 November 1822, derived from Sophocles' *Electra*. This Greek tragedy also featured in the visual arts of the time. The followers of Jacques-Louis David competed annually for the Prix de Rome by painting neo-classical scenes. Between 1801 and 1821 the prescription was always from the *Iliad*, ancient historians, the Old Testament and Ovid, but suddenly in 1822 it was 'Oreste et Pylade', and in 1823 that familiar Sophoclean scene, 'Egisthe, croyant retrouver le corps d'Oreste mort, découvre celui de Clytemnestre'.[38]

Bayley's prologue drew connections between the classical sub-ject-matter and the continuing struggle in Greece by arguing that the drama at Athens used 'to spread by scenic arts the Patriot flame'. The epilogue makes an allusion to the 'suffering Greeks'.[39] The play emphasizes the role of the people of Argos in the uprising

---

[36] *The Drama*, 5 (1823), 40.   [37] Frenzel (1962), 484.

[38] In subsequent years other Sophoclean scenes were chosen: *Antigone* in 1825, *Philoctetes* in 1838, and *Oedipus Tyrannus* in 1843, 1867, and 1871. See Harding (1979), 32, 91–4.

[39] The prologue and epilogue do not appear in the first published version (Bayley (1825*a*)), or in any other edition. They are quoted from the manuscript in the Larpent Collection (Bayley (1824)).

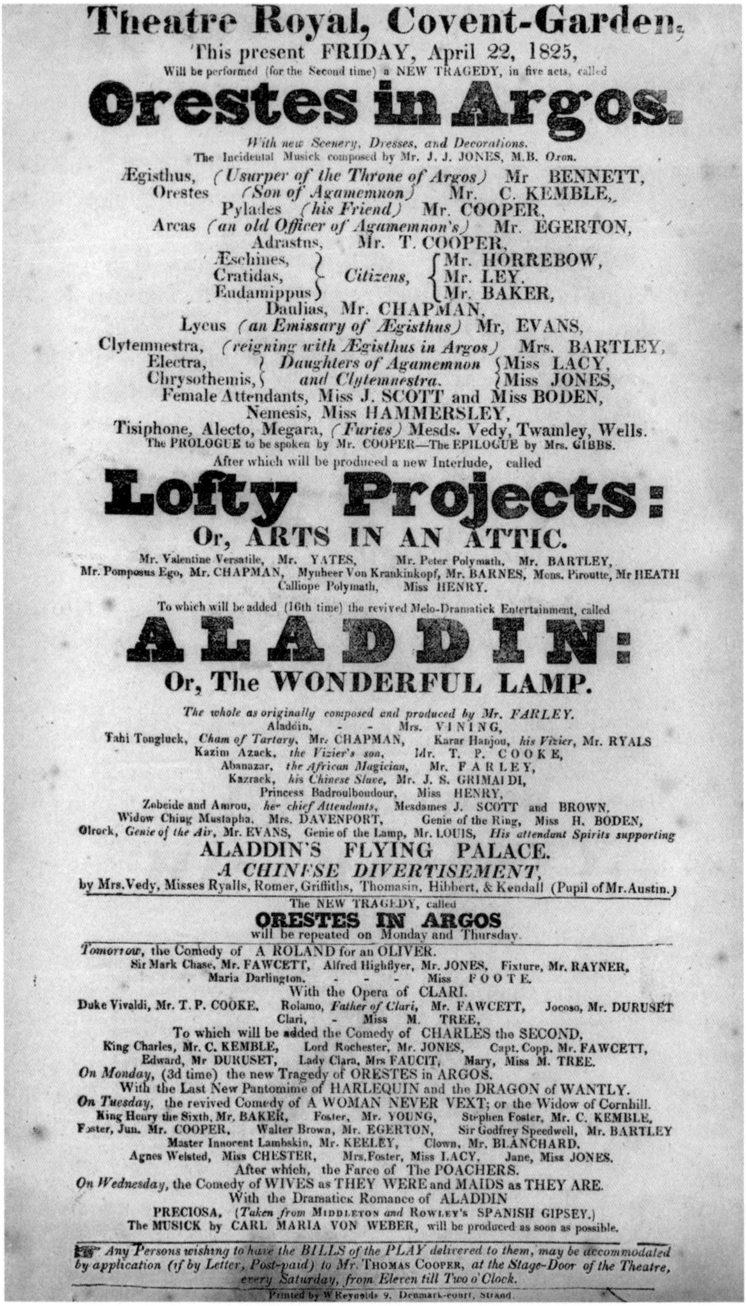

Theatre Royal, Covent-Garden.
This present FRIDAY, April 22, 1825,
Will be performed (for the Second time) a NEW TRAGEDY, in five acts, called
Orestes in Argos.
With new Scenery, Dresses, and Decorations.
The Incidental Musick composed by Mr. J. J. JONES, M.B. Oxon.
Ægisthus, *(Usurper of the Throne of Argos)* Mr BENNETT,
Orestes *(Son of Agamemnon)* Mr. C. KEMBLE,
Pylades *(his Friend)* Mr. COOPER,
Arcas *(an old Officer of Agamemnon's)* Mr. EGERTON,
Adrastus, Mr. T. COOPER,
Æschines, Cratidas, Eudamippus, *Citizens,* Mr. HORREBOW, Mr. LEY, Mr. BAKER,
Daulias, Mr. CHAPMAN,
Lycus *(an Emissary of Ægisthus)* Mr, EVANS,
Clytemnestra, *(reigning with Ægisthus in Argos)* Mrs. BARTLEY,
Electra, Chrysothemis, *Daughters of Agamemnon and Clytemnestra.* Miss LACY, Miss JONES,
Female Attendants, Miss J. SCOTT and Miss BODEN,
Nemesis, Miss HAMMERSLEY,
Tisiphone, Alecto, Megara, *(Furies)* Mesds. Vedy, Twamley, Wells.
The PROLOGUE to be spoken by Mr. COOPER—The EPILOGUE by Mrs. GIBBS.
After which will be produced a new Interlude, called
Lofty Projects:
Or, ARTS IN AN ATTIC.
Mr. Valentine Versatile, Mr. YATES, Mr. Peter Polymath, Mr. BARTLEY,
Mr. Pomposus Ego, Mr. CHAPMAN, Mynheer Von Krankinkopf, Mr. BARNES, Mons. Piroutte, Mr HEATH
Calliope Polymath, Miss HENRY.
To which will be added (16th time) the revived Melo-Dramatick Entertainment, called
ALADDIN:
Or, The WONDERFUL LAMP.
The whole as originally composed and produced by Mr. FARLEY.
Aladdin, - - Mrs. VINING,
Tahi Tongluck, *Cham of Tartary,* Mr. CHAPMAN, Karar Hanjou, *his Vizier,* Mr. RYALS
Kazim Azack, *the Vizier's son,* Mr. T. P. COOKE,
Abanazar, *the African Magician,* Mr. FARLEY,
Kazrack, *his Chinese Slave,* Mr. J. S. GRIMALDI,
Princess Badroulboudour, Miss HENRY,
Zobeide and Amrou, *her chief Attendants,* Mesdames J. SCOTT and BROWN,
Widow Ching Mustapha, Mrs. DAVENPORT, Genie of the Ring, Miss H. BODEN,
Olrock, *Genie of the Air,* Mr. EVANS, Genie of the Lamp, Mr. LOUIS, *His attendant Spirits supporting*
ALADDIN'S FLYING PALACE.
A CHINESE DIVERTISEMENT,
by Mrs. Vedy, Misses Ryalls, Romer, Griffiths, Thomasin, Hibbert, & Kendall (Pupil of Mr. Austin.)
The NEW TRAGEDY, called
ORESTES IN ARGOS
will be repeated on Monday and Thursday.
Tomorrow, the Comedy of A ROLAND for an OLIVER.
Sir Mark Chase, Mr. FAWCETT, Alfred Highflyer, Mr. JONES, Fixture, Mr. RAYNER,
Maria Darlington. - - - Miss FOOTE.
With the Opera of CLARI.
Duke Vivaldi, Mr. T. P. COOKE, Rolamo, *Father of Clari,* Mr. FAWCETT, Jocoso, Mr. DURUSET
Clari, - Miss M. TREE,
To which will be added the Comedy of CHARLES the SECOND,
King Charles, Mr. C. KEMBLE, Lord Rochester, Mr. JONES, Capt. Copp. Mr. FAWCETT,
Edward, Mr DURUSET, Lady Clara, Mrs FAUCIT, Mary, Miss M. TREE.
On Monday, (3d time) the new Tragedy of ORESTES in ARGOS.
With the Last New Pantomime of HARLEQUIN and the DRAGON of WANTLY.
On Tuesday, the revived Comedy of A WOMAN NEVER VEXT; or the Widow of Cornhill.
King Henry the Sixth, Mr. BAKER, Foster, Mr. YOUNG, Stephen Foster, Mr. C. KEMBLE,
Foster, Jun. Mr. COOPER, Walter Brown, Mr. EGERTON, Sir Godfrey Speedwell, Mr. BARTLEY
Master Innocent Lambskin, Mr. KEELEY, Clown, Mr. BLANCHARD,
Agnes Welsted, Miss CHESTER, Mrs. Foster, Miss LACY, Jane, Miss JONES.
After which, the Farce of The POACHERS.
On Wednesday, the Comedy of WIVES as THEY WERE and MAIDS as THEY ARE.
With the Dramatick Romance of ALADDIN
PRECIOSA, (*Taken from* MIDDLETON *and* ROWLEY'S SPANISH GIPSEY.)
The MUSICK by CARL MARIA VON WEBER, will be produced as soon as possible.
Any Persons wishing to have the BILLS of the PLAY delivered to them, may be accommodated by application (if by Letter, Post-paid) to Mr. THOMAS COOPER, *at the Stage-Door of the Theatre, every Saturday, from Eleven till Two o'Clock.*
Printed by W Reynolds 9, Denmark-court, Strand.

FIGURE 10.1 Contemporary playbill for Peter Bayley's *Orestes in Argos* at Covent Garden, 1825.

against Ægisthus, and Arcas, the *paidagōgos* figure, is central to the 'revolt | against the tyrant'.[40] Although Bayley's tragedy uses Alfieri, Voltaire, and the version by Shirley discussed above in Ch. 6, the major source is *Electra*. One of the reviewers even called Bayley a 'translator' of Sophocles, and compliments him for greater fidelity to the Greek than either Voltaire or Crébillon.[41]

The production was praised for Charles Kemble's performance as Orestes (Fig. 10.2) and for the effectiveness of the recognition scene,[42] but its primary impact seems to have been visual. The theatre designers put considerable work into the classical scenery for Bayley's play (Fig. 10.3).[43] The stage directions for the opening of the second act required the representation of the tomb of Agamemnon, the palace of the Pelopidae, and 'Argos in the distance—not too remote', while Aegisthus' death scene required numerous pillars. It was set in 'A large court of the Palace, with colonnade, entrances to various apartments, baths &c.'[44]

This brief theatrical revival of Sophocles contributed to the irrevocable changes in public expectations of the playhouses which marked the 1820s, and were to prepare the ground for the introduction of all the glories and excesses of Victorian spectacular theatre. At Drury Lane, for example, there is no mention of classic scenes at all in its 1819 inventory, but by 1829 the Covent Garden sale catalogue includes quite a number, quite possibly including items from Bayley's *Orestes*. There were three palace scenes in the Doric style, the Ionic, and the Corinthian respectively, along with a forum, an Ionic palace, a Roman hall, an Ionic hall, and a Corinthian street. As Rosenfeld argues, this new type of classical idiom was important as the *only* new style to be introduced into the English theatres in the first few decades of the nineteenth century. Not only the three adapted Greek tragedies but several other new plays of the 1820s had Greek or Roman themes, allowing the representation of ancient palaces and religious buildings: *Leonidas, King of Sparta* boasted a remarkable temple of Hercules.[45] New technologies were developed for satisfying the audience's appetite for the representation of antique buildings. In 1824 the ingenious

---

[40] Bayley (1825a), 49.　　[41] Anon. (1825), 372.　　[42] Ibid. 373.
[43] Rosenfeld (1981), 150, 174–6.　　[44] Bayley (1825a), 12.
[45] Rosenfeld (1981), 176. This play was probably a version of Michel Pichat's *Léonidas*, a tragedy performed in Paris at the Théâtre Français in 1825, with Talma in the title role. See further Athanassoglou-Kallmyer (1989), 57–9 with fig. 26.

FIGURE 10.2   Thomas Woolnoth, *Mr. C. Kemble as Orestes*, frontispiece
to Dolby's British Theatre edition of Peter Bayley's *Orestes in Argos*
(1825).

DOLBY'S BRITISH THEATRE.

———

ORESTES IN ARGOS.

T. Jones, Del.   White, Sculpt.

Orestes. Where lurks the murderous and sensual beast?
Ha! art thou found! Ye Gods, I thank you!—Die—
Die—a thousand deaths in one!

ACT V. SCENE 4.

FIGURE 10.3   Henry White, engraving of the climax of Peter Bayley's
Orestes in Argos (1825).

eidophusikon was used for only the second time at Drury Lane in William Moncrieff's melodrama *Zoroaster*, and the views it offered extended upwards of forty-eight breathtaking feet. Along with the Egyptian pyramids and Vesuvius erupting, they displayed the Temple of Apollinopolis Magna and the Colossus of Rhodes.

If John Kemble had been associated with authentic set design, and his sister Sarah Siddons had begun, towards the end of her career, to experiment with attitudes and drapes derived from Greek statuary,[46] their rather younger brother Charles will always be remembered for his contribution to the development of theatrical costuming. Indeed, historians of theatre have traditionally dated the birth of modern costuming in Britain to the medieval realism of his 1823 production of *King John*, two years prior to *Orestes in Argos*.[47] Kemble's enthusiasm was fed by Levacher de Charnois's lavishly illustrated *Recherches sur les costumes et sur les théâtres de toutes les Nations tant anciennes que modernes* (1790), and above all Thomas Hope's *Costumes of the Ancients* (London, 1809), a compendium of illustrations based on ancient paintings to be seen on the vases Hope collected. The edition of Bayley's play published in the popular series *Dolby's British Theatre* provided illustrations and descriptions of the costumes. Miss Lacy's Electra wore an austere 'slate-coloured cotton long dress, and drapery', while Kemble's Orestes sported a

lilach-coloured fine cloth short tunic, embroidered with black around the bottom; black belt, with white embroidery; white hat worn on his back; white square robe, embroidered with lilach, the colour of the tunich; white sandals, flesh legs and arms.[48]

Those 'flesh legs and arms', implying authentic Greek semi-nakedness, were an innovative feature. Edward Fitzball, the author of *Antigone; or, the Theban Sister*, later recalled that

the first time I saw naked feet represented, (in silk fleshings, of course,) was in a Greek tragedy, 'Orestes', at Covent Garden Theatre, and many people disliked the appearance, although it should have reminded them of some of the finest statues in the world; but English taste was very squeamish.[49]

---

[46] Pentzell (1967), 214–19.   [47] See Lily B. Campbell (1918), 213–15.
[48] Bayley (1825*b*), p. ix. The reaction was similar to the shock caused by the revealing toga which Talma had worn when playing the role of Brutus in Paris in 1789.
[49] Fitzball (1859), i. 69.

Even though these Sophoclean experiments of the 1820s were born out of a combination of archaeologism and the exciting new experience of enacting episodes from the real-life drama unfolding in Greek-speaking lands, it was Kemble's taste for antiquarian glamour that was to prove the most dominant strain in the British encounter with the ancient Greek stage over the remainder of the nineteenth century. White fabrics, pastel drapery, sandals, fleshings, the illusion of naked limbs, marble shoulders, sculptural metaphors, the eroticization of the actor's physique—all these were to become dominant elements in the language in which Greek theatre was discussed and imitated, especially after the lustrous Helen Faucit's (almost) bare-shouldered realization of *Antigone* in 1845 (see Ch. 12).

Before this book's narrative moves to that crucial production, however, it must first linger on the political scene just long enough to consider the impact of the change of government that followed the general election of 1830, and the consequent Great Reform Act, upon a young alumnus of Reading School. Thomas Talfourd spent his early adulthood engaged in studying law, pursuing radical causes, and reviewing the archaeologically sophisticated theatre of the 1820s. In the next chapter it will be worth bearing in mind that it was Talfourd who objected to Horn's *Dirce* because he held such passionate views, nourished by the continuing struggle in Greece, about the appropriate way to put on stage the freedom-loving offspring of Thermopylae and Marathon.

Talfourd's Ancient Greeks in the Theatre of Reform

A THEATRICAL HIT

It is 26 May 1836. Covent Garden theatre is packed with prominent writers, including Charles Dickens, Robert Browning, Richard Hengist Horne, William Wordsworth, Walter Savage Landor, Mary Russell Mitford, and John Forster. Politics and high society are well represented—Lord Melbourne, Lord Chief Justice Denman, Lord Grey, Lady Blessington. One literary man realizes that the theatre is thronged 'with an audience the like of which, in point of distinction', he has 'never seen in an English theatre'.[1]

They have gathered for the first night of Thomas Talfourd's *Ion*, a new star vehicle for the actor William Macready, incomparable as Coriolanus and Richard III. The excitement has been fanned by Talfourd's enterprising pre-circulation of the play to shrewdly selected eminent persons. Mr Cathcart, an actor, is 'so devoted to his art' that he has walked from Brighton to London to be present.[2] Macready, in ancient Greek costume, assumes the role of the foundling priest Ion and to rapturous applause leads the cast in an emotionally compelling enactment of a story set in heroic Argos (see Fig. 11.1). Like Euripides' Ion and Sophocles' Oedipus, Talfourd's Ion discovers that he is the hereditary monarch of his country: the difference is that this nineteenth-century Ion founds a republic and commits suicide.

Ion represents a remarkable moment in the history of British Hellenism's manifestations in the theatre. By the 1830s, when the Whigs returned to power after nearly fifty years in opposition, the theatre-going public had all but forgotten the adaptations of Greek tragedy which had entertained them during the Whig ascendancy of the eighteenth century, and the taste for which had been

---

[1] Macready (1912), i. 469; Robinson (1872), ii. 176, i. 214.
[2] Mary Russell Mitford (1872), ii. 261.

"In your presence
For now I feel you nigh, I dedicate
This arm to the destruction of the king
And of his race."

FIGURE 11.1   Martha Macready, *Macready as Ion* (1836).

fleetingly revived in the early 1820s. They were by now accustomed to seeing ancient Greece theatrically represented by the settings of stuntmen's spectaculars, like the hippodramatist Andrew Ducrow's *The Taming of Bucephalus, the Wild Horse of Scythia; or, the Youthful Days of Alexander the Great*, which had enthralled audiences at Astley's in the late 1820s.[3] *Ion*, together with Talfourd's other play inspired by Greek tragedy, *The Athenian Captive* (1838), was to constitute the last significant use of Greek tragedy on the professional stage for a radical political purpose until the Edwardian era. The only other successful nineteenth-century plays to draw their plots from ancient Greece or Rome were James Knowles's *Caius Gracchus* (1815) and *Virginius* (1820), which had both dramatized Roman themes.[4] Talfourd's plays, much the most radical theatre pieces of their time, were direct responses to it: in 1836 the country could still feel the enthusiasm for change which had resulted in the great Reform Act of 1832. Moreover, both their leading actor and their author were committed reformers. Macready was an ardent republican, and Talfourd a radical MP, committed to universal suffrage.[5]

Both Talfourd's 'ancient Greek' tragedies feature the deposition of a tyrannical hereditary monarch: by 1830 the words 'despotism' and 'tyranny' had been applied by both Whigs and radical democrats to the Tory administration around King George IV, who had incurred odium during the Queen Caroline scandal, and had never recovered popular support. When the incompetent William IV was crowned in 1830, he enjoyed a brief spell of popularity, but soon became disliked by both the working and the liberal middle classes, now hungry for change.

Reformers of the parliamentary system had by 1836 made progress. In 1828 Nonconformists had been allowed to qualify for public office by the repeal of the Test and Corporations Act; this was followed in 1829 by the Catholic Emancipation Act. Decades of Tory rule were ended by their defeat in the House of Commons in 1830, following a general election in which the two main issues of the campaign had been reform of parliament and the ending of

---

[3] British Museum playbills 170; see Saxon (1978), 147.

[4] Ernest Reynolds (1936), 118 n. 1.

[5] See Armstrong (1993), 154: 'much the most radical plays of this time were being written by Thomas Noon Talfourd'. See also the notice of Talfourd's elevation to the Bench in *ILN* 15, no. 382 (28 July 1849), 52 col. 3.

slavery. The great Reform Act of 1832, which had taken fifteen turbulent months to be passed by the Lords following its first introduction to parliament by Lord John Russell, had nearly doubled the size of the electorate. In 1833 slavery was ended. Other reformist legislation had followed quickly.

Most contemporary writers approved of the changes, and looked to the past for an genealogy of reform; after the Whigs' return to office in 1830 they sought historical precedents for a party which had been excluded from power for nearly half a century.[6] Some found them in the Renaissance, in sixteenth-century Protestants, or in the Roundheads of the seventeenth-century English Civil War. But Talfourd located the antecedents for constitutional reform and for the denunciation of slavery in archaic Greece.

Talfourd's tragedies were disregarded throughout much of the middle and later twentieth century.[7] Evaluated according to purely aesthetic criteria, the neglect is understandable. The poetry is derivative, the heroes implausibly selfless. But in his day Talfourd had the reputation of a foremost dramatist; in *A New Spirit of the Age* (1844) Richard Hengist Horne included an extended discussion of Talfourd, thus implicitly putting his achievements on a level with those of Dickens, Wordsworth, Tennyson, and Carlyle.[8] Leigh Hunt addressed no fewer than three sonnets to the author of *Ion* in the *New Monthly Magazine*, and the play was so popular amongst the reading public that it ran through two private and four public editions by 1837 (many more subsequently),[9] in addition to German and American editions.

Moreover, contemporary sources concur that the first night of *Ion* was a triumph. Some even thought that 'the Elizabethan age had returned, and that the old dramatists had returned in the

[6] Llewellyn (1972), 64.

[7] The play was still regarded as an important work of literature by some into the first four decades of the twentieth century: it was the subject of a Leipzig University dissertation by Saschek (1911), and before the Second World War an American academic, Robert S. Newdick, was writing two books on Talfourd (n.d. *a*, *b*). The undated and unpublished typescripts are housed in Reading Public Library and have been a useful source of factual information.

[8] Horne (1844), i. 245–60.

[9] The first public edition was *Ion, a Tragedy* (London, 1835), followed by the second edition (1835), the third (1836), and fourth (1837). *The Athenian Captive* was less widely read, enjoying only one solo publication (*The Athenian Captive, a Tragedy* [London, 1838]), although regularly appearing in collections of Talfourd's works.

person of Talfourd'.[10] *Ion*'s success inspired other historical tragedies: Browning's dramatic career began with his *Strafford*, in
1837. This play was composed directly for Macready, and it was at
the first-night party celebrating *Ion* that Browning broached with
him the possibility of this tragedy on English history.[11] Even
fashionable high society loved *Ion*: Macready continued to perform until at least the autumn of 1837, and one man of the theatre
recalls 'the unceasing rattle of the numerous carriages, bringing
aristocrat after aristocrat, to witness the triumph'.[12] Reviews
record such 'storms of applause as rarely trouble the stagnant
atmosphere of an English theatre'.[13] *Ion* received the undoubted
honour of a detailed dramatic travesty by Frederick Fox Cooper,
which was performed at the Garrick Theatre in November 1836,
and, with an almost entirely female cast, at the Queen's Theatre,
Whitechapel, in December.[14] The title role in the tragedy was
also taken by Talfourd's son Frank in front of distinguished
guests at a drawing-room production, in 1848, the same year
that undergraduate friends of Frank at Oxford were the first
nineteenth-century men to defy their university's ban on theatrical
performances by staging *Ion* at Brasenose College.[15]

Yet *Ion* was also seen as a heavyweight stage play of lasting
stature: amongst other London revivals, the play was performed
at Sadlers Wells in 1852 and 1861.[16] Unfortunate boys born in the
late 1830s risked being christened 'Ion'; passages from *Ion* were
translated by Samuel Butler's schoolboys at Shrewsbury into
Greek iambics.[17] It was still familiar in France in 1849,[18] and its
republican message made it popular in the USA, where it enthralled the Eliot Professor of Greek Literature at Harvard,

---

[10] Robinson (1872), i. 214; ii. 176; Brain (1904), 92–3.
[11] Miller (1953), 53–9.   [12] Macready (1912), i. 318; Fitzball (1859), ii. 97.
[13] *The Athenaeum*, no. 448 (28 May 1836), 386.
[14] Cooper (1836). See Nicoll (1952–9), iv. 283. *Ion Travestie* went to great lengths
to send up Macready's appearance and style of acting, with wild, carrot-coloured
wig and a comically erect posture. See Cooper (1836), 'Costumes' and notes on p. 8.
[15] Robinson (1872), ii. 288; 'The fight for the drama at Oxford', *The Oxford
Times*, 10 Sept. 1887.
[16] Thomas Noon Talfourd (1841–52), entry for 27 Apr. 1852; Newdick (n.d. *a*), 32.
[17] e.g. Ion Trant, a Cambridge undergraduate in 1859: see Burnand (1880), 186.
On the Shrewsbury iambics see British Museum Add. MS 34589 f. 325; Newdick
(n.d. *a*), 14–15.
[18] See Milsand (1849), 838: '*Ion* fut applaudi; et, entre les pièces modernes, on en
citerait peu qui se soient aussi bien maintenues au répertoire.'

Cornelius C. Felton, who was reminded of 'a long-lost work of Sophocles'.[19] It was performed in New York by December 1836, and often revived there until 1857.[20] Talfourd's brother Field (an artist known for the portrait of Elizabeth Barrett Browning which adorns the cover of most editions of her poems), saw it in Buffalo in 1853;[21] Mary Anderson starred as Ion in Boston in 1877 and 1881.[22] Professional performances were not uncommon in the USA at the turn of the twentieth century.[23]

THE PROVINCIAL BREWER'S SON

Talfourd was a humorous, sweet-tempered, and popular man, loved by some better remembered writers, especially Charles Dickens (see Fig. 11.2, Daniel Maclise's affectionate caricature of Talfourd, composed shortly after his triumph with *Ion*). Readers may have encountered him in the disguise of the innocent Tommy Traddles in *David Copperfield*; his children Frank and Kate gave their names to two youngsters in *Nicholas Nickleby*. He and his eccentric wife Rachel (the devout daughter of John Towill Rutt, a Nonconformist minister; she despised fashion and doted on cats) hosted famous dinners in their London residence at 56, Russell Square. These were attended by guests such as Douglas Jerrold, William Thackeray, Macready, Daniel Maclise, Mary Russell Mitford, and John Forster, the 'mutual friend' of many of Dickens' circle.[24] The parties were remembered for the presence of swarming children.

Talfourd's own grandfather was a Nonconformist minister in Reading; his father, a brewer, was also religious. Although Thomas attended the Protestant Dissenters' grammar school in Mill Hill for two years (1808–10), his most formative period was spent at Reading School under Dr Valpy. It was here that Talfourd, who became head boy, discovered his love of Greek tragedy. The performances of Greek drama so delighted him that he continued to promote them

---

[19] Felton (1837), 486.   [20] T. Allston Brown (1903), i. 49, 393, 427, 493.
[21] *Buffalo Commercial*, 23 May 1853.   [22] Newdick (n.d. *a*), 32.
[23] Ibid. 33.
[24] Cumberland Clark (1919), 10–11, 20. See also Fig. 11.2, from Bates (1873), 194. Talfourd also edited the works of Lamb and wrote standard essays on Dennis and Rymer: see Anon. (1854). For further details of Talfourd's life and achievements outside the theatre, see *ODNB* liii. 735–7 (Edith Hall).

FIGURE 11.2   Thomas Noon Talfourd by Daniel Maclise (published 1873).

as an adult by reviewing them in the national press. He later claimed that it was Dr Valpy and his theatrical productions that had awakened within him the admiration for classical drama that lay behind the genesis of his *Ion*.[25] Although there does not seem to have been a staged performance of *Ion* at Reading school, Talfourd probably encountered the play via Gilbert Wakefield's 1794 school selection of Greek tragedies, with notes, from which Dr Valpy must have taught (see Ch. 9). Wakefield's second volume contained *Ion*, *Philoctetes*, and *Eumenides*.[26] On the other hand Talfourd is most unlikely to have read the two relatively recent German experiments with *Ion*, since, despite his radical outlook, he remained a doggedly provincial patriot.[27] He was proud of his inability to speak any foreign languages, was an enthusiast for English food and drink, and by 1836 had only left Britain on a single occasion, for a brief business trip to Portugal in 1818.[28]

Talfourd also developed at Reading School his enthusiasm for good causes, precociously publishing *Poems on Various Subjects* (1811), including 'The Education of the Poor', a biblical tragedy entitled 'The Offering of Isaac', and a pamphlet against the use of the pillory.[29] His family's poverty prevented his attending university; instead he chose a career in law (he eventually became a judge), combined with literature and reformist politics. His democratic idealism is evident from the speech he delivered to 'thunderous' applause at Reading town hall after the Peterloo Massacre in 1819, using an allusion to Greek mythology to make his point:[30]

Free and open discussion is the Promethean heat, without which the noblest constitution would be useless...The tombs of the victims at Manchester must become altars on which the friends of liberty must swear eternal union.[31]

---

[25] Thomas Noon Talfourd (1844), 3–4.

[26] Talfourd may also have read William Whitehead's *Creusa* (see Ch. 5), and there is also just possibly some connection with mysterious watercolour sketches for a putative production of Euripides' *Ion* by the English architect and classical perspectivist Joseph Michael Gandy, painted in around 1820, and now housed in the Getty Research Library Special Collections.

[27] On Johann Jakob Bodmer's narrative poem *Kreusa* (1777), and August Wilhelm von Schlegel's adaptation *Ion*, a drama first performed at Weimar, under Goethe's direction, in January 1802, see Franke (1939), 14–15, 134–42.

[28] See *ODNB* liii. 736.

[29] Brain (1904), 72–5.

[30] Ibid. 86.

[31] Quoted from the *Reading Mercury*, of 1819, ibid. 84–5.

Talfourd was first elected Member of Parliament for Reading in 1835; he was re-elected on the accession of Queen Victoria in 1837 and once again in 1847. His political career was devoted to philanthropy: in 1837, encouraged by Wordsworth, he delivered a crucial speech in a debate preceding the introduction of the 1842 Copyright Act (popularly known as 'Talfourd's Act'), which helped the indigent relations of deceased writers. This earned him the gratitude of Charles Dickens, who applauded the initiative in the touching dedication to *The Pickwick Papers* (1837). Talfourd was also responsible for the pathbreaking Custody of Infants Act, 'conferring on unhappy wives, separated from their husbands, a right to have a sight of their children'.[32] This piece of legislation, along with Talfourd's important contribution to the 1843 repeal of the Theatrical Patents Act, will become significant below, in Ch. 14.

Talfourd's rise from poverty-stricken provincial obscurity to attendance at the dinner parties of the London elite astonished his contemporaries, including the diarist Henry Crabb Robinson.[33] For Talfourd was a grammar-school boy from (at best) the lower middle class, who appropriated the ancient Greeks—*without* a university education—in the cause of reform. He was a literary analogue of those new men, often nonconformists enriched by trade, who began in the 1830s to patronize Classics and fine arts, thus usurping the aristocracy's control of culture.[34] This process had begun two decades earlier, as Graeco-Roman antiquities had accumulated at the British Museum. By 1830 ordinary people could visit one of the richest repositories of such objects in the world, and this was crucial to the creation of a cultured middle class.[35] Certainly it required familiarity with the statuary of the Parthenon for Talfourd's audience to visualize his Ismene in *The Athenian Captive*, kneeling 'At stern Minerva's inmost shrine', 'with an arm as rigid | As is the giant statue' (I. i). Certainly it

---

[32] Robinson (1872), i. 214.

[33] Ibid. ii. 174 (entry for 8 May 1836): 'In the evening called at Talfourd's. He was gone to dine with Lord Melbourne. I knew Talfourd when he was a young man studying the law, unable to follow the profession but by earning money as a reporter.... He now dines with the Prime Minister. I must add a more upright and honourable man never existed.'

[34] Frank Davis (1963), 13–14.

[35] See Grewal (1990), 209. On the impact on British Romantic poets of the Elgin marbles and Greek sculpture generally, see Larrabee (1943), especially the discussion of Byron and Shelley (149–203).

took a grasp of art history to appreciate the critic who in 1844 defined the effect of *Ion*'s old-and-new classicism as that of an austere Doric temple at Athens filled with the 'elegant statues of Canova'.[36]

If Talfourd discovered that mythical Greeks could be as modern and elegant as Canova's artworks, he also saw that they could be as sympathetic as the characters in popular fiction. Contemporary literature was increasingly stressing the ordinary and the domestic, especially in the popular comic writing of Dickens and Thackeray. But the new interest in bourgeois domesticity seeped even into interpretations of 'heroic' subject-matter, leading to a fascination with the family life of historical personages such as Charles I,[37] or even archaic heroes such as Talfourd's Ion, who is given a home life of affectionate intimacy with his foster-father and his adoptive sister Clemanthe, played with an impressive aura of piety by Ellen Tree (see Fig. 11.3).

Talfourd's lively, elegant, domesticated ancient Greeks are symptomatic of the contemporary reaction against the elite's control of classical education. Talfourd was an intimate friend and collaborator of Edward Bulwer (in 1836 they edited Hazlitt together). In the preface to *The Last Days of Pompeii* (1834), Bulwer (he had not yet renamed himself Bulwer-Lytton) complains that the northern imagination has been alienated from the classical age 'by the scholastic pedantries which first acquainted us with their nature', and proposes that it is a better plan 'to people once more those graceful ruins. To reanimate the bones . . . to traverse the gulph of eighteen centuries . . .'.[38] In *Ion* the audience traversed a 'gulph' of twenty-five centuries, and realized that the ancient Greeks were animate, sentient humans just like them. A perception running through the reactions is that *Ion*'s classicism was offering something palpably warmer—more human and lifelike—than any classical tragedy before. Dramatists had usually written

as if the Greeks and Romans of other days were stiff, passionless, and bloodless, as the statues which represent them. This is not the case with 'Ion', which was a beautiful and interesting specimen of life, as doubtless it passed in the days of Ion's existence.[39]

---

[36] Horne (1844), i. 254–6.   [37] Stein (1987), 72.
[38] Bulwer (1834), pp. vii, v.   [39] Fitzball (1859), ii. 96–7.

FIGURE 11.3   Ellen Tree as Clemanthe in the original production of
Talfourd's *Ion* at Covent Garden (1836).

The play also reflects the influence upon Talfourd of romantic
Hellenism. His poetry overflows with the literary images which the
Romantics had absorbed into their mental landscape of Hellas: the
glimmering moonbeams, lonely fanes, white columns, and
saddening cypress by the Cephisus proliferate as much in Talfourd
as in Lord Byron's *Curse of Minerva* (1812).[40] But Talfourd had
also learnt from Keats, and from Shelley's translations and adaptations of Greek texts, that Greek mythology need not be merely

[40] Levin (1931), 33.

ornamental. It could be used as a potent arena for the exploration of social and political concerns. Talfourd was attached to Shelley's writings: a few years after his own 'Grecian' tragedies he was successfully to defend *Queen Mab* against an attempt to censor it on the ground of its alleged atheism.[41] Although *Ion* feels more mythical, while *The Athenian Captive* tends to the pseudo-historical, both Talfourd's tragedies are insistently future-focused, envisaging utopias in a brave new world after the fall of tyrants: this was a use of Greek myth and ancient Greek heroes derived from Shelley's interest in the implications of the Greek past for an impending new golden age.[42] Greek literature, for Talfourd, revealed from the past a potentiality for people to live in utopian freedom, a potentiality which could therefore be realized once again in the future. As Shelley had put it,

What the Greeks were, was a reality, not a promise. And what we are and hope to be, is derived, as it were, from the influence and inspiration of those glorious generations.[43]

ION AND THE GREAT REFORM ACT

Ion is a five-act drama in pleasantly archaizing iambic pentameters with a simple plot. The foundling hero has been fostered by a priest of Apollo at Argos. The city is being oppressed by a cruel king, Adrastus, and is suffering from a plague. It transpires in Act II from an oracle that Apollo requires a republic:

> Argos ne'er shall find release
> Till her monarch's race shall cease.

But Ion discovers that he is of the 'monarch's race', for Adrastus is his father. After Adrastus has been assassinated Ion must commit suicide in order that Argos may 'find release'.

Talfourd's story fuses the foundling priest-king from Euripides' *Ion* with the plague-bringing king from Sophocles' *Oedipus Tyrannus*; the motif of the patriotic youth's suicide owes something to Euripides' *Phoenician Women*. In the exciting recognition scene

---

[41] Thomas Noon Talfourd (1841).

[42] Webb (1982), 25–6. On Shelley's 'regenerative' view of history, including ancient Greek history, see Kucich (1996).

[43] David Lee Clark (1966), 219.

(IV. i), the reconciliation of the dying king Adrastus with his long-lost son Ion recalls the endings of both *Hippolytus* and *Trachiniae*. The play's title is designed to draw attention to its classical heritage; Talfourd wrote that it was Euripides' *Ion*

which gave the first hint of the situation in which its hero is introduced—that of a foundling youth educated in a temple, and assisting in its services; but otherwise there is no resemblance between this imperfect sketch and that exquisite picture.[44]

This disclaimer is not entirely true. Several features have been absorbed from the Euripidean prototype, especially a certain sweetness of atmosphere and the moral probity of its hero: Ion in Talfourd is only forced into wrongdoing because it is justified in the name of a higher principle. There are also echoes in terms of detail: Ion was abandoned in a sacred grove, just as Euripides' hero had been left by his mother in a place of religious significance.

Yet the play's most important influences are Sophocles' Theban plays. Like several English radicals before him (see Ch. 8), Talfourd saw in *Oedipus Tyrannus* the concept of the plague-bringing hereditary dynasty of kings, who must be destroyed in the cause of their citizens' welfare. *OT* also supplied the opening sequence at the temple of Apollo: Agenor, an old sage of Argos, laments the plague afflicting the city (I. i). Ion first encounters the tyrannical monarch Adrastus when delivering a message from the sages of Apollo, just as Creon in the *OT* arrives with news from the Delphic oracle; Adrastus responds to the news of Ion's arrival much as Oedipus responds to Tiresias' prophecies, with a paranoid accusation that the sages are 'sophist traitors' bent on deposing him. Oedipus swears to root out the slayer of Laius, who turns out to be himself: Ion swears to shed the blood not only of the tyrant Adrastus but of any child he might have fathered, since that 'is needful to the sacrifice | My country asks' (III. ii).

Antigone lies behind Ion's encounter with Adrastus, which has been forbidden on pain of death. The old king, shunned by his foremost citizens and courtiers, has locked himself away and banned all visits by his subjects, thus transparently imitating the dissolute seclusion into which George IV had retired in the late 1820s. The youthful Ion shares numerous features with Antigone:

---

[44] Thomas Noon Talfourd (1844), 7–8.

he has disobeyed the tyrant's edict, is convinced that he is defended by the 'strengths of heaven', and that he is opposing Adrastus' temporary human law with 'the eternal law' (II. i). Adrastus, in turn, is modelled on Creon, the archetypal tyrant in *Antigone*: Talfourd was devoted to this play, in which he may have performed at Reading School in 1812.

Talfourd also loved *Oedipus at Colonus*, remarking, in an essay on the theory of tragedy, 'how reconciling and tender, yet how awful, the circumstances attendant upon the death of Œdipus!'[45] This synthesis of tenderness and awe informs the inexorable sense of duty and piety driving Ion towards parricide (which in the event is avoided) and subsequently towards his own death. Talfourd called this compulsion

> the idea of *fascination*, as an engine by which Fate may work its purposes on the innocent mind, and force it into terrible action most uncongenial to itself, but necessary to the issue.[46]

This 'fascination' is a peculiarly Romantic concept, shared, amongst others, with the philhellene Byron: late in his short life he had described his own magnetic attraction—physical and spiritual—to Greece and her liberation as a 'maddening fascination'.[47]

Talfourd was fortunate in his actors. Macready apart, John Vandenhoff was excellent in the role of Ion's despotic father Adrastus. Vandenhoff was a Latin scholar and former classical teacher,[48] whose interest in classical subject-matter later resulted in his famous realization of the role of Creon in Sophocles' *Antigone* at Covent Garden (1845; see Ch. 12). He was an old-fashioned actor, regarded as 'the last prominent tragedian of the Kemble school, having a good deal of the stately carriage and bold outline of his predecessor'; in the role of Adrastus his 'pathetic bursts', in contrast with his repressed dignity, were apparently 'very telling'.[49]

For Adrastus is no two-dimensional tyrant: the play emphasizes the essential humanity even of royalty. Ion pities Adrastus,

---

[45] Thomas Noon Talfourd (1850*a*), 21–8 at p. 26.
[46] Thomas Noon Talfourd (1844), 8.
[47] See Byron's fragmentary 'Last Words on Greece', with Levin (1931), 50: 'What are to me those honours or renown | Past or to come, a new-born people's cry? | . . . | Such is this maddening fascination grown | So strong thy magic or so weak am I.'
[48] Vandenhoff (1860), 30–1.
[49] Marston (1888), i. 22.

however despotic, because he is 'childless, friendless, and a king'
(I. i); Adrastus only developed into a bitter, cruel old man because
of a series of emotional deprivations in his youth. Yet Adrastus is
clearly now a Tory renegade. In 1836 the audience must have been
acutely aware of recent legislation designed to regulate working
conditions for the labouring classes, such as the Factory Act of
1833, and the Poor Law Amendment Act of 1834, intended to
fight rural poverty. Against this backdrop Adrastus' expressed
views on the lower orders associated him with the Tory landowners (despite their intermittent crocodile tears over the industrial workers employed by their Whig opponents), with whom
Talfourd and Macready were in such disagreement. Adrastus des-
pises 'artizans', believing them to be gullibly vulnerable to dema-
gogues, and his opinion of the agricultural labourer is as low. In a
familiar type of Tory rant, he says he has never been prepared to be
accountable to

> the common herd,
> The vassals of our ancient house, the mass
> Of bones and muscles framed to till the soil
> A few brief years, then rot unnamed beneath it. (II. i)

Adrastus is a cynical, bitter, arbitrary relic of an ancient Greek
ancien régime, prophetically aware that he is 'sad heritor' of 'a great
race of kings' whose 'doom is nigh' (II. i). He is thus like the
protagonists of the numerous apocalyptic and anxiety-laden 'last
of the race' novels produced in this period, from James Fenimore
Cooper's *The Last of the Mohicans* (1826) to Bulwer's *The Last
Days of Pompeii* (1834);[50] he is also like Creon in *Antigone*, in that
he knows that if his power (and the monarchy itself) is to last he
must apply the laws he has decreed even if he is reluctant to do so
(II. i):

> Or the great sceptre which hath sway'd the fears
> Of ages, will become a common staff
> For youth to wield, or age to rest upon,
> Despoil'd of all its virtues.

The full political thrust of the play is not revealed until the final
scene of the last act (V. iii). The scene is set in the great square of

---

[50] On which see Stafford (1994), especially the chapter on Bulwer (ch. 10).

the city: 'on one side a Throne of state prepared,—on the other an Altar,—the Statues decorated with garlands'. The 'Priests, Sages, and People' process onto the stage, followed by Ion 'in royal robes. He advances amidst shouts, and speaks'. For the new king of Argos has a four-point plan to announce for its constitutional reform.

Benthamite Utilitarians believed that law is 'not antecedent to the state, but the making of it the proper activity of the state';[51] in *Ion* the theatre-going public of the 1830s could enjoy watching a complex constitutional overhaul being undertaken in the city-state of ancient Argos. First, to Agenor, the trusted old sage who brought him up, Ion entrusts the overseeing of appointments to legislative bodies and the judiciary. These officials are to be good and sympathetic men. Ion instructs him,

> To rule our councils; fill the seats of justice
> With good men not so absolute in goodness
> As to forget what human frailty is;
> And order my sad country.

At the time of the production of *Ion* appointments to the judiciary had become a red-hot issue. It had been agreed in 1835 that municipalities were to have a bigger say in the selection of their Justices of the Peace, and throughout 1836 Whig Justices of the Peace were elected in town and country, much to the chagrin of Tory magistrates. *Ion* reflects this concern with the administration of justice, and installs a fairer system at Argos: *The Athenian Captive* implies the impossibility of a fair judicial system under a corrupt constitution in the murder trial which constitutes Act V. The solution is to import some noble-minded young Athenians to supervise the proceedings (IV. iii)!

Step two in Ion's constitutional overhaul is to disband and exile the army. The maintenance of a standing army had in reality long been a contentious political issue, but there is even a hint here of an anti-imperialist sentiment: Crythes, Captain of the Royal Guard, is shocked at Ion's demilitarization of the state, and asks him,

> Dost intend
> To banish the firm troops before whose valour
> Barbarian millions shrink appall'd . . . ?

---

[51] Llewellyn (1972), 9.

The empire which the Whigs inherited in 1830 already included a large dependency in India, a foothold in the south of Africa, and the plantation colonies of the West Indies where slavery was not ended until 1833, but many radicals were now as reluctant as Ion to extend the dominions.

Ion's third step is to outlaw monarchy and transfer sovereignty to the Argives themselves.

> Never more
> Let the great interests of the state depend
> Upon the thousand chances that may sway
> A piece of human frailty! Swear to me
> That you will seek hereafter in yourselves
> The means of sovereign rule.

Ion is prepared to envisage that a state with large territories might need the unifying symbol of a ruler: Argos, not being large,

> Needs not the magic of a single name
> Which wider regions may require to draw
> Their interests into one.

But even this lone concession to royalty is couched in conditional terms ('*may* require'). Ion sees monarchy's function not as to govern or legislate, but solely to provide the unifying focus of a single figurehead for a plurality of regions. The issue of the size of the democratic city-state may have more to with the series of acts of 1835, following the Municipal Corporations Commission, which brought about the experience of radical democracy at least on a local level. Local politics now gave the British people their first heady taste of representative democracy in which the franchise was not based on property qualifications.

Ion is shortly to secure his fourth guarantee that after his death,

> the sovereign power shall live
> In the affections of the general heart,
> And in the wisdom of the best.

Despite the (probably deliberate) poetic vagueness of this prescription, it is difficult not to read Ion's final clause as a dramatic legitimization of the 1832 Reform Act; the sovereign power is to exist in the 'affections of *the general heart*', implying the universal male suffrage for which William Cobbett had already been calling in the 1820s and for which Talfourd campaigned. The 'wisdom of the best' probably means the elected representatives of the sovereign population. Talfourd was certainly on the radical wing of the Whig administration, but believed that the middle classes had something special to offer the newly enfranchised masses: he was to distance himself from the more extreme Chartists at the end of the decade.

Thus Ion's constitutional overhaul seems to entail not an entirely levelled society, but one in which all classes share sovereignty and coexist in harmony. The state is to be governed 'tenderly' and 'by simple laws'; 'all degrees' are to be 'moulded together as a single form'. This utopian prescription is the product of a time when writers from Benjamin Disraeli and Thomas Carlyle to Elizabeth Gaskell were noticing the fragmentation of society into separate interest groups.[52] In archaic Argos Ion solves the problem by inviting those very artisans and agricultural labourers whom Adrastus had despised to partake in the sovereignty of this idyllic, kingless state.

Ion, as the last king of Argos, now stabs himself to death. He has delivered the Argives from tyranny and plague; as their last ever constitutional monarch he dies to secure their freedom from monarchy. Talfourd had refused to contemplate using any actor other than William Macready, and he was fortunate that Macready (who was pursued by aspiring playwrights) agreed to take on the play: the public's renewal of interest in serious drama from around 1830 was a direct result of his performances at Covent Garden. After careful rehearsal, detailed in his diary, he gave a brilliant performance on the first night. He was particularly pleased with his characterization of 'the devotion of Ion to the destruction of Adrastus . . . and in the last scene',[53] that is, in the two most blatantly political sequences. Given the importance of individual star actors to the theatre of this period,[54] and Macready's own attraction to the role of Ion, it is important to appreciate how the identity of the actor must have augmented the political meaning of the play in performance.

---

[52] Ibid. (1972), 14.
[53] W. C. Macready (1912), i. 318. See Fig. 11.1 above, in which Ion swears to slay Adrastus.
[54] See Emeljanow (1987), 5 and 12: it was 'Macready's encouragement that brought temporary fame to writers like Talfourd'.

Childhood privations caused by his father's imprisonment had led this Rugby-educated middle-class boy to become an ardent republican. He loathed the monarchy with an unusual intensity: his diary records the bitterness with which in 1847 he spurned an invitation from Queen Victoria to perform passages to her from the English translation of 'Mendelssohn's' *Antigone* (on which see the next chapter).[55] He banned the phrase 'lower classes', insisting that they be called 'poorer classes'.[56] As actor-manager of Covent Garden from 1837 he incurred odium in the highest places by allowing Anti-Corn-Law meetings to be held in the theatre.[57] Throughout his career he chose roles which allowed him to impersonate 'the defender of the Hearth, Home, and the People against the brutality of tyrants', and to pour out 'the zeal and heat of his own political convictions',[58] including James Knowles's stirring *Virginius* (1820).[59] Watching this republican actor playing a Greek hero who dies to put an end to a corrupt royal family must have been quite an experience.

Ion enacts the transference of power in Argos from the aristocracy to the middle and (to a lesser extent) working classes, and a change in value-system from heredity to meritocracy; in *The Athenian Captive* power is transferred from a lawless tyrant to a young, moderate monarch, with the idealized democratic Athens on the horizon. Ancient Greece thus provides a theatrical context for the fictive replaying of the history of the 1830s, which had seen near-revolution, radical reform, and finally an accommodation with a new, young, domesticated monarch.

ATHENS AND ARGOS IN THE 1830S

The last years of Tory rule in the 1820s had seen the Greek revolt and the birth of an independent Greece. The Romantics' association of *ancient* Greece with their more vaguely conceptualized 'liberty' was lent concrete form by the Greek War of Independence.[60] As we have seen in the previous chapter, the war itself provided material for the popular stage, but it also stimulated the drawing of parallels between ancient Greek struggles for liberty

---

[55] Macready (1912), ii. 301.   [56] Marston (1888), i. 65.
[57] Horne (1844), ii. 119.   [58] Shattock (1958), 5.
[59] Emeljanow (1987), 12–13; Shattock (1958), 2, 5, 23.
[60] See Jenkyns (1980), 15; Tsigakou (1981), 46–7.

and the modern Greek dream of liberation from Turkish domination. Yet this very war stopped what little tourism had previously
operated in Greece,[61] making the country a peculiarly blank canvas
on which romantic radicals like Talfourd could inscribe their
utopian and reformist fantasies. The great 'oath' scene in which
his Ion swears to take up arms in the cause of liberty, for example,
is informed by the classical models provided by the pagan Leonidas
at Thermopylae and by the oath of the Horatii, familiar from Whitehead's tragedy *The Roman Father* (see pp. 129, 141) and above all
from David's already famous painting *Le Serment des Horaces*
(1784). But a more immediate reference is the 'oath' theme popular
amongst painters responding in the 1820s to the Greek uprising, for
example Michel Philibert Genod's *The Oath of the Young Warrior*.
The Greek youth portrayed is a pious Christian, swearing on his
weapon as he departs to confront the Turkish infidel.[62]

In the 1830s ancient Greece was an ideological minefield. One
year after *Ion*, and one year before *The Athenian Captive*, Talfourd's friend Bulwer published part of his history of Athens,
commenting that 'the history of the Greek Republics has been
too often corruptly pressed into the service of heated political
partisans'.[63] The partisans to whom he referred included William
Mitford (no relation of Mary Russell Mitford), whose conservative
The History of Greece (the first volume was published in 1784), a
massive account from the perspective of Tory landowners, had
indicted Athenian democracy. It had consequently 'more than
anything else legitimized the use of Athenian history as a vehicle
for debating in detail the wisdom and viability of modern democratic government'.[64] Mitford's interpretation of Athenian history
was to dictate the parameters of the debate and find its way into
encyclopaedias and textbooks beyond the middle of the nineteenth
century, certainly until the first volume of Grote's pro-Athenian
and pro-democratic account was published in 1846.[65]

But ranged against the anti-democratic critique of classical
Athens was the adulation of her democracy expressed by radical

---

[61] Pemble (1988), 48.   [62] See Athanassoglou-Kallmyer (1989), 19–20.

[63] Bulwer (1837), i, p. viii.

[64] For the fundamental account of Mitford, Grote, and the debate over the
Athenian constitution see Turner (1981), 192–244. See also A. Momigliano's inaugural lecture, 'George Grote and the study of Greek history', delivered at University College, London in 1952, and published in Momigliano (1969), 56–74.

[65] On the conflicting British attitudes to Greek history in this period, see also the
more recent discussion by Jennifer Tolbert Roberts (1994), 229–304.

British supporters of the French revolution: Tom Paine's followers, for example, had included in the repertoire of liberty songs
they sang at their meetings an ode based on the old Athenian song
in praise of the tyrannicides Harmodius and Aristogeiton.[66] Views
of ancient Athens had been implicated in the movement for reform
in the 1820s and early 1830s: Thomas Arnold's edition of Thucydides, published between 1830 and 1835, draws parallels between William Cobbett and the ancient Athenian demagogue
Cleon;[67] the year before the production of *Ion* saw the publication
of the first volume of Bishop Connop Thirlwall's eight-volume
History of Greece, (1835–44), which was not pro-Athenian, but
whose moderation 'implicitly neutralized Athens as a stock weapon
in the conservative armoury'.[68]

Talfourd carved out an ambiguous path for his Ion, aligning
himself with those who applauded the ancient democracies while
holding back from explicit advocacy of republicanism itself (neither the word 'republic' nor 'democracy' is ever actually used). Ion
is no hardbitten regicide: he regards actual assassination as permissible only if 'the audible voice of Heaven' calls an individual to
'that dire office' (I. i). Ion prefers to encourage insurrection by
speeches consisting of 'words which bear the spirits of great deeds |
Wing'd for the Future; which the dying breath of Freedom's
martyr shapes as it exhales...' (I. i). But evidence that *Ion* was
certainly perceived in 1836 to be a radically political drama comes
from the comic parody by Frederick Fox Cooper staged late in that
year. Cooper published an essay with *Ion Travestie*, in which he
remarks that the tragedy's sentiments were all 'on the side of
liberty... Liberalism "goes the whole hog".' In the travesty the
character of Irus is conceived as a black slave, who has suffered
terrible treatment, but celebrates the reforms about to be enacted
in Argos by singing (24–5) that now he is at last 'emancipate' he can
'get into de parliament | And represent de nation!'

It is most significant that Talfourd transfers the political focus
altogether from Athens to Argos. One of the attractions of the

[66] See Woodcock (1989), 27. The Athenian song was translated and the English
ode composed by the republican Sir William Jones, the great oriental scholar
associated with the experiments with Greek tragedy in the 1770s at Stanmore
School, discussed above (Ch. 8).
[67] Turner (1981), 209.
[68] Ibid. 211.

semi-fictive context of archaic Argos must have been its very vagueness: although this city-state was democratic during some parts of the classical period, little is known of earlier Argive politics, which made Talfourd's idea of a constitutional overhaul reasonably believable. But more importantly, in Euripides the foundling Ion is revealed to be the true-born king of *Athens*, not only with a *hereditary* right to the throne, but since a god (Apollo) is his father, with an absolute *divine* right to rule. In Talfourd's play Ion kills himself rather than perpetuate a corrupt monarchy: Athens itself, against the background of William Mitford and Tom Paine, might have been too nakedly political a setting, but Ion's suicide must have been especially significant to those who knew the Euripidean prototype.

SLAVERY, SHELLEY, AND UTOPIA

The political trajectory of *The Athenian Captive* is similar to that of *Ion*: it portrays a Greek people's revolt against an autocrat (in this case named Creon), and his destruction. But a major difference between the two tragedies is that the republican tenor of *Ion* is replaced in *The Athenian Captive* by a less constitutionally specific appeal for 'liberty'. Corinth remains a monarchy, even if it is implicitly presented as inferior to the democratic Athens whence arrives the play's hero (Thoas played by Macready). Yet it can hardly be irrelevant that Talfourd's second and considerably less anti-monarchical 'Greek' play was produced at the Haymarket in August 1838, a year *after* the death of William IV and the young Queen Victoria's accession. In *The Athenian Captive* a corrupt old monarch in Corinth is replaced by a virtuous young one, as if to echo the hopes of the liberal British middle classes in respect to their youthful new queen.

The plot entails the arrival at Corinth of Thoas, an Athenian prisoner of war (with a Euripidean name) who does not know that he is the long-lost son of the Corinthian tyrant Creon and his wife, an Athenian aristocrat. Thoas is enslaved, kills Creon, finds out his true identity, and kills himself to prevent his accidental act of parricide from polluting the people. He leaves them in the benevolent hands of Creon's young son Hyllus. The echoes of Athenian tragedy are louder even than in *Ion*, especially during the assassination of Creon, in which the offstage death-cries typical of regicidal scenes in Greek theatre are imitated. Euripides' *Ion* was again an inspiration: *The Athenian Captive* opens at a temple where a priest watches the flight of the birds (the opening line is 'Wheel through the ambient air, ye sacred birds'), and when Thoas' mother Ismene recognizes the illegitimate son whom she bore in lonely maidenhood in Athens (III. ii), the language is reminiscent of the mother-son recognition scene in Euripides' *Ion*.

Creon is named after the Corinthian king in Euripides' *Medea*, and the Corinthian setting, the pervasive eulogy of Athens, and Creon's speech in which he exiles his son Hyllus are all suggestive of that tragedy. Another influence is Sophocles' *Electra*: Creon's son Hyllus is injured in the chariot race at the Corinthian games, and the messenger describes the accident in lines inspired by the Sophoclean *paidagōgos*' false messenger speech reporting the death of Orestes in the chariot race at the Pythian games. In one scene Creusa addresses the urn containing her dead father's ashes (IV. i), which is rendered more profound if the contrast with its prototype in Sophocles' *Electra* is held in mind. But Thoas' 'mad' scene after he kills Creon (III. iii), the brother–sister bond between Creusa and Hyllus, and the intensity of the relationship between Thoas and Hyllus, are imitations of the deranged Orestes' relationships with Electra and Pylades in at least five Greek tragedies. These include Euripides' *Orestes*, which Talfourd had seen in the performance at Reading School in 1821 (see Ch. 9).

Although the overtly anti-monarchical tone of *Ion* is missing from *The Athenian Captive*, Athens, which has no sovereign, is once again idealized: the focus has shifted from the idealization of a system (people's sovereignty) to idealization of a specific place. Talfourd taps directly into a now traditional image of Athens, the hugely potent 'ideal city of the mind',[69] the Athens Shelley had described in *Hellas* (1822) as 'Based on the crystalline sea | Of thought and eternity' (698–9). Creon once raped Ismene, an Athenian patrician, whose loveliness and grace he ascribes to her Athenian provenance (I. i). Nostalgic for home, Thoas cries (I. i),

> I seem
> Once more to drink Athenian ether in

[69] Webb (1982), 3.

> And the fair city's column'd glories flash
> Upon my soul.

When Ismene asks him how, though only a soldier, he learnt to think loftily, he responds (III. ii),

> From Athens;
> Her groves; her halls; her temples; nay, her streets
> Have been my teachers.

Had he been raised anywhere else, he says, as an orphan he would have been 'rude'. But the education provided by Athenian civic life had proved sufficient even to a poor orphan, raised by 'an old citizen' who lived (like Electra's husband in Euripides' *Electra*) in a lowly hut.

When Creon insults Athens at the victory feast, Thoas risks his life to defend his city's name. He goes into a state of what Hyllus calls 'ecstacy' and 'frenzy' as he characterizes Athens as 'the purest flame the gods | Have lit from heaven's own fire'. He continues,

> 'Tis not a city crown'd
> With olive and enrich'd with peerless fanes
> Ye would dishonour, but an opening world
> Diviner than the soul of man hath yet
> Been gifted to imagine—truths serene,
> Made visible in beauty, that shall glow
> In everlasting freshness . . .
> . . . on the stream of time, from age to age
> Casting bright images of heavenly youth
> To make the world less mournful.

Like Walter Savage Landor's Pericles in *Imaginary Conversations* (1824) and many ancient Greeks in nineteenth-century English literature, Thoas speaks very much in the future tense: 'A Victorian might try to imagine himself as an ancient Greek, but the Greek that he became tended to be one strangely obsessed with the future.'[70] The 'pure beauty' of Athens, 'the Queen of cities', we are assured, will be responsible for 'empearling starless ages' (IV. ii). Salamis remains in the future: Asia will at some time invade with her ships, but they will be swept away 'As glittering clouds before the sun-like face | Of unapplianced virtue' (IV. ii; 'unapplianced probably means 'natural'). There is a good deal more of

---

[70] Jenkyns (1980), 53.

this prophetic Athenophilic mysticism; in prison Thoas comforts himself (unironically) with 'airy visions' of Athens' future greatness. When he philanthropically kills himself, to curb his parricidal pollution,[71] his dying words request that he be returned (v. i):

> To the city of my love;
> Her future years of glory stream more clear
> Than ever on my soul. O Athens! Athens!

Talfourd was not the only radical provincial politician who saw a connection between the democratic society whose creation the reforms of the 1830s had made possible and the glories of Periclean Athens. In 1832 the man who had played the crucial role in the drawing up of the terms of the bill was John Lambton, first Earl of Durham, known to his constituents as 'Radical Jack'. When he died prematurely, the monument that local businessmen erected in 1844 to dominate the early Victorian skyline at Penshaw (between Durham and Sunderland) was a proud replica of the Athenian Theseion, symbol of Pericles' building programme and of Athenian democracy in its prime (see Fig. 11.4).

The bill to abolish slavery was passed in 1833; another political strand in the play is its denunciation of slavery, as suffered at Corinth by the (apparently) ordinary Athenian Thoas. He refuses to take off his helmet in front of the king, and when offered the choice of slavery or death, responds, 'Dost dare | Insult a son of Athens by the doubt | Thy words imply?' The play's most theatrically powerful feature is the contrast between Thoas' first armoured, helmeted entry in Act I and his second, in a slave's garb, in Act II. When Lycus, the wicked slave-master comes to give him servile dress, Thoas laments,

> Must an Athenian warrior's free-born limbs
> Be clad in withering symbols of the power
> By which man marks his property in flesh...?

Macaulay, at least, would have had something to say about Talfourd's idealization of Athens and his implication that slavery was not a problem there: in his essay on the Comte de Mirabeau (July 1832) he criticizes those revolutionary leaders who chant rhapsodies

---

[71] This was the performed conclusion, for which Macready was largely responsible; Talfourd had planned that Thoas should persuade Hyllus to kill him. The original ending is printed as an appendix in Talfourd (1844), 264–8.

FIGURE 11.4 The Penshaw Monument, near Sunderland.

to Athenian democracy while forgetting about Athenian slavery.[72] But Talfourd did really mean it: the *Reading Mercury* of 5 May 1838 reports that he spoke with considerable passion on the subject of 'Negro Emancipation' at a public meeting in his constituency. The action of the play throughout underlines the equality of all members of mankind and the inhumanity of slavery, especially in the friendship between Hyllus and Thoas, which transcends superficial markers of status and race, and Hyllus' fantasy that he and Thoas can exchange clothes and thus erase the social boundary dividing them.

NONCONFORMIST ION

Talfourd, born in the eighteenth century, retained an affection for neoclassical tragedy and its practitioners: he was just old enough to have been mightily impressed by Mrs Siddons at the end of her

[72] See Clive (1989), 109.

career in 1812.[73] He also owed much to Joseph Addison's *Cato*, that
manifesto of Whiggish patriotism first produced at Drury Lane in
1713 and subsequently becoming a staple of the eighteenth- and
early-nineteenth-century staged historical imagination.[74] Talfourd
had seen Kemble in the starring role, and had himself performed
the play in private theatricals.[75] Like Addison's Cato, both Talfourd's classical heroes commit suicide in the name of the common
good, and the parallel was sensed by the shrewder of his contemporaries: Horne saw *Ion* as profiting from the legacy of *Cato*, but
substituting for pity, terror, and the intellectual force of eighteenth-
century tragedy, 'a moral power' which induces in its audience
admiration and spiritual edification.[76]

For Talfourd's theatrical ancient Greeks simultaneously look
both forwards and backwards.[77] His choice of a poetic diction
with echoes of Elizabethan forms is a symptom not so much of
retrogressive archaism as of the contemporary sense that the
greatest traditions of tragedy in English were currently being
revived.[78] It seemed to Talfourd that plays like Knowles's *Virginius* (1820) and Mary Russell Mitford's *Rienzi* (1828) marked a
definite revival of tragedy in England, superior to anything since
the age of Shakespeare. And in Talfourd's important contribution
to the regeneration of the national drama with his ancient Greeks
he can be seen as representing an emergent trend in the ideas which
underpinned the new era.[79]

In his influential study of Victorian Hellenism, Frank Turner
has argued that one reason for the attractiveness of the Greeks to
nineteenth-century Britons is precisely the newness of the link. To
appeal to Greece

was to appropriate and domesticate a culture of the past with which there
had been, particularly in Britain, a discontinuous relationship. And that
very discontinuity may have been part of the attraction for nineteenth-

---

[73] Newdick (n.d. *b*), 13.   [74] See Culler (1985), 11.
[75] Unidentified cutting, Thomas Noon Talfourd (n.d.), col. 9.
[76] Horne (1844), i. 254–5.
[77] On Talfourd's pivotal position see also Sharma (1979), 158.
[78] Ibid. 157, arguing that the lucidity of his style is a marked improvement on
Browning's dramatic versifying, and that it was the main cause of Talfourd's
triumph with *Ion* on the stage.
[79] On Talfourd's role in revivifying serious theatre, see Bulwer's dedication to
him of *The Lady of Lyons* in his *Dramatic Works* (Bulwer (1863), 106).

century writers who regarded much of their own experience as discontinuous with the recent past.[80]

While the evidence assembled in the earlier chapters of this book suggests that Turner is overstating his case in arguing that Britain's relationship with ancient Greek culture could be described as 'discontinuous', there is no doubt that there was a *perception* amongst the newly bourgeois that their identification with the Greeks was innovative. For the new middle class in the new reformed Britain, of which Talfourd was a 'left-of-centre' ideological spokesman, to give voice to the Greeks was precisely to revel in what Humphry House famously dubbed their sense of being a '*parvenu* civilization'.[81] It was, they felt, to counter the continuous Latinate line which the crowned heads of Europe could trace to ancient Rome.

The perceived newness of the resuscitated voice of the ancient Greeks was connected with their perceived youth. Talfourd saw in Greek tragedy the importance of its *youthful* figures:

> ...how rich a poetic atmosphere do the Athenian poets breathe over all the creations of their genius! Their exquisite groups appear in all the venerableness of hoar antiquity; yet in all the distinctness and in the bloom of unfolding youth.[82]

Ion's first night was also Talfourd's forty-fourth birthday, but if he was not himself as strikingly young as the great Romantic poets had been when they had their poems (and mostly died), he could make his heroes like them. In both his Hellenizing plays the contrast between the obsolete tyranny and the new, reformed society is symbolized by a stark generation gap between ageing monarchs and their vigorously idealist young sons.

Ion did have detractors. Macaulay wrote from Calcutta on 25 July 1836 that there was both 'too much and too little of the antique about it...Ion is a modern philanthropist, whose politics and morals have been learned from the publications of the Society for the Diffusion of Useful Knowledge.'[83] He had a point: Ion is philanthropically given to visiting the worthy poor. He risks his own health spending 'The hours of needful rest in squalid hovels |

---

[80] Turner (1989), 61.
[81] This was in a broadcast entitled 'Are the Victorians coming back?'. See House (1955), 93.
[82] Thomas Noon Talfourd (1850), 26.
[83] Cit. Newdick (n.d. *a*), 34–5.

Where death is most forsaken' (I. ii). George Darley reviewed the play negatively in *The Athenaeum*,[84] and the trajectory of his attack is obviously political. He feels that a levelled society without exceptional individuals cannot hope to produce serious 'true' drama: 'Where are the models to draw from, when individuality is lost in the sameness of civilization?' He objects to the play's 'languishing' poetry, 'insipidities' of character, domestic emotions and 'feminine' sweetness. It is one instantiation of the modern 'perpetual hymn and hosanna about the altar of social love', and marred by Ion's 'methodistical cant', in particular his Wesleyan claim of divine protection (I. ii):

> But they who call me to the work can shield me,
> Or make me strong to suffer.

Darley is correct about the religiosity of Talfourd's Greeks. Both plays, alongside their democratic political thrust, reflect Talfourd's own Nonconformist background, and the influence upon him of his Dissenting wife Rachel, by featuring independent-minded priestly figures with profound moral authority.[85] Turner has argued that one of the reasons why some nineteenth-century writers found Greece so attractive an arena for working out their own identity was that Christianity—rightly or wrongly—seemed easier to reconcile with Greek polytheism than with what they understood of Roman religion. It was much easier 'to interpret Greek religion as an earlier stage of a human perception of the divine that was in certain respects compatible with ... Christianity'.[86] Talfourd's heroes are both charismatically Christlike and unshakeable in their religious convictions.

But the Nonconformist spirituality of Talfourd's heroes, however eccentric it may seem in hindsight, was actually one of the most distinctive features of their author's Romantic reformist Hellenism. There is nothing comparable in the eighteenth-century adaptations of Greek tragedy discussed earlier. Talfourd offered his audiences sentimentalized Shelley plus a large dose of Methodism. Phocion in

---

[84] Darley (1836). It is striking that this negative literary discussion of the play was published in the same issue of *The Athenaeum* as the ecstatic review of the first performance at Covent Garden (see above, n. 13).

[85] Sharma (1979), 155–6. Talfourd himself claimed, in the fascinating account of the genesis of *Ion* published in the 1844 edition of his collected plays, to have been deeply affected in his early youth by Hannah More's 'sacred dramas' on biblical themes: Thomas Noon Talfourd (1844), 10.   [86] Turner (1989), 76.

Ion is the son of the high priest of Apollo: he refuses to kneel to Adrastus, announcing in superbly Nonconformist manner that he has studied in a school

> where the heart
> In its free beatings 'neath the coarsest vest,
> Claims kindred with diviner things than power
> Of kings can raise or stifle (II. iii).

To a son of Athens like Thoas slavery is unendurable, because it would be 'foulest treachery to the god within' to indulge the will to live in 'the vain spasms of the slavish soul'. Thoas has also joined an ancient temperance movement, scornfully spurning wine when there is the serious business of liberty to worry about (II. i).

Ion was known as much for its religious commitment as its political radicalism: Horne wrote that it appealed to 'the *conscientiousness* of its audience', as a 'mixture of the pure Christian principle of faith and love with the Greek principle of inexorable fate.'[87] It seems that the religious dimension was most apparent when the role of Ion was taken—as it often was—by a woman as a 'breeches' role. Nothing awed by Macready's identification with the part, the redoubtable Ellen Tree exchanged Clemanthe's muslin and ringlets for Ion's tunic and sandals, and took the play to the Haymarket. She was so impressive at conveying the hero's 'purity, nobility, and self-sacrifice', that 'at the close, the spectator withdrew reverentially as after a religious observance'.[88] Another woman to impress in the role of Ion was Charlotte Cushman, the first American actress ever to win international fame (see Fig. 11.5); she was a disciple of Macready's energetic but controlled style of acting, and her performances during the London season in 1845–6 earned her a reputation as tragic actress second to none except Helen Faucit (who took over from Ellen Tree the role of Clemanthe in *Ion* shortly after its premiere (see Fig. 11.6), and is a central interest of the next chapter). Judging from the sketch in the *Illustrated London News* of Cushman's performance as Ion at the Haymarket in February 1846, she had closely modelled it on Macready's definitive realization of the role (compare Fig. 11.1).

Talfourd's works have partly disappeared from the scene because of the tendency amongst historians of literature to regard the

---

[87] Horne (1844), i. 254–5.   [88] Marston (1888), i. 219.

MISS CUSHMAN, AS "ION," AT THE HAYMARKET THEATRE.

FIGURE 11.5   Charlotte Cushman as Ion, Haymarket Theatre (1846).

1830s as an infertile wasteland lying between the Romantics and the Victorians. With a few exceptions, such as Tennyson's first volume and some early Dickens, little from this decade is ever now even read. The main reason is precisely the self-consciously political tone of much of the writing, an inevitable consequence of the rapid social and political changes taking place. In his book *The Spirit of Reform*, Brantlinger writes of the 'intense excitement and expectation of further radical changes or of social dissolution' characterizing the early 1830s, and of the self-consciously 'improving' quality of the literature that this decade produced.[89] Talfourd's choice of ancient Greek *content* may have distinguished him sharply from the other theatrical writers of his day. But his reformist *message* was absolutely typical of the contemporary theatre. In the 1830s drama become a context for self-consciously 'improving' sentiments equal to that provided by fiction and periodicals.

[89] Brantlinger (1977), 11–12, 19.

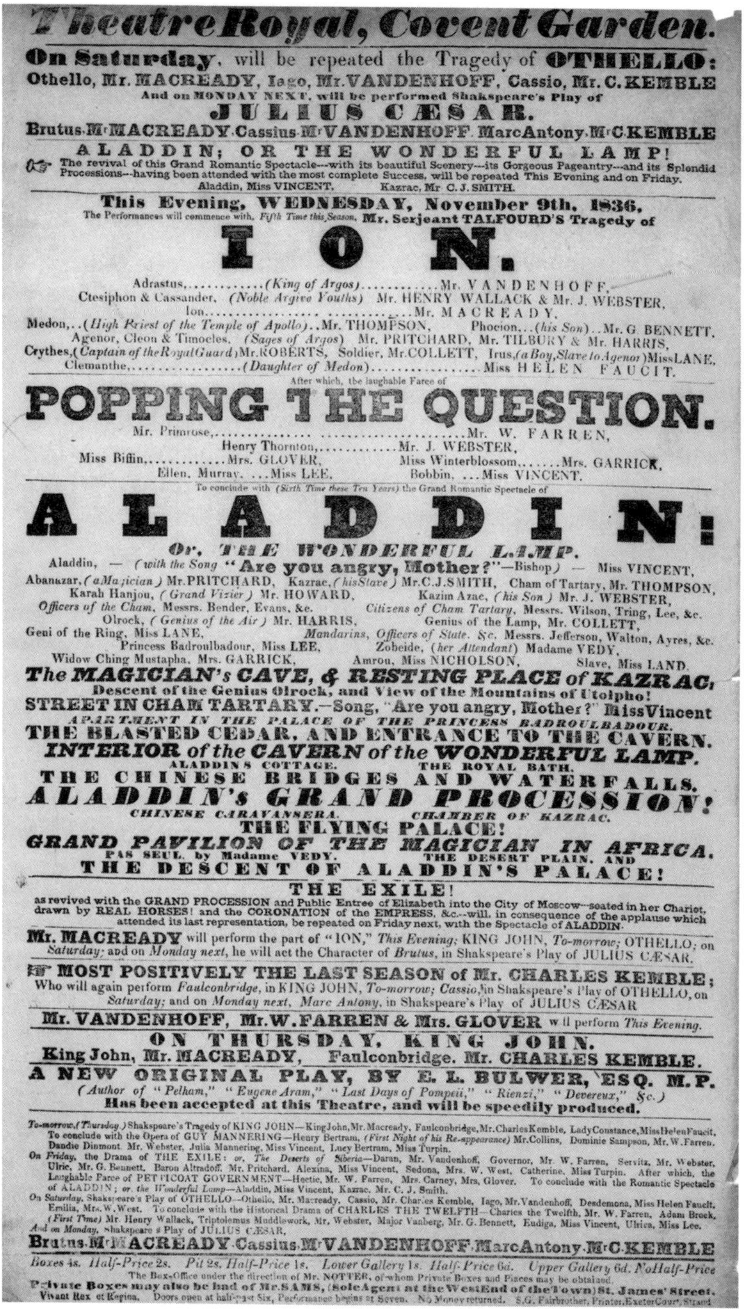

Theatre Royal, Covent Garden.

On Saturday, will be repeated the Tragedy of **OTHELLO:**
Othello, Mr. MACREADY, Iago, Mr. VANDENHOFF, Cassio, Mr. C. KEMBLE
And on MONDAY NEXT, will be performed Shakspeare's Play of
JULIUS CÆSAR.
Brutus, Mr. MACREADY. Cassius, Mr. VANDENHOFF. MarcAntony, Mr. C. KEMBLE

ALADDIN; OR THE WONDERFUL LAMP.
The revival of this Grand Romantic Spectacle---with its beautiful Scenery---its Gorgeous Pageantry---and its Splendid Processions---having been attended with the most complete Success, will be repeated This Evening and on Friday.
Aladdin, Miss VINCENT. Kazrac, Mr C. J. SMITH.

This Evening, WEDNESDAY, November 9th, 1836.
The Performances will commence with, *Fifth Time this Season,* Mr. Serjeant TALFOURD's Tragedy of

ION.

Adrastus,...........(*King of Argos*)...........Mr. VANDENHOFF,
Ctesiphon & Cassander, (*Noble Argive Youths*) Mr. HENRY WALLACK & Mr. J. WEBSTER,
Ion..................................Mr. MACREADY,
Medon,...(*High Priest of the Temple of Apollo*)..Mr. THOMPSON, Phocion...(*his Son*)..Mr. G. BENNETT,
Agenor, Cleon & Timocles, (*Sages of Argos*) Mr. PRITCHARD, Mr. TILBURY & Mr. HARRIS,
Crythes,(*Captain of the RoyalGuard*)Mr.ROBERTS, Soldier, Mr.COLLETT, Irus,(*a Boy,Slave to Agenor*)MissLANE,
Clemanthe,...............(*Daughter of Medon*)...............Miss HELEN FAUCIT.

After which, the laughable Farce of

POPPING THE QUESTION.

Mr. Primrose,..Mr. W. FARREN,
Henry Thornton,................Mr. J. WEBSTER,
Miss Biffin,.......Mrs. GLOVER, Miss Winterblossom,.......Mrs. GARRICK,
Ellen, Murray, ...Miss LEE, Bobbin, ...Miss VINCENT.

To conclude with (*Sixth Time these Ten Years*) the Grand Romantic Spectacle of

ALADDIN:

Or, THE WONDERFUL LAMP.
Aladdin, — (*with the Song* "Are you angry, Mother?"—Bishop) — Miss VINCENT,
Abanazar, (*a Magician*) Mr. PRITCHARD, Kazrac, (*his Slave*) Mr.C.J.SMITH, Cham of Tartary, Mr. THOMPSON,
Karab Hanjou, (*Grand Visier*) Mr. HOWARD, Kazim Aznc, (*his Son*) Mr. J. WEBSTER,
Officers of the Cham, Messrs. Bender, Evans, &c. Citizens of Cham Tartary, Messrs. Wilson, Tring, Lee, &c.
Olrock, (*Genius of the Air*) Mr. HARRIS, Genius of the Lamp, Mr. COLLETT,
Genii of the Ring, Miss LANE, Mandarins, Officers of State. &c. Messrs. Jefferson, Walton, Ayres, &c.
Princess Badroulbadour, Miss LEE, Zobeide, (*her Attendant*) Madame VEDY,
Widow Ching Mustapha, Mrs. GARRICK, Amrou, Miss NICHOLSON, Slave, Miss LAND.
The MAGICIAN's CAVE, & RESTING PLACE of KAZRAC,
Descent of the Genius Olrock, and View of the Mountains of Utolpho!
STREET IN CHAM TARTARY.—Song, "Are you angry, Mother?" Miss Vincent
APARTMENT IN THE PALACE OF THE PRINCESS BADROULBADOUR.
THE BLASTED CEDAR, AND ENTRANCE TO THE CAVERN.
INTERIOR of the CAVERN of the WONDERFUL LAMP.
ALADDIN'S COTTAGE. THE ROYAL BATH.
THE CHINESE BRIDGES AND WATERFALLS.
ALADDIN's GRAND PROCESSION!
CHINESE CARAVANSERA. CHAMBER OF KAZRAC,
THE FLYING PALACE!
GRAND PAVILION OF THE MAGICIAN IN AFRICA.
PAS SEUL, by Madame VEDY. THE DESERT PLAIN, AND
THE DESCENT OF ALADDIN'S PALACE!

THE EXILE!
as revived with the GRAND PROCESSION and Public Entree of Elizabeth into the City of Moscow---seated in her Chariot, drawn by REAL HORSES! and the CORONATION of the EMPRESS, &c.--will, in consequence of the applause which attended its last representation, be repeated on Friday next, with the Spectacle of ALADDIN.

Mr. MACREADY will perform the part of "ION," This Evening; KING JOHN, To-morrow; OTHELLO; on Saturday: and on Monday next, he will act the Character of Brutus, in Shakspeare's Play of JULIUS CÆSAR.

MOST POSITIVELY THE LAST SEASON of Mr. CHARLES KEMBLE;
Who will again perform Faulconbridge, in KING JOHN, To-morrow; Cassio, in Shakspeare's Play of OTHELLO, on Saturday; and on Monday next, Marc Antony, in Shakspeare's Play of JULIUS CÆSAR.

Mr. VANDENHOFF, Mr. W. FARREN & Mrs. GLOVER will perform This Evening.

ON THURSDAY, KING JOHN.
King John, Mr. MACREADY, Faulconbridge, Mr. CHARLES KEMBLE.

A NEW ORIGINAL PLAY, BY E. L. BULWER, ESQ. M.P.
(*Author of* "Pelham," "Eugene Aram," "Last Days of Pompeii," "Rienzi," "Devereux," &c.)
Has been accepted at this Theatre, and will be speedily produced.

To-morrow,(Thursday) Shakspeare's Tragedy of KING JOHN—King John,Mr.Macready, Faulconbridge,Mr.CharlesKemble, LadyConstance, LadyHelenFaucit, Dandie Dinmont. Mr. Webster, Julia Mannering, Miss Vincent, Lucy Bertram, Miss Turpin.
To conclude with the Opera of GUY MANNERING—Henry Bertram, (*First Night of his Re-appearance*) Mr.Collins, Dominie Sampson, Mr. W.Farren,
On Friday, the Drama of THE EXILE! or, The Deserts of Siberia—Daran, Mr. Vandenhoff. Governor, Mr. W. Farren, Servitz, Mr. Webster, Ulric, Mr. G. Bennett, Baron Altradoff. Mr. Pritchard, Alexina, Miss Vincent, Sedona, Mrs. W. West, Catherine, Miss Turpin. After which, the Laughable Farce of PETTICOAT GOVERNMENT—Hector, Mr. W. Farren, Mrs. Carney, Mrs. Glover. To conclude with the Romantic Spectacle of ALADDIN; or, the Wonderful Lamp—Aladdin, Miss Vincent, Kazrac, Mr. C. J. Smith.
On Saturday, Shakspeare's Play of OTHELLO—Othello, Mr. Macready, Cassio, Mr. Charles Kemble, Iago, Mr. Vandenhoff, Desdemona, Miss Helen Faucit, Emilia, Mrs. W. West. To conclude with the Historical Drama of CHARLES THE TWELFTH—Charles the Twelfth, Mr. W. Farren, Adam Brock, (*First Time*) Mr. Henry Wallack, Triptolemus Muddlework, Mr. Webster, Major Vanberg, Mr. G. Bennett, Eudiga, Miss Vincent, Ulrica, Miss Lee.
And on Monday, Shakspeare's Play of JULIUS CÆSAR.

Brutus, Mr. MACREADY. Cassius, Mr. VANDENHOFF. MarcAntony, Mr. C. KEMBLE

Boxes 4s. Half-Price 2s. Pit 2s. Half-Price 1s. Lower Gallery 1s. Half-Price 6d. Upper Gallery 6d. NoHalf-Price
The Box-Office under the direction of Mr. NOTTER, of whom Private Boxes and Places may be obtained.
Private Boxes may also be had of Mr. SAMS, (Sole Agent) at the WestEnd of the Town) Mr. James' Street.
Vivant Rex & Regina. Doors open at half-past Six, Performance begins at Seven. No Money returned. S.G. Fairbrother, Printer, ExeterCourt, Strand

FIGURE 11.6 Contemporary playbill for Talfourd's *Ion* at Covent Garden (1836), after Helen Faucit took over the role of Clemanthe from Ellen Tree.

THE DREAM OF A POLITICAL STAGE

With the more popular stage presentations *Ion* also shares a sense of imminent apocalypse, a feeling that civilization was approaching a moment of radical change. Deep resonances were found in the idea of lost empires, lost civilizations of the past, especially those which had come to a spectacular end: stage adaptations of Bulwer's novel *The Last Days of Pompeii* abounded, and it was one of the most popular subjects of panoramas during the 1830s and 1840s.[90] But the 'lost civilization' theme in Talfourd is subordinate to the ideals of patriotism and democracy, also at the centre of Browning's political plays; even Browning's love dramas emphasize the moral motifs of service and sacrifice.[91] In the dramas of Talfourd's friend Douglas Jerrold, in particular, reformist themes prefiguring those of Dickens's fiction had been explored since the late 1820s. Jerrold's plays portray the plights of petit bourgeois and working-class characters, oppressed by dastardly aristocrats, just as Ion and Thoas think they are commoners, and are persecuted by kings. Jerrold's famous *Black-Eyed Susan* (1829), and other politicized melodramas such as *The Press Gang* and *The Factory Girl* were, by the early 1830s, staples of the popular theatre; *The Golden Calf* (1832) attacks those who honour money and social status.[92]

Politics were thus being placed at the centre of culture. Bulwer was behind the 1832 Select Committee of Enquiry into the legal foundations of the theatre, which had criticized the Lord Chamberlain's prerogative of dramatic censorship; he believed that literature needed a propagandist voice. In his non-fictional study *England and the English* (1833), he argues against political censorship of theatre, whose main function he saw as the protection of the nobility by preventing 'political allusions'. He acidly concludes that 'to see our modern plays, you would imagine there were no politicians amongst us'.[93] In contrast, he invokes the ancient Athenians:

the theatre with them was political... Thus theatrical performance was to the Athenian a newspaper as well as a play. We banish the Political from the stage, and we therefore deprive the stage of the most vivid of its actual

---

[90] Altick (1978), 181–2, 323.   [91] Sharma (1979), 2–3.
[92] This section owes much to Brantlinger (1977), 26. See also Walter Jerrold (1914), ii; Emeljanow (1987), 21–55.
[93] Bulwer (1833), ii. 141–2.

sources of interest. At present the English, instead of finding politics in the stage, find their stage in politics.[94]

As if in response to his friend's challenge, Talfourd consciously created a theatrical performance imitating Athenian theatre in which he could put those exciting contemporary politics back onto the English stage.

Talfourd thought literature should ideally not be used for the expression of narrowly *party* political sentiment. In a discussion of Hazlitt in the *Edinburgh Review*, he had once written that dramatists ought to respect all members of their audiences, which invariably consist both 'of men of all parties, and men of no party'.[95] He shared with Carlyle and Dickens an advocacy of social reform which basically assumed that social reform presupposed *moral* reform: institutions could best be changed by altering human nature.[96] Yet feelings ran so high in the decade of reform that Talfourd's ancient Greeks in *Ion* and *The Athenian Captive*, while modelled on the characters in extant Athenian tragedy, do deliver speeches closely echoing the constitutional debates in the newspapers of the 1830s, and do express views which imply that they would have been extremely unlikely to vote Tory. But they are warm and sympathetic human beings, acting nobly and speaking eloquently in the name of improving the condition of their peoples and the reform of their body politic. With Thomas Talfourd's emotional and idealized Hellenic heroes, as impersonated by Macready, not only the theatre but the ancient Greeks it represented had indeed once again become political.

---

[94] Ibid. 141.

[95] Talfourd, 'Hazlitt's lectures on the drama' (first published in *The Edinburgh Review*), in Thomas Noon Talfourd (1850), 68–73, at p. 69.

[96] See Brantlinger (1977), 2, 4–5, 11.

Antigone with Consequences

SOPHOCLEAN DREAMERS

In recollections of his Dublin boyhood, published in 1902, the elderly Irish writer and theatre critic Percy Fitzgerald confessed to a recurring dream. In 1846, when still a teenager, he had witnessed the ravishing Helen Faucit performing the leading role in Sophocles' *Antigone*. More than half a century later Fitzgerald wrote that the 'classical vision haunted my boyish dreams for weeks, and does still . . . It seemed some supernatural figure lent temporarily to this base earth. Never since have I understood in the same way the solemnity of the Greek play'.[1] What kind of theatrical experience could have made such an impact on an adolescent male psyche that it informed his fantasies for more than a half a century? In this chapter's exploration of the consequences of *Antigone*'s appearance on the stages of Britain and Ireland in the 1840s, an unprecedented degree of hyperbole will everywhere be apparent in the responses of its adulatory spectators.

The impact made by Talfourd's *Ion* on the London imagination had inevitably raised once again the issue of whether the texts of Greek tragedy themselves could successfully be performed. In 1837, the year after *Ion*, Talfourd's friend Bulwer asked himself exactly this question. He felt that Aeschylean drama was wholly unsuitable, its formal, declamatory style requiring not actors but mere 'reciters'. On the other hand, says Bulwer,

When we come to the plays of Sophocles, we feel that a new era in the drama is created, we feel that the artist poet has called into full existence the artist actor. His theatrical effects are tangible, actual—could be represented tomorrow in Paris—in London—everywhere.[2]

Bulwer's view now seems oddly prescient. Although he personally failed to persuade Macready to produce a play called *The Murder*

---

[1] Percy Fitzgerald (1902), 26–7.   [2] Bulwer (1837), ii. 590–3.

of Clytemnestra (probably Sophocles' *Electra*) in 1838,[3] almost all Sophocles' tragedies would indeed be performed in Britain, un-adapted, before the end of the nineteenth century. It is even more striking that within less than a decade of Bulwer's statement, Sophocles' *Antigone* should have been fully staged not only in Paris and London but in Potsdam, Berlin, Hamburg, Frankfurt, Vienna, Dublin, Edinburgh, and even New York.

In 1845 there was a seismic shift in the British public's relation-ship with Greek tragedy. The cause was an unprecedented pro-duction at Covent Garden of Sophocles' *Antigone* in English translation (not adaptation), to music by Mendelssohn. This pro-duction had far-reaching consequences for British theatrical and cultural life, consequences which were to inform not only the developments explored in this chapter, but much of the material discussed in all the remaining chapters of the book. *Antigone* has been an overwhelmingly popular play in the modern world. It has been staged on hundreds of occasions, and has also stimulated several adaptations (by Brecht and Anouilh, among others) so significant that they have themselves become 'Classics' of the repertoire. It is therefore at first sight surprising to find that *Antigone* was never performed in Britain during the seventeenth and eighteenth centuries, except latterly in the form of Italian opera; Francesco Bianchi's *Antigona* was actually first performed in England at the King's Theatre in 1796.[4] One reason for the neglect of *Antigone* was the unimportance to its heroine of her relationship with Haemon, her betrothed: as even Bulwer acknow-ledged, if *Antigone* were to be staged, it might be desirable to have 'more reference to her lover'.[5] But the main reason why *Antigone* had made so little impact on the British imagination before the nineteenth century was that there was no significant French model for British dramatists to imitate: Corneille, Racine, and Voltaire had none of them attempted to adapt this tragedy. For the first time in the narrative traced in this book, the credit for discovery of a Greek drama as a text suitable for performance on a modern British stage must be given, unquestionably, to German-speaking culture.

---

[3] Macready (1912), i. 472.
[4] See the English translation of Lorenzo da Ponte's libretto in Bianchi (1796).
[5] Bulwer (1837), i. 551.

The ancient Greek tragedian most likely to be chosen for the privilege of a fully staged English-language performance was always Sophocles. He had been the most influential in the late seventeenth century, the first to be edited by an Englishman, and the first to be translated in full into the English language. His *Oedipus* and *Electra*, as we have seen, had far-reaching implications for the eighteenth-century London stage and for Shelley's and Talfourd's late Georgian responses to Greek tragedy. But it was his exaltation by German Romantics (in the poetry of Goethe and of Hölderlin, whose translation of *Antigone* was published in 1804, and above all in August Wilhelm Schlegel's influential lectures on Greek tragedy, first published in English translation in 1815) which had led, by the 1830s, to Sophocles' enjoyment of the status of 'best' ancient tragedian in Britain. He was thought to occupy the ideal middle ground 'between' Aeschylean primal ruggedness and Euripidean wordy decadence. He was 'a pure Greek temple' in contrast to Aeschylus' 'Gothic Cathedral'.[6] He was regarded as 'sublime', 'ideal', his plays exemplars of classical perfection comparable with the statues created by the master sculptor contemporary with him, Phidias; his chorus was deemed to represent Schlegel's 'ideal spectator', the serene, mournful but emotionally distanced witness to the tragic crises suffered by monarchs and noblemen.[7]

PRUSSIAN *ANTIGONE*

Although Talfourd's *Ion* prepared the ground, the immediate stimulus behind the Covent Garden staging of *Antigone* was undoubtedly German admiration for the play. The British interest in cultural developments in German-speaking countries was connected with the Queen's marriage in 1840: in 1841 the Prince Consort, a deep admirer of the Prussian kingdom, had been invited by Sir Robert Peel to chair the Royal Commission on the promotion of the Fine Arts in Britain. Indeed, the so-called Mendelssohn *Antigone*, along with a translation of the *Oedipus at Colonus* for which Mendelssohn had also composed a musical accompaniment,

---

[6] Edward FitzGerald (1889), i. 190.
[7] On the concept of the ideal 'Spectator', which Schlegel found in the pseudo-Aristotelian *Problems*, see further Hall (1999e), 96 n. 1.

were to enjoy royal command performances at Buckingham palace and Windsor Castle throughout the years 1848 to 1850.[8]

It is in the context of the young Queen Victoria's recent union with a committed advocate of the achievements of German culture that the Covent Garden management chose to imitate an important Potsdam production of 1841, overseen by Friedrich Wilhelm IV, who dreamed of a renaissance of Greek tragedy in the heart of the Kingdom of Prussia. For in Germany in the late eighteenth century, nationalist fervour had fuelled long-standing resentment against French neoclassicism and the dominantly Roman/Latin lens through which Greek culture had been viewed; one manifestation of that had been the pre-eminence enjoyed by the French neoclassical adaptations of Greek drama. This nationalism, combined with developments in both classical scholarship and in the theatre, led eventually to a revival of Greek tragedy that was to spread throughout the whole of Europe. When German classical scholarship first sought, in the late eighteenth century, to encompass all aspects of the ancient world within its range of study, it found a keen audience amongst members of an intelligentsia in search of a model upon which to base their own ideas. And since many German cities were able to enjoy permanent standing theatres from the late eighteenth century onwards (long before any comparable institutions existed elsewhere in Europe), the stability of the profession entailed an unprecedented respectability and increasing vitality. Goethe took over the Hoftheater in Weimar in 1791, giving Europe for the first time a theatre which was, generally speaking, free from the whims of public taste and able to experiment in the staging of Greek tragedy in verse translations.

Whilst the French plays had been designed primarily to improve on the Greek originals by extending the emotional range of the material, and English adaptations had often provided commentary on political ideas and events, the productions at the Hoftheater sought to capture the 'universal' in Greek tragedy and usher it into the world of Goethe's Weimar. Goethe's own enthusiasms were evidently not shared by all: A. W. Schlegel's adaptation of *Ion* (produced early in 1802) failed to satisfy the Weimar audiences;

---

[8] See Cole (1859), ii. 46. William Bartholomew once again supplied the English translation: see Bartholomew (1850).

and Johann Friedrich Rochlitz's abbreviated and inelegant adaptation of *Antigone* (early in 1809) was strongly criticized by classical scholars. But the Weimar experiment is still of some (albeit indirect) significance. For even if Schlegel's version of *Ion* proved unsuccessful, it was his lectures on Greek tragedy between 1809 and 1811 that first established the high status accorded to the Greek plays throughout Europe in the nineteenth century. Moreover, by staging the Rochlitz version of *Antigone*—its infelicities notwithstanding—Goethe had introduced the public to the Greek tragedy that was to remain pre-eminent in the German-speaking theatre, and indeed in the European theatre as a whole, throughout the second half of the century.

It was the production of Sophocles' own *Antigone* that opened at the Hoftheater in the Neues Palais in Potsdam on 28 October 1841 that secured the pre-eminence of the play in the nineteenth-century European repertoire. It is generally referred to as the Mendelssohn *Antigone* on account of the orchestral introduction and the musical settings of the sung choral odes and the 'melodramatic' parts of the dialogue (i.e. 'sung-dramatic', from the Greek *melos*, 'song'), which were composed by the rising star of the Prussian Conservatory and the European concert hall, Felix Mendelssohn-Bartholdy. He saw himself as in some sense 'restoring' the authentic musical dimension to the play, originally provided by music, now lost, which had nevertheless been composed by none other than the tragedian Sophocles himself. But the production was in fact a collaborative undertaking overseen by Friedrich Wilhelm IV. The translation, which was by Johann Jakob Christian Donner, was both accurate and lucid as well as being metrically complex; the classical scholar August Boeckh of Berlin University had been called in as philological adviser. The play was performed in the Vitruvian theatre in the palace, and the responsibility for the staging fell largely to Ludwig Tieck, who sought to avoid all those illusionist techniques that had predominated in the realism of Goethe's Weimar stage, with its detailed costumes, elaborate sets, mirrors, and special effects.

The choice of *Antigone* was by no means fortuitous, since the tragedy had been central to the development of post-Kantian German philosophy. It had fundamentally informed both Hegel's dialectical view of history and the specific themes of his *Phenomenology*: nation-state versus family, legislative fiat versus traditional ethics. Hegel's pupils had already applied to contemporary politics their master's ideas of the 'moral community' (*sittliche Gemeinschaft*) that for Hegel constituted the Greek polis. And here, in the intellectual excitement of Friedrich Wilhelm IV's Prussia, there was to be no better illustration of that 'moral community'.

That is not to imply, however, that the production offered a Hegelian interpretation of the play *tout court*, in which the claims of Creon and Antigone were antithetically balanced, or that it was simply an apology for Creon, as has sometimes been claimed.[9] For not only were the collaborators in the production themselves of diverse political persuasions, but the Potsdam audience's open-minded outlook would have made them as likely to have been in sympathy with Antigone as with Creon.[10]

This extraordinary *Antigone* was transferred to several German theatres, scored a success at the Paris Odéon, and proved a sensation when it was produced in London in early January 1845. The English translation was made from Donner's German text (not Sophocles' Greek) by William Bartholomew.[11] From London it was taken by John Vandenhoff's son George to New York, where it was much less successful (see below). The Potsdam *Antigone* and its imitations were billed everywhere as the first ever attempts to resuscitate this ancient play on the modern stages of Europe and America, and attracted 'learned and unlearned alike'.[12] Despite its failure, even the New York *Antigone* was important as an early example of a European production of Greek tragedy beginning to become a truly international phenomenon by being exported across the Atlantic: its only certain British precedent was Ellen Tree's first American tour with Talfourd's *Ion*, which she acted, for example, at the Park Theater in New York on 3 February 1837.[13]

ANTIGONE AT COVENT GARDEN

Part of the appeal of the British première of *Antigone* was the identity of the two actors taking the roles of Creon and Antigone.

[9] George Steiner (1984), 182.
[10] See Steinberg (1991), 141–2; Flashar (1991), 74–5.
[11] Bartholomew (1845).
[12] Stirling (1881), i. 161–2.
[13] T. Allston Brown (1903), i. 49.

John Vandenhoff, fêted a few years previously for his performance
as another ancient Greek autocrat, Adrastus in the Haymarket
production of Talfourd's *Ion*, kept Greek tragedy in the family
by playing Creon to the Antigone of his own daughter Charlotte.
They were both highly praised. The scene which seems to have
made the greatest impact, to judge from the reviews and the
cartoons in *Punch* shortly afterwards (18 January), was precisely
the confrontation of the arrested Antigone with her tyrannical
uncle (see Fig. 12.1). Yet Creon was notable for his 'great dignity',
his 'powerful and melodious voice';[14] he was admired for his
portrayal of Creon's 'stern and rugged passions', especially in his
'desolation of grief' at the end of the play.[15] Charlotte Vandenhoff,
whose solemn vocal delivery was much admired, played Antigone
with 'the highest intelligence', especially in the difficult enunciation of speech through the music in the fourth scene (which
required her to say words such as 'woe' with feeling and frequently).[16] The performance was wildly applauded, and the run
was extended for another month, resulting in no fewer than forty-
five performances (an exceptional success in those days). These
made a considerable profit. A young American undergraduate at
Cambridge, Charles Bristed, recalled later,

I went down to London . . . to see *Antigone*, which was just then one of the
lions, and received with a *furore* that showed how extensively Classical
tastes are diffused among the educated classes in England. One interesting
effect of the acting on a modern stage of this ancient play was, that it
brought out the points, and showed how far Sophocles wrote for the
galleries.[17]

For despite the popularity of other music by Mendelssohn in
London at the time, the reviewers were surprised to find that the
play itself, in performance, upstaged the music.

   The sixty poorly rehearsed chorus-members performed badly, at
least on the first night, and the *Punch* cartoon depicting the chorus
was more acerbic than the cartoons depicting the other performers
(Fig. 12.2). It suggested that the chorus' costumes had entirely
failed to conceal their true identities as early Victorian oratorio
singers; an amused Mendelssohn wrote to his sister to describe
the cartoon. He was also astonished that the London production

---

[14] Marston (1888), i. 21.   [15] *ILN* 6, no. 140 (4 Jan. 1845), 10.
[16] Ibid.   [17] Bristed (1852), 234.

FIGURE 12.1 *Punch* cartoon illustrating Antigone under arrest by guards (1845).

FIGURE 12.2 *Punch* cartoon illustrating the chorus of the 'Mendelssohn *Antigone*' (1845).

had pandered to popular taste by inserting a ballet to accompany the ode to Dionysus.[18] Yet the tragedy itself, at least according to the reviewer in *The Times*, was 'triumphantly successful':

[18] Wyndham (1906), ii. 177.

Up to seven o'clock last night the general belief was that the tragedy would be a failure unless indeed it was saved by Mendelssohn's music. How the wise have been deceived! The music, as executed last night, proved detrimental, whilst the tragedy itself has been most triumphantly successful. Far from the chorus saving the tragedy, the tragedy has saved itself in spite of the chorus.[19]

The Covent Garden *Antigone* did have a few critics. Macready, motivated primarily by envy at its popularity, described it as 'low, provincial rant and extravagant pantomime. If this be the representation of a Greek play the Athenians must have had a wretched taste.'[20] But Londoners now enthusiastically shared that taste: a feature in the *Illustrated London News* devotes much space to a plan of Greek theatre, a bust of Sophocles, and a 'scene from "Antigone"', explained as 'that wherein "Antigone" is brought by the guards, and acknowledges having buried the corpse of her brother'.[21]

The strength of the public interest is partly rooted in the precise historical context. The costumes were of conscious antiquarian correctness, and John Macfarren's painted proscenium, depicting what was a knowledgeable approximation to the *frons scaenae* of a Roman imperial theatre, was the result of extensive research into archaeological publications. It was an unprecedented theatrical masterpiece of minute antiquarianism, the product of a period newly interested in reconstructing and recording in a precise and scientific way the archaeology of the past (see Fig. 12.3). This development is reflected in the close relationship between Classics and early photography: two of the earliest daguerreotypes in existence record the Roman forum in 1840 and a Pompeian scene: they are attempts 'to capture antiquity with the tools of the machine age'.[22] The inventor of photography as we know it, William Fox Talbot, was a classical and Oriental scholar who had won the Porson prize at Cambridge for translating some of *Macbeth* into Greek: one of his first pictures was of a bust of Patroclus, taken in 1840: two further pictures of this bust were published in his collection of 'photogenic drawings', which began to appear just the year before the Covent Garden *Antigone*.[23] It is revealing to find reviewers, whose expectations of historical sets were being

[19] *The Times*, 3 Jan. 1845, quoted in Little (1893), 67.
[20] Macready (1912), ii. 289.
[21] *ILN* 6, no. 142 (18 Jan. 1845), 45.
[22] Buckland (1980*a*), 117, 189.
[23] Buckland (1980*b*), 61, 81.

SCENE FROM "ANTIGONE," AT GOVENT GARDEN THEATRE.

FIGURE 12.3   Antigone, arrested by guards, is brought before Creon. Scene from *Antigone* at Covent Garden, January 1845. Reproduced from *ILN* 6, no. 142 (18 January 1845), 45.

transformed by the invention of photographic media, anxious to show off their own classical knowledge. They begin to complain about tiny anachronistic details, such as the Roman (rather than Greek) appearance of the sandals.[24]

ANTIGONE IN DUBLIN

In Britain it was not only the London stage which succumbed to this unique production. Indeed, the actress who later became most

[24] *ILN* 6, no. 140 (4 Jan. 1845), 10.

firmly identified with the role in the public memory was not the neurasthenic Charlotte Vandenhoff of the London production, but Helen Faucit, a slightly older, warmer, and more graceful figure, who took *Antigone* to Dublin and Edinburgh. Faucit was the outstanding English tragic actress of her generation (she had learnt much of her craft from Macready) and a great beauty. In striking contrast to her American rival, Charlotte Cushman, who was notoriously masculine in voice and appearance, when Faucit acted in tragedy she was almost universally acknowledged, by women and men alike, as representing the ideal of perfect womanhood. Indeed, despite her own parents' scandalous divorce, the example Faucit set in her own personal life, both as a young woman and in her excellent marriage to Theodore Martin (later Prince Albert's official biographer), did much to make it possible for respectable women to think about entering the acting profession.

Faucit was the daughter of an accomplished actress, Harriet Faucit, and John Savill Faucit, the author of the musical version of *Oedipus Tyrannus* performed at the West London Theatre in 1821 (see above, Ch. 8). Their slender, dark-haired daughter had made her name in the roles of lovely young heroines—Shakespeare's Juliet, Miranda, and Rosalind, Otway's Belvidera in *Venice Preserved*, Julia in Sheridan Knowles' *The Hunchback*, and the sweet Clemanthe in Talfourd's *Ion*. Perhaps it was involvement in Talfourd's work that had originally inspired her longstanding interest in Greek tragedy, and had prompted Macready to give her a copy of Schlegel's *Dramatic Literature* to read when she was bedridden in 1840.[25]

Having conquered Paris in 1844, where she made a point of studying the ancient sculptures in the Louvre, Faucit witnessed the Covent Garden *Antigone* in January 1845 in the company of John Calcraft, the manager of the Theatre Royal, Dublin. After immersing herself in the study of Greek tragedy with Theodore Martin, the scholarly admirer she was later to marry, she immediately agreed to take the play to Dublin, where she performed it on 22 February and nine further times in the next few weeks.

The Dublin theatre was capacious enough for the raised Greek stage, complete with Ionic pillars, 'authentic' tripods, and a set containing no fewer than five doors. In the centre was placed the

---

[25] Macready (1912), ii. 40.

door reserved for the entrances of Creon (played by Calcraft). The inflated tone of the reviews and other records of the production indicate that Faucit's personal performance was a towering triumph. She excited all who watched her by managing to convey both a cool, abstract sense of the apprehension of a mournful destiny, and a physical, tactile, loving intimacy. The consistent theme in the ecstatic Dublin press is her reconciliation of the formal, classical ideal with warm humanity and emotion. Faucit's 'classical' poses and gestures, her elegant limbs framed in flowing drapery, were captured in the portrait (see Fig. 12.4) and sketches by Sir Frederick Burton, the Director of the National Gallery, and impressed every commentator.[26]

She seems to have been an acceptable object of sublimated (and not always so sublimated) male sexual desire, and certainly made a particular impact on boys and young men, including the adolescent Percy Fitzgerald whose recollections opened this chapter. She became the fashionable rage and attracted several Irish suitors. Thirty-five distinguished gentlemen, members of the Royal Irish Academy and the Society of Ancient Art, presented Faucit with a Graeco-Roman brooch, and publicly thanked her for advancing the study of the Greeks in Dublin 'by creating love and admiration' for their art.[27] In December of the same year she also starred in seven performances of *Antigone* in Edinburgh, where the production had been eagerly awaited in the city which already regarded itself as the 'Athens of the North'. The actor John Coleman fell passionately in love with her extraordinary 'beauty of face and form... combined with those rare gifts—beauty of mind and purity of soul'. He adored her as a 'goddess', admiring her 'Grecian type of beauty... the sloping and majestic shoulders, the virginal bust, and the arms lost to the Venus de Milo'.[28]

INTELLECTUAL REVERBERATIONS

Faucit's performance in Edinburgh was witnessed by Thomas de Quincey, who was inspired to write a fulsome essay on the subject. The terms in which this piece was composed illuminate the reasons why Antigone spoke so loudly to the public sensibility of this

---

[26] Carlyle (2000), 144–7; she reproduces the sketches on p. 145.
[27] Theodore Martin (1900), 145–58.
[28] Coleman (1904), 328–9.

early Victorian decade. Faucit's realization of the role chimed
perfectly in tune with the contemporary view of ideal womanhood,
and did much to ensure for the next half century that Antigone
maintained the status of 'the supreme woman figure in the whole
range of Greek tragedy', as a female educationist was still describing her in 1903.[29] Although Faucit had been discriminating in her
use of classical poses, making them part of a fluid sequence of
movements and deliberately avoiding static tableaux,[30] de Quincey
was fascinated by the statuesque aspect of the performance. He
drew recurrent parallels between Faucit's 'attitudes' and Greek
statuary or between Faucit's flesh and marble. He described ec-
statically the moment when the heroine first appeared on stage:

Then suddenly—O heavens! what a revelation of beauty!—forth stepped,
walking in brightness, the most faultless of Grecian marbles, Miss Helen
Faucit as Antigone. What perfection of Athenian sculpture! The noble
figure, the lovely arms, the fluent drapery! What an unveiling of the ideal
statuesque! Is it Hebe? Is it Aurora? Is it a goddess that moves before us?
Perfect she is in form; perfect in attitude.[31]

The Victorian theatrical aesthetic was of course obsessed with the
equation of statues and beautiful women (especially dead or dying
women), to an extent brilliantly demonstrated by Gail Marshall in
her recent study of nineteenth-century actresses and the 'Pygmalion' motif, whose cover illustration portrays none other than Frederick Burton's portrait of Helen Faucit acting Antigone
(Fig. 12.4).[32] The descriptions of Faucit's performance as Antigone
provide the first truly extended examples of the sculptural simile
which was later to suffuse the discourse around, for example, the
early academic Greek plays which will be discussed later in Chs.
15–16. This simile helped to sustain the more generic parallel
drawn between Greek tragedy and the art of sculpture. De Quincey
argues that while indigenous English tragedy has the colour and
realism of paintings, the Greek conception of tragedy 'is a breathing
from the world of sculpture . . . What we read in sculpture is not
absolutely death, but still less is it the fulness of life.'[33]

For if Antigone was proof that Greek tragedy was aesthetically
sculptural, she was also evidence that it was ethically scriptural.

---

[29] Fogerty (1903), p. xii.   [30] Carlyle (2000), 143.
[31] De Quincey (1863), 225.   [32] Marshall (1998).
[33] De Quincey (1863), 217.

FIGURE 12.4 Frederick Burton's portrait of Helen Faucit in the role of Antigone (1845).

She offered the early Victorians the possibility of reconciling maidenly Christian piety with brutal pagan mythology. In a telling passage, de Quincey apostrophizes Sophocles' Antigone as 'Holy heathen, daughter of God, before God was born . . . idolatrous, yet

Christian lady'.[34] The identification of the Victorian conscience, founded in Christianity, with Antigone's virtue is crucial. It underlies the tenor of most of the many poems on the subject of this heroine composed in the aftermath of the Mendelssohn *Antigone*, including Margaret Sandbach's *Antigone* in her high-minded collection *Aurora* (1850), and George Meredith's *Antigone* in his *Poems* (1851), where the entombed heroine speaks apocalyptically to her sister Ismene of martyrdom and redemption.

The Covent Garden *Antigone* also happened to coincide with the early days of the Brownings' courtship and in particular with Elizabeth Barrett's planning of her verse novel *Aurora Leigh*. The heroine speaks as a High Victorian 'cultural prophet inscribing a secular scripture' when she so clearly echoes Antigone's distinction between temporal, contingent, man-made law and the timeless, universal imperatives:[35] Aurora writes of poets as

> Of the only truth-tellers now left to God,
> The only speakers of essential truth,
> Opposed to relative, comparative,
> And temporal truths . . . (1. 859–62)

These ideas also prefigure Robert Browning's appropriation of Greek tragic ethics (as represented in his case by Euripides) to prefigure his own spiritually advanced and esoteric version of Christianity, above all in book 10 of *The Ring and the Book*, where Euripides rises from the dead in order to defend his ethical system, as a 'pagan', in the new court of Roman Christianity.

Matthew Arnold was impressed by Helen Faucit as Antigone, and in his 1849 poem *To a Friend* names as his chief intellectual prop—more important even than Homer or Epictetus—the tragedian Sophocles:

> . . . whose even-balanced soul
> From first youth tested up to extreme age,
> Business could not make dull, nor passion wild;
> Who saw life steadily, and saw it whole;
> The mellow glory of the Attic stage,
> Singer of sweet Colonus, and its child.[36]

---

[34] Marshall (1998), 204–5.

[35] McSweeney (1993), p. xxxii. The following quotation from *Aurora Leigh* is on p. 29 of McSweeney's edition.

[36] Arnold (1986), 53. In *Dover Beach* (1867), Arnold depicts Sophocles listening to the sounds made by the Aegean sea, and hearing in them 'the turbid ebb and flow | Of human misery' (ll. 15–18).

In the same year he also published *Fragment of an Antigone*, which proposes a lyric dialogue between Haemon and the chorus, at the ethical centre of which lies the opposition between 'obedience to the primal law, | Which consecrates the ties of blood,' and the 'good' that each individual man 'selects' for himself.[37] Arnold certainly also had a performance by Helen Faucit in mind when he wrote his Hellenizing tragedy *Merope* (1858), for he tried hard to persuade the actress to perform the role.[38] In another famous Victorian 'closet' Greek tragedy, Swinburne's *Atalanta in Calydon* (1865), although Althaea is primarily modelled on Aeschylean queens, she nevertheless turns into Antigone as she laments the death of her brothers, who, unlike her husband and son, can never be replaced.[39]

The long essay that de Quincey wrote about Faucit also shows that the Mendelssohn *Antigone* engaged with the Victorians' emergent metaphysical sense of the gloom and glory of their destiny, of a fate as inexorable as the machines on which the industrial revolution had been built, of a *march* of history that was simultaneously progressive and fraught with tragic suffering. This was fundamentally different from the upbeat Whig teleological vision of history. The Whig aetiology of British liberty had dominated much of the eighteenth century's interpretation of Greek tragedy, and vestigial signs of it can be seen as late as Talfourd's *Ion*. How different is the note sounded by de Quincey when, from the entire corpus of Greek tragedy, he deems that no scene 'towers into such affecting grandeur as this final revelation, through Antigone herself, and her own dreadful death, of the tremendous wo [*sic*] that destiny had suspended over her house'. Through watching *Antigone* de Quincey had apprehended Greek tragedy's essential 'breathless waiting for a doom that cannot be evaded . . . the inexorable rising of a deluge'.[40]

If *Antigone* seemed to chime with High Victorian ideas of the feminine, the beautiful, the pious, the virtuous, and the ineluctably destined, it also offered fruitful material for the social and political ruminations of many intellectuals, notably George Eliot. Referring to an 1850 revival of the Mendelssohn *Antigone* at Drury Lane, her essay 'The *Antigone* and its Moral' shows that she discerned in the

---

[37] Arnold (1986), 20.
[38] See the letter from Arnold cit. Theodore Martin (1900), 256.
[39] Swinburne (1901), 66: 'Who shall get brothers for me while I live? | Who bear them? Who bring forth in lieu of these?'
[40] De Quincey (1863), 205, 217–18.

play precisely the type of arduous, complicated social process that mirrors those she depicts in her novels, a struggle for civilization 'between elemental principles and established laws by which the outer life of man is gradually and painfully being brought into harmony with his inward needs'. Far from being a simplistic defence of Antigone's insistence on her principles, however valid they are, Eliot sees the play as portraying the inevitable *cost* of enlightenment, civilization, and progress: 'Reformers, martyrs, revolutionists, are never fighting against evil only; they are also placing themselves in opposition to a good—to a valid principle which cannot be infringed without harm . . . make a new road, and you annihilate vested interests; cultivate a new region of the earth, and you exterminate a race of men'.[41] Here *Antigone* is heard to resonate not only with the victims of the industrial revolution at home, but with those of the British empire overseas. The figure of Antigone was deeply to inform several of her subsequent novels, above all her treatment of Maggie Tulliver's attitude to familial responsibilities in *The Mill on the Floss* (1860), the moral tensions of *Romola* (1863), and Dorothea in *Middlemarch* (1871–2). In the way that the Covent Garden *Antigone* brought Greek tragedy—its social and domestic conflicts, its sense of inexorable fate, its synthesis of mournfulness and magnificence, its dialogue between individual subjectivity and collective consciousness—into the forefront of the Victorian psyche, it is scarcely possible to overestimate its subterranean impact on the social vision not only of Eliot, but also, subsequently, on the works of other novelists including W. Francis Barry (whose *The New Antigone* was published in 1887), and, much more significantly, almost every book ever written by Thomas Hardy.

THEATRICAL REPERCUSSIONS

Antigone did not produce an immediate revival of other Sophoclean tragedies on the British stage, despite its cult status and the hopes that enthusiasts such as Bulwer continued to nurture. By

---

[41] See Eliot (1856), reprinted in Pinney (1963), and, most conveniently, in Rosemary Ashton (1992), 243–6. 'The *Antigone* and its Moral' began life as a notice of a school edition of *Antigone* with English notes, but outgrew its original function. The Drury Lane revival to which she refers, which featured John Vandenhoff, was reviewed in *The Athenaeum*, no. 1175 (4 May 1850), 482.

December 1845 he was proposing to Macready a version of Sopho-cles' *Oedipus Tyrannus*, with choruses along the lines of the Men-delssohn experiment, and by the following February the Italian composer Saverio Mercadante had agreed to write the music to accompany them. But when Macready read the manuscript, he rejected it almost out of hand because he felt it lacked 'simplicity of style and picturesqueness and *reality*'.[42]

Almost all the people who had profited from the Antigone craze attempted to cash in on what was felt—incorrectly, as it turned out—to be a lasting new fashion for serious Greek theatre. The Covent Garden management revived Talfourd's *Ion* in the same season, and Haymarket followed suit the following year.[43] William Bartholomew, the author of the English text for *Antigone*, at-tempted to repeat the success it had achieved with a version of a play by August von Kotzebue from 1812. *The Ruins of Athens; A Dramatic Masque*, to music by Beethoven, opened at the Princess's Theatre in Oxford Street in March 1846. It is set in the early nineteenth century, thus anachronistically assuming that Greece is still under Ottoman domination.

Minerva is chained to a rock in Greece, awaiting liberation; two enslaved Greeks, improbably named Helen (a descendant of Mil-tiades!) and Hector, sing a lament beneath the ruins of the Athen-ian acropolis, now a Turkish mosque. Mercury tells Minerva that she must move to a new country: after rejecting the possibility of migrating to Rome, they select an isle where 'the relics of our fanes | Are honoured and adored by Freedom's sons'. This, it transpires, is Britain. The last scene depicts the façade of the Royal Exchange, the Bank of England, and a statue of the Duke of Wellington; here Minerva is introduced to a procession of characters from Shake-spearean drama, and consequently decides to move forever to London and crown a statue of Shakespeare with an olive wreath. The musical numbers include choruses by 'Priests and Priestesses of Apollo', a hymn to Mahomet sung by dervishes, and the patri-otic conclusion depicting the witches from *Macbeth* apostrophiz-ing the Greek goddess:

[42] Macready (1912), ii. 313, 322, 338, 340.
[43] Stirling (1881), i. 61–2; *ILN* 8, no. 199 (21 Feb. 1846), 133.

> Hail, Minerva,
> In Ancient Greece, Athena of th' Athenians:
> And here, and *now*, Britannia of the Britons!

Nothing could more clearly equate ancient Greek theatre and the contemporary London stage than the conflation of Minerva with Britannia.[44]

Bartholomew dedicated the published version of his *Antigone* to Charlotte Vandenhoff, in gratitude for helping to make his name, and the original Antigone never forgot her moment of triumph at Covent Garden. She was later responsible for a spectacular version of *Alcestis*, performed to Gluck's music with Sir Henry Bishop conducting, at St James's Theatre in 1855 (see Ch. 15). But a more immediate theatrical repercussion was felt, once again, in Ireland. In November 1846 Helen Faucit and John Calcraft attempted to build on their triumphant Dublin *Antigone* by staging a second Greek tragedy featuring a persecuted virgin, Euripides' *Iphigenia in Aulis*. This time the play was proudly billed as offering the first *original* production of a Greek tragedy in Ireland. Calcraft composed an English translation by synthesizing several different versions, and cast himself as Agamemnon. Faucit successfully extracted the maximum pathos out of Iphigenia's predicament, without succumbing to sentimentality, when (as *The Freeman's Journal* for Monday, 30 November put it) she appeared 'a suppliant at her father's feet, and shuddering with horror at that gloom and dark uncertainty that awaited her'. She was rewarded with showers of flowers and standing ovations, in contrast with poor Mrs Ternan's Clytemnestra, who was criticized for lack of dignity (perhaps using her own toddler Ellen as the infant Orestes had caused its particular problems). The orchestra and oratorio-style chorus performed a score by the theatre's musical director, Richard Levey. Like many directors before and since, Calcraft ameliorated the psychological harshness of the play by using the more comfortable (and post-Euripidean) alternative denouement in which Iphigenia is replaced by a deer and whisked off to safety by the goddess Artemis, thus exonerating her father from his crime. Calcraft offered his audience what *The Freeman's Journal* described as 'a magnificent tableau', involving Agamemnon's

---

[44] See Bartholomew (1846).

departing galley and 'the Grecian fleet wafted by a favouring gale from the winding bay of Aulis'.[45]

Although plans to take *Iphigenia* to Edinburgh did not materialize, the role, it has been argued by Faucit's recent biographer, was important to her development as an actress. It gave her further scope to experiment with consciously sculptural effects, an experience that she later found invaluable, especially when tackling the role of Hermione in *The Winter's Tale*. In the famous statue scene the marble-like Faucit was in 1847 regarded as spellbinding; the role of the self-sacrificing young maiden also powerfully affected her newly serene realization of the role of Shakespeare's Juliet.[46]

Antigone itself continued to capture the public imagination long after the productions of 1845. That it had become a byword for serious theatre in Britain is amply illustrated by the fact that in 1867, when Albert Joseph Moore was commissioned to paint a frieze to go above the proscenium at the new Queen's Theatre, in Long Acre, the subject he chose was 'An ancient Greek audience watching a performance of "Antigone" by Sophocles'.[47] In March 1859 there was a colossal performance at Crystal palace of Sophocles' *Oedipus at Colonus*, with a choir and orchestra performing Mendelssohn's music to this second Sophoclean play. It was not a great success, but when Edith Heraud performed the Mendelssohn *Antigone* a few weeks later, on 9 April, before ten thousand people, she did it 'with such beautiful elocution and passionate expression that the assemblage were moved as well as delighted.'[48] Geneviève Ward performed with rather more success in the same venue, in both *Antigone* (December 1875) and *Oedipus at Colonus* (June 1876).[49] Over the next decade she also performed Antigone in Dublin and even toured Australia with it. She made *Antigone* all the rage in Melbourne in 1885, where her performance was voluntarily supported by no fewer than ninety-five members of the local Philharmonic Society.[50]

[45] *The Freeman's Journal*, Monday, 30 Nov. 1846; hearty thanks to Norma Macmanaway and especially Charles Benson for help with research in Dublin.

[46] Carlyle (2000), 172–3.

[47] Geoffrey Ashton (1992), 61–4.

[48] *ILN* 34, no. 963 (5 Mar. 1859), 226; no. 969 (16 Apr. 1859), 379. Edith Heraud also performed *Antigone* at St James's Hall: Edith Heraud (1898), 125.

[49] Gustafson (1881), 126; *ILN* 68, no. 1922 (27 May 1876), 511.

[50] Ward and Whiting (1918), 62, 117–20.

In 1850 the English Ambassador in Athens had asked for the Mendelssohn *Antigone* to be staged on Sophocles' native soil, but it was not until December 1867 that the play was finally performed, in the translation of Alexander Rangavis, in the Odeion of Herodes Atticus in Athens. Despite the fact that earlier audiences had found Mendelssohn's music both baffling and disappointing by turns, it was the music that was to remain popular the longest and was the main attraction in revivals towards the end of the century; it is even recommended in the first monumental English-language edition of Sophocles, begun in the 1880s, which earned its author Richard Jebb the chair of Greek at Cambridge and a knighthood into the bargain.[51] It was not uncommon to find new productions using Mendelssohn's score, even productions of other Greek plays; when Sophocles' *Electra* was performed by the young women of Girton College, Cambridge, in 1883, the accompanying music was Mendelssohn's compositions for *Antigone*, played on the pianoforte. As late as 1903 the redoubtable Elsie Fogerty published a special edition of *Antigone* for use in girls' schools, and prescribed Mendelssohn's music as if it were a compulsory ingredient of any performance, helpfully informing her readers that it is available from the publishers Novello, at the price of four shillings.[52] It is difficult to find corners of the globe where the music was not still being heard in the last years of the nineteenth century. It was performed more than once in New Haven, Connecticut, and was studied as the subject of Leipzig dissertation by a US citizen, who then published it in Washington, DC.[53] Even Stanislavsky, when he mounted a production of *Antigone* in 1899 at the Moscow Art Theatre, chose Mendelssohn's music to complement the naturalistic details of the actors' performances.

ANTIGONE TRAVESTIED

After all the praise and extravagant rhetoric bestowed on the Mendelssohn *Antigone* it is almost refreshing to discover the acerbity with which Edgar Allan Poe reviewed the 1845 production, by some actors from England, at Palmo's Opera House in

[51] Cf. Campbell (1891), 318; and Jebb (1900), p. xlii: 'To most lovers of music Mendelssohn's *Antigone* is too familiar to permit any word of comment here.'
[52] On the Girton *Electra* see Hall (1999a), 291–6; Fogerty (1903), p. xxxii.
[53] Little (1893), 50.

Chamber's Street, New York. He was appalled. The stage was far too small, the design was shoddy and absurdly anachronistic, and the singers who performed the choruses were completely unrehearsed. Although the musical score was beautiful, the play itself was crude and unperformable. The 'imperfection' of its dramatic development proved, to Poe, only Sophocles' artistic immaturity— the 'dramatic *inability* of the ancients'. Indeed, the very idea 'of reproducing a Greek play before a modern audience, is the idea of a pedant and nothing beyond'.

Like any serious dramatic performance that goes badly wrong, the Palmo's *Antigone* was hilarious. As Poe says, 'of the numerous school-boys who were present on the opening night, there was *not one* who could have failed to laugh in his sleeve'.[54] It was reported that at one performance a wit in the audience threw darts at the messenger's shield, which was painted with concentric black and white rings and thus bore an unfortunate resemblance to a dartboard. The wit succeeded in scoring a bull's eye at what should have been the emotional climax of the play, and 'the absurdity of the entire piece burst upon the audience, who hailed the descent of the curtain with unrestrained mirth and laughter'.[55] Just for once the performers and even the harshest critics were in agreement. The young English actor-manager who played Creon, George Vandenhoff (son and brother of the Covent Garden Creon and Antigone, John and Charlotte Vandenhoff), later admitted that he had himself found it almost impossible not to laugh at the chorus: 'a parcel of goat-headed, goat-bearded old fellows, in Grecian robes, with spectacles on nose, confronting me, within the proscenium, opening wide their mouths, and baa-a-ing at me'.[56]

The point of the comic tale of the fate of *Antigone* in New York is rather more serious than it seems. It is a general rule of live theatre that the more elevated the text, the more uproarious the result if the elevation is not sustained in performance. It was partly because it took itself, its solemnity, and its archaeologism so seriously that plans were born to exploit the *comic* potential of the 1845 *Antigone* as soon as it had opened in London. A brilliant rhymed, poetic synopsis of the play appeared in *Punch* almost immediately to accompany the cartoons reproduced in Figs. 12.1–2; the

---

[54] Poe (1845), 132.   [55] T. Allston Brown (1903), i. 341.
[56] Vandenhoff (1860), 245.

depiction of Antigone as a naughty child who has been apprehended by the stage police may suggest that some members, at
least, of the Covent Garden audience may have found not only the
chorus but the play's central characters somewhat comical. The
synopsis extends over two full pages, and a sense of its flavour can
be gleaned from these lines describing Creon's conduct at the
tragedy's conclusion:

> He's getting exceedingly sick of his life,
> When to add to his sorrow the corpse of his wife
> Is shown through an opening made at the back
> Of the stage, and his mind is of course on the rack:
> He goes from the scene with a heart-rending cry,
> As everyone fancies, to languish and die.

The man responsible for this piece was almost certainly Mark
Lemon, the magazine's founding editor, and it gave rise to a
rumour that he was preparing a burlesque on the tragedy for the
Adelphi theatre.[57] In the event Lemon's burlesque was not staged,
perhaps because of the speed with which a rival, the gifted Edward
Leman Blanchard, produced his brilliant *Antigone Travestie*. In
the 1830s, when Frederick Fox Cooper's *Ion Travestie* had
followed hard on the heels of Talfourd's neoclassical *Ion* (see Ch.
11), Blanchard had written songs for the saloon theatres he frequented. Later he was responsible for the annual pantomimes at
Drury Lane between 1852 to 1888, which earned him the title
'father of British pantomime'. But he was also the undisputed
father of burlesqued Greek tragedy, for he established his career
in February 1845 with his innovative response to the smash hit at
Covent Garden: it is frustrating that his detailed dairies are miss-
ing for the exact period during which this piece was conceived and
performed.[58]

For if one important consequence of the Mendelssohn *Antigone*
in Britain was the discovery that Greek tragedy could be staged,
another was the concomitant discovery that the conventions of
Greek tragedy, if burlesqued, were extremely funny. There had
been occasional burlesques of classical mythology before, notably
James Planché's *Olympic Revels* (1831), written for the opening

---

[57] *Punch*, 8 (18 Jan. 1845), 42–3; see *ILN* 6, no. 142 (18 Jan. 1845), 43.
[58] Blanchard (1891), i. 40. He was involved at this time in extensive household
removals.

night of the Olympic Theatre; the new manager, Madame Vestris, had sustained the role of Pandora. *Ion Travestie* had burlesqued a late Georgian tragedy deriving from a Greek tragedy, although without many of its formal conventions such as the chorus. There had even been rare experiments in burlesquing Greek tragedy for reading purposes.[59] But it was only in 1845 that Blanchard discovered in the form and conventions of performed Greek tragedy itself an inspirational source for the popular stage.

The burlesque opened at the New Strand Theatre at the beginning of February. Blanchard may have got the idea of burlesquing *Antigone* from the satirical parody *Antigone in Berlin* with which Adolf Glassbrenner had mocked the Prussian mania for things in Greek in the aftermath of the Potsdam production. But the English-language travesty is wholly original and draws on a purely indigenous strand in British theatre and musical comedy. Its setting was 'a parody on the old Greek theatre, in the shape of the outside of Richardson's show'; at the end the cast crouched under umbrellas outside it, to escape divine vengeance in the form of a shower of rain.[60] John Richardson, now dead, had been an important impresario associated particularly with Bartholomew Fair: his touring productions offered a diet of variety acts, abridged melodramas, and 'panoramic views'. This form of fairground theatre, which often parodied serious drama as performed at the licensed theatres, was a vital medium for the dissemination of drama in and beyond London during the early nineteenth century. The portable theatre whose setting Blanchard's *Antigone Travestie* imitated was an unusually large booth with detachable fittings, an elevated platform, and an interior stage with crimson curtains.[61]

By choosing this setting Blanchard was commenting on the role of his own travesty in bringing such a quintessentially highbrow art-form as Greek tragedy to a wider, more popular audience. The work is thoughtfully titled, perhaps reminiscent of *Ion Travestie*, but also placing it in the tradition of the torrent of earlier 'classical' travesties inaugurated by Paul Scarron's *Virgile travesti* of 1648; travesty, according to comic theorists, is the subcategory of

---

[59] See e.g. Styrke (1816); Anon. (1843).

[60] *ILN* 6, no. 145 (8 Feb. 1845), 91.

[61] Altick (1978), 173; Banham (1995), 921. Thanks to Dave Gowen for researching this.

burlesque which recasts a particular work, usually of high style, in an aggressively familiar register.[62]

Antigone Travestie has never been published. The only known copy is the manuscript in the collection of Lord Chamberlain's plays housed in the British Library.[63] It is a close and hilarious burlesque of the Sophoclean tragedy. The cast consists of Creon, Antigone, Ismene, a guard, Tiresias (an astrologer), 'Hermon' instead of Haemon, a chorus and a chorus-leader. It ends happily. Antigone and Hermon play tricks with nooses in the cave, and appear alive at the end; Hermon's rebellion against his father is compounded by a conviction for debt. But otherwise it closely follows the Sophoclean plot, parodying the memorable passages, with the addition of several songs to be sung to popular tunes. It was regarded as belonging to 'the broad rather than the polished school of extravaganza', but was also thought to be 'exceedingly well written, and not a passing topic of the day is let off without a joke or allusion.'[64] The production was enhanced by the great comedian Harry Hall as Creon, commended by Blanchard himself.[65]

The opening scene features Antigone bemoaning her fate: 'Ah me! What griefs are mine, much more than I can bear; | Perhaps Ismene wouldn't mind a share.' Antigone clearly imitates the 'translationese' of the Anglicized Covent Garden tragedy: she bemoans her 'catalogue of woes | With lots of evils'. Creon has scenes modelled on his Sophoclean 'inauguration' speech and encounter with the guard. The intimacy with the original becomes even closer in Antigone's argument with Creon, which addresses the issue of gender. Creon rebukes her, 'Oh woman, woman!', and she responds 'Don't insult our sex. | Vivat regina now—not vivat rex': Victoria had ascended the throne only eight years previously, in 1837. Yet since Antigone was a 'drag' role, played by Mr. G. Wild, the gender dynamics here must have been complicated.

At Covent Garden massive applause had greeted Haemon's stirring rebuke of his father, 'That is no state where only one man rules':[66] Blanchard's travesty developed the theme. 'A king's no king who spoils a subject so', said 'Hermon', adding 'It's but

[62] See e.g. Jump (1972), 2.   [63] Add. MSS 42982, fos. 166–173.
[64] *ILN* 6, no. 146 (15 Feb. 1845), 110.   [65] Blanchard (1891), i. 202, n.2.
[66] Bristed (1852), 234–5.

hard lines, when only one man rules.' Another highlight was the Tiresias scene, recognizably sub-Sophoclean, including Tiresias' accusation, 'You've been and cast one living in a tomb'; the scene concluded with a Tiresias–Creon duet, to the well-known tune of *The Gypsey King*. This musical number synthesizes the traditional 'swagger' and the 'laughing song':

> Oh, I am the Gypsey King
>> And not such a King as thee.
> Your conduct is not the thing
>> And that you will presently see.
> Your empire will be knocked down
>> And your lands will your enemies seize.
> They won't leave the king half a crown,
>> So your majesty do as you please.

The refrain is shared by Tiresias and Creon, singing respectively 'I am' and 'You are' . . . 'the gypsey King—ha! Ha! Yes I am/he is the gypsey king.'

Some of the humour emerges from updated references to hailing cabs, taking trains, and emigrating to New South Wales. But most derives directly from parody of Greek theatrical conventions: it requires a familiarity with Greek tragedy which many of its audience had only recently acquired through witnessing the serious Covent Garden *Antigone*. The chorus self-referentially explain to the audience that they 'fill up the dialogue when it a little porous is. | And let slip the meaning . . .'. Antigone, condemned to the cave, sings a solo exploring the idea of being buried alive, much as she does in Sophocles; yet Blanchard's Antigone self-consciously promises the audience, 'Even there I can behave as a heroine should rave'.

THE INVENTION OF GREEK TRAGIC BURLESQUE

In sending up Greek tragedy Blanchard's *Antigone Travestie* struck a vein of humour that was to continue to be mined for another three decades. The satirical press now used parodic versions of the Greek tragic chorus in a variety of contexts. Some weeks later, for example, parliament was bitterly divided over the Maynooth Bill, which proposed to raise the grant given from

London to support this Catholic seminary in Ireland. The difficult position in which Sir Robert Peel found himself was likened in an article in *Punch* 'to the situation of the heroes in Greek tragedy, whose proceedings were the subject of alternate abuse and praise from the chorus'; these conflicting comments duly appear in a choral ode divided into 'Maynooth strophes' and 'anti-Maynooth anti-strophes'. The Maynooth ode is adorned with a cartoon, depicting prominent politicians wearing Greek costumes and holding top hats (see Fig. 12.5). It is strikingly similar to the cartoon of the *Antigone* chorus published earlier that year (see Fig. 12.2).[67]

Only a month after Blanchard's travesty there appeared a stunning burlesque on the theme of Medea, 'in every way calculated to foster the taste for the Greek drama, called up by the revival of "Antigone"' and 'concocted by Messrs. Planché and Euripides.'[68] James Robinson Planché's *The Golden Fleece* opened at the Haymarket on Easter Monday, 24 March 1845. It benefited from Priscilla Horton's legs in breeches as Jason, and from the incomparable wife-and-husband team of Madame Vestris and Charles Mathews, as Medea and the chorus respectively. They toured with this pathbreaking piece until late 1847.[69]

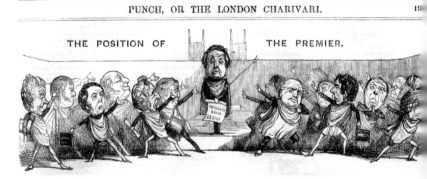

FIGURE 12.5 *Punch* cartoon showing Sir Robert Peel torn by the Maynooth controversy (1845).

[67] *Punch*, 8 (3 May 1845), 191.   [68] *ILN* 6, no. 152 (29 Mar. 1845), 200.
[69] Appleton (1974), 159–61.

Planché's burlesque is unusual in not being inspired by a play that was currently in the repertoire of the London theatres. Instead it is the Austrian trilogy *Das Goldene Vlieβ* of Franz Grillparzer that lies behind Planché's play. Grillparzer's version, with its sympathetic portrait of Medea, had enjoyed enormous popularity elsewhere in Europe.[70] But the fact that Planché should have chosen to write a burlesque of a play that was largely unknown to a London audience is not as foolhardy as it may at first appear. Members of the audience may not have been familiar with the details of the story of Medea, but many would have very recently become acquainted with the formal elements of Greek tragedy, and especially with its chorus, through the Covent Garden *Antigone*. Planché would have had particular reason for following the fortunes of the German *Antigone*, since as early as 1838 he had been approached by Mendelssohn himself to write the libretto, but his lengthy correspondence with the composer had come to nothing.[71]

Planché chose to distinguish between 'burlesque' and his own 'extravaganzas' by claiming that burlesque was 'the broad caricature of a tragedy', whilst extravaganza was 'the whimsical treatment of a poetical subject'.[72] It seems to have been the degree to which he took his original seriously, combined with no small amount of finesse, that secured his leadership in the field, and set exacting standards for his successors. If 'polysyllabic loquacity' could be claimed to be the hallmark of burlesque,[73] then Planché combined such linguistic pyrotechnics with ingenious allusiveness.

As a leading founder of the British Archaeological Association in 1843, Planché was at the forefront of the movement towards historical accuracy in scenic and costume design; and the extravaganzas he put on with Eliza Vestris at the Olympic have rightly been considered to be the forerunners of the naturalistic plays of the 1880s onwards.[74] It was partly the much-admired archaeological accuracy of the Mendelssohn *Antigone* at Covent Garden that made Planché choose a Greek subject for his extravaganza in 1845, so that he was able, amongst other things, to comment on its style of presentation.

[70] See Macintosh (2000a), 12–14.   [71] Roy in Planché (1986), 31.
[72] Planché (1901), 268.   [73] Cf. Trussler (1994), 238 on Victorian farce.
[74] Booth (1969–76), v. 14.

The Golden Fleece was commended for its light-hearted imitation of the Covent Garden *Antigone*'s earnest authenticity: it was played 'on the raised Greek stage' boasting a bilingual English and Greek inscription on the pediment, and 'the concluding effect' featured Medea rising *ex machina* from Corinth in a chariot 'drawn by two Fiery Dragons amidst the clouds'.[75] The first part was based on Apollonius' *Argonautica* (see Fig. 12.6), and the second on Euripides' tragedy *Medea*. But it used a chorus (in the lone form of Mathews) throughout; the playbill makes several comic references to the Covent Garden *Antigone*. It says that Mathews represents 'the whole body of the Chorus, rendering at least fifty-nine male voices entirely unnecessary'.[76] Medea, abandoned by Jason, sings a lament to the tune of 'The Fine Young English Gentleman' (quoted at greater length in Ch. 14), which

SCENE FROM THE EXTRAVAGANZA OF " THE GOLDEN FLEECE," AT THE HAYMARKET THEATRE.

FIGURE 12.6 Tableau portraying Jason and Medea escaping on the Argo at the end of part 1 of Planché's *The Golden Fleece* (1845).

[75] See Planché (1845), 30.   [76] Prefixed to Planché (1845).

intertextually refers directly to the production which had begun the 'Grecian' craze:

> He leaves me to darn his stockings, and mope in the house all day,
> While he treats *her* to see 'Antigone', with a box at the Grecian play.

It is easy to disparage burlesques, underestimating the virtuosity of the best of the actors. Charles Mathews's performance as the Chorus in *The Golden Fleece* was admired by the most serious of theatrical critics: he was particularly commended for his quickness, easy elegance, and what we would call 'deadpan' ability to let the incongruous clash between the gravity of the material and the levity of the performance speak, hilariously, for itself. He was especially remembered for the manner in which he sang a silly song beginning 'Fol de riddle lol' completely straight, without grimace or wink, at a tense moment in the action.[77]

The next year saw Planché attempting to repeat the success of *The Golden Fleece* with a remarkable Easter entertainment at the Haymarket, based on an ancient Greek comedy. *The Birds of Aristophanes: A Dramatic Experiment in one Act, being an humble attempt to adapt the said "Birds" to this climate, by giving them new names, new feathers, new songs, and new tales* stands virtually alone in the history of the British stage before the twentieth century as an attempt to make commercial theatre out of the texts of Old Comedy (see Fig. 12.7). *Birds* may have been chosen because of its famous bird-noises and low level of obscenity, although Planché may also have been aware that Goethe had staged this play in late eighteenth-century Weimar. Planché's piece makes witty reading: the playbill advertised the settings as 'Apex of a woody mountain, whereon is held the parliament of Birds', followed by 'The high court of Olympus, with *poses plastiques* of the principal deities' (on this type of spectacle see above, p. 30): it boasts that besides the King of the Birds, and Priscilla Horton as the nightingale, there will appear 'other birds by a flock of auxiliaries from the zoological gardens'.

The costumes were 'in exquisite taste', the 'stage itself was cleverly platformed into a rocky model of the ancient Greek stage, backed . . . by modern scenery', and Horton's performance earned her the title of 'the most graceful burlesque actress on the

---

[77] George Taylor (1989), 71–2.

SCENE FROM THE NEW CLASSIC BURLESQUE OF " THE BIRDS OF ARISTOPHANES," AT THE HAYMARKET THEATRE.

FIGURE 12.7   Scene from Planché's burlesque *The Birds of Aristophanes* (1846).

stage'. Her 'beautiful voice' was 'heard to great advantage in the incidental parodies'.[78] The impressive music comprised tunes by Handel, gavottes, and a delicious trio between the Nightingale, Euelpides, and Peisthetaerus in their updated personae of Jackanoxides and Tomostyleseron ('Hellenized' forms of the proverbial Jack Noakes and Tom Styles). The tune was *Mocking Bird*; the chorus incorporated words from Aristophanes' famous 'bird-noise' refrain:

> *Toro toro toro tinx,*
> *Kickabau, kickabau,*
> *Toro toro toro, loli lolink.*

The targets of the humour included ugly new urban architecture, hazardous financial speculations of 'joint-stock company direct-

[78] *ILN* 8, no. 207 (18 Apr. 1846), 253.

ors', and the current craze for building railways. The equivalent of the inhabitants of Cloudcuckooland, men who dream impossible dreams, are the proponents of a Channel Tunnel: as the chorus sing in a ditty entitled 'Parabasis',

> Why should not the fowls in the air build a palace,
> When there's hope of a submarine railway to Calais?

Yet this play was not a success with the public: one reviewer pronounced it 'too good—too good, at least, to elicit shouts of laughter from a general audience. Nothing can be more polished or witty than the writing; but in some instances the writing was too esoteric.'[79]

Planché later complained that his intention had been to ascertain 'how far the theatrical public would be willing to receive a higher class of entertainment than the modern *Extravaganza* of the English stage . . . To open a field—not for myself alone—but in which much abler men might give the reins to their imagination and their wit in a dramatic form, unfettered by the rules and conventions of a regular Comedy, and assisted to any extent by Music and Decoration.'[80] In his memoirs he was more explicit: he was trying to 'open a new stage-door by which the poet and the satirist could enter the theatre without the shackles imposed upon them by the laws of the regular drama'. He contemplated no less an ambitious scheme than 'to lay the foundation for an Aristophanic drama, which the greatest minds would not consider it derogatory to contribute to'.[81] The ultimate problem was that making comedy out of comedy was not the way of the early Victorians: the whole point of the laughter in burlesque was that it parodically reworked an elevated prototype.

Greek tragedy began to be given a comic spin even outside the theatre in the immediate aftermath of the 1845 Covent Garden *Antigone*. Thackeray began writing *Vanity Fair* in mid-February 1845, when he returned to London from a long trip abroad to find the Covent Garden *Antigone* at the height of its success. The novel began to appear in 1847. At the same time he began to draw the sketches to accompany the text in the form of wood engravings.[82]

---

[79] Ibid.   [80] 'Preface' to Planché (1846), 4–5.   [81] Planché (1872), ii. 80.
[82] On the chronology of the novel and the sketches, see D. J. Taylor (1999), 220, 260–1, and Catherine Peters (1987), ch. 7. Recent critics have acknowledged the importance of the Clytemnestra engraving to the reader's experience of *Vanity Fair* (see e.g. Jadwin 1993), but the connection between it and the Covent Garden

In chapter 51 the indomitable Becky Sharp attends some fashionable charades, given by Lord Steyne at Gaunt House, his stately
home. The first and second charades are orientalizing fantasies
with Turkish settings; the third moves, however, to ancient
Greece, and features Becky as Clytemnestra, murdering Agamemnon to the sound of music from *Don Juan*, her eyes 'lighted up with
a smile so ghastly, that people quake as they look at her.' The
charade ends with Lord Steyne's pun: 'Mrs Rawdon Crawley
was quite killing in her part.' This is followed by the narrator's
comment that, in front of the excited Prince of Wales, 'Becky
laughed; gay, and saucy looking, and swept the prettiest little
curtsey ever seen.' Thackeray illustrates this moment with an
engraving (see Fig. 12.8).[83] The financially embarrassed adventur-
ess, dressed as a Greek tragic heroine whose bare-shouldered
costume and simple hairstyle are clearly modelled on those worn
by Antigone as played by both Charlotte Vandenhoff and Helen
Faucit, was sexily saluting none other than the excited Prince
Regent. This scene therefore sums up all the essential features of
classical burlesque—the conjunction of the high tragic plot with
operatic or ballad-operatic music, puns, sauciness, pretty women,
and frolics that challenged, even as they failed to erase, huge
disparities in class and status.

The American Charles Bristed who went to see the Mendelssohn *Antigone* was a politically conscious young man, touchingly
idealistic about the brave new republic in his homeland. His account of his days at Cambridge often reveals his astonishment at
the political apathy, class snobbery, and casual brutality against
servants and women he found in England. He was perplexed that
the audience of *Antigone* brought down the house at Haemon's
famous line, 'That is no state where only one man rules', because
he perceived the British to be apolitical and characterized by an
extreme acceptance of social hierarchy.[84] Perhaps Bristed's confusion offers another clue as to the reason why Greek tragedy burlesqued, rather than played straight, was to prove the dominant
mode of its presentation in the next few decades. Classical bur-

---

Antigone has not been drawn. For fuller discussion of this and the other, quite
different Clytemnestra engraving in *Vanity Fair*, where Becky Sharp resembles
Medea rather than Antigone, see Macintosh (forthcoming).

[83] Thackeray (1968), 596–7.   [84] See Bristed (1852), 234–5.

FIGURE 12.8   *The Triumph of Clytemnestra*, plate depicting Becky Sharp dressed for a drawing-room charade inspired by Aeschylus' *Agamemnon* (1867).

lesque was fun and apparently anodyne, but its very particular comedic world, as the next chapter will argue, offered the class-ridden audiences of mid-Victorian London an imaginative environment whose implicit politics were rather less innocuous than they seemed.

13

The Ideology of Classical Burlesque

CLASSICS AND CLASS

Several important books published over the last few decades have illuminated the diversity of ways in which educated nineteenth-century Britons used ancient Greece and Rome in their art, architecture, philosophy, political theory, poetry, and fiction.[1] The picture has been augmented by Christopher Stray's study of the history of classical education in Britain, in which he systematically demonstrates that however diverse the elite's responses to the Greeks and Romans during this period, knowledge of the classical languages served to create and maintain class divisions and effectively to exclude women and working-class men from access to the professions and the upper levels of the civil service.[2] This opens up the question of the extent to which people with little or no education in the classical languages knew about the cultures of ancient Greece and Rome.

One of the most important aspects of the burlesques of Greek drama, to which the argument turned towards the end of the previous chapter, is their evidential value in terms of the access to classical culture available in the mid-nineteenth century to working- and lower-middle-class people, of both sexes, who had little or no formal training in Latin or Greek. For the burlesque theatre offered an exciting medium through which Londoners— and the large proportion of the audiences at London theatres who travelled in from the provinces[3]—could appreciate classical material. Burlesque was a distinctive theatrical genre which provided entertaining semi-musical travesties of well-known texts and stories, from Greek tragedy and Ovid to Shakespeare and the *Arabian Nights*, between approximately the 1830s and the 1870s.[4] With the

---

[1] See Jenkyns (1980), (1991); Turner (1981); Vance (1997).
[2] Stray (1998).
[3] See Percy Fitzgerald (1870), 15–16.
[4] See Nicoll (1955), iv. 133–54, and Schoch (2002).

important but rare exceptions of the productions studied else-where in this book,[5] during these decades neither ancient drama nor serious drama on ancient Greek and Roman themes was much performed in Britain. This was noticed with some pleasure by Charles Dickens, himself praised by Karl Marx for ousting the hoary nobility from their centre place in imaginative literature, and substituting impoverished working people.[6] Dickens's antipathy to the Greek and Roman classics was connected both with his particular model of indigenous radicalism and with his conven-tional mid-nineteenth-century taste for farce, sentimentality, and melodrama.[7] He wrote to Bulwer-Lytton in 1867 that the public of their day could only be induced to go and see a Greek play in the form of burlesque: moreover, 'a Greek name and breakdown nigger-dance [the (to us shocking) term for a type of musical frolic characteristic of the mid-nineteenth-century popular theatre] have become inseparable'.[8] Dickens was scarcely exaggerating: classical burlesques were so popular that in some years several new examples came before the public. In 1865, for example, the London playhouses offered no fewer than five new classical bur-lesques: these featured Pirithous, the ancient mariner Glaucus, and Echo and Narcissus, along with the *Odyssey* and the Aeschyl-ean *Prometheus Bound*.[9]

Burlesques often opened at holiday times, when they reached large audiences: in the 1850s it was estimated that over 60,000 people visited the London theatres and places of amusement each Boxing Night alone.[10] In this era, which invented the traditional British pantomime, it was unremarkable for at least one Christmas entertainment in any year to have a classical setting. In 1859 the theatregoer could choose to watch a treatment of one of the panto-mime themes still familiar today, such as Robin Hood (Drury

---

[5] The exceptions include Talfourd's *Ion* in the 1830s, the 'Mendelssohn *Antig-one*', and some tragedies derived from *Medea*.

[6] See Demetz (1967), 45.

[7] See van Amerongen (1926), 72.

[8] Letter of 25 Oct. 1867, cit. van Amerongen (1926), 72.

[9] F. C. Burnand, *Pirithoüs, the Son of Ixion* (New Royalty Theatre, April); F. T. Trail, *Glaucus; or, a Fish Tail* (Olympic Theatre, July); Henry J. Byron, *Pan; or, The Loves of Echo and Narcissus* (Adelphi Theatre, April); F. C. Burnand, *Ulysses* (St James's Theatre, April); Robert Reece, *Prometheus; or, the Man on the Rock* (New Royalty Theatre, December).

[10] Ritchie (1857), 17.

FIGURE 13.1   Scene from Robert Brough's burlesque *The Siege of Troy*, (1859).

Lane) or Little Red Riding Hood (Covent Garden), but at least one reviewer regarded them as outclassed by Robert Brough's 'ambitious' burlesque of the *Iliad* (Lyceum), entitled *The Siege of Troy* (Fig. 13.1).[11]

The burlesque theatre transcended class barriers. Unlike virtually all other professionals, actors were recruited from across the class spectrum.[12] Theatre audiences also included the proletariat: in 1859 as many as 60,000 individuals attended the plebeian Standard Theatre in the East End of London—at the time the largest theatre in Britain—to witness John Heraud's tragedy *Medea in Corinth* (on which see Ch. 14).[13] One censorious commentator describes the audience of burlesque as a mixture of 'vapid groundlings who take stalls, and, with vacant mind, "guffaw" over the poor antics they come to see' and the fashionable 'swell of our day'.[14] The Adelphi Theatre was associated with raucous burlesques,

[11] *ILN* 34, no. 953 (1 Jan. 1860), 10–11; Robert Brough (1858).
[12] Tracy C. Davis (1991), 3.
[13] Allan Stuart Jackson (1993), 65, 68, 123–4.
[14] Percy Fitzgerald (1870), 150.

popularly known as 'Adelphi Screamers', and with the unruly fans of Mr Edward Wright, a drag actor specializing in transvestite roles such as Medea in Mark Lemon's *Medea; or a Libel on the Lady of Colchis* (1856).[15] The Grecian Saloon in Shepherdess Walk, off what is now the City Road, which could seat 700 members of the urban and suburban working and lower middle classes, specialized in firework displays, cosmoramas, grotto scenes, statuary, and colonnades.[16] It was home to John Wooler's *Jason and Medea* (1851), which was held to have been 'nicely got up, but very vulgar in dialogue'.[17]

Henry Morley, Professor of English Literature at University College, London, wrote in the early 1850s:

There is a large half-intelligent population in London that by bold puffing can be got into a theatre. It numbers golden lads and lasses as well as chimney sweeps.[18]

Yet the audience also often included this worthy academic. For at the other end of the spectrum the big West End theatres attracted spectators including people of much higher social class and education, and burlesque in such contexts could be extremely sophisticated. George Henry Lewes (George Eliot's partner) recalled the performances of the suave public-school-educated Charles Mathews, at the time of his famous realization of The Chorus in James Robinson Planché's *The Golden Fleece* (1845), as characterized by grace, elegance, and 'delightful airiness'. Mathews had been 'the beau-ideal of elegance' whose costumes were studied by young men of the town 'with ardent devotion'.[19] An engraving by 'Phiz' beautifully captures the mixed constituents of the audience in the 1850s: in the stalls sit the middle classes, in the boxes the most affluent of families, and in the gallery the standing hordes of the working classes.[20] At the end of the period for classical burlesque, when it was partly replaced by a taste for light opera and Gilbert and Sullivan, the singer Emily Soldene recalled with pleasure that it had been her privilege 'to earn the applause of all ranks', from members of the royal family 'to the coster and his wife of Whitechapel'.[21] Most

---

[15] Ritchie (1857), 205.   [16] Pearsall (1973), 27.
[17] Wooler (1851); Blanchard (1891), i. 86.   [18] Morley (1866), 23.
[19] Lewes (1875), 62.
[20] The engraving is reproduced in Pearsall (1973), 67. See also Booth (1977), 101.
[21] Soldene (1897), 299.

classical burlesques would have found their ideal spectator in the man who enjoyed the topical satire and cartoons in the magazine *Punch* (founded in 1841), which was ostensibly aimed at the educated bourgeoisie, but was particularly appealing to the more aspirational members of the lower middle class. His education in the Classics would have been similar to that inflicted on one theatregoer during his childhood in the 1840s, when a governess made him merely learn 'parrot-wise' from the old Eton Latin grammar and from a couple of books on ancient myth and history.[22] Those who loved the theatre for the most part simply accepted burlesque as one of the range of entertainments on offer: theatre-going diarists tend to record accounts of serious performances of Shakespeare alongside those of burlesque without any sign that one was inherently superior to the other.[23]

Despite its wide appeal, classical burlesque has been almost completely neglected by scholars since William Davenport Adams's important study of burlesque, written at the end of the nineteenth century.[24] There are at least three reasons for the lack of research. First, written sources are sparse: with the significant exception of Dickens, the famous works of the great Victorian writers usually ignore the entertainments offered to the urban masses, whose social stratification lay between solid middle-class prosperity and hopeless poverty.[25] Secondly, classical burlesques have slipped through a chasm yawning at the place where academic disciplines fail to meet. For modern students of the Victorian theatre, with little education in Classics, burlesques of Ovid or Homer are uninviting. Scholars of English literature, on the other hand, have regarded all burlesque as inferior and ephemeral, significant only as a symptom of the decadence of Victorian theatre. As for classicists, even those interested in nineteenth-century reception, few have even been aware of the existence of the genre, except possibly in one of its last manifestations, *Thespis, or the Gods Grown Old*, the first work on which W. S. Gilbert and Arthur Sullivan collaborated (see below). Thirdly, the problem has been exacerbated by the inaccessibility of many of the mid-Victorian

---

[22] Francillon (1914), 45–6.
[23] e.g. Clement Scott (1892).
[24] W. Davenport Adams (1891). He identifies 'mythological' (i.e. classical) burlesque as the most significant of burlesque's subspecies, and devotes his first major chapter to it.
[25] See Bradley (1965), p. viii.

burlesques, which were either published in (now) rare series such as *The Acting National Drama* or *Lacy's Acting Edition*, or not published at all. The unpublished burlesques discussed below (there are others) have been consulted in the Lord Chamberlain's collection of manuscript plays, housed in the British Library. The creation of this important research resource was one of the few positive by-products of censorship in the British theatre.[26]

Yet the dozens of theatrical entertainments on Graeco-Roman themes produced in the mid-nineteenth century demand attention, since they show that knowledge of Classics was more widely disseminated across all social strata than has been recognized. For the sake of simplicity this discussion includes in the category 'burlesque'—also known as 'burletta'—[27] many pieces which styled themselves 'extravaganzas'. The founding father of the genre, James Robinson Planché, saw 'burlesque' as the systematic comic rewriting of a particular work of literature, to be distinguished from the 'extravaganza', which was a theatrical spectacular only *based* on a familiar story.[28] But in practice the boundaries are impossible to maintain: self-styled extravaganzas included extended parodies of familiar texts, while self-styled burlesques, which often contained lavish spectacle, could depart considerably from their textual archetype. By 1870 a comic theorist remarked that nobody—managers, authors, actors, or audience—could define burlesque, much less describe it: if pressed, they would say it used 'low dresses' (i.e. lower-class clothing), and was 'a thing made up of dancing and jokes and an old story'.[29]

THE ORIGINS OF CLASSICAL BURLESQUE

To the long tradition of burlesque of elevated texts in English belonged such important dramas as Beaumont and Fletcher's *Knight of the Burning Pestle* (1611), which burlesqued chivalric

---

[26] On censorship in the British theatre see Macintosh (1995) and Chs. 4 and 18, this volume.

[27] See Nicoll (1952–9), i. 137–9; the term 'burletta' originally referred to a dramatic work which included a sufficient number of songs to allow it to be performed at one of the minor unlicensed theatres. These theatres were not permitted to stage all-spoken drama until the Theatrical Patents Act was repealed in 1843, but circumvented the ban by including songs amongst the spoken drama.

[28] Planché (1872), ii. 79–80. Decades later, W. Davenport Adams (1891) suggested the same distinction between extravaganzas and burlesques, which he saw as 'definite and deliberate travesties of subjects previously existent' (pp. v f.).

[29] Percy Fitzgerald (1870), 150–1.

themes in the theatre, and Henry Fielding's burlesque of the high tragic style, *Tom Thumb* (1730), subsequently renamed *The Tragedy of Tragedies; or, The Life and Death of Tom Thumb the Great* (1731).[30] The musical component of burlesque, however, owed more to eighteenth-century ballad opera, which featured proletarian characters, breakneck comic routines, and the wealth of traditional British popular song. The earliest of these was John Gay's *The Beggar's Opera*, first produced at Lincoln's Inn Fields in 1728. The element of spectacle in Victorian classical burlesque was in turn related to the fairground entertainment of the eighteenth century, which had included spectacular enactments of scenes deriving from classical mythology (including Greek tragedy; see above, Ch. 2), such as *Hero and Leander*, with scenery and machinery representing 'the sea, Leander and Hero, Tritons, Neptunes, and mermaids', a standard entertainment at St Bartholomew's Fair in the East End of London.[31] In Ch. 2 it was argued that there was one attempt to perform a musical, spectacular, and also parodic version of a particular Greek tragedy in the eighteenth century— Lewis Theobald's *Orestes* of 1731.[32] Yet it was also suggested that the more influential eighteenth-century antecedents of the Victorians' distinctive classical burlesques were undoubtedly the classical 'burlettas' of the Irish playwright Kane O'Hara, whose *Midas* was still known and admired by nineteenth-century writers including Planché and his successor W. S. Gilbert: as late as 1870 *Midas* was held to be universally familiar.[33]

The authors of mid-Victorian classical burlesque also share a debt to the irreverent rhyming subversion of classical themes favoured by Lord Byron. He had written a parodic six-line translation of the opening of Euripides' *Medea* (June 1810), beginning: 'Oh how I wish that an embargo | Had kept in port the good ship Argo!'; in *Don Juan* he had further explored the rhyming potential of the name *Argo* by rhyming it with *cargo* and even with *supercargo*.[34] The identical rhyme occurs in the nurse's 'prologue' to Part II of Planché's seminal *The Golden Fleece* (1845), which fundamentally influenced the direction taken by its genre:

[30] Mackinlay (1927), 203–5.   [31] Stirling (1881), i. 15.
[32] See above, pp. 54–60.   [33] Percy Fitzgerald (1870), 149–50.
[34] *Don Juan* 2. 66, 14. 76. See Lord Byron (1994), 34, 657, 813.

> O, that the hull of that fifty oared cutter, the Argo,
> Between the Symplegades never had passed with its cargo![35]

Moreover, Byron had translated a popular modern Greek ballad, *Maid of Athens*, to which the refrain was Ζωή μου, σᾶς ἀγαπῶ ('My Life, I love you'); Planché used this refrain in a duet in *The Golden Fleece*.[36] The continuing influence of Lord Byron's works is reflected in the self-conscious quotation from *Don Juan* (canto 1, st. 201) which opens the preface to Francis Burnand's *Venus and Adonis; or, the Two Rivals & the Small Boar* (Haymarket 1864):

> I've got new mythological machinery
> And very handsome supernatural scenery.[37]

These lines both define classical burlesque and exemplify its style. It incorporated mythical themes, elaborate theatrical machinery, stunning visual effects (often set in supernatural contexts such as Olympus or Hades), and was written virtually throughout in brazenly doggerel rhyming verse.

Planché had been writing burlesques since 1818, but had to wait until 1831 to succeed with a burlesque upon a classical theme, his *Olympic Revels*, the foundation text of the mid-nineteenth-century classical burlesque. Loosely related to Hesiod, it was inspired by George Colman's story *The Sun-Poker*, and, under its original title *Prometheus and Pandora*, had been rejected by different theatres. But when the indomitable actress-manager Madame Vestris took over the Olympic Theatre, intending to attract the *beau monde* with a new kind of elegant burletta similar to French vaudeville, she turned to Planché. His innovative piece, with its locally allusive new title, assured her success. The effects were charming (the exquisitely pretty Vestris as Pandora emerged from a trap door), and the music eclectic but elegant. While Pandora sang songs based on Swiss yodelling melodies, in order best to display her coloratura, Jupiter and the other gods sang to rousing music from Mozart's *Marriage of Figaro*, Weber's *Der Freischütz*, Auber's *Masaniello*, and Rossini's *William Tell*.[38] Planché also attributed the success enjoyed by *Olympic Revels* to the decision to costume it in elegant recreations of ancient clothing—a decision which was to affect the whole future of the genre—rather than in the absurd

---

[35] Planché (1845), 20.   [36] Lord Byron (1994), 34; Planché (1845), 14.
[37] Burnand (1864).   [38] Appleton (1974), 64–9.

clown-like uniform previously conventional in burlesque. Prometheus, for example, was dressed in a 'Phrygian' cap, tunic, and
trousers, instead of the traditional 'red jacket and nankeens, with a
pinafore all besmeared with lollipop.'[39] The next piece on which
Planché and Vestris collaborated, *Olympic Devils* (Christmas
1831), was even more successful, especially the elaborate special
effect which concluded in the Bacchantes' *sparagmos* of Orpheus'
body, and the floating of his head down the river Hebrus.[40]

GREEK TRAGEDY IN A NEW ELECTRIC LIGHT

Over the next forty-five years dozens of burlesques on classical
themes were performed on the London stage. They drew on ancient sources—especially epic and tragedy—which would have
been encountered by the authors at school or university. But
many filled out their storylines from Lemprière's famous classical
dictionary, a book to which the scripts often make explicit reference.[41] Burnand's *Venus and Adonis*, for example, recommends
that fuller information on the *dramatis personae* can be found in
the 'celebrated dictionary of Dr. Lemprière'.[42]

The *Odyssey* was a staple of the genre, and the *Iliad* was the
source of Brough's *The Siege of Troy*, whose huge cast of Greeks,
Trojans, and Immortals was supplemented by 'Camp Followers,
Policemen, Thieves, Philosophers and Poets'. This burlesque also
draws on Shakespeare's *Troilus and Cressida*, but much of it requires familiarity with the *Iliad*; even the cast list includes Homeric epithets in both Greek and English for characters including
Nestor and Hector. The action includes parodies of famous Iliadic
scenes, such as Achilles' argument with Agamemnon from book 1,
Hector, Andromache, and Astyanax (in a perambulator) from book
6, Achilles' arming scene, and the death of Hector, upon which
Achilles typically comments,

> I'll for my chariot run,
> And drag him, tied behind it, round the city.
> 'Twill be effective, though perhaps not pretty![43]

---

[39] Planché (1872), i. 179–80.   [40] Appleton (1974), 68–9.
[41] Lemprière (1788).   [42] Burnand (1864), 3.
[43] Robert Brough (1858), 2–3, 4–12, 23–4, 29, 43.

It is highly likely that Brough was inspired to send up the *Iliad* by the earnestness of William Gladstone's massive three-volume *Studies on Homer and the Heroic Age*, published earlier in 1858 and widely discussed.

Epics from later antiquity were also burlesqued: it was the third and fourth books of Apollonius' *Argonautica* that inspired the first half of Planché's *The Golden Fleece*; the witty playbill claimed that Part I was

founded on the third and fourth books of 'the Argonautics', a poem by the late Apollonius Rhodius Esq., principal Librarian to his Egyptian Majesty, Ptolemy Evergetes, professor of Greek poetry in the Royal College of Alexandria.[44]

The attention to Apollonius is particularly strict in Æetes' instructions concerning the yoking of the bulls and the sown men, and in Medea's speech to Jason about the magic salve.[45] Part II, however, was a parody of Euripides' *Medea*. Planché's brilliant burlesque, as will be seen in the next chapter, was to inspire several imitations throughout the history of the genre. The popularity of Ovid's *Metamorphoses* will also become apparent. Two examples are Francis Talfourd's *Atalanta, or the Three Golden Apples, an Original Classical Extravaganza* (Haymarket 1857), which drew on books 8 and 9, and *Pluto and Proserpine; or the Belle and the Pomegranate. An Entirely New and Original Mythological Extravaganza of the 0th Century* (Haymarket 1858), inspired by book 6. The *Aeneid* also produced a famous burlesque, Burnand's *Dido* (St James's Theatre, 1860).

Although only one burlesque of an Aristophanic comedy seems to have been attempted in performance, Planché's *The Birds of Aristophanes* (1846), the works of all three Greek tragedians were regularly burlesqued.[46] Aeschylus was favoured by Robert Reece in *Agamemnon and Cassandra; or, The Prophet and Loss of Troy* (Liverpool, Dublin, and Portsmouth, 1868), which featured a witty encounter in Agamemnon's bathroom, and in *Prometheus;*

---

[44] Reproduced at the front of Planché (1845).
[45] Ibid. 7, 11.
[46] There had been considerable precedent on the French stage for the burlesquing of neoclassical adaptations of Greek and Senecan tragedy (on burlesques of serious works inspired by *Medea* see below, Ch. 14), but very much less for the straightforward burlesque of ancient plays to be found after the Mendelssohn *Antigone*.

FIGURE 13.2   Fanny Reeves in the title role of Robert Reece's extravaganza *Prometheus; or the Man on the Rock!* (1865).

or, the Man on the Rock! (New Royalty Theatre, London, 1865; see
Fig. 13.2). Some of the other tragedies burlesqued during this
period were Euripides' *Medea*, *Iphigenia in Aulis*, *Bacchae* and
Alcestis, and Sophocles' *Oedipus* and *Antigone*. In order to acquire
a true flavour of the burlesque approach to Greek tragedy, it may
be useful to dwell briefly upon a particularly clever example, Frank
Talfourd's popular *Electra in a New Electric Light*. This was one of
the Easter entertainments offered to London theatre-goers in
1859. Talfourd, despite deeply upsetting his father by failing to
graduate from Christ Church, Oxford as a result of debt and
debauchery, was a student of Classics in possession of a 'gay and
brilliant intellect'.[47]

During the 1850s the electric carbon-arc, which delivered an
unprecedentedly brilliant light, began to be installed in London
theatres.[48] Talfourd's title refers to the first occasion on which the
carbon-arc was used in a sustained manner in a British theatre, in
Paul Taglioni's ballet *Electra* at Her Majesty's Theatre on 17 April

---

[47] *The Athenaeum*, no. 1794 (15 Mar. 1862), 365.
[48] Rees (1978), 65, 68–9, 72–4; Bergman (1977), 178–80.

1849. The ballet was subtitled *The Lost Pleiade*, for Taglioni's electric Electra was unconnected with Sophocles: she was the Electra of ancient cosmology, the Pleiad and mother of Dardanus, whose frequent invisibility as a star is explained by her conceal-ment of her eyes at the sight of the ruins of Troy (Ovid, *Fasti* 4. 31–2, 174, 177–8).[49] Taglioni's ballet culminated in Electra's ascent as a star, 'so brilliant and far-piercing' that it stunned the audience, completely eclipsing the effect of gas.[50] But despite this reference to a previous theatrical hit, Talfourd's new electrified Electra was indeed the Sophoclean heroine.

The burlesqued *Electra* was 'really a magnificent affair', as the *Illustrated London News* opined.[51] It required at least a rudimen-tary knowledge of Sophocles' tragedy in order to understand the jokes. The famous scenes are humorously recreated: Electra's dialogues with Chrysothemis, her conflict with her mother, the news that Orestes has died after falling from his curricle, the urn scene (comically substituting a tea-urn), and Electra's recognition of her brother. But love interests supplement the plot, along with a wrestling match, a balletic *divertissement*, and star musical turns including that staple of the popular theatre, the 'laughing song', delivered as a trio to the tune *Rose of Castile* by Ægisthus, Orestes, and Pylades.[52]

The scenery commissioned by the manager of the Haymarket, John Buckstone, outstripped all opposition: 'Palatial chambers, sacred groves, curtained galleries, city squares, banqueting halls, are all finely painted and admirably set.'[53] The costumes, according to the droll playbill, were 'derived from most Authentic sources'.[54] The stage directions to the eyecatching fifth act illus-trate the updated classicism typical of the mid-Victorian Greek tragic burlesque:

The Stage is crowded with PEOPLE *engaged in various pursuits—Some are looking at the exhibition of a classical 'Punch and Judy' . . . others are engaged*

---

[49] This Electra had come to represent the sun, and had figured in the masque by Ben Jonson offered as King James I's 'Entertainment in passing to his Coronation' on 15 Mar. 1603. See Herford, Simpson, and Simpson (1941), viii. 107.

[50] Rees (1978). 67; Guest (1972), 139, 143 n. 3, 159.

[51] *ILN* 34, no. 971 (30 Apr. 1859), 419.

[52] Francis Talfourd (1859), 23–4.

[53] *ILN* 34, no. 971 (30 Apr. 1859), 419.

[54] Reproduced in Francis Talfourd (1859), 1–5.

witnessing the performance of a Strolling Company of ACTORS *on a Thespian cart.*[55]

This play-within-a-play is symptomatic of the burlesque stage's tendency to provide a self-conscious commentary upon the very genre which it is subverting. When Nemesis rises in the final scene, she delivers a lecture on ancient theatrical practice:

> I really cannot tell if all of you
> Recall the old Greek rule of stage propriety—
> Which was—the audience having had satiety
> Of crime displayed and vengeance on it willed,
> Upon the stage the actors were *not* killed,
> But by some fanciful poetic means
> Were decently disposed of—off the scenes.[56]

The middle and lower-class audience, even if it knew nothing about Greek tragedy at the beginning of Talfourd's *Electra*, certainly knew something by its end.

The theatre of burlesque warmed to the heroines of Greek tragedy: Talfourd's Electra, played by Miss Eliza Weekes, is central to this play, just as Alcestis had dominated Talfourd's other burlesque of Greek tragedy, *Alcestis* (Strand Theatre, 1850; see Ch. 15).[57] The burlesque audiences relished transvestism, and three other appealing young women played Chrysothemis, Orestes, and Pylades. This 'constellation of beauty and vivacity... could not fail of extraordinary effect'.[58] But the burlesque actresses needed to be more than pretty faces. The play involves a breathtaking acceleration of punning lines. When Electra enters in scene 1, '*her hair dishevelled, her dress torn and disarranged, shoes unsandaled and down at heel*', she begins to lament,

> Another day has passed, and yet another
> Brings with its light no tidings of my brother.[59]

Remarking self-consciously that she resembles a 'classic heroine', she turns to the subject of her unkempt hair in a manner only the industrial revolution can illuminate:

---

[55] Reproduced in Francis Talfourd (1859), 29–30.   [56] Ibid.34.
[57] Francis Talfourd (1850).   [58] *ILN* 34, no. 971 (1859), 419.
[59] Francis Talfourd (1859), 11.

These locks of gold, when servants on me waited,
Used to be carefully *electra-plaited*,
Now all dis-*sheffield* down my shoulders flow.[60]

Electra's prominence is not due to any deeper understanding of our tragic heroine. Talfourd's uncritical adoption of the burlesque genre's stereotypical caricature of the henpecking wife in his characterization of Clytemnestra suggests that this is no feminist reading of Sophocles' play.[61] But in Weekes Talfourd had an actress of virtuoso verbal agility, and it was her skill in singing, dancing and delivering the fast-falling puns beneath the electric carbon-arc which his audience prized.

Long ago the ancient dramatist Aristophanes used father–son conflicts to symbolize the contemporary struggles between traditional and iconoclastic ideologies. The nineteenth century offers us a real father–son relationship encapsulating the difference between the old and new ways of putting ancient Greek tragedies on the stage. The young Frank Talfourd was magnetically attracted to Greek tragic burlesque: he was a close friend of its inventor, Blanchard, and became one of its best exponents. The attraction must have been partly Oedipal: we recall that Frank Talfourd's father Thomas, a radical MP, had been author of the important 1836 tragedy *Ion*, a serious political appropriation of ancient drama in the theatre of reform. But his dissolute son Frank, sent down from Oxford to a bohemian lifestyle in London, produced some of the most irreverent of all the Victorian burlesques of Greek tragedy, thus saucily knocking the ancient Greek theatre from the very pedestal onto which his public-spirited Georgian father had elevated it.

CLASSICS AND POPULAR CULTURE

A reviewer of Talfourd Junior's *Electra in a New Electric Light* felt it was unnecessary to recount the plot, for 'the classical story is, we may take for granted, well known.'[62] Another noticed that the audience of Henry Byron's *Orpheus and Eurydice* (Strand Theatre, 1864) 'readily appreciated his classical allusions as well as the more direct fun with which his scenes abounded'.[63] These sources sug-

---

[60] Ibid. 12. [61] But see below, Ch. 15, for his burlesque of Euripides' *Alcestis*.
[62] *ILN* 34, no. 971 (30 Apr. 1859), 419.
[63] *ILN* 44, no. 1239 (2 Jan. 1864), 19.

gest that a regular spectator of any social class, even if he or she had never read a book, could theoretically have been acquainted with the contents of the major ancient epics, with at least some Greek tragedies, and with perhaps a dozen stories out of Ovid's *Metamorphoses*. But there were limits: when F. T. Trail attempted a burlesque of Ovid's unfamiliar account of the ancient marine-dwelling Glaucus in *Metamorphoses* 13–14, a reviewer said it would not succeed, 'being a burlesque of the classic story, which is not so well known as many of the subjects caricatured by modern playwrights.'[64]

A standard feature of burlesque was the display of Greek lettering, usually in the form of a placard or inscription bearing an English phrase simply transliterated into the Greek alphabet. This was presumably intended to tempt the spectators into practising their skill in deciphering it. Thus in Burnand's *Venus and Adonis* Mercury waved a placard at Paphos railway station, reading:

ΠΑΦΟΣ ΑΝΔ ΒΑΧ ΦΟΡ ΑΡΦ Α ΚΡΟΥΝ[65]

A little knowledge of Homeric Greek also enhanced the pleasure in attending. In Burnand's *Ixion; or, the Man at the Wheel* (Royalty Theatre, 1863), three Thessalian revolutionaries are called *Tonda-pameibomenos* ('Answering him') *Prosephe* ('he addressed'), and *Podasokus* ('swift-footed') respectively, between them comprising one of the more famous of all Iliadic formulae. The programme to Burnand's *Patient Penelope; or, The Return of Ulysses* (Strand Theatre, 1863) reproduced quotations from the *Odyssey* (the set, representing Penelope's room, was also decorated with various scenes from Greek myth to be serially identified by the audience).[66]

A few Greek tag phrases are part of the genre's poetic repertoire: in *The Golden Fleece* Planché punctuated one quartet with such lexical items as *To kalon, Eureka!*, and *pros Theōn*.[67] But puns in Latin, requiring only the most elementary knowledge and no formal schooling in the language, are more frequent. A typical example is Pluto's self-admonition during a quarrel with Persephone in Byron's *Orpheus*: 'The *suaviter in modo* dropped must be | In

---

[64] *ILN* 47, no. 1324 (15 July 1865), 47.   [65] Burnand (1864), 28.
[66] Burnand (1863*a*), 2–3.   [67] Planché (1845), 8.

favour of the *fortiter in re*.[68] Burnand's *Venus and Adonis* plays on the words *non est*, on *unus* for 'one', on *os* for 'countenance', and, more adventurously, in one dialogue:

> *Venus* Oh, lost Adonis! he for whom I pant, is ...
> *Jupiter*   ... *confessio amantis?*
> *Venus* Yes! *a man 'tis!*[69]

Occasionally much more elaborate quotations from Latin occur, which can only have spoken to those who had actually studied Latin at school. When Theseus confronts the minotaur in Planché's *The Marriage of Bacchus* (Lyceum, 1848), he addresses him thus:

> *Monstrum horrendum et informe ingens,*
> Prepare to get the soundest of all swingeings![70]

But even the quotations from classical authors tend to be part of a small repertoire of phrases from Horace, Ovid, or Virgil, similar to that deployed in parliamentary debate at the time. In the burlesque theatre the effect was to debunk the practice, which was in fact already waning: Gladstone was considered old-fashioned because of his predilection for quoting Latin.[71]

Doggerel rhyming verse was burlesque's chosen poetic medium: Planché self-deprecatingly described the hilarious effect of his classical burlesques as attributable to 'persons picturesquely attired speaking absurd doggerel'.[72] Puns were essential. Even the stage directions, some of which were reproduced in the programmes, strove for punning effect; scene 1 of B.J. Spedding's *Ino; or, The Theban Twins* (Strand Theatre, 1869) was set in 'The Gardens of Athamas at Thebes. Showing the Haughty-Culture of the Greeks'.[73] Amongst the favoured verbal tricks was alliteration, evident in the title of Edward Nolan's *Iphigenia; or, The Sail!! The Seer!! And the Sacrifice!!* (1866). The genre is marked by an arch self-consciousness of its own conventions and enjoys disrupting the dramatic illusion it half-heartedly creates: in Brough's *The Siege of Troy* Homer is the war correspondent of *The Times* newspaper, discovered spying in the Greek camp. He is armed with a telescope, a notebook, and a pencil, in order to record proceedings

---

[68] Henry J. Byron (1863), 22.   [69] Burnand (1864), 18, 19, 24, 26.
[70] Planché (1879), iii. 240.   [71] Watson (1973), 17–21.
[72] Planché (1872), i. 180.   [73] Spedding (1869), 9.

for his forthcoming epic.[74] The ghost of Euripides, similarly, engaged in a dialogue with the ghost of Polydorus in Cranstoun Metcalfe's *Hecuba à la Mode; or, The Wily Greek and the Modest Maid*, to lament 'the way my plays | Are murdered by these actors nowadays'.[75]

SONG AND SPECTACLE

Song was central to burlesque, which drew not only on favourite tunes from familiar operas, but also on the vast repertoire of ballads, nursery rhymes, and formulaic genres of popular song in the English language.[76] The last group (later to be plundered by Gilbert and Sullivan) included the 'laughing song', the catalogue or 'patter' song, the 'swagger' where a (male) character introduced himself, and songs about stock subject-matter such as drinking, the weather, or nostalgia.[77] The classical burlesques simply adapted their material to this conventional music: in Burnand's *Arion; or, The Story of a Lyre* (Strand Theatre, 1872), the mythical singer's presence on the pirate boat inspires a breathtaking series of parodies from opera, including a chorus 'We've come to kill Arion', sung to a famous tune from Giacomo Meyerbeer's *Les Huguenots* (1836).[78] In Brough's *The Siege of Troy* Ulysses, in a Scottish accent, sings a formulaic catalogue-song about piling up chariots with loot, to the well-known Scottish tune of *Bonny Dundee*.[79] The tone of the musical dimension of the genre is beautifully exemplified by Planché's *The Deep Deep Sea; or, Perseus and Andromeda; an Original Mythological, Aquatic, Equestrian Burletta* (Olympic Theatre, 1833), which used book 4 of Ovid's *Metamorphoses*. Handel's appropriately titled *Water Music* was used throughout, but at the climactic moment where Perseus (Madame Vestris) entered *ex machina* on Pegasus, clutching Medusa's head, the tune to which (s)he sang the following ditty was

---

[74] Robert Brough (1858), 8.   [75] Metcalfe (1893), 14.
[76] Many of there were collected in the three-volume songbook published by Jones & Co., *The Universal Songster, or Museum of Mirth* (London, 1835). See also Bratton (1975).
[77] Disher (1955), 25–46.
[78] Burnand (1872), 13–15.
[79] Robert Brough (1858), 418.

the universally familiar *Ride a Cock Horse*, a famous English nursery rhyme:

> Ride a wing'd horse,
> The country across.
> I've killed an old woman,
> Both ugly and cross;
> Ringlets of vipers hung down to her toes.
> Her name was Medusa, as all the world knows.[80]

The equally important dance routines were a central part of burlesque.[81] One reviewer of Planché's 1832 Olympic extravaganza *The Paphian Bower; or, Venus and Adonis* was so struck by the brevity of some of the female costumes that he recommended, only half-facetiously, that the Bishop of London intervene.[82] The prominent female legs of burlesque were connected with the convention of transvestism (see Figs. 13.2 and 13.3). It became customary in burlesques, classical or otherwise, to use an attractive actress as a mythical hero or fairy-tale prince (Vestris as Orpheus), and the Queen's Theatre production of Fredrick Fox Cooper's burlesque of Talfourd's *Ion* in 1836 used actresses for all the male roles, while a man played the heroine, Clemanthe. Thenceforward the female breeches role became a standard feature.[83] It was the burlesque (and pantomime) theatre's analogue of the *danseuse en travesti*, the ballerina who began to usurp the male romantic lead in the *corps de ballet* in both Paris and London from 1830 onwards. It has been argued that this development reflected the transformation of ballet from a courtly entertainment to fit the tastes of the market-place and a new bourgeois and sub-bourgeois public—broadly the same public who enjoyed burlesque.[84]

Some burlesques were more marked by mildly naughty jokes than others; Reece's *Prometheus*, for example, described Jove as 'erratically erotic', and apparently encouraged its leading actress to assume sexually suggestive poses from her 'bondage' on the rock. But some of the women who played male parts in burlesque were considerable performers. Two of the most famous legs of all belonged to Priscilla Horton, but she had performed in reputable productions of Shakespeare (she was the definitive Ariel of her day), and possessed a

---

[80] Planché (1879), i. 155–6.   [81] Fletcher (1987), 9–33.
[82] Cited in Appleton (1974), 74.
[83] Fletcher (1987), 22; Garber (1993), 176.   [84] Garafala (1993), 96.

FIGURE 13.3   Annie Bourke as Mercury in Robert Reece's extravaganza
Prometheus; or the Man on the Rock! (1865).

remarkable contralto capable of the most difficult opera, heard to
great advantage as the nightingale in Planché's *The Birds of Aristophanes*. She took numerous male roles in classical burlesque, from
Jason in *The Golden Fleece* to Oedipus in the Brough brothers'
'wildly inventive' *Sphinx* (Haymarket, 1849: Fig. 13.4).[85] Indeed,

---

[85] Stedman (1969), 2–3 and n. 6. William and Robert Brough (1849).

SCENE FROM THE NEW EXTRAVAGANZA OF "THE SPHINX," AT THE HAYMARKET THEATRE.

FIGURE 13.4   A scene from the Brough brothers' extravaganza *The Sphinx* (1849).

by the 1850s, both female-to-male and male-to-female transvestism was routine in burlesque. Older female roles, such as Clytemnestra or Medea, began systematically to be taken by men.[86] The male impersonation of women had emerged from the even lowlier subculture of the public houses, the circus, and the transvestite demi-monde around the fringes of popular culture associated with sexual relations between men.[87]

Henry Morley gave a revealing account of the success of the female breeches roles when recording his response (or that which he thought would be expected of him) to Burnand's *Ixion*:

The whole success of the piece was made by dressing up good-looking girls as immortals lavish in display of leg, and setting them up to sing and dance, or rather kick wretched burlesque capers.[88]

---

[86] The most famous male transvestite star of all was Frederick Robson of the Olympic, whose performance as Medea in 1856 was legendary. See further Ch. 14.
[87] Senelick (1993), 82–5.   [88] Morley (1866), 7.

This distinguished professor also professed revulsion at the effect of burlesque transvestism: Miss Pelham in *Ixion*, he writes, looks hideous with beard and moustache, and 'the woman in her [should] rise in rebellion', while the Hon. Lewis Wingfield, who dressed 'in petticoats and spoke falsetto as Minerva', was guilty of conduct unbecoming in a gentleman.[89] But Morley's professed revulsion did not prevent him from attending burlesques, for his diaries record his reactions to them alongside his records of evenings spent watching the works of Shakespeare and Racine.

Dancing and transvestite costumes contributed to one of the most important dimensions of this type of theatre—as of all Victorian entertainment—the element of spectacle. The ancient myths provided numerous opportunities for extravagant visual stunts.[90] Writers and scenery designers of burlesque competed with their rivals at other theatres for the biggest gasp of wonder and approval at their lavish scenery: a reviewer notes that in Byron's *Orpheus* (Fig. 13.5), for which Mr Fenton had created the scenery:

At the sound of his [Orpheus'] lyre all obstacles vanish, rocks part, and a temple appears, the beauty of which caused Mr Fenton to have an ovation... This classical burlesque cannot fail of being a great success.[91]

At the end of Spedding's *Ino* the heroine appears from the sea, mounted on a dolphin, and announces she is now a goddess; this conclusion was imitated by Burnand in his *Arion*, when the hero ascended to the Milky Way on a dolphin while strumming his lyre.[92]

A manager famous for lavish spectacle was John Buckstone, incumbent of the Haymarket theatre from 1853, when Planché wrote *Mr Buckstone's Ascent of Parnassus* to celebrate his appointment. This piece featured nine muses and puns on the 'Hellenic' names of the London theatres (the Olympic, the Grecian, the Lyceum, etc.). The frequent changes of spectacular scenery (for which research in Pausanias was conducted) included representations of Mount Parnassus from a distance, Delphi, the Castalian Spring, the haunt of Pan, and the summit of Parnassus itself.[93]

---

[89] Morley (1866).
[90] For a brilliant discussion of the reasons behind the Victorian taste for theatrical spectacle see Booth (1981), especially 1–29.
[91] *ILN* 44, no. 1239 (2 Jan. 1864), 19.
[92] Spedding (1869), 46; Burnand (1872), 32.
[93] Planché (1879), iv. 263–4, 291.

FIGURE 13.5   Domestic conflict in Henry Byron's burlesque *Orpheus and Eurydice* (1864).

Physical routines borrowed from the circus and sporting competitions were also regularly featured. In Lemon's *Medea* Jason has a boxing match with Orpheus, and is also a skilled acrobat and knife-swallower; in Talfourd's *Electra* Orestes, played by a young woman, has a wrestling match with Lycus much praised by the press.[94] Burnand's *Pirithoüs, the Son of Ixion* (New Royalty Theatre, 1865) included a centauromachy performed by a horse-back circus troupe; the Hades tableau in the final scene displayed Tantalus in a bath, Sisyphus as an acrobat, kicking a large ball uphill, and Ixion turning his wheel.[95]

THE INSOUCIANCE OF CLASSICAL BURLESQUE

An important factor in the ideological workings of classical burlesque is the social and educational background of the genre's

[94]   British Library Add. MS 52960 L, 6; *ILN* 34, no. 971 (30 Apr. 1859), 419.
[95]   Burnand (1865).

authors. The majority were somewhat rebellious or disaffected members of the middle class, and the term 'bohemian' is regularly found in the description of their lifestyles by contemporaries, notably in the cases of Talfourd, Burnand, and Blanchard.[96] The 'decadent' authors of classical burlesque however fall into two identifiable groups. Some of them are from relatively prosperous families, and had nominally studied Classics at university. At Balliol College, Oxford, in the 1850s, Robert Reece had produced two farces 'to the horror of the authorities'.[97] Francis Burnand, the son of a well-to-do London stockbroker, was educated at Eton and Cambridge (where he was much involved in comic theatricals), and flirted with a career in the church or the law. But when he fell out with his father and left university, a career in the popular theatre became an economic necessity.[98] As we have already seen, 'Bohemian' Frank Talfourd failed to graduate from Christ Church, Oxford after running up huge debts.[99]

The scholarly antiquarian Planché, who had not attended university, was decidedly conventional and by no means disaffected. But among the burlesque writers there were other, more rebellious non-university men, who must have encountered Classics at school. Henry Byron, although the son of the British consul in Haiti, became an actor before he was twenty after failing in the middle-class professions of medicine and law.[100] The brothers William and Robert Brough (like Thomas Talfourd) were the offspring of a provincial brewer. Although they were educated at a private school in Newport, Wales, their fortunes were blighted when their father's business failed through his enthusiasm for radical causes. Robert, the more talented writer, worked as a clerk before finding success in the theatre. But he had apparently inherited his father's politics, publishing in 1859 the satirical *Songs of the Governing Classes*, written from a radical perspective.[101]

Yet the mildly rebellious authors of classical burlesque did not use it as a platform for radical politics. The truth is that the social

---

[96] See e.g. on Talfourd, Burnand (1904), 387; on Blanchard, *DNB* xxii. 216.
[97] Adderley (1887).
[98] Burnand (1904), i. 322.
[99] See Thomas Talfourd (1841–54), entries for Friday, 26 Oct. and Monday, 3 Dec. 1849.
[100] Jim Davis (1984), 1–32.
[101] *ODNB* vii. 967–8.

ferment and reforming zeal of the theatre of the 1830s, which, in the wake of the Great Reform Act of 1832 had permitted experimentation even with republican ideas,[102] was replaced soon after the accession of Queen Victoria in 1837 with a much more conservative stance, apparently unquestioned in burlesque. Nolan's *Agamemnon at Home; or, The Latest Particulars of that Little Affair at Mycenae* (1867) actually goes out of its way to criticize political radicals currently demonstrating for parliamentary reform.[103] In addition, this piece is even more unpleasantly racist than most burlesques,[104] although jokes about 'niggers' were part of the genre's standard repertoire. It is of course significant that *Agamemnon at Home* was performed not in the popular theatre of London or Liverpool but on the amateur stage of the ever-conservative Oxford University. But a similar conservatism marks some of the great hits of the London stage, including Burnand's *Ixion*, in which much humour is created at the expense of the 'radicals' of ancient Thessaly, loosely modelled on French revolutionaries. Ixion's anti-monarchical wife is followed by a 'Crowd of Red Republicans, Unread Republicans . . . appropriately crowned with mob caps'.[105] One of the revolutionaries, Tondapameibomenos, suggests some revolutionary violence against King Ixion:

> Let us break all the windows, and make plain
> The 'Rights of Man,' by reference to *Paine*.[106]

Yet the red revolutionaries of ancient Thessaly come to an ineffectual end, casually struck motionless by Mercury when their humorous potential has been exhausted. The burlesque theatre may have had its subversive dimension, but *explicit* political radicalism was alien to it.

Nevertheless, burlesque occasionally implies a mild sympathy for reform in its audience, especially in the works of Frank Talfourd (the son of Thomas Talfourd, MP for Reading and a staunch supporter of universal male suffrage).[107] Apollo laments in the prologue to his burlesque of Euripides' *Alcestis* that people do

[102] One of the more important of such writers was Francis Talfourd's father Thomas (see Ch. 11).
[103] Nolan (1867), 12.
[104] Ibid. 23.
[105] Burnand (1863*b*), 2.
[106] Ibid. 8.
[107] See *ILN* 15, no. 382 (28 July 1849), 52 and above, Ch. 11.

not believe in the gods any more, or worship at Delphi's altars: all they can talk about these days is 'the Rights of Persons'.[108] There is a vaguely cynical attitude towards politicians, apparent in, for example, Talfourd's burlesque of Sophocles' *Electra*. Here the corrupt tyrant Ægisthus is characterized as a cynical manipulator of the people of Argos. He explicitly makes fun of monarchs' tendency to use speeches composed by their ministers.[109] Burlesque's position on women is also ambivalent. Domineering wives are stock characters (usually played by men). The most terrifying is Ino in Spedding's *Ino*, who batters her husband Athamas, 'a wretched hen-pecked member of the matrimonial band'. He confides to his guest Æetes that

> A week or two of our connubial fights
> Would teach you what is meant by women's rights.[110]

Yet several burlesques do take the side of women in ancient myth—even of Medea—and this must, at least in part, be a response to the female component of the audience (see Ch. 14).[111]

The subversiveness of the genre, however, was expressed more by its tone and stance than by its explicit content. To burlesque any 'classic' text is of course slightly subversive. But to travesty the very content of the education which divided the classes and fostered the elite, in front of a distinctively cross-class audience, was a complex procedure of some ideological potency. The insouciant attitude of the generation of burlesque writers in the 1850s and 1860s is clear from their subtitles, which self-consciously indicate disrespect for their sources: Talfourd's *Alcestis; the Original Strong-Minded Woman: a Classical Burlesque in One Act* (Strand Theatre, 1850) was further brazenly subtitled *a most shameless misinterpretation of the Greek Drama of Euripides*. Classical burlesque is thus related to the serious critiques of classical education which serious-minded intellectuals were publishing at

---

[108] Francis Talfourd (1850), 'Prologue'. Since Talfourd disliked both religion and his father's political earnestness, the satire may be on both the Established Church (which stressed duties and distrusted rights) and liberal politics (fashionable froth having obscured eternal verities).

[109] Francis Talfourd (1859), 6, 7, 37.

[110] Spedding (1869), 9–10.

[111] Although women certainly attended classical burlesques, as well as acting in them, unfortunately no source seems to be known which records a woman's responses to this type of theatre in any detail.

the time,[112] and to the humorous accounts to be found in the works of the comic prose writers. When Charles Dickens, for example, read his novels aloud in public recitations, he slightly adapted them to heighten their dramatic effect. In the eighth chapter of *Nicholas Nickelby*, the schoolmaster Squeers tells the pupils to whom he teaches English spelling and philosophy, that a horse is 'a quadruped; and quadruped's Latin'. But in the performance version, Dickens added to this speech of Squeers a denunciation of training in the ancient tongues: '. . . or Greek, or Hebrew, or some other language that's dead and deserves to be'.[113] Thackeray, in the persona of M. A. Titmarsh, describes a journey to Athens, and includes a hilarious attack on conventional adulation of antiquity. Titmarsh regards the ten years of Classics he endured as 'ten years' banishment of infernal misery, tyranny, arrogance'. In Attica he was visited by the Greek muse, and explains that he could not effect any reconciliation with her because he read her poets 'in fear and trembling; and a cold sweat is but an ill accompaniment to poetry'. Ancient History was 'so dull . . . that when the brutal dulness of a schoolmaster is superadded to her own slow conversation, the union becomes intolerable'. People only 'say they are enthusiastic about the Greek and Roman authors and history, because it is considered proper and respectable'.[114]

There was a particularly strong opposition perceived between Classics as it was experienced in schools and universities, and the delights of the popular theatre. Renton Nicholson (see further below) composed a song in 1853 to advertise the Drury Lane Pantomime, whose words are supposed to be sung by young men released from the classroom and lecture hall:

> Let Homer be banished, and Virgil laid down,
> Academics be blowed,—we have come up to town . . .
> The schoolmaster's at home, his pupils abroad;
> Who cares for his cane? And who cares for his Rod?[115]

Burnand, similarly, records a conversation with the 'short, wizened, dried-up elderly' Vice-Chancellor of Cambridge University, from whom he asked permission to stage three burlesques at Cambridge in the 1850s. The Vice-Chancellor misunderstood his

---

[112] Stray (1998), 83–113.   [113] See van Amerongen (1926), 47.
[114] Thackeray (1846), quoted from Thackeray (1903), 272, 276.
[115] Bradley (1965), 314. Cf. Ch. 16 n. 18.

request, assuming that by 'staging a play' the young undergraduate before him must have meant a Greek or Latin drama.[116] The account implies that serious ancient theatre represents the establishment, while burlesque is the medium of smart young rebels— even though they were officially students of Classics.

The classical burlesques often make explicit their authors' own resentment about their pedantic education: in Vincent Amcotts's *Ariadne: or, The Bull! The Bully!! And The Bullion!!* (1870), Theseus' studious friend Mentor loses his treatise on Greek verbal roots, which has fallen 'overboard'. Theseus suggests that *all* 'classic authors' be thrown overboard:

> Away with Latin, Greek, and all such stuff,
> For I've been *over bored* with them enough.[117]

In a similarly satirical vein, Minerva in Burnand's *Ixion* wants to reject Ganymede's application for the post of Olympian butler on the ground of his poor classical education:

> For his situation
> We want competitive examination;
> How can he hand about the drinks that *we* brew
> Unless he knows his Latin, Greek, and Hebrew?[118]

Perhaps the most powerful example is constituted by the finale of Burnand's *Venus and Adonis*. Adonis sings a 'spelling' song about the burlesqued ancient poet, Ovid:

> *Adonis* (spelling):   O, V, *ov*; I, D, *id*—
>   OVID was his name!

To which the ensemble (Pluto, Jupiter, Venus, Mercury, Vulcan, Adonis) respond:

> Marked by cane
> Very plain,
> Each young swain
> Laughs again,
> When he sees
> METAMORPHOSES
> Right in the middle of the play bill, oh![119]

---

[116] Burnand (1880), 7–17.   [117] Amcotts (1870), 8.
[118] Burnand (1863*b*), 18.   [119] Burnand (1864), 50.

The burlesque thus reminds its audience of the corporal punishment attendant in schools upon the deciphering of Ovid, and points up the pleasure to be derived from revisiting the text of the Latin epic in the theatre of burlesque laughter. For Burnand, who at Eton had been made truly miserable by Greek and Latin, later recalled the great popularity of his burlesque *Dido*, which in 1860 ran for no fewer than eighty nights. He meditated that in conceiving this assault on the *Aeneid*, 'perhaps I was taking revenge on the Classics'.[120]

CLASSICAL BURLESQUE AS CULTURAL APPROPRIATION

It is possible to see in the complex ideology of classical burlesque a witty subversion of classical education, with all that might imply for an audience including many people who had no access to the privileges such an education conferred. Yet even if they were ostensibly repudiating Classics, burlesques were simultaneously *appropriating* the subject for their audience. Nineteenth-century classical burlesque belongs to that sub-category of burlesque literature which comic theorists identify with travesty—the 'low burlesque' of a particular work or story achieved by treating it 'in an aggressively familiar style'.[121] Such a 'familiar' treatment paradoxically implies a form of cultural ownership. The authors of classical burlesque liked to display their knowledge of Classics to their audiences, but it seems that these audiences enjoyed the sense of cultural possession which their own familiarity with some aspects of Classics, derived from or affirmed in burlesque, then bestowed upon them. Victorians of all classes were, as Pearsall has put it, sentimental and aesthetically conservative, but they were also sharp, cynical, and knowing;[122] the subversively 'knowing'— even conspiratorial—tone of burlesque was similar to that of the slightly later Victorian phenomenon of the music hall.[123] There is an emphasis in classical burlesque on 'knowing' the details about ancient culture, distinguishing Greek from Latin names, and pointing out anachronisms. In *The Golden Fleece* Medea complains

---

[120] Burnand (1904), i. 144–7, 366.   [121] Jump (1972), 2.
[122] Pearsall (1973), 15.
[123] See Bailey (1994); cf. Schoch (2002) on Shakespeare.

that Eros is 'vulgarly called Cupid'; in Lemon's *Medea* Creon says
that Medea cannot follow a new career as a Vestal Virgin, as
Glauce suggests, because Vestals 'will be Roman institutions, |
Not Grecian'.[124]

The mock-erudite tone of classical burlesque is also apparent in
its semi-serious instruction in details of ancient mythology, which
often takes the form of a rhyming, punning, adaptation of an article
in Lemprière's 1788 dictionary. In Planché's *The Marriage of
Bacchus* (Lyceum, 1848), Daedalus sang a 'patter song' which
escorted the audience on a breakneck journey through classical
history and myth, with lines about Homer, Hannibal, Cato,
Plato, Aeneas, Sardanapalus, Dido, Caesar, and Priam.[125] In Burnand's *Venus and Adonis* Vulcan sings a 'catalogue' song enumer-
ating Jove's love affairs, 'There's Semele, Leda, Europa, Callisto,'
etc.[126]

Several classical burlesques mused knowingly upon ancient
stage conventions. Planché's 1845 *The Golden Fleece* was
prompted by the important production of Sophocles' *Antigone*,
accompanied by Mendelssohn's music and a sixty-strong male
chorus, which had been a huge success at Covent Garden that
season.[127] Charles Matthews, Planché's 'Chorus', explained:

> Friends, countrymen, lovers, first listen to me;
> I'm the Chorus: Whatever you hear or see
> That you don't understand, I shall rise to explain—
> It's a famous old fashion that's come up again.[128]

By twenty years later, in December 1865, when Planché's adaptation of Offenbach, *Orpheus in the Haymarket*, played at the Haymarket, the figure of Public Opinion could affirm in the prologue
that everyone, whatever their social background, now knew what a
Greek chorus did:

> On this occasion I enact the Chorus.
> There's not an urchin in this learned age,
> But knows that on the old Hellenic stage
> The Chorus told the audience all the plot,
> Whether there was one in the play, or not.[129]

---

[124] Planché (1845), 9; Lemon (1856), 13.   [125] Planché (1879), iii. 248–9.
[126] Burnand (1864), 13.
[127] On the important Covent Garden *Antigone* see Ch. 12.
[128] Planché (1845), 5.   [129] Planché (1879), v. 239.

Similarly, in Talfourd's *Electra* the audience heard about the Greeks' preference for keeping violence off stage. This brilliant burlesque also featured a play-within-a-play, 'the performance of a Strolling Company of ACTORS on a Thespian cart', thus confirming in Talfourd's audience their knowledge about the origins of Greek tragedy in the pre-classical era.[130]

CLASSICAL BURLESQUE AS SELF-DEFINITION

Yet alongside such passages, which reinforce a sense of familiarity with pleasurable aspects of ancient culture, one of the most distinctive features of classical burlesque was its creation of humour out of anachronistic references to the contemporary world of the audience. In the eighteenth century comic writing for the stage had ridiculed its characters; Victorian comedy, on the other hand, deliberately avoided overt malice, and emphasized amiability and fellow feeling between writer and character. From the 1840s onwards the primary source of wit and humour was regarded as incongruity—the arbitrary juxtaposition of dissimilar ideas and material—which was seen as giving rise not to an 'insolent' but to a 'congenial' sense of superiority.[131] There was a beautifully stark incongruity in juxtaposing classical myths with references to hailing cabs, or making Admetus smoke the cigars to which he is addicted in Talfourd's burlesque *Alcestis*. Indeed, in 1870 Percy Fitzgerald argued that in mythological burlesque of the type pioneered by Planché, mirth is produced precisely by 'a transposition of the subject matter into, or its contrast with, some inappropriate time or condition'. The successful burlesque humorist would try to

reproduce his old Romans and Greeks as nearly as possible with the weaknesses and conditions of our everyday life . . . knowing how inconsistent such old manners and customs are with present habits, he will exaggerate the former so as to make the discordance more startling.[132]

Reviewers therefore often compliment authors who write burlesques in which 'the theme is classical, but scarcely the spirit of

---

[130] Francis Talfourd (1859), 29–30. See further Hall (1999*a*).
[131] Robert Bernard Martin (1974), 17, 22.
[132] Percy Fitzgerald (1870), 154–5.

SCENE FROM THE NEW EXTRAVAGANZA OF "PAN," AT THE ADELPHI THEATRE.—SEE PRECEDING PAGE.

FIGURE 13.6   Landscape featuring the statue of Pan, in Henry Byron's extravaganza *Pan; or, the Loves of Echo and Narcissus* (1865).

the piece', an approving contemporary description of Byron's clever *Pan; or, the Loves of Echo and Narcissus* (Adelphi Theatre, 1865, see Fig. 13.6);[133] and the outstanding success of the Brough brothers' *The Sphinx* was a result precisely of its contrast of 'authentic' classical scenery and costumes with the smart, contemporary, updated riddles which Œdipus had to solve.[134] Examples could be multiplied. A highlight of Wooler's *Jason and Medea* was Chiron's song about the Great Exhibition of that year; in the second scene of Frank Sikes's *Hypermnestra* (Lyceum Theatre 1869), the Danaids play croquet in the Argive palace garden; a woman in Burnand's *Arion* walks strangely because of her 'Grecian bend'—an allusion to a shape of profoundly *un*-Greek corseted female costume fashionable at the time.[135]

---

[133] *ILN* 46, no. 1310 (15 Apr. 1865), 359.
[134] *ILN* 14, no. 3566 (14 Apr. 1849), 244–5.
[135] Wooler (1851), 27; Sikes (1869), scene 2; Burnand, (1872), 21: see Barton (1937), 462. On 'Greek' fashions see further Ch. 16.

The presence in London of the Metropolitan Police Force, established as recently as 1829, features prominently in burlesque: in Talfourd's *Alcestis* the imported figure of Polax the Policeman, lover of Alcestis' nurse, 'is habited in a classic dress, with the exception of his hat, cape, and staff, which are those of a modern policeman'.[136] In Sikes's *Hypermnestra* Danaus is arrested by Mercury and an attendant policeman.[137] Other modern social developments were deliberately inserted into the classical milieu; in Amcotts's *Pentheus* (1866), inspired by Euripides' *Bacchae*, Pentheus threatens Bacchus with compulsory membership of the temperance movement, and a vow of abstinence;[138] in Brough's *The Siege of Troy* Helen is 'the divorced wife of Menelaus, married, under the new act, to Paris', a reference to the great Divorce Act of 1857 (on which see further below, Ch. 14).[139]

There was a particularly pervasive tendency to refer to modern technology. In Amcotts's *Pentheus* Bacchus, when asked during the earthquake if the gas is exploding, observes:

> To talk of gas so long before its age
> Is really *making light* of history's page.[140]

The Theseus of the same author's *Ariadne* points out that diving-bells 'aren't yet invented'.[141] The audiences seem to have found intrusive references to modern forms of vehicular transport quite hilarious. In Spedding's *Ino* the Greek heroine pushes her twins in a perambulator; in a burlesque *Jason and Medea* Jason's war-chariot is drawn by Theseus and Pirithous riding bicycles instead of horses; in Amcotts's *Ariadne* Theseus arrives in Crete by steam-boat.[142] Burlesque betrays a particularly strong obsession with railways: in Blanchard's *Antigone Travestie* of 1845, Creon's response to his problems is to imagine taking the next train out of Thebes and emigrating to New South Wales; Planché's *The Birds*

---

[136] Francis Talfourd (1850), 12.

[137] Sikes (1869), 62.

[138] Amcotts and Anson (1866), 16.

[139] Robert Brough (1858), 2. See also H. J. Byron (1863), 28, where Proserpine declares she wants to sue for a divorce from Pluto on the ground of infidelity (he has kissed 21 girls). In Burnand's *Venus and Adonis* the audience is informed that Juno has won a formal separation from Jove, who used to beat her, on the grounds of 'cruelty and base desertion': Burnand (1864), 9.

[140] Amcotts and Anson (1866), 39.

[141] Amcotts (1870), 8.

[142] Spedding (1869), 13; Addison and Howell (1878), 4; Amcotts (1870), 7.

of Aristophanes (1846) satirizes plans to build a cross-Channel railway tunnel; Lemon's *Medea* features a scene at Corinth Railway Station.[143]

So why did the Victorians conjure up this bizarre theatrical world where mythical Greeks and Romans mingled with policemen and modern railway stations? They were of course interested in all previous periods of history—in the medieval era, the Renaissance, and the epoch of revolution—as much as in Graeco-Roman antiquity. Yet it was as no simple 'mirror' that they used any period of the past. Their historical consciousness was a mode of *self*-consciousness involving a complex dialectical process by which analogy became awareness of *difference*. As Culler concludes, when the Victorian Age looked into the mirror of history,

it saw not merely itself reflected but also the whole panorama of the past... Indeed, in the course of looking to the past it became conscious of the distinctive characteristics of the present.[144]

For the newly 'historicist' outlook of the Victorian era gave rise to the idea of 'modernity' as it is now understood. It was through thinking with history and 'classic' authors that the Victorians became conscious of the meaning of their own modernity, the characteristics of their age. The conscious modernization involved in burlesque helped audiences to conceive what made them different from people of the past. The newly created image of the scientifically advanced, modern, urban society was constructed out of symbols of what the Greeks and Romans did *not* share with modernity—the policemen and steam engines central to the Victorians' metropolitan self-image.

THE VICTORIANS AND COMIC EXPRESSION

The burlesque of classical texts and myths must ultimately be placed in the context of the Victorians' profound taste for comedy, to which their dominant sense of affluence and progress seems to have provided a special backdrop:[145] it was during the nineteenth century that it became socially unacceptable to be thought lacking a sense of humour, and the English sense of humour became an

---

[143] Blanchard (1845); Planché (1846), 17; Lemon (1856), 7.
[144] Culler (1985), 284.   [145] Henkle (1980), 4–5.

important part of English self-definition. Indeed, with the exceptions of the Irish and the Americans, all other nations were
regarded as existing in a state of humourless darkness.[146] Gilbert
Abott à Beckett took pains to defend the contemporary taste for
comic expression, even in works of instruction, as in his *The Comic
History of Rome* (1852), although he is aware that 'Comic Literature' is still despised in certain quarters, 'since that class of writing
obtained the popularity which has especially attended it within the
last few years'.[147] This entertaining volume is enhanced by the
engraved illustrations by John Leech, which express perfectly the
spirit—and probably the direct influence of the scenic design—of
theatrical classical burlesque.

The taste for humorous rewriting of classical stories penetrated
middle-class private theatricals. In 1865 two famous writers of
burlesque co-published a collection 'Specifically Written for Performance in the Theatre-Royal Back Drawing-Room'. Only one,
William Brough's *Robin Hood*, has a non-classical theme. The
others are his *Phaeton; or, Pride Must Have a Fall*, and Burnand's
Orpheus; or, the Magic Lyre, Sappho; or, Look Before You Leap!,
and *Boadicea the Beautiful; or, Harlequin Julius Caesar and the
Delightful Druid*.[148] The book contains amusing instructions for
the achievement of special effects: the sound of Phaeton's chariot
crashing could be created by throwing flat-irons, bootjacks,
candlesticks, kitchen pokers, and a full coal-scuttle from a tea-
tray to the floor; Charon in *Orpheus* would look good in a sou'-
wester; there are suggestions for how to paint a scene-cloth
depicting the Leucadian Rock from which Sappho can leap.[149]

Staged burlesque was also popular in elitist contexts. St John's
College, Oxford, mounted several classical burlesques in the 1860s
with an all-male cast, including Nolan's infantile send-up of Aeschylus' *Agamemnon*, entitled *Agamemnon at Home*.[150] Meanwhile,

---

[146] Robert Bernard Martin (1974), 6, 36; Cobbe (1863).
[147] See à Beckett (1852), p. v. This author also wrote burlesques for the theatre.
[148] Brough and Burnand (1865). This chapter has dealt with burlesques of
classical myths, but many others staged scenes from ancient history, including the
lives of Alexander the Great and Cleopatra, and from Bulwer's novel *The Last Days
of Pompeii*.
[149] Brough and Burnand (1865), 35, 40, 78. See Margaret Reynolds (2000),
250–43.
[150] Nolan (1867). The humour relies entirely on jokes at the expense of women
and 'niggers', and lacks all the refined wit, puns, rhymes, and literary allusiveness
which graced the superior examples of this genre.

at Balliol College, a much funnier undergraduate reading Classical Moderations followed by Modern History was writing a burlesque of Euripides' *Bacchae*, an adaptation of Offenbach's *La Belle Hélène*, and an Ovid-inspired burlesque *Ariadne*.[151] The ban on theatrical performances at Oxford University at this time meant that these classical burlesques had to be staged 'more or less surreptitiously'.[152]

Yet the spirit of classical burlesque was omnipresent: undergraduates and even their superiors were using varieties of parody and burlesque in privately circulated texts which, paradoxically, were *confirming* their membership of their elite. This practice can be dated to at least as early as a puerile 1816 burlesqued translation of Euripides' *Alcestis*, done line-by-line, as its author explains, with numerals printed to 'help' its readers through the Greek of Gaisford. Its comic rhymes and scatological humour are plainly aimed at teenage boys seeking to alleviate the boredom of ploughing through the original tragedy.[153] In 1843 an undergraduate at Oxford published a self-styled burlesque of Aeschylus' *Persians* entitled *The Chinaid*, in which his stated object was 'to invest with absurdity' his classical model. The recent Opium Wars suggested replacing Xerxes with Chinyang, the Emperor of China, and his chorus with opium-addicted court mandarins. About fifty per cent of the text is fairly accurate translation of the original.[154] Similar in spirit is Trevelyan's updated version of Aristophanes' *Wasps*, which is replete with esoteric references to fellow members of his Cambridge university clique, their alcoholic japes, and confrontations with the police.[155] Even the Very Revd Henry Longueville Mansel, Dean of Christ Church, Oxford, chose classical burlesque in a parody of Aristophanes' *Clouds* when he wanted to

---

[151] *Pentheus*: Amcotts and Anson (1866); *Fair Helen*: Amcotts (1866); *Ariadne*: Amcotts (1870).

[152] A handwritten inscription, dated 1907, on the cover of the Bodleian Library's copy of Amcotts's *Fair Helen* (1866) records that 'In those days the drama was cultivated, more or less surreptitiously, in Oxford by a set of men of whom Amcotts was a leading member'. On Oxford undergraduate theatricals see further Ch. 15.

[153] Styrke (1816). At the end the chorus address the reader, expressing their hope that he has enjoyed it, 'Whether you read the *Greek*, or smudge, twitter and smirk | At the blithe, jolly version of *Issachar Styrke*' (p. 97). See further Ch. 15.

[154] Anon. (1843).

[155] Trevelyan (1858), 8.

satirize the political and religious controversies afflicting Oxford University.[156]

In an important study of the all-pervasiveness of the comic spirit in Victorian culture, Roger Henkle defines the Victorians' 'comic attitude' as the avoidance of the upsetting aspects of a subject, or a reduction in the consumers' confrontation with its social implications.[157] This is exactly what the burlesques of ancient myth and literature did with their harsher aspects. The 'moral distancing' in the burlesque theatre was partly made possible by the impersonation of young men by women, which allowed the audience to recognize and empathize with the (often famous) player, and thus to distance themselves from the fictitious character she was impersonating. Orestes the murderer and vindictive Olympian rapists are rendered innocuous, even charming, by being played by exaggeratedly 'feminine' women.[158] But more importantly, the incest, death, murder, rapine, and deviation from socially acceptable forms of behaviour so fundamental to classical mythology are ruthlessly censored in burlesque. In those dealing with Medea, her children are either not killed at all, or are revivified by her magic. In *The Siege of Troy* even Hector comes back to life after his duel with Achilles. In Talfourd's *Electra* the hero Orestes is spared the guilt of actually killing his mother and uncle. Sappho burlesques always followed the pattern set by the ancient variant of her tale in which she was infatuated with a man named Phaon (see above all Ovid, *Her.* 15), by 'correcting' her sexuality. In Burnand's *Dido*, the unbearable emotional pain of *Aeneid* book 4 is transformed into an undignified squabble between a male drag actor as Dido and Anna over Eneas, their Trojan beau, played by an attractive young woman.[159]

The writers of comedy and comic theorists were aware that their era was inimical to tragic drama. Some even blamed burlesque for the dearth of serious drama during this period, arguing that it was precisely the taste for burlesque of highbrow works which had led to the blurring of the line between true drama and low entertainment.[160] Some killjoy members of the literary and intellectual elite despised and avoided burlesque altogether. An obituary of Frank

---

[156] Mansel (1873), 395–408.   [157] Henkle (1980), 4–6.
[158] George Taylor (1989), 140.   [159] *ILN* 36, no. 1017 (18 Feb. 1860), 155.
[160] Percy Fitzgerald (1870), 142, 251.

Talfourd in *The Athenaeum* regrets that he 'left the world with little or no adequate witness of his powers—the travestie and burlesque in which he revelled showing but one, and that the poorer, side of his gay and brilliant intellect.'[161] In 1870 a writer who dreamed of a superior type of comedy disdains the intellects of the spectators of burlesque, lamenting that the genre now failed to tickle the brain, for the actresses 'acting Hector and Achilles only delight the eye'.[162]

In the late 1860s and early 1870s commentators became increasingly restive about the state of comic writing, especially writing for the stage. They yearned for more intellectual wit and less amiable sentimentality in their humour. The more perspicacious of them could see that the burlesque seam was exhausted, and the well of inventiveness, especially when it came to puns, had been drained dry.[163] Burlesque's death knell is sounded by a reviewer of Burnand's burlesque of *Antony and Cleopatra* in 1873, who describes the performance as thoroughly inane:

The fact is that burlesque has been done to death, and the attempt to raise it from an occasional entertainment into a permanent institution must ultimately fail.[164]

The public agreed, for burlesques—certainly classical burlesques—die out at this time, except, indeed, for the 'occasional entertainment' at small or private theatres, such as Metcalfe's clever burlesque of Euripides' *Hecuba*, performed privately as late as 1893.[165]

The pivotal moment was the first work on which Gilbert and Sullivan collaborated, *Thespis, or the Gods Grown Old* (1871). It includes numerous features typical of the classical burlesque: the pseudo-Greek comic names (Thespis' travelling players include Timidion, Tipseion, Preposteros, and Stupidas), young women in tights impersonating Olympian gods, Thespis' enumeration in Act I of Jove's sexual scandals with Danaë, Leda, and Europa, and his recitation of the entry under 'Apollo' in Lemprière's classical dictionary.[166] Indeed, it is possible to read the libretto of *Thespis*

---

[161] 'Our Weekly Gossip', *Athenaeum*, no. 1794 (15 Mar. 1862), 365.
[162] Percy Fitzgerald (1870), 150–1.
[163] Robert Bernard Martin (1974), 17, 38; Percy Fitzgerald (1870),149–99.
[164] *ILN* 63, no. 1776 (13 Sept. 1873), 239.
[165] Metcalfe (1893), performed at Vestry House, Anerley.
[166] Rees (1964), 71, 93, 162, 134.

as a self-conscious satire on the conventions of the genre of the classical burlesque. Thespis, for example, is aware that the Victorian theatre had preferred its classics in burlesque form, declaring that as an actor he is rarely called upon to act the role of Jupiter these days, for 'In fact we don't use you much out of burlesque.'[167] *Thespis* was unsuccessful—too clever, it seems for its audience, who failed to understand either the more obscure classical allusions or the self-conscious commentary on the genre intended by its authors.[168] It was to be with *Trial by Jury*, which had a contemporary setting, that they were to make their name. Although they adopted various settings for the subsequent works, from the Japan of *Mikado* to the Venice of *Gondoliers*, they never again put the Graeco-Roman world before their audience. Other authors simultaneously abandoned the rhyming, punning subversion of classical mythology which had entertained London audiences for several decades: by 1888, and George Hawtrey's *Atalanta* (Strand Theatre), even the hallmark rhyming couplets of traditional burlesque had been abandoned in favour of up-to-date idiomatic prose dialogue.[169]

Such 'Hellenism' as did appear in Gilbert and Sullivan's subsequent operettas was totally different from that of the burlesque theatre—it was the pretentious Hellenism of the Aesthetic movement, which they mocked in *Patience* in 1881. The Aesthetes were by the late 1870s turning for inspiration less to medieval sources and more to Graeco-Roman statuary and the paintings of Alma-Tadema,[170] which certainly contributed to the death of classical burlesque. Watching popular entertainers dressed up as ancient Greeks perhaps seemed less hilarious than watching progressive members of the educated classes doing so in all seriousness.[171]

A related development was the new fashion for academic Greek plays, beginning with the *Agamemnon* performed in Greek at Oxford in 1880 (see Chs. 15 and 16). By the 1890s 'Classical theatricals' indubitably meant academic Greek plays; an anonymous comedy *Our Greek Play*, performed in 1892, sends up an

---

[167] Ibid. 120. See also the 'metatheatrical' chorus in Act I, where the chorus sing, 'Here's a pretty tale for future Iliads and Odyssies, | Mortals are about to personate the gods and goddesses.'
[168] See Baily (1973), 38–9.
[169] Mackinlay (1927), 214.
[170] Ormond (1968), 38.   [171] See Stella Mary Newton (1974), 58.

erudite curate who organizes a 'Greek play' at his local stately home.[172] The fun in this piece is no longer at the expense of the conventions of classical literature, as in the burlesque theatre, but of a new convention—the contemporary fashion for serious performances of classical tragedies.

CLASSICS BEYOND THE ELITE

Burlesque was by no means the only medium of entertainment through which uneducated people had access to classical culture in the nineteenth century. There were other types of popular diversion which treated the classics with more or less insouciance. Extensive use of a kind of Latin, for example, characterized the famous 'Judge and Jury Society' run at the Garrick's Head Hotel in Bow Street, London, by the publican, Renton Nicholson. This society conducted subversive mock trials based on celebrated cases of the day. The half-educated Nicholson had himself spent time in gaol, and was thus familiar with judicial Latin.[173] The trials had a working-class tenor, for Nicholson liked trials involving the private lives of aristocrats, bestowing upon them new titles such as the Hon. Viscount Limpus versus the Hon. Priapus Pulverton.[174] The female parts were acted by male transvestites, and Nicholson, who always acted the judge, entertained his demotic audience by extemporizing in streams of amateur Latin, especially when summarizing what an observer denounced as the 'filthy particulars' of the cases.[175]

Working-class access to classical myth and history included the entertainments offered by travelling showmen. The famous Billy Purvis took his booth theatre around the circuit of northern racetracks, in which he displayed phantasmagorias illustrating scenes from classical mythology, such as Neptune in his car with Amphitrite and Tritons; Purvis's troupe of actors also performed paraphrases of plays on classical themes, including *The Death of Alexander the Great*, which had been the sub-title of Nathaniel Lee's famous *The Rival Queens* of 1677.[176] The most famous of all early circus performers, Andrew Ducrow, specialized in 'hippo-

---

[172] Anon. (1892).
[173] Bradley (1965), pp. xi, 250–1, 291.
[174] Charles Douglas Stuart and Park (1895), 8–10.
[175] Ritchie (1857), 80.   [176] Bowman (1875), 137; Mayer (1971), 27–34.

dramatic' enactments of Hercules' labours, of Alexander the Great taming Bucephalus, of the rape of the Sabine women, and Roman gladiators in combat.[177] Most of these were performed at Astley's Theatre in London, which was heterogeneous in its clientele: it had a large working-class audience, and yet middle-class families also took their children.[178] In the unlikely event of any of the audience becoming bored during the action, they could raise their eyes to the ceiling (renovated in 1858), adorned with pictures of Neptune, Diana, Cybele, Apollo, Dawn, and Venus, all riding chariots drawn by appropriate animals (peacocks for Venus, deer for Diana).[179]

A telling source for the variety of avenues by which the Londoner in the 1840s had access to classical mythology is the diary of Charles Rice, by day a lowly porter at the British Museum, guardian of celebrated Graeco-Roman antiquities for the middle and upper classes, but by night a tavern singer in the public houses of central London. On 19 February 1840, at the Adam & Eve in St Pancras Road, he was engaged to put his knowledge of ancient sculpture to profitable use by delivering notices accompanying Mr Lufkeen's delineation of *The Grecian Statues*, a series of acrobatic poses based on classical statuary (a routine originally popularized by Ducrow), including 'Hercules wrestling with the Nemean Lion'.[180] Lufkeen and Rice were entertaining people from the lowest income bracket, but the work of the more famous Ducrow was also acceptable to middle-class taste: one educated reviewer could compare his athletic poses with the work of ancient Greek sculptors:

What god-like grace in that volant movement, fresh from Olympus ... to convert his frame into such forms ... as the Greek imagination moulded into perfect expression of the highest state of the soul, *that* shows that Ducrow has a spirit kindred to those who in marble made their mythology immortal.[181]

Yet this form of entertainment, in other contexts, soon developed pornographic associations. From the 1840s onwards well-developed female models in skin-tight 'fleshings' could be seen in the popular *poses plastiques*, in which they imitated naked

---

[177] Saxon (1978), 73, 109, 47.   [178] East (1971), 37.
[179] *ILN* 33, no. 946 (20 Nov. 1858), 488, 490.   [180] Senelick (1997), 44–5.
[181] Quoted in East (1971), 37.

classical statues for the delectation of audiences which contemporary critics regarded as including the 'worst sort' of person.[182] *Tableaux vivants* such as *Diana Preparing for the Chase*, at Liverpool's Parthenon Rooms in 1850, provided a narrative of eroticized female beauty in which proletarian sexual voyeurism was legitimized by the use of classical mythology.[183] One of the more important directors of such events was the same enterprising Renton Nicholson of the 'Judge and Jury' society, who hired working-class girls to enact scenes from classical myth which he accompanied with mock-learned 'lectures'.[184] A contemporary critic regarded Renton's *poses plastiques* as morally reprehensible, and was displeased that women were allowed to join the audience.[185]

Public house entertainment, circuses, hippodrama, fairground theatre, and *poses plastiques* would all, therefore, bear further investigation to see what they can tell us about the uses of classical culture by the population beyond the educated elite in nineteenth-century Britain. But none of these diversions was as ideologically complex, as rich, and as challenging to the modern interpreter as the dazzling, cheeky, and surprisingly erudite phenomenon of the mid-Victorian classical burlesque. For this important genre of popular theatre transcended narrow class interests, repudiated classical education and yet at the same time appropriated the more pleasurable parts of its contents for ordinary people, and helped them define their modernity. Our picture of nineteenth-century classicism in Britain will therefore surely remain incomplete until the burlesque theatre takes its place as a serious subject of study alongside the canon of great literary responses to the Greeks and Romans produced by and for the classically educated elite.

---

[182] See Holström (1967); Altick (1978), 345–9; George Taylor (1989), 47.
[183] Tracy C. Davis (1991), 125.   [184] Bradley (1965), 298–9.
[185] Ritchie (1857), 80.

14

Medea and Mid-Victorian
Marriage Legislation

PROBLEMATIC MEDEA

Euripides' Medea has penetrated to parts of modernity most mythical figures have not reached. Since she first rolled off the printing
presses half a millennium ago, she has inspired hundreds of performances, plays, paintings, and operas.[1] Medea has murdered her
way into a privileged place in the history of the imagination of the
West, and can today command huge audiences in the commercial
theatre. Yet in Britain, at least, her popularity on the stage is a
relatively recent phenomenon. Medea has transcended history
partly because she enacts a primal terror universal to human
beings: that the mother-figure should *intentionally* destroy her
own children. Yet this dimension of the ancient tragedy was until
the twentieth century found so disturbing as largely to prevent
unadapted performances. On the British stage it was not until 1907
that Euripides' *Medea* was performed, without alteration, in English translation (see Ch. 17).

   Although Medea's connection with the British stage goes back to
at least the 1560s, when Seneca's *Medea* was performed at Cambridge University,[2] she only exerted a subterranean influence on
Renaissance, Jacobean, and Restoration tragedy.[3] It is instructive
to contemplate the reaction to Simon Mayr's opera *Medea in
Corinto*, which caused a stir at the King's Theatre in London in

---

[1] For the growing literature on the reception of Medea see e.g. Mimoso-Ruiz
(1982), Uglione (1997), Clauss and Johnston (1997), 3–5; Hall, Macintosh, and
Taplin (2000).
[2] Boas (1914), appendix 4.
[3] For the probable influence of Seneca's *Medea* on Shakespeare, see Purkiss
(1996), 259. Lines and sentiments identical to some in Euripides' *Medea* are spoken
by both Livia and Isabella in Thomas Middleton's *Women Beware Women* (c.1620)
and Joyner's *The Roman Empress* (1670); see above p. 11 n. 28. The anonymous
female author of a tragedy featuring an oriental murderess acted at Lincoln's Inn
Fields in 1698 knew Euripides' *Medea*: 'A Young Lady' (1698), 49.

1826–8 as a result of the performance of Giuditta Pasta in the title role.[4] British audiences were able to tolerate 'unnatural' deeds of violence more happily in the opera house (especially if the performances were in Italian) than in the English-speaking theatre. But even in Meyer's opera, Medea's culpability is diminished by having her conceive her barbarous plans under pressure from Egeo (Aegeus).[5] Henry Crabb Robinson saw Pasta in 1828, and recorded that the effect of the murder scene was 'overpowering'. He wondered what a great tragedienne might have made of the role, while observing that of all 'Grecian fables' this particular one 'has never flourished on the English stage'.[6]

Robinson had a point. Euripides' Medea had presented an almost impossible challenge to eighteenth-century sentiment, which abhorred mothers who intentionally killed their children (see Ch. 3). The only successful British *Medea* in that century was Richard Glover's, performed at Drury Lane in 1767, in which Medea was redesigned as a near-perfect mother sent temporarily insane. But another reason why Glover's play was a success was that Act III offered the audience a spectacular sorcery scene of the type which they enjoyed in ballets. The most famous Medea-entertainment was Jean-Georges Noverre's stunning ballet *Médée*, first performed at the Württemberg court in 1762, and subsequently enjoying tours to Vienna, Warsaw, Paris, Italy, St Petersburg, and England. Noverre drew on Euripides and Seneca, but his Medea (unlike Glover's) was a truly superhuman witch, with awesome magical powers. This ballet was popular at the King's Theatre in London, where Continental entertainments featuring the 'supernatural' configuration of Medea continued to be performed until the beginning of the nineteenth century.[7]

Yet Medea was nearly invisible in the British theatre for several decades. It was only after 1845, and especially 1856, that a stream of dramas on the theme began to flow and did not dry up until the late 1870s. If the virginal Theban Antigone was the Greek tragic

---

[4] Edward FitzGerald, letter of 16 June 1872, in FitzGerald (1889), i. 340

[5] Anon. (1826). The audience was provided with an Italian text and facing English translation; in the latter he was called 'Œgeus' (ibid. 13, 19, etc.).

[6] Robinson (1872), ii. 56. On Pasta's performance see Margaret Reynolds (2000), 132–6, with fig. 10.

[7] Noverre (1804), pp. iii f.; Roberdeau (1804), 34 and n.; Guest (1972), 150.

figure who dominated the 1840s and early 1850s (see Ch. 12), by 1857 she had relinquished ground to the abandoned mother from Colchis. The heroine who represented the sanctity of familial ties was displaced by the one who represented their desecration. An exemplary female who excited admiration gave place to one who inspired at best pity and at worst revulsion. Medea was everywhere—in serious spoken tragedy, witty sung burlesque, and proletarian spectacular. She appeared in venues ranging from the elegant Olympic to the downmarket Grecian Saloon. For the first time in this book a single Greek tragedy produced, within the space of a few years, a greater number of separate performed adaptations in English than any other Greek tragedy inspired during the entire period 1660–1914.

In this chapter we shall discuss no fewer than nine different Medea dramas performed in Britain between 1845 and the 1870s, introducing numerous women performers who impersonated Medea (several of them foreigners, like Euripides' Black Sea heroine), along with a handful of men. But above all we shall seek to explain the causes—and some effects—of this mid-Victorian theatrical epidemic. Sudden interest in a myth previously regarded as troublesome demands explanation, and it will be found in thinking about changes in the social perception of the actress, in conventions of theatrical transvestism, and in the early appearance of 'feminist' ideas about women's need for independence, prefiguring by decades those more commonly associated with the New Woman of Ibsen's dramas. The Victorian burlesque Medea did things few heroines in other imaginary contexts could yet dare or achieve— she extracted herself, triumphantly, from a ruined marriage, while succeeding in keeping her sons alive, or cunningly coerced her husband into mending his ways, or took the initiative to correspond with her love rival over financial arrangements, or argued with cogency, wit, and panache that women's lot was iniquitous. Tragic dramatists, on the other hand, used more sombre means to show how all the economic and legal cards were stacked against women like Medea, who therefore deserved pity rather than condemnation. The story of the Victorian Medea is sufficiently complicated to require relating in chronological sequence, partly because the plays tend to comment on their predecessors in a self-conscious intertextual manner. But the shape of the narrative is above all determined by the most important reason for the centrality of Medea at this time: the passing of an epochal series of new laws regulating matrimony.

THE IMPOSSIBILITY OF DIVORCE

It now seems astonishing that divorce was not a live issue in mainstream English culture until the middle of the nineteenth century, when the law of divorce still followed the canon law derived from Rome. All other Protestant countries in Europe, including Scotland, and in the American colonies, had long made legal provision for divorce. Yet it was not possible in England except by a private Act of Parliament, an extremely unusual measure available only to the very rich and almost exclusively to men.[8] Its rarity is illustrated by the Archbishop of Canterbury's lament in 1809 that the divorce rate had risen to a scandalous three a year![9] Along with the absence of a divorce law, the eighteenth century gave fathers absolute rights to custody of children of a marriage, regardless of which spouse was at fault and regardless of the age of the children. Fathers could also ban all contact between children and their mothers. This situation explains why Euripides' Medea, who is determined that her husband is to have no power over their children, had to be so radically altered before the nineteenth century. It would have made much more unpalatable viewing in such an ideological environment than in fifth-century Athens, where divorce was practised, even if, as Medea complained, it was not 'respectable' for women (236–7).

By the 1830s, however, humanitarians were at last questioning the absolute right of fathers to bar mothers from all access to their children, and the case of the celebrated Caroline Norton swung public opinion in mothers' favour. Norton, as the beautiful granddaughter of the dramatist Richard Brinsley Sheridan, came from a family that has been encountered several times in the course of this book. She had her children forcibly removed by her jealous husband, who in 1836 accused no lesser man than the Prime Minister, Lord Melbourne, of adultery with his wife. Although the jury dismissed the case, Mr Norton cruelly exercised his right to bar his wife from all access to her children until they reached the age of majority.[10] In

---

[8] Shanley (1981–2), 357.   [9] Wolfram (1987), 147.
[10] Shanley (1989), 22–5; Chedzoy (1992), 170–3.

1837 the radical MP for Reading, Thomas Talfourd (see Ch. 11), introduced the Infant Custody Act. It was passed in 1839, at last making it possible for women to receive custody of children under seven, and visitation rights thereafter. The Act is now seen as a watershed; for the first time it 'stripped traditional unlimited patriarchal authority from the father', and heralded all the reforming acts concerned with divorce and women's property which were to follow.[11] It also precipitated a debate on marriage and women's rights which was to increase in importance over the next decades.

Talfourd's patron Lord Brougham tried to reform divorce procedure in 1844.[12] But there were fears that it would lead to the impoverishment of abandoned wives and children. The debate in parliament certainly informed various passages in the first of the nineteenth-century Medea plays, Planché's *The Golden Fleece; or, Jason in Colchis and Medea in Corinth*. This important drama, based on Grillparzer as well as Euripides and first performed in 1845 following the Mendelssohn *Antigone* (see Ch. 12), inaugurated a tradition of entertainments based on the Medea myth which lasted throughout the period of matrimonial legislation, culminating in *Jason and Medea: A Ramble after a Colchian* in 1878. Influenced by Planché's play, this burlesque was performed at the Garrison Theatre in Woolwich toward the end of the fashion for Classical burlesque.[13] Planché's *The Golden Fleece* was itself regularly revived after its first production in 1845, not least because of the increasing topicality of Medea's predicament.

THE ENTERPRISING MEDEA OF THE ENGLISH *GOLDEN FLEECE*

When the New Woman emerged in the drama at the end of the nineteenth century, one of the arenas in which she had been prefigured in reality was, ironically enough, the acting profession. The idea (not of course historically confined to Victorian Britain) that the prima donna enjoyed unusual freedom was widely expressed in women's fiction, journals, and memoirs,[14] and the actress seems to have enjoyed a similarly privileged and/or

---

[11] See Stone (1995), 178.
[12] See 'Divorce', *The Law Review*, 1 (1844–5), 353–81.
[13] Addison and Howell (1872).   [14] Rutherford (1992).

exceptional status. One such example was the acting career of Helen Taylor (stepdaughter of John Stuart Mill and daughter of Helen Taylor Mill), which she pursued from the 1850s onwards in order to secure her independence. Helen Faucit, the famous Dublin and Edinburgh Antigone, even managed to combine fame with domestic stability. One of the most striking features of Planché's *The Golden Fleece* is the interplay between the dominant, powerful figure of Medea the heroine, and the social identity of the prominent actress-manager, Eliza Vestris, who played her.

Vestris had become the first woman to manage a London theatre when she took over management of the Olympic Theatre in 1831. Together with Planché, Vestris had staged the first of the classical burlesques that were to prove so popular during the course of the century (see Chs. 12 and 13); and her dark features and exotic (Regency) past as a diva in Italian opera made her a suitable choice for Medea, whom she played 'according to the approved style of dishevelled tresses and severe costume'.[15] But it was not only her previous professional appearances as prima donna that marked her out as a free woman; she could also be said to embody the independence of mind and body that the role of Medea entailed in her professional life beyond the stage. In her first curtain speech at the Olympic she proudly proclaimed:

> Noble and gentle—matrons—patrons—friends!
> Before you here a ventr'ous woman bends!
> A warrior woman—that in strife embarks
> The first of all dramatic Joan of Arcs.
> Cheer on the enterprise thus dared by me!
> The first that ever led a company.[16]

Madame Vestris (as she was somewhat reverentially and exotically known) took the part of Medea in Planché's *The Golden Fleece*, but as a regular actress in burlesque, her most common role was the breeches part. In Planché's extravaganza she played opposite Priscilla Horton as Jason, who (as we have seen) was like Madame Vestris renowned above all for her shapely legs.[17] The reluctance on the part of Victorian journalists to mention male impersonation in interviews with the actresses has led commentators to wonder whether this signals its relative unimportance or its perilous

---

[15] *ILN* 6, no. 152 (29 Mar. 1845), 200.   [16] Cited by Auerbach (1987), 58.
[17] Fletcher (1987), 9.

nature.[18] It may well be that '[t]ransexual casting was one way to give women the sort of mythic adventures [others imagined]'.[19] For like the New Woman of the 1890s, when Priscilla Horton performed in Planché's burlesque of *Medea*, she wore unfeminine garb: not male attire, but a costume that was symbolically different from the voluminous Victorian petticoats. Therefore the burlesque actress was not only a woman of independent means through her pursuit of a career: by being clad in a costume that foreshadowed the famous knickerbockers of the *fin de siècle*, she enjoyed a freedom of movement that the normally restricted female body could never hope to share.

The recent Theatre Regulation Act of 1843 had concerned itself, amongst other things, with the dangers inherent in the ambiguity of cross-dressed roles. It has been suggested that it may be possible to see a subversive consciousness at play beyond the evident sex-appeal of the male impersonations.[20] If we look at *The Golden Fleece*—and indeed the other burlesques of *Medea* where men too (to borrow Froma Zeitlin's phrase) 'play the Other'[21]—it is clear that there is, at least on some occasions, a serious manipulation of Victorian gender boundaries in the cross-dressed roles, which raises questions that come to dominate the stage at the turn of the century (see Ch. 17).

If Medea the outsider transgressed boundaries, so too did Madame Vestris; but unlike her Greek persona, Eliza Vestris crossed boundaries with pioneering spirit and apparently without blame.[22] For the success of *The Golden Fleece* was partly due to the piquancy of its casting of a publicly celebrated couple, soon to be married (the second time for Madame Vestris)—the exotic foreigner and Charles Mathews, an English public-schoolboy—as Medea and The Chorus respectively.[23]

In a rewrite of the plot, Medea turns out to have deceived both chorus and audience by merely pretending to have 'flogged' her boys. Planché, as he explains in his Argument to the play, has chosen to 'redeem the character of the unfortunate heroine' and follow the historian Aelian in maintaining that the Euripidean account of Medea's infanticide was written following a bribe

---

[18] Bratton (1992), 87.   [19] Fletcher (1987), 31.
[20] Bratton (1992), 88; Senelick (1993), 82.   [21] Zeitlin (1996).
[22] Appleton (1974).   [23] Ibid. 159–61; George Taylor (1989), 71–2.

from the Corinthians, who were themselves the guilty party.[24]
Like Grillparzer, Planché chooses to inform his audience of the
pre-history of Medea in order to present her case in the most
sympathetic light. In Part I not only do we see Jason's utter
dependency on Medea for his early successes, we also learn that
it was Jason, not Medea, who killed Apsyrtus when he 'Let fly a
blow that would have felled an ox— | Black'd both his precious
eyes, before so blue, | And from his nose the vital claret drew'.[25]

   Planché, with his male chorus of one, has of necessity done away
with the 'Women of Corinth' speech, replacing the general complaint of the Euripidean Medea with an account of personal griev-
ance sung to the tune of 'The Fine Young English Gentleman'.
This Medea has to put up with her absentee husband, who abandons her and the children to a dubious fate in cramped lodgings,
whilst he is happily ensconced in the palace, lavishly entertaining
his royal mistress. But this poor Medea (because of the absence of
divorce legislation) cannot be shot of her thankless burden:

> He leaves me to darn his stockings, and mope in the house all day,
> Whilst he treats *her* to see 'Antigone', with a box at the
>   Grecian play,
> Then goes off to sup with Corinthian Tom, or whoever,
>   he meets by the way,
> And staggers home in a state of beer, like
>   (I'm quite ashamed to say)
> A fine young Grecian gentleman,
> One of the classic time.[26]

Moreover, Planché's male Chorus, far from being sympathetic to
Medea's plight, delivers a deeply misogynistic view of the perils of
Cupid on a young man's heart in the place of the Euripidean ode in
praise of moderation.[27]

   However, Planché's handling of the events of the plot would
seem to fly in the face of the Chorus's assessment. Not only does
his Medea draw the line at internecine killing, but she has little
difficulty in winning over the audience to her side with an adversary in Jason, who is a drunken, cowardly, and serial philanderer.
And when she turns to the audience in the last moments of the play
to appeal to the Grand Jury—a punning plea, both to continue the

---

[24] Aelian, *Historical Miscellany* 5. 21.   [25] Planché (1845), 158.
[26] Ibid. 161.   [27] Ibid. 167–8; cf. Euripides, *Medea* 627–62.

theatrical run and to reach a judicial settlement in favour of the wronged woman—there is little doubt that the audience's sympathies are expected to lie with her.[28]

At the end of *The Golden Fleece* Medea triumphs in the sense that she takes the children, alive and well, off to Athens in her chariot. But on the other hand she is the abandoned, ill-used wife, watching her husband alienated from herself and his children by his passion for Glauce. The drama thus explores, in a comic vein, the plight of wives should divorce become accessible to husbands who had tired of them. When Jason is annoyed with Medea's nagging, she says that he threatens her with 'getting a Scotch divorce'.[29] For while Jason would have found it virtually impossible to divorce Medea in England, divorce was already cheaply available in Scotland on the grounds of both adultery and desertion.[30] Marital breakdown is thus explicitly figured in *The Golden Fleece* as a contentious issue, even while its powerful leading actress was known to be about to enter matrimony with its leading actor. By 1850 the more general issue of women's status—'the woman question', as it was called—began to dominate public debate;[31] it was decided to set up a Royal Commission to investigate the problem of the non-existent divorce law.

MEDEA AT THE GRECIAN SALOON

The inauguration of the Royal Commission on Divorce in 1850 is reflected in the spectacular entertainment by Jack Wooler, *Jason and Medea: A Comic. Heroic. Tragic. Operatic. Burlesque-Spectacular Extravaganza*, performed at the proletarian Grecian Saloon in 1851.[32] Like the plays by Grillparzer and Planché, Jack Wooler's *Jason and Medea* begins with the events narrated in the third book of Apollonius Rhodius' epic *Argonautica*. Whereas Planché comically alludes to the stage conventions of Greek tragedy when he avoids enacting the capture of the fleece ('You'll think, perhaps, you should have seen him do it | But 'tisn't classical—you'll hear, not view it'),[33] Wooler chooses to entertain his audience with the very spectacles that Planché so tantalizingly

---

[28] Planché (1845), 170–1.   [29] Ibid. (1845), 20–1.   [30] Stone (1995), 351.
[31] Cvetkovich (1992), 46; Christopher Parker (1995), 2.   [32] Wooler (1851).
[33] Planché (1845), 155.

denies. Act I alone shifts from the clouds above Olympus, to a rocky and desolate island (where the Argonauts have landed), to the city of Æetes (with the Euxine Sea behind), all with the help of Mercury's wand. It then moves on to Hecate's temple at Medea's behest ('Melt tower and town! Rise, Hecate's shrine! behold!'),[34] before passing through the Field of Mars, the dragon's lair and ending up at the port from which the Argo escapes.

However, as with Planché's treatment of the myth, the most notable effect of including the background to the events in Corinth is to enhance Medea's case. At the end of Act I, when Jason has overcome the dragon with Medea's aid, he proclaims, parodying a Byronic rhyme:[35]

> The fleece is mine—and it shall ever be a
> Pledge of my passion for my own Medea.

But as soon as they arrive in Colchis, the philanderer takes the decision to break his pledge, to the popular tune of 'Jeanette and Jeanot':

> Come conscience—I have loved you full a year
> One can't be constant constantly my dear.[36]

Yet Wooler's Medea has shown herself to be a match for male tyranny from the first act, when she sings a song in defiance of her father's threats of restraint:

> If all girls had my spirit—they wouldn't thus be done—
> I'd rather wed our butcher boy than ever be a nun.[37]

Jason in Corinth seems to have forgotten Medea's powers of sorcery, which enabled her to stage manage events for him in Act I, and which assist her now in melting towers and towns, and conjuring devils in a darkened wood. Like Grillparzer's Medea, Wooler's heroine is pushed to the limits by the savage cruelties of a Jason, who deliberately flaunts his latest conquest. Even Creusa pities

[34] Wooler (1851), 287.

[35] See Lord Byron (1970), 34: 'Translation of The Nurse's Dole in the *Medea* of Euripides' (June 1810): 'Oh how I wish that an embargo | Had kept in port the good ship Argo! | Who, still unlaunch'd from Grecian docks, | Had never pass'd the Azure rocks; | But now I fear her trip will be a | Damn'd business for my Miss Medea'; cf. above, pp. 356–7.

[36] Wooler (1851), 290, 299.

[37] Ibid. 28.

Medea's public humiliation, although her pity comes too late to avoid the wrath of Medea, who contrives for her a combusted, onstage end. This Medea merely kills her rival, not her own (here absent) children. Triumphant Medea magics herself away into the ether with the help of a white sheet, leaving a cursing Jason to fall and fatally crack his head. In the final moments of Wooler's play she re-emerges at the back of the stage in a chariot, agreeing to revive Jason with the Golden Fleece if he will only take her back as wife. The revived Jason ends the play with these utterly implausible lines:

> My own dear Medea, all your grief is past
> You were my first love and shall be my last.[38]

Marriage here at all costs is to be favoured over desertion, because in 1851 an abandoned Medea still had no future whatsoever. Like Planché, Wooler here offers to some extent a patriarchal study of a woman *in extremis*, in which the masculinity of her adversary is however somewhat muted and compromised by the fact that Jason is a breeches role. In the final analysis, Wooler's extravaganza evades the plight of the separated wife, attempting to negate the real social implications of the ancient myth, by reuniting Jason and Medea at its conclusion.

LEGOUVÉ'S *MEDEA* (1856)

When the bill which was finally to introduce divorce arrived in parliament in 1856, feminists and their male supporters agitated feverishly. First, they drew attention to the sexual double standard implied by the bill's differential treatment of possible grounds for divorce for men and for women, and secondly, they pointed out the terrible hardship caused by married women's inability to hold property in their own name. On marriage a man assumed all legal rights over his wife's property. Worse, he owned any property she assumed thereafter, including earnings, rents, and income. This led to the iniquitous situation in which even abandoned wives were forced to hand over their money for the remainder of their lives. They were also debarred from remarriage since divorce was impossible. The debate continued throughout 1856 and both sessions

---

[38] Ibid. 308.

of 1857, becoming more impassioned as the months wore on. The bill came, correctly, to be perceived as a measure which would alter the legal status of women in an unprecedented manner.[39] And during the years 1856–7, Medea, the abandoned wife and mother of Greek myth, became one of the most ubiquitous heroines on the London stage.

If Grillparzer's Medea lurked behind the burlesques of Planché and Wooler, in 1856–7 it was partly a Franco-Italian conception of the heroine that fuelled the topical enthusiasm for her plight. In June 1856 the *diva* Adelaide Ristori brought an Italian translation of Ernest Legouvé's new tragedy *Medea* to the Lyceum (Fig. 14.1). Legouvé's play spoke directly to the hearts of the London public, now so exercised by the reporting of the parliamentary debate on divorce, precisely because, as one reviewer noted, Legouvé had made the ancient heroine much more accessible, tender, and pitiable. He had eschewed 'the grandeur of the Euripidean heroine' and had 'contented himself with the domestic interest of her misfortunes. The deserted wife, the distressed mother, alone remained'.[40]

Legouvé's three-act French adaptation draws on Euripides, although diluting Medea's responsibility for the deaths of her sons. She kills them, but her motive is changed to an altruistic desire to prevent the Corinthians from subjecting them to a crueller death when they discover that she has murdered Jason's new wife. Legouvé aimed to do for Medea what Racine had done for Euripides' Iphigenia and Phaedra; he defined his work as 'collaboration' by a 'temporary partner' with the original Greek man of genius.[41] The tragedy was written for Madame Rachel, the famous French actress whose performance in Racine's *Phèdre* was held in international awe. But Rachel rejected the role of Medea on the ground that this heroine was 'unnatural', despite Legouvé's amelioration of her crime.[42]

Indeed, the role of Medea repelled many actresses, who feared that her reputation might become confused with their own. Legouvé, frustrated, offered the part to Adelaide Ristori, Rachel's

---

[39] Shanley (1989), 158.

[40] *ILN* 29, no. 811 (19 July 1856), 65. The reviewer was probably John Heraud (see below).

[41] Legouvé (1893), ii. 47–8.

[42] Geneviève Ward and Whiting (1918), 187.

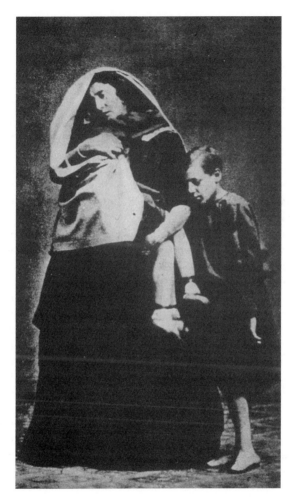

FIGURE 14.1   Adelaide Ristori as Medea with her children, in Ernest Legouvé's adaptation, *c.*1856.

Italian rival, who had also hitherto avoided acting Medea. She explained to her public the reason why she had rejected the *Medea* of 1814 by the Duca della Valle:

Nature having gifted me with a high sense of maternal love . . . I could not present such a monstrosity on the stage, and in spite of the pressing requests of my managers to interpret that role I was unable to overcome my aversion to it.[43]

But she agreed to do the Legouvé version, because he 'had discovered a way to make the killing of the children appear both just and necessary'.[44] Indeed, throughout the last part of Legouvé's play, there is never any doubt that Medea's love for her children exceeds her hatred for Jason. Ristori took her impersonation of Medea all over the globe, along with her other virtuoso roles—Marie Antoinette and both queens (althouth not simultaneously) in Schiller's *Maria Stuart*. But Medea was the heroine she invariably performed on tour, in Spain, Portugal, North America, Argentina, and Brazil in addition to the most famous production in London in the summer of 1856.[45]

Ristori was tall and statuesque, with chestnut hair, and acted Medea in an imitation chiton and long blue cloak (Fig. 14.2). She was proud of the 'attitudes' she struck, for which she had studied the Niobe groups in the Uffizi Museum in Florence.[46] Her Medea was admired by all who enjoyed neoclassical theatre, including George Henry Lewes, who later wrote that the actress 'completely conquered' him in the role: 'The exquisite grace of her attitudes, the mournful beauty of her voice, the flash of her wrath and the air of supreme distinction which seems native to her, gave a charm to this performance which is unforgettable'.[47]

MARK LEMON'S LIBELLED LADY

Medea had appeared in French burlesques since at least the early eighteenth century; Cherubini's opera *Médée* (1797) alone had inspired three parodies.[48] It is this tradition that lies behind the

---

[43] Ristori (1907), 175.   [44] Ibid.

[45] Ibid. 42–3, 59, 72, 80, 107. The translation, by Joseph Montanelli, was published to accompany Ristori's London performance, offering a parallel English version by Thomas Williams: *Medea: A Tragedy in Three Acts* (London, 1856).

[46] Ristori (1907), 179–81.

[47] Lewes (1875), 44, 145.

[48] Medea had been the anti-heroine in the parody of Longepierre's *Médée* by Dominique and Biancolelli, *La Méchante Femme* (1728); the Cherubini burlesques were C. Sewrin's *La Sorcière* (27 March), P. A. Capelle and P. Villiers's *Bébé et Jargon* (Théâtre Montasier, 28 March) and Citizen Bizet and H. Chaussier's *Médée ou l'Hôpital des fous* (Théâtre de l'Ambigu, 15 April). See Travers (1941), 27, 111; Macintosh (2000a), 12, (2000b), 84.

ADELAIDE RISTORI AS MEDEA

FIGURE 14.2 Adelaide Ristori as Medea striking an attitude, in Ernest Legouvé's adaptation, *c*.1856.

appearance, shortly after Legouvé's tragedy had opened to great acclaim at the Théâtre Italien in Paris on 8 April 1856, of the burlesque of Cogniard, Grange, and Bourdois entitled *La Médée en Nanterre* (Théâtre des Variétés, 9 June). It is the multilingual layers of the performance—that a French version of a Greek

tragedy is now being performed in an Italian translation in Paris—
that provide the source of much amusement. Similarly, the fact
that the London audience was being treated to an Italian translation of a French version of a Greek tragedy did not escape the wit
of English writers. Two burlesques reacting to Ristori's play
opened simultaneously on 14 July. The one at the Adelphi was
by Mark Lemon, the editor of *Punch*, and was entitled *Medea; or, a
Libel on the Lady of Colchis*. In its prologue Creon explains:

> If your Italian scholarship's complete
> And you can pay a guinea for your seat
> Go, and applaud an artist truly grand
> And don't be proud because you understand.
> But if your stock of choice Italian's small
> And the wife wants the guinea towards her shawl
> You're better where you are—You'll get a notion
> Of what has thrown the town into commotion.
> While our Medea here is doubly strong
> It's twice as moral, and not half as long.[49]

That Lemon's Medea is 'twice as moral' is open to doubt, but it is
true that his audience is being offered a remarkably close rendering
of Legouvé's version, albeit in another key.

But there the similarities between the French burlesque and
Lemon's seem to end. In *La Médée en Nanterre* the characters
are all attached to a circus troupe, with Créon as the manager of
the acrobats and Créuse as the high-wire dancer; Médée is a
fortune-teller and Jason earns his living as a fairground wrestler.[50]
Whilst Lemon's acrobatic and knifethrowing Jason bears more
than a passing resemblance to his French counterpart, the two
English burlesques generally enjoy a much closer relationship
with their tragic sources.

Lemon's protagonist is hardened by the experience of poverty
and toil, and has little demonstrable feeling for the children. When
Jason says that the children 'weigh immensely on my mind',
Medea complains:

> And so they ought, for it's three years old chap
> Since for those kids you've paid a single rap—
> It's difficult to say what brats were made for
> Unless to teach us 'Children must be paid for.'[51]

---

[49] Lemon (1856), 1.   [50] Mimoso-Ruiz (1978), 485.
[51] Lemon (1856), 26.

After Jason has threatened Medea with deportation (he cannot afford the £2,000 necessary for a divorce) and claimed custody of the children, Medea begins to execute her revenge. When Glauce comes to warn Medea of her imminent deportation, the princess's altruistic motives are misconstrued by Medea, whose avenging hand fatally daubs her victim's cheeks with black (poisonous) face-paint. When the police arrive with a warrant for Medea's arrest, Jason announces his intention of sending the children to boarding school. Medea calls the boys over to bid them farewell, and in a startling and unprecedented *coup de théâtre*, she stabs them both onstage for all to see:

> Stay stop a word or two
> Children come hither I am sent away
> And therefore I have only this to say
> That if your father thinks he's served me out
> He'll alter his opinion I've no doubt—
> As witness this and this. [*Stabs children there and now*][52]

The 'moral', to which the Prologue refers, is the deeply ironic coda that is self-consciously appended to Lemon's play. Jason unconvincingly claims to Medea:

> Yes, had you kept this business off your hands
> And like Griselda bowed to my commands,
> I had forgiven you for my past desertion
> And spent my life with you without coercion.[53]

Medea apologizes for any 'aggravation' she has caused, pays reparation by restoring both Glauce (with the aid of a damp towel) and her boys (by ordering them to 'look alive'). She is then miraculously united in embrace with Jason, proclaiming her own (significantly unreciprocated) undying love.

Whilst Lemon's play apparently raises questions merely to sidestep them in the final moments, what is new in his burlesque is an attempt to provide an exploration of, as well as an explanation for, the hardening of feelings in Medea. The burlesque explores the social reality which Medea would encounter if abandoned in Victorian London rather than archaic Corinth. Medea has been forced into training her children in pickpocketing because 'one's vile husband no allowance makes'.[54] Jason threatens to have her

---

[52] Ibid. 16.   [53] Ibid. 17.   [54] Ibid. 6.

arrested, and demands she agree to a divorce, saying he will only support the children if she does so. Even the comic defence of Lemon's Medea by Orpheus in Act I has its serious edge:

> A woman's face grows haggard who reflects
> All day upon her husband's base neglects.
> And it don't mend her temper to consider
> That tho' a wife she's lonely as a widder.
> As for the other charges you have filed
> My classical Lothario—draw it mild.[55]

Indeed, the plot of Lemon's burlesque hit too close to home. And although Wright was noted as one of the finest comedians of his generation, as a male performer impersonating Medea, he played all too naturalistically. One reviewer remarked that in Mr Wright's Medea the audience saw only 'the wronged wife, the wretched woman, demanding sympathy, and forbidding laughter'.[56] Divorce, after all, was not yet a possibility in England.

ROBERT BROUGH'S BEST OF MOTHERS

The partisan subtitle of the other British burlesque of the Legouvé–Ristori tragedy that year, which opened at the Olympic, was *The Best of Mothers, with a Brute of a Husband*. Its author, Robert Brough, thus located it contentiously within the debate about the abuse of women by home-abandoning husbands. Even the programme announced its connection with legislative controversy: the setting of Scene i, 'A Palace near Corinth', is described as staging the 'Factitious Opposition to a Proposed Measure for Legalizing Marriage with a Non-Deceased Wife's Rival.'[57] Orpheus defends Medea: 'When wives are bad, the husbands are to blame', warning Jason that his intention is illegal and amounts to bigamy; but Jason is defiant, telling the minstrel that 'the marriage tie's no noose to me'.[58]

Like Lemon, Brough places great emphasis on the penury to which Medea and the children have been reduced, as they too are

---

[55] Lemon (1856), 5.   [56] *ILN* 29, no. 811 (19 July 1856), 65.

[57] For the programme see Robert Brough (1856). The joke refers to yet another legislative controversy concerned with marriage, the long-running attempt to remove the ban on a man marrying his deceased wife's sister. Bills on this issue had been debated and defeated in both 1849 and 1856. See Shanley (1989), 41.

[58] Robert Brough (1856), 8–10.

forced to beg for their survival. Medea's begging patter starts as a
rewrite of the 'Women of Corinth' speech before taking on a life of
its own, in which the pathos engendered almost eclipses the comic
realization that Medea is offering a kind of confidence trick to the
passers-by:

> My Grecian friends, with deep humiliation
> I stand in this disgraceful situation,
> Though unaccustom'd publicly to speak,
> I have not tasted food since Tuesday week.
> Three sets of grinders out of work you see,
> Through the invention of machinery.
> A landlord, as inclement as the weather,
> Has seiz'd our flock bed—we were out of feather.
> Shoeless and footsore, I've through many lands
> Walked, with this pair of kids upon my hands.
> The tear of infancy requests you'll stop it—
> (*looking round*) Bother! there's no one looking at us—drop it![59]

Jason subsequently explains to her that he will permit her to
remarry anyone that she pleases, for 'Our separation equals a
divorce'. The burlesque enacts in ancient Corinth the type of
scenario which many feared the divorce bill, if made law, would
precipitate. Jason insists that Medea must send him the boys as
soon as they are old enough to educate, a reference to the right
fathers had to custody over the age of 7. In the event this burlesque
saves the lives of both Creon's new bride and Medea's children,
while leaving anxiously suspended the issue of Medea's future. But
Creusa promises that she will ensure that Medea gets permanent
custody of the children, and that she receives sufficient money.
The women thus find a way around the problems inflicted on them
by men.[60]

   If we seem to be discussing too earnestly the social significance
of what was an inherently light-hearted comic genre, it is important to be aware that the Victorians themselves took it seriously.
The Medea burlesques are often discussed alongside the Italian-
language tragedy as if there were little generic difference between
the performances. Indeed, what is striking about English tragedy
and burlesque in general at this time is the extent to which the
separate genres become intermeshed in the minds of audiences.

---

[59] Ibid. 11.   [60] Ibid. 22–3, 33.

George Henry Lewes's comments on Ristori's performance, partially quoted above, are illustrative in this regard. Lewes recalls of a revival of this production that when Ristori 'conquered' him in the role of Medea, 'the conquest was all the more noticeable, because it triumphed over the impressions previously received from Robson's burlesque imitation'.[61] The inference, of course, is that Lewes did not see Ristori as Medea during her first London tour, whereas he had seen and been overwhelmed by the burlesque performance of Robert Brough. But since Robson's performance is here cited alongside that of a leading tragedienne of the European stage, Lewes's comments are also testimony to the power and seriousness of Robson's burlesque interpretation of the role. And the illustrations bear testimony to the uncanny resemblances between the two actors as they performed Medea (compare Fig. 14.3 with 14.2 above).

Elsewhere Lewes explains the success of a revival of Planché's *The Golden Fleece* with reference to the extraordinary self-discipline of the actors, who were able to engender both hilarity and credulity in the audience at one and the same time. Burlesque, in Lewes's formulation, is rooted in the real world; and he maintains that the finest of burlesque acting can 'show that acting burlesque is the gross personation of a character, not the outrageous defiance of all character; the personation has truth, although the character itself may be preposterously drawn.'[62] The degree of seriousness attached to burlesque by the 1850s can also be gauged by the fact that Cambridge undergraduates, according to Burnand, found it difficult to distinguish between tragedy and burlesque. Burnand recalls of his fellow thespians in the Amateur Dramatic Club:

... at that time [Lent Term 1854] we probably mistook tragedy for burlesque, and burlesque for tragedy ... we were constantly seeing Robson ... when in his burlesque he touched the very boundary line of tragedy ... [63]

In Brough's play, the penury of the deserted wife is underlined in what is initially a hilarious begging scene. The younger of Jason and Medea's sons wears a placard round his neck with the word 'orphans' in four 'languages': first transliterated into the Greek alphabet ($\phi\alpha\theta\epsilon\rho\lambda\epsilon\varsigma$), then translated into French (*Orphelins*), Italian (*Orfani*), and English respectively. And at one point, Medea is

---

[61] Lewes (1875), 166.   [62] Ibid. 70.   [63] Burnand (1880), 23.

FIGURE 14.3   Frederick Robson as Medea, in Robert Brough's *Medea;*
*or, the Best of Mothers with a Brute of a Husband, c.*1856.

driven to distraction by the plurality of linguistic options available to her for revenge:

> 'Sangue! sangue! Straziar spezzar suo cuore.'
> Which means, translated, something red and gory.
> 'Unche di spaventos atroce strano'
> —Murder in Irish! No—Italiano!
> 'Ai! Ai! Dia mow Kephalas flox owrania,
> 'By-ee tiddy moi zeen èté Kurdos'—
> Stop, that's Euripides!
>> 'Du sang! du sang!'
> 'Briser torturer son cœur—oui!'
>> That's wrong!
> I've got confused with all these versions jinglish—
> Thunder and turf!—And even that's not English.[64]

A closely related source of the humour in Brough's burlesque was precise parody of the conventions of Ristori's Italian school of acting, for Robson found his own route to the 'melodramatic abandonment or lashing-up to a certain point of excitement' he shared with his model. Ristori went to see Robson, and commented, 'Uomo straordinario', as well she might.[65] For Robson indeed took the role of Medea more seriously than might have been expected in a burlesque star, and was admired by the most intellectual of playgoers, including Henry Morley, Professor of English at University College, London, whose account sits alongside his reviews of important productions of Shakespeare. Morley praises Robson's 'wonderful burlesque of Medea, wherein he seems to have reached the climax of success in personating jealousy by a wild mingling of the terrible with the grotesque.'[66] Burnand, writing some years after the early performances, recalls Robson's 'best days at the Olympic', when he took the parts of Shylock and Medea with equal conviction.[67] Robson's Medea was actually considered more truly tragic than Ristori's by some educated spectators, including Charles Dickens:

It is an odd but perfectly true testimony to the extraordinary power of his performance (which is of a very remarkable kind indeed) that it points the badness of Ristori's acting, in a most singular manner, by bringing out what she does and does not do. The scene with Jason is perfectly terrific;

---

[64] Robert Brough (1856), 25.   [65] Sands (1979), 77; Sala (1864), 49.
[66] Morley (1866), 95–9, 159 (entry dated 1 Nov. 1856).
[67] Burnand (1880), 22–3.

and in the manner in which the comic rage and jealousy does not pitch itself over the float at the stalls is in striking contrast to the manner in which the tragic rage and jealousy does. He has a frantic song and dagger dance, about two minutes long altogether, which has more passion in it than Ristori could express in fifty years.[68]

In the Dublin performance 'the passionate display of histrionic power . . . well-nigh appalled by its terrible earnestness and desperation.' Robson's *Medea* was 'sublime in its savage intensity, and life-like and human in its commonplace features'. He portrayed 'the tigerish affection with which she regards the children she is afterwards to slay . . . through the medium of doggerel and slang, with astonishing force and vigour'.[69]

Robson won more sympathy for Medea than any previous actor on the British stage. Perhaps the audience found it easier to deal with Medea's challenge to conventional notions of femininity when the actor impersonating her was a man. Yet Robson's passion as Medea was touching and surprisingly 'real':

Mr Robson was the *Medea* of vulgar life; and, in the climax of the interest, he passed out of the burlesque altogether . . . with an earnestness that dissipated all mockery, and made every heart in the house thrill with painful sympathy.[70]

Indeed there are constant shifts in tone and register that reflect the human and superhuman sides of Medea herself. She pursues vengeance with Marlovian gusto, but only after being been driven to the limits of endurance by the supremely arrogant Jason, who pronounces his intention to strip her of her children as well as her marital status:

> Medea (*giving vent to her suppressed passion*)
> Now drop it! I can't stand it any longer!
> Oh, gods celestial and gods infernal!
> Oh, powers of mischief—dark and sempiternal!
> Demons above, and deities below,
> I ask ye sternly—isn't this a go?[71]

---

[68] Dickens (1965–2002), viii. 171, to Macready, 8 Aug. 1856.
[69] *The Freeman's Journal*, cit. Sands (1979), 79; Sala (1864), 19, 49.
[70] *ILN* 29, no. 811 (19 July 1856), 65.
[71] Robert Brough (1856), 23.

She tries to smother her feelings for her children at their farewell, and (as with Legouvé's version) is reduced to a state of despair and hurt at the possibility that Creusa has poisoned their hearts against their mother. When she reads the note that they have brought from Creusa, which promises to restore the children and to give her money, the stage direction describes her *'wholly overcome by this sympathy, stands trembling—crushing the letter in her hand; then she falls sobbing on her knees, embracing her two children, who have knelt on each side'*. The author's note to the acting edition of the text at this point instructs all the characters that 'the action must be conducted [from now on until the end] . . . as in tragedy'.[72]

In direct imitation of the French version, as Brough's Medea hears the rabble approaching, she enfolds her children in her robes to protect them. When Creon threatens to seize the boys, it is already too late as *'Medea is seen standing alone, on steps . . . quivering with emotion—reeking knife in her hand . . .'*. Then the tragedy finally gives way to wish-fulfilment with the dagger turning into a jester's bauble as Medea is on the verge of killing Jason, and with Creusa being brought back on stage miraculously revived.

However, what is different about Medea's final speech in comparison with the endings of Wooler's and Lemon's plays, is that Brough's coda is not simply deeply ironic; it is a flagrant denial of any such attempts to rewrite the story of Medea. Brough's heroine turns to the audience in the final moments of the play, flanked by her revived children, and exclaims:

> What can a poor, lone, helpless woman do—
> Battled on all sides—but appeal to you?
> (*To audience*) My plot destroyed—my damages made good.
> They'd change my very nature if they could.
> Don't let them—rather aid me to pursue
> My murd'rous career the season through;
> Repentance is a thought that I abhor,
> What I have done don't make me sorry for.[73]

Behind the traditional plea for the audience's support is an unequivocal call for endorsement of all that the New Woman was later to stand for: 'They'd change my very nature if they could. | Don't let them' cries Medea, there on the London stage, some sixty-two years before women over the age of thirty were finally

---

[72] Ibid. 33 and n.   [73] Ibid. (1856), 34.

granted the vote. Robert Brough, who had in the previous year published satirical, radical verse with his Songs of the 'Governing Classes',[74] is deliberately situating Medea at the forefront of the early campaign for women's independence. And that his burlesque spoke to a whole generation of theatre-goers, and not just those who had seen Ristori's performance, is borne out by the numerous revivals of the play in the late 1850s and well into the 1860s, where the role of Medea attracted star performers other than Robson.[75]

THE MOTHER'S TRAGEDY

The last group of Medea plays to emerge, however, were in every sense tragic dramas, and the heroine was in these invariably played by a woman. The first overlapped with the very last, tortuous debates about the divorce bill, which continued to grind through parliamentary debates into 1857, itself competing for attention in the newspaper columns with the sensational trial of one of the most famous of all Victorian murderesses, Madeleine Smith. Smith had conducted a secret relationship with Pierre Émile L'Angelier; under Scots law at that date their intercourse, following an engagement to marry, itself constituted marriage. When her father sought to marry her to someone else, L'Angelier threatened to inform him of the facts; instead he died of poison, almost certainly at her hands. But a verdict of not proven was returned after a brilliant defence by John Inglis, Dean of the Faculty of Advocates; the press and the public overwhelmingly supported her, seeing her as taking 'righteous revenge against an exploitative seducer'.[76] This reaction shows how much women's vulnerability to men—even if it led them to murder—was now informing opinion.

The Divorce and Matrimonial Causes Act was finally passed at the end of the long, hot August of 1857.[77] In legalizing divorce for ordinary people, it remains the most important landmark in British marriage law. It also slightly lessened the unfairness women faced by giving them more equal access to divorce (although full equality

---

[74] See Robert Brough (1890).

[75] Notably the actor-manager of the Grecian Theatre, George Conquest, who appeared in a popular revival in 1861. See Hackney Archives Department, Playbill no. 467.

[76] Hartman (1985), 52–4.

[77] For a detailed account see Shanley (1989), 35–44.

was not secured until 1923), and protecting women's property and earnings from seizure by their former husbands. Once a man had abandoned his wife he could no longer expropriate her money. Custody of children could also now be awarded to the mother if the court saw fit (which in practice rarely happened). Medea would now theoretically, at least, be able to keep the children if she could persuade a judge it was in their interests; she could also remarry or earn money without interference from her former husband.[78] But the Act also made it much easier for the Jasons of the world to leave their wives for new partners, and to abandon their responsibilities towards their offspring.

The details of these legislative measures were being finalized in the summer of 1857, when Sadler's Wells staged John Heraud's *Medea in Corinth*. This offered a London public drawn from across the class spectrum the first of what was to become a series of mid-Victorian tragic *Medea*s in English. More systematically than even Brough's burlesque, Heraud's tragedy subjects the issues surrounding the divorce bill to agonizing scrutiny through the medium of the myth of Medea. Heraud, a liberal Huguenot by descent, and a frequent guest of Carlyle,[79] was convinced that ordinary people's sensibilities could be educated by the theatre. He had led the campaign for the Repeal of the Theatrical Patents Act in 1843, which had broken the stranglehold of the patent theatres, making it possible to produce serious spoken drama at theatres other than Drury Lane, Covent Garden, the Haymarket, and the Theatre Royal in each provincial town. He had been supported in this by his friend Thomas Talfourd, the instigator of the Infant Custody Bill.[80]

Heraud's major occupation was drama critic of the *Illustrated London News*, but he also wrote two other plays putting the position of women at the centre of the agenda, *Videna; or, the Mother's Tragedy* (Marylebone Theatre, 1854), and *Wife or no Wife* (Haymarket, 1855). He educated his daughter Edith enthusiastically, encouraging her to read Schelling and Shakespeare in her early

---

[78] The Act would have transformed the life of Helen Faucit's mother Harriet, who had always been the breadwinner of the family. After the failure of her marriage she was condemned to live not only in poverty but 'in sin' with her new partner, and her subsequent children suffered terribly from the stigma of illegitimacy. See Carlyle (2000).

[79] *ODNB* xxvi. 648–9.

[80] Edith Heraud (1898), 91.

teens. She starred in her father's 1857 *Medea* at Sadler's Wells, and recalled that this version, which used far more Euripides than Legouvé, 'was acknowledged by the public press to be superior to those that had preceded it'.[81] The audience were greatly excited by her 'singularly powerful acting', and the production was transferred to Liverpool.[82]

Besides other productions, two years later Heraud's *Medea* was revived at the thoroughly demotic Standard Theatre on Shoreditch High Street in the East End. After renovations in 1850 and 1854, the Standard had the largest capacity of any auditorium in Britain; it could seat five thousand, two thousand more than Drury Lane or Covent Garden. The audiences included the poorest residents of London, who needed to pay only 3*d.* for the gallery. The fantastic success of the theatre in the 1850s inspired spectators to arrive on trains from up to twenty miles away. The manager, John Douglass, was determined to bring theatrical Classics to the masses; in 1854–5 he staged Shakespeare and *The Duchess of Malfi*. *Medea*, starring Edith Heraud, was part of this highbrow programme, and scored one of Douglass's two great successes in 1859, running for twelve nights.[83] This means that it was seen in that year alone by up to 60,000 individuals.

Edith Heraud commented later on the unexpected success enjoyed by the adapted ancient play in the theatre of the ordinary working people of London:

... one of the weekly papers remarked that it was surprising that a play of Greek origin should be acted at the East End—that it should be understood, and its sentiments frequently applauded. Another triumph ... another instance of the good effected by the repeal of the Patents. Not only was the Shakespearian and poetic drama enthusiastically welcomed by the million, but the severer Greek tragedy was kindly accepted and appreciated by them. Of the truth of my father's theory that the stage was the popular educator, what further proof was needed?[84]

That the sentiments in Heraud's tragedy on the theme of Medea were 'frequently applauded' is hardly surprising given the climate of the 1850s, when divorce and the iniquities suffered by women

[81] Ibid. 128–9.
[82] *ILN* 31, no. 873 (15 Aug. 1857), 163; *ILN* 31, no. 876 (29 Aug. 1857), 219.
[83] Allan Stuart Jackson (1993), 6, 112, 124.
[84] Edith Heraud (1898), 128–9.

and children had remained at the top of the agenda consistently since the Royal Commission was inaugurated in 1850.

Heraud transparently transfers contemporary discussion of divorce and women's rights to the context of ancient Corinth. Jason is in love with Creusa, but also wants custody of the children. Creon asks Jason what he is going to do about Medea. Jason replies, 'I publicly repudiate and divorce her', and asks Creusa to adopt the children.[85] Aegeus, in this version the voice of reason, is mindful that the paternal prerogative over custody is no longer uncontestable: he responds to Jason by asking him if he would defy

> The angry curses of a wronged wife?
> The malice of a deserted mother?
> Her children's cries, from her caresses snatched?[86]

The potential disadvantages of divorce for women are scrutinized in a discussion between Medea and Jason, which draws heavily on the Euripidean interchanges between these estranged spouses. Jason begs Medea to grant him a divorce, to 'immolate' herself for the sake of the children. Greece has apparently already passed a Divorce Act, because Jason says to his wife, 'By our laws, divorce is not | As perjury regarded'. But Medea apparently opposes the improvement of access to divorce to philandering husbands:

> Laws—laws—laws!
> But justice so regards, who would not
> Women should suffer more than man the wrongs
> Of man's inconstancy.[87]

Jason responds by asserting his rights over the custody of children, who will 'find paternal refuge | 'Neath Creon's palace-roof'. But Medea delivers a scornful tirade expressing the wrongs of women under Greek (English) law:

> 'Tis safely planned.
> Ingenious, too. Again your man-made laws,
> Framed to suppress the rights of subject woman,
> By nature meant to know but a first love,
> Formed like the swan to be one only mate.
> Therein our sex is nobler far than yours ...
> My boys, you say, will dwell in royal halls,
> But what, meanwhile, will be the mother's doom?[88]

---

[85] John Heraud (1857), 17–18.   [86] Ibid. 18.   [87] Ibid. 20–5.
[88] Ibid. 22.

Like most Victorians, Heraud's Medea believes in women's 'natural' monogamy. In the mid-eighteenth century women's sexual appetite had often been seen as potentially voracious (see above, Ch. 3, pp. 89–90); by 1840, however, it had become the common sense of the middle classes that nature had bestowed upon men and women essentially different bodies and psychologies but complementary roles.[89] Yet she also supports women's rights, for the speech draws attention to two injustices which the 1857 Act was intended to alleviate—father's absolute rights to children over seven, and the blighted, manless future of separated women. Jason is not allowed to retain rights over the sons, for Aegeus intervenes:

> Let him who loveth not
> His offspring be the first to tear away
> The children from the mother.[90]

Jason then allows Medea to take *one* of the boys, although in the event, terrified by their mother's strange behaviour, they both choose to go with Creusa.

Like Legouvé's version, Heraud's allows Medea to kill the children to save them from the Corinthians, but she blames Jason more emphatically for their deaths. Heraud's tragedy was successful in staging an English-language tragedy derived from Euripides' *Medea* because it was a provocative response to its times. It continued to excite audiences at more minor venues, and to enjoy revivals for years at both the Standard and at Sadler's Wells: it was almost certainly Heraud's version of Euripides' tragedy which was still being 'daringly presented' by 'the dignified Jennie Maurice' at Sadler's Wells in 1873.[91]

THE SUBJECTION OF WOMEN AND THE MURDER OF CHILDREN

The divorce act of 1857 still left women with unequal access to divorce, for which they could only apply on the ground of adultery *aggravated* by incest, bigamy, or cruelty, while men could divorce their wives on the ground of adultery alone. But the small steps

---

[89] Davidoff and Hall (1987), 149.
[90] John Heraud (1857), 31.
[91] *ILN* 61, no. 1714 (13 July 1872), 43; Arundel (1965), 164.

which the act had taken to equalize men's and women's rights provoked the reconsideration of marriage which remained a prominent feature of public discourse throughout the next two decades,[92] and affected the nature of the fictions and myths through which the Victorians defined themselves. Even the myth of Perseus, Medusa, and Andromeda, consistently popular in Victorian art and literature, began to be interpreted and represented in subtly different ways: in the middle of the century it had offered an archetypal image of idealized patriarchal marriage, counterpoising vanquished female wildness and idealized feminine acquiescence. But gradually the roles of Medusa and Andromeda altered, as marriage became seen as 'a less definitive way to tame woman's dangerous power.'[93]

Women's rights received fresh support in the outburst of reforming activity following John Stuart Mill's election to the House of Commons in 1865 and the publication of his important essay (written in 1861), *The Subjection of Women*, in 1869.[94] In this essay Mill is almost certainly echoing Euripides, *Medea* 233–4 when he writes that 'the wife is the actual bond-servant of her husband', yet worse than a slave because she is unable to turn down the 'last familiarity' of her husband.[95] This decade saw the beginnings of serious campaigning for women's suffrage, and feminists pressing for women's rights to property and child custody. As a result, the Married Women's Property Acts of 1870 and 1882 made it possible for every married woman to make a will without her husband's agreement, and to hold property in her own name: the Infant Custody Acts of 1873 and 1886 gave mothers additional rights to appeal for custody of their children.[96] It is interesting to see the widening gap at this time between (male) academic writing on Medea, and the progressive female authors who were reassessing her from a sympathetic standpoint. A learned editor of *Medea* could in 1873 still inform his schoolboy readers that Euripides disliked women, who included

persons with base and evil minds, persons whose profligacy was shameful, whose daring was great, whose ability to plot and intrigue for mischief was

---

[92] Shanley (1981–2), 356.   [93] Munich (1989), 32–7.
[94] For a recent edition with useful introduction, notes, and bibliography see Mansfield (1980).
[95] Ibid. 55, 57.
[96] Shanley (1989), 14.

unequalled. The quality remains to some extent in the race to the present day, as we see in the use of women as spies &c. by Russia.[97]

As late as 1887 a male translator of *Medea* excises Medea's first monologue 'with an eye to the dramatic effect'.[98] Yet the (uncut) translation of Mill's associate Augusta Webster, a prominent campaigner for women's suffrage and education, was published in 1868, and in her poetic monologue *Medea in Athens* the heroine insightfully comments on her relationship with Jason.[99] Webster was persuasive: the reviewer of her translation in the *Athenaeum* can now write:

> . . . the subject, if not grand, is one of general interest, being confined to no time, place or class of society. It is also one which a lady might naturally be expected to handle with success as she must be able to enter fully in to the feelings of the unfortunate heroine in her distressing condition.[100]

Similarly, in *Adam Bede* (1859) George Eliot compares Hetty Sorrel, a victim of seduction and an infanticide, with Medea; in *Felix Holt* (1866) the analogy with Mrs Transome, whom her former lover Jermyn wishes to sever from her son, is ironically developed.[101]

Medea continued to appear regularly on the London stage, in both burlesques and tragedies, throughout this period of hectic legislation. Parliamentary debates were of course not the sole explanation. By the 1860s sensational murder trials, especially those involving women motivated by revenge, had become a public fascination. Yet even this development was connected with social change. Criminologists have perceived a pattern whereby murders by women during this period were increasingly practised for reasons connected less with a desire for respectability or with life-threatening poverty, but with 'new—and disappointed—expectations about their status and rights within marriage'.[102] Women were ardent followers of the twists and turns of the trials. Robert Altick has remarked upon the 'striking Victorian paradox'

---

[97] John Hogan (1873), p. xxv.

[98] Blew (1887), p. ix.

[99] Webster (1868), (1870), 1–13. See Hardwick (1997), 2–4. On Webster's political activity see Leighton (1992), 164–201.

[100] *Athenaeum*, no. 2135 (26 Sept. 1868).

[101] Jenkyns (1980), 115–17, 125–7, Hurst (2003), 103–37.

[102] Hartman (1985), 263.

whereby middle-class women, brought up to pride themselves on the delicacy of their sensibilities, and to faint at the thought of drowning a kitten, revelled in the gory details of murder trials.[103]

Similar fascinations mark the fiction of the period. The 'fad genre' of the 1860s and early 1870s was sensational fiction, related to stage melodrama; important examples were Mary Elizabeth Braddon's *Lady Audley's Secret* (1862), Wilkie Collins's *The Woman in White* (1860), and Ellen Wood's *East Lynne*, first serialized in the *New Monthly Magazine* in 1860.[104] The success of these novels, many of which were written by women, rested on their assertive heroines, and their display of 'female anger, frustration, and sexual energy',[105] all of which were of course also offered by the story of Medea. Lady Audley is a golden-haired murderess. Isabel Vane in *East Lynne* is the archetypal heroine of sensationalized 'maternal melodrama', which squeezed every drop of emotion out of mothers' separations from their offspring:[106] locked in a loveless marriage and obsessed by her husband's adultery, she actually abandons her children. For the female protagonists of this fiction are often depicted as escaping from their families and repudiating conventional ideals of motherhood and femininity through 'illness, madness, divorce, flight, and ultimately, murder'.[107] Medea perhaps no longer seemed so very different from other heroines in popular culture.

Another issue which made Medea seem relevant was anxiety about child-killing. Victorian fiction and melodrama had always enjoyed dwelling on the lachrymose deaths of children (one need think only of Little Nell),[108] but child-murder was different. In the early 1860s the public was stunned to learn that no fewer than 298 coroners' verdicts of wilful murder of children found dead on the streets of London were given between 1855 and 1860. Scores of children's corpses—mostly infants—were found abandoned in the city every year, and in 'The Function of Criticism at the Present Time' (1864), Matthew Arnold cites a case of alleged

---

[103] Altick (1970), 42.
[104] Cretkovich (1992), 15–22. For a discussion of *Lady Audley's Secret* see Bernstein (1997), 73–103.
[105] Showalter (1977), 182.
[106] Cvetkovich (1992), 112–13.
[107] Showalter (1997), 182–3.
[108] Auerbach (1990), 24, 96. For a comprehensive study, see McDonagh (2003).

infanticide as a reminder of the realities that reside behind self-satisfied myths about Victorian culture.[109] The Infant Life Protection Act of 1872 tried to curb the inordinately high number of infant deaths; a serious debate was under way whether these children died because of their mothers' poverty or culpable irresponsibility.[110]

It is in this context that tragedies on the theme of Medea remained popular: they were almost all adaptations, like Heraud's, of Euripides combined with Legouvé. The durability of Legouvé's version was a result of its compatibility with nineteenth-century notions of femininity. One reviewer (perhaps Heraud) noted approvingly that Legouvé had tried to 'humanize' the terrifying heroine,

and to bring her and her acts within the sphere of our moral sentiments. He is careful from the beginning to make her exhibit the feelings of maternity to an excessive degree; and attributes the catastrophe to a revolt of those feelings. . . . There is in this a natural motive supplied, wanting in the original story.[111]

Legouvé was felt to have 'improved' on Euripides by making Medea's primary motive the 'natural' one of maternal love, rather than the apparently 'unnatural' reactions to her faithless spouse of sexual jealousy, wrath, or vindictiveness.

The barbarian heroine became part of the repertoire of touring female virtuoso actresses, and thus was often played in London by appropriately foreign performers. In 1861, for example, two different actresses played versions of Legouvé's tragedy at major London theatres. The American Matilda Heron did not impress in her own English-language version at the Lyceum in April of that year; she alienated her audience by her stiff, Continental, style of acting. Edward Blanchard felt it 'very bad'.[112] But the smaller, gentler Avonia Jones, described variously as American or Australian, did rather better at Drury Lane in November.[113]

[109] Shanley (1989), 87, 90; Arnold (1986), 145–6.
[110] Hoffer and Hull (1984); see also Rose (1986), 35–45.
[111] *ILN* 28, no. 804 (7 June 1856), 619.
[112] *ILN* 38, no. 1086 (27 Apr. 1861), 389; Heron (1861); Blanchard (1891), i. 256; see also *ILN*, loc. cit.
[113] *ILN* 39, no. 1116 (9 Nov. 1861), 469; Blanchard (1891), i. 263.

MEDEA IN THE 1870S

The most exotic actress to appear as Medea after Ristori was Madame Francesca (Fanny) Janauschek, of Central European provenance, who starred in a version of Grillparzer's, rather than Legouvé's, treatment at the Haymarket in 1876. In her performance the emphasis was much less upon the divorce issue. Medea's ethnicity had not been a preoccupation of the earlier Victorian theatre (although it is possible that there was a racial element in the ruse employed by Medea in Mark Lemon's 1856 burlesque, where she had daubed her rival's complexion with toxic black paint).[114] Yet Janauschek's interpretation of Grillparzer's trilogy (which was written against a background of pogroms in Austria) now spoke to contemporary experiences of empire rather than to issues of gender, for she emphasized the barbarous, oriental character embodied in Grillparzer's Hasidic Medea, contrasted with the civilized Creusa. This version never even asks whether the children might prefer to be with their natural mother rather than with Jason's white-skinned new bride: Jason insists, and Creusa agrees, that the children self-evidently must not 'grow to manhood in a | Foreign, barbarous clime'.[115] This type of Medea consistently attracted the painters of the period, who neglected Euripides' abandoned mother in favour of the visual potential offered by the exotic sorceress of the *Argonautica* and her derivatives in, for example, Charles Kingsley's *The Heroes* (1855) and William Morris's *Life and Death of Jason* (1867).[116] Madame Janauschek's failure to present herself as her husband's victim may have been one reason for her unpopularity, and she further estranged an audience used to sympathizing with Medea by the declamatory style she favoured. This went down well in Germany, Austria, and Russia, but was disliked in England.[117]

For in tragedy the British wanted a pretty Medea whom they could pity. The curious flipside of Victorian sexism, which was confused about women's competence as moral agents, was the reluctance to find them criminally responsible for infanticide.

---

[114] Lemon (1856), 16 (see also above, p. 407).
[115] Anon. (1876), 21. For Grillparzer's Hasidic Medea see Macintosh (2000*a*), 13–14, 19–21.
[116] Kestner (1989), 40, 45, 55–6, 170.
[117] Maude (1903), 161–2.

Between 1849 and 1877 only three female child-murderers suffered capital punishment in Britain, the most famous being a real-life Medea. Ann Lawrence's execution caused a sensation in 1864, after she vented her rage on her four-year-old son when she found that her lover was unfaithful.[118] Lawrence died because she was too like Euripides' vindictive Medea and too unlike Legouvé's altruistic mother. The Victorians needed Medea to be a tender model of maternal devotion, and favoured the lovely young Isabel Bateman in the role, which she performed with remarkable success in William Gordon Wills's tragedy *Medea in Corinth* in the summer of 1872 at the Lyceum.[119] An engraving appeared in the *Illustrated London News* (Fig. 14.4), significantly reassuring its readership that Bateman 'shines in the display of motherly emotion'.[120]

John Heraud, as drama critic of the *Illustrated London News*, compared Wills's play, his own, and Euripides', objecting with some justification that Wills's rhetoric was florid.[121] Yet his play was admired by others: a 'distinguished' critic complimented him on the way he had 'skilfully remoulded the matter afforded him by Euripides, and...ably fitted the action to the requirements and the condition of the modern stage'.[122] For Wills had indeed 're-moulded' the play to create an emotional drama which spoke to his audience's concerns about divorce. This adaptation is unusual (and perhaps more true to the way in which Euripides' play was understood by its original audience of Athenian males) in presenting both spouses as individuals with understandable problems. Medea speaks scornfully of Jason's hypocritical use of arguments from the children's welfare to disguise his own self-interested motives, 'mouthing here of love and care paternal, | The interests of thy children as thy motives'. Yet Jason is stranded in a loveless marriage to a heathen, a 'barbarian cursed of our Gods, | And by our Grecian laws I may divorce her'. Creon, however, has read the

---

[118] Rose (1986), 76–7; see also Patrick Wilson (1971). One Rebecca Smith had been executed in 1849 after admitting to killing no fewer than eight of her children (Rose, 76).

[119] Blanchard (1891), ii. 414. Bateman was born in America and came to England in her teens. For a less favourable review, see Cook (1883), 214–17.

[120] *ILN* 61, no. 1715 (20 July 1872), 65.

[121] *ILN* 61, no. 1714 (13 July 1872), 43.

[122] Unfortunately this critic is not named in the source citing these words, which is Freeman Wills (1898), 90.

FIGURE 14.4   Isabel Bateman as Medea (1872).

1857 Divorce Act, and warns Jason that he cannot divorce Medea, who has committed no fault, without her consent, 'For this is vital in our Grecian law'.[123]

[123] W. G. Wills (1872).

The last important Victorian Medea was Geneviève Ward, an American-born artist, educated in Europe (Fig. 14.5). One of her first tragic roles was Medea, whom she acted in a version of Legouvé's tragedy in Dublin, Liverpool, Hull, and London between 1873 and 1876. Her performance was enhanced by her contralto voice, stately figure, and intelligence.[124] Ward certainly saw the connections between Medea and the contemporary debates about women's rights, which during the 1870s had begun to focus on the issue of marital violence. This led to the passing in 1878 of the Matrimonial Causes Act, which added assault to the grounds on which a woman could legally separate from her husband. Ward asked herself how Medea would react if she was the victim of battering, and assumed that she would not have tolerated the kind of everyday abuse meted out to working-class British women by their husbands. In one production the 4-year-old daughter of the property man was to play Medea's younger child, but became frightened. Ward reports that her mother endeavoured to soothe her, 'a sad-faced woman, who probably accepted all hardships and ill-usage from her lawful master as meekly as Medea fiercely resented her wrongs'.[125]

PREFIGURATIVE MEDEA

Performances of plays about Medea disappeared at the time of the passing of the last pieces of significant Victorian marriage legislation in the early 1880s. This period coincided with the transformations in attitudes to Greek tragedy which are to be the subject of the next two chapters—they entailed the death of classical burlesque, a growing dislike of the neoclassical school of adaptation exemplified by Legouvé, and academic experiments with performing Greek drama, unadapted, in the ancient language. The outrageous Medea did not appeal to those who selected the plays for

[124] Gustafson (1881), 119, 130.
[125] Geneviève Ward (1881), 127–8. Another American, Charles Bristed, who studied Classics at Cambridge in the 1840s, was scandalized by the treatment of women in England. It was the standard practice of English gentlemen, he writes, to abuse working-class women sexually, and he has seen more brutality to women than in any other European country except Russia. 'The cases of aggravated assault and battery upon women that come before the London police-magistrates are positively startling in number and degree' (Bristed (1852), 347 and n.)

FIGURE 14.5   Geneviève Ward, *c.*1875. Reproduced courtesy of the APGRD.

educational productions: suitable pedagogical models of femininity were identified in *Alcestis* or *Antigone*.

In subsequent chapters it will also be seen that the burlesqued and tragic Medeas of the mid-Victorian era prefigured the appearance of the New Woman on the British stage at the end of the nineteenth century. Far from being an interloper from Scandinavia, prototypes for this New Woman, so widely associated with Ibsen, are there in the mid-Victorian British plays based on *Medea*. But the burlesque Medea, in particular, is far from simply the traditional victim of melodrama; on the contrary, as is typical of the heroines of the burlesque tradition that adopted her so readily, she has cunning, resolve, and experience behind her that enable and indeed force her to break out of the traditional Victorian feminine mould. Collectively these mid-Victorian Medeas are also the ancestors of the Edwardian Medea adopted by the Suffragettes (see below, pp. 511–19) and of the many hundred Medeas to have argued their cases on the stages of the world since the Women's Liberation Movement of the early 1970s.

There have been many productions over the last three decades, including the commercial successes achieved by Diana Rigg in the 1990s and Fiona Shaw in the third millennium. When the story of Medea's recent stage appearances comes to be written, connections will be drawn between the upsurge of interest in Euripides' tragedy and legislative activity around sex discrimination, equal pay, equal opportunities, divorce, child custody, and, more recently, wives' retaliation against abusive husbands. But Medea's relationship with legislative change has had a rather longer history. By the end of the Victorian era she was already a veteran, having spent over half a century in the vanguard of the campaign for women's emancipation.

15

Page versus Stage: Greek Tragedy, the Academy, and the Popular Theatre

Eduard Devrient, the actor who took the part of Haemon in the Potsdam premiere of the Mendelssohn *Antigone* in 1841, refers to the pivotal nature of the production:

The ancient tradition shifted with this performance out of the narrow world of bookish study into the wide open ground of live art, accessible to all.[1]

Whilst the impact of the Mendelssohn *Antigone* in Britain was enormous and long-lasting, its consequences were in many ways different from those of the German-speaking world. It did not lead in any unequivocal sense to Greek tragedy being immediately transported 'into the wide open ground of live art, accessible to all'. There were in its wake, as we have already heard, a number of serious productions of *Medea*, whose success and 'accessibility' would have been unimaginable without the collective memory of the 1845 *Antigone*. The fact that a French version of an ancient Greek play being performed in Italian on the London stage with Legouvé's *Medea* should have aroused such genuine interest (and the burlesque responses to this are further testimony to this) can only be explained with reference to the 1845 precedent; and equally, the 'vernacular' *Medea* of John Heraud, which was in many ways 'accessible to all' with its long run at the Standard Theatre,[2] cannot be considered independently of the Mendelssohn *Antigone*.

However, as with the Legouvé *Medea*, there was no easy transition from page to stage consequent on this milestone *Antigone*. It resulted instead in the invention and development of the hugely popular form, the Greek tragic burlesque (see Ch. 12).

---

[1] Cited in Fischer-Lichte (1999a), 4.

[2] See Ch. 14; and for the social diversity of the audience at the Standard and other East End theatres, see Davis and Emeljanow (2001), 52–4.

As Theodore Alois Buckley, Fellow of St John's College, Oxford, points out wryly in the none too laudatory preface to his two-volume translation of Euripides' extant plays, just as Aristophanes surpassed Euripides in the fifth century so now it is the burlesque writer rather than the tragedian who holds sway in the theatre in Britain. Writing in 1850, Buckley observes truculently:

If the reader discover the painful fact that the burlesque writer is greater than the tragedian, he will perhaps also recollect that such a literary relation is, unfortunately, by no means confined to the days of Aristophanes.[3]

It was not until the 1870s that the British theatre could be said to have caught up with the German-speaking world in its relationship to Greek tragedy. It was only, then, for example that a British classical scholar of Boeckh's standing was to involve himself in a production (albeit now an amateur one) of an ancient Greek play, when Professor Lewis Campbell began his series of performances in St Andrews and Edinburgh together with Professor and Mrs Fleeming Jenkin. And it was only some thirty years later that a British academic was to lend his expertise to a professional production of a Greek play, when Gilbert Murray's translations began to be performed at the Court and Savoy Theatres in London from 1907 onwards (see Ch. 17). This is not to say that there had been no performance tradition within the academy (on the contrary, Samuel Parr's school theatricals at Stanmore and Richard Valpy's at Reading are testimony to the vigour of that tradition); but there had been no serious involvement in the performance of Greek plays within British universities since the Renaissance. The prohibitions on performance in general in Oxford have already been mentioned (Ch. 12); and around the middle of the nineteenth century, there are clear signs that young classical scholars at both Oxford and Cambridge, including at least two who went on to become celebrated burlesque writers, Frank Talfourd and A. C. Burnand, felt acutely frustrated with these prohibitions.

In this chapter we seek to explain why Greek tragedy came into vogue in the 1880s. As Pat Easterling, Chris Stray, and Mary Beard have shown,[4] the changes in the classical curriculum towards

---

[3] Buckley (1850), 'Preface'.
[4] Easterling (1999), 27–48; Stray (1998), 149–54; and more generally, Beard (2000), *passim*.

the end of the century were most influential in this regard. The increasing understanding of the ancient world in its entirety—the move away from a narrowly philological understanding of antiquity and an embrace of what was termed *Altertumswissenschaft* in Germany—although slower to take root in Britain than elsewhere in Europe, dictated the developments in the British classical curriculum in the 1880s. By now the general interest in classical archaeology beyond the academy (afforded especially by high-profile excavations that were closely documented in the national press) was formally acknowledged with the endowment of Chairs in the subject within the universities. Furthermore, the arrival of women within higher education, whose school curriculum had often included the enactment of ancient plays, cannot be excluded from any attempt to explain the extraordinary efflorescence of performance of Greek plays at this time.

However, developments in the professional theatre also made that flowering possible. The rise of Naturalism was in many ways indebted to the attention to acute detail pioneered by Planché in his burlesques of Greek tragedy; and the revivals of Greek plays, despite their evident parallels with and influence on other deliberately non-naturalistic performance styles (notably Symbolism), need to be considered in relation to theatrical Naturalism. Frank Benson, who had performed Clytemnestra in the 1880 production of *Agamemnon* at Balliol College, Oxford, immediately recognized a common endeavour, when he was inspired by the 1881 visit to Britain of the Saxe-Meiningen Company to take his own company on tour with the *Oresteia* in 1883.[5] Indeed, it was very much an awareness of theatrical developments elsewhere in Europe at this time—and the consequent realization that Britain needed to find ways of matching these—that also led to experiments with Greek tragedy. When the Comédie-Française visited the Gaiety Theatre in 1879 for a season, Matthew Arnold was sufficiently riled by the contrasts between the French and the British theatrical traditions to call for a serious English national theatre.[6] Shortly after, when Lewis Campbell saw the French tragedian, Jean Mounet-Sully in the role of Oedipus, he asked himself: 'Why can we not

---

[5] On the impact of the Saxe-Meiningen Co. on Benson, see Stokes (1972), 35 n.; Trewin (1960), 30.

[6] Arnold (1879); Stokes (1972), 4.

have the like of this in England?'[7] And even if it was to be some years before a professional company would mount a similarly successful production in England, Campbell's efforts in Scotland began the laying of the foundations for such a production.

Not surprising, then, any attempt to explain why Greek tragedy became so fashionable in Britain from the 1880s onwards must delineate a confluence of factors both within and beyond the academy—the widening of the classical curriculum, the inclusion of women, as well as the broader developments within the professional theatre which allowed for both the power of the burlesque and fostered an interest in music drama. But it is, above all, the result of the interplay between popular and high-brow culture during this period—in a crude sense, between stage and page—a relationship (though largely agonistic) that has very often been overlooked. It is Robert Browning, who had vainly tried his fortunes on the professional stage only to lose out to writers of burlesque and melodrama, who provides in many ways the catalyst for the change with his 'page'-based engagements with Greek tragedy. For Browning's reworkings of Greek tragedy, especially his *Alcestis* and his transcript of the *Agamemnon*, acted as the spur for the next generation to make Greek tragedy (as Devrient claimed happened much earlier in the German-speaking world) 'accessible to all'. And just as Buckley's plaint in 1850 presupposes a negative corollary between the tragedian and the burlesque writer in the popular theatre, we find that corollary reversed once Euripides, Aristotle's 'most tragic' of writers, regains respect within the academy in no small measure through Browning's pioneering efforts to champion his cause.

THE POWER OF BURLESQUE: ALCESTIS AND THE STRONG-MINDED WOMAN

In the same year that saw the appearance of Theodore Alois Buckley's edition of translations of Euripides' nineteen extant tragedies, which included his admonition that burlesque writers may well exceed in power and magnitude those who produce the 'serious' drama, a burlesque was mounted at the Strand Theatre that may well have lent credence to his observation. For the play

[7] Lewis Campbell (1891), 328.

was based on Euripides' *Alcestis* and was composed by the classically educated Frank Talfourd to considerable commendation. Talfourd's burlesque of *Alcestis* was not the first such attempt in
English: he may well have known the 1816 burlesque version of
the play by Issachar Styrke, designed to provide the reader of the
1806 Oxford Greek school edition of Gaisford with an amusing
(and not entirely reliable) crib, with line references to the Greek
text appearing alongside his burlesque (see Ch. 12). With its numerous interpolations and deliberate misrepresentations, Styrke's
edition was clearly not to be relied upon by any Greekless student.
Nor with its often lame doggerel does it pretend to any literary
value. But what does make Styrke's burlesque worthy of some
serious consideration, however, is the fact that it can be considered
to provide an early example of the counterview to the ennobling
tendency in portrayals of Admetus (as had been seen, for example,
in Thomson's Edward and Eleonora; see Ch. 4). Although Styrke's
alternative view merely highlights aspects already inherent in the
Euripidean prototype, it becomes increasingly common in nineteenth-century burlesque versions, which anticipate (and perhaps
even determine) twentieth-century readings of Euripides' play.
And it was undoubtedly the generic disturbances in this play,
which made the task of the burlesque writer a particularly easy one.

Talfourd's version was subtitled 'the Original Strong-Minded
Woman . . . a shameless misinterpretation of the Greek drama of
Euripides', and with its brazenly upfront and wayward Alcestis it
was indeed a far cry from the Euripidean prototype. Talfourd's
Alcestis has every reason to give up on Admetus and go off with
Death:

> For life with him was nothing but a curse
> And though I took him 'for better or for worse'.
> The world can't surely wonder I forsook him, for
> I found him such a deal worse than I took him for.[8]

Yet whilst Talfourd's Alcestis is 'a shameless misinterpretation' of
her Greek prototype, his representation of Admetus merely mag-
nifies embryonic traits discernible in Euripides. Talfourd's Admetus is not only an excessively self-regarding buffoon, 'weak in
intellect'[9] and strong on self-satisfaction; he is also a financial

---

[8] Francis Talfourd (n.d.), 15.   [9] Ibid. 1.

incompetent who has run up debts with Orcus/Death that he is unable to repay. Alcestis may as well 'do the heroine'[10] and die in this version, because an impecunious marriage for a woman in mid-Victorian Britain was little short of a death sentence.

Although Talfourd's burlesque is unusual in not being tied to a particular production of a Greek play, it is clearly responding to a number of classically inspired productions—serious and burlesque—at this time in London that gained their importance in the light of pressing political and social issues. As we have seen in the previous chapter, the debate about divorce legislation in England lent profound resonance to numerous mid-Victorian burlesque productions of *Medea*, in which Euripides' protagonist is rendered an abandoned wife rather than monstrous infanticide. Consideration of the marital state had led to regular recourse to the Euripidean tragedy of marital breakdown from at least the 1830s, and the debate inevitably led in turn to that other Euripidean exposé of marital relations, the *Alcestis*.

The highly popular early-nineteenth-century poet, Felicia Hemans, obliquely engaged with that debate in 1831, when she chose to render into English Alcestis' leave taking of her family. Eight years before the passing of the Infant Custody Act (granting mothers custody over children under seven years in the event of separation or divorce), Hemans, who was herself an abandoned wife, translated Act I, Scene ii of Alfieri's 1798 version, *Alceste*, in which the dying mother reminds her husband of the woeful negligence of newly married fathers and the perils that await children at the hands of those who are not their birth-mothers. It was Frank Talfourd's father, Thomas Noon Talfourd, who would be been responsible for this first important piece of legislation in the emancipation of women (see Ch. 13). Here some twelve years later in the younger Talfourd's burlesque, we find Alcestis publicly scrutinizing the institution of marriage itself, pronouncing after her resurrection at the end to the popular air of 'Roisin the Beau':

> We have come to a happy conclusion—
> A happy conclusion?—Who knows!
> Kind friends don't destroy the illusion
> But let all be *couleur de rose*![11]

---

[10] Ibid. 10.   [11] Ibid. 27.

If Talfourd senior had chosen to comment upon the politics of the decade following the Reform Bill of 1832 with a 'serious' rewrite of Euripides' *Ion*, his son (in tune with a generation for whom, in Buckley's terms, 'the burlesque writer is greater than the tragedian') chose to push the boundaries of the debate about marriage in the serio-comic form that was holding sway on the mid-Victorian stage.

Heroic tragedy had enjoyed a brief revival in the 1830s with the plays of Bulwer-Lytton and Thomas Talfourd (see Ch. 10); and in the hands of these playwrights, the 'domestication' of the ancients had perhaps reached its limit. But with the advent of serious burlesques of Greek tragedy, the traditional burlesque weapon of domesticating in order to deflate is used to more than comic effect. Frank Talfourd's burlesque version gives us an intriguing insight into a period in theatre history when 'serious' drama in English rarely left the page. What is striking about this and other burlesques is not so much that they kept a memory of Greek tragedy alive on the British stage at this time, but that they did so to a broadly based audience; an audience, moreover, that included those who went on to become involved in the 1880s revivals.

As we have already heard, the playwright, and editor of *Punch*, F. C. Burnand claims with hindsight that he and his fellow undergraduates at the time found it difficult to distinguish between tragedy and burlesque (see Ch. 14). Whilst Talfourd's Alcestis might not have boasted a performance to match Frederick Robson's in Brough's *Medea; or, the Best of Mothers with a Brute of a Husband* some six years later (1856), it did (like Brough's version) enjoy numerous revivals with Frank himself (who had made his theatrical debut at the Henley Regatta as Lady Macbeth) in the part of Alcestis (Fig. 15.1).[12]

However, it is important to stress that at their most successful, the burlesques at this time were barely distinguishable from (and, on occasions at least, clearly able to outstrip) the very objects they sought to travesty. If Robson could outperform the Italian tragedi-

---

[12] His presumed relation W. Talfourd also appeared in the 1851 revival at the Royal Soho Theatre in the part of Orcus (see the details on the playbill in Fig. 15.1). There were also revivals in 1850 in New York, for which see T. Alliston Brown (1903), i. 287, who refers to a production of *Alcestis* in September 1850 at Mitchell's Olympic, 'a very popular place of entertainment', and then in London in 1853; see Talfourd (n.d), which cites the prologue from the revival on 24 Nov. 1853. For Talfourd's undergraduate theatricals, see Mackinnon (1910), 21–7.

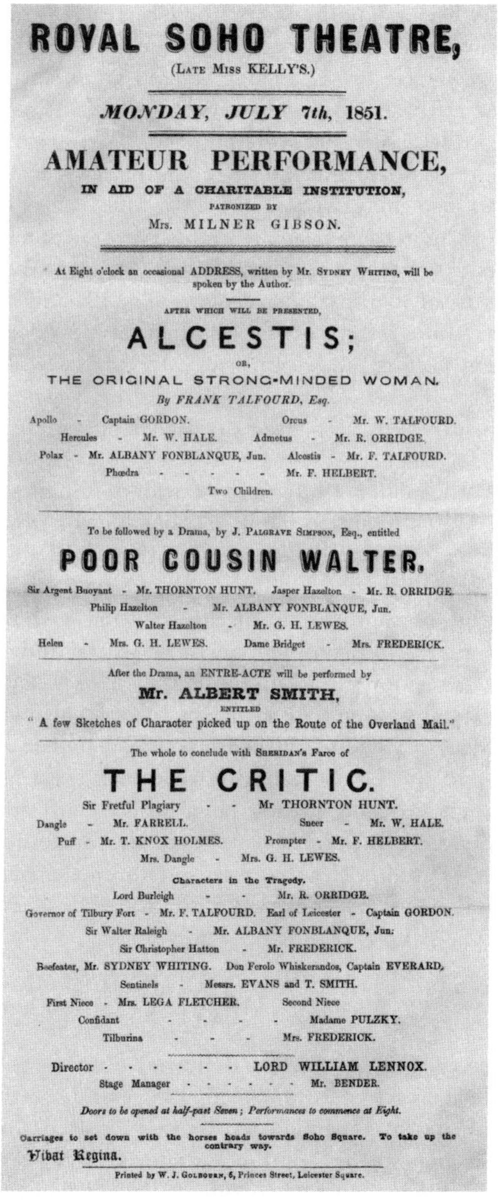

ROYAL SOHO THEATRE,
(LATE MISS KELLY'S.)

MONDAY, JULY 7th, 1851.

AMATEUR PERFORMANCE,
IN AID OF A CHARITABLE INSTITUTION,
PATRONIZED BY
Mrs. MILNER GIBSON.

At Eight o'clock an occasional ADDRESS, written by Mr. SYDNEY WHITING, will be spoken by the Author.

AFTER WHICH WILL BE PRESENTED,

ALCESTIS;
OR,
THE ORIGINAL STRONG-MINDED WOMAN.
By FRANK TALFOURD, Esq.

Apollo	Captain GORDON.		Orcus	Mr. W. TALFOURD.
Hercules	Mr. W. HALE.		Admetus	Mr. R. ORRIDGE.
Polax	Mr. ALBANY FONBLANQUE, Jun.		Alcestis	Mr. F. TALFOURD.
Phædra				Mr. F. HELBERT.

Two Children.

To be followed by a Drama, by J. PALGRAVE SIMPSON, Esq., entitled

POOR COUSIN WALTER.

Sir Argent Buoyant	Mr. THORNTON HUNT.	Jasper Hazelton	Mr. R. ORRIDGE.
Philip Hazelton	Mr. ALBANY FONBLANQUE, Jun.		
Walter Hazelton	Mr. G. H. LEWES.		
Helen	Mrs. G. H. LEWES.	Dame Bridget	Mrs. FREDERICK.

After the Drama, an ENTRE-ACTE will be performed by

Mr. ALBERT SMITH,
ENTITLED
" A few Sketches of Character picked up on the Route of the Overland Mail."

The whole to conclude with SHERIDAN's Farce of

THE CRITIC.

Sir Fretful Plagiary - - Mr THORNTON HUNT.

Dangle	Mr. FARRELL.	Sneer	Mr. W. HALE.
Puff	Mr. T. KNOX HOLMES.	Prompter	Mr. F. HELBERT.
Mrs. Dangle	Mrs. G. H. LEWES.		

Characters in the Tragedy.

Lord Burleigh			Mr. R. ORRIDGE.
Governor of Tilbury Fort	Mr. F. TALFOURD.	Earl of Leicester	Captain GORDON.
Sir Walter Raleigh	Mr. ALBANY FONBLANQUE, Jun:		
Sir Christopher Hatton	Mr. FREDERICK.		
Beefeater, Mr. SYDNEY WHITING.	Don Ferolo Whiskerandos, Captain EVERARD,		
Sentinels	Messrs. EVANS and T. SMITH.		
First Niece	Mrs. LEGA FLETCHER.	Second Niece	
Confidant			Madame PULZKY.
Tilburina			Mrs. FREDERICK.

Director	LORD WILLIAM LENNOX.
Stage Manager	Mr. BENDER.

Doors to be opened at half-past Seven; Performances to commence at Eight.

Carriages to set down with the horses heads towards Soho Square. To take up the contrary way.

Vivat Regina.

Printed by W. J. GOLBOURN, 6, Princes Street, Leicester Square.

FIGURE 15.1   Playbill for a revival of Frank Talfourd's *Alcestis; or, the Original Strong-Minded Woman* (1851).

enne Adelaide Ristori, perhaps the English theatre should attempt Greek tragedy *au naturel* after all. Indeed, it may well have been in part Talfourd's burlesque challenge that led to the serious production of *Alcestis*, which was mounted at St James's Theatre in 1855. If the commercial theatre was often quick to seize upon that potential, the undergraduate generation bought up on Robson at the Olympic and elsewhere was particularly well placed to foster it. Brough seized upon the burlesque's ability to cross generic boundaries (for his instructions to his actors to transport the burlesque into the realms of its elevated target see Ch. 13) and the younger generation of undergraduates in the audience (who flocked down to London from Oxford and Cambridge to catch Robson and his contemporaries at the Adelphi Theatre in the Strand) were very obviously inspired by this example to go on to mount serious productions of the tragedies themselves some years later. Burnand's fellow thespian in those early years of the Amateur Dramatic Club, John Willis Clark, became responsible for organizing the early productions in Cambridge in the 1880s. And although Burnand himself was enjoying a successful career as a burlesque playwright in London at the time of the revivals of Greek plays at Cambridge, he was a prominent member of the audience on the first night of Greek plays in London in the 1880s (see Ch. 16).

These classically trained undergraduates were also undoubtedly best placed to recognize further connections between the classical burlesques and the Greek plays. With Greek tragedy's combination of speech and song having been only recently rediscovered with the Mendelssohn *Antigone*, it was the burlesque (with its fusion of words and music) that was best equipped, paradoxically, to initiate audiences into the form of the original.

MUSIC THEATRE: HENRY SPICER'S ALCESTIS (1855)

Talfourd's burlesque of *Alcestis* followed Planché in his *Golden Fleece*, in its paratragic response to the operatic tradition. The Great Exhibition of 1851 had led to an increased sophistication amongst members of the London audiences, who were now often drawn from a wider (and often foreign) constituency.[13] Here in

---

[13] Davis and Emeljanow (2001), 197 ff.

Talfourd's burlesque, Lully's famous passage in Act 4 of *Alceste*, 'Il faut passer tôt ou tard!', with a comic Charon is parodied by Talfourd in the duet between Orcus and Alcestis as they sink down through the trap door in the stage to the air of 'My skiff is on the shore'. And five years later when Henry Spicer's *Alcestis* was performed at St James's Theatre, one of Spicer's main concerns was to bring the music of Gluck's *Alceste* to the audience's attention (Fig. 15.2). Henry Morley, the close friend of Charles Dickens and later Professor of English at University College London, who was present on the opening night, attributes the play's success in equal measure to the enduring appeal of its subject, to the classical acting of Charlotte Vandenhoff in the title role, and to Gluck's choruses.[14]

It was not just the presence of Charlotte Vandenhoff (who played the first Antigone, see Ch. 12) that alluded to the Mendelssohn *Antigone* at Covent Garden ten years earlier. Spicer's use of a chorus of sixteen singers—eight male and eight female voices—recalls the (admittedly much larger) chorus of that performance.[15] Spicer's play owes more than a passing debt to Hippolyte Lucas's version seen at the Odéon in Paris some eight years earlier, and on some occasions is no more than a translation from the French.[16] Lucas's Act I owes much in its turn to Act I of the libretto to the French version of Gluck's opera by Marie-François-Louis Gand Leblanc Du Roullet; and the choral music by Antoine Elwart was no doubt inspired by the Mendelssohn example that had caused an equal stir when it was staged in Paris in 1844. However, Spicer makes it clear in his prologue that he is not adopting a classical set—in other words, he is deliberately eschewing the staging employed at Covent Garden in 1845 for the Mendelssohn *Antigone* that was generally considered to be the first attempt at replicating a Greek theatre in recent theatre history (see Ch. 12). Spicer comments:

The fixed 'scena', with its three entrances, the chorus, oscillating between pit and stage; the curtain lowered not lifted, at the commencement of the play etc. etc these details, though more acceptable to the classic eye,

---

[14] Morley (1866), 107.

[15] In the Potsdam premiere, by contrast, there were only 15 chorus members.

[16] Lucas (1847), pp. vii f. Pheres has no role in either Lully's *Alceste* (1674) or Handel's *Admeto, rè di Tessaglia*; and more importantly, he is omitted from the more recent Italian (1767) and French (1776) versions of Gluck's *Alceste*.

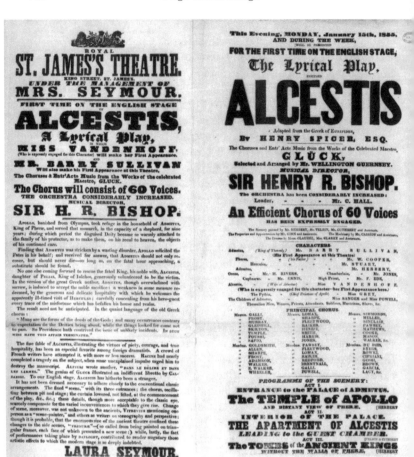

FIGURE 15.2   Playbill for Henry Spicer's *Alcestis* (1855).

scarcely compensate for the varied inconveniences to which they give
rise.[17]

What Spicer wanted, and felt that the 'classic' set would deny him,
was the freedom (that he noted was even available to the ancients) to
follow the essentially modern operatic tradition in its change of
scene. Like Gluck before them, both Lucas and Spicer adopt a

[17] Spicer (1855), p. iv.

three-act structure for their play: they begin outside the palace of Admetus and the temple of Apollo, before moving inside the palace for the death scene; and they end up outside the city at night, by Alcestis' tomb and the Cave of Death. Unlike the Mendelssohn *Antigone* and unlike the Legouvé *Médée*, which came to London the following year, Spicer's *Alcestis* was indeed no authenticating revival; it was instead a well-intentioned attempt to wed the aural aesthetics of Greek drama to the visual expectations of Victorian melodrama. Indeed when Orcus appears in 'growing lurid light' from his cave in Act III, approaches the tomb and is suddenly confronted by Heracles before their off-stage tussle in the cave, the audience at St James's were being treated to on-stage spectacle, to which the mid-nineteenth century spectator was accustomed. The image, largely through the operatic tradition, was to remain powerful enough to serve as the subject for Lord Leighton's painting 'Hercules Wrestling with Death for the Body of Alcestis' (*c.*1869–70).[18]

However, unlike Talfourd's burlesque, Spicer's *Alcestis* is not a version to expose the trials and tribulations of the marital state; it is, if anything, a version that promotes the value of marital fidelity at a time when its frequent absence was coming under public scrutiny. Numerous debts notwithstanding, it is the changes made by Spicer in his version which are significant; and in most cases, the slight alterations made by Spicer to Lucas's play are done with a view to reducing the domestic touches in the French and making it more faithful to the Greek of Euripides.

Spicer clearly did not wish to reproduce the Euripidean irony in his presentation of Admetus; instead in marked opposition to the burlesque tradition, he sets out to improve upon the Euripidean prototype. Spicer's Admetus (unlike Euripides' protagonist) does not himself actively seek a willing substitute for his own death: it is Alcestis here who does the seeking, convinced that: 'You will not, shall not, perish.'[19] Even before her search turns out to prove vain,

---

[18] For another study of the figure of Alcestis in the visual arts around this time see Burne-Jones's 'Love Leading Alcestis' (1863; sketch Ashmolean Museum, Oxford; watercolour Birmingham City Museum and Art Gallery, no. 13'04). Much earlier, Edward Hodges Baily had won the Royal Academy's gold medal in 1811 for a model of a sculptural group 'Hercules restores Alcestis to Admetus': *EB*[11] iii. 221.

[19] Spicer (1855), 8. Spicer is following the operatic tradition, and especially Wieland's libretto for Anton Schweitzer's music, which was staged in Weimar in 1773. See L. P. E. Parker (2003), 12–15.

Admetus expresses his doubts that anyone will be found willing to relinquish the pleasures of life for another. This is an Admetus who is not only principled; he is prescient as well.

When Spicer's Alcestis enters in the last throes of life, we are never allowed to forget that this is a marriage born of love not convenience. Alcestis urges Admetus:

> Untwine
> Thy loving grasp, dear husband. Lay me down
> Here, at thy feet. All strength hath left me now,
> Mine eyes are gathering darkness. [*sinks down on couch*][20]

And with the early arrival of Hercules in Act I—when it is only Admetus' fate that has been determined and needs to be kept from the untimely guest—even the 'deception' required is far less potentially ambiguous, since it is only his own fate that the king needs to deny. Hippolyte Lucas had followed Alfieri in redeeming Pheres in his version,[21] but Spicer goes a step further in removing Admetus' father from the play altogether until the very last scene. Here Pheres arrives in the final moments of the play wondering why Admetus had kept everything from him, adding how he himself would have been a fitter ransom.[22] With Admetus' reply: 'Well I knew | You would so deem it, father',[23] the audience of Spicer's play never have to doubt Admetus' integrity, and by implication the appropriateness of the reunion of man and wife at the end of the play. To confirm the legitimacy of the remarriage, Spicer's Alcestis is granted a voice, and after greeting the earth and Thessaly, calls out:

> O, Admetus
> Clasp me, again, thy wife, twice wedded . . .[24]

ALCESTIS ON THE PAGE

It was in part because such spectacles were so commonplace in nineteenth-century theatre that the next important *Alcestis*, Robert Browning's *Balaustion's Adventure* (1871), was never

---

[20] Spicer (1855), 13.   [21] Lucas (1847), pp. vii f.   [22] Spicer (1855), 22.
[23] Ibid. 23.   [24] Ibid. 22.

designed for the stage at all.[25] But Browning also wrote the work in part because he felt audiences were being denied direct access to Euripides himself: ever since Schlegel's damnation of Euripides in his *Lectures on Drama* at the beginning of the century, classical scholarship had denounced the tragedian as decadent, dangerous, and wordy.[26] And as we have seen, all recent stage versions of Euripides' tragedies were mediated by other competing and/or 'improving' sources (Spicer's *Alcestis* by way of Hippolyte Lucas; and the *Medea*s in subsequent years by way of both Legouvé and Grillparzer); and in the case of Talfourd's burlesque, what was on offer was 'a shameless misinterpretation' of the Greek prototype. By the time Browning published *Balaustion's Adventure* in 1871, he had long given up on the professional stage. Indeed, he had come round to the Aristotelian view expressed by Balaustion, the narrator of his version: 'Who hears the poem . . . sees the play.'[27]

In Browning's dramatic monologue, Balaustion tells how, following the disaster of the Sicilian Expedition, she was able to save herself, her compatriots, and the good name of Athens by reciting Euripides' *Alcestis* to an audience of Syracusans. Balaustion's solo rendering of the play includes her commentary on the action, and closely charts the progress of Admetus from selfish bungler to worthy hero. At the death-bed of Alcestis, Balaustion perceptively comments:

> So he stood sobbing: nowise insincere,
> But somehow child-like . . . none heard him say,
> However, what would seem so pertinent,
> 'To keep this pact, I find surpass my power:
> Rescind it, Moirai! Give me back her life,
> And take the life I kept by base exchange!'[28]

---

[25] There were a number of other poems about Alcestis around this time: in 1859 a revised edition of *The Hellenics* by Walter Savage Landor appeared, which included the dramatic dialogue entitled 'Hercules, Pluto, Alcestis, Admetus'; more closely contemporary with Browning is the Pre-Raphaelite fascination, exemplified in the Burne-Jones sketch and watercolour, in William Morris's poem 'The Love of Alcestis', in part 3 (vol. ii) of his epic *Earthly Paradise* (1868; Browning heavily criticized it) and in Francis Turner Palgrave's 'Alcestis: A Poem' in his collection *Lyrical Poems* (1871).

[26] On 19th-c. scholarly reception of Euripides, see generally Michelini (1987); and Behler (1986), 335–69.

[27] Robert Browning (1940), 9. For Browning's early career in the theatre, see James Hogg (1977).

[28] Robert Browning (1940), 23.

Similarly the scene between Admetus and Pheres is admirably explicated with the illuminating observation that : 'So, in old Pheres, young Admetos showed, | Pushed to completion: and a shudder ran, | And his repugnance soon had vent in speech.'[29] At the end of this scene, Balaustion observes that after Pheres had left, Admetus was ' . . . Only half-selfish now, since sensitive . . . ';[30] and henceforth he begins to grow in stature until he is worthy of his wife in the resurrection scene:

> Able to do, now, all herself had done,
> Risen to the height of her: so hand in hand,
> The two might go together, live and die.[31]

Browning's version of *Alcestis* is not simply an account of the growth in Admetus' moral statue; it is more importantly an account of the creative process itself, with Balaustion as the poet/maker, who can alter her audience's perceptions of both herself and her fellow crew members, and the subjects of her narrative through her power as narrator.

'One thing has many sides',[32] she reminds her audience; and she uses this as a cue to offer a (second) completely new version of Euripides' play, in which an enlightened Admetus rules (unlike his ancestors) for his people alone. When it becomes evident that this new, much improved Admetus is to die, Alcestis makes a deal with Apollo to allow her husband to live and to continue his good work. When Admetus finds out about the terms of the deal, he vainly refuses to accept on the grounds that ' . . . we two prove one force and play one part | And do one thing'; and since '[thou] . . . wast to me as spirit is to flesh', it is the flesh that must die.[33] However, when this 'spiritual' side of their union does perish with Alcestis' demise, 'her whole soul entered into his'.[34] And with Persephone's refusal to grant Alcestis residence in the underworld on the grounds that now, as Admetus' soul, she cannot die while he is alive, we are offered a metaphysical affirmation of marital endurance.

Despite and even because of the evident biographical echoes of Browning's version—with the deceased Elizabeth Barrett Browning being conflated with both Alcestis (as eternal partner) and Balaustion, the Kore figure (as poet/maker)—*Balaustion's*

---

[29] Ibid. 37.   [30] Ibid. 43.   [31] Ibid. 62.   [32] Ibid. 65.
[33] Ibid. 68.   [34] Ibid. 70.

Adventure acted as the catalyst for a revival of interest in the paradigmatic perfect wife. When the Irish playwright, John Todhunter wrote his stage version of *Alcestis* eight years later, his debt to Browning is made explicit with a direct quotation ('Still, since one thing may have so many sides...one might mould a new | Admetos, new Alkestis') serving as epigraph to the play. And Todhunter begins his play as if it were an attempt to translate Balaustion's second retelling of *Alcestis* into dramatic form. In Act I, Scene i, we watch the final throes of Admetus' utopian rule in Thessaly being overshadowed first by Alcestis' presentiments and finally by heavenly portents.

The debt, or rather homage, to Browning here in Todhunter's play in many ways determined its subsequent history as closet drama.[35] However, despite its Greek subject, Todhunter's late nineteenth-century *Alcestis* owes more to Shakespeare in both its mood and language than it does to Greek tragedy. As Todhunter himself points out in his Preface, he had not intended to write a Greek play at all; his Thessaly bears as much resemblance to its real setting as Shakespeare's Bohemia did to the real Bohemia; and his introduction of the (underdeveloped) subplot concerning the relationship between Aegle and Hercules in Act I, no less than his choric street scene at the start of Act II, aligns his play with Shakespeare and the British tradition.

Yet Todhunter's debts are not just to Browning and Shakespeare. After Alcestis has duly pledged herself as substitute to Apollo, her revivifying kiss of Admetus gestures towards Thomson's eighteenth-century version (see Ch. 4). And with Admetus' irrationally violent reaction to Alcestis' altruistic act—'Thou hast not play'd | The whore with death?'[36]—the 'realist' burlesque presentation of Admetus the ingrate immediately comes to mind,

---

[35] Todhunter's play does not appear to have been staged: it was not used in either of the two productions of *Alcestis* in 1910–11, both productions associated with the University of London. The first, by students of Bedford College and University College on 16–19 Feb. 1910 in South Villa, Regent's Park, used a translation by the Vice-Provost of Eton, Dr Warre-Cornish (see Ch. 17 nn. 107, 129); the second, staged by William Poel (Ch. 17) in December 1911 (Marble Hall, Imperial Institute, South Kensington), used a translation by Francis Hubback of Trinity College, Cambridge. This production was also staged in the Little Theatre, London University, 3–9 Jan. 1912 and then later in April 1914 for the Religious Dramatic Society in the Ethical Church, Bayswater.

[36] Todhunter (1879), 54.

as well as the irascible Leontes of Shakespeare's *The Winter's Tale*.
Indeed, this Admetus has much to learn from his wise wife; but
unlike his comic counterparts, he is a king who ruled over a utopian
Thessaly, and at least has the capacity to learn. Alcestis urges him
to live and to love the sun, and to appreciate his second birth as she
will appreciate hers in the air. Above all, Todhunter's Admetus
must learn to accept her gift of life as a mother to a son:

> Thou art my child
> Pledged to live bravely for me, or I die
> In vain and Death stands victor.[37]

After the death of Alcestis, Admetus' education proper begins as
he too learns the importance of parenthood in the cloyingly sentimental encounters he has with his children (II. ii, III. iii). Here in
the scene with Pheres, there are no indignities, only Admetus'
asides, which show how hard he finds it to bear condolence.
After his eventual reunion with Alcestis, there is a celebration of
Love which recalls the operatic tradition; but this is clearly a
celebration of the power of familial (as opposed to strictly conjugal)
love. Todhunter provides us with an Admetus with promise rather
than any unimpeachable performance; and it is this qualified heroism in Admetus alone that is to make Euripides' play and modern
reworkings of it of interest to audiences in the post-Ibsenite world
of the new century (see Ch. 17).

FROM PAGE TO STAGE: ARCHAEOLOGY AND
THE VIEWING CULTURE

In the same year as Browning's *Balaustion's Adventure*, the
scholar-poet Lewis Campbell wrote a shorter poetic reworking of
Euripides' tragedy entitled 'Admetus and Alcestis'.[38] Although the
poetic tradition of including the figure of Alcestis in verse cannot
be considered independently from Miltonic veneration (see Ch. 4),
the timing of Campbell's own short version (dated 27 September
1871) would imply at least a partial response to Browning's dramatic monologue. Although Campbell was later to express some
doubts about Browning's reworkings of the classics—even later
confessing to a preference for Tennyson's work—he never doubted

---

[37] Ibid. 64.   [38] Lewis Campbell (1914), 5–8.

Browning's seriousness as a classical scholar.[39] And his use of the three separate poetic voices here—the narrative voice as well as those of Alcestis and Admetus—would imply that Campbell (like other poets of his generation) had learnt much from Browning's development of the dramatic monologue.

In many ways, like Todhunter, Campbell's poem is responding to Balaustion's invitation to her audience to 'mould' the main characters anew. In Campbell's version, as in Balaustion's second retelling, Admetus is here redeemed by the fact that 'He had loved life for noble ends' and did not (unlike his Euripidean counterpart) seek Alcestis as a substitute. Too late does Admetus discover her secret compact with Apollo; and following her death, he begins, albeit reluctantly at first, 'to labour amid ceaseless pain'.[40] But slowly 'the humbled monarch' finds he is guided by a strong aspiration: 'Oh loved too late! if thee I may not see, | Let me be worthy still of following thee!'[41] Just as the spirit of Browning's Alkestis had entered into Admetos, so now Campbell's peerlessly benign ruler is guided by 'the mystic effluence of his guiding star | The promise of his future, felt from far'.[42]

Campbell's 'Admetus and Alcestis' was by no means the last time that he was to respond to Browning's engagements with Greek tragedy. Like Browning, he was committed to the desire to bring Greek tragedy to a wider audience; but unlike the older Browning, Campbell was enthralled by the theatre, and sought to bring the ancient plays to new audiences through the medium of performance. Campbell expressed on more than one occasion his genuine excitement at seeing the raw reactions of students and others upon their first encounters with Greek drama. One notable response he records was that of the novelist, Robert Louis Stevenson, who upon rehearsing for the part of the messenger in Sophocles' *Trachiniae* (for a production mounted in Edinburgh and later at St Andrews in 1877) was overwhelmed by his first glimpse of what he felt was the evident superiority of Sophocles' powers even

---

[39] See Campbell's comments in 'The Higher Humanism', ibid. 332: '... Mr Browning's classicism is almost pedantically displayed. But this is excusable, because Mr Browning was an enthusiastic Greek scholar'; and for his preference for Tennyson see his letter of 16 Apr. 1907 printed ibid. 434.

[40] Ibid. 7.

[41] Ibid. 8.

[42] Ibid. 8.

to Shakespeare's.[43] Campbell's translations of both Sophocles and later Aeschylus, although often originally prompted by the occasion of local performance, were eventually to have a much wider impact. In an obituary of Campbell in the *Cornhill Magazine* in December 1908 by one of his close colleagues, Leonard Huxley, we hear how a poet-scholar like Campbell may well meet 'with a smaller measure of scholarly appreciation in this country than he might well have expected' on account of his translations. Huxley, however, adds by way of ample compensation:

Nevertheless, he has a way of coming into his own at last. How many thousands in recent years have had revealed to them the essential spirit of Greek tragedy, and have joined in a special revival of the threatened classics simply from hearing or reading these poets' translations of the poets, while the conscientious prose of the grammarian passes them by, and is only used for textual study.[44]

Since 1863 Campbell had been Professor of Greek in the University of St Andrews and together with his wife, Frances Pitt Campbell, and with the help of Mrs Baynes (wife of Thomas Spencer Baynes, editor of the ninth edition of the *Encyclopaedia Britannica*) he had formed first The Shakespeare Society and later the Students Dramatic Society. By the 1870s and throughout the 1880s, the readings and plays directed by Campbell were the 'main features of the social circle' in St Andrews and Edinburgh; and for Stevenson, at least, these theatricals provided the only excitement during his undergraduate years in Edinburgh.[45] The Campbells' principal friends in Edinburgh were Professor and Mrs Fleeming Jenkin, who shared their passion for ancient Greece and for the theatre; Mrs Jenkin was considered 'an amateur actress of unusual capacity'.[46] Fleeming Jenkin was a professor of engineering at the University of Edinburgh, and the young Stevenson was one of his pupils. From 1873 onwards, Jenkin staged a number of Greek plays in translation in his private theatre at 3 Great Stuart Street, Edinburgh.[47] In 1877 when Stevenson took the part of messenger in Sophocles' *Trachiniae*, Mrs Fleeming Jenkin was Deianeira in Campbell's translation. This was a Sophoclean play

---

[43] e.g. ibid. 193.   [44] Ibid. 452–3.
[45] Eve Blantyre Simpson (1898), 208–9.
[46] Leonard Huxley in Lewis Campbell (1914), 461.
[47] Fleeming Jenkin had earlier directed *Frogs*, see Baker-Penoyre (1898), ii. 324.

close to Campbell's heart, and one which he claimed to have defended against the false imputations of Schlegel (as Browning was to do with Euripides) since at least 1848;[48] and now in 1877 the *Trachiniae* could, in effect, 'defend' itself in a performance of Campbell's translation.

Jenkin was particularly interested in the ancient world in its entirety and spent much time researching the costumes and sets for his productions (Fig. 15.3).[49] In this sense, he was very much in tune with the spirit of the age which followed the excavations in southern Europe with great interest. *The Illustrated London News*, which like *Punch* was launched in the 1840s, reached a circulation of 140,000 copies per week by 1852, with at least three readers per copy.[50] It gave over large amounts of space to photographs and line drawings of archaeological sites; and throughout February and March of 1877 there was intensive coverage of Schliemann's excavations at Mycenae. On 24 February 1877, in an account of the discovery of the so-called 'Death Mask' of Agamemnon, we detect a bizarre shift in register as the correspondent's highbrow reportage gives way to mundane trivia:

... and if his brother was like him it is little to be wondered at that Helen should have preferred Paris.[51]

With such a degree of domestication, it was impossible not to feel involved in the events of the House of Atreus as they were unfolding in front of the reader's eyes.

In a letter of 1876 Browning said he intended to publish his own version of Aeschylus' *Agamemnon* with photographs of Schliemann's recent excavations at Mycenae; and as Tony Harrison has pointed out, there is a definite 'craggy'-ness about Browning's language in his translation.[52] In *Balaustion's Adventure* Browning had sought to offer Euripides' *Alcestis* to his audience with a running commentary; in the final section of his *Aristophanes' Apology* (1875), he had offered Euripides' *Heracles Furens* to his reader without any commentary whatsoever—it was, so to speak, Euripides pure and simple, for a generation whose Euripides had

---

[48] Letter of 29 Mar. 1905 in Lewis Campbell (1914), 419.
[49] Jenkin (1887), esp. 35–44.
[50] See Altick (1989), 146. I am indebted to Debbie Challis for this reference.
[51] *ILN* 70, no. 1963 (24 Feb. 1877), 185.
[52] Harrison (2002), 14–15.

FIGURE 15.3 Drawing by Fleeming Jenkin illustrating the correct draping of the ancient Greek female *peplos* (1874).

been beset by mediators.[53] And now with the publication of his *Agamemnon*, Browning was situating himself on the opposite side to Matthew Arnold in the hotly contested current theoretical debate about translation that had been granted both prominence and intensity by Arnold in his lectures 'On Translating Homer' (1861–2). In marked contrast to Arnold's ideal of elevated domestication, Browning sought to convey the spirit of Aeschylean tragedy through pushing the English language to its limits, writing (as he proclaimed in the Preface) in 'as Greek a fashion as English will bear' without doing it 'violence'.[54] With his adoption of Greek syntax, Browning clearly explored the potential of the English language in ways remarkably similar to those being tested by that other (at the time unknown) Balliol poet, Gerard Manley Hopkins.[55] Most, however, found Browning's transcript (as he called it) 'unreadable' (Augusta Webster claimed that at least Aeschylus' text remained to guide the hapless reader); and it is significant that when Fleeming Jenkin reviewed it in *The Edinburgh Review* in 1878, he claimed that its main shortcomings derived from its fundamental unperformability.[56]

It was, perhaps, inevitable that Campbell's efforts then turned towards producing a 'performable' translation of the *Agamemnon* for his next production with Fleeming Jenkin, which took place in Edinburgh in May 1880, one month before the much more famous production of the play in ancient Greek performed in the hall of Balliol College, Oxford. That the Oxford *Agamemnon* was mounted at Balliol was, similarly, inevitable, given the very close ties that existed between Campbell and Benjamin Jowett, Master of the College since 1866.[57] Campbell had been at Balliol as an undergraduate with a prestigious Snell Exhibition, which was designed to bring bright young Scotsmen to the College. Jowett's time as Master at Balliol (and later as Vice-Chancellor of

---

[53] See Riley (2005) for an excellent account of *Aristophanes' Apology* as an attempt to offer the reader an unmediated taste of Euripides.

[54] On the 19-c. debate about translation generally, see Hardwick (2000b), 23–42; on Browning's translation, see Matthew Reynolds (2003).

[55] Harrison (2002), 11 also notes the parallels between Hopkins and Browning. Hopkins's poetry was not published until 1918, and it is significant that when he tried to publish his work during his lifetime, he met with strong resistance on the grounds on its unreadablity.

[56] Webster (1879), 66–79; Jenkin (1878), 409–36.

[57] On Jowett, generally, see Prest (2000), 159–169.

the University) was characterized by his commitment to widening access in accordance with the Scottish higher education model; and with the arrival of the highly intelligent young Exhibitioner Campbell at Balliol in 1849, began a lifelong intellectual and social partnership between them. Campbell, like Browning, was later made Honorary Fellow of Balliol; and the bronze memorial plaque erected in Campbell's memory by the chapel door in the college proclaims: 'For more than forty years the friend of Benjamin Jowett and of Balliol'.

When Jowett had heard of Campbell's appearance as Antony alongside Mrs Fleeming Jenkin's Cleopatra in a production of Shakespeare's *Antony and Cleopatra* in May 1879 (just over a year before the Oxford *Agamemnon*), he had joined others in sending Campbell a 'chaffing' letter.[58] Jowett's later concern that a proposed tour of the Oxford *Agamemnon* might be deleterious to the characters involved would suggest that he was especially anxious about potential hostility from those for whom all theatricals were immoral and/or dangerous. In Oxford these anxieties were particularly associated with cross-dressed performances following a scandal in 1869–70, when an Oxford undergraduate well known for his performances in drag was charged with 'obscenity' in London.[59] Whatever the reason for Jowett's 'chaffing' letter to Campbell upon hearing of his former pupil's performance as Antony—whether it stemmed from the apparent indecorum of a Professor of Greek consorting on the stage with the wife of a fellow Professor or not—Campbell's defence of amateur theatricals *per se* must have been sufficiently robust. For the following year when Jowett was approached about a Balliol production by two New College undergraduates, Frank Benson (who went on to become the famous actor-manager) and the Hon. W. N. Bruce, he readily agreed to allow a performance of the *Agamemnon* in Greek to take place in the hall at Balliol.

Oscar Wilde claimed that he had first suggested the project, and that he had allocated the parts and designed the costumes and the scenery.[60] There may well be more than a grain of truth in this,

---

[58] Huxley in Lewis Campbell (1914), 461; and more generally, see Shepley (1988).
[59] Mackinnon (1910), 59; and for the London scandal of 1869–70, see Carpenter (1985), 14.
[60] Ellmann (1987), 101–102.

even though Benson never mentions Wilde's involvement, and even though there are other claims that the scenery used a drawing by the late Burne-Jones and that the costumes were designed by Professor W. B. Richmond.[61] What is significant about these claims, of course, is the fact that retrospectively, at least, the undoubted success of the 1880 *Agamemnon* made it worthy of close association. Indeed Wilde's close friend, Rennell Rodd (who went on to appear in *The Story of Troy* in London 1883) assisted with the painting of the scenery; and Wilde himself remained a keen observer of the 1880s revivals, even if he did not participate in person (see Ch. 16).

The 1880 Balliol *Agamemnon* became the first production of a Greek tragedy in the original language to receive serious critical consideration since the Renaissance; and there was a clear attempt in Oxford to reflect aspects of the ancient theatre that were compatible with modern expectations (for this reason, there were no masks). In that sense this was no 'archaeologizing' production *tout court*; as one satisfied reviewer put it, the set and costumes were instead suggestive of antiquity 'and that is sufficient'.[62] The two-fold division of the stage space (as with the 1845 *Antigone*) was designed to keep actors and chorus separate (Fig. 15.4); and the music was composed by the organist of Magdalen, Walter Parratt, for the beginning of the parodos alone, and consisted of a few austere bars. The choral delivery was controversial, with the alternation between monotone recitation and dialogue among the Chorus members generally not deemed a success.[63] The acting parts, by contrast, were much praised with Benson as Clytemnestra, W. L. Courtney (later the theatre critic of the *Daily Telegraph*) as the watchman, and W. N. Bruce as Agamemnon. Benson especially earned critical plaudits, which are surely acknowledged (if not actually being celebrated) in the painting of Clytemnestra by John Collier of 1882.[64]

The production as a whole was much acclaimed by leading figures of the day, and it went on to be performed at Eton,

---

[61] Mackinnon (1910), 61.

[62] *Cambridge Review*, 9 Feb. 1881.

[63] See Mackinnon (1910), 60–1; and the otherwise favourable review in the *Cambridge Review*, loc. cit.

[64] Collier's *Clytemnestra*, in the Guildhall Art Gallery, London, is reproduced in Macintosh, Michelakis, Hall, and Taplin (forthcoming, eds.).

FIGURE 15.4 Final scene of the *Agamemnon* in Balliol Hall, Oxford, (1880).

Harrow, and Winchester; it was also performed for three nights at St George's Hall in London, where it was seen by an enthusiastic George Eliot, and no lesser luminaries than Henry Irving and Ellen Terry, who were eventually to become Benson's employers at the Lyceum Theatre in 1882. Browning, whose controversial translation had propelled Aeschylus' text into the critical limelight, and who had been an Honorary Fellow of Balliol since 1867, was appropriately in the audience on the first night in Oxford as Jowett's guest. And the Oxford *Agamemnon* led to a renewed interest in Aeschylus' play and in Browning's translation, in particular, with the general public (during a performance in Cambridge the subsequent year) reportedly struggling to follow the Greek with Browning's abstruse *Agamemnon* on their knees.[65]

---

[65] *Cambridge Review*, loc. cit.

WOMEN IN THE ACADEMY

Benson was responsible for numerous revivals of the Oxford production; and with his own company, he went on to tour Australia and the colonies with a production of the *Oresteia* (see Fig. 15.5), which led in turn to new productions of Aeschylus' *Agamemnon* being performed in the English-speaking world (notably in Sydney in 1886). Greek drama was all the rage in the 1880s, and it was arguably the *Alcestis*—as had been the case at the beginning of the century (see Ch. 4)—that was considered the most suitably edifying of Greek plays for school productions. Indeed the choice of the *Agamemnon* as the inaugurating play in Oxford was not always (despite Schliemann's excavations) considered an obvious choice. One reviewer commented:

> ... it would have been wiser to begin with a drama which is less intensely lyrical and has more psychological interest than the *Agamemnon*, such, perhaps, as the *Medea* of Euripides, the *Antigone* of Sophocles.[66]

FIGURE 15.5 Scene from *Eumenides* from Frank Benson's touring production of the *Oresteia* (1905).

[66] Ibid.

If the choice of *Agamemnon* was in large measure due to the fascination with the discoveries at Mycenae and Hissarlik and the debate engendered by Browning's transcript, then the increasing interest in the 'psychological' Greek plays—and especially those plays with strong female roles—was very closely related to the growing participation of women in educational establishments.

Campbell and his wife were deeply committed to the education of women before it became a 'popular' rallying point; and without their involvement, St Leonard's School for girls in St Andrews would not have come into existence at that time.[67] After having watched a performance of the *Antigone* in his own translation at the school in June 1903, Campbell explained that some thirty years previously when he had begun work on the translation, he had imagined 'some [female] élève of the Higher education imperson- ating Antigone', adding that now his intended performers had finally given his text life.[68] And when Alan Mackinnon, the found- er of the Oxford University Dramatic Society, comments on the impact of the 1880 *Agamemnon* in Oxford as a whole, he writes:

The excitement spread even to North Oxford, and fluttered the dovecotes of the Woodstock and Banbury roads, where the educated lady was in those days really a new woman, and this form of 'education made pleas- ant,' an excellent opportunity to make a trial of strength, with a first exhibition of newly-acquired culture.[69]

Despite Mackinnon's somewhat scoffing tone, his New Woman hungry for more of this 'newly acquired culture' was to have a significant impact on the performance history of ancient plays over the next two decades (see Ch. 17).

Before joining the Lyceum Theatre in 1882, Benson was invited by the newly appointed Headmaster of Bradfield College, the Revd Herbert Branston Gray, to stage a performance of *Alcestis* at the school. The choice of Alcestis in a boys' school no doubt stemmed from the Miltonic privileging of the play for pedagogic purposes; but it was also Browning's reworking that kept Euripi- des' play very much in vogue.[70] The Headmaster took the part of

---

[67] See Edward Caird (Jowett's successor at Balliol) in 1893, in Lewis Campbell (1914), 470.

[68] Ibid. 405–6.

[69] Mackinnon (1910), 60.

[70] In the first part of the 20th c., the *Alcestis* continued to be performed by schools, and especially girls' schools. And when Bournemouth Girls' High School

Admetus, but the participation of both Benson (as Apollo) and Courtney (as Heracles) provided an evident link with the earlier Oxford *Agamemnon*. The production is particularly significant in hindsight because it led eventually to the establishment of regular triennial productions of Greek plays at Bradfield from 1890 onwards, when the open-air Greek theatre, modelled on the theatre at Epidaurus, was completed. Together with the Greek plays at Oxford and at Cambridge from 1882, the Greek play at Bradfield College in Berkshire was to become another notable date in the social calendar.[71]

In 1886, when a number of productions of Greek plays in London became involved in the campaign to broaden women's education (see Ch. 16), the girls of Queen's College, Harley Street (founded by the Christian Socialist F. D. Maurice in 1848) performed the *Alcestis* in a production deemed by the reviewer in *The Graphic* (18 December 1886) to be 'the first representation in London of a Greek play by lady students' (Fig. 15.6). Three years previously Girton College, the newly founded women's college at the University of Cambridge, had staged its pioneering production of Sophocles' *Electra*, dubbed by the *Illustrated London News* 'the first time that a Greek drama was acted by women',[72] with Janet Case as an extremely powerful Electra. The significance of the event did not go unmarked: the front page of *The Graphic* carried an engraving of a sketch of Electra and the chorus.[73] Janet Case's performance earned her the part of Athena two years later in the Cambridge production of the *Eumenides*—an unparalleled achievement until well into the twentieth century, when women were finally allowed to perform in the Cambridge Greek play.[74]

produced the play in 1903, they used a version that included excerpts from Browning's *Balaustion's Adventure* (and the music by Henry Gadsby, which had been especially written for the Queen's College production of *Alcestis* in London in 1886).

[71] See Duncan Wilson (1987), 107 for a sense of the cultural significance of the Bradfield Greek play in the first decade of the 20th c. The *Alcestis* received its first production in Bradfield's Greek theatre in 1895 and it remained (together with *Antigone* and the *Agamemnon*) in the repertoire until the First World War, being performed again in 1904 and 1914.

[72] *ILN* 83 (1883), 527.

[73] See further Hall (1999*a*), 291–5.

[74] See Easterling (1999), 28–30.

FIGURE 15.6 A performance of *Alcestis* at Queen's College, Harley Street, London (1886).

In 1887 the Oxford University Dramatic Society (OUDS) used a similarly cross-gendered casting in their production of *Alcestis* in ancient Greek. Prohibitions on men assuming female roles at Oxford (set down by Jowett himself as Vice-Chancellor) led to the part of Alcestis being played with mixed success by the then increasingly notable classical scholar, Jane Harrison, who happened to be giving a course of lectures in Oxford at the time. Harrison's performance (somewhat curtailed owing to her refusal to appear as a corpse in the middle of the play) received a mixed response, with critics assuming that her 'scholarship ... out-stripped her dramatic power'.[75] However, despite the apparent shortcomings of Harrison's performance, the production as a whole proved enormously popular and played to full houses enabling OUDS to rid itself of its financial crisis for the first time.

One of the striking features of the production was the set and the costumes, purchased from John Todhunter,[76] whose play *Helena*

[75] See Mackinnon (1910), 129–30.
[76] For details of the sale of the set, see the Todhunter Papers, University of Reading, MS 202/1/1, fos. 362–7.

in Troas had been produced the previous year in London, and which was arguably one of the most important stagings of a classically inspired play in the last part of the nineteenth century (see Ch. 16). *Helena in Troas* had been performed at Hengler's Circus in a Greek-style theatre, especially designed for the production by the architect, E. W. Godwin. It was W. L. Courtney, by now at the *Daily Telegraph*, who funded the 1887 *Alcestis;* but it was Todhunter who oversaw the initial set design and 'induced them to board over the stalls for the chorus'.[77] And in marked contrast to previous productions of ancient plays, on this occasion the chorus of fifteen male voices, which sang to C.H. Lloyd's music for flute, clarinet and harp, was deemed a great success. However, despite acquiring the Godwin set, this was (far less than the *Agamemnon* of 1880) no archaeological production. In many respects it recalled the melodramatic staging of Spicer's 1855 *Alcestis* at St James's Theatre in London, with Death entering via a trap-door enfurled in steam, and Apollo making his precarious entry on trick wires.

Attending the Greek play in Oxford was for most audience members (as was the case in London with Todhunter's *Helena in Troas*) a fashionable event. Indeed the bewildered response of the reviewer from *Punch* to what was more than a dose of highbrow academic fare may well have been representative (Fig. 15.7). Under the title ' "Very Original Greek at Oxford" by an Untutored Correspondent', the reviewer explained:

Though I have not had a classical education, yet I have had a very fair theatrical one, and I remembered the title years ago at, I think, the Haymarket.[78]

Although this particular reviewer is hiding behind a mask of ignorance—he was in fact the classically trained and highly successful burlesque playwright, F. C. Burnand—his claim to having been brought up on classical burlesque would no doubt have been widely shared by audience members (the reference here is undoubtedly to Talfourd's *Alcestis*, and its revivals). Now being offered Greek drama *au naturel* for the first time, many members of the audience inevitably responded favourably to those landmarks in the production that had been imported from high Victorian melodrama.

[77] Todhunter to Herbert Horne, 27 Nov. 1887 (Todhunter Papers, University of Reading, MS 202/1/1).
[78] *Punch*, 92 (28 May 1887), 264.

Classic Costume revived at
Oxford.

FIGURE 15.7   *Punch* cartoon 'Classic Costume Revived at Oxford' (1887).

Two years later, a graduate of Girton wrote an article entitled 'Greek Plays at the Universities' in the magazine *Woman's World* (1888), in which she maintains that the *Alcestis* is a suitable choice of play for women to perform:

What could be more touching than the picture of the self devotion of Alcestis in obedience to her ideal of wifely duty, or the gradual unfolding of the character of Admetus under the influence of sorrow?[79]

Euripides' play concerning the perennial themes of death and marital fidelity is clearly being promoted as the perfect pedagogical tool. But by now the world of academe is no longer screened from the broader social considerations that are being aired on the professional stage in London. And with the knowledge that the editor of *Women's World* was in fact the playwright, Oscar Wilde, it would not be wide of the mark to infer that 'the gradual unfolding of the character of Admetus under the influence of sorrow' was not

[79] 'A Graduate of Girton' (1888), 127.

entirely devoid of ironic intent. Whilst the choice of the *Alcestis* for performance in a girls' school or within a women's college might assuage even the most ardent anti-feminist with its subject-matter, with its ironic portrait of Admetus, Euripides' play (as was to be the case with so many Greek plays over the next two and a half decades) could equally well provide ample food for thought for the emergent New Woman.

16

London's Greek Plays in the 1880s:
George Warr and Social Philhellenism

On 13 and 15 May 1886 at 9 p.m. 'The Story of Orestes', billed as 'An abridged English version of the Oresteian Trilogy of Aeschylus', was performed in the Prince's Hall, Piccadilly, under the patronage of the Prince and Princess of Wales. The proceeds of these two performances, together with those from a series of scenes of tableaux from Homer entitled *The Tale of Troy* on the afternoon of 14 May, formed 'a contribution towards a University Endowment Fund, with the object of enabling King's College and University College, London, to extend and cheapen the higher collegiate education, with a view to qualify them for the functions of a Teaching University'.[1]

The following week, a rival production of a new classically inspired play by John Todhunter, *Helena in Troas*, took place at Hengler's Circus, Argyll Street. The proceeds from Todhunter's play went to the equally deserving charitable cause, the newly founded British School of Archaeology at Athens, and the event similarly attracted the patronage of the Prince and Princess of Wales.[2]

A survey of the two cast lists may not ring many bells to those acquainted with the London stage in the 1880s (Mr and Mrs Beerbohm Tree and Hermann Vezin—all in *Helena in Troas*—are the only professional actors), but to those interested in the history of classical scholarship and the history of the performances of Greek drama in particular, they provide a rich mine. Surprising

---

[1] There is a copy of the programme attached inside the British Library copy of Warr and Crane (1887).

[2] A copy of the programme is in the production file at the Theatre Museum, London. Todhunter had offered the proceeds to the British School a year earlier. See Richard Jebb's letter to Todhunter, 11 Feb. 1885: 'I am extremely obliged to you for the kind gift of your drama, 'Helena in Troas', and not less for the proposal that it should be performed for the benefit of the British School at Athens.' [MS 202/1/1, fos. 310–13, Reading University Library]. For an account of the production, see Stokes (1972), 52–6.

collocations of names are found: from Todhunter's list, we find the artist Louise Jopling together with the former art student, Constance Wilde (better known as Mrs Oscar Wilde) both acting as assistants to Helen;[3] in *The Story of Orestes*, we find Eugénie Sellers (better known under her later married name, Eugénie Strong, and in her capacity as assistant director of the British School in Rome)[4] listed as an Argive Maiden alongside Dorothy Dene (the model for Sir Frederic Leighton's last major paintings), who took the part of Cassandra.[5]

The Hengler's Circus event was clearly distinguished from the performances at the Prince's Hall both on account of its superior venue and the professionals among its cast members. But what is striking about both productions is the calibre and range of expertise contributing behind the scenes. In the case of Todhunter's play, it was the presence of the architect turned stage-designer E. W. Godwin that guaranteed public attention. Godwin's Greek theatre in the Vitruvian mould had been expressly designed for the production; and with its circular *orchestra* and central *thymele* neatly fitted into the circus arena at Hengler's, it included a raised stage in accordance with the prevailing archaeological orthodoxy.[6] Despite the anachronistically intrusive curtains—a point that did not escape the reviewer for *Punch*[7]—the set was widely admired, even by those who had misgivings about both the play and the production (Fig. 16.1).[8]

For the performances at the Prince's Hall, it was the engagement of such luminaries from the art world as Sir Frederic Leighton, E. J. Poynter, G. F. Watts, and Walter Crane for the designing of

---

[3] See Jopling (1925), 179–80.

[4] For a fascinating account of the life of Eugénie Strong and her relationship to Jane Harrison, see Beard (2000).

[5] For a brief account of Dene's life and her relationship to Leighton, see Christopher Wood (1983), 75–9 and below, pp. 482–4.

[6] This remained the prevalent view until 1896, with the publication of Dörpfeld and Reisch (1896).

[7] See *Punch*, 90 (19 May 1886), 261: 'the curtains rise,—a concession to modernism, surely vexing to the classical souls of Professors Godwin and Todhunter . . .'.

[8] The *Punch* reviewer's comments (loc. cit.), the tone notwithstanding, are fairly representative of the detractors: 'I hope the British School of Archaeology at Athens has profited considerably more than I have by the performance of Mr Todhunter's *Helena in Troas* . . . [Nonetheless] Mr Godwin, FSA . . . has to be congratulated on his success in reproducing the most perfect imitation of a Greek theatre ever seen in London.'

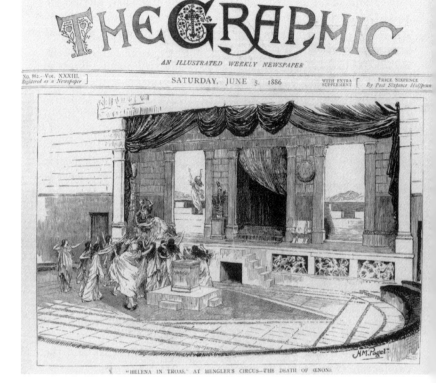

FIGURE 16.1   Scene from John Todhunter's *Helena in Troas* (1886).

the scenery and tableaux that secured public recognition of the seriousness of the endeavour (Fig. 16.2).[9] But perhaps the most intriguing of all of those involved behind the scenes is the somewhat shadowy figure of Professor George Charles Winter Warr, the man responsible for the abridgement of Aeschylus' trilogy and the author of *The Tale of Troy*, and the mind and body behind the production as a whole.

Warr had been at King's College since 1874 when he joined the Department of Classics as a lecturer, and he had been promoted to

---

[9] The tableaux had already been staged before in 1883 in Warr's *The Tale of Troy*. See Hearnshaw (1929), 318; Beard (2000), 37–53; and below, pp. 466–7.

FIGURE 16.2 Scene depicting Clytemnestra awakening the Furies in George Warr's *The Story of Orestes* (1886).

the Chair of Classical Literature in 1881.[10] Since the performances at the Prince's Hall were very much his own creation, it is not too far from the truth to refer to this seemingly fringe event in May 1886 as King's College's first attempt to bring Aeschylus' trilogy to the general public. Indeed, the rehearsals for the Chorus, at least, took place in the Music Room of the Ladies' Department of the College in Kensington.[11] In this chapter we seek to retrieve

[10] The bald details of Warr's life can be gleaned from *Who was Who 1895–1915*, i (6th edn. 1988); Ball and Venn (1913); and Venn (1954), s.v. Warr, George Charles Winter.
[11] *See Minutes of the Meeting of the Executive Committee of the Ladies' Department*, 16 Feb. 1886, 10–11 (King's College London Archive, KW/M2). The production of a Greek play has been an annual event at King's since 1953, and since 1988 has formed a part of the London Festival of Greek Drama.

Warr from the wings, so to speak, and to give an idea of the multifarious nature of 1880s social philhellenism.

GEORGE WARR

Warr had also been responsible in some senses for staging King's first Greek play some three years earlier in 1883 when *The Tale of Troy* was given two ancient-Greek and two English-language performances in a private theatre in the home of Lord and Lady Freake, in South Kensington. Lord Freake, a member of King's College Council, had offered his house to Warr after his fellow members had refused to allow women to perform in the Great Hall in the College. Since Warr had decided to mount the production of *The Tale of Troy* in order to provide funds for a permanent site for the Ladies' Department of King's College in Kensington, there was considerable irony and no small amount of wilful obstruction in the Council's decision.[12]

In other quarters, the worthy cause to which the production's proceeds were destined worked very much in Warr's favour; the 1883 cast list included Mr and Mrs Beerbohm Tree as Paris and Helen respectively, as well as Mrs Andrew Lang, J. K. Stephen, and Lionel Tennyson amongst its members. Maud Tree (née Holt, and former pupil of Queen's College, Harley Street, where she had learnt Greek and made her début in a Greek tragedy) later recalled 'a beautiful collie, the gift of Professor George Warr, who christened him Argus, in remembrance of one of our feats [in his play]'.[13] Indeed, Godwin (who was then drawing up plans for his own Greek theatre) was sufficiently interested in the project not only to attend the English language performance of the play, but also to accompany Beerbohm Tree to Cromwell House on at least

---

[12] Hearnshaw (1929), 318. See *Minutes of the Executive Committee of the Ladies' Department of King's College*, 31 May 1883, 101–2 (King's College, London Archive KW/M1), which, in addition to congratulating Warr 'upon the eminent success which had crowned his labours', also refers to the desire to stage repeat perform- ances in the Great Hall at King's and the need to enlist Lord Freake's help in this matter; and the *Minutes* of 8 June (106–7) again refer to hopes for performances at the College in the Autumn. Lord Freake's death shortly after this no doubt meant that persuading the Council was an unlikely prospect (cf. Hearnshaw (1929), 439).

[13] For Maud Tree's early years at Queen's College, see Foulkes (1997), 154, 163; for her memories of Warr, see Mrs Beerbohm Tree, ' "Herbert and I": A Trivial, Fond Record' in Beerbohm (*c.*1918), 21.

three occasions to watch him take part in the rehearsals; and Godwin referred to 'these representations...[as] among the greatest artistic delights ever provided for London society.'[14]

By 1886 the picture had altered considerably, with Warr's performances upstaged in many ways by the professionalism surrounding *Helena in Troas*. But despite the evident superiority of the Argyll Street project, there was clearly some anxiety on Todhunter's part, when he wrote to Godwin on 18 May: 'Warr wants to have our theatre for a performance of his "Orestes"!!! He is going to write to you on the subject. Of course he *must* not get it for love or money. Fancy him muddling with his amateurs over our stage.'[15] And behind Todhunter's acerbic comments lurks more than a tinge of insecurity about a perceived rival: Todhunter, it should be recalled, had failed altogether in getting his first attempt at a classically inspired play, his *Alcestis* of 1879, on the stage (see Ch. 15).

The distinguished classical scholar Jane Harrison, who took the part of Penelope in the 1883 production and who was to take the part of Alcestis at Oxford the following year (see Ch. 15), is said to have spoken of Warr with hindsight as 'a Mr Pickwick' unable to contain a 'bevy of high-spirited beautiful young ladies who rustled and "bussled" on every side'.[16] And Todhunter's picture of Warr 'muddling' over the stage with his 'amateurs' in 1886 may well echo Harrison's view. Furthermore, Warr's frustrated attempts to silence the voluble enthusiasm for Dorothy Dene's performance as Cassandra did not escape the mordant wit of the reviewer from *Punch*:

A graceless youth knocked his stick against the floor. The Professor leaped to his feet: 'How dare you do it! No applause!' Whereat their Royal Highnesses roared with laughter, the schoolmaster conquered, the Orestian Trilogy dragged its slow length along...[17]

---

[14] See Godwin's diary, 22 May–6 June 1883 inclusive (V&A Archive of Art and Design, AAD 4/8–1980); and the (unsourced) article by Godwin in the E. W. Godwin Collection, Theatre Museum, Box 2: Programmes and Cuttings.

[15] Todhunter to Godwin, 18 May 1886 (E. W. Godwin Collection, Theatre Museum, Box 8: *Helena in Troas*/Misc. Correspondence).

[16] I am indebted to both Mary Beard and Chris Stray for this reference, which comes from the Mirrlees Notebook and draft biography, Harrison Papers, Box 15, Newnham College, Cambridge. The account of the 1883 theatricals is partly based on Elinor Paul's letter and diary written *c*.1934. See Beard (2000), 183 n.15.

[17] *Punch*, 90 (19 May 1886), 261.

Whilst Warr's efforts would appear on the one hand to lend support to Harrison's picture of the bumbling professor, the reviewer's comments here (as with Harrison's assessment) are not free of
hauteur. And although the term 'schoolmaster' in this context must
be measured alongside the headline to the review, 'The Schoolmaster Abroad'—a direct allusion to comments by the distinguished founder of London University, Lord Brougham[18]—a
derogatory note is clearly sounded. Warr had made the bizarre
written request in the programme for the audience to refrain
from applause during the performance; and his interventions,
however comical, clearly reflect a somewhat misguided effort on
his part to get the audience to *listen* to Aeschylus' words rather
than simply *view* the play as a series of *tableaux vivants*.

Indeed, Harrison's simple-minded Pickwickian character turns
out to have been a remarkably energetic and multifaceted person-
ality. Warr was primarily a scholar, with impeccable academic
credentials, winning the prestigious Porson Prize as an undergraduate at Cambridge in 1868, and placed third in the First
Class of the Classical Tripos in 1869.[19] His published work, moreover, demonstrates that he was fully engaged with the latest developments in his field. Harrison may well have found his theatricals
faintly amusing, but he found much of note in her work; and in his
commentary on the *Oresteia* that accompanied his translation in
1900, he credits her insights on numerous occasions.[20]

Following a 'most distinguished' record at the Royal Institution
School Liverpool and an equally distinguished undergraduate
career at Cambridge, he joined the Classics Department at
King's after a brief spell teaching at St Paul's and elsewhere.[21] It

---

[18] Cf. Brougham's speech at the London Mechanics' Institute, 1825: 'Look out,
gentlemen, the schoolmaster is abroad!'

[19] Other honours and prizes at Cambridge listed in Venn (1954) include,
Tancred Scholar (1865), First Bell Scholar (1866), Foundation Scholar at Trinity
(1867), Member's Prize (1868), Winchester Reading Prize (1869). See further the
testimonials on Warr in the Archives at University College, London (Classics, 1876,
M–W), written in support of his double application for the Chairs of Greek and
Latin respectively in 1876.

[20] Warr (1900), 186, 190, 200, 204 refers to two articles by Harrison in *Journal of
Hellenic Studies*, one in vol. 19 and another in vol. 20; and on 215, he refers to her
introduction and commentary in *Mythology and Monuments of Ancient Athens*
(London, 1890). In the preface, p. xi, he also expresses his debt to recent research
by Harrison, Verrall (usually in dissent), Wilamowitz, and Wecklein.

[21] A. T. Brown (1924), 58 cites the Revd James Lonsdale's memory of George
Warr and his elder brother Henry (who became a distinguished barrister on the

was most probably connections from his own school days that secured him the lectureship at King's London in 1874: a former Assistant Master at the Royal Institution, the Rev. James Lonsdale, had only relatively recently vacated the Chair of Classical Literature in 1870.[22]

Warr had been elected Fellow of Trinity College, Cambridge, in 1870, four years before the King's appointment, but he had not been admitted to the Fellowship after declining to take the oath of allegiance to the Church of England. His involvement in the Movement for the Abolition of University Tests during 1871, which successfully sought to overturn the ruling that members of the Church of England alone were able to matriculate, seemed inevitable. This principled act of dissent was clearly one that radically changed his predicted life pattern. His tutor from his Cambridge years, Robert Burn refers to it in his testimonial written in support of Warr's double application for the Chairs of Greek and Latin at University College, London in 1876:

I regret very much that his conscientious scruples, for which I have the highest respect, should have prevented him from accepting a Fellowship, and I feel that Cambridge thereby lost a scholar who would have been a valuable teacher and lecturer in Classics.[23]

During his early years in London, Warr had been at the heart of the Liberal establishment as Secretary to the Cobden Club; and connections made at this time clearly proved helpful and longlasting. Gladstone was President in 1870, and the Prime Minister's attendance at one of the Greek performances of Warr's *The Tale at Troy* some years later, in 1883, may well have owed something to their work together in the Club.[24] It was during this time that Warr

---

Northern circuit) as being amongst the Revd William Dawson Turner's 'most distinguished pupils'. Warr also taught at Trinity College, Cambridge in 1871, and from 1872 at Garrick Chambers, where he prepared pupils for the classical papers in the Indian Civil Service examinations (a duty he continued to perform during his time at King's). See too Hearnshaw (1929), 310–311.

[22] Hearnshaw (1929), A. T. Brown (1924).

[23] Testimonial dated 12 Apr. 1876 (Archives, n. 17). Cf. Warr's comments in his letter of application dated 28 Apr. 1876: 'It is recorded in the Cambridge University Calendar that I was elected but not admitted a Fellow of Trinity College in 1870. I should state that I declined admission on the ground of the sectarian tests which were then in force.'

[24] There appears to be some confusion about the dates of Warr's period of office: according to Venn (1954) and *Who was Who* (1988), he was Secretary 1869–73;

made the acquaintance of the artist, Walter Crane, who designed the Cobden bookplate in 1875; and in 1887, in an extremely handsome two volume edition of the performance texts of both *The Tale of Troy* and *The Story of Orestes* and the musical accompaniment, Crane's engravings of the tableaux and the set designs were reproduced.[25]

Warr's political radicalism had clearly been fostered during his years at the Royal Institution, under the tutelage of the liberal Broad Church headmaster and former pupil of Thomas Arnold, the Revd William Dawson Turner. Turner, who spent the last years of his life working in London hospitals for the poor, was believed during his years as headmaster to have discreetly kept many free places for promising but impoverished pupils.[26] Warr shared Dawson's principles, with his own passionate commitment during his career to extending the access of higher education to include members of the lower middle and working classes as well as to women. He became involved in the North of England Council for the Higher Education of Women, and gave a series of 'highly esteemed' lectures 'to the working people and others' in Rochdale.[27] He played a central role in the formation of the London Society for the Extension of University teaching in 1876, which led to University lecturers taking their learning to the suburbs and allowing women to attend their classes for the first time. In 1879 Warr was lecturing on Ancient History at the ladies' department in South Kensington; and he was at the forefront of the campaign to set up a permanent college for the higher education of women, to be known as King's College for Women. As we have heard, the 1883 production of *The Tale of Troy* was mounted to raise funds for the new building in South Kensington; and in 1888 Warr arranged for a share of the profits for *Echoes of Hellas* to be donated to the Ladies Department of the College.[28]

whereas Brock (1939), 82, lists 1873–77. For Gladstone's attendance at *The Tale of Troy*, see Hearnshaw (1929), 492.

[25] For Crane's bookplate, see Brock (1939), 24; for the performance texts, see Warr and Crane (1887).

[26] A. T. Brown (1924), 31.

[27] See the testimonial from James Stuart, Professor of Mechanism and Applied Mechanics in the University of Cambridge, 17 Apr. 1876 (Archives, n. 17).

[28] The net proceeds of the performances amounted to an impressive £652. 19*s.* 6*d.* Other contributors included Anna Swanwick (£30), Gladstone (£100), F. W. Maitland (£5), Lord Freake (£100), Miss M. Gurney, John Ruskin (5 gns.). See

In the 1880s with his productions of Greek plays, Warr shows himself to be a deft mediator between the visual, theatrical, literary and musical worlds, with friends and acquaintances in pre-eminent circles. It is tempting to see his schooldays as having prepared him for this unusually broad brief: the Royal Institution in Dawson Turner's time was as keen on equipping its pupils with a detailed knowledge of modern as well as ancient culture, with modern languages playing as prominent a part in the school curriculum as Latin and Greek. A recurrent emphasis in the testimonials submitted by Warr's referees for his application for the Chairs of Greek and Latin at University College, London is the breadth of his learning in modern as well as ancient literature; and the range of literary allusion in his work would appear to bear this out.[29] Another unusual strength of The Royal Institution in Turner's time was the art department, with the so-called 'drawing boys' forming an élite group. As a prizewinner for drawing on at least one occasion, Warr would have had his picture exhibited on Speech Day together with the school's 'Roscoe' collection of Italian and Flemish masters.[30]

It seems to have been the influence of Warr's main partner in the 1883 production, Charles Newton (keeper of Greek and Roman Antiquities at the British Museum from 1861 to 1885 and Yates Professor of Classical Archaeology at University College, London from 1880 to 1888) that led to the involvement of members of the artistic establishment such as Leighton, Poynter, and Watts.[31] But it must be recalled that Warr had already known Walter Crane, at least, for some years; and his own, by no means inconsiderable background in the visual arts, must have made him unusually well-placed to co-ordinate such a large-scale collaborative project.

As scholar, radical, and socialite of sorts, then, Warr's wide-ranging agenda invites comparison, perhaps, with the life of his younger contemporary, the much better known, and rather more

The Calendar of King's College, London for 1886–7 (London 1886), 99. For *Echoes of Hellas*, see *Minutes of the Executive Committee of the Ladies' Department of King's College* 4 May 1888, 37 (King's College, London Archive, KW/M2).

[29] See e.g. the comments of Arthur Holmes (dated 1872), Henry Jackson, and Herbert Kynaston (both 1876; above, n. 17). In his commentary on the *Oresteia* (London, 1900), there are frequent references to Milton, Shakespeare, Tennyson, and others.

[30] A. T. Brown (1924), 37.

[31] Hearnshaw (1929), 492.

distinguished, classical scholar Gilbert Murray. Clearly Murray's marriage into the Howard family elevated him into a sphere that Warr could only glimpse, but never enter (see further Ch. 17). Warr's own social separation from the South Kensington circles that the Greek productions put him in touch with no doubt lurks behind Jane Harrison's image of the bumbling Mr Pickwick, and behind the patronizing tone of some of the reviews of the 1886 production.[32] Moreover, in marked contrast to Murray's upwardly mobile marriage, Warr's own marriage to Constance Emily, daughter of Thomas Keddy Fletcher of Union Docks, Limehouse, in 1885 was probably a socially ambiguous match for the son of a Liverpool clergyman. Although it is uncertain whether Constance was one of Warr's Extension students, it would be safe to infer that her family circumstances were not dissimilar to those of the students who attended the extension lectures at Toynbee Hall and elsewhere in the 1880s.[33]

Such noticeable social divisions notwithstanding, Murray and Warr shared common ground. Murray's first translations of Greek plays—the 1902 volume of Euripides' *Hippolytus, Bacchae*, and Aristophanes' *Frogs* that so impressed George Bernard Shaw and his contemporaries (see Ch. 17)—appeared as Volume III in a series of verse translations, with commentaries and notes for English readers, that was edited by Warr himself. Warr's own (unabridged) translation of the *Oresteia* formed the first volume in 1900; and in the Preface, his opening remarks convey popularizing sentiments that Murray would have no doubt endorsed. Warr writes:

Considering the obvious advantages offered by the combination of translation with commentary, it is strange that the field of Greek and Roman

[32] For Murray, see Francis West (1984) and Duncan Wilson (1987). For Harrison's comments, see n. 16 above. Note that at this point Warr is cast as a gauche bachelor, but within two years he will have married Constance Fletcher. Cf. further the tone of the testimonials written for William Wayte, who was appointed Professor of Greek in 1876 after Warr's unsuccessful application. Whereas Warr's referees have only known him in a professional capacity, Wayte's referees have often known him personally since their time together at Eton (Archives, n. 17).

[33] King's College Archive contains no lists of extension students. For a profile of the students at Toynbee Hall in the mid 1880s, see *Toynbee Hall, Whitechapel: Second Annual Report of the Universities Settlement in East London* (Oxford, 1886), *passim*; and the comment (p. 6) that in 1884 all the major newspapers were full of accounts of life in the East End.

literature has been so far neglected in this respect that the classics—the basis of literary education in our schools and colleges—are still, so to speak, sealed books for all but students of Greek and Latin. By those who do not possess the key to the originals they are read, if at all, with little real appreciation, while it is to be feared that the majority even of those who have acquired the key at much expense of time and labour make hardly any subsequent use of it.

The difficulty seems to be met most simply and directly, not only for the 'English reader', but for the more or less instructed student, by thoroughly annotated translations, giving to the latter the means of widening the area of his early reading and following it up in after life, so to make the ancient literature a permanent possession. Translations on these lines from the Greek have the further recommendation that they go far to fill the gap and bring continuity into the classical work of the 'modern side' which is restricted to Latin.[34]

For Warr, translation (together with commentary) was vital to widen the audience of the ancient texts; it served not only to educate the Greekless reader, but also (as he was more than made aware when he prepared students for the Indian Civil Service examinations)[35] those public school boys whose grasp of Greek remained limited and/or non-existent since they had remained on the 'modern side' and learnt only Latin at school.

In his commentary Warr chooses to cite *Prometheus Bound* in a translation by Augusta Webster; this is no doubt significant given Webster's radical agenda in her translations from the Greek, together with her high degree of scholarship.[36] But it is important, above all, to situate Warr alongside the other rather better remembered pioneers in the area of translation, Richard Jebb and especially Lewis Campbell (see Ch. 15). And what is notable about their translations, as with Murray's to come, is that they either derive directly from the recent revivals, or (as with Jebb's primarily scholarly and pedagogical translations) they reflect at the very least a new awareness of an essentially performative context.[37]

---

[34] Warr (1900), pp. ix f.

[35] See n. 21 above; and the testimonial from William Baptiste Scoones, Garrick Chambers (24 Apr. 1876): 'The students... are young men... drawn from the upper Forms of the public schools but occasionally backward and requiring much guidance...' (Archives, n. 17).

[36] Warr (1900), pp. xlvii–xlix. For Webster, see Hardwick (2000*a*), 68–81.

[37] Jebb's translations of Sophocles, with text, commentary, and translation were published from 1883 to 1895, and Lewis Campbell's *A Guide to Greek Tragedy for*

WHY THE *ORESTEIA*?

In the Introduction to Warr's translation of the *Oresteia*—though we should note that it was written some ten or so years after his production—we find a striking account of the trilogy:

> ... we see in the story of Cassandra the history of the 'Sybil'—the woman with that faculty of divination, which the Greeks as well as the Teutons had discovered in the female sex—crushed out by the Delphic priesthood. The same jealousy, which denied honour and worship to women, is felt in Apollo's ruling that the mother is naught, that the father's blood alone runs in the child's veins, that a mother's blood may be shed by her son, provided he is absolved with that of a pig by a man 'who expiates for bloodshed'. The triumphant plea of Athena, that she was born without a mother, reflects the same hostility. She herself is, in a sense, the counterpart of the Delphic divinity—another embodiment of the Hellenic masculine intellect imposing its ordinances with a quasi-sacerdotal authority.[38]

Notwithstanding that Warr is writing in the wake of the English discovery of Ibsen and in the early waves of the women's suffrage movement, his commentary seems decidedly strident in tone ('masculine intellect imposing its ordinances with a quasi-sacerdotal authority'). It is not, moreover, without passing resemblance to the early-nineteenth-century evolutionary reading of the play by J. J. Bachofen in *Das Mutterrecht* (1821), who argued that the trilogy enacted the historical overthrow of a matriarchy by a patriarchal system of order.

That Warr chose to highlight the theme of gender in the trilogy in terms remarkably familiar to late twentieth-century ears is by no means surprising in the light of his feminist sympathies during his time at King's. It also seems clear from his comments why he chose to represent aspects of the three Aeschylean plays, rather than, as had been the trend previously, perform one play in its entirety. For him, the trilogy is concerned with the ascendance of this 'Hellenic masculine intellect', and to break it up into its constituent parts is to obscure this important message. Indeed, in a written response to a damning review of his play in *The Athenaeum*, which objected

---

English Readers appeared in 1891. For Jebb's interest in revivals, see his introductory comments to each of the volumes.

[38] Warr (1900), pp. xlii f.

primarily to the cramped stage conditions at the Prince's Hall, Warr countered the reviewer's objections to his abridgement in precisely these terms: 'My object has been to rescue the Trilogy from the dislocation to which it has hitherto been subjected.'[39] For Warr, as his comments in the 1900 edition of his translation confirm, the meaning of the *Oresteia* can only be broached through contemplation of its full trilogic sweep.

However, there were other less urgently radical reasons that would have also prompted his decision to mount a production of the *Oresteia*. Ever since Schlegel's lectures on Greek drama reached the English public through translation in 1815, Aeschylus had enjoyed the reputation of being a kind of honorary Shakespeare: a rugged, towering genius. Indeed, Aeschylus's strength was increasingly deemed to be his very deviation from the classical ideal formulated by Winckelmann. For Ruskin, for example, Aeschylus shared with Shakespeare the grotesque element that he admired in Gothic architecture.[40] By 1886 in a review of a concert of Stanford's music for the 1885 Cambridge *Eumenides*, the writer looks to Aeschylus as a guide needed in a venal age. He refers to the poet's

passionate sympathy for the noblest types of human character . . . and his profound belief in the inevitable and inexorable Nemesis which waits upon wrong doing . . . a faith which in this opportunistic age of shifty politics and harum-scarum morality seem to be fast dying out altogether. The other day 'Orestes' [meaning 'The Story of Orestes'] was ably impersonated and rapturously received at Cambridge . . . [41]

But perhaps equally important, the Victorian privileging of Homer should be invoked in order to account for Warr's choice of the *Oresteia*. The frieze of the Albert Memorial (1871–2) gives more space to Homer than to Shakespeare; and Homer has clearly toppled the native artistic giant by 1891, with Shakespeare humbly deferring to his ancient Greek master in a *Punch* cartoon.[42] Gladstone famously set aside two tables in his library, one for Homer and one for the Bible; and he wrote four studies on Homer in which

[39] *The Athenaeum*, no. 3057 (29 May 1886), 725 in response to no. 3056 (22 May 1886), 690.

[40] Ruskin (1851–3), iii, ch. 3, para. 67; Jenkyns (1980), 88.

[41] *Pall Mall Gazette*, 17 May 1886, 3–4.

[42] *Punch* (1891). Thanks to Chris Stray for drawing this to our attention; see further Turner (1981), 135–86.

he argued his belief in the historical reality of the poems: *Homeric Synchronism* (1876) drew on Schliemann's recent discoveries at Hisarlık to corroborate his thesis. Schoolboys knew of Homer either directly or through popular anthologies, and in the visual arts scenes from the Homeric epics were standard. And the Homeric world is both privileged and domesticated in this late Victorian context: in Alma-Tadema's *A Reading from Homer* (1885), for example, we find the 'classical' figures lounging around in what is essentially (as Richard Jenkyns has pointed out) a Victorian drawing-room, albeit one with marble furniture.[43]

It is hardly surprising, then, that Warr's first attempts in 1883 to involve his students from the Extension classes at King's in drama should have focused on Homer. Although the 1883 cast of *The Tale of Troy* contained even more socialites than we find in the revivals of 1886—in 1883, Sitwells, Mrs Andrew Lang, and Mrs Bram Stoker appear amongst other notables—Warr's original intention had been for a predominantly, if not exclusively, student-based project; and his efforts to stage the play in the college bear this out.[44]

A privileging of Homer also accounts, in part at least, for the early choice of tragedies for performance in Greek at Oxford and Cambridge from 1880 onwards, when the Trojan War and its aftermath predominated. As we saw in the previous chapter, the first such production was the *Agamemnon*, performed at Balliol in 1880; Cambridge followed with the *Ajax* in 1882 and the *Eumenides* in 1885. In the same year, F. R. Benson, the organizer of the 1880 Oxford *Agamemnon*, now a professional actor, mounted a touring production of the *Oresteia* with his Shakespeare Company which proved enormously popular, both at home and abroad.[45] And Todhunter's *Helena in Troas* (published before the 1886 production) enacts the events between the ending of the *Iliad* and the start of Euripides' *Trojan Women*. Warr's choice, then, of the most obviously Greek tragic 'sequel' to the Homeric epics, the *Oresteia*, as the basis for his second dramatic performance was a natural one.

---

[43] Jenkyns (1991), 239.

[44] See above, n. 11.

[45] The Company performed *The Orestean* [sic] *Trilogy of Aeschylus* at the New Theatre, Cambridge for 6 nights in May/June 1885 (Programme in Cambridge Greek Play Archive). See further Trewin (1960), 143–44.

TRAGEDY AND ARCHAEOLOGY

In the previous chapter, we have spoken of the power of the classical burlesque at its best to enable it to rival (and on occasions at least to outstrip) the very objects it sought to travesty. Moreover, the burlesque, with its fusion of words and music, went some way towards giving its audiences an idea of the form of the original. But Greek tragic burlesques did not simply recapture the form of the Greek plays. They were also at the forefront of the movement towards historical accuracy in scenic and costume design. J. R. Planché, who has already been mentioned as the author of a highly successful burlesque *The Golden Fleece*, was also a leading founder of the British Archaeological Association in 1843 (a splinter group from the Society of Antiquaries). The extravaganzas he put on with Eliza Vestris at the Olympic were in many ways forerunners of the Naturalistic plays of the 1880s. But they can equally well be seen as forerunners of the revivals of Greek tragedies in the 1880s; and the fact that the most important stage designer of the late nineteenth century, and the designer of Todhunter's *Helena in Troas*, E. W. Godwin, was a disciple of Planché bears this out.

From 1869 the restored Roman theatre at Orange in Provence played host to productions by the Comédie-Française; and Godwin was at the forefront of British experiments with alternative, classically inspired, performance spaces. He had been involved in 1884 and 1885 in open-air productions in Surrey,[46] and it was now a desire to replicate the ancient Greek performance space that had led him to Hengler's Circus. In an article that formed part of a series on 'Archaeology on the Stage' in the *Dramatic Review*, Godwin advocates that critics should ignore the action of the play, and 'give undivided attention to the external [*sic*] of architecture and costume'.[47] When reviewers comment on Todhunter's play, it is very often as if they were adhering to Godwin's dictates: it is the set and costume that command their attentions almost to the exclusion of the play-text proper. Jane Harrison's extravagant praise of Todhunter's play in a letter to the playwright's wife is representative:

---

[46] See Stokes (1972).   [47] *Dramatic Review*, 8 Feb 1885.

I was little prepared for the vision of beauty that met our eyes on Monday. The chorus seated against the white marble is a sight I shall never forget.[48]

And when a reviewer comments on *The Story of Orestes*, praise is given to the overall effect of scenic design:

Very great care, moreover, had evidently been taken, and several of the tableaux were as effective as any scene from a Greek play yet performed here. The sleeping furies about Orestes, in their flame-coloured garments and green serpentine headdresses, their faces covered with cleverly contrived masks, were first-rate, and whether their leader was a man or a woman nobody could be sure.[49]

It was Schlegel, of course, who maintained that Greek tragedy was sculptural, and this observation was nowhere more keenly felt than in the 1880s. The revivals at Cambridge were closely linked with the rise of archaeology as a discipline.[50] In 1884 the new university museum, which contained a collection of 600 or so plaster casts of Greek and Roman sculptures, was officially opened. Todhunter's play was not unique in being mounted in aid of the newly established British School of Archaeology at Athens; a planned production of Sophocles' *Antigone* at Bradfield College in 1886/7, which never in fact materialized, similarly intended its proceeds to go to the British School in Athens.[51]

The 1880s revivals of Greek tragedy were veritable *Gesamtkunstwerke*. Whilst it was the music that endured in the public memory in the long run in the case of the Mendelssohn *Antigone*, at the time of its first appearance at Covent Garden in 1845 it was the scenery and costumes that impressed audiences (see above). So with the 1880 revivals: there may well have been subsequent concerts of the music that had been written expressly for the productions—as was the case with Stanford's music for the *Eumenides* at Cambridge in 1885, which was performed at the third Richter concert in 1886[52]—but again, it is the visual dimension of

---

[48] Todhunter Collection, University of Reading Library (Ms 202/1/1, fos. 327–30).

[49] *Pall Mall Gazette*, 14 May 1886, 3.

[50] Easterling (1999), *passim*; Beard (2000), 37–53.

[51] Letter to Oscar Browning from N. B. Gray, 21 May 1886 (Oscar Browning Papers, King's College Cambridge; a copy deposited by Chris Stray is in the Archive of Performances of Greek and Roman Drama, University of Oxford).

[52] *The Academy*, 29, no. 733 (22 May 1886), 371; *Pall Mall Gazette*, 18 May 1886, 3–4.

the productions that predominates in the reviews of the 1880s plays. As Martin Booth has persuasively argued, Victorian stage spectacle and stage pictorialism are very much a product of what was essentially a 'viewing' culture.[53] Audiences went to the theatre to see enactments of famous paintings—genuine *tableaux vivants*. And Louise Jopling's comments on her role in the Godwin–Todhunter production are revealing in this regard:

> for the pediment, I was instructed [by Godwin] to drape and seat, half a dozen figures in the same attitudes as those on the frieze of the Parthenon. The poor things had to remain without moving during the whole time the play was in progress. They were attired in unbleached calico draperies, which simulated the white marble, just tinged with age, wonderfully well.[54]

Warr's productions, then, are very much in tune with these broader concerns of the period. But it was clearly his coup (with the help of Newton) in securing the services of the most highly regarded members of the British art world that made his productions significant to London society. The assistance of Charles Waldstein, who was Secretary to the Cambridge Greek Play,[55] was also a valuable asset in dealing with the art establishment. Waldstein's work on Phidias and Ruskin gave him obvious stature amongst the members of the Royal Academy. As the Academicians had sought to capture the classical world on canvas, they were now equally eager to participate in the general attempt to recreate its drama on the stage; and Alma-Tadema had already been to Cambridge to see the *Ajax* in 1882.[56] If nineteenth-century stage history is in large measure an account of the art of perfecting stage pictorialism, the paintings of this period in turn seem increasingly to invoke the stage. But as Mrs Tree recalled many years later of the 1883 production, it was, above all, the actors who 'all loved to be the willing slaves of all the great artists of the day'.[57]

SOCIAL HELLENISM VERSUS THE NEW WOMAN

That George Warr could make such inroads into high society at this time was substantially due to the increasingly fine line between

---

[53] Booth (1981), 1–29. See further Altick (1978), *passim*.
[54] Jopling (1925), 289.   [55] Easterling (1999), 32.   [56] Ibid. 38.
[57] Mrs Beerbohm Tree in Beerbohm (*c*.1918), 18.

aesthetic and what one might term social Hellenism. In 1884 the
Argyll Street store of Messrs Liberty & Co. mounted an exhibition
of 'artistic and historical' costumes designed by no lesser authority
than E. W. Godwin himself; and in an account of the show in the
Pall Mall Gazette, the social, scholarly, and aesthetic spheres
coalesce:

[the historical costumes] are more for fancy dresses than everyday wear, as
our climate will scarcely allow ladies to wear the garment of ancient
Greece, however picturesque they may look in the background of soft
silks which drape the walls of the exhibition rooms.... The first was a
Greek robe... from a vase in the British Museum *c.*350 BC; the second,
third and fourth also Greek costumes of different periods, imitated from
vases at the British Museum.[58]

This was a time when leading artists enjoyed almost unprecedented social-standing and wealth. Sir Frederic Leighton was the
most extreme example of the well-heeled, well-connected painter
of the period: in the last decade of his life he was granted a peerage
(the only English artist ever to have received the honour), and after
his death he was given full funeral honours at St Paul's. But he was
not alone in his receipt of public recognition: successful artists
often appeared in magazines and books, amidst the grandeur of
their vast, opulent studios.[59] In 1885 the Royal Academy hosted a
ball where the ladies went attired in Greek chitons with fillets in
their hair.[60] The diary section of the *Pall Mall Gazette* wittily and
tartly captures this social Hellenism in its report of the first performance of Todhunter's play a year later:

Argyll Street was dumbfounded at the sight of the smart people who
besieged the doors of Hengler's Circus yesterday afternoon... Sir Frederick [*sic*] Leighton was there, a spruce Olympian; Miss Fortescue looked
like an artist's model as she passed the President... and rank, wealth and
beauty were all represented. 'How pretty, dear! but oh, this nasty incense!'
'Quite too charming' 'How those flowing draperies would become me,'
'Are they not just a little—you know?' and so on.[61]

---

[58] *Pall Mall Gazette*, 2 May 1884.
[59] Wood (1983), 30–32. Leighton's own studio was so large that he was able to
host musical concerts there.
[60] Gaunt (1952), 144.
[61] *Pall Mall Gazette*, 18 May 1886, 3.

Warr's 1883 production at Lord and Lady Freake's home, Cromwell House, spawned the phrase 'South Kensington Hellenism'; and by 1886 many reviewers had grown weary of the distinct class of Liberty-gowned ladies who flocked to the Greek plays (see Fig. 16.3). *The Academy*'s reviewer of the May 1886 plays caustically dismisses the new fashion as 'that Hellenic craze which has succeeded the craze for blue and white china, and which, so far as the general public is concerned, will last

FIGURE 16.3   Fashion plate advertising 'Hellenic' couture (1888).

as long.'[62] The reviewer was a little wide of the mark when he predicted the imminent passing of social philhellenism: it was still sufficiently alive a decade later, in 1896, to provide the target for Gilbert and Sullivan's *The Grand Duke*. And as late as 1910, Lady Diana Cooper can still refer to the Greek rage in evening dress.[63]

But the classically inspired changes in fashion were by no means entirely associated with upper-class frivolity. The Healthy and Artistic Dress Union, which advocated dress reform in close association with the political emancipation of women, promoted the Greek style as well. In 1893 in the first issue of its journal *Aglaia*, the title page by the designer Henry Holiday (who also worked on the 1883 and 1886 productions of Warr) showed three Victorian women in Greek robes; and there were illustrations in the inside pages showing the contrasts between ancient, medieval, and modern dress by Holiday and Warr's close associate Walter Crane. Other names from the 1880s revival—Louise Jopling and G. F. Watts—also lent themselves in support of the Healthy and Artistic Dress Union.[64]

It would, of course, be erroneous to claim that the revivals of the 1880s afforded in any sense a manifestation of what George Bernard Shaw was provocatively to label in 1891 the 'unwomanly woman', better known by the slightly later coinage the 'New Woman' (see Ch. 17). But it is equally important not to overlook the fact that Frederic Leighton lent his support to *The Tale of Troy* because of his keen interest in the idea of a Ladies' Department at King's College.[65] And his (apparently innocent) relationship with his model Dorothy Dene, who took the part of Cassandra in *The Story of Orestes*, is in some ways confirmation of his feminist sympathies.

The 'discovery' of Dene from the public's point of view really began with her appearance in Warr's play, when she received glowing reviews for her performance as Cassandra. She had turned down a 'merely walking character' in Todhunter's play, and rightly so, it seems, since the reviewers were unanimous in their praise of her interpretation of a difficult, major role:

The chief feature of the performance was the remarkable acting of Miss Dorothy Dene as Cassandra. We are inclined to think it was the best piece

---

[62] *The Academy*, 29, no. 734 (29 May 1886), 386–7.   [63] Wood (1983), 30.
[64] Ibid. 29–30.   [65] Hearnshaw (1929), 492.

of acting... that we have seen from an English actress for a long time. Miss Dene has great personal charm, but nobody expected from her a performance so powerful, so finished, and so self-controlled. It was not the least Greek, but we do not hesitate to anticipate from it a high position for her on the English stage.[66]

In the *Illustrated London News* she is praised for being 'lost in the passion of her personation', for playing 'Cassandra with real fire...'. In the estimation of the reviewer, Dene 'is evidently an artist of considerable promise'; and her interpretation of the role, her ability to lose her 'identity in the character... and [be]... absorbed in the contemplation of a great subject', is considered exemplary and an object lesson from which the professional players in the production (namely the Trees) could learn.[67]

If the discovery of Dene began with her interpretation of the role of Cassandra in Warr's play, her 'discovery' by the art world had begun some time earlier in 1879, when she was introduced to Leighton and Watts as a model for portrait studies.[68] From a poor East End background, she confided to Leighton her ambition to be an actress; and it was Leighton who had funded her training and followed her acting career enthusiastically. She does not appear to have enjoyed much success on the stage after her startling performance as Cassandra, but she remained in the public eye as Leighton's principal model for all his major paintings in the final decade of his life.

In a fascinating study of Victorian actresses and the myth of Pygmalion and Galatea, Gail Marshall sees the relationship between Leighton and Dene as representative of what she terms the nineteenth-century Galatea-aesthetic.[69] Dene is Leighton's Galatea, desired and desirable in her sculptural state; and her acting career significantly ended following the death of her benefactor. One might infer much from the Dene–Leighton example about the questionable morality of the Pygmalion role—one that Shaw was to probe somewhat later in his play of that name.[70] Born as the East

---

[66] *Pall Mall Gazette*, 14 May 1886, 3.
[67] *ILN* 88, no. 2412 (22 May 1886), 524. Cf. the engraving of Dene in contemporary dress alongside the review of the play in *Punch*, 90 (19 May 1886), 245.
[68] For an account of Dene's life, see Wood (1983), 75–9.
[69] Marshall (1998), 172.
[70] Leonée Ormond has also suggested that Leighton's relationship with Dene lies behind Shaw's play. See ibid. 216 n. 84.

End girl Ada Alice Pullen, she was then transported into the heights of fashionable London society as 'Dorothy Dene' by her benevolent, patriarchal benefactor, only to discover that 'origins' still matter even in the most seemingly egalitarian circles. Dene found this out most cruelly when Walter and Mary Crane, both professed socialists, nevertheless broke off their son's engagement to her on class grounds.[71] Not only, then, are Dene's experiences clear evidence of the perils of re-fashioning an individual in an unchanged world, they are also representative, as Marshall demonstrates, of an important aspect of the 'viewing' culture and its treatment of actresses in general.

Lily Langtry rose to stardom in the last quarter of the nineteenth century in large measure on account of her looks, and she had not unsurprisingly been the first choice for the part of Helena in Todhunter's play.[72] Oscar Wilde is said to have taken her under his wing—rather as Leighton had done with Dene—when she expressed a desire to learn more about the ancient world, and about ancient Greece in particular. Wilde regularly attended Sir Charles Newton's lectures at King's College, London with Langtry in 1881, and it is said that students would wait outside the building and cheer when the social luminaries emerged from their cab. On one occasion during Newton's lecture, Langtry is said to have sat facing the audience as a living example of Attic beauty. She was deemed to possess the small upper lip and rounded chin that was so highly valued in Greek sculpture, and her beauty as much as (or even more than) her acting ability accounted for her success on the stage.[73]

As Marshall says of Victorian actresses in general, they have the sculptural metaphor imposed upon them; and the desirability of the actress lies precisely in the fact that it is the male gaze that determines the sexual potential of the otherwise inanimate body.[74] In the 1880s, with increasing anxieties about homosexuality and male effeminacy following the increase in information about birth control and the attendant drop in the birth rate in the previous decade, feminine virtues of all kinds were promoted. Marshall sees

---

[71] Wood (1983), 78.

[72] She features prominently in the Prospectus to *Helena in Troas* (Godwin Collection, Theatre Museum, Box 8: *Helena in Troas*/Misc. Correspondence).

[73] Ellmann (1987), 70; Wood (1983), 30. See further Beatty (1999).

[74] Marshall (1998), 1–7.

this desire to promote the feminine aspect in what was feared an increasingly effeminate society to lie behind the rise of the social standing of the actress during this period.[75]

That the actress is granted life and potency through the male spectator's gaze is felt nowhere more keenly than in accounts of the 1880s revivals of Greek plays. The drama critic of *The Academy* makes the following observations about Todhunter's play:

But the chief charm as well as the chief novelty lay in the part of the chorus, upon whose training no pains had been spared. Their singing, we have been told, was technically not free from blame; but it would be impossible to pick any other fault in the performance. Though there was no attempt at dancing, their intricate windings over the orchestra, their rhythmical waving of their bare arms, and the grace of the white garments, strangely affected the imagination.[76]

Even though this particular chorus does not appear to have done what a Greek chorus would be expected to have done—namely sing *and* dance—it is still considered to have given a near faultless performance. The languor of the writer's last few lines here, to-gether with the neat counterpoint between the potentially erotic 'bare arms' and the chaste 'grace of the white garments', leaves the reader in no doubt as to how this particular reviewer's imagination was 'strangely affected'. And the detractors of the Godwin–Todhunter endeavour metaphorically tear back the garments and expose the play as a vehicle for shameless titillation of the male spectator. Here is the *Illustrated London News*:

Society is ransacked for comely maidens, with stately figures and classical profiles, to patter about marble pavements with sandalled feet, and to meander around the thymele, or altar, perfumed with incense ... and there has been a generous display of classically modelled neck and white arm.[77]

No doubt it was the potentially highly charged nature of the audience-actor dynamic in revivals of Greek plays that led to the prohibitions on cross-dressed roles at Oxford, where men were not allowed to take women's roles. This led to Jane Harrison's being invited to take the part of Alcestis in the 1887 production of

---

[75] Ibid. 92–4; see also Dowling (1994).
[76] *The Academy*, 29, no. 733 (22 May 1886), 370.
[77] *ILN*, no. 3056 (22 May 1886), 524.

Euripides' play (which as we heard in the previous chapter coincidentally employed the set designed by Godwin for *Helena in Troas* the previous year).[78] And Cambridge's prohibitions on women taking part in the Greek play (which with one notable exception in 1885, when Janet Case of Girton played Athene in the *Eumenides*, lasted until 1948,[79] when women became members of the University) may well have had more to do with the dangers inherent in what Marshall calls the Galatea-aesthetic than it did with the status of women within the university.

It would, perhaps, be unfair to reduce these revivals to vehicles for the purposes of demeaning their female participants. In some senses the plays were simply hijacked by a social elite unwilling or unable to appreciate any deeper significance behind the occasions. Warr's comments on Athena's embodying 'the Hellenic masculine intellect imposing its ordinances with a quasi-sacerdotal authority',[80] for example, do not seem to have struck any reviewer of *The Story of Orestes* as either significant or relevant to the play. For many critics, as we have seen, it is the equally (or indeed more) important peripheral action that commands their attention.

These productions, it seems, may well be best understood as being, like Warr himself, thoroughly representative of the 1880s in general—a culture in transition. Warr was a radical who rubbed shoulders with the Establishment. But unlike Crane, for example, he seems to have lived by his principles in his work and personal life. The 1880s revivals are poised on the threshold of a new era that was to recognize that going back was the only sure way to go forward. And it is interesting to hear what one such pioneer waiting in the wings, the poet-playwright, W. B. Yeats has to say about one of these revivals. Although he did not see *Helena in Troas*, Yeats knew the play well and recognized the importance of the 1886 production in the development of modern drama:

[Todhunter's] sonorous verse, united in the rhythmical motions of the white robed chorus, and the solemnity of the burning incense, produced a semi-religious effect new to the stage.[81]

Without the 1880s experiments of Warr and his contemporaries—experiments indeed with all their vagaries—the next

---

[78] Carpenter (1985), 44–5.   [79] Easterling (1999), 28.
[80] Warr (1900), pp. xlii f.   [81] Yeats (1989), 36.

generation would never have taken the bold leaps into extending the range of modern drama in English that they went on to take. Yeats's dance dramas from 1914 onwards drew no less on Greek tragedy than they did on Japanese Noh drama; and his collaborator, Gordon Craig, the son of E. W. Godwin, acknowledged his parentage most significantly in his reverence for his father's understanding of classical Greece. This should be reason enough to write Warr back into theatre history, and to restore his efforts and those of his students at King's College, London, to the public memory.

17

The Shavian Euripides and the Euripidean Shaw: Greek Tragedy and the New Drama

In an essay entitled 'The Womanly Woman' published in *The Quintessence of Ibsenism* (1891), George Bernard Shaw refers to the quickly fading romantic ideal following completion of the marriage ceremony. Shaw informs us that:

The wife finds that her husband is neglecting her for his business; that his interests, his activities, his whole life except that one part of it to which only a cynic referred before her marriage, lies away from home; and that her business is to sit there and mope until she is wanted. Then what can she do? If she complains, he, the self-helper, can do without her; whilst she is dependent on him for her position, her livelihood, her place in society, her home, her very bread ... [1]

A little further on in the essay, Shaw goes on to compare the sites of endurance that await each party:

The domestic career is no more natural to all women than the military career is natural to all men; and although in a population emergency it might become necessary for every able-bodied woman to risk her life in childbed just as it might become necessary in a military emergency for every man to risk his life in a battlefield, yet even then it would by no means follow that the child-bearing would endow the mother with domestic aptitudes and capacities as it would endow her with milk. [2]

In 1891 Shaw's unnamed paradigm is, of course, Nora Helmer from Ibsen's *The Doll's House,* which had only recently received its first London production two years earlier in 1889. But the details of these passages—the wandering husband versus the encaged wife; the collocation of childbed and battlefield—bear more than a passing resemblance to Medea's famous 'Women of Corinth' speech in Euripides' tragedy. And when Shaw approaches the climax of his excursus, it is as if it is the example of Medea herself,

---

[1] Shaw (1986), 59.   [2] Ibid. 60.

the paradigmatic transgressor of duty, that is pointing the 1890s woman towards abandonment of the myth of the 'womanly woman'. Shaw writes:

> ... unless woman repudiates her womanliness, her duty to her husband, to her children, to society, to the law and to everyone but herself, she cannot emancipate herself...[3]

The links between Medea and the New Woman were regularly made from the 1890s onwards, and it was the 'discovery' of the radical 'Women of Corinth' speech that made those connections both pertinent and possible. All previous adaptations in England, which drew on either the Seneca, Grillparzer, or Legouvé models had omitted that speech; and it may well have been this serious omission that led to Augusta Webster's decision to publish her much admired translation of *Medea* in 1868 (Ch. 14).

The perceived affinities between the Medea of 'Women of Corinth' speech and the manifesto of the New Woman, however, were not always seen as positive. The writer Mary Coleridge comments on the parallels in a diary entry of 1894 with more than a tinge of disapproval:

> Medea is thoroughly fin de siècle; says she would rather go into battle three times than have a baby once, pitches into men like anything. But there's too much Whitechapel about her. How are you to be seriously interested in a woman who has murdered her father [*sic*] and boiled her father-in-law before the play begins? So different from the gentle Phaedra, and the wonderful Antigone and Helen.[4]

Opponents of the New Woman, however, were to receive their most prominent advocate in 1895, when Max Nordau in *Degeneration* provided, amongst other things, a sharp riposte to the advocates of the Ibsenite 'unwomanly woman'. Nordau explains:

> With Ibsen woman has no duties and all rights. The tie of marriage does not bind her...Woman is always the clever, strong, courageous being; man always the simpleton and coward. In every encounter the wife is victorious, and the man flattened out like a pancake...With Ibsen she has even overcome her most primitive instinct—that of motherhood—and abandons her brood without twitching an eyelid when the caprice seizes her to seek satisfactions elsewhere.[5]

---

[3] Ibid. 61.
[4] Mary E. Coleridge (1910), 235. Thanks to Isobel Hurst for this reference.
[5] Nordau (1895), 412.

Nordau's nominal defier of duty is again Nora Helmer, but as with
Shaw, he could equally well be offering his reader a commentary
on the last two encounters between the Euripidean characters of
Jason and Medea.

The links between Euripides and Ibsen were regularly commented upon at the beginning of the new century. The theatre
manager and critic J. T. Grein described Euripides in 1904 as 'the
poet Ibsen of his day'.[6] Similar views hailed from academic circles
with Lewis Campbell describing Euripides as 'Ibsenist' in a letter
to a friend early in 1906.[7] The previous year, in the preface to his
translation of Euripides *Electra* (1905), Gilbert Murray had
pointed to similarities between Euripidean and Ibsenite psych-
ology. Indeed for Murray, Euripides was an honorary contemporary: 'I almost feel he expresses my own beliefs: rational, liberal,
humane, feminist.'[8]

Moreover, with the Scandinavian Euripides receiving his most
prominent and successful champion in Britain in the person of
George Bernard Shaw, it was perhaps inevitable that Shaw himself
came to be seen as the Euripides of the English-speaking world.
Following the study by Gilbert Norwood entitled *Euripides and
Shaw* in 1921, which focused primarily on their common interest
in the drama of ideas, the perceived links between Euripides and
Shaw became commonplace. But the association was being made
much earlier: an author of a book on Euripides published in 1911
opens with these questions:

That Euripides is a 'modern' requires no proof. Does he not, with Prof.
Gilbert Murray for interpreter, find his natural place on our stage by the
side of our newest and brainiest dramatists? Is he not familiar to all Fleet
Street as the 'Greek Ibsen,' the 'Attic Shaw'? Are not his plays an inex-
haustible mine of tags for the Feminist and other workers for Great
Causes?[9]

However prevalent these observations were at the time, discussion of such interconnections today is generally confined to questions of what the moderns did to the ancients. In other words, it is
not Euripides' influence on either Shaw or Ibsen that is deemed

---

[6] *Sunday Times*, 29 May 1904, 6.
[7] Lewis Campbell (1914), 423, letter of 30 Jan. 1906.
[8] Cit. Francis West (1984), 69.
[9] Salter (1911), 9.

significant, but the ways in which Euripidean scholarship of the time was influenced by responses to the contemporary playwrights.[10] Here in this chapter, by contrast, the focus will be on the various and important ways in which Greek drama exerted a profound influence on the modern play of ideas; and we shall see how the concept of the Euripidean Shaw is not just tenable, but central to an understanding of Shaw's play of 1905, *Major Barbara*.

We have already seen the extent to which the forebears of the New Woman can be found in the mid-century burlesques of *Medea* (Ch. 14). We have also seen the ways in which a generation brought up on burlesques of Greek tragedy went on to become involved in the amateur revivals of Greek tragedies in Edinburgh, Oxford, Cambridge, and London from the 1870s onwards (Chs. 15 and 16). Shaw is, perhaps, the most interesting link with these two earlier phases of Greek tragedy's production history in Britain. As a theatre critic in late-Victorian London, he had ample opportunity to learn about the mechanics of Victorian comic forms.

Shaw's close friend and colleague at the Court Theatre was the classicist Gilbert Murray; and Murray was the major source of Shaw's ideas on Greek tragedy as Shaw himself was quick to acknowledge. Later in his life, he explained: 'Thanks mainly to Gilbert Murray, I know as much as anyone need know of the ancient Greek drama.'[11] The Shavian Euripides, as we will see in this chapter, is really Murray's Euripides. And Shaw was no doubt amused to learn that Murray owed his first name to his mother's uncle, who was the father of the formidable and witty lyricist W. S. Gilbert. Gilbert himself was widely acknowledged as the true successor to the father of the classical burlesque, J. R. Planché; and now, in a sense, the mantle is being passed on as Shaw finds out, through his close contacts with Murray, how the burlesque tradition can be developed for serious political ends. If the classical burlesque died a death around 1870 (see Ch. 13), it was now at the turn of the century being reincarnated in the Shavian play of ideas. Many years later in 1933, when Murray published his study on

---

[10] See, e.g. Lloyd-Jones (1982), 195–214, esp. 199–201 for the influence of Ibsen on Wilamowitz's scholarship.

[11] Holroyd (1988–92), iii. 400.

Aristophanes, he significantly dedicated it to Shaw: 'lover of ideas and hater of cruelty, who has filled many lands with laughter and whose courage has never failed.'[12]

MURRAY AND SHAW

It was largely on account of Granville Barker's productions of Murray's translations at the Court Theatre from 1904 onwards that the Greek example became widely known in Britain. When Frank Benson returned with his company from their tour in 1905, it was Barker's theatrical experiments with Murray's version of the *Hippolytus* that led him to seek a London venue for his own production of the *Oresteia*.[13]

The influence of Murray's translations on Shaw's oeuvre in formal terms was extensive: in his play *Getting Married*, and to some extent in Act III of *Major Barbara*, Shaw's avoidance of formal act divisions is an obvious debt to the Greek example; and in his resistance to the formal ending of the 'well-made' play in favour of plays whose dénouements very often look towards the future, Shaw clearly has the aetiological endings of numerous ancient plays in mind. But it was also the content of certain ancient plays, as they were mediated through Murray, that was to have a profound effect on Shaw's creative aesthetic.

Theatre historians may well have overlooked the influence of Greek drama on the Shavian play of ideas, but Shaw chose to make his debt to the leading expert on classical drama explicit. In the epigraph to *Major Barbara* (1905), Shaw writes:

NB The Euripidean verses in the second act of *MB* are not by me, nor even directly by Euripides. They are by Professor Gilbert Murray, whose English version of *The Bacchae* came into our dramatic literature with all the impulsive power of an original work shortly before *MB* was begun. The play, indeed, stands indebted to him in more ways than one.[14]

Shaw's deep respect for Murray's literary skills and for his translations of Greek drama, in particular, remained unchanged throughout his life despite obvious changes in public taste. Although

[12] Murray (1933), p. v.

[13] Benson's *Oresteia* was eventually staged at the suburban Coronet Theatre in March 1905. See *The Academy*, 68, no. 1714 (11 Mar. 1905), 242–3.

[14] Shaw (1960).

T. S. Eliot's damning criticism of Murray's translations in his essay 'Euripides and Mr Murray' has now become orthodoxy, on its first appearance in *Arts and Letters* in 1920,[15] Eliot's essay did little damage to Murray's reputation as a fine translator for his age. But twenty years later, when Murray's translations had been falling from fashion for at least a decade, and his values no longer seemed to suit the times, Shaw made the extraordinary claim that the translations were the only works from the turn-of-the-century flowering of theatre in English that were likely to survive.[16]

Shaw's debt to Murray at this point in his career, at least, cannot be overstated; and in many ways, Murray's role is analogous to the one played by Nietzsche to Wagner some years earlier. It may well be by no means fortuitous to invoke the Nietzsche–Wagner relationship in this context, particularly since Shaw himself was both fascinated by and indebted to them both in his own career. In 1898 when he was working on *The Perfect Wagnerite* (1898), an interpretation of Wagner's *Ring* cycle, he was living down the road from Murray in Surrey; and in 1903 Shaw spoke of Schopenhauer and Nietzsche as being 'among the writers whose peculiar sense of the world I recognise as more or less akin to my own'.[17]

It is important to stress that Shaw never assumed towards Murray anything like the kind of lofty, rather patronizing role of the (elder) Wagner towards the (young) Nietzsche;[18] on the contrary, their personal relationship was one of mutual respect and remained so throughout their lives.[19] Instead, it is the intellectual stimulus and authority that Murray was able to offer Shaw that resembles Nietzsche's influence on Wagner. In both cases classical scholars were able to provide theatre practitioners with ideas that were already starting to coalesce in the dramatists' own minds. The Murray–Shaw relationship may not be as famous (nor indeed as infamous) as the German counterpart, but it was definitely more enduring and more profitable in the long term. Without Shaw, Murray would not have gained the kind of access to and 'inside'

---

[15] T. S. Eliot (1950), 46–50.

[16] Francis West (1984), 100.

[17] Holroyd (1988–92), ii. 3–4; and for the quotation, see Shaw Papers, British Museum, 1931–2.

[18] For a full discussion of the Nietzsche–Wagner relationship, see Silk and Stern (1981).

[19] See Holroyd (1988–92), index, s.v. Murray, Gilbert.

knowledge of the professional theatre that he needed; and more importantly perhaps, without Murray, Shaw would not have been as adventurous, nor have offered such serious intellectual challenges, at this stage in his career.

Productions and readings of particular Greek plays can be seen to have had, in retrospect, inordinate influence on the subsequent history of ideas. The most notable example is Freud's attendance at the famous Comédie-Française production of *Oedipus Rex* in the 1880s, with Jean Mounet-Sully in the title role, which can now be seen to have been responsible for shaping twentieth-century definitions of self (see Ch. 18). And although nothing can quite match that event, there are at least two occasions when readings of Gilbert Murray's translations of Euripides' plays can also be seen, in retrospect, to have had wide-ranging consequences in the twentieth century. The first is the impact that Murray's reading of his translation of the *Hippolytus* at Newnham College, Cambridge, in February 1901 had on Bertrand Russell's philosophical system.[20] The second is Murray's reading of a selection of his translations later that year at a Fabian Society meeting, when Shaw was so overwhelmed that he urged Murray to seek immediate publication.[21]

In 1902 Murray's translations of the *Hippolytus*, *Bacchae*, and *Frogs* were published as the third volume in the pioneering series edited by George Warr (see Ch. 16), which combined translation with an introduction and commentary. Murray's experience in preparing lectures for his students during his time as Professor of Greek at Glasgow from 1889 had led him to share with both Campbell and Warr a concern for the need of the wide availability of good translations (see Chs. 15 and 16). Following his retirement on the grounds of ill-health from the Chair of Greek at Glasgow in 1899, Murray was to spend the next five years making Euripides' plays available to a range of different audiences: to scholars (through his Oxford Classical Text edition of the plays);[22] to readers without Greek (through his published translations); and eventually, through the productions of his translations on the professional stage, to a wide theatre-going public throughout Britain and the English-speaking world. Just as Shaw the dramatist was being introduced to new audiences at the Court Theatre

---

[20] Monk (1996), 135–8.   [21] Francis West (1984), 72.
[22] See Easterling (1997).

through Barker's productions of his plays, so Barker with Murray's mediation was introducing the same people to Euripides at the special matinée performances. And if the London venue was in Sloane Square, the rural retreat around Churt, Hindhead, and Haslemere in Surrey—where Murray, Shaw, and Barker all had houses for a time—made that extraordinary interchange of ideas and energy not just possible but intensely fruitful.

MURRAY'S *HIPPOLYTUS*

Two years after the publication of Murray's first collection of translations, the *Hippolytus* was staged by Barker in May 1904 at the Lyric Theatre. Barker, who had written and produced several plays based on New Women, was keen to mount the ancient myth of Phaedra, the would-be adulterous/incestuous step-mother. Barker himself had worked closely with the theatre producer William Poel; and most of his actors had either worked with Poel, or (like Poel) trained with Benson's company. Here at the Lyric Theatre, the production was generally received with 'polite encouragement',[23] although Max Beerbohm, a great admirer of the Bradfield Greek play and also a notorious anti-feminist, not surprisingly objected to the fact that the indoor space and proscenium arch at the Lyric reduced the play to a 'modern story'. For Beerbohm, the attraction of Euripides and his contemporaries was not their contemporary resonances; instead it was (despite Murray's 'excellent' translation) their very distance from the real (both linguistic and thematic) that gave them value for modern audiences.[24]

For most commentators, however, it was felt that Barker's production had marked a watershed in British theatre. For the none too disinterested critic William Archer (his company, the New Century Theatre, had co-sponsored the production with the Stage Society), *Hippolytus* in Murray's translation had restored 'beauty and deep poetic feeling' to the theatre.[25] And the diplomat and poet Wilfrid Scawen Blunt recorded in his diary: 'At the end of [the production] we were all moved to tears, and I got up and did what I never did before in a theatre, shouted for the author,

---

[23] Kennedy (1985), 23.   [24] *Saturday Review*, 4 June 1904, 716.
[25] Holroyd (1988–92), ii. ii. 96.

whether for Euripides or Gilbert Murray I hardly knew.'[26] Both Arthur Bourchier at the Garrick Theatre and the producer William Poel were keen to stage the play. But whilst *Hippolytus* was in production at the Lyric, Sophocles' *Electra* was being performed by Greek actors with moderate success at the Court Theatre; and Barker, who had earned plaudits not simply for his role in the direction of the *Hippolytus*, but also for his appearance as the messenger, learnt that the leaseholder of the Court Theatre had expressed a desire to produce Greek plays on a regular basis.[27]

This fortuitous timing led to the start of the extraordinary flowering of productions of Euripides and the New Drama in the first public theatre to stage 'serious' plays, when Barker began his partnership with the business manager Paul Vedrenne at the Court Theatre in October 1904. Both Shaw and Murray were staunch supporters of the theatre, together with a motley collection of Fabians, feminists, and avant-garde theatre practitioners. Their support did not just take the form of supplying plays for performance: they were also on occasions ready to offer considerable financial support to this daring enterprise.[28]

The revival of the *Hippolyus* at the Court Theatre opened on 18 October; and if Beerbohm had bemoaned the confines of the modern theatre space at the Lyric, now on an even smaller stage, the original chorus of eight women was increased to twelve plus the leader, Florence Farr, who accompanied with the strains of her psalteries. Even though Farr's chanting had particularly impressed W. B. Yeats, both Barker and Murray grew to dislike what they felt was her precious 'art for art's sake' approach.[29] But whatever the shortcomings of certain aspects of the production, the *Hippolytus* was generally considered to be a success; and when it was revived in March 1906, it was advertised in the popular pictorial weekly, the *Bystander* with the disclaimer: 'You will like it without any necessity of posing as an earnest student of the drama.'[30] Greek tragedy, thanks to the combined efforts of Murray and Barker, was no longer the exclusive preserve of the private theatres in the English-speaking world; and Euripides, in particular, was now truly 'popular'.

---

[26] Holroyd (1988–92), ii. ii. 97.   [27] Ibid. 97.   [28] Kennedy (1985), 24.
[29] For an account of the problems experienced by Barker and Murray with the chorus in general, see ibid. 42–4.
[30] *The Bystander*, 11 Apr. 1906, 72.

MURRAY'S *BACCHAE*

What impressed Shaw, in particular, about Murray's 1902 collection of ancient plays was his translation and commentary upon the *Bacchae*, and the extent to which the play (in Murray's reading) explored religious experiences and questions of moral identity in terms remarkably similar to Shaw's own. Through Shaw's acquaintance with Murray's *Bacchae*, he discovered how classical scholarship could illuminate twentieth-century political concerns. Like Shaw, Murray had been led to believe by his Irish ancestry that religion could never be considered independent of politics.[31]

In the Introductory Essay to the 1902 volume, Murray concluded that the main message of Euripides' *Bacchae* was that:

The kingdom of Heaven is within you—here and now. You have but to accept it and live with it—not obscure it by striving and hating and looking in the wrong place.[32]

The play, according to Murray, was offering a simple, liberating message that the godhead is within you. Murray, it should be recalled, was writing against the nineteenth-century view of Dionysus as a kind of proto-Christ with Euripides, the lifelong atheist, now recanting at the end of his life. But Murray was also writing in contradistinction to contemporary readings of the play (by Wilamowitz, Verrall, and Norwood) that hailed Pentheus as the embodiment of reason duped by the mountebank Dionysus.

In Murray's Introductory Essay, we find an interesting collocation of Dionysus, the pagan ('the God of all high emotion, inspiration, intoxication'[33]), with Dionysus, the proto-Christ ('He has given man Wine, which is his Blood and a religious symbol'[34]). Although it is clearly Murray's own teetotalism that prevents him from resisting the nineteenth-century Christianizing tendencies of his subject entirely, much of what Murray has to say about Dionysus is new and very close to the discussions of the Cambridge Ritualists and Jane Harrison's work in particular.[35] Whilst the

---

[31] See Jean Smith and Toynbee (1960), 25–6 for Murray's account of his Irish ancestry.

[32] Murray (1902), p. lxvi.

[33] Ibid., p. lix. Cf. Easterling (1997). We are indebted to Professor Easterling's close reading of the passage in the next couple of sentences.

[34] Murray, loc. cit.

[35] Easterling (1997).

content is clearly in line with developments close to home, the terminology on occasions shows a surprising similarity to discussion much further afield. When Murray states that '...he [Dionysus] gave to the Purified a mystic Joy, surpassing in intensity that of man, the joy of a god or a free wild animal',[36] it is the Nietzschean echo that resounds through his words. In marked contrast to his debt to Jane Harrison whom he gratefully acknowledges in the Preface ('On points of ancient religion I have had the great advantage of frequent consultation with Miss J. E. Harrison'[37]), any debt to Nietzsche would have to go unacknowledged. For not only would it have involved a severe break with the classical establishment as a whole, it would also have precipitated a breach with his much-respected and highly valued colleague, Wilamowitz, whose authorship of the first devastating review of *The Birth of Tragedy* had guaranteed Nietzsche's ostracism.[38]

It was not until 1908 that Murray's *Bacchae* received its premiere at the Court Theatre, when it was staged not by Barker, but by his former mentor William Poel. Barker was away in Ireland at the time, and his wife Lillah McCarthy (who was prevented by Vedrenne from starring in her husband's productions) took the opportunity to ask Poel to stage the *Bacchae* with herself as Dionysus. Poel had admired Murray's *Hippolytus*, but found his translations generally and his *Bacchae* in particular, distinctly non-dramatic.[39] He agreed to the project only on the condition that Murray allow him to take certain liberties with his translation. Although Murray had gallantly agreed, when he eventually saw what Poel had done not just to his translation, but above all to the text of Euripides, he refused to allow the production to run beyond the first two matinées. It was not simply the highly static nature of the production (the seated chorus of Maenads moved only once throughout the entire two hours!) that concerned Murray; it was primarily because Poel's Verrallesque reading of the play had removed all the mysticism surrounding Dionysus (what Poel felt were the Euripidean 'digressions'), and had reduced the play to a 'rational' satire *tout court*.[40]

---

[36] Murray (1902), pp. lix f.   [37] Ibid., p. vii.
[38] Silk and Stern (1981), 95–109.   [39] Speaight (1954), 168.
[40] Ibid. 173. It is important to stress that although Murray's scholarship differed in many ways from Verrall's own, they were in fact close friends, having met originally in Switzerland in 1894, one year before Verrall's highly influential and deeply controversial study entitled *Euripides the Rationalist* (1895).

That Murray's *Bacchae* had to wait until 1908 for its first production was, perhaps, not surprising since Shaw's *Major Barbara*
of 1905 (which was the first play expressly written for production
at the Court Theatre) was in many ways a reworking of his version
in its first two acts. And with its clear allusions to Aristophanes'
Frogs in its third act, *Major Barbara* can be considered a tribute to
that 1902 volume of Murray's translations, which had so enthralled Shaw in 1901.

THE SHAVIAN EURIPIDES

The understated Nietzschean echoes in Murray's reading of the
Bacchae would have been both obvious and exciting to Shaw; and
Murray's liberating interpretation of the play struck a particularly
strong chord in Shaw for whom the only solution to society's ills
was to rely on strident action—the Shavian socialist must be a
realist and grapple with reality, rather than resort to idealized
visions of that reality. That Murray had translated a play about
religion, if not any conventional 'religious' play, was of especial
interest to Shaw. In his conclusion to the 'Preface to *Major Barbara*', he writes:

At present there is not a single credible established religion in the world.
That is perhaps the most stupendous fact in the whole world.[41]

Like the *Bacchae*, Shaw's play explores one recent 'alternative'
to the established religions; and like the *Bacchae*, which Murray
had shown to be no mere denunciation of the Dionysiac religion,[42]
Shaw's treatment of the Salvation Army is not without sympathy
and respect. Shaw was not the first to recognize the links between
the Army of Christ founded by William Booth in 1878 and the
Dionysiac cult of ancient Greece. In 1894, Mary Coleridge had
observed:

There is much more real religion in the *Bacchae* of Euripides [than, for
example, in the *Life of Dr Pusey*], which is simply glorious—a sort of Greek
Salvation of Army business, all drums and cymbals and ecstasy . . . There's
no real tipsiness as far as I can make out. The Hallelujah lasses get
drunk on the wine of the spirit, not the wine of the grape.[43]

[41] Shaw (1960), 49.   [42] Murray (1902), pp. liv ff.
[43] Coleridge (1910), 233.

That Shaw was not alone in making these connections makes his own case in the preface that much more topical and convincing; but unlike Coleridge, Shaw is not just interested in the 'ecstatic' affinities. For him, it is the political parallels that matter. Although at the end of his play, the Army of Christ is shown ultimately to be no different from the established religions Shaw so vehemently rejected, he is at pains to stress its apparent links with the ancient cult of Dionysus.

In its populist appeal, and even in its militant fight against poverty, the Salvation Army resembles the tyrants' religion that came to unsettle the orthodoxy of the oligarchs in the archaic Greek world. The tambourines, trumpets, and drums carried by the soldiers of Christ as they process through the East End of London are clearly seen by Shaw to be akin to the trappings of the dancing Maenads of ancient Greece (see Fig. 17.1). Cusins, the collector of religions, explains to Undershaft in Act II:

It is the army of joy, of love, of courage ... It picks the waster out of the public house and makes a man of him: it finds a worm wriggling in a back kitchen, and lo! a woman! Men and women of rank too, sons and daughters of the Highest. It takes the poor professor of Greek, the most artificial and self-suppressed of human creatures, from his meal of roots, and lets loose the rhapsodist in him; reveals the true worship of Dionysos to him; sends him down the public street drumming dithyrambs.[44]

Like the Dionysiac faith, the gospel of the Army is in some senses the great leveller, a truly democratic religion. But although Shaw himself was genuinely moved by the Army's bands and singing,[45] he is at pains to emphasize its political shortcomings. As with the mystery cults at the end of the fifth century BC, the army's gospel merely provides an escape from the evils of reality, blunting the insurrectionary tendencies amongst the masses with the promise, not of a heaven on earth, but bliss in eternity. What had attracted Shaw to the Dionysiac—the message that 'The kingdom of Heaven is within you'[46]—is not ultimately to be found through the Salvation Army. As Shaw says in the 'Preface' of 1906, the Army will very soon lose its radical edge and join the ranks of other established churches.[47]

---

[44] Shaw (1960), 93–4.   [45] Cf. ibid. 29 and Holroyd (1988–92), ii. 108.
[46] Murray (1902), p. lxvi.   [47] Shaw (1960), 30.

4 [SUPPLEMENT.] **THE SKETCH.** DEC. 13, 1905

THE SALVATION ARMY ON THE STAGE :
"MAJOR BARBARA," AT THE COURT.

1. MR. OSWALD YORKE AS BILL WALKER. 2. MR. GRANVILLE BARKER AS ADOLPHUS CUSINS.
3. MISS WYNNE MATTHISON AS MRS. BAINES. 4. MISS ANNIE RUSSELL AS BARBARA UNDERSHAFT. 5. MISS DOROTHY MINTO AS JENNY HILL.
6. MR. LOUIS CALVERT AS ANDREW UNDERSHAFT. 7. MR. DAWSON MILWARD AS CHARLES LOMAX.

Photographs by E. H. Mills.

FIGURE 17.1 'The Salvation Army on the Stage' in Shaw's *Major Barbara* (1905).

For the true modern counterpart to Dionysus—Murray's cold, savage, and inhuman god[48]—Shaw found the brazen capitalist, arms manufacturer, Andrew Undershaft. Like Dionysus, Undershaft—the underminer, the mineshaft[49]—defies normal categories and boundaries. The destructive/creative entrepreneur had numerous real-life models, the two most notable being Alfred Nobel, the patentee of dynamite in 1867, who subsequently endowed the Peace Prize in 1901, and Friedrich Alfred Krupp, the Prussian cannon-king, whose paternalistic welfare system for workers in Essen was admired world-wide, but who some thirty years on was to be a prominent Nazi sympathizer. The Greek god, Dionysus, embodied Shaw's concept of the Life-force: energy without morality; a potential for both good or evil, depending on what its recipient decides to do with it. We create, as Pentheus does to some extent, either a god or a devil in accordance with how we use the divine energy, or the Life-force. And Undershaft's chilling amorality makes him the modern embodiment of that energy.

Like the *Bacchae*, *Major Barbara* is in this sense a play about the contrasts and contradictions inherent in certain religious experiences. Throughout the 'Preface', Shaw highlights the confusions that result from these contradictions: the Salvation Army officer and the theatre-goer are really kindred spirits yet both fail to recognize each other, one denouncing the other as a reveller, the other as a killjoy.[50] And although Shaw does not spell out the Dionysiac connection, it is as celebrants of the Greek god that they are, in fact, one: they each worship Dionysus, yet in each case they worship him in one of his different guises. And for Shaw, for whom means are often starkly at odds with ends (for example he maintained that socialism could be secured through arch individualism; liberation, very often as here, through mass destruction), the Dionysiac experience became a kind of metaphysical equivalent of the Shavian dialectic.

If this is Euripides speaking through Murray to the urgent needs of the modern world, Murray's contribution (as we have seen in

---

[48] Murray (1902), pp. liv–lvi.

[49] The Greek verb κατασκάπτω—noun κατασκαφή—meaning 'to undermine' may well lie behind 'Undershaft', especially since it is often translated as 'to raze'. Although it is not used in *Bacchae*, it is regularly used to describe the effects of an earthquake.

[50] Shaw (1960), 24.

the epigraph to the play) is fully acknowledged by Shaw. The biographical parallels between Murray and Cusins in the play are regularly noted; but the Euripidean/Shavian play is Murray's creation in other ways too. For Murray did not simply provide Shaw with intellectual stimulus for *Major Barbara*; he also provided him with help during the composition itself.[51] Act III proved particularly taxing for Shaw, and although he completed the first two acts with relative ease, the last act was subject to numerous rewrites before the play was produced in November 1905.

After Shaw had completed a first full draft of Act III, he visited Murray's house in Oxford in October to seek his approval. The Murrays and Granville Barker (who was also present) expressed their disappointment at what they felt was the outright victory of the Undershaft principles. Murray offered Shaw more dialogue to strengthen Cusins's case; and although none of Murray's dialogue appears to have been incorporated into the final version, his suggestion that Undershaft should become more of a representative of cosmic forces than a free agent is clearly heeded:[52] Undershaft in *Major Barbara* is more god than man in the last act, less a debater, and more of an impersonal presence. He has become, under Murray's direction, what Shaw himself had told the actor, Louis Calvert, earlier that year that Undershaft should be, 'diabolical, subtle and gentle, self-possessed, powerful and stupendous.'[53]

The ostensible reason for Shaw's visit to the Murrays' house for a reading of the play was to avoid offence to the family.[54] According to one of Murray's biographers,[55] Shaw failed to prevent offending the women in Murray's family, who did not take kindly to having aspects of their personal lives caricatured on the stage. There are, however, as with Undershaft, numerous models for the Shavian characters; and it is, perhaps, pertinent to invoke Shaw's comments in this regard:

One never really makes portraits of people in fiction. What happens is that certain people inspire one to invent fictitious characters for them, which is quite another matter.[56]

[51] See Albert (1968), 123–40; and Dukore (1981), pp. xv–xix.
[52] Duncan Wilson (1987), 110. [53] Holroyd (1988–92), ii. 106.
[54] Ibid. 108. [55] Francis West (1984), 104.
[56] Holroyd (1988–92), ii. 104.

Lady Britomart, with her libertarian Whig principles and personal despotism, is clearly 'inspired' by Murray's formidable mother-in-law, the Countess of Carlisle;[57] and the real-life separation of the Earl and Countess of Carlisle undoubtedly lies behind the Britomart–Undershaft relationship. Moreover, Shaw is said to have jokingly told Murray that he had considered calling his play *Murray's Mother-in-Law*.[58] In the case of Barbara there are numerous possible sources: Beatrice Webb appears the most likely candidate, the rich man's daughter whose conscience took her to experience life at the hard edge in the East End of London,[59] but some critics have found both the actress Eleanor Robson and Murray's own wife, Lady Mary, in the character.[60] In the case of Cusins, Murray himself was the primary inspiration (although elements of the actor Granville Barker and King Gustavus Adolphus of Sweden are evident too).[61] When Cusins recalls his gift of a gun to a former pupil who went to fight for the Greeks against the Turks, Shaw is drawing on a real-life incident when Murray gave a revolver to his pupil H. N. Brailsford in 1897 for the same reason.[62] Murray was clearly flattered rather than offended by his portrait; and the inclusion of the comment from Stephen when the play was in rehearsal, 'Cusins is a very nice fellow, certainly: nobody would ever guess that he was born in Australia',[63] is surely confirmation of the fact that the connections with Murray were to be both deliberate and obvious. That the name Cusins suggests the relative 'cousin' as well is perhaps a reminder that Adolphus' position in the play is related to the playwright's own.[64] Like Cusins, Shaw is faced with the problem of how the intellectual can engage effectively with the world.

If Cusins represents Shaw's ideal position, it is, perhaps, important to stress that Undershaft, in the opinion of a number of commentators, represents rather too many aspects of the Shavian position in practice.[65] And it is this somewhat unholy alliance that has led to problems of interpretation from the start. Like Milton before him, and many others since, Shaw takes the devil's party, the line goes, with rather too much readiness and zeal. Beatrice

---

[57] Grene (1984), 85.   [58] Francis West (1984), 100; Holroyd (1998), 107.
[59] Holroyd (1988–92), i. 263, ii. 101.   [60] e.g. Francis West (1984), 104.
[61] Holroyd (1988–92), ii. 107–8.   [62] Duncan Wilson (1987), 110.
[63] Dukore (1981), xviii.   [64] Holroyd (1988–92), ii. 108.
[65] See esp. Grene (1984), 84–100.

Webb found the ending a chilling example of 'the triumph of the unmoral';[66] and according to another commentator, Shaw's evident admiration for Undershaft leads to a dilution of the Cusins case and a profound imbalance in Act III.[67] A detailed survey of the play with reference to its source, however, together with some reference to Murray's biography, will show that these problems are far from insurmountable.

EURIPIDES VS. DIONYSUS: *MAJOR BARBARA* AND THE 1902 VOLUME

That Shaw may have intended his play to have been a version of the *Bacchae*, and not simply a play inspired by Euripides' tragedy, seems clear from early drafts.[68] Cusins at first was conceived as a twin to Cholly Lomax with the name of Dolly Tankerville (a would-be Pentheus perhaps); and although Tankerville disappeared from the plan once Shaw began writing, Pentheus' role is there, at least in embryonic form, in the person of Stephen when he refuses to join the participants of the Army ritual at the end of Act I and remains alone in the library. Like Murray in the 1902 Introductory Essay,[69] Shaw would have found Pentheus' position untenable; and in accordance with Shavian dialectics, it was much more important to find a serious contender to meet the Dionysiac force. If Cusins is no Pentheus, which Greek character is he based upon? From Act III onwards he is referred to as Euripides by Undershaft. What Shaw is offering us at the end of his play, it would seem, is his own version of another play in the 1902 volume, Aristophanes' *Frogs*. And with the *Bacchae* lying behind its first two acts, and the *Frogs* behind its third, *Major Barbara* becomes a tribute to the 1902 volume.

The echoes of the *Bacchae* in Act I are thematic and straightforward; with Act II the debt is explicit and rather more intriguing. In this act there are a series of encounters which resemble the scenes between Pentheus and Dionysus in Euripides' play. The

---

[66] Cited by Holroyd (1988–92), ii. 101.

[67] Grene (1984), 95–100.

[68] Cf. Thorndike (with Casson) (1960), 157: 'It does seem possible that Shaw planned *Major Barbara* as a Euripidean drama...'.

[69] Murray (1902), pp. lvi f.

first is Barbara's near spell-binding effect on Bill Walker which is only prevented by the interruption of Cusins's drum roll.[70] This episode is clearly designed to confirm her Undershaft inheritance: Barbara's spiritual powers are as considerable as her father's, just as earlier, her organizational skills had proved as effective as those of her mother. The spell-binding scene proper[71] is divided into two parts: in the first part Undershaft has the first and last word as he confidently expounds his religion to the would-be anthropologist, Cusins, and ends on a resounding 'yes', whose cadence, as Shaw notes, 'makes a full close in the conversation'.[72] But the Undershaft position of superiority finally gives way to one of equality when he recognizes an affinity with Cusins at the end of round two:

Cusins. The business of the Salvation Army is to save, not to wrangle about the name of the pathfinder. Dionysos or another what does it matter.
Undershaft [*rising and approaching him*] Professor Cusins: you are a man after my own heart.
Cusins. Mr Undershaft: you are, as far as I am able to gather, a most infernal old rascal; but you appeal very strongly to my sense of ironic humour.
Undershaft mutely offers his hand. They shake.[73]

Just as Dionysus at line 811 in Euripides' *Bacchae* sees a weakness (which is really an affinity) in Pentheus at an analogous point in the play, when Pentheus expresses his desire to spy on the Maenads, so too the affinity perceived by Undershaft here might well be construed as a kind of moral flaw in Cusins as he confesses for the first time to endorsing any means for noble ends ('... Dionysos or another what does it matter'[74]). Cusins remains horrified by his pact with the devil (Mephistopheles, Machiavelli, he calls him following the almost ritual handshake here), but Undershaft's power over Cusins seems absolute: 'Dionysos Undershaft has descended. I am possessed', he tells the appalled Barbara at the end of the act.[75]

In Act III the new relationship of equals between Undershaft and Cusins is confirmed by Cusins's new title, Euripides. Like the first part of the *Frogs*, the first part of the act constitutes the preparation for the descent to Hades—Perivale St Andrews is

---

[70] Shaw (1960), 91.   [71] Ibid. 75–98.   [72] Ibid. 57.   [73] Ibid. 95.
[74] Ibid.   [75] Ibid. 109–10.

envisaged as a kind of hell on earth. During the *agōn* in Act III
Cusins now resembles the robust and confident Euripides of Aristophanes' play as he skilfully bargains for his salary and conditions
of employment with Undershaft.[76] When he claims that Undershaft is powerless after all being run by the cannon-works rather
than running it himself ('I have more power than you, more will.
You do not drive this place: it drives you...'[77]), this discovery
reduces the Shavian Dionysus to the level of his Aristophanic
counterpart. From now on there is no serious debate between
Euripides and Dionysus ('...Bah! you tire me, Euripides, with
your morality mongering', he adds after some vain attempt to
regain his position of ascendancy[78]). Having tired of reason, all
that is left to Undershaft are his piercing eyes and heady rhetoric
with which he tries to hypnotize Barbara.[79]

In this Shavian rewrite of the *Frogs*, Euripides has won the
argument. And when Cusins and Barbara are left alone together
towards the end of the play we see the extent of their victory:
Cusins's strength is revealed in his realization that 'all power is
spiritual', and that power for good necessarily entails the power for
evil as well;[80] and Barbara espouses the essence of the Dionysiac
message when she proclaims that 'There is no wicked side: life is all
one.'[81] Their way of life, Barbara declares, is 'through the raising
of hell to heaven and of man to God, through the unveiling of an
eternal light in the Valley of The Shadow'.[82] Perivale St Andrews,
the hell on earth, will become through their guidance a heaven on
earth: death will not be an end in itself, but a way towards a new,
better way of life. The message that Murray found in the *Bacchae*,
that 'The kingdom of Heaven is within you', will be revealed
through the tutelage of Cusins and Barbara. If Perivale St
Andrews and its inhabitants are to undergo a rebirth of the kind
that Murray and his fellow Cambridge Ritualists found in the
Dionysiac religion, Cusins's rebirth as the new Undershaft represents the victory of the new year-daemon over his predecessor.

That Cusins and Barbara will successfully rise to the challenge
set by Undershaft to make war on war by taking over the cannon-
works, and that they will run it according to their own principles,
seems certain. Undershaft might think he still sets the agenda

---

[76] Ibid. 137–9.   [77] Ibid. 139.   [78] Ibid.   [79] Ibid. 140.
[80] Ibid. 150.   [81] Ibid. 151.   [82] Ibid. 152.

when he has the last word and orders Euripides to start work at six the following morning, but the silence of Cusins is surely one of hopeful dissent rather than silent submission.[83] Undershaft, like Dionysus, may well remain powerful and diabolical in human terms until the end of the play, but the combined strengths of Cusins and Barbara (Mind and Spirit respectively) have guaranteed that the wildness of Dionysus has now been held in check as it was through institutions and rituals during the fifth century BC in Athens.

MAKING WAR ON WAR: *TROJAN WOMEN*

Murray's subsequent career in the League of Nations Society (from 1915), the League of Nations Union (from 1918) and then the League of Nations itself (from 1920) showed just how successful he was in making war on war. But Shaw's stage direction at the start of *Major Barbara* describing Cusins as 'a most implacable, determined, tenacious, intolerant person'[84] on his first appearance was not unrelated to Murray's public conduct at the very beginning of the century.

In response to his increasing revulsion against the events of the Boer War, Murray had published an essay in *The International Journal of Ethics* in 1901, arguing that the interaction between states on an international level is subject to none of the moral restraints that apply within an individual community. Powerful nations, he maintained, inevitably sink into subhuman, barbaric treatment of their enemies and rivals.[85] His opposition to the war, founded in moral conviction that the Boers had justice on their side, led him to sponsor the South African Conciliation Committee (which recognized that European imperialism in Africa was the root cause of the crisis) and to give the then significant donation of £100 to the Boer Women and Children's Hardship Fund.[86]

It can be no coincidence that only the second Euripidean play staged by Barker, in Murray's translation, was *The Trojan Women*.

---

[83] Shaw (1960), 153.   [84] Ibid. 62.

[85] Murray (1901), where it is described as an 'expression of the feelings of the Liberal minority during the Boer War'.

[86] Duncan Wilson (1987), 73–4. It is important to stress that Murray's opposition to the war was on ethical-liberal humanitarian grounds and not, as was the case with socialists such as Walter Crane, fuelled by revolutionary anti-imperialism. See Kaarsholm (1989).

After testing the response to the play by reciting extracts from the translation to the Socratic Society of Birmingham in November 1904, Murray was delighted when the play was given eight matinée performances at the Royal Court in April of the following year. The production, however, was not as successful as the 1904 *Hippolytus*. Murray said that it was too harrowing, and one critic found the play 'too monotonously painful, and in the scenes of the child, positively heartbreaking.'[87] But Max Beerbohm criticized it, rather, for being far too 'penitential'.[88] Indeed, the stance of the play, implicitly sympathetic to the Boers, must have been troublesome. Murray's old Oxford friend Leonard Hobhouse, a committed Liberal thinker, could not even bear to watch it. On 5 May, a week after the last performance of *Trojan Women*, Hobhouse wrote to Murray explaining why. The reason was simple: the production was too chillingly reminiscent of the suffering of the Boers at British hands. This particular play 'revived troubles that lie too near'.[89]

Leonard Hobhouse's politics were shared by his sister Emily, to whom he was very close. It had been Emily Hobhouse who had made history by her exposure of the scandal of the South African concentration camps. In late 1900, her attention had been drawn to the plight of the Boer women and children, dying in great numbers of disease and starvation in the camps, which the British had built to house them after destroying their houses and property by Lord Kitchener's famous 'scorched earth' policy. It was her tour of the camps south of Bloemfontein in 1901 that alerted other British liberals to the near-genocidal level of suffering. When she returned, she went to see the leader of the opposition, Henry Campbell-Bannerman, and poured out to him for two hours 'the detailed horrors of those camps, the desperate condition of a burnt-out population... the people deprived of clothes, bedding, necessities, the semi-starvation in the camps, the fever-stricken children lying upon the bare earth... the appalling mortality.' Campbell-Bannerman was outraged, and continually muttered while she spoke, 'methods of barbarism, methods of barbarism'. On 14 June, he delivered one of the most famous political speeches of the twentieth century, which instantly became known as his

---

[87] *TLS* 14 Apr. 1905, 21. [88] *The Saturday Review*, 22 Apr. 1905, 520–1.
[89] Letter cited in Duncan Wilson (1987), 106 with n. 15.

'Methods of Barbarism' speech after the famous words he used to denounce the governmental policy of interning Boer women and children, resulting in a death-rate of nearly half the internees: 'When is a war not a war? When it is carried out by methods of barbarism in South Africa.'[90]

Of all Greek tragedies only *Trojan Women* and *Hecuba* present their audience with women and children deported to prisoner-of-war camps while their homes burn. Only *Trojan Women* features the corpse of a tiny child in such a camp. And from all the ancient literature, only *Trojan Women* contains the line which could have inspired Campbell-Bannerman's famous phrase, when Andromache, the mother of that tiny child, bitterly denounces the 'Greek inventors of methods of barbarism' (*Tro.* 764). This paradoxical apostrophe was famous already in antiquity, and had been much quoted ever since.

Whether or not Campbell-Bannerman was consciously reminding his political audience of Euripides' play, that speech must have reminded Murray of *Trojan Women*. His version and its 1905 production were certainly seen by the Edwardians as exemplifying his bold 'pro-Boer' political stance.[91] That the Boer War was a major impetus behind the Court Theatre *Trojan Women* is also suggested by the absence of any previous performance history for this tragedy. Since the Renaissance always in *Hecuba*'s shadow, *Trojan Women* had been singled out for particular derision by A. W. Schlegel. When Berlioz wanted to write an opera about the fall of Troy, he chose not Euripides but the *Aeneid* as his source. It took the Boer War, and Gilbert Murray's idiosyncratic reading of Euripides, to make the *Trojan Women* socially resonant.

The 1905 *Trojan Women* also had a major impact on discussion of Euripides in the academy. Perhaps the single most important book about Euripides ever written, Murray's *Euripides and his Age*, first published in 1913, contained interpretations of the plays resulting from his experiences of translating them and seeing them staged in Edwardian London. He interprets *Trojan Women* as a protest play in which Euripides denounced the imperialist policies and cruelty of his fellow Athenians towards the popula-

---

[90] For the quotations from Emily Hobhouse and Campbell-Bannerman, see the chapter 'Methods of Barbarism' in John Wilson (1973), 342–56.
[91] Salter (1911), 9.

tions of Greek communities who had rebelled against the Athenian empire, especially the islanders of Melos in 416 BC.[92] This pathbreaking interpretation was born out of Murray's own equation of the Athenian and British empires, and of Troy with the Transvaal: he might just as well have been speaking of the Unionist government as the ancient Athenians when, in the 'Introductory Note' to the published translation, he described the state as 'now entirely in the hands of the War Party', and 'engaged in an enterprise which, though on military grounds defensible, was bitterly resented by the more humane minority'.[93] This specific act of identification went on to inform not only the many pacifist and anti-imperialist performances which took place during the twentieth century, but every single scholarly discussion of the play. Academics must always either agree with Murray or argue against his view. The 1905 *Trojan Women*, if not particularly successful as theatre, thus provides an outstanding example of the necessity of excavating performance history in order to illuminate not only intellectual history, but scholarly controversies within the Classical academy.

SUFFRAGETTE *MEDEA*

The discovery of the New Woman, as we have seen, was coincident with the discovery of Euripides' *Medea* and in particular Medea's 'Women of Corinth' speech. The Barker production of Murray's translation of *Medea*, which opened on 22 October 1907, was the fourth of his pathbreaking productions of Euripides' tragedies and it followed the *Electra* which opened on 16 January 1906. The *Medea*, staged at the Savoy Theatre, was deliberately performed against the upsurge of public interest in the movement for women's suffrage.

In 1907 Gilbert Murray was a Fellow of New College, Oxford, before his appointment to the Regius Chair of Greek in 1908. Although he was later to distance himself from the militant wing of the women's suffrage movement, he had supported its aim since 1889. He believed that the ancient Greeks were 'the first nation

---

[92] Murray (1913), 126–36.
[93] Murray (1905), 6. 'Unionist' was the name of the combined Conservative and Liberal Unionist party.

that realized and protested against the subjection of women',[94] and the actress Sybil Thorndike recalled him saying that *Medea* 'might have been written' for the women's movement.[95] Barker's enthusiasm for *Medea* is even less surprising, since he had both written and staged controversial plays offering radical social commentary, especially on women's issues, from the beginning of his career. By the time *Medea* opened he had been informed of the banning of his own play *Waste*, due to follow *Medea*: the censor required the deletion of references to an abortion, saying that the author must 'moderate and modify the extremely outspoken reference to the sexual relations'.[96] But another reason for the choice of *Medea* in 1907 was the new performance venue: with the company's move to the more capacious Savoy, Barker was anxious (as he explained in a letter to Murray in the early summer) to find 'something sensational' with which to open there.[97]

Murray and Barker may have been influenced by the success of Max Reinhardt's Berlin production of *Medea*, in Wilamowitz's translation, in 1904.[98] But the political climate must also have made *Medea* an attractively 'sensational' choice. In 1906 Emmeline Pankhurst had moved the Women's Social and Political Union (WSPU) from Manchester to London and inaugurated the movement for women's suffrage. The Liberal Party's landslide victory in the 1906 general election gave the movement hope that its goals were attainable. The first Women's Parliament met at Caxton Hall in February 1907, and in March Willoughby Dickinson's Private Member's Bill, which would have given the vote to some women, provoked a divisive debate. The bill was defeated, sparking a huge demonstration by women of all classes. The first mass arrests of suffragettes shocked the public: no fewer than sixty-five served sentences in Holloway Prison.[99]

Support for the movement grew rapidly throughout 1907, when thousands of meetings were organized, and the Qualification of Women Act, which enabled women to sit on borough and county councils, whetted the appetite for suffrage.[100] The campaign inspired Barker in April of that year to produce the first of the whole series of suffrage plays which flourished on the commercial stage

---

[94] Duncan Wilson (1987), 9.   [95] Thorndike (1936), 74.
[96] Purdom (1955), 54–70.   [97] Salmon (1986), 239.
[98] Flashar (1991), 124–6.   [99] Atkinson (1996), 127.
[100] Pankhurst (1931), 223; David Morgan (1975), 46.

until 1914, *Votes for Women*, by the Ibsen-influenced Elizabeth Robins, who was on the governing committee of the WSPU.[101] Barker had told its author that he was 'strongly prejudiced in favour of its subject'.[102] This impassioned piece was staged at a suffragette meeting in Trafalgar Square, described by one reviewer as 'the best stage managed and original scene we have had in the theatre for many a day'.[103]

That for Barker there was a clear continuum between such social realist drama and Euripidean tragedy is evidenced in this production not least by his handling of the crowd scenes, which was strikingly reminiscent of his staging of the Greek chorus in his recent productions at the Court.[104] And when University College London and Bedford College mounted a joint production of Euripides' *Medea* in Greek at the Botanical Garden of University College on 13–15 June 1907, the topical resonances did not go unmarked.[105] This was the first of a number of productions staged under the auspices of Bedford College in aid of the Women's College's Building Fund; and the first in which Ethel Abrahams was to star to considerable acclaim. Abrahams, together with many members of the cast and committee, was to remain a tireless campaigner on behalf of women's rights; and her performance in the part of Deianira in Sophocles' *Trachiniae* at the Court in 1911 earned praise from no lesser activist than Emily Davison, who in her review in the campaigning paper *Votes for Women* found that 'The anti-suffragist argument that women do not fight receives its criticism in this play.'[106]

---

[101] Stowell (1992), 2–5, 9–30.

[102] Cit. ibid. 12 from the Vedrenne–Robins correspondence at the Harry Ransom Humanities Research Centre, University of Texas at Austin.

[103] *ILN* 130, no. 3547 (13 Apr. 1907), 546.

[104] Kennedy (1985), 59–60.

[105] See especially the review in the *Daily News*, 14 June 1907.

[106] Although there was a performance of the *IT* in Greek as early as 1887, it was in the early 20th c. that the productions of Greek plays were mounted in aid of the Building Fund. Sophocles' *Electra* was performed on 15–17 July 1909 at the Aldwych Theatre in Campbell's translation, with Miss E. Calkin as Electra; *Alcestis* was performed on 16–19 Feb. 1910, in English in South Villa, Regent's Park, with Ethel Abrahams as the eponymous heroine in a translation by Gerald Warre Cornish; and the *Trachiniae* was staged at the Court Theatre on 6–8 July 1911, directed by G. R. Foss with Abrahams as Deianira in Campbell's translation. Abrahams was also the author of *Chiton and Himation. Greek Dress: A Study of the Costumes Worn in Ancient Greece* (London, 1908). Emily Davison's review of *Trachiniae* was in *Votes for Women*, 14 July 1911.

The acting version of the London University *Medea* included Murray's very recently published translation facing the ancient Greek.[107] Both Murray and Barker were keen supporters of the Bedford Greek plays; and it may well have been the success of the Bedford experiment that confirmed their choice of play for October at the Savoy, when the actress Edyth Olive emerged from her house in Corinth and lectured the audience on the injustices suffered by women at the hands of men (Fig. 17.2). One reviewer remarked on how surprisingly 'human' *Medea* was for an ancient play, and complimented Olive on winning the audience's sympathy, despite looking 'so bizarre with her dark complexion and hair and her reddish robes' and her 'intense' declamation.[108] She was well supported by Hubert Carter as Jason and Lewis Casson as the messenger, fresh from a role in *Votes for Women*, and also from performing the Ghost of Darius in his own symbolist production of *The Persians* in a prose translation by B. J. Ryan at Terry's Theatre in April.[109]

Medea not only offered the authority of classical drama to a contemporary cause, but can be understood, like *Votes for Women*, as one of the founding dramas in the prolific genre of suffragette plays and songs which were placed before the public from 1907 onwards.[110] In *Euripides and his Age*, Murray writes of Euripides both in a fifth-century context and in Edwardian Britain:

To us he seems an aggressive champion of women; more aggressive, and certainly far more appreciative, than Plato. Songs and speeches from the *Medea* are recited today at suffragist meetings.[111]

Medea did indeed become intimately associated with the suffragettes: after the London production, passages from the play formed part of the repertoire of special texts—especially monologues and poems—that members of the Actresses' Franchise League prepared for performance at suffragette meetings from the most elegant of upper middle-class suburbs to the East End

---

[107] There is a copy of the acting version of the text, with the parallel text of Murray (1906) in the Bedford College Archive in the Royal Holloway, University of London Archives (PP1/4/3/5).
[108] *ILN* 131, no. 3575 (26 Oct. 1907), 588.
[109] *ILN* 130, no. 3546 (6 Apr. 1907), 518. See Devlin (1982), 43.
[110] See the catalogue in Atkinson (1992), 65–6.
[111] Murray (1913), 32.

FIGURE 17.2   Edyth Olive as Medea (1907).

of London.[112] The passages must have included Medea's first monologue and the strophic pair on the misogyny of man-made myths (410–30), which Murray described as celebrating 'the coming triumph of Woman in her rebellion against Man'.[113]

---

[112] Holledge (1981), 60–1, 80–1.   [113] Murray (1906), 86.

Edyth Olive had won the role despite opposition from Lillah McCarthy, and despite Murray's own intervention.[114] McCarthy was a notable suffragette, later becoming the Vice-President of the Actresses' Franchise League,[115] and often marched under the League's banner, which sported ancient Greek masks of tragedy and comedy (Fig. 17.3).[116] Barker, meanwhile, had reservations about Olive, whom he had previously described as 'morally hoydenish, full of ideals and illusions . . . she is essentially girlish in her movements and in the particular abandon which characterizes her methods'.[117] Bernard Shaw had also cruelly described her, after her realization of the crazed Cassandra of *Trojan Women*, as too warm and vulgar to be cast as a ravishable virgin.[118] But these qualities had been more successful in the roles of the protagonist of Murray's translation of *Andromache*, produced by the Stage Society in 1901,[119] of the sympathetic Clytemnestra of Euripides' *Electra*, and above all the sexually driven Phaedra in the *Hippolytus*. On the strength of these performances she won the part of Medea.

Medea shared with the burgeoning genre of suffrage drama a serious examination of the issue of motherhood, now seen as both the principal element in the regulation of female sexuality and a source of feminine power.[120] Nevertheless, the play was found disturbing. *The Graphic* doubted the plausibility of Medea's calculating infanticide. 'Were she sane', the reviewer argued, her concern for her children would have had to stem her anger. But Medea, of course, is so sane that she informs the audience that while she knows perfectly well that what she is going to do is wrong, her anger makes her do it (1078–9—in Gilbert Murray's translation, 'Yea, I know to what bad things | I go, but louder than all thoughts doth cry | Anger').[121] The reviewer insists that although we have to admire the 'tremendous quality' of Medea's hatred, 'we are not able to feel that it is a living possible hatred'. Medea's actions are simply 'not convincing as the outcome of the situation in which she is placed'.[122]

---

[114] Kennedy (1985), 29.   [115] Tickner (1987), 130; Pankhurst (1931), 284.
[116] Tickner (1987), 254.
[117] Letter to Murray, 14 Dec. 1904, in Salmon (1986), 231.
[118] West (1984), 93.   [119] Murray (1900), West (1984), 293–5.
[120] Stowell (1992), 4–5.   [121] Murray (1906), 61.
[122] *The Graphic*, 26 Oct. 1907, 567.

FIGURE 17.3   Banner of the Actresses' Franchise League (*c*.1911).

This view of Euripides' *Medea* had been prevalent until the twentieth century. In 1893 even the most liberal of Ibsenite critics, William Archer, is unable to support an emotionally charged report of infanticide on the stage, when Florence Bell and Elizabeth Robins' play *Alan's Wife* was produced anonymously.[123] But some now saw maternal infanticide in a different light. Murray himself regarded Medea's child-killing as realistic:

Euripides had apparently observed how common it is, when a woman's mind is deranged by suffering, that her madness takes the form of child-murder.[124]

Cicely Hamilton, a prominent author of suffragette drama, attacked the idealization and mystification of the mother–child bond in her polemical tract *Marriage as Trade* (1909). She reveals that she has frequently heard women, both in informal conversation and special meetings, discussing the death sentence for maternal infanticides. Hamilton has been surprised to discover that the sympathy 'invariably and unreservedly' lay on the side of the mother.[125]

Sylvia Pankhurst recalled how the great stirring of social conscience in 1906 had led to economically privileged women noticing the hardships of women in the lower classes: 'Women raised above the economic struggle by wealth and leisure, and the relatively small number of successful professional women', including 'the few actresses and musicians at the top of their tree', began to feel solidarity with the 'starved and exploited members of their sex'.[126] The focus was on a number of tragic cases of poor women 'which in other days might have passed unnoticed', but were now used to point the moral of women's inferior status:

Daisy Lord, the young servant sentenced to death for infanticide; Margaret Murphy, the flower-seller, who, after incredible hardships, attempted to poison herself and her ailing youngest child ... Julia Decies, committed to seven years' penal servitude for throwing vitriol at the man who betrayed and deserted her; Sarah Savage, imprisoned on the charge of cruelty to her children for whom she had done all that her miserable poverty would permit. By reprieve petitions, by propaganda speeches and articles, the names and the stories of these unfortunates were torn from their obscurity, to be branded upon the history of the women's movement of their day.[127]

[123] Gardner (1992), 9.   [124] Murray (1906), 94.
[125] Hamilton (1909), 210–13.   [126] Pankhurst (1931), 225–6.   [127] Ibid.

The dismal crimes of these modern Medeas—infanticide, violence against their husbands, child abuse—were now seen as caused by their social status. Even intentional child-murder by women was now being seen as connected with male irresponsibility: like Daisy Lord and Margaret Murphy, Medea could now kill her children with premeditation and be given, at least in the progressive theatre, a sympathetic hearing.

If Medea could now be herself in full tragic guise for the first time on the British stage, how did her anti-self Alcestis fare in the climate of increasingly radical suffragism? With her overwhelming sense of duty to her husband and her children, she of course confirmed rather than undermined what Shaw termed the myth of the 'Womanly Woman'. In marked contrast to Medea and the other strong female roles from Euripidean drama which regularly appeared on the stage in Barker's productions of Murray's translations from 1904 onwards, Alcestis hardly surprisingly never made an entry under Barker's direction. Although there were two productions of this Euripidean play between 1910 and 1911—one in aid of the Bedford College Building Fund and the second under the direction of Barker's mentor, William Poel—both of these were informed, more or less, by Verrall's ironic reading of the play.[128] Indeed, only a deliberately ironic and deceptive wife (who does not indeed die) was plausible in the Ibsenite world of strong, independent women.

It is, moreover, significant that Murray, with his close association with the New Drama, did not translate *Alcestis* until 1915. Whilst the Verrall–Poel solution was (consciously or not) an over-bold attempt to impose the plot of Shakespeare's *Winter Tale* upon Euripides' drama, Murray's interpretation of the *Alcestis* was rather more straightforward. For him, it was the work of a young playwright; it was, he continued, '. . . as if more enjoyment and less suffering had gone to the making of the *Alcestis* than to that of the

---

[128] After seeing the production in aid of the Bedford College Building Fund in February 1910 in Gerald Warre Cornish's translation, Poel asked a Cambridge graduate called Francis Hubback (who was to die in the First World War) to write him a version. The play was performed in December 1910 on the Grand Staircase at London University, and revived in January 1911 at the Little Theatre, London, and at the Ethical Church, Bayswater in April 1914. For details, see Speaight (1954), 170–8.

later plays.'[129] Against the background of the campaign for
women's suffrage, Euripides' drama of the selfless and ultimately
silent wife seemed somehow irrelevant and, perhaps, even deeply
unhelpful, except of course to those who might hail the Greek
heroine as the ideal 'Womanly Woman' against whom the New
Woman was being defined.

[129] Murray (1915), p. xvi. Barker did, however, have plans to stage *Alcestis* on an
American tour in 1914, but these failed to materialize. See Kennedy (1985), 181.

18

Greek Tragedy and the Cosmopolitan Ideal

We can understand Pericles better than we understand
Palmerston.

G. Norwood, Euripides and Shaw *(London, 1911)*, 2.

Some time in early 1915, after several years of direct involvement
in the Cambridge Greek play, John Sheppard of King's College,
Cambridge, concludes the Preface to his translation of *Oedipus
Tyrannus* with the following comment: 'If you doubt whether in
these days Greek tragedy still matters, you may learn the answer in
Paris.'[1]

The 'answer' to which Sheppard is referring is the startling
performance of *Œdipe Roi* by the then legendary *tragédien* of the
Comédie-Française, Jean Mounet-Sully. Mounet-Sully had been
responsible for reintroducing Sophocles' play into the repertoire of
the Comédie-Française in 1881, and between then and the time of
Sheppard's comment in 1915 Mounet-Sully had made in excess of
100 appearances in the title role. His fame as Oedipus had spread
throughout Europe, as the French troupe toured the continent
bearing the civilization of France, and more particularly acting as
custodians of ancient Greek drama. In 1899, after the company
had performed *Œdipe Roi* in the Theatre of Dionysus in Athens
under the aegis of the French Archaeological Society in Athens,
Mounet-Sully's carriage was unhitched from its horses and borne
aloft by a jubilant crowd through the streets of Athens: 'Long live
Mounet-Sully! Long live France!' chanted the ecstatic crowd. And
similar cries greeted him in Romania.[2] Nation and star actor become
inseparable in the minds of foreign audiences: Oedipus was reincarnated as an honorary Frenchman, or, more importantly,

---

[1] Sheppard (1920), p. xi.
[2] See Mounet-Sully (1917) generally; Sideris (1976), 148–58 on his reception in
Greece; and Lolière (1907), 396 for Romania.

through the power of Mounet-Sully's interpretation of Sophocles' tragic role, Oedipus had become Everyman.

Owing to the disruption of the war years, Sheppard's own translation of *Oedipus Tyrannus* did not in fact appear in print until 1920, some four years after the death of Mounet-Sully at the age of 75 years old. But give or take these few years, what is especially striking about Sheppard's comment is that he is referring to a production of a Greek play that first appeared in the repertoire of the Comédie-Française over fifty years previously. Although the great Mounet-Sully had not appeared in those early performances from 1858 onwards—Geffroy, the acclaimed successor to the leading actor of the revolutionary years, Talma, took the part of Oedipus—and despite some notable changes to the set and minor changes to the chorus in the 1881 revival, the *Œdipe Roi* which Sheppard saw in Paris was essentially the same as the *Œdipe Roi* that opened on 18 September 1858 in the translation of the poet and playwright Jules Lacroix.

For Sheppard, then, Mounet-Sully's performance was proof that Greek tragedy still mattered; and the formal beauty of the production demonstrated to him that 'Greek drama, not bolstered up by sensationalism, and not watered with sentimentality, has power to hold and move a modern audience.' The French production, in Sheppard's view, stood in stark contrast to the 'lavish, barbaric, turbulent' production of *Oedipus Rex* directed by the celebrated Austrian director, Max Reinhardt, which had opened at Covent Garden in London in January 1912.[3] According to Sheppard, Reinhardt's actors:

raged and fumed and ranted, rushing hither and thither with a violence of gesticulation which in spite of all their effort, was eclipsed and rendered insignificant by the yet more violent rushes, screams and contortions of a quite gratuitous crowd.[4]

Sheppard was not alone in objecting to the crowd of about a hundred extras that was used in the London production (see Fig. 18.1), some of whose members literally invaded the audience's space as they entered through the auditorium. What offended Sheppard most was that Reinhardt's production was a kind of 'total theatre' assaulting the audience's senses on every level; and

---

[3] Sheppard (1920), pp. x f., ix.
[4] Ibid., p. ix.

FIGURE 18.1 John Martin-Harvey as Oedipus in Max Reinhardt's *Oedipus Rex* (1912).

instead of clarity—as had been the case with the Mounet-Sully production—Reinhardt brought only obscurity, summed up best, according to Sheppard, by the palace at the opening of the play that was a 'black cavern of mystery'.[5]

Reinhardt's production, which had opened in Munich in September 1910, had originally used the German translation of Hugo von Hofmannstahl. Hofmannstahl had already provided the libretto for Strauss's *Elektra* (1909), which had shocked and enthralled audiences by showing Greek myth as savage and primitive.[6] And here in the production of *Oedipus Rex*, audiences were being offered further evidence of Nietszchean-inspired insights into the ancient Greek world, with the collective Dionysiac

---

[5] Ibid. Cf. the reviewer in *The Theatre Journal*, 14 (1911), 56–60, who noted the symbolic significance of the use of light and darkness in the production: 'Out of the darkness into which they [the chorus] disappear comes all the ill-fortune that besets Oedipus, bit by bit, until finally, overwhelmed by an accumulation of tragedies, blind, powerless and deserted, he is driven into the darkness himself, followed by the same mob, which does not even touch him now, for fear of pollution.'

[6] Goldhill (2002), 108–77.

experience being held somewhat precariously in check by the Apolline action on the raised platform.

That the Reinhardt production defined itself in opposition to the French *Œdipe Roi* was undoubtedly the case. Lillah McCarthy (who had played Dionysus in Poel's *Bacchae* in 1908; see Ch. 17) and who took the part of Jocasta in the London production of the German/Austrian play, comments in her memoirs that the Comé-die-Française production

was cold, classical. Chorus: two women dressed in French classical style. No movement, the figures of the actors motionless, carved in marble. Nothing lived in it except Mounet-Sully, for whose superb acting no praise would be extravagant, but oh! for a Reinhardt to breathe into the other actors breath of life.[7]

Lillah herself received plaudits for her performance as Jocasta (see Fig. 18.2); and whilst the startling performance of John Martin-Harvey in the title role did earn him praise from many quarters, his earlier experience as a star in melodrama seems to have denied him the *gravitas* accorded to his French counterpart. Whilst Mounet-Sully's movements and gestures earned him wide acclaim, for Martin-Harvey, it was his voice that attracted attention: in the Nietzschean equation that the Reinhardt production so vividly represented, the individual had been subsumed by the overwhelming Dionysiac collective.

That the classical establishment in Britain and elsewhere in Europe in the first part of the century should have favoured the French over the German/Austrian production is hardly surprising given the ostracism afforded to Nietzsche and Nietzschean-inspired scholarship at this time.[8] Moreover, it would not be wide of the mark to claim that the hero-centred readings of Greek tragedy, which were to last for at least the first half of the twentieth century, are linked in important ways to Lacroix's version of *Œdipe Roi* as it was mediated through the powers of Mounet-Sully. But there is some irony, although perhaps no coincidence, in the fact that it is France—the country best known for its championing of the collective over the individual in the political realm—that should have chosen to celebrate the embattled Greek hero, crushed through his own noble endeavour. Yet there is perhaps

---

[7] McCarthy (1933), 302.
[8] See Silk and Stern (1981).

FIGURE 18.2 Edmund Dulac, *Lillah Borne by the Wings of Love from the Wings of the Stage* (c.1921).

even greater irony in the fact that it was this French production that afforded that much more famous Austrian, Sigmund Freud, the opportunity to explore the individual psyche,[9] just at the time when many of his compatriots were beginning to be wooed by the exponents of the ideology of the collective that was to take its most pernicious form in the first half of the twentieth century.

In the previous chapter we saw how the content of Greek tragedy influenced the modern play of ideas; here in this chapter, we see how the formal features of the ancient example were to provide inspiration to modern theatre practitioners. If Barker had had reservations about the chorus in his early productions of Euripides (see Ch. 17), once he had travelled to Berlin to see the rehearsals for Reinhardt's *Oedipus Rex* in the Zirkus Schumann in 1910, he found a model to emulate. Two months after the *Oedipus Rex* appeared at Covent Garden in January 1912, Barker staged Murray's *Iphigenia in Tauris* at the Kingsway Theatre; and for the first time not only were the choral groupings and delivery to his satisfaction, they also delighted those members of his audience who had been similarly initiated with the help of the European model.

However, the Reinhardt example, as Sheppard himself is partly acknowledging in his preface of 1915, was to carry with it perils as well as potentialities. Not least was Reinhardt's 'people's theatre', with its inclusive agenda in terms of class and physical spatial relations, eventually reformed and deformed as it served as the model for the Nazi mass rallies in the 1930s.[10] But in the first decade of the twentieth century in London, the perils of Reinhardt's 'people's theatre' were conceived less in terms of its political than its moral potential.

The insistence on the physicality of the performer—the naked bodies which steamed through the darkened auditorium carrying torches at the opening of the play—provoked horrified reactions amongst the audience members accustomed to view stage action safely contained behind the proscenium arch. Mounet-Sully's gestures may have been greatly prized, and he may well have made his final dramatic exit through the auditorium, but his acting style was always essentially sculptural (Fig. 18.3). In the French production the body was merely a means of conveying the cerebral and the

---

[9] For the impact of this production on Freud, see Ernest Jones (1953), 194.
[10] Fischer-Lichte (1999*b*).

FIGURE 18.3   H. Bellery-Desfontaines, engraving of Jean Mounet-Sully as Oedipus in the Comédie-Française production of *Œdipe Roi*.

emotional qualities of the protagonist; whereas in the Reinhardt production the sheer physical presence of the actors was a central part of the performance.

For Reinhardt, as was the case for the pioneers of modern dance who both admired and in turn influenced his work, movement (as opposed to voice) was the prerequisite for the performer. The dance experiments of both Isadora Duncan and Maud Allan at the beginning of the century were hailed as revivals of the 'totality' of ancient Greek dance, combining expressive qualities with a religious/spiritual and educative function. For many critics, W. B. Yeats's famous (and somewhat later Duncan-inspired) question 'How can we know the dancer from the dance?'[11] was a measure of this 'modern/ancient' pattern of movement. But whilst this new corporeality initially engendered amazement within the audience, it also eventually brought moral outrage and scandal. Neither Duncan nor Allan was able to sustain her high status as 'serious' dancers in the post-war world; and this was in no small measure on account of their own personal tragedies. But their eclipse from high cultural circles was also symptomatic of the Anglo-Saxon world's retreat from its brief rapprochement with European culture and what came to be perceived as the 'cosmopolitan' corporeality that Reinhardt's theatre had so demonstrably embodied.

UNDER THE BLUE PENCIL

The Edwardian era ushered in a new Europeanization, which led in many (essentially patriarchal) circles to a nostalgia for a 'healthier' time, when 'modern' problems (often of a sexual nature) did not exist. New frank discussion about gender roles and sexuality in general fuelled these anxieties, as they had done in the last two decades of the nineteenth century.[12] The English retreat from what was increasingly considered to be European cosmopolitan decadence was, perhaps, best illustrated during this period with reference to its instutionalized moral custodians, and not least its theatre censor, the Lord Chamberlain.[13]

The Theatre Regulation Act of 1843, which gave the Lord Chamberlain the power to ban any play (old or new) and to rescind

---

[11] Yeats, 'Among School Children', *The Tower* (1928), in Yeats (1962), 130.
[12] Hynes (1968), 132–71.
[13] Ibid. 212–53.

any licence already granted, was generally implemented with reference to moral rather than political criteria. Under Section 14 of the Act, the Lord Chamberlain had the power to stop any performance in the interest of 'good manners, decorum or the public peace'.[14] However laughable this may seem to us, it must be remembered that Victorian audiences themselves jealously guarded the notion of strict public morality, and thus perceived the powers to protect that morality as necessary rather than as a repressive measure.

What was, however, perceived to be increasingly absurd about the legislation during the last quarter of the nineteenth century was the fact that an individual—in theory the Lord Chamberlain himself, in practice his Assistant, the Examiner of Plays—should be granted absolute authority over matters of decency and decorum. And not only did the Lord Chamberlain's right of silence continue to prove irksome to individual playwrights whose plays were refused a licence (as had been William Shirley's experience with his *Electra* in 1762; see Ch. 6); it was also increasingly resented that no questions at all relating to the Lord Chamberlain's decisions could be made in the House of Commons because his name appeared on the Civil List. Furthermore, the unsystematic and often inconsistent method that the Examiners of Plays adopted in their work turned more and more writers towards active opposition. When Granville Barker's new play *Waste*, which dealt with the dalliance of a married politician, was denied a licence in 1907, the playwright-director spearheaded a counteroffensive against the Censor. On 29 October *The Times* published a letter signed by Barker and other prominent opponents of the Censor including Shaw, Yeats, Synge, and Gilbert Murray highlighting the absurdities of the system; and eventually in 1909 a Joint Select Committee of the House of Lords and the House of Commons was set up to investigate the state of theatre censorship in Britain.

Although between 1895 and 1909 out of some 8,000 plays submitted for licence only thirty were banned,[15] amongst the thirty was Sophocles' *Oedipus Tyrannus*, which was being widely read by schoolboys and had been performed by undergraduates at Cambridge in 1887. A measure of the arbitrary and inconsistent nature

---

[14] On the 1843 Act, see Fowell and Palmer (1913), 373. On stage censorship in Britain generally, see de Jongh (2000).

[15] Findlater (1967), 79.

of the licensing procedure at this time is the fact that the Examiner of Plays from 1895 to 1911, George Alexander Redford, consistently refused to license Sophocles' play, and yet happily granted a licence to Aristophanes' *Lysistrata*, a comedy that was considered sufficiently ribald for subsequent Examiners to deny it a licence on a number of occasions during the interwar period.[16]

The experience of Sophocles' play at the hands of the British censor can be charted from 1886 onwards, when the campaign to abolish theatre censorship began to gather momentum. As we saw in Ch. 1, the incest and parricide had been deemed problematic from at least 1808, when Scott referred to the 'incestuous passion, [which] carries with it something too disgusting for the sympathy of a refined age'.[17] When the Shelley Society mounted a production of Shelley's controversial play about incest, *The Cenci*, at the Grand Theatre, Islington, some seventy years after it was written, the subject-matter was deemed indelicate even if the play itself was seen as an interesting period piece. An editorial in *The Era* insists that just because Greek drama has become very voguish,

> ... we must beware of mistaking a passing craze for a national artistic development. It would not do (to take a parallel instance) to suppose that because *The Cenci* has been placed on the stage and listened to with attention, not to say avidity, by a mixed audience of old men, young men, and maidens, that our public taste in matters of morality had become sufficiently degraded to permit of the sin of incest forming a common and acceptable motif for a modern drama.[18]

Indeed there were others, as we will see, who deemed the 'public taste in matters of morality' to be so delicate that the inclusion of 'the sin of incest' in any drama was problematic.

When the Shelley Society thrust *The Cenci* into the limelight, they established a similarly high profile for Sophocles' tragedy on account of their shared treatment of incest. And from 1886 until 1910, when Sophocles' play was finally granted a licence after much public pressure—*The Cenci* had to wait until 1922 to receive one—the fates of these two plays were inextricably linked, featur-

---

[16] See the letter from Barker to Murray dated August 1910 in Purdom (1955), 113: 'You know I suppose that the Little Theatre opens with the Lysistrata—blessed by Redford.'

[17] Walter Scott (1808), vi. 121.

[18] *The Era*, 22 May 1886. See Ch. 16 for the taste for 'Greek' plays in London at this time.

ing prominently in almost every important debate concerning theatrical censorship. Furthermore, it may be argued that it was the eventual prising apart of the two plays that led to the dilution of the case against censorship in 1910, when the increasingly splintered opposition was left without a *cause célèbre* around which to rally.

The linking of the plays was perhaps inevitable given that both plots involved incest and parricide. Although Shelley drew on Sophocles' *Electra* as well during his composition of *The Cenci* (see Ch. 6), in the Preface to the published edition of the play, he refers to the Oedipus plays, although he himself refrains from pointing to the obvious thematic parallels.[19] And the members of the Shelley Society followed his example in their Prologue (written by the author of *Alcestis* and *Helena in Troas*, John Todhunter), similarly invoking the Sophoclean precedent without drawing explicit parallels between the two plays.[20] Furthermore, a glance at the Evidence given to the Joint Select Committee in 1909 shows that not only had the twinning of the plays become habitual by this time, but that the two playwrights were now enlisted in the cause against censorship as well.[21] When the playwright Henry Arthur Jones was unable to attend the Joint Select Committee to give evidence in person, he issued a vitriolic pamphlet in which Sophocles and Shelley had become bywords for the absurdity of the licensing system. Jones writes: 'Thus the rule of Censorship is "Gag Shelley! Gag Sophocles! License Mr Smellfilth! License Mr Slangweazy!" . . .'[22]

---

[19] Although Shelley does not refer explicitly to their thematic parallels, he was fully aware that such parallels would not be missed. Thomas Love Peacock, who had vainly submitted the play to Covent Garden at Shelley's request, doubted whether *The Cenci* would have been granted a licence anyway because other treatments of incest (including Dryden and Lee's *Oedipus*) had been banned from the stage in recent times. See Woodberry (1909), pp. xxxiii–xxxv.

[20] See A. and H. B. Forman's Introduction to Shelley (1886). As well as his *Alcestis* and *Helena in Troas* (on which see Chs. 15 and 16 respectively), Todhunter had also written a study of Shelley in 1880.

[21] See *Censorship and Licensing* (1910), *passim*.

[22] Jones's pamphlet, written in the form of a letter to Herbert Samuel, Chairman of the Joint Select Committee, is reprinted in *Censorship and Licensing* (1910), 199–203 (quotation p. 201). Perhaps the most notorious figure behind the Slangweazy tendency is none other than the future Examiner of Plays, Charles H. E. Brookfield. His play, *Dear Old Charlie* (an adaptation of Eugène Labiche and Alfred-Charlemagne Delacourt's 1863 *Célimare, Le Bien Aimé*) is invoked in the

It is extremely difficult to assemble the evidence for the case for censoring Sophocles' play, particularly since the evidence given by George Redford, Examiner of Plays, to the Joint Committee in 1909 is terse, to say the least. Redford was asked why a version of the *Oedipus* by the *Daily Telegraph* drama critic (and former Oxford don who was involved in the 1880 *Agamemnon* at Balliol; see Ch. 15), W. L. Courtney, had been refused a licence. When asked by Mr Harcourt if an alleged impropriety had led to the banning of Courtney's version whilst the *Oedipus* of Dryden and Lee was apparently exempt from such strictures, Redford replied: 'Mr Courtney's version was submitted and it was considered; Mr Dryden's version was not considered.'[23] Harcourt's line of enquiry here is an attempt to ascertain the extent to which precedent determined the fate of newly submitted plays. And it is clearly precedent in the case of *Oedipus Tyrannus* that is affecting its fortunes at the hands of the censor. For the analogy with *The Cenci*, and the refusal of a licence to Oscar Wilde's *Salomé* in 1893—Wilde's play remained unlicensed until 1931—meant that any play dealing with incest in any shape or form was deemed indecent and unfit for stage representation.[24]

It may seem incredible to us that Sophocles' tragedy can be reduced to a play about incest *tout court*, but anxieties concerning consanguineous sexual relations had become increasingly acute throughout the first few years of the century culminating in the passing of The Punishment of Incest Act of 1908. Before 1908—with the exception of the interregnum years (see Ch. 1), and in marked contrast to Scotland, where incest had been a crime since 1567—incest in England and Wales had been dealt with by the ecclesiastical courts, despite numerous attempts to make it a criminal offence.

---

evidence to the Joint Select Committee as an example of the inconsistencies in the censorship (ibid. 93). *Dear Old Charlie* was licensed for performance at the Vaudeville Theatre, where it played for 92 performances from 2 Feb. to 21 Mar. 1908. The play caused considerable offence on account of its apparent amorality in its depiction of a serial cuckolder, who causes considerable consternation to the two husbands he has cuckolded, when he decides to settle down and get married to a new lover.

[23] Ibid. 68.

[24] There were other plays involving incestuous relationships that were also banned at this time: thus Gabriele D'Annunzio's *La città morta*—which Eleonora Duse had tried to stage in London—was denied a licence in 1903.

The new legislation of 1908 undoubtedly lurks behind the ludicrously 'literalist' reading of Sophocles' tragedy proffered by the Examiner of Plays, which can be found in the copy of Murray's translation of *Oedipus Tyrannus* that was submitted to the Lord Chamberlain's Office in November 1910. On the first page, in the list of *dramatis personae*, Jocasta is described as '*Queen of Thebes; widow of Laius, the late king and now wife to Oedipus*'. '*Now wife to Oedipus*' is underlined in blue pencil—the only such underlining in the text—and the reason for this becomes clear from Redford's comment in his letter to Lord Spencer, the current Lord Chamberlain. Redford writes:

I have read the Gilbert Murray version. In many respects it differs from Mr Courtney's treatment, but it follows the classic story throughout, and the character of Jocasta 'now wife of Oedipus', is represented and the well known situations of the play are retained.[25]

Redford's comments are overwhelmingly naïve—indeed by implying that a version of Oedipus without Jocasta would be permissible, he might as well be asking for a Hamlet without the ghost; but when the Comptroller of the Lord Chamberlain's Office, Douglas Dawson, wrote to members of a recently formed Advisory Board to seek their advice concerning the Murray translation, he broadly adopted Redford's terms. Dawson writes:

Some years previously a translation of the same drama was made by Mr W. L. Courtney and was refused a licence for stage performance on the ground that it was impossible to put on the stage in England a play dealing with incest. There was a precedent for the action which the Lord Chamberlain took on this occasion in the refusal of successive Lord Chamberlains to license 'The Cenci'.[26]

So jealously did they guard their role as the custodians of public morality that the incumbents of the Lord Chamberlain's Office were in danger of confusing representation with imitation. For as Henry Arthur Jones wryly observed at the time:

Now, of course, if any considerable body of Englishmen are arranging to marry their mothers, whether by accident or design, it must be stopped at once. But it is not a frequent occurrence in any class of English society.

---

[25] George Alexander Redford to Lord Spencer, 10 Nov. 1910, Lord Chamberlain's Plays' Correspondence File: *Oedipus Rex* 1910/814 (British Library).
[26] Douglas Dawson to Sir Edward Carson, 11 Nov. 1910, ibid.

Throughout the course of my life I have not met more than six men who were anxious to do it.[27]

It is surely this shift in attitudes towards incest that accounts for the marked change in Murray's scholarship on Sophocles' play. In 1897 in *Ancient Greek Literature*, Murray reads the incest motif in the play literally complaining that 'Sophocles is always harping on it [the incest] and ringing the changes on the hero's relationships, but never thinks it out...'.[28] But by 1911 in the Preface to his translation, and all too consciously aware of the ban on the play (owing to the over-literal readings of the Censor) that has only just been lifted, Murray apologizes for his earlier view and offers an anthropological explanation of the incest: now, in his estimation, the characters of Jocasta and Oedipus bear some traces of the Earth Mother and the Medicine King respectively.[29]

DEFYING THE BAN

As efforts had been made to stage Shelley's *The Cenci*, attempts were underway to stage *Oedipus Tyrannus* in London. The first attempt seems initially, at least, to have been unrelated to any political campaigning. In 1904 Sir Herbert Beerbohm Tree— inspired by Mounet-Sully—sent his Secretary at His Majesty's Theatre, Frederick Whelen, to ask Redford about the possibility of mounting a production of Sophocles' tragedy in London. Despite the precedent of the undergraduate production in Cambridge in 1887, Redford said that a London production was out of the question.[30]

---

[27] Cit. Fowell and Palmer (1913), 275 n. 1. One of those 'six or seven' may well have been Shaw, who confessed to Murray to committing mother–son incest in his own 'dream world': 'I very seldom dream of my mother...but when I do, she is my wife as well as my mother. When this first occurred to me (well on in my life), what surprised me when I awoke was that the notion of incest had not entered into the dream: I had taken it as a matter of course that the maternal function included the wifely one; and so did she. What is more, the sexual relation acquired all the innocence of the filial one, and the filial one all the completeness of the sexual one...if circumstances tricked me into marrying my mother before I knew she was my mother, I should be fonder of her than I could ever be of a mother who was not my wife, or a wife who was not my mother.' Cited in Holroyd (1988–92), i. 20.

[28] Murray (1911, 239); and for comment, Easterling (1997), 119.

[29] Murray (1911), p. v.

[30] *Censorship and Licensing* (1910), 68.

Tree's informal inquiry led to a flurry of activity. First and most significantly, W.B. Yeats seized the opportunity to use the ban as a means of putting the Abbey Theatre in Dublin on the theatrical map of the English-speaking world when it opened at the end of the year. The Lord Chamberlain's Office had no jurisdiction in Dublin; and it was recognized by the founders of the Abbey that there could be no more effective beginning to a national theatre's career than to stage a play which would enable the theatre to go down in history as the champion of intellectual freedom: Ireland would liberate the classics from the English tyranny. When Yeats announced the establishment of the Abbey Theatre in 1904, he added:

Oedipus the King is forbidden in London. A censorship created in the eighteenth century by Walpole, because somebody has [*sic*] written against election bribery, has been distorted by a puritanism which is not the less an English invention for being a pretended hatred of vice and a real hatred of intellect. Nothing has suffered so many persecutions as the intellect, though it is never persecuted under its own name.[31]

Yeats's interpretation of Redford's 'real hatred of intellect' masquerading behind a 'pretended hatred of vice' is highly apposite because comical treatments of unorthodox sexual relations were routinely licensed by the Lord Chamberlain's Office. And the banning of Sophocles' tragedy was confirmation for Yeats that England was the mean-spirited stifler of the intellect that Ireland would proudly defy.

Almost immediately, Yeats wrote to Murray asking him to write a translation of Sophocles' play for the newly founded Irish theatre.[32] Murray was working on Euripides at the time and had been since late 1890s; he found Sophocles conventional in comparison;[33] and as we have already heard, he had deep misgivings about Sophocles' handling of the incest theme in the *Oedipus Tyrannus*. He wrote to Yeats, declining his invitation on the grounds that the play was 'English-French-German...all construction and no spirit', with 'nothing Irish about it'.[34] However, Yeats's letter clearly opened up new areas of concern to Murray:

[31] Yeats, 'Samhain: 1904' in Yeats (1962), 131–2.
[32] Yeats to Murray, 24 Jan. 1905 in the Bodleian Library, reprinted in Clark and McGuire (1989), 8–9.
[33] Easterling (1997), 119; and see Ch. 17.
[34] Murray to Yeats, 27 Jan. 1905 in Finneran, Harper, and Murphy (1977), i. 145–6.

I am really distressed that the Censor objected to it. It ought to be played not perhaps at His Majesty's by Tree, but by Irving at the Lyceum, with a lecture before . . . and after. And a public dinner. With speeches. By Cabinet Ministers.[35]

The banning of such a significant play, according to Murray, should be taken to heart by the British establishment. And, indeed, some years later when he had completed his own translation of Sophocles' proscribed tragedy, Murray (then Regius Professor of Greek at Oxford) appropriately became the person to take the play to the heart of the establishment, when it was his play that was used in the celebrated Reinhardt production at Covent Garden in 1912.

While Yeats was trying to find a suitable translation for an Abbey production, Shaw's *The Shewing up of Blanco Posnet* fell victim to the stringencies of the Lord Chamberlain's Office in 1907, and it was decided to stage his play at the Abbey as well.[36] Although Shaw's play went ahead successfully (despite threats from the Lord Lieutenant of Ireland to revive his powers of censorship), the plan to stage *Oedipus Tyrannus* lost some of its initial force when campaigns in London to produce the play looked as if they would upstage those at the Abbey.[37] And it was not until 1926, after Yeats had completed his version of the play, that the Abbey Theatre finally staged Sophocles' tragedy.

Another actor-manager, John Martin-Harvey, had (like Sir Herbert Tree) been inspired by Mounet-Sully's performance as Oedipus; and it was Martin-Harvey who had approached Courtney to produce a free version of the play.[38] As a former classical scholar with an intimate knowledge of the professional stage, Courtney was an ideal choice. But despite his impeccable credentials, Courtney's version was (as we have seen) denied a licence by Redford. So significant was the ban that the rejected play was submitted as evidence before the Joint Select Committee in 1909; and its presence guaranteed that a high profile was granted to Greek tragedy in general, and Sophocles' play in particular throughout the proceedings of the Committee.

---

[35] Murray to Yeats, 27 Jan. 1905 in Finneran, Harper, and Murphy (1977), 145.
[36] Findlater (1967), 101–2; Clark and McGuire (1989), 14–5.
[37] Clark and McGuire (1989), 17–18.
[38] Martin-Harvey (1933), 391–403.

Robert Harcourt, the Member of Parliament who had introduced the Theatres and Music Halls Bill designed to abolish censorship, was determined to keep the Sophoclean scandal at the forefront of the Committee's concerns. Even Sir Herbert Tree, who (like most actor-managers of the time) was against abolition *per se*, none the less admitted under Harcourt's assiduous questioning that the Lord Chamberlain's stance over the *Oedipus Tyrannus* was clearly mistaken.[39] When the half-million-word report on the Committee's findings and recommendations appeared in November 1909, the frequency with which references to Sophocles' play occurred made it inevitable that a production would be mounted in London before too long.

By the middle of 1910, two leading theatre managers were planning to stage *Oedipus Tyrannus*.[40] Sir Herbert Tree, undeterred by Redford's previously negative response, was again hoping to mount a production at His Majesty's Theatre; and Herbert Trench, the new Manager of the Theatre Royal in the Haymarket, had approached Murray for his almost completed translation of Sophocles' tragedy.[41] Murray's involvement in the 1909 campaign, together with his close friends and colleagues, Barker and Shaw, had undoubtedly led him to a temporary rejection of Euripides in favour of a translation of Sophocles' now notorious play. When Trench sent Murray's translation to the Lord Chamberlain's Office, Redford was all set to return it to Trench with the customary rejection based on precedent. When Redford wrote to the Lord Chamberlain for his seal of approval, he added:

Mr Trench and Dr Gilbert Murray are opponents of the office, and no doubt desire to make capital out of a prohibition of an ancient Greek classic so familiar to every school boy etc etc.[42]

It was these words that must have sounded a warning to the Lord Chamberlain's Comptroller, Douglas Dawson, for he acted swiftly, telling Redford to inform Trench that the play was under review. Murray's translation was to be granted the dubious dis-

[39] *Censorship and Licensing* (1910), 74.
[40] See the Barker–Murray correspondence in Purdom (1955), 99–102.
[41] See Murray to Barker, 6 Aug. 1910 in Purdom (1955), 112.
[42] Redford to Lord Spencer, 11 Nov. 1910. Lord Chamberlain's Plays' Correspondence File: *Oedipus Rex* 1910/814 (British Library).

tinction of being the first play to be referred to the newly appointed Advisory Board.[43]

All the members of the Board felt that a ban would be hard to sustain, although the retired actor-manager Sir John Hare recommended that 'the greatest caution should be exercised and the matter very seriously and deliberately considered in all its bearings before a licence is granted.'[44] Professor Walter Raleigh from Oxford, however, injected some common sense into the debate when he pointed out—as neither side for obvious political purposes had done before—that 'any supposed analogies' with *The Cenci* 'should [not] be allowed to have weight' because the treatment of incest in both plays is of such a different order and degree.[45]

The recommendations of the Advisory Board were heeded and Murray's translation of Sophocles' play, entitled *Oedipus, King of Thebes*, was finally granted a licence on 29 November 1910. And perhaps by no means coincidentally, on the same day the Lord Chamberlain's Office issued a licence for Strauss' opera, *Salome*, which used Wilde's play (albeit in the German translation of Hedwig Lachmann) as the basis for the libretto, and the opera was performed a few days later at the Royal Opera House, Covent Garden on 8 December.

THE GERMAN/AUSTRIAN OEDIPUS

Not only had the greatest barrier to a performance of Sophocles' play in London now been removed. News too from Germany of an exciting production of *Oedipus Tyrannus* by the celebrated Austrian theatre director Max Reinhardt, gave an even greater impetus to the British campaign. In October 1910, Granville Barker had gone to Berlin to see the production, which had just transferred from Munich, where it had opened at the Musikfesthalle in September, and wrote enthusiastically to Murray about what he had seen.[46] Since Trench, a slow mover, seemed ever less likely actu-

---

[43] Dawson to Redford, 11 Nov. 1910; same to Sir Edward Carson, 11 Nov. 1910, ibid. The other members of the Board were Sir Squire Bancroft, Sir John Hare, Professor Walter Raleigh, and S. O. Buckmaster.

[44] Sir John Hare, ibid.

[45] Professor Walter Raleigh, 22 Nov. 1910, ibid.

[46] Purdom (1955), 114–15.

ally to mount the production he had agitated for,[47] the attention of directors, actors, and theatrical impresarios alike towards the end of the year was fixed on the Reinhardt production that played thirty times to rapturous audiences in the Zirkus Schumann in Berlin. In mid-February 1911, Reinhardt's emissary Ordynski came to London saying that Reinhardt himself wanted to stage a London production using Murray's translation.[48] Although negotiations conducted on Murray's behalf by Frederic Whelen to produce the play at the Kingsway Theatre fell through with the death of the financier, by the end of July there were firm plans for a production of the *Oedipus* in January 1912 at Covent Garden, with Martin-Harvey in the leading role and Barker's wife, Lillah McCarthy, as Jocasta. Because the original production used the free version of Hugo von Hofmannstahl, Murray's translation had, in the event, to be slightly adapted by Courtney. In the programme note to the play, the production was hailed as 'the first performance of the play in England since the seventeenth century',[49] a clear allusion to Dryden and Lee's *Oedipus* of 1678, and an oblique reference to the earlier ban. Although this was factually inaccurate—it ignores all revivals of the Dryden and Lee version, Faucit's *Oedipus* (see Ch. 8) and the Cambridge production of 1887—it is not (as we have seen) without some foundation.

Reinhardt was already renowned for his direction of crowd scenes, but in the *Oedipus Rex* he put those skills to a severe test by directing a crowd of 300 extras who represented the citizens of Thebes, together with a chorus of twenty-seven Theban Elders (there were fewer in the chorus in London). But it is misleading to focus exclusively on the monumental aspects of the production because the naturalistic acting was particularly noteworthy— Reinhardt himself had trained at the Deutsches Theater under the so-called father of stage naturalism, Otto Brahm; and Hoffmanstahl's version, no less than Lacroix's, focused on the individual suffering of Oedipus.

There were three performance levels in Reinhardt's production—the space at the front of the auditorium for the crowd, the palace steps for the chorus, and the front of the palace itself for the

[47] Ibid. 116.

[48] Duncan Wilson (1987), 165.

[49] A copy of the programme is in the Production File to the *Oedipus Rex* in the Theatre Museum, Covent Garden. The note is written by F. B. O'Neill.

actors—and the infringements of those separate performance levels at points of high tension were particularly noteworthy. Most striking was the opening of the play, which broke with the conventional relationship between performers and spectators absolutely when the vast crowd surged through the darkened auditorium, reminding *The Times* critic of 'some huge living organism'.[50] A murky blue light broke through the darkness, partially revealing the chanting, groaning crowd; and after a strong yellow light had been cast over the altar and steps, the entry of Oedipus from the central doors, dressed in a brilliant white gown, was captured in spotlight. If the Mounet-Sully production had downplayed the Theban context in order to highlight the sufferings of Oedipus in his relations with the gods, Reinhardt's Nietzschean-inspired production emphasized the extent to which those individual (Apolline) sufferings had to be seen against a background of the general (Dionysiac) suffering of the Chorus. The highly spectacular ending (Nietzschean in spirit and strictly non-Sophoclean), when Oedipus made his cathartic exit from Thebes groping his way through the audience, was deemed so effective that it led some members of the audience to avert their gaze as he passed them by. Certainly there were aspects of the staging that came in for criticism—most notably the dumbshow that surrounded the messenger-speech—but few who saw the production failed to be impressed by the sheer scale and grandeur of the formal patterns of movement.

London audiences were overwhelmed by what they saw, and although certain aspects of the production were denounced, the performances of Martin-Harvey and Lillah McCarthy were unanimously praised; and Martin-Harvey continued to tour with the play for many years after the event, winning for himself the same distinction as his hero Mounet-Sully of being a truly great Oedipus. Amongst the criticisms levelled at the production was that audiences were being offered undiluted Reinhardt rather than pure Sophocles, and this particular barb led Gilbert Murray to make a spirited defence of Reinhardt and his production in a letter to *The Times*:

After all Professor Reinhardt knows ten times as much about the theatre as I do. His production has proved itself: it stands on its own feet, something

---

[50]   *The Times*, 16 Jan. 1912, 10.

vital, magnificent, unforgettable. And who knows if the more Hellenic production I dream of would be any of these?[51]

Reviews of the production remained curiously silent about the play's recent history at the hands of the British censor. Shortly after the opening of the Reinhardt production, Barker drew attention to this serious omission in a letter to *The Times*:

Sir,—Public memory is short. In no review of the production of *Oedipus Rex* at Covent Garden has it been recalled that until a year ago this was a forbidden play. But neither has any critic even suggested that it is a thing unfit to be seen. This is a famous case against the Censorship. It is, as it were, brought to trial, and judgement goes by default. Why have the Lord Chamberlain's champions, eager to support him in principle, never a word to say in defence of any of his important acts? Here is a chance for them; and if they feel it is one to be missed, will they not in fairness offer a vicarious apology to the public and the theatre, who have been for several generations wantonly deprived of their property in this play?—Yours etc.[52]

Even though no theatre critic found Sophocles' play 'a thing unfit to be seen', there were some people who clearly did. When Martin-Harvey took the Reinhardt production on a tour around Britain in 1913, the Manager of the New Theatre in Cardiff (no less a person than the brother of George Redford, former Examiner of Plays) refused to allow *Oedipus* to be performed in his theatre, and Martin-Harvey and his company had to find an alternative venue.[53]

Oedipus Tyrannus may have been finally freed but the British stage was to remain under the shadow of the censor for another fifty years. The new Examiner of Plays was even more stringent than his predecessor, and his high-handedness provoked a petition that was presented to the King on 11 June 1912 with the signatures of over sixty dramatists. In the petition, the recent success of Reinhardt's *Oedipus Rex* was held up as evidence of the absurdity of the system of censorship. The statement avers:

That the Lord Chamberlain's Department by working on custom and not on ascertainable results has been grossly unjust to managers, authors and the public, and has cast discredit on the administration of the Department by its treatment of classical plays, and of plays in which scriptural charac-

---

[51] *The Times* , 23 Jan. 1912, 8.   [52] *The Times,* 18 Jan. 1912, 9.
[53] Martin-Harvey (1933), 490.

ters appear, as may be instanced by the repeated refusals to many managers of a licence for Sophocles' great play *Oedipus Rex*, which now, at last permitted, has been produced with every indication of public approval.[54]

However strong a statement of protest the petition contained, a censored *Oedipus Tyrannus* had clearly been a far more effective weapon against the Lord Chamberlain's Office than a liberated one could ever be. Moreover, Barker's concerns, expressed to Murray in 1910 before the ban on *Oedipus* was lifted, were proving prophetic. Barker had written:

My fear is that the Lord Chamberlain means to scotch opposition by making as many concessions as he can—we—the general body of opposers—are so rottenly divided on the question of principle—that it would be an easy job if he had the wit to set about it. Personally one will be glad to see the *Oedipus* through but—at once—everyone will bless the name of the committee and say that nothing more need be done.[55]

Redford may not have had sufficient 'wit' to scotch the opposition single-handedly; but by implying in his letter to the Lord Chamberlain that the Sophoclean tragedy was the opposition's trump card, he had unwittingly guaranteed his Office's survival for some more years. For by withdrawing the *Oedipus Tyrannus* from the fray, the Lord Chamberlain had deftly wrongfooted the opposition; and the British stage had to wait until the 1960s for its freedom.

The history of Greek tragedy on the British stage is thus closely interwoven with the history of British stage censorship. Thomson's adaptation of the *Agamemnon* in 1738 was one of the first plays to challenge the authority of the Lord Chamberlain's Office (see Ch. 4). And had *Oedipus Tyrannus* remained on the list of proscribed plays a year or so longer, it may well be that a London production of Sophocles' tragedy would have been mounted to celebrate that Office's demise.

COSMOPOLITANISM, CORPOREALITY, AND COLLECTIVITY

Two months after the Reinhardt *Oedipus Rex* had opened at Covent Garden, Barker's production of *Iphigenia in Tauris* was

---

[54] The petition is quoted in full in Fowell and Palmer (1913), 374–6.
[55] Purdom (1955), 116.

mounted at the Kingsway Theatre. Critics were quick to see the imprint of Reinhardt on the production.[56] These two ancient plays that had been dominant in the Restoration and early eighteenth centuries (see Chs. 1 and 2) and which for various reasons had disappeared from the British stage for many decades, finally returned to the repertoire. Now, however, at the beginning of the twentieth century it is not so much the individual who provides the focus for the director/adapter: instead, we find a new anthropological approach in the reworkings of these tragedies, which places equal emphasis upon the collective.

Barker, it should be recalled, had attended the *Oedipus* rehearsals both in Berlin and London; and he had helped his wife Lillah McCarthy prepare for her part as Jocasta in London. In Barker's production, she was now a statuesque and dignified Iphigenia surrounded by primitive peoples with savage practices. In previous productions, Barker had demonstrated the power of Greek tragedy in the modern world with reference, primarily, to its content (see Ch. 17); but now he had found ways of effectively representing those of its formal characteristics that could be accommodated within the proscenium arch theatre. As had been the case with Reinhardt's *Oedipus Rex* at Covent Garden, Barker built a forestage out over the (admittedly smaller) orchestra pit and front three rows of the stalls at the Kingsway Theatre, upon which the chorus of eleven captive women danced. Here and unlike in earlier productions, both on account of their dark purple costumes and the new larger choral space, the chorus was no longer a permanently static, and occasionally intrusive presence: instead it faded in and out of the action in accordance with the dictates of the plot.[57] And when Barker went on later in the year to stage the same production in the Greek theatre at Bradfield College, not only did it transpose easily, it made Barker feel that he would never do Greek plays 'in a stuffy theatre again'. During the First World War, he took the production to America, where it was staged together with *Trojan Women*, in various outdoor venues to great acclaim. It was this tour that established Lillah McCarthy, who

---

[56] See J. T. Grein, *Sunday Times*, 24 Mar. 1912, 12 : '...it is Reinhardt's spirit that hovers over the whole picture'.

[57] For a detailed account of the production, see Kennedy (1985), 119–21.

played both Iphigenia and Hecuba, as the leading Edwardian tragedienne (see Fig. 18.4).[58]

Finding new spaces meant devising new patterns of movement for the performers. In July 1910, in a journal called *The Mask*, Godwin's Greek theatre at Hengler's Circus in 1886 (see Ch. 16) was proclaimed as seminal in theatre history, with Godwin himself having 'fathered the new movement in the European theatre'.[59] The anonymous author of the article was none other than *The Mask*'s editor, Edward Henry Gordon Craig, the illegitimate son of the actress Ellen Terry and Godwin himself. In part Craig is of course trying to establish his own (literal) genealogy in this article, but since this former Bradfield pupil went on to become one of Europe's most influential stage-designers in the first part of the century, his acknowledgement of the importance of the designer in the modern theatre is significant. Craig had no time for Poel's Elizabethan revivalism nor for the Court productions of Euripides.[60] He rightly saw that unless the appropriate spaces and levels were found in the theatre, the movement patterns of the performers would be severely hampered. Indeed, movement, in his schema, had primacy over the spoken word: the father of the dramatist, he argued, was the dancer.[61]

Craig's fascination with the dancer was in reality at this time an obsession with one particular dancer, the pioneer of what is now called 'Modern Dance', Isadora Duncan. He had met Duncan in 1904 and had found in her bare-footed, tunic-clad dance performances the corporeal correlative to what he had been seeking to capture with his set designs. Duncan had begun her career in

---

[58] Barker to Murray in Purdom (1955), 144. Before the three afternoons at Bradfield, 11–13 June, the production was mounted on 4 June for a matinée performance at Tree's request at His Majesty's Theatre as part of the annual Shakespeare Festival. On the American tour in 1915 the company performed in the Yale Bowl, 15 May; Harvard Stadium, 18 May; Piping Rock Country Club on Long Island, around 25 May; College of the City of New York, 31 May and 5 June; the University of Pennsylvania, 8 June; Princeton University, 11 June. See Kennedy (1985), 212–13.

[59] John Semar (pseudonym for Edward Gordon Craig), 'A Note on the Work of E. W. Godwin' *The Mask*, 3 (July 1910), 53.

[60] 'Balance' (pseudonym for Edward Gordon Craig), 'A Note on Masks', *The Mask*, 1, 1908, 11.

[61] Craig, 'The Art of the Theatre. The First Dialogue' (1905), repr. in full in Craig (1911), 137–82 (quotation p. 140).

FIGURE 18.4   Lillah McCarthy as Hecuba in *The Trojan Women* (1915).

Europe as an extra with Benson's company,[62] but turned increasingly towards solo dance performances in aristocratic private houses in Paris and London, accompanied by her mother on the

[62] Isadora Duncan (1928), 50. There is some confusion about the date of her first meeting with Craig. I follow Duncan in her memoir with 1904. Their daughter Deirdre was born in 1905.

piano. She drew inspiration from Greek sculptures and depictions on Greek vases, as well as from the example of the celebrated Japanese dancer Sadayakko, whom Duncan had admired at the 1900 Exhibition in Paris.[63] But like many others of her generation, she records her most powerful memory as a spectator in the theatre as being the night she saw Mounet-Sully (in what she describes as an otherwise uninspired 'Greek revival' production) in the part of Oedipus.[64] Some years later, Duncan relates how dressed as a Maenad at a fancy dress ball in Paris, she somewhat over-daringly danced with a Greek-robed Mounet-Sully: 'I danced with him all the evening', Duncan explains, 'or at least I danced about him, for the great Mounet disdained modern dance steps, and it was bruited about that our conduct was extremely scandalous.'[65]

After a visit to Greece with her brother in 1903, she took a group of young Greek boys with her on tour across Central Europe.[66] Together with the singing boys, Duncan danced the odes from Aeschylus' *Suppliants* with mixed success to audiences in Vienna, Budapest, Berlin, and Munich. Some years later in 1915, she mounted a full-scale production of *Oedipus Rex* in her studio in New York, with thirty-five actors, eighty musicians, and a hundred singing voices, with herself and her pupils performing as the dancing chorus, and her brother Augustin Duncan in the title role.[67] But most of her work remained on a much smaller scale and consisted of a series of dances designed to mirror the workings of the soul; in Duncan's formulation, the dancer dances the music (rather than *to* the music) 'a music heard inwardly, in an expression

---

[63] Isadora Duncan (1928), 54; and for the impact of Sadayakko's dancing generally in the west, see Downer (2003).

[64] Isadora Duncan (1928), 68.

[65] Ibid. 164. The tone here highlights the self-consciously romantic nature of the memoir (billed on the 1996 paperback edition as 'The uninhibited autobiography of the woman who founded modern dance'). For comment in this regard, see Goldhill (2002), 115–20.

[66] Isadora Duncan (1928), 100–3. Her brother, Raymond, who married Penelope, sister of the Greek poet Angelos Sikelianos, 'went Greek' and insisted all his family wear Greek costume even in adverse climes. This resulted in the notorious incident of his arrest in New York on grounds of child cruelty.

[67] Isadora Duncan (1928), 226. Duncan also devised an *Iphigenia*, which consisted of scenes taken from Euripides' *Iphigenia in Aulis* and *Iphigenia in Tauris*, danced to Gluck's music, which she performed in Amsterdam 1905, and New York 1908–9.

of something out of another, profounder world. This is the truly creative dancer; natural but not imitative, speaking in movement out of himself and out of something greater than all selves.'[68]

Apart from the inevitable reservations from certain quarters about her scantily clad appearance, and notwithstanding the very real objections from many quarters about her personal life (which involved in the early years having a child out of wedlock with Craig), Duncan's art form was generally recognized as being an expression of the 'purity' and 'innocence' of the Arnoldian Greek. For the avant-garde theatre practitioners, however, it provided a radical break with the tyranny and restrictions of the past. For Nijinsky, for example, the star of Les Ballets Russes, Duncan 'dared to put liberty to movement; she has opened the door of the cell to the prisoners.'[69]

In this sense the very 'corporeality' of the Reinhardt *Oedipus Rex* of 1910–12 was part of a broader European concern to emphasize the sheer physicality of the performer;[70] and through watching some of the developments in dance from the beginning of the century, some members of the English audience had been prepared (if not always ready) for Reinhardt's assault. In 1911 following the London premiere of Les Ballets Russes under Diaghilev's direction, *The Times* drama critic commented:

Alas! Many pleasant illusions have been shattered thereby, many idols tumbled from their pedestals; we have grown up terribly fast and lost the power of enjoying things that pleased our callow fancies only a month or two ago.[71]

In the Britain of 1911, audiences had never before seen such bright and lavish costumes; never before had dancers danced with such energy and physicality; and Nijinksy, then the lover of Diaghilev, was the embodiment of the raw energy and power that became associated with the Company.[72]

---

[68] Isadora Duncan (1920).

[69] Nijinsky, cited in Kurth (2001), 248.

[70] The work of Émile Jacques-Dalcroze, whose system of eurhythmics was made public from at least 1903 and which he later developed further together with the theorist and designer Adolphe Appia at Hellerau in Germany from 1911 to 1914, is another important illustration of the confluence of ideas in European theatre at this time.

[71] *The Times*, 5 Aug. 1911, 9.

[72] In May 1912, a few months after the Reinhardt *Oedipus*, Nijinsky went on to break moral as well as balletic convention with his twelve-minute ballet,

However, it was perhaps Maud Allan, in some ways a follower of Duncan's art, who had prepared London audiences most. For unlike Duncan, Allan performed in public spaces, most notably at the Palace Theatre in London, where she had been consistently topping the bill since 1908. Like Duncan, Allan was also from San Francisco, and came to Europe to make her career. For Allan, in the early years, this meant studying the piano in Berlin; but after seeing Duncan's barefooted performances, Allan had turned to dance without any formal training. She had also been inspired by Reinhardt's work, notably his production of Wilde's *Salomé*, which she had seen at the Neues Theater in Berlin in 1902.[73]

It is surprising in some ways that Duncan should make no mention of her compatriot in her memoirs for Allan was, perhaps, her most talented offspring. But the eventual controversy and scandal surrounding Allan—both with regard to her dance of *Salome* and the allegations of sexual deviancy which she unsuccessfully challenged in court in 1918 (see further below)—no doubt also played a part. However, it may well have been the fact that Allan succeeded in outstripping the doyenne of Modern Dance in the eyes of certain critics that accounts for Duncan's studied silence about her. J. T. Grein, for example, claimed to detect a new emotionality in Allan's performances, which enabled her to outrival Duncan.[74] It was undoubtedly the case that Allan had enjoyed a greater following in London at the Palace Theatre than Duncan ever managed to secure with her narrowly based, socially elite audiences in the private houses of the rich.

After Edward VII had seen Allan perform in Marienbad in 1907, he approached the manager of the Palace Theatre, Alfred Butt, who was in search of a 'high-art' act to replace the popular and risqué 'living pictures' that had finally been banned by the London County Council in 1907.[75] From 1908 Allan performed at the Palace Theatre to very wide audiences, including the Prime Minister's wife, Margot Asquith, who was one of her most admir-

---

L'Après-midi d'un faune, which culminated in a simulated orgasm that sent shock-waves through Parisian high society.

[73] Tydeman and Price (1996), 140.
[74] *Sunday Times* and *Sunday Special*, 8 Mar. 1908.
[75] Walkowitz (2003), 342.

ing fans.[76] Allan can be said to have played a significant role in establishing the pre-First-World-War dance craze in England, which led to a flurry of ballet schools being set up, to Greek-inspired movement classes being taught widely both at school and as part of the women's health reforms in general, and eventually to the tea dances and dinner dances that flourished at the Grand Hotels in London.[77]

As with Duncan, critics noted how when the musically trained Allan danced, she was 'music made visible'.[78] She could have danced straight off a Greek vase, freeing herself from the regularities of the vase depiction and transporting the onlooker back to a Golden Age (see Fig. 18.5).[79] According to the drama critic of *The Telegraph*, W. L. Courtney, who had spent at least the previous twenty-five years engaging with questions concerning Greek tragedy in performance (see Ch. 15), Allan's dancing was 'part of that rhythmical motion which philosophy tells us lies at the basis of all created things, and is an imitation of the law of the universe.'[80] For another, she symbolized the revolt against the repression of the 'top-hat' culture, against which Shaw and Ibsen had railed; and she served as the living example of the Nietzschean liberating powers of music.[81] Just as the women's health reforms, aided by the Directoire fashion designs by Paul Poiret, had gone to 'war on the corset', so now Allan (as Duncan herself) was setting the trend in the new 'liberating' fashion of the day. When Max Beerbohm had reviewed Barker's *Hippolytus* at the Lyric in 1904, he had identified the corsets under the costumes of some members of the chorus as a 'symbol' of all that was wrong with this intrinsically 'un-Greek' revival.[82] Behind Beerbohm's criticism, no doubt, lies some admiration for the liberating tunic of Duncan (as an anti-feminist, he would presumably only have tolerated this in a

---

[76] There were rumours over many years of a lesbian relationship between Allan and Margot Asquith (as well as rumours of her relationship with the Prime Minister, Herbert Asquith). These were to come to the fore during 1918. See Tydeman and Price (1996), 80–1; and Goldhill (2002), 121–9 on one of Allan's admirers, Lady Constant Stewart Richardson.

[77] Walkowitz (2003), 336. See Watts (1914) for an example of the serious 'hellenizing' of the women's exercise movement.

[78] Walkley ([1911]).

[79] Renaud ([1911]). Renaud was an American critic from San Francisco.

[80] Courtney ([1911]).

[81] Haden Guest ([1911]).

[82] *Saturday Review*, 4 June 1904, 716.

Mavd Allan
and
Her Art

FIGURE 18.5   Frontispiece to *Maud Allan and Her Art* ([1911]).

'theatrical' context), which was soon to be popularized in London by Allan's Greek-inspired costumes on stage at the Palace Theatre.

In the same year which saw a particularly static production of Murray's *Bacchae* under the direction of William Poel, in which the chorus of four moved only once during the entire production (see Ch. 17), one reviewer was overwhelmed when he saw Maud Allan dance as a 'reeling Bacchante', making her whole body and even her skin move.[83] But however 'Greek' many of her dances were, it was her *Vision of Salome* for which Allan became most celebrated.[84] Yet even here, it was Allan's ability to dance an oriental dance with a freshness that was deemed 'Greek' in spirit, and which removed any dangerously Wildean exoticism from the oriental subject-matter, that earned her acclaim in wide quarters.

But whilst defenders of her art always sought to emphasize an 'Anglo-Saxon purity' that they detected in her dancing, Allan's performances both on account of their slightly ambiguous venue (the Palace never shook off its sleazy Soho image) and their (albeit remote) association with Wildean deviant sexuality meant that they were never entirely free from taint (Fig. 18.6). Moreover, as had been the case with the British premiere of the Strauss *Elektra*,[85] and now with the premiere of the (albeit censored) Strauss *Salome* in 1910, Allan found herself on the fringes of what was increasingly seen to be cosmopolitan, and more particularly German/Jewish decadent voluptuary.[86] And later during the war in 1918, when the Dutch/Jewish Grein sought to organize a tour of a production of *Salome* at the Court directed by his wife and starring Allan in the title role, there was a vehement right-wing and anti-Semitic backlash. The production was mounted to serve as a propaganda exercise sponsored by the Ministry of Information designed to promote British culture, and the fact that what was deemed a 'Jewish' production should be seeking to represent 'British' culture caused outrage in certain circles.[87] Although this particularly unsavoury episode falls beyond the time-span of this book, it is worthy of a brief mention, not least because

---

[83] *Daily Mail*, 7 Mar. 1908.
[84] See Tydeman and Price (1996), 140 ff.
[85] Goldhill (2002), 137–77.
[86] Walkowitz (2003), 373–6; and generally, see Hynes (1968), esp. 254–306.
[87] Tydeman and Price (1996), 79–86.

FIGURE 18.6   Portrait of Maud Allen in *Maud Allan and Her Art* ([1911]).

it has some (albeit indirect) bearing on Sheppard's comments with which this chapter began.

In an excoriating article entitled 'The Cult of the Clitoris', the independent right-wing, anti-Semitic MP Noel Pemberton Billing attacked Allan as a representative of the sexual vice of the cosmopolitan (now read 'German/Jewish') world which was seeking to undermine the 'healthy' English nation.[88] The imputation was clear: Allan was being publicly labelled a lesbian, and the earlier rumours and hints in the American press of an intimate relationship between her and the former Prime Minister's wife made her especially sensitive to the slander.[89] Foolishly and despite much advice to desist, Allan insisted on suing Billing and was forced to endure a shameful ordeal during which she was cast as the disloyal, idle, and pleasure-seeking woman, who had both precipitated, and was now undermining, the war. Allan stood little chance now that civilian hysteria against anything remotely German was sweeping the country. Central to the defence case was the claim that Allan's *Vision of Salome* fostered a cult amongst transvestites; and with the testimony of the now married and 'respectable' 48-year old, former lover of Wilde, Lord Alfred Douglas, whose 'piety' attendant on his conversion in 1911 to Roman Catholicism appeared to make him an even more 'reliable' witness, the jury heard that the play written by Douglas's former lover was fundamentally immoral. By continuing to enact such immoral subject-matter and by her own alleged personal conduct, notwithstanding the scandal of her brother's guilt and execution many years earlier,[90] Allan was damned by association and lost her claim against Billing.

This tragic end to an otherwise starry career had, it would seem, wide implications for the performance of Greek tragedy in Britain throughout the twentieth century. In 1912, following the success of the Reinhardt *Oedipus Rex* and Barker's *Iphigenia in Tauris*, Les Ballets Russes made their second tour to London. This pivotal year in the London theatre[91] saw the publication of Huntly Carter's *The New Spirit in Drama and Art*, in which Carter

[88] Kettle (1977), 18–19.
[89] Walkowitz (2003), 373–6.
[90] Allan's brother Theodore had been found guilty of murdering two women and had been executed in San Francisco in 1898. In 1910 this family secret was 'outed' in the American press. See Walkowitz (2003), 243.
[91] Kennedy (1985), 153.

identified the 'New Spirit' as artistic internationalism. Internationalism very soon, of course, brought with it other anxieties on the political front; and the brief 'awakening' of Britain that had begun during the early years of the first decade of the century was shortly to be eclipsed.[92]

When the Cambridge don John Sheppard recoils from the 'lavish, barbaric, turbulent' aspects of the Reinhardt production in his Preface in early 1915, his response is symptomatic of what we can now see as a general retreat from the continental/German performance culture in Britain at this time. Furthermore, the increasing association in British culture of dance with decadence, which culminated in the trial of Maud Allan, was clearly deep-rooted and of longstanding. The post-war British classical establishment's apparent lack of interest in the ancient dancing chorus, in marked contrast to its unerring focus on the ancient tragic 'hero', may well be a product of this crude, late Edwardian association. If Barker had finally managed to find a way in 1912 to stage his chorus through Reinhardt's example, in the post-War world there was a general retreat in performance terms to those early years at the Court. Indeed, as was the case with the British censor, the strides made during the Edwardian summer were never to be fully recovered until the last quarter of the twentieth century. Just as the Lord Chamberlain's Office finally lost its powers in 1968, so Greek tragedy at that time began to enjoy a new lease of life in Britain as it had done at the beginning of the century.[93] And now in the last part of the twentieth century it was the Greek chorus in particular that came alive once more on the British stage, when once again 'foreign' (now Asian) models began to show British directors new ways of performing an ancient chorus.

[92] Hynes (1968).
[93] See Hall, Macintosh, and Wrigley (2004).

Chronological Appendix

(compiled by Amanda Wrigley)

This appendix attempts to list chronologically all the performances referred to in the text of this book, including those of plays not inspired by
Greek tragedy. Also included are a handful of planned performances
which never made it to the stage, and some films. The great majority of
entries refer to plays inspired by Greek tragedy, and so a *Medea* can be
understood to draw on the Euripidean play; Senecan versions appear as
'Seneca's *Medea*'. Explanations are offered when the title of a play gives
little or no indication of the ancient model from which it draws, and also
when more than one ancient model has been used.

Each entry attempts to offer information on the date of performance, the
title and text of the work, the people involved in its realization, the
venue(s) at which it played, and the theatre company. All dates refer to
premieres unless otherwise stated. The year is stated in modern style
throughout, although this was not formally adopted in England until
1752: so, 25 January 1672 is given instead of 25 January 1671 or 1671/2.
All British dates before 1752 are Old Style, others New Style from 1582.

This information has been drawn by the authors from a wide range of
sources. Particularly useful reference works include: A. Nicoll (1959), *A
History of English Drama, 1660–1900* (Cambridge: Cambridge University
Press); E. L. Avery, C. B. Hogan, A. H. Scouten, G. W. Stone, and
W. Van Lennep (1965–8, eds.), *The London Stage, 1660–1800: A Calendar
of Plays, Entertainments and Afterpieces*...(Carbondale, Illinois: Southern Illinois University Press); S. Sadie (ed.; 1992), *The New Grove Dictionary of Opera* (London: Macmillan).

1559 × 1560	*Hecuba*; performed at Trinity College, Cam- bridge.
1559 × 1560	Seneca's *Oedipus*; in a translation by Alexan- der Neville (an undergraduate at Trinity); performed at Trinity College, Cambridge.
1560 × 1561	Seneca's *Medea*; performed in Latin at Trinity College, Cambridge.
late 1566	*Jocasta*; an English language drama, derived from Euripides' *Phoenician Women* via Ludovico Dolce's Italian *Giocasta*, by

George Gascoigne and Francis Kinwelmershe; performed at Gray's Inn, London,
during the Christmas revels.

by 1567   *Horestes*; a play by John Pikeryng drawing on
medieval versions of the Orestes story; performed in London.

1571   *Persians*; performed in a private house
belonging to Italian nobility on Zante.

early 1580s   *Antigone*; probably in Thomas Watson's Latin
translation; performed at St John's College,
Cambridge.

1609 × 1619   *The Tragedie of Orestes*; an original English-
language play by Thomas Goffe drawing on
Euripides' *Orestes*, Seneca's *Agamemnon*
and *Thyestes*, William Shakespeare's
Hamlet, and Sophocles' *Electra*; performed
at Christ Church, Oxford.

1613   *Bonduca*; by Francis Beaumont and John
Fletcher.

1632   *Roxana*; by William Alabaster; performed at
Trinity College, Cambridge.

early 1637   *Le Cid*; by Pierre Corneille; performed at the
Théâtre du Marais, Paris.

25 January 1659   *Œdipe*; an adaptation of Sophocles and Seneca
by Pierre Corneille; performed at the Hôtel
de Bourgogne, Paris; with Floridor in the
title role.

1659   *Pylade et Oreste*; a tragedy, probably based on
Iphigenia among the Taurians, by Coqueteau
la Clairière; performed in France; Molière's
company.

7 November 1667   *The Tempest*; an adaptation of William Shake-
speare's play by William Davenant and
John Dryden; performed at Lincoln's Inn
Fields, London; the Duke's Company.

1667   *Andromaque*; a play by Jean Racine drawing on
Euripides' *Andromache*, Seneca's *Troades*,
and Virgil's *Aeneid* III; performed in
France.

4 February 1668   *Horace*; a version of Pierre Corneille's *Horace*
by Katherine Philips; performed at Court.
(On 16 January 1669 the King's Company

	acted the play at the first Drury Lane theatre on Bridges Street, London.)
c. August 1670	*The Roman Empress*; a play by William Joyner drawing on *Oedipus Tyrannus*, Euripides' *Hippolytus* and *Medea*; performed at the first Drury Lane theatre on Bridges Street, London; the King's Company.
19 January 1674	*Alceste, ou Le triomphe d'Alcide*; an opera composed by Jean-Baptiste Lully; libretto by Philippe Quinault; performed at the Opéra, Palais Royal, Paris.
c. August 1674	*Andromache*; an adaptation of Racine's *Andromaque* by John Crowne; performed at the Dorset Garden Theatre, London; the Duke's Company.
1674	*Iphigénie en Aulide*; an adaptation by Jean Racine; performed in the gardens at Versailles.
1675	*Iphigénie*; an adaptation of *Iphigenia in Aulis* by Michel Le Clerc and Jacques de Coras; performed in Paris.
1 January 1677	*Phèdre*; adaptation of *Hippolytus* and Seneca's *Phaedra* by Jean Racine; performed at the Hôtel de Bourgogne, Paris.
12, 18 January 1677	*The Destruction of Jerusalem by Titus Vespasian* (parts I and II); by John Crowne; performed at Drury Lane, London; the King's Company.
12 May 1677	*Circe*; an adaptation of *Iphigenia among the Taurians* by Charles Davenant; prologue written by John Dryden; with music composed by John Bannister; with Mary Betterton as Iphigenia and Thomas Betterton as Orestes; performed at the Dorset Garden Theatre, London; the Duke's Company. Revived frequently until 1706 (with Henry Purcell's music replacing that of Bannister *c*.1685); see also under 11 April 1719.
12 December 1677	*All for Love; or, The World Well Lost*; a reworking by John Dryden of Shakespeare's *Antony and Cleopatra*; performed at Drury Lane, London; the King's Company.

by November 1678	*The Destruction of Troy*; a play by John Bankes drawing on Seneca's *Troades*; performed at the Dorset Garden Theatre, London; the Duke's Company.
c. mid-November–mid-December 1678	*Oedipus*; by John Dryden and Nathaniel Lee; with Thomas Betterton as Oedipus, Samuel Sandford as Creon, and Mary Betterton as Jocasta; performed at the Dorset Garden Theatre, London; the Duke's Company.
1678	*Il tempio di Diana in Taurica*; a 'festa musicale' composed by Antonio Draghi; libretto by Nicolò Minato; performed in Vienna.
c. April 1679	*Troilus and Cressida; or, Truth Found Too Late*; a reworking of Shakespeare's play by John Dryden; performed at the Dorset Garden Theatre, London; the Duke's Company.
c. March 1680	*Thyestes*; an adaptation of Seneca's play by John Crowne; performed at Drury Lane, London; the King's Company.
9 January 1683	*Phaéton*; an opera composed by Jean-Baptiste Lully; libretto by Philippe Quinault; performed at Versailles.
late April 1688	*Darius, King of Persia*; by John Crowne; with Elizabeth Barry as Barzana; performed at Drury Lane, London; the United Company.
1691	*Athalie*; by Jean Racine; performed at the girls' boarding school of Saint-Cyr near Versailles.
13 October 1692	*Oedipus, King of Thebes*; by John Dryden and Nathaniel Lee; a revival with music for the incantation scene composed by Henry Purcell; Samuel Sandford as Creon mistakenly wounded George Powell as Adrastus; performed in London, either at the Dorset Garden Theatre or at Drury Lane; the United Company.
20 February 1697	*The Mourning Bride*; by William Congreve; with Anne Bracegirdle as Almeria; performed at Lincoln's Inn Fields, London;

	Betterton's Company. Revived in 1755 at Drury Lane.
1697	*Oreste et Pylade*; by François Joseph de Lagrange-Chancel; performed in Paris.
1697	*The Unnatural Mother*; a play with echoes of *Medea* by an anonymous woman; performed at Lincoln's Inn Fields, London; Betterton's Company.
March 1698	*Phaeton; or, The Fatal Divorce*; an adaptation of Philippe Quinault's *Phaéton* and Euripides' *Medea* by Charles Gildon; with Frances Mary Knight as Althea, the Medea figure; performed at Drury Lane, London; Rich's Company.
c. December 1699	*Iphigenia*; an adaptation of *Iphigenia among the Taurians* by John Dennis; with Elizabeth Barry as the Scythian Queen and Anne Bracegirdle as Iphigenia; performed at Lincoln's Inn Fields, London; Betterton's Company.
c. December 1699	*Achilles; or, Iphigenia in Aulis*; an adaptation of Racine's *Iphigénie en Aulide* by Abel Boyer; with Frances Mary Knight as Clytemnestra; performed at Drury Lane, London; Rich's Company.
c. April 1701	*Love's Victim; or, The Queen of Wales*; a play drawing on *Alcestis* by Charles Gildon; performed at Lincoln's Inn Fields, London.
1702	*Électre*; a tragedy by H. Longepierre; performed in Paris.
23 December 1705	*Ulysses*; by Nicholas Rowe; performed at the Queen's Theatre, London.
21 April 1707	*Phædra and Hippolitus*; an adaptation of *Hippolytus* by Edmund Smith; with Thomas Betterton as Theseus, Booth as Hippolitus, and Elizabeth Barry as Phædra; performed at the Queen's Theatre, London.
31 May 1708	*The Persian Princess; or, The Royal Villain*; by Lewis Theobald; performed at Drury Lane, London.
1708	*Électre*; a tragedy by Prosper Jolyot de Crébillon; performed at the Comédie Française, Paris.

5 February 1709	*Appius and Virginia*; by John Dennis; performed at Drury Lane, London.
17 March 1712	*The Distrest Mother*; by Ambrose Philips; with Mrs Oldfield as Andromache; performed at Drury Lane, London.
5 April 1712	*Créuse l'athénienne*; an opera composed by Louis de Lacoste; libretto by Pierre-Charles Roy; performed at the Opéra, Palais Royal, Paris.
14 April 1713	*Cato*; by Joseph Addison; performed at Drury Lane, London.
5 January 1714	*The Victim: or, Achilles and Iphigenia in Aulis*; a re-writing by Charles Johnson of Boyer's adaptation of Racine's *Iphigénie en Aulide* (see under December 1699 above); with Frances Mary Knight as Clytemnestra and Mary Anne Porter as Iphigenia; performed at Drury Lane, London.
1 April 1714	*Oedipus Tyrannus*; in ancient Greek; performed by Mr Low's Scholars at Mile End Green, London.
18 November 1718	*Œdipe*; by Voltaire; performed at the Comédie Française, Paris.
7 March 1719	*Busiris, King of Egypt*; by Edward Young; performed at Drury Lane, London.
11 April 1719	*Circe*; an opera composed by J. E. Galliard; John Rich's revival of Davenant's adaptation of *Iphigenia among the Taurians* (see under 12 May 1677); performed in Lincoln Inn's Fields, London.
1719	A play by Plautus; directed by Thomas Sheridan (Snr); performed at Sheridan's School, Capel Street, Dublin.
1720	*Hippolytus*; in ancient Greek; directed by Thomas Sheridan (Snr); performed at Sheridan's School, Capel Street, Dublin.
1720 × 1726	*Philoctetes*; in ancient Greek; directed by Thomas Sheridan (Snr); performed at Sheridan's School, Capel Street, Dublin.
22 January 1722	*Love and Duty; or, The Distress'd Bride*; by John Sturmy; performed at Lincoln's Inn Fields, London.

23 January 1722	Terence's *Eunuchus*; in Latin; performed by the King's Scholars at Westminster School, London.
23 January 1722	*Iphigénie en Aulide*; probably that by Jean Racine; performed at the Haymarket Theatre, London.
1722	*Oedipus Masque*; a masque with music by J. E. Galliard and libretto by John Dryden and Nathaniel Lee; performed at Lincoln's Inn Fields, London.
18 January 1723	*Phædra and Hippolitus*; a revival of Edmund Smith's adaptation of *Hippolytus*; with Mrs Seymour as Phædra (except in the May performance when the role was taken by Mrs Boheme); performed at Lincoln's Inn Fields, London.
23 April 1723	*The Fatal Legacy*; an adaptation of Racine's *La Thebaïde* and Euripides' *Phoenician Women* by Jane Robe; with Mrs Boheme as Jocasta and Mrs Bullock as Antigona; performed at Lincoln's Inn Fields, London.
10 December 1723	*Oedipus Tyrannus*; in ancient Greek; directed by Thomas Sheridan (Snr); performed by Sheridan's pupils at the King's Inn's Hall, Dublin.
1723	*L'Oreste*; an opera composed by Benedetto Michaeli; Italian libretto by G. Barlocci; performed in Rome.
14 January 1726	*Apollo and Daphne; or, the Burgomaster Trick'd*; by Lewis Theobald; performed at Lincoln's Inn Fields, London.
2 February 1726	*Hecuba*; by Richard West; with Mary Anne Porter in the title role; performed at Drury Lane, London.
3 December 1726	*Phædra and Hippolitus*; a revival of Edmund Smith's adaptation of *Hippolytus*; with Mary Anne Porter as Phædra; performed at Drury Lane, London.
1726	*Oreste*; an adaptation of *Iphigenia among the Taurians* by Giovanni Rucellai; performed at the Collegio Clementino, Rome.
31 January 1727	*Admeto, re di Tessaglia*; an opera composed by G. F. Handel; libretto adapted from

	A. Aureli's *Antigona delusa da Alceste*; performed at the King's Theatre, London.
13 February 1727	*The Rape of Proserpine*; by Lewis Theobald; with music composed by J. E. Galliard; performed at Lincoln's Inn Fields, London.
1727	Terence's *Adelphi*; directed by Thomas Sheridan (Snr); performed at Sheridan's School, Capel Street, Dublin.
1728	*La méchante femme*; a parody of H. Longepierre's *Médée* by Dominique (= Pierre François Biancolelli); performed at the Théâtre Italien, Paris.
1728	a Greek play; directed by Thomas Sheridan (Snr); performed at Sheridan's School, Capel Street, Dublin.
10 February 1729	*Themistocles, the Lover of His Country*; a tragedy by Samuel Madden; performed at Lincoln's Inn Fields, London.
28 February 1730	*Sophonisba*; a tragedy by James Thomson; Drury Lane, London.
24 April 1730	*Tom Thumb: A Tragedy* … (from 1731 known as *The Tragedy of Tragedies; or, The Life and Death of Tom Thumb the Great*); a burlesque by Henry Fielding; performed at the Haymarket Theatre, London.
11 December 1730	*The Tragedy of Medæa*; by Charles Johnson; with Mary Anne Porter in the title role; performed at Drury Lane, London.
c.1730	Terence's *Andria*; with William Whitehead in a female role; performed at Winchester School.
3 April 1731	*Orestes*; an adaptation of *Iphigenia among the Taurians* by Lewis Theobald; with James Quin as Thoas, Lacy Ryan as Orestes, and Elizabeth Buchanan as Iphigenia, accompanied by dancers including Marie Sallé; performed at Lincoln's Inn Fields, London.
October 1731	*Cato*; by Joseph Addison; performed by pupils at Reading School, Berkshire.
before 1732	*Oedipus*; by John Dryden and Nathaniel Lee; a revival with Thomas Elrington as Oedipus; performed in Dublin.

10 February 1733	*Achilles*; a ballad opera composed by John Gay; performed at Covent Garden, London.
20 August 1733	*The Tuscan Treaty; or, Tarquin's Overthrow*; an English language tragedy by William Bond; performed at Covent Garden, London.
14 January 1734	*Pygmalion*; a ballet choreographed and danced by Marie Sallé; performed at Covent Garden, London.
25 November 1734	*Junius Brutus*; by William Duncombe; performed at Drury Lane, London.
18 December 1734	*Oreste*; a *pasticcio* opera, based on *Iphigenia among the Taurians*, composed by G. F. Handel; with an anonymous Italian libretto adapted from G. Barlocci's *L'Oreste*; performed at Covent Garden, London.
16 April 1735	*Athalie*; by Jean Racine; a revival at the Haymarket Theatre, London.
13 April 1737	*Eurydice Hiss'd; or, A Word to the Wise*; a play by Henry Fielding drawing on Aristophanes' *Frogs*; performed at the Haymarket Theatre, London.
6 April 1738	*Agamemnon*; an adaptation by James Thomson from Aeschylus and Seneca; with James Quin as Agamemnon, Mary Anne Porter as Clytemnestra, and Susannah Maria Cibber as Cassandra; performed at Drury Lane, London.
27 March 1739	*Edward and Eleonora*; James Thomson's adaptation of *Alcestis* which was to have been acted on this day at Covent Garden, but whose performance was forbidden by the Lord Chamberlain. It received its premiere on 18 March 1775 (see below).
19 November 1740	*Oedipus, King of Thebes*; an opera composed by Thomas Arne; libretto by John Dryden and Nathaniel Lee; performed at Drury Lane, London.
2 April 1744	*Oedipus, King of Thebes*; by John Dryden and Nathaniel Lee; a revival with the blind Michael Clancy as Tiresias; performed at Drury Lane, London.
5 January 1745	*Hercules*; an oratorio composed by G. F. Handel; libretto by Thomas Broughton drawing

	on *Trachiniae*; performed at the King's Theatre, London.
20 March 1745	*Alfred the Great, King of England*; a masque with music by Thomas Arne and libretto by James Thomson and David Mallett; performed at Drury Lane, London.
6 February 1749	*Mahomet and Irene*; by Samuel Johnson; with Hannah Pritchard as Irene; performed at Drury Lane, London.
6 January 1750	*Edward the Black Prince; or, The Battle of Poictiers*; by William Shirley; performed at Drury Lane, London.
24 February 1750	*The Roman Father*; an adaptation of Corneille's *Horace* by William Whitehead; with David Garrick as Horatius and Mary Ann Yates as Horatia; performed at Drury Lane, London. Much revived at Drury Lane and Covent Garden.
16 April 1750	*The Sacrifice of Iphigenia*; an 'entertainment'; with music composed by Thomas Arne; performed at the New Wells, London Spa.
1750	*Oreste*; an adaptation of Sophocles' *Electra* by Voltaire; with Mlle Clairon in the title role; performed in Paris.
28 November 1751	*Phædra and Hippolitus*; a revival of Edmund Smith's adaptation of *Hippolytus*; with Hannah Pritchard as Phædra; performed at Drury Lane, London. Revived at Drury Lane with Pritchard (but some other changes of cast) in 1752, 1754, and 1757.
1752	*Les Héraclides*; by Jean-François Marmontel; (probably) performed in France.
6 March 1753	*Phaedra and Hippolytus*; an opera composed by Rose Ingrave; libretto by Edmund Smith; performed in Dublin.
1 December 1753	*Boadicea*; by Richard Glover; with Hannah Pritchard in the title role; performed at Drury Lane, London.
20 April 1754	*Creusa, Queen of Athens*; an adaptation of *Ion* by William Whitehead; with Hannah Pritchard in the title role, Maria Macklin as Ilyssus (the Ion figure), and David Garrick as Aletes; performed at Drury Lane,

	London. Revived at Drury Lane with Pritchard and Macklin (but some other changes of cast) in 1755, 1757, 1758, and 1759.
7 November 1754	*Phædra and Hippolitus*; a revival of Edmund Smith's adaptation of *Hippolytus*; with Mrs Woffington as Phædra; performed at Covent Garden, London. Revived later at Covent Garden with Woffington (but some other changes of cast) in 1756.
1754	*Phædra and Hippolitus*; a revival of Edmund Smith's adaptation of *Hippolytus*; performed at the Theatre Royal, Bath.
10 January 1755	*Oedipus, King of Thebes*; by John Dryden and Nathaniel Lee; a revival with Thomas Sheridan (Jnr) as Oedipus and Mrs Woffington as Jocasta; performed at Covent Garden, London.
27 July 1761	*The Wishes; or, Harlequin's Mouth Opened*; a comedy by Richard Bentley; performed at Drury Lane, London.
11 December 1761	*Hecuba*; an adaptation by John Delap; with Hannah Pritchard in the title role; performed at Drury Lane, London.
20 April 1762	*Creusa, Queen of Athens*; William Whitehead's adaptation of *Ion*; with Sarah Lennox (later Lady Bunbury) in the title role; performed at Holland House, London.
November 1762	*Electra*; this Sophoclean adaptation by William Shirley was refused a licence for the stage by the Lord Chamberlain.
1762	*Médée et Jason*; a ballet choreographed by Jean-Georges Noverre; with music composed by Jean-Joseph Rodolphe; libretto by Noverre; first performed at the Württemberg court, before transferring to the Hoftheater, Stuttgart, in 1763.
22 February 1764	*Midas*; a burletta in English on the myth of Midas and the ass's ears by Kane O'Hara; performed at Covent Garden, London.
20 February 1766	*The Clandestine Marriage*; by David Garrick in collaboration with George Colman; performed at Drury Lane, London.

12 July 1766	*The Sacrifice of Iphigenia*; a ballet; with music composed by Thomas Arne; performed in Richmond.
24 March 1767	*Medea*; by Richard Glover; with Mary Ann Yates as Medea; performed at Drury Lane, London. Revived with Yates in 1768, 1769, and 1771.
3 March 1768	*Oithóna*; a dramatic poem taken from *Ossian* performed as a libretto to an opera composed by F. H. Barthelemon; performed at the Haymarket Theatre, London.
2 February 1769	*Caractacus*; a play by William Mason with a plot modelled on *Oedipus at Colonus*; recited as part of 'An Attic Evening's Entertainment' at the Haymarket Theatre, London. The play received its first London staging on 6 December 1776 (see below).
13 March 1769	*Orestes*; Thomas Francklin's adaptation of Voltaire's *Oreste*; with Mary Ann Yates as Electra; performed at Covent Garden, London. Revived in October 1774 (see below).
1769	*Die Hermannschlacht*; by Friedrich Klopstock; performed in Germany.
26 February 1772	*The Grecian Daughter*; by Arthur Murphy; with Ann Barry as Euphrasia; performed at Drury Lane, London.
21 November 1772	*Elfrida*; a play by William Mason with echoes of *Philoctetes*, *Trachiniae*, *Hippolytus*, and *Phoenissae*; with music composed by Thomas Arne; performed at Covent Garden, London. The play was subsequently revived in London and the provinces.
6 February 1773	*The Golden Pippin*; a burletta in English by Kane O'Hara on the story of Paris and Oenone; performed at Covent Garden, London.
23 February 1773	*Alzuma*; a play by Arthur Murphy drawing on Sophocles' *Electra*; with music composed by Thomas Arne; performed at Covent Garden, London.
28 May 1773	*Alceste*; Singspiel composed by Anton Schweitzer; libretto by Christoph Martin

	Wieland; performed at the Hoftheater, Weimar.
15 October 1774	*Electra*; a revival of Thomas Francklin's adaptation of Voltaire's *Oreste*, with a new prologue and epilogue by David Garrick; set designed by Phillippe de Loutherburg; with Mary Ann Yates as Electra, but otherwise a largely different cast from the March 1769 production (see above); performed at Drury Lane, London.
1774	*Masque of the Druids*; by John Fisher; performed at Covent Garden, London.
18 March 1775	*Edward and Eleonora*; James Thomson's adaptation of *Alcestis*, altered and produced by Thomas Hull; with Ann Barry as Eleonora and Hull as Gloster; Covent Garden, London. (This was the first performance; the planned 1739 premiere had been banned by the Lord Chamberlain.)
20 March 1775	*Medea*; by Richard Glover; with Mary Ann Yates as Medea, and otherwise a largely new cast; performed at Drury Lane, London. Revived in 1776.
25 May 1775	*Oreste et Électre*; a ballet choreographed by Simonin Vallouis; with Vallouis as Oreste and his wife as Électre; performed at the King's Theatre, London.
1775	*Oedipus*; by John Dryden and Nathaniel Lee; a revival with Mrs Bellamy as Jocasta; performed in London.
6 December 1776	*Caractacus*; a play with a plot modelled on *Oedipus at Colonus* by William Mason; with music composed by Thomas Arne; performed at Covent Garden, London. This, the play's first London staging (following the 30 March 1764 premiere at the Crow Street Theatre, Dublin, and the recitation in London in February 1769; on the latter see above), was followed by a tour of the provinces.
1776	*Œdipus Tyrannus*; in ancient Greek; performed by Samuel Parr's pupils, with Joseph Gerrald in the title role, at Stanmore School, Middlesex.

1776	*Trachinians*; in ancient Greek; performed by Samuel Parr's pupils at Stanmore School, Middlesex.
1777	*Codrus*; by Dorning Rasbotham; performed in Manchester. Revived the following year (see below).
23 March 1778	*Iphigenia; or, The Victim*; Thomas Hull's adaptation of Abel Boyer's *Achilles* and Charles Johnson's *The Victim*; performed at Covent Garden, London.
1778	*Codrus*; by Dorning Rasbotham; performed in Manchester (a revival of the previous year's production, on which see above).
25 March 1779	*Medea*; by Richard Glover; with Mary Ann Yates as Medea, and otherwise a cast largely similar to the production of 20 March 1775 (see above); performed at Drury Lane, London.
18 January 1780	*Agamemnon*; in Henri Panckoucke's French translation of James Thomson's *Agamemnon*; performed in Paris.
26 June 1780	*Phædra and Hippolitus*; a revival of Edmund Smith's adaptation of *Hippolytus*; with Mrs Crawford as Phædra; performed at Covent Garden, London.
1780	*Die Vögel*; an adaptation of Aristophanes' *Birds* written and directed by Johann Wolfgang von Goethe; performed in Weimar.
1780s	*Oedipus*; by John Dryden and Nathaniel Lee; a revival with John Philip Kemble as Oedipus; performed in London.
17 February 1781	*The Royal Suppliants*; an adaptation of *Heraclidae* by John Delap; with a prologue by Hester Thrale; performed at Drury Lane, London.
1782	*The Wishes; or, Harlequin's Mouth Opened*; a revival of Richard Bentley's July 1761 comedy (see above); performed in Ireland.
29 April 1783	*Creusa in Delfo*; an opera composed by Venanzio Rauzzini; libretto by G. Martinelli; performed at the King's Theatre, London.

9 March 1786	*The Captives*; a loose adaptation of *Helen* by John Delap; performed at Drury Lane, London.
1789	*Iphigenia in Tauride*; an opera composed by Tommaso Traetta; libretto by M. Coltellini; performed at the private house of Mrs Blaire, London.
October 1791	Plautus' *Aulularia*; in Latin; directed by Richard Valpy; performed by pupils at Reading School, Berkshire.
26 March 1792	*Medea*; by Richard Glover; with Mrs Pope as Medea; performed at Covent Garden, London.
9 April 1792	*Medea's Kettle: or, Harlequin Renovated*; an anonymous harlequinade (not based on the tragedy); with Mrs Dighton as Medea; performed at Sadler's Wells, London.
23 April 1793	*Iphiginia in Auliede; or, The Sacrifice of Iphiginia*; a ballet choreographed by Jean-Georges Noverre; performed at the King's Theatre, London.
7 April 1796	*Iphigenia in Tauride*; an opera composed by Christoph Willibald Gluck; libretto by N. F. Guillard, translated by Lorenzo da Ponte; performed at the King's Theatre, London (English premiere).
24 May 1796	*Antigona*; an opera composed by Francesco Bianchi; libretto by Lorenzo da Ponte; performed at the King's Theatre, London.
22 October 1796	*Edward and Eleonora*; a revival of James Thomson's adaptation of *Alcestis*; with Sarah Siddons as Eleonora and John Philip Kemble as Edward; performed at Drury Lane, London.
13 March 1797	*Médée*; an opera composed by Luigi Cherubini; libretto by François-Benoît Hoffman; performed at the Théâtre Feydeau, Paris.
27 March 1797	*La Sorcière*; a parody of Cherubini's *Médée* by C. Sewrin; performed in Paris.
28 March 1797	*Bébé et Jargon*; a parody of Cherubini's *Médée* by P. A. Capelle and P. Villiers; performed at the Théâtre Montasier, Paris.

15 April 1797	*Médée ou l'Hôpital des Fous*; a parody of Cherubini's *Médée* by 'Citizen' Bizet and H. Chaussier; performed at the Théâtre de l'Ambigu, Paris.
5 floréal year V (24 April 1797)	*Agamemnon*; Louis Jean Népomucène Lemercier's adaptation of Aeschylus and Seneca; with Françoise Vestris as Clitemnestre; performed at the Théâtre de la République, Paris.
October 1797	Plautus' *Amphitryo*; in Latin; directed by Richard Valpy; performed by pupils at Reading School, Berkshire.
12 February 1798	A pageant on British history, including scenes from William Shirley's *Edward the Black Prince*, James Thomson's *Edward and Eleonora*, and William Mason's *Caractacus*, which took place at Covent Garden, London.
21 July 1798	*Cambro-Britons*; by James Boaden, with some songs written by George Colman the younger; with new music by Samuel Arnold; performed at Haymarket Theatre, London.
1799	*Oracle of Delphi*; a mythological pantomime; performed at Sadler's Wells, London.
early 19th century	*Les Perses*; probably a French adaptation; perhaps performed at Jassy, in the court of Alexandros Morouzis, Phanariot Prince of the Danubian principality of Moldavia.
January 1802	*Ion*; an adaptation by August Wilhelm von Schlegel; directed by Johann Wolfgang von Goethe; performed in Weimar.
October 1806	*Oedipus Tyrannus*; in ancient Greek; directed by Richard Valpy; performed by pupils at Reading School, Berkshire.
30 January 1809	*Antigone*; an adaptation by Johann Friedrich Rochlitz; directed by Johann Wolfgang von Goethe; performed in Weimar.
October 1809	*Alcestis*; in ancient Greek; directed by Richard Valpy; performed by pupils at Reading School, Berkshire.
October 1812	Passages from (?) *Antigone*; in ancient Greek; directed by Richard Valpy; performed by pupils at Reading School, Berkshire.

October 1815	Passages from *Medea* and Homer; in ancient Greek; directed by Richard Valpy; performed by pupils at Reading School, Berkshire.
1817	Recitations of de la Harpe's version of *Philoctète* and Euripides' *Iphigenia in Tauris*; performed by Talma at the Opera House concert room.
28 February 1818	*Philoctetes*; a modern Greek adaptation by Nikolaos Pikkolos; performed by the Phanariot community in Odessa.
October 1818	*Heracles*; in ancient Greek; directed by Richard Valpy; performed by pupils at Reading School, Berkshire.
1820	*Virginius*; by James Knowles.
(?) February 1821	*Antigone; or, The Theban Sister*; a tragedy by Edward Fitzball drawing on Sophocles' *Antigone* and Euripides' *Phoenician Women*; performed at the Theatre Royal, Norwich.
5 March 1821	*The Daughters of Danaus and the Sons of Aegyptus; or, Fifty Weddings and Nine and Forty Murders*; by Thomas John Dibdin; performed at the Surrey Theatre, London.
June 1821	*Dirce; or, The Fatal Urn*; an opera composed by Charles Horn (the first all-sung English opera); with Eliza Vestris as Cerinthus; performed at Drury Lane, London.
June 1821	*Oreste*; a French adaptation by Jean Marie Janin; performed at the Théâtre Français, Paris.
October 1821	*Orestes*; in ancient Greek; directed by Richard Valpy; performed by pupils at Reading School, Berkshire.
1 November 1821	*Oedipus: A Musical Drama in 3 Acts*; by John Savill Faucit; performed at the Royal West London Theatre, London.
1821	*Das Goldene Vließ*; an adaptation of *Medea* by Franz Grillparzer; performed at the Burgtheater, Vienna.
1821	*The Greeks and the Turks; or, The Intrepidity of Jemmy, Jerry, and a British Tar*; a 'Melo-Drama' (musical drama) by C. E. Walker; performed at the Coburg Theatre, London.

19 October 1822   *Ali Pacha; or, The Signet Ring*; a 'Melo-Drama' (musical drama) by John Howard Payne; performed at Covent Garden, London.

7 November 1822   *Clytemnestre*; a play by Alexandre Soumet drawing on Sophocles' *Electra*; performed at the Odéon, Paris.

March 1823   *Julian*; by Mary Russell Mitford; performed at Covent Garden, London.

11 August 1823   *Antigone; or, The Theban Brothers*; a reworking, described as a 'Melo-Drama' (musical drama), of Edward Fitzball's play drawing on Sophocles' *Antigone* and Euripides' *Phoenician Women* (see above under February 1821); performed at the Surrey Theatre, London.

November 1823   *Lazaria the Greek; or, The Archon's Daughter*; a 'Melo-Drama' (musical drama); performed at the Coburg Theatre, London.

December 1823   *Petraki Germano; or, Almanzar the Traitor*; by J. Dobbs.

October 1824   *Alcestis*; in ancient Greek; directed by Richard Valpy; performed by pupils at Reading School, Berkshire.

1824   *The Revolt of the Greeks; or, The Maid of Athens*; performed at Drury Lane, London.

20 April 1825   *Orestes in Argos*; a play by Peter Bayley drawing on Sophocles' *Electra*; with Charles Kemble in the title role; performed at Covent Garden, London.

1825   *Léonidas*; by M. Pichat; with Talma in the title role; performed at the Théâtre Français, Paris.

c.1825   *Leonidas, King of Sparta*; probably a translation of M. Pichat's *Léonidas* (see above under 1825); probably performed in London.

July 1826   *The Siege of Missolonghi; or, The Massacre of the Greeks*; performed at Astley's Amphitheatre, London.

1826   *Medea in Corinto*; an opera by Simone Giovanni Mayr; libretto by Felice Romani; with Giuditta Pasta in the title role; performed at

	the King's Theatre, London. Revived regularly until 1850.
October 1827	*Hecuba*; in ancient Greek; directed by Richard Valpy; performed by pupils at Reading School, Berkshire.
1827	*Britons at Navarino*; a musical drama by H. M. Milner; performed at the Coburg Theatre, London.
May 1828	*Creon the Patriot*; by J. Smith; performed in Norwich.
9 October 1828	*Rienzi: A Tragedy*; by Mary Russell Mitford; performed at Drury Lane, London.
1828	*The Mufti's Tomb; or, The Turkish Misers*; an extravanganza; performed at Astley's Amphitheatre, London.
1829	*The Suliote; or, The Greek Family*; performed at Drury Lane, London.
late 1820s	*The Taming of Bucephalus, the Wild Horse of Scythia; or, the Youthful Days of Alexander the Great*; by Andrew Ducrow; performed at Astley's Amphitheatre, London.
3 January 1831	*Olympic Revels; or, Prometheus and Pandora*; a burlesque by James Robinson Planché; with Eliza Vestris as Pandora; performed at the Olympic Theatre, London.
26 December 1831	*Olympic Devils; or, Orpheus and Eurydice*; a burlesque by James Robinson Planché; performed at the Olympic Theatre, London.
June 1832	*Lord Byron in Athens; or, The Corsair's Isle*; an anonymous musical; performed at Sadler's Wells, London.
26 December 1832	*The Paphian Bower; or, Venus and Adonis*; a burlesque by James Robinson Planché; performed at the Olympic Theatre, London.
26 December 1833	*The Deep, Deep Sea; or, Perseus and Andromeda; An Original Mythological, Aquatic, Equestrian Burletta*; a burlesque drawing on book 4 of Ovid's *Metamorphoses* by James Robinson Planché; with G. F. Handel's *Water Music*; with Eliza Vestris as Perseus; performed at the Olympic Theatre, London.

26 May 1836

Ion; by Thomas Talfourd; with William Macready as Ion and John Vandenhoff as Adrastus; performed at Covent Garden, London.

9 September 1836

Ion Travestie; a burlesque of Talfourd's *Ion* by Frederick Fox Cooper; performed at the Garrick Theatre, London.

14 December 1836

Ion; by Thomas Talfourd; with G. Jones in the title role; performed in New York.

December 1836

Ion Travestie; a burlesque of Talfourd's *Ion* by Frederick Fox Cooper; with an all-female cast; performed at the Queen's Theatre, Whitechapel, London.

3 February 1837

Ion; by Thomas Talfourd; with Ellen Tree in the title role; performed at the Park Theater, New York.

4 August 1838

The Athenian Captive; by Thomas Talfourd; with Helen Faucit as Creusa and William Macready as Thoas; performed at the Haymarket Theatre, London.

28 October 1841

Antigone; in a German translation by Johann Jakob Christian Donner; with music composed by Felix Mendelssohn; performed at the Hoftheater, Neues Palais, Potsdam.

1841

Antigone in Berlin; a German language burlesque by Adolf Glassbrenner; performed in Germany.

1844

Antigone; a new production of the 1841 Potsdam *Antigone* (see above), in a French translation by Paul Meurice and Auguste Vacquérie; with music composed by Felix Mendelssohn; performed at the Odéon, Paris.

2 January 1845

Antigone; in William Bartholomew's translation of Donner's German translation; directed by Edward Stirling; with music composed by Felix Mendelssohn; with Charlotte Vandenhoff in the title role and John Vandenhoff as Creon; performed at Covent Garden, London.

4 February 1845

Antigone Travestie; a burlesque of the January 1845 *Antigone* at Covent Garden written by Edward Leman Blanchard; with G. Wild in the title role and H. Hall as Creon;

performed at the New Strand Theatre, London.

February 1845   *Antigone*; in William Bartholomew's translation of Donner's German translation; directed by John Calcraft; with music composed by Felix Mendelssohn; with Helen Faucit in the title role and Calcraft as Creon; performed at the Theatre Royal, Dublin. The production toured to Palmo's Opera House, New York, in April 1845 (with George Vandenhoff, John's son, as Creon); to Edinburgh in December 1845; and to the Haymarket Theatre, London, in August 1846; returning to Dublin in October 1846.

24 March 1845   *The Golden Fleece; or, Jason in Colchis, and Medea in Corinth*; a burlesque by James Robinson Planché; with Eliza Vestris as Medea, Priscilla Horton as Jason, and Charles Mathews as the Chorus; performed at the Haymarket Theatre, London, and touring Britain from January to June 1847.

February 1846   *Ion*; by Thomas Talfourd; with Charlotte Cushman in the title role; performed at the Haymarket Theatre, London.

March 1846   *The Ruins of Athens: A Dramatic Masque*; a masque with music by Beethoven and libretto by William Bartholomew adapted from August von Kotzebue; performed at the Princess's Theatre, London.

18 April 1846   *The Birds of Aristophanes*; a burlesque by James Robinson Planché; performed at the Haymarket Theatre, London.

28 November 1846   *Iphigenia in Aulis*; a version written and directed by John Calcraft; with music composed by Richard Levey; with Helen Faucit in the title role and Calcraft as Agamemnon; performed at the Theatre Royal, Dublin.

16 March 1847   *Alceste*; by Hippolyte Lucas; with music composed by Antoine Elwart; performed at the Odéon, Paris.

25 April 1848   *Theseus and Ariadne; or, The Marriage of Bacchus*; an extravaganza by James Robinson

	Planché; performed at the Lyceum Theatre, London.
1848	*Ion*; by Thomas Talfourd; with Francis Talfourd as Ion; a private performance at Brasenose College, Oxford.
1848–1850	*Antigone*; a recital of William Bartholomew's translation; with music composed by Felix Mendelssohn; performed at Buckingham Palace and Windsor Castle.
1848–1850	*Oedipus at Colonus*; a recital of William Bartholomew's translation; with music composed by Felix Mendelssohn; performed at Buckingham Palace and Windsor Castle.
17 April 1849	*Electra: The Lost Pleiade*; a ballet choreographed by Paul Taglioni (unconnected with Greek tragedy); performed at Her Majesty's Theatre, London.
1849	*Sphinx*; a burlesque by the brothers Robert and William Brough; performed at the Haymarket Theatre, London.
1850	*Alcestis, the Original Strong-Minded Woman: A Classical Burlesque in One Act*; a burlesque by Francis Talfourd; performed at the Strand Theatre, London.
1850	*Antigone*; a revival of the 1845 *Antigone* at Covent Garden (see above); with John Vandenhoff as Creon; performed at Drury Lane, London.
1850	*Diana Preparing for the Chase*; a *tableau vivant* in the Parthenon Rooms, London.
1850	*Ion*; by Thomas Talfourd; performed at Covent Garden, London.
25 August 1851	*Jason and Medea*; an extravaganza by John Pratt Wooler; performed at the Grecian Saloon, London.
1851	*Alcestis, the Original Strong-Minded Woman: A Classical Burlesque in One Act*; a burlesque by Francis Talfourd; with W. Talfourd as Orcus; performed at the Royal Soho Theatre, London.
1851	*Ion*; by Thomas Talfourd; performed at the Haymarket Theatre, London.

1852	*Ion*; by Thomas Talfourd; performed at Sadler's Wells, London.
28 March 1853	*Mr Buckstone's Ascent of Parnassus*; by James Robinson Planché; performed at the Haymarket Theatre, London.
1853	*Ion*; by Thomas Talfourd; performed in Buffalo, NY.
1854	*Videna; or, The Mother's Tragedy*; by John Heraud; performed at the Marylebone Theatre, London.
15 January 1855	*Alcestis*; an adaptation by Henry Spicer; with music for the choruses composed by Christoph Willibald Gluck; Charlotte Vandenhoff in the title role; performed at St James's Theatre, London.
1855	*Wife or no Wife*; by John Heraud; performed at the Haymarket Theatre, London.
18 April 1856	*Medea*; in an Italian translation of Ernest Legouvé's French adaptation; with Adelaide Ristori as Medea; performed at the Théâtre Italien, Paris, and touring Europe (see under June 1856 below).
9 June 1856	*La Médée en Nanterre*; a burlesque of Legouvé's adaptation (see above under April 1856) by Cogniard, Grange, and Bourdois; performed at the Théâtre des Variétés, Paris.
June 1856	*Medea*; in an Italian translation of Ernest Legouvé's French adaptation; with Adelaide Ristori as Medea; performed at the Lyceum Theatre, London (see under 18 April 1856 above).
14 July 1856	*Medea; or, A Libel on the Lady of Colchis*; a burlesque of Legouvé adaptation (see above under June 1856) by Mark Lemon; with Edward Wright in the title role; performed at the Adelphi Theatre, London.
14 July 1856	*Medea; or, The Best of Mothers, with a Brute of a Husband*; a burlesque of Legouvé's adaptation (see above under June 1856) by Robert Brough; with Frederick Robson in the title role; performed at the Olympic Theatre, London.

1857	*Atalanta; or, The Three Golden Apples, an Original Classical Extravaganza*; a burlesque drawing on books VIII and X of Ovid's *Metamorphoses* by Francis Talfourd; performed at the Haymarket Theatre, London.
1857	*Medea in Corinth*; an adaptation by John Heraud; with Edith Heraud in the title role; performed at Sadler's Wells, London, later transferring to Liverpool.
18 September 1858	*Œdipe Roi*; in a French translation by Jules Lacroix; with Edmund Geffroy in the title role; performed at the Théâtre Français, Paris, by the Comédie Française. See also under 9 August 1881.
27 December 1858	*The Siege of Troy*; a burlesque of Homer's *Iliad* by Robert Brough; performed at the Lyceum Theatre, London.
1858	*Pluto and Proserpine; or, The Belle and the Pomegranate. An Entirely New and Original Mythological Extravanganza of the 0th Century*; a burlesque by Francis Talfourd drawing on book 5 of Ovid's *Metamorphoses*; performed at the Haymarket Theatre, London.
March 1859	*Oedipus at Colonus*; a recital of an English translation; with music composed by Felix Mendelssohn; performed at Crystal Palace, Sydenham.
9 April 1859	*Antigone*; a recital of an English translation; with music composed by Felix Mendelssohn; with Edith Heraud in the title role; performed at Crystal Palace, Sydenham.
25 April 1859	*Electra; In a New Electric Light*; an extravaganza by Francis Talfourd based on Sophocles' play; directed by John Buckstone; with Eliza Weekes in the title role; performed at the Haymarket Theatre, London.
1859	*Medea in Corinth*; an adaptation by John Heraud; with Edith Heraud in the title role; performed at the Standard Theatre, London.

*c.*1859	*Antigone*; with music composed by Felix Mendelssohn; with Edith Heraud in the title role; performed at St James' Hall, London.
1860	*Dido*; a burlesque of Virgil's *Aeneid* by F. C. Burnand; performed at St James's Theatre, London.
April 1861	*Medea*; Matilda Heron's version of Legouvé's adaptation; with Heron in the title role; performed at the Lyceum Theatre, London.
5 November 1861	*Medea*; a version of Legouvé's adaptation; with Avonia Jones in the title role; performed at Drury Lane, London.
1861	*Ion*; by Thomas Talfourd; performed at Sadler's Wells, London.
1861	*Medea; or, The Best of Mothers, with a Brute of a Husband*; a revival of Robert Brough's burlesque of Legouvé's adaptation (see under June 1856); with George Conquest in the title role; performed at the Grecian Theatre, London.
7 May 1862	*Les Perses*; performed by students of Rhetoric in a seminary in Orleans, France.
September 1863	*Ixion; or, The Man at the Wheel*; a burlesque by F. C. Burnand; performed at the Royalty Theatre, London.
1863	*Patient Penelope; or, The Return of Ulysses*; a burlesque by F. C. Burnand; performed at the Strand Theatre, London.
1864	*Orpheus and Eurydice*; a burlesque by Henry Byron; performed at the Strand Theatre, London.
1864	*Venus and Adonis; or, The Two Rivals & the Small Boar*; by F. C. Burnand; performed at the Haymarket Theatre, London.
23 December 1865	*Prometheus; or, The Man on the Rock!*; a burlesque by Robert Reece; performed at the New Royalty Theatre, London.
26 December 1865	*Orpheus in the Haymarket*; a burlesque by James Robinson Planché adapted from Hector Crémieux's libretto to Jacques Offenbach's *Orphée aux enfers*; performed at the Haymarket Theatre, London.

1865	*Pan; or, The Loves of Echo and Narcissus*; by Henry Byron; performed at the Adelphi Theatre, London.
April 1865	*Pirithoüs, the Son of Ixion*; by F. C. Burnand; performed at the New Royalty Theatre, London.
30 June 1866	*Helen; or, Taken from the Greek*; a loose adaptation by F. C. Burnand of Jacques Offenbach's *La belle Hélène*; performed at the Adelphi Theatre, London.
21 November 1866	*Antony and Cleopatra*; a burlesque by F. C. Burnand; performed at the Haymarket Theatre, London.
1866	*Iphigenia; or, The Sail! The Seer!! And the Sacrifice!!!* a burlesque by Edward Nolan; performed during Commemoration at Oxford; St John's College Amateurs, Oxford.
1866	*Pentheus*; a burlesque inspired by Euripides' *Bacchae* by Vincent Amcott and W. R. Anson; performed in Oxford.
1866	*Fair Helen: A Comic Opera*; an adaptation by Vincent Amcott of Offenbach's *La belle Hélène*; performed in Oxford.
7 December 1867	*Antigone*; in a modern Greek translation by Alexander Rangavis; with music composed by Felix Mendelssohn; performed at the Herodes Atticus Theatre, Athens.
1867	*Agamemnon at Home; or, The Latest Particulars of That Little Affair at Mycenæ*; a burlesque by Edward Nolan; performed during Commemoration at Oxford; St John's College Amateurs, Oxford.
13 April 1868	*Agamemnon and Cassandra; or, The Prophet and Loss of Troy!*; a burlesque by Robert Reece; performed at the Prince of Wales Theatre, Liverpool, later travelling to Dublin and Portsmouth.
March 1869	*Hypermnestra; The Girl of the Period*; by Frank Sikes; performed at the Lyceum Theatre, London.
1869	*Ino; or, The Theban Twins*; a burlesque by B. J. Spedding; performed at the Strand Theatre, London.

1870	*Ariadne; or, The Bull! The Bully!! And the Bullion!!!*; a burlesque inspired by Ovid by Vincent Amcott; performed in Oxford.
26 December 1871	*Thespis; or, The Gods Grown Old*; by W. S. Gilbert and Arthur Sullivan; performed at the Gaiety Theatre, London.
8 July 1872	*Medea in Corinth*; by William Gorman Wills; with Isabel Bateman in the title role; performed at the Lyceum Theatre, London.
1872	*Arion; or, The Story of a Lyre*; a burlesque by F. C. Burnand; performed at the Strand Theatre, London.
1873 × 1876	*Medea*; a version of Legouvé's adaptation; with Geneviève Ward in the title role; performed in Dublin, Liverpool, Hull, and London.
December 1875	*Antigone*; with music composed by Felix Mendelssohn; with Geneviève Ward in the title role; performed in London.
June 1876	*Oedipus at Colonus*; with Geneviève Ward as Antigone; performed in London.
1876	*Medea*; an adaptation of *Medea* by Franz Grillparzer; with Francesca Janauschek in the title role; performed at the Haymarket Theatre, London.
1877	*Ion*; by Thomas Talfourd; with Mary Anderson in the title role; performed in Boston and Philadelphia, USA. Revived in 1881.
before 1873	Aristophanes' *Frogs*; directed by Fleeming Jenkin; performed in Edinburgh.
1877	*Trachiniae*; in a translation by Lewis Campbell; produced by Fleeming Jenkin; with Mrs Fleeming Jenkin as Deianeira and Robert Louis Stevenson as Messenger; performed at Fleeming Jenkin's Private Theatre, Edinburgh, and later revived at the Town Hall, St Andrews.
6 June 1878	*Jason and Medea: A Ramble after a Colchian*; an anonymous burlesque influenced by Planché (see under March 1845); performed at the Garrison Theatre, Woolwich.
May 1880	*Agamemnon*; in a translation by Lewis Campbell; produced by Fleeming Jenkin;

	performed at Fleeming Jenkin's Private Theatre, Edinburgh.

3 June 1880   *Agamemnon*; in ancient Greek; with music composed by Walter Parratt; with Frank Benson as Clytemnestra and W. N. Bruce as Agamemnon; performed at Balliol College, Oxford, with further performances that year at three public schools and St George's Hall, London, and in January 1881 at Cambridge.

1881   *Alcestis*; in ancient Greek; produced by Frank Benson; with Benson as Apollo; performed at Bradfield College, Berkshire.

9 August 1881   *Œdipe Roi*; in a French translation by Jules Lacroix; with Jean Mounet-Sully in the title role; performed at the Comédie Française, Paris, followed by an extensive tour and revivals throughout Europe. See also under 18 September 1858.

29 November 1882   *Ajax*; in ancient Greek; performed at St Andrew's Hall, Cambridge; University of Cambridge.

15 October 1883   *Agamemnon*; produced by Frank Benson; performed in Cambridge, followed by a national tour; F. R. Benson's Dramatic Company, England.

1883   Sophocles' *Electra*; directed by Ethel Sargant; with music composed (for *Antigone*) by Felix Mendelssohn; with Janet Case in the title role; performed at Girton College, Cambridge.

1883   *The Tale of Troy*; a series of tableaux from Homer by George Charles Winter Warr, delivered in ancient Greek and in English on different nights; with Jane Harrison as Penelope, and Mr and Mrs Beerbohm Tree as Paris and Helen respectively; performed at a private theatre at Cromwell House (the home of Lord and Lady Freake), South Kensington, London.

May 1885   *The Orestean* [sic] *Trilogy of Aeschylus*; in English translation; produced by Frank Benson; performed at the New Theatre,

	Cambridge, followed by a tour; F. R. Benson's Dramatic Company, England. The production toured to the provinces later in 1904.
1885	*Antigone*; with Geneviève Ward in the title role; performed in Melbourne.
1885	*Eumenides*; in ancient Greek; with music composed by Charles Villiers Stanford; with Janet Case as Athena; performed at St Andrew's Hall, Cambridge; University of Cambridge.
13 May 1886	*The Story of Orestes*; a version of the *Oresteia* by George Charles Winter Warr, with set designs by Frederick Leighton, E. J. Poynter, E. H. Watts, and Walter Crane; with Dorothy Dene as Cassandra; performed at Prince's Hall, Piccadilly, London.
14 May 1886	*The Tale of Troy*; a revival in English of the 1883 production, comprising a series of tableaux from Homer by George Charles Winter Warr; performed at Prince's Hall, Piccadilly, London.
17 May 1886	*Helena in Troas*; an imitation of a Greek tragedy by John Todhunter; with Mr and Mrs Beerbohm Tree as Paris and Oenone, and Hermann Vezin as Priam; set designed by E. W. Godwin; performed at Hengler's Circus, London.
14 June 1886	*Agamemnon*; in ancient Greek; performed at the University of Sydney.
December 1886	*Alcestis*; with music composed by Henry Gadsby; performed at the Queen's College, London by pupils of the school.
1886	*The Cenci*; a play by Percy Bysshe Shelley drawing on Sophocles' *Electra* and *Oedipus Tyrannus*; performed at the Grand Theatre, Islington, London; the Shelley Society.
18 May 1887	*Alcestis*; in ancient Greek; directed by Alan Mackinnon; set designed (for the May 1886 *Helena in Troas*) by E. W. Godwin; with Jane Harrison in the title role; performed at the New Theatre, Oxford; Oxford University Dramatic Society.

1887	*Iphigenia among the Taurians*; in ancient Greek; performed at Bedford College, London.
1887	*Oedipus Tyrannus*; in ancient Greek; with music composed by Charles Villiers Stanford; performed at St Andrew's Hall, Cambridge; University of Cambridge.
1888	*Atalanta*; a prose burlesque by George Hawtrey; performed at the Strand Theatre, London.
19 October 1889	*Persians*; in a modern Greek translation by Alexandros Rizos-Ragavis; directed by Demetrius Kokkos; performed in Athens.
6 November 1890	*Antigone*; translated by Robert Whitelaw; with music composed by Felix Mendelssohn; performed at Crystal Palace, Sydenham.
November 1890	*Ion*; in ancient Greek; with music composed by Charles Wood; performed at St Andrew's Hall, Cambridge; University of Cambridge.
1890	*Antigone*; in ancient Greek; performed at Bradfield College, Berkshire.
1 May 1893	*Hecuba à la Mode; or, The Wily Greek and the Modest Maid*; by C. Metcalfe; performed at Vestry House, Anerley.
1894	*Iphigenia in Tauris*; in ancient Greek; performed at St Andrew's Hall, Cambridge; University of Cambridge.
14 February 1895	*The Importance of Being Earnest*; by Oscar Wilde; performed at St James's Theatre, London.
1895	*Alcestis*; in ancient Greek; performed at Bradfield College, Berkshire.
1899	*Antigone*; directed by Stanislavsky; with music composed by Felix Mendelssohn; performed at the Moscow Art Theatre.
February 1901	*Hippolytus*; a reading by Gilbert Murray of his own translation at Newnham College, Cambridge.
1901	A reading by Gilbert Murray of a selection of his own translations of *Bacchae*, *Hippolytus*, and Aristophanes' *Frogs*; performed at a Fabian Society meeting, St Pancras, London.

1902	*Salome*; by Oscar Wilde; directed by Max Reinhardt; performed at the Neues Theater, Berlin.
June 1903	*Antigone*; in a translation by Lewis Campbell; performed at St Leonard's School, St Andrews, by pupils of the school.
1903	*Alcestis*; an English adaptation of Euripides, with excerpts from Browning's *Balaustion's Adventure*; with music composed by Henry Gadsby; performed at Bournemouth Girls' High School, by pupils of the school.
after 1903	the odes from Aeschylus' *Suppliants*; danced by Isadora Duncan, accompanied by a singing chorus of boys; performed across central Europe, including Vienna, Budapest, Berlin, and Munich.
May 1904	Sophocles' *Electra*; performed by Greek actors at the Court Theatre, London.
May 1904	*Hippolytus*; in a translation by Gilbert Murray; directed by Granville Barker; with Barker as Henchman and Edyth Olive as Phaedra; performed at the Lyric Theatre, London; New Century Company, England.
18 October 1904	*Hippolytus*; in a translation by Gilbert Murray; a revival of Granville Barker's May 1904 production at the Lyric Theatre (see above); with Barker as Henchman; performed at the Court Theatre, London; under Vedrenne–Barker management.
November 1904	*The Trojan Women*; a reading by Gilbert Murray of extracts of his own translation; performed at the Socratic Society of Birmingham.
1904	*Alcestis*; in ancient Greek; performed at Bradfield College, Berkshire.
1904	*Medea*; in a German translation by Ulrich von Wilamowitz-Moellendorff; directed by Hans Oberländer and Max Reinhardt; performed at the Neues Theater am Schiffbauerdamm, Berlin.
11 April 1905	*The Trojan Women*; in a translation by Gilbert Murray; directed by Granville Barker; with Edyth Olive as Cassandra, Edith

	Wynne-Matthison as Andromache, and Marie Brema as Hecuba; performed at the Court Theatre, London.
28 November 1905	*Major Barbara*; by George Bernard Shaw; with Granville Barker (at first, but not from January 1906) as Cusins/Euripides/ Gilbert Murray; performed at the Court Theatre, London.
1905	*Iphigenia*; scenes taken from *Iphigenia in Aulis* and *Iphigenia in Tauris* danced by Isadora Duncan; with music composed by Christoph Willibald Gluck; performed in Amsterdam. Revived in New York in 1908-1909.
16 January 1906	Euripides' *Electra*; in a translation by Gilbert Murray; directed by Granville Barker; with Edith Wynne-Matthison as Electra and Edyth Olive as Clytemnestra; performed at the Court Theatre, London.
26 March 1906	*Hippolytus*; a revival of Granville Barker's October 1904 production (see above); with Granville Barker as Henchman; performed at the Court Theatre, London.
March 1907	*The Persians*; in a translation by B. J. Ryan; directed by Lewis Casson; with Casson as the ghost of Darius; performed at Terry's Theatre, London.
13 June 1907	*Medea*; in ancient Greek; with Ethel Abrahams in the title role; performed at the Botanical Garden, University College London; University College London and Bedford College.
22 October 1907	*Medea*; in a translation by Gilbert Murray; directed by Granville Barker; with Edyth Olive in the title role, Hubert Carter as Jason, and Lewis Casson as the Messenger; performed at the Savoy Theatre, London; under Vedrenne–Barker management.
1908	*Bacchae*; in a translation by Gilbert Murray; produced by William Poel; with Lillah McCarthy as Dionysus; performed at the Court Theatre, London.
25 January 1909	*Elektra*; an opera composed by Richard Strauss; libretto by Hugo von Hof-

	mannsthal; directed by Georg Toller; with Frau Krull in the title role; performed at the Hoftheater, Dresden.
15 July 1909	Sophocles' *Electra*; in a translation by Lewis Campbell; with E. Calkin in the title role; performed at the Aldwych Theatre, London, in aid of Bedford College's Building Fund.
16 February 1910	*Alcestis*; in a translation by Gerald Warre Cornish; with Ethel Abrahams in the title role; performed at the South Villa, Regent's Park, London, in aid of Bedford College's Building Fund.
19 February 1910	*Elektra*; an opera composed by Richard Strauss; libretto by Hugo von Hofmannsthal; with Edyth Walker in the title role; performed at Covent Garden, London.
25 September 1910	*Oedipus Tyrannus*; in a German version by Hugo von Hofmannsthal; directed by Max Reinhardt; performed at the Musikfesthalle, Munich, followed by a run at the Zirkus Schumann, Berlin and a European tour (for the English language production see under 1912 below); Deutsches Theater Company, Germany.
8 December 1910	*Salomé*; an opera by Richard Strauss; libretto by Oscar Wilde, in a German translation by Hedwig Lachmann; performed at the Royal Opera House, Covent Garden, London.
December 1910	*Alcestis*; in a translation by Francis Hubback; produced by William Poel; performed on the Grand Staircase at London University, and later at the Little Theatre, London, in January 1911.
6 July 1911	*Trachiniae*; in a translation by Lewis Campbell; directed by G. R. Foss; with Ethel Abrahams as Deianeira; performed at the Court Theatre, London, in aid of Bedford College's Building Fund.
15 January 1912	*Oedipus Rex*; in a translation by Gilbert Murray of Hugo von Hofmannsthal's German version; directed by Max Reinhardt; with John Martin-Harvey as Oedipus

and Lillah McCarthy as Jocasta; performed at Covent Garden, London (for the German language production see under 25 September 1910 above).

19 March 1912   *Iphigenia in Tauris*; in a translation by Gilbert Murray; directed by Granville Barker; with Lillah McCarthy as Iphigenia; performed at the Kingsway Theatre, London (also performed on 4 June at His Majesty's Theatre; and, with Granville Barker as Orestes, on 11 June at Bradfield College, Berkshire); the McCarthy-Barker Company, England.

February 1914   *Acharnians*; directed by Cyril Bailey; performed at the New Theatre, Oxford; Oxford University Dramatic Society.

April 1914   *Alcestis*; a revival of the December 1910 production of Francis Hubback's translation (see above); produced by William Poel; performed at the Ethical Church, Bayswater; Religious Dramatic Society.

1914   *Alcestis*; in ancient Greek; performed at Bradfield College, Berkshire.

1915   *Oedipus Rex*; directed and choreographed by Isadora Duncan; with Duncan and her pupils as the Chorus; performed at Isadora Duncan's studio, New York.

15 May 1915   *Iphigenia in Tauris*; in a translation by Gilbert Murray; directed by Granville Barker; with Lillah McCarthy as Iphigenia; performed in Yale University's Bowl, and touring to Harvard University (18 May), the Piping Rock Country Club, Long Island, New York (*c*.25 May), the College of the City of New York (31 May and 5 June), the University of Pennsylvania (8 June), and Princeton University (11 June); the McCarthy-Barker Company, England.

19 May 1915   *Trojan Women*; in a translation by Gilbert Murray; directed by Granville Barker; with Lillah McCarthy as Hecuba and Edith Wynne-Matthison as Andromache; performed at Harvard University, and touring to the College of the City of New

	York (29 May and 2 June), the University of Pennsylvania (9 June), and Princeton University (12 June); the McCarthy-Barker Company, England.
7 December 1926	*Oedipus the King*; in a translation by W. B. Yeats; directed by Lennox Robinson; with music composed by Robinson; with Frank J. McCormick as Oedipus and Eileen Crowe as Jocasta; performed at the Abbey Theatre, Dublin.
summer 1953	*The Confidential Clerk*; by T. S. Eliot; directed by Martin E. Browne; performed at the Edinburgh Festival.
1965	*Persians*; directed by Karolos Koun; performed in Greece; Theatro Technis, Greece.
10 September 1992	*Medea*; in a translation by Alistair Elliot; directed by Jonathan Kent; with Diana Rigg in the title role; performed at the Almeida Theatre, London, later transferring to New York; Almeida Theatre Company, England.
1995	*Mighty Aphrodite*; a film which parodies both *Oedipus Tyrannus* and *Hippolytus*; directed by Woody Allen; USA.
September 1998	*Samson Agonistes*; a play by Milton drawing on *Oedipus at Colonus*; directed by Barrie Rutter; with Rutter as Samson; performed at the Viaduct Theatre, Halifax; Northern Broadsides, England.
23 January 2000	*Oreste*; a *pasticcio* opera, based on *Iphigenia among the Taurians*, composed by G. F. Handel; anonymous Italian libretto adapted from G. Barlocci's *L'Oreste*; directed by Anthony Besch; performed at the Linbury Studio Theatre, Covent Garden, London; English Bach Festival Opera.
6 June 2000	*Medea*; in a translation by Kenneth McLeish; directed by Deborah Warner; with Fiona Shaw in the title role; performed at the Abbey Theatre, Dublin, and transferring to London in 2001 and New York in 2002; Abbey Theatre, Republic of Ireland.

December 2000   *Alceste*; a masque with music by G. F. Handel and libretto by Tobias Smollett; directed by Tom Hawkes; performed at the Linbury Studio Theatre, Covent Garden, London (the first performance at this venue, following the 1989 world premiere in the Banqueting House, Whitehall, London); English Bach Festival Opera.

2001   *AI: Artificial Intelligence*; a film directed by Steven Spielberg; USA.

Bibliography

à Beckett, Gilbert Abbott (1852). *The Comic History of Rome* (London).

'A Graduate of Girton' (1888). 'Greek Plays in the Universities', *Woman's World*, 1: 121–8.

'A Young Lady' (1698). *The Unnatural Mother, the Scene in the Kingdom of Siam* (London).

Abrahams, Ethel B. (1908). *Greek Dress* (London).

Ackermann, Rudolph, et al. (1809). *Microcosm of London; or, London in Miniature*, 3 vols. (London).

Adams, George (1729). *The Tragedies of Sophocles, Translated from the Greek*, i (London).

Adams, W. Davenport (1891). *A Book of Burlesque: Sketches of English Stage Travestie and Parody* (London).

Adderley, J. G. (1887). 'The Fight for the Drama at Oxford', *Oxford Times*, 10 September 1887 (cutting in file *Oxford University Dramatic Society*, i (1884–1926), Bodleian Library, Oxford).

Addison, J., and Howell, J. (1878). *Jason and Medea: A Ramble after a Colchian. A Classical Burlesque* (British Library Add. MS 53203 M).

Albert, S. P. (1968). ' "In More Ways Than One": *Major Barbara*'s Debt to Gilbert Murray', *Educational Theatre Journal*, 20: 123–40.

Alfieri, Vittorio (1810). *Memoirs of the Life and Writings of Victor Alfieri, Written by Himself*, English translation, 2 vols. (London).

Altick, Richard D. (1970). *Studies in Scarlet* (New York).

——(1978). *The Shows of London* (Cambridge, MA, and London).

——(1989). 'English Publishing in 1852', in Altick (ed.), *Writers, Readers, and Occasions: Selected Essays on Victorian Literature and Life* (Columbus, OH), 141–58.

Amcotts, Vincent (1866). *Fair Helen: A Comic Opera* (Oxford and London).

——(1870). *Ariadne; or, The Bull! The Bully!! And the Bullion!!! A Classical Burlesque* (London).

——and Anson, W. R. (1866). *Pentheus: A Burlesque in Three Acts. Founded to a Certain Extent on the 'Bacchæ' of Euripides* (Oxford).

Amerongen, J. B. van (1926). *The Actor in Dickens: A Study of the Histrionic and Dramatic Elements in the Novelist's Life and Works* (London).

Anderson, Robert (1795, ed.). *The Works of the British Poets, with Prefaces Biographical and Critical*, xi (London).

Anon. (1714*a*). *Electra, A Tragedy. Translated from the Greek of Sophocles* (London).

——(1714*b*). *Ajax of Sophocles. Translated from the Greek, with Notes* (London).

——(1723). *An Abstract of the Lives of Eteocles and Polynices: Necessary to be perused by the Spectators of the New Tragedy, called, The Fatal Legacy* (London).

——(1726). *Reflections upon Reflections. Being Some Cursory Remarks on the Tragedy of Hecuba in Answer to the Pamphlet on that Play* (London).

——(1752). *Remarks on Mr. Mason's Elfrida, in Letters to a Friend* (London).

——(1760). *The Tendencies of the Foundling Hospital in its Present Extent* (London).

——(1761). *The Rise and Progress of the Foundling Hospital Considered* (London).

——(1762). *Occasional Thoughts on the Study and Character of Classical Authors ... with Some Incidental Comparisons of Homer and Ossian* (London).

——(1773). 'The Origin of Tragedy in Scotland', *The Scots Magazine*, 35 (January), 41–2.

——(1799). *The Battle of the Nile: A Dramatic Poem on the Model of the Greek Tragedy* (London).

——(1806). 'Reading School Play. Triennial Visitation', *Reading Mercury and Oxford Gazette*, 44, no. 2334 (Monday, 20 October), 3, col. 2.

——(1808). *A Description of Caractacus. A Grand Ballet of Action in Three Parts. Written by Thomas Sheridan, Esq. The Action under the Direction of Mr D'Egville* (London).

——(1809). 'Reading School Play', *Reading Mercury and Oxford Gazette*, 47, no. 2491 (Monday, 23 October), 3, col. 2.

——(1812). 'Triennial Visitation', *Reading Mercury and Oxford Gazette*, 90, no. 4692 (Monday, 26 October), 3, col. 3.

——(1815). 'Triennial Visitation', *Reading Mercury and Oxford Gazette*, 93, no. 4848 (Monday, 23 October), 3, col. 1.

——(1825), 'Orestes in Argos', *The Drama*, 7: 372–3.

——(1826). *Medea in Corinto (Medea in Corinth). A Tragic Opera in Two Acts. The Music by the Celebrated Meyer. The Translation in Easy Verse* (London).

——(1827), 'Triennial Visitation', *Reading Mercury and Oxford Gazette*, 105, no. 5563 (Monday, 22 October), 3, col. 2.

——(1834). 'Coleridge's Poetical Works', *Blackwood's Edinburgh Magazine*, 36, no. 227 (October), 542–70.

——(1843). *The Chinaid, or the 'Persae' of Aeschylus Burlesqued* (Oxford).

—— (1854). 'Mr Justice Talfourd', *The Literary Gazette and Journal of Belles Lettres, Science, and Art*, no. 1939 (28 March), 254–5.

—— (1876). *Medea* (a tragedy in English derived from the French play by E. Legouvé and performed at the Haymarket; British Library Add. MS 53167 E).

—— (1892). *Our Greek Play* (British Library Add. MS 55505 L).

—— ([1911], ed.). *Maud Allan and Her Art*, souvenir programme (London).

Appleton, William (1974). *Madame Vestris and the London Stage* (New York and London).

Armstrong, Isobel (1993). *Victorian Poetry: Poetry, Poetics and Politics* (London and New York).

Arnold, Matthew (1879). 'The French Play in London', *The Nineteenth Century*, 5: 242–3.

—— (1986). *Matthew Arnold: A Critical Edition of the Major Works*, ed. Miriam Allott and Robert H. Super (Oxford).

Arundel, Dennis (1965). *The Story of Sadler's Wells 1683–1964* (London).

Ashby, Stanley (1957). 'The Treatment of the Themes of Classical Tragedy in English Tragedy between 1660 and 1738' (Ph.D. diss., Harvard).

Ashton, Geoffrey (1992). *Catalogue of Paintings at the Theatre Museum, London* (London).

Ashton, Rosemary (1992, ed.). *George Eliot: Selected Critical Writings* (Oxford and New York).

Athanassoglou-Kallmyer, Nina (1989). *French Images from the Greek War of Independence 1821–1830* (New Haven and London).

Atkinson, Diane (1992). *Suffragettes in the Purple, White, and Green: London 1906–14* (London).

—— (1996). *The Suffragettes in Pictures* (Stroud).

Aubignac, François Hédelin, abbé d' (1657). *La Pratique du théâtre* (Paris)

—— (1684) *The Whole Art of the Theatre*, English translation of above (London).

Auerbach, Nina (1987). *Ellen Terry: Player in Her Time* (London and Melbourne).

—— (1990). *Private Theatricals: The Lives of the Victorians* (Cambridge, MA, and London).

Axton, Marie (1982) (ed.). *Three Tudor Classical Interludes* (Cambridge).

Ayres, Philip (1997). *Classical Culture and the Ideal of Rome in 18th-Century England* (Cambridge).

Babbitt, Irving (1919). *Rousseau and Romanticism* (Boston).

Bailey, Peter (1994). 'Conspiracies of Meaning: Music-Hall and the Knowingness of Popular Culture', *Past & Present* 144: 138–70.

Baily, Leslie (1973). *Gilbert and Sullivan and their World* (London).

Bainbridge, Beryl (2001). *According to Queeney* (London).

Baker, David Erskine (1763). *The Muse of Ossian: A Dramatic Poem of Three Acts, Selected from the Several Poems of Ossian the Son of Fingal. As it is Performed at the Theatre in Edinburgh* (Edinburgh).

Baker, Sir Richard (1643). *A Chronicle of the Kings of England, from the Time of the Romans Government unto the Raigne of our Soveraigne Lord, King Charles* (London).

Baker-Penoyre, J. ff. (1898). 'School Plays in Latin and Greek: An Historical Study with some Observation on the educational value of acting, and on the recent revival of Greek Drama in Schools', *Special Reports on Educational Subjects*, 2, C. 8943. Board of Education (London).

Bakhtin, Mikhail (1986). 'Response to a Question from the *Novy Mir* Editorial Staff', English translation by Vern W. McGee, in Caryl Emerson and Michael Holquist (eds.), *Speech Genres and Other Late Essays* (Austin, TX), 1–7; first published as 'Smelee pol'zovat'sya vozmozhnostyami' ('Use Opportunities More Boldly') in *Novy mir*, vol 46, no. 11 (November 1970), 237–40.

Balderston, Katharine (1942, ed.). *Thraliana*, i (Oxford).

Ball, W. W. Rouse, and Venn, J. A. (1913). *Admissions to Trinity College, Cambridge*, v: *1851–1900* (London).

Ballaster, Ros (1996). 'The First Female Dramatists', in Helen Wilcox (ed.), *Women and Literature in Britain 1500–1700* (Cambridge), 267–90.

Banham, Martin (1995, ed.). *The Cambridge Guide to Theatre* (Cambridge).

Barnett, Dene (1987). *The Art of Gesture: The Practices and Principles of 18th Century Acting* (Heidelberg).

Barrell, John, and Guest, Harriet (2000). 'Thomson in the 1790s', in Terry (ed.), 217–46.

Barrière, François (1846–81, ed.). *Bibliothèque des mémoires relatifs à l'histoire de France* (Paris).

Bartholomew, William (1845). *An Imitative Version of Sophocles' Tragedy Antigone, with its Melo-Dramatic Dialogue and Choruses, as Written and Adapted to the Music of Dr. Felix Mendelssohn Bartholdy by W. Bartholomew* (London).

——(1846). *The Ruins of Athens. A Dramatic Masque* (London).

——(1850). *The Choral Lyrics, with Intermediate Recitations, written and adapted by W. Bartholomew, to Illustrate the Music of Sophocles' Tragedy 'Oedipus Coloneus', as Composed by Felix Mendelssohn Bartholdy* (London).

Barton, Lucy (1937). *Historic Costume for the Stage* (London).

Bates, William (1873, ed.). *A Gallery of Illustrious Literary Characters (1830–1838), Drawn by the Late Daniel Maclise R.A.* (London).

Bayley, Peter (1824). *Orestes, A Tragedy in Five Acts* (British Library Add. MS 42865, fos. 157–273).

——(1825*a*). *Orestes in Argos* (London).

——(1825*b*). *Orestes in Argos*, in *Dolby's British Theatre* (London).

Beard, Mary (2000). *The Invention of Jane Harrison* (Cambridge, MA, and London).

——(2002). *The Parthenon* (London).

Beattie, James (1776). 'An Essay on Poetry and Music as they Affect the Mind', in *Essays* (London), 3–317.

Beatty, Laura (1999). *Lillie Langtry: Manners, Masks and Morals* (London).

Beaumont, Cyril W. (1934). *The French Dancers of the 18th Century: Lamargo, Sallé, Guimard* (London).

Beerbohm, Max (*c*.1918). *Herbert Beerbohm Tree: Some Memories of Him and his Art* (London).

Behler, Ernst (1986). 'A. W. Schlegel and the 19th-century Damnatio of Euripides', *Greek, Roman, and Byzantine Studies*, 27: 335–69.

Bell, William Boscowan (1823). *The Queen of Argos: A Tragedy in Five Acts* (London).

Bénézit, E. (1999). *Dictionnaire critique et documentaire des Peintres Sculpteurs Dessinateurs et Gravures, nouvelle édition*, ed. Jacques Busse (Paris).

Bentley, Richard (1761). *The Wishes; or, Harlequin's Mouth Opened* (Larpent Coll. 199, F 253/85).

Bergman, Gösta M. (1977). *Lighting in the Theatre* (Stockholm and Totowa, NJ).

Bernbaum, Ernest (1958). *The Drama of Sensibility* (Gloucester, MA).

Bernstein, Susan (1997). *Confessional Subjects: Revelations of Gender and Power in Victorian Literature and Culture* (Chapel Hill, NC, and London).

Bevis, Richard (1988). *English Drama: Restoration and Eighteenth Century: 1660–1789* (Harlow).

Bianchi, Francesco (1796). *Antigona: A New Serious Opera in Two Acts. To Be Performed at the King's Theatre, Hay-Market. The Music, Composed, Here, by Bianchi* (London).

Biet, Christian (1994). *Œdipe en monarchie: tragédie et théorie juridique à l'âge classique* (Paris).

Binder, Gerhard (1964). *Die Aussetzung des Königskindes: Kyros und Romulus* (Beiträge zur klassischen Philologie, 10; Meisenheim am Glan).

Binns, J. W. (ed.) (1981). *Renaissance Latin Drama in England* (Hildesheim and New York).

Blanchard, E. L. (1845). *Antigone Travestie* (British Library Add. MS 42982, F 166–73).

——(1891). *The Life and Reminiscences of E. L. Blanchard*, ed. Clement Scott and Cecil Howard, 2 vols. (London).

Blew, William John (1887). *Medea, from the Tragedy of Euripides* (London).

Boaden, James (1798). *Cambro-Britons, an Historical Play in Three Acts* (London).

Boas, Frederick S. (1914). *University Drama in the Tudor Age* (Oxford and London).

Bockett, B. B. ('Oliver Oldfellow') (1857). *Our School: or, Scraps and Scrapes in Schoolboy Life, with Illustrations by William McConnell and Others* (London).

Boehrer, Bruce Thomas (1992). *Monarchy and Incest in Renaissance England: Literature, Culture, Kinship and Kingship* (Philadelphia).

Boileau Despréaux, Nicolas (1674). *Œuvres diverses du sieur D—, avec le Traité du sublime, ou du merveilleux dans le discours, traduit du grec de Longin* (Paris).

Bond, Richmond P. (1932). *English Burlesque Poetry 1700–1750* (Cambridge, MA).

Booth, Michael R. (1969–76). *English Plays of the Nineteenth Century*, 5 vols. (Oxford).

——(1977). 'East End and West End: Class and Audience in Victorian London', *Theatre Research International*, 2: 98–103.

——(1981). *Victorian Spectacular Theatre 1850–1910* (London).

Bosker, A[isso] (1930). *Literary Criticism in the Age of Johnson* (Groningen and The Hague).

Bowers, R. H. (1949). 'William Gager's Oedipus', *Studies in Philology*, 46: 141–53.

Bowman, Daniel (1875). *The Life and Adventures of Billy Purvis* (Newcastle).

Boyer, Abel (1694). *The Complete French Master* (London).

——(1699). *The Royal Dictionary: In Two Parts* (London).

——(1700). *Achilles: or, Iphigenia in Aulis. A Tragedy* (London).

——(1714). *The Victim; or, Achilles and Iphigenia in Aulis: A Tragedy. As it was Acted at the Theatre-Royal, in Drury-Lane. The Second Edition. To which is added, an Advertisement about the late Irregular Reviving of this Tragedy* (London).

——(1737, ed.). *The Political State of Britain*, no. 54 (London).

Braddon, Mary Elizabeth (1860). *Lady Audley's Secret* (London).

Bradley, John L. (1965, ed.). *Rogue's Progress: The Autobiography of 'Lord Chief Baron' Nicholson* (London).

Brain, John A. (1904). 'An Evening with Thomas Noon Talfourd', in *Berkshire Ballads and Other Papers* (Reading), 67–110.

Brantlinger, Patrick (1977). *The Spirit of Reform: British Literature and Politics, 1832–1867* (Cambridge, MA, and London).

Bratton, J. S. (1975). *The Victorian Popular Ballad* (London/Totowa, NJ).

——(1992). 'Irrational Dress', in Gardner and Rutherford (eds.), 77–91.

Brewer, John (1976). *Party Ideology and Popular Politics at the Accession of George III* (Cambridge).

——(1979–80). 'Theatre and Counter-Theatre in Georgian Politics', *Radical History Review*, 22: 7–40.

Bridwell, E. Nelson (1971). *Superman from the Thirties to the Seventies* (New York).

Bridges, Emma, Hall, Edith, and Rhodes, P. J. (forthcoming, eds.), *Cultural Responses to the Persian Wars* (Oxford).

Brissenden, R. F. (1974). *Virtue in Distress: Studies in the Novel of Sentiment from Richardson to Sade* (London and Basingstoke).

Bristed, Charles (1852). *Five Years in an English University*, 2nd edn. (New York).

Broadus, Edward Kemper (1921). *The Laureateship* (Oxford).

Brock, C. J. L. (1939). *A History of the Cobden Club* (London).

Brooke, Henry (1739). *Gustavus Vasa, The Deliverer of his Country* (London).

Brough, Robert (1856). *Medea; or the Best of Mothers, with a Brute of a Husband. A Burlesque* (London).

——(1858). *The Siege of Troy: A Burlesque in One Act* (Winchester).

——(1890). *Songs of the 'Governing Classes' and Other Lyrics Written in a Seasonable Spirit of 'Vulgar Declamation'*, 2nd edn. (London).

Brough, William, and Brough, Robert (1849). *The Sphinx* (London).

——and Burnand, F. C. (1865). *Beeton's Book of Burlesques* (London).

Brown, A. T. (1924). *Some Account of the Royal Institution School, Liverpool* (Liverpool).

Brown, John (1763). *A Dissertation on the Rise, Union, and Power, the Progressions, Separations, and Corruptions, of Poetry and Music* (London).

Brown, T. Allston (1903). *A History of the New York Stage from the first performance in 1732 to 1901*, 3 vols. (New York).

Browning, Elizabeth Barrett (1994). *The Works of Elizabeth Barrett Browning* (Wordsworth edn., Ware).

Browning, Robert (1940). *Poems and Plays*, iv: *1871–1890*, ed. M. M. Bozman (London).

Brumoy, Pierre (1730). *Le Théâtre des Grecs*, 3 vols. (Paris).

——(1785–9). *Le Théâtre des Grecs*, 2nd edn., with notes by Guillaume Dubois Rochefort, François Jean Gabriel de La Porte du Theil, and [Prévost], 13 vols. (Paris).

Brunkhorst, Martin (1999). 'Das Experiment mit dem antiken Chor auf der modernen Bühne (1585–1803)', in Pieter Riemer and Bernhard Zimmermann (eds.), *Der Chor im antiken und modernen Drama* (Stuttgart and Weimar, 1999), 171–94.

Buchanan-Jones, John (1966, ed.). *The Remains of Thomas Hearne (Reliquiæ Hernianæ), Being Extracts from his MS Diaries, Compiled by Dr. John Bliss* (London and Fontwell).

Buckland, Gail (1980*a*). *First Photographs* (London).

—— (1980*b*). *Fox Talbot and the Invention of Photography* (London).

Buckley, Theodore Alois (1850). *The Tragedies of Euripides*, 2 vols. (London).

Bulwer, Edward Lytton, later Bulwer-Lytton, first Baron Lytton (1833). *England and the English*, 2 vols. (London).

—— (1834). *The Last Days of Pompeii* (London).

—— (1837). *Athens: Its Rise and Fall*, 2 vols. (London).

—— (1863). *Dramatic Works* (London).

—— (2004). *Edward Bulwer Lytton, Athens: Its Rise and Fall*, ed. Oswyn Murray (London).

Burden, Michael (1994). *Garrick, Arne, and the Masque of Alfred: A Case Study in National, Theatrical, and Musical Politics* (Lewiston, NY, and Lampeter).

Burian, Peter (1997). 'Tragedy Adapted for Stages and Screens: the Renaissance to the Present', in Easterling (ed.), 228–83.

Burke, Edmund (1790). *Reflections on the Revolution in France* (London).

Burnand, F. C. (1863*a*). *Patient Penelope: or, the Return of Ulysses* (London).

—— (1863*b*) *Ixion; or, the Man at the Wheel* (London).

—— (1864). *Venus and Adonis: or, the Two Rivals & the Small Boar. Being a Full, True, and Particular Account, Adapted to the Requirements of the Present Age, of an Ancient Mythological Piece of Scandal* (London).

—— (1865). *Pirithoüs, the Son of Ixion* (London).

—— (1872). *Arion; or, The Story of a Lyre* (London).

—— (1880). *The 'A. D. C.': Being Personal Reminiscences of the University Amateur Dramatic Club, Cambridge* (London).

—— (1904). *Records and Reminiscences, Personal and General*, 2 vols. (London).

Burnell, Henry (1659). *The World's Idol: A Comedy written in Greek by Aristophanes, translated by H.H.B.* (London).

Burns, Landon C. (1974). *Pity and Tears: The Tragedies of Nicholas Rowe* (Salzburg).

Butler, Samuel (1896). *Life and Letters of Samuel Butler 1790–1840*, 2 vols. (London).

Byron, George, Lord (1994). *The Works of Lord Byron* (Wordsworth edn.; Ware).

Byron, Henry J. (1863). *Orpheus and Eurydice; or, the Young Gentleman who Charmed the Rocks* (London).

Calcraft, John William (1847). *Iphigenia in Aulis: A Tragedy, From the Greek of Euripides, as Presented in the Theatre of Bacchus, at Athens, circa B.C. 430. Adapted to the Modern Stage*, 3rd edn. (Dublin).

Campbell, Hilbert H. (1976). *James Thomson (1700–1748): An Annotated Bibliography of Selected Editions and the Important Criticism* (New York and London).

Campbell, Lewis (1891). *A Guide to Greek Tragedy for English Readers* (London).

——(1914). *Memorials in Prose and Verse of Lewis Campbell*, with a preface by Frances Pitt Campbell (London).

Campbell, Lily B. (1918). 'A History of Costuming on the English Stage between 1660 and 1823', *University of Wisconsin Studies in Language and Literature*, 2: 87–223.

Campbell, Thomas (1834). *Life of Mrs. Siddons*, 2 vols. (London).

Cannan, Paul D. (1994). 'New Directions in Serious Drama on the London Stage, 1675–1678', *Philological Quarterly*, 73: 219–42.

Cannon, Garland (1970, ed.). *The Letters of Sir William Jones*, 2 vols. (Oxford).

Cannon, John (1972). *Parliamentary Reform 1640–1832* (London).

Carlisle, Nicholas (1818). *A Concise Description of the Endowed Grammar Schools in England and Wales*, 2 vols. (London).

Carlyle, Carol Jones (2000). *Helen Faucit: Fire and Ice on the Victorian Stage* (London).

Carpenter, Humphrey (1985). *O.U.D.S.: A Centenary History of the Oxford Dramatic Society* (Oxford).

Caryl, John (1691). *Sir Salomon; or, the Cautious Coxcomb, A Comedy* (London); first published 1671.

Castle, Terry (1995). *The Female Thermometer: Eighteenth-Century Culture and the Invention of the Uncanny* (New York and Oxford).

Censorship and Licensing (1910). *Censorship and Licensing (Joint Select Committee) Verbatim Report of the Proceedings and Full Text of the Recommendations with an Appendix containing further statements by Mr G.Bernard Shaw, Mr Henry Arthur Jones, Mr Charles Frohman etc and Articles from 'The Stage'* (London).

Chalmers, Alexander (1807, ed.). *The British Essayists*, xl (London).

——(1810). *The Works of the English Poets from Chaucer to Cowper*, 21 vols. (London).

Chedzoy, Alan (1992). *A Scandalous Woman: The Life of Caroline Norton* (London).

Chénier, Marie-Joseph de (1818). *Œdipe-Roi*, in *Théâtre*, 3 vols. (Paris), iii.

Chevalier, Noel (1995, ed.). *The Clandestine Marriage, By David Garrick & George Colman the Elder* (Peterborough, ON).

Clark, Cumberland (1919). *Dickens and Talfourd* (London).

Clark, David Lee (1966, ed.). *Shelley's Prose*, corrected edn. (Albuquerque, NM).

Clark, D. R., and McGuire, J. B. (1989). *W. B. Yeats: The Writing of Sophocles' King Oedipus* (Philadelphia).

Clark, George Somers (1790). *Oedipus, King of Thebes, A Tragedy from the Greek of Sophocles: translated into Prose with Notes, Critical and Explanatory* (Oxford).

Clarke, M. L. (1945). *Greek Studies in England 1700–1830* (Cambridge).

Clauss, James J., and Johnston, Sarah Iles (1997, eds.). *Medea* (Princeton).

Clifford, James L. (1947, ed.). *Dr Campbell's Diary of a Visit to England in 1775* (Cambridge).

Clive, John (1989). 'Macaulay and the French Revolution', in Crossley and Small (eds.), 103–22.

Coats, Alice M. (1975). *Lord Bute: An Illustrated Life of John Stuart, Third Earl of Bute* (Princes Risborough).

Cobbe, F. P. (1863). 'The Humour of Various Nations', *Victoria Magazine*, 1 (July), 194.

Cole, John William (1859). *The Life and Theatrical Times of Charles Kean, F.S.A.*, 2 vols. (London).

Coleman, John (1904). *Fifty Years of an Actor's Life* (London).

Coleridge, Mary E. (1910). *Gatherered Leaves from the Prose of Mary E. Coleridge with a Memoir by Edith Sichel* (London).

Coleridge, Hartley (1836). *The Worthies of Yorkshire and Lancashire* (London).

Colley, Linda (1989). 'Radical Patriotism in Eighteenth-Century England', in Samuel (ed.), 169–87.

——(1992). *Britons: Forging the Nation 1707–1837* (New Haven).

Collins, Wilkie (1860). *The Woman in White* (London).

Collins, William (1765). *The Poetical Works*, ed. J. Langhorne (London).

Colman, George (1783). *The Art of Poetry; an Epistle to the Pisos. Translated from Horace, with Notes* (London).

Congreve, William (1753). *The Works*, 3 vols. (London).

Conolly, L. W. (1976). *The Censorship of English Drama 1738–1824* (San Marino, CA).

Constable, W. G. (1927). *John Flaxman 1755–1826* (London).

Cook, Dutton (1883). *Nights at the Play*, vol. i. (London).

Cooke, William (1775). *The Elements of Dramatic Criticism* (London).

Cooper, John J. (1923). *Some Worthies of Reading* (London).

Cooper, John Gilbert (1755). *Letters Concerning Taste*, 2nd edn. (London).

Corbett, Charles (1744). *A Catalogue of the Library of Lewis Theobald, Deceased* (London).

Courtney, W. L. ([1911]). 'An Interpretative Dancer', in Anon. ([1911], ed.).

Cowling, Jane (1993). 'An Edition of the Records of Drama, Ceremony and Secular Music in Winchester City and College, 1556–1642' (diss. Southampton).

Craig, Edward Gordon (1911). *On the Art of the Theatre* (London).

——(1677). *The Destruction of Jerusalem by Titus Vespasian. In Two Parts* (London).

Crossley, Ceri, and Small, Ian (1989, eds.). *The French Revolution and British Culture* (Oxford and New York).

Crowne, John (1675). *Andromache: A Tragedy* (London).

——(1681). *Thyestes: A Tragedy* (London).

——(1688). *Darius, King of Persia: A Tragedy* (London).

Crump, Galbraith Miller (1962, ed.). *The Poems and Translations of Thomas Stanley* (Oxford).

Crusius, Otto (1888). 'Stesichoros und die epodische Composition in der griechischen Lyrik', in *Commentationes Philologae quibus Ottoni Ribbeckio . . . congratulantur discipuli Lipsienses* (Leipzig), 3–22.

Culler, A. Dwight (1985). *The Victorian Mirror of History* (New Haven and London).

Cunningham, Hugh (1989). 'The Language of Patriotism', in Samuel (ed.), 57–89.

Cunningham, John E. (1950). *Theatre Royal: The History of the Theatre Royal, Birmingham* (Oxford).

Cvetkovich, Ann (1992). *Mixed Feelings: Feminism, Mass Culture, and Victorian Sensationalism* (New Brunswick, NJ).

Dacier, André (1692). *La Poétique d'Aristote: Traduite en français avec des remarques d'André Dacier* (Paris).

——(1693). *Tragédies grecques de Sophocle traduites en François, avec des notes Critiques, & un Examen de chaque pièce selon les règles du Théâtre* (Paris).

——(1705). *Aristotle's Art of Poetry. Translated from the Original Greek, according to Mr Theodore Goulston's edition, together with Mr Dacier's notes translated from the French* (London).

Dakin, Douglas (1972). *The Greek Struggle for Independence, 1821–1833* (London).

Dallas, R. C. (1823). *Adrastus: A Tragedy* (London).

Dalton, Richard (1751). *A Collection of Fifty-Two Engraved Plates from Drawings by Richard Dalton of Antiquities in Sicily, Greece, Asia Minor and Egypt* (London).

Dalzel, Andrew (1821). *Substance of Lectures on the Ancient Greeks and on the Revival of Greek Learning in Europe* (Edinburgh).

Daniel, Samuel (1594). *The Tragedie of Cleopatra* (London, revised 1601).

Darley, George (1836). review of T. N. Talfourd's *Ion* in *The Athenaeum*, 9, no. 448, pp. 371–3 (Saturday, 28 May).

Darter, William Silver (1888). *Reminiscences of Reading, by an Octogenarian* (Reading).

Davenant, Charles (1677). *Circe, a Tragedy as it is Acted at his Royal Highness the Duke of York's Theatre* (London).

Davidoff, Leonore, and Hall, Catherine (1987). *Family Fortunes: Men and Women of the English Middle Class 1780–1850* (London).

Davies, Rowland (1856). *The Journal of the Very Rev. Rowland Davies* (Camden Society, 68; London).

Davies, Thomas (1780). *Memoirs of the Life of David Garrick Esq.*, 2 vols. (London).

—— (1784). *Dramatic Miscellanies*, 3 vols. (Dublin).

Davis, Frank (1963). *Victorian Patrons of the Arts* (London).

Davis, Jim (1984, ed.). *Plays by H. J. Byron* (Cambridge).

—— and Emeljanow, Victor (2001). *Reflecting the Audience: London Theatregoing, 1840–1880* (Hatfield).

Davis, Tracy C. (1991). *Actresses as Working Women: Their Social Identity in Victorian Culture* (London and New York).

Décembre-Alonnier, Joseph (1975). *Dictionnaire de la Révolution Française 1789–1799*, 2 vols. (Paris).

Defoe, Daniel (1719). *The Life and Strange Surprizing Adventures of Robinson Crusoe* (London).

Delap, John (1762). *Hecuba a Tragedy* (London).

—— (1781). *The Royal Suppliants. A Tragedy*, 2nd edn. (London).

—— (1786). *The Captives* (Larpent Coll. F 253/340/1–3).

Demetz, Peter (1967). *Marx, Engels, and the Poets: Origins of Marxist Literary Criticism*, 2nd edn., English translation (Chicago and London).

Dennis, John (1693). *The Impartial Critick: or, some Observations upon a late Book, entitled A Short View of Tragedy, written by Mr Rymer* (London).

—— (1698). *The Usefulness of the Stage to the Happiness of Mankind. To Government, and To Religion. Occasioned by a Late Book written by Jeremy Collier M.A.* (London).

—— (1700). *Iphigenia a Tragedy, Acted at the Little Lincolns-Inn-Fields* (London).

—— (1702). *The Monument: A Poem Sacred to the Immortal Memory of the Best and Greatest of Kings, William the Third, King of Great Britain* (London).

—— (1704a). *Liberty Asserted* (London).

—— (1704b). *The Grounds of Criticism in Poetry* (London).

—— (1939–43). *The Critical Works* (Baltimore).

Denvir, Bernard (1984). *The Early Nineteenth Century: Art, Design, and Society 1789–1832* (London).

Derry, Warren (1966). *Dr. Parr: A Portrait of the Whig Dr. Johnson* (Oxford).

Devlin, Diana (1982) *A Speaking Part: Lewis Casson and the Theatre of his Time* (London).

Di Maria, Salvatore (1996). 'Toward an Italian Dramatic Stage: Rucellai's *Oreste*', *MLN* 111: 123–48.

Dickens, Charles (1965–2002). *The Letters of Charles Dickens*, ed. Graham Storey et al., 12 vols. (Oxford).

Dickinson, H. T. (1977). *Liberty and Property: Political Ideology in Eighteenth-Century Britain* (London).

Disher, Maurice (1955). *Victorian Song* (London).

DNB = Dictionary of National Biography, 2nd edn., 22 vols. (London, 1908–9).

Dobrée, Bonamy (1932, ed.). *The Letters of Philip Dormer Stanhope, 4th Earl of Chesterfield* (London).

Doddington, George Bubb (1809). *The Diary of the Late George Bubb Doddington*, 4th edn. (London).

Doran, John (1888). *'Their majesties' servants': Annals of the English Stage from Thomas Betterton to Edmund Kean*, rev. Robert W. Lowe, 3 vols. (London).

Dörpfeld, Wilhelm, and Reisch, Emil (1896). *Das griechische Theater* (Athens).

Dowling, Linda (1994). *Hellenism and Homosexuality in Victorian Oxford* (Ithaca, NY, and London).

Downer, Leslie (2003). *Madame Sadayakko: The Geisha Who Seduced the West* (London).

Downie, J. A. (1994). *To Settle the Succession of the State: Literature and Politics, 1678–1750* (Basingstoke and London).

Drake, Nathan (1798). *Literary Hours* (London).

Draper, John W. (1924). *William Mason: A Study in Eighteenth-Century Culture* (New York).

Droulia, Loukia (1974). *Philhéllenisme: ouvrages inspirés par la guerre de l'indépendance grecque 1821–1833. Répertoire bibliographique* (Athens).

Dryden, John (1970). *Selected Criticism*, ed. James Kinsley and George Parfitt (Oxford).

—— (1984). *The Works of John Dryden: Plays* Vol. XIII: *All for Love, Oedipus, Troilus and Cressida*, ed. Maximillian E. Novak (Berkeley and Los Angeles).

—— and Davenant, William (1670). *The Tempest, or The Enchanted Island: A Comedy* (London).

Dudden, F. Homes (1952). *Henry Fielding: His Life, Works, and Times*, i (Oxford).

Dukore, B. F. (1981). *Major Barbara: A Facsimile of the Holograph Manuscript* (New York and London).

Duncan, Isadora (1920). *The Philosopher's Stone of Dancing* (London).

——(1928). *My Life* (London).

Duncan, William (1753). *Caesar's Commentaries* (London).

East, John M. (1971). 'Andrew Ducrow: The World's Greatest Equestrian Performer', *Theatre Quarterly*, 1: 37–9.

Easterling, P. E. (1997). 'Gilbert Murray's reading of Euripides', *Colby Quarterly*, 23: 113–27.

——(1997, ed.). *The Cambridge Companion to Greek Tragedy* (Cambridge).

——(1999). 'The Early Years of the Cambridge Greek Play', in Christopher Stray (ed.), *Classics in 19th and 20th Century Cambridge: Curriculum, Culture and Community* (= *PCPS* suppl. 24; Cambridge), 27–47.

——and Hall, E. (2002, eds.). *Greek and Roman Actors: Aspects of an Ancient Profession* (Cambridge).

EB^{11} = *Encyclopaedia Britannica*, 11th edn., 29 vols. (Cambridge, 1910–11).

Eccles, F. Y. (1922). *Racine in England* (Oxford).

Edwards, Catharine (1996). *Writing Rome: Textual Approaches to the City* (Cambridge).

——(1999, ed.). *Roman Presences: Receptions of Rome in European Culture 1789–1945* (Cambridge and New York).

Egger, Émile (1862). 'Une représentation des "Perses" au palais épiscopal d'Orléans', *Bulletin de la Société des Antiquaires de France*, 44–5.

Eliot, George (1856). 'The Antigone and its Moral', *The Leader*, 29 March, 306.

Eliot, T. S. (1950). 'Euripides and Mr Murray', in *Selected Essays* (London), 46–50.

——(1954). *The Confidential Clerk* (London).

Ellmann, Richard (1987). *Oscar Wilde* (Harmondsworth).

Emeljanow, Victor (1987). *Victorian Popular Dramatists* (Boston).

Erasmus, Desiderius (1506). *Euripidis Poetae nobilissimi Hecuba et Iphigenia* (Paris).

Erffa, Helmut von, and Staley, Allen (1986). *The Paintings of Benjamin West* (New Haven and London).

Essick, Robert N. (1983, ed.). *William Blake: Catalogue* (Princeton).

Etienne, Robert, and Etienne, Françoise (1992). *The Search for Ancient Greece: New Horizons*, English translation (London).

Euben, J. Peter (1986). 'The Battle of Salamis and the Origins of Political Theory', *Political Theory*, 14: 359–90.

Ewans, Michael (forthcoming). 'Agamemnon's Influence in Germany: From Goethe to Wagner', in Macintosh, Michelakis, Hall, and Taplin (forthcoming, eds.).

Ewbank, Inga-Stina (forthcoming). 'Striking Too Short at Greeks', in Macintosh, Michelakis, Hall, and Taplin (forthcoming, eds.).

Faucit, J. Savill (1821). *Oedipus, A Musical Drama in Three Acts. Compiled, Selected, and Adapted from the Translations from the Greek of Sophocles by Dryden, Lee, Corneille, and T. Maurice, Esq.* (London).

Feather, John (1988). *A History of British Publishing* (London).

Felton, Cornelius C. (1837). 'Ion, A Tragedy in Five Acts', review article no. 8 in *The North American Review*, 44: 485–503.

Ferris, Lesley (1993, ed.). *Crossing the Stage: Controversies on Cross-Dressing* (London and New York).

Field, William (1828). *Memoirs of the Life, Writings and Opinions of the Rev. Samuel Parr LL.D.*, 2 vols. (London).

Fielding, Henry (1730). *Tom Thumb: A Tragedy*, 2nd edn. (London).

—— (1731). *The Tragedy of Tragedies; or, The Life and Death of Tom Thumb the Great* (London).

—— (1742). *The History of the Adventures of Joseph Andrews*, 2 vols. (London).

—— (1749). *The History of Tom Jones, A Foundling* (London).

—— and Young, William (1742). *Plutus. The God of Riches. A Comedy. Translated out of the Original Greek* (London).

Findlater, Richard (1967). *Banned: A Review of Theatrical Censorship in Britain* (London).

Fines, John (1967). 'Dr. Richard Valpy, Headmaster of Reading School' (unpublished typescript, Reading Public Library).

Fink, Zera S. (1945). *The Classical Republicans: An Essay in the Recovery of a Pattern of Thought in Seventeenth Century England* (Evanston, IL).

Finneran, R. J., Harper, G. Mills, and Murphy, W. M. (1977, eds.). *Letters to W. B. Yeats*, 2 vols. (London).

Firth, C. H., and Rait, R. S. (1911). *Acts and Ordinances of the Interregnum 1642–1660*, ii (London).

Fischer-Lichte, Erika (1999*a*). 'Between Text and Cultural Performance: Staging Greek Tragedies in Germany', *Theatre Survey*, 40: 1–30.

—— (1999*b*). 'Invocation of the Dead, Festival of Peoples' Theatre or Sacrificial Ritual? Some Remarks on Staging Greek Classics', in Savas Patsalidis and Elizabeth Sakellaridou (eds.). *(Dis)Placing Classical Greek Theatre* (Thessaloniki), 251–63.

—— (2004). 'Thinking about the Origins of Theatre in the 1970s', in Hall, Macintosh, and Wrigley (eds.), 329–60.

Fisk, Deborah Payne (2000, ed.). *The Cambridge Companion to English Restoration Theatre* (Cambridge).

Fiske, Roger (1986). *English Theatre Music in the Eighteenth Century*, 2nd edn. (Oxford).

Fitzball, Edward (1821). *Antigone; or, The Theban Sister* (Larpent Coll. F 254/649/1–4).

——(1859). *Thirty-Five Years of a Dramatic Author's Life*, 2 vols. (London).

FitzGerald, Edward (1889). *Letters and Literary Remains*, ed. William Aldis Wright, 3 vols. (London/New York).

Fitzgerald, Percy (1870). *Principles of Comedy and Dramatic Effect* (London).

——(1902). *Recollections of Dublin Castle and Dublin Society. By a Native* (New York).

Flashar, Hellmut (1991). *Inszenierung der Antike: das griechische Drama auf der Bühne der Neuzeit* (Munich).

Fletcher, Kathy (1987). 'Planché, Vestris, and the Transvestite Role: Sexuality and Gender in Victorian Popular Theatre', *Nineteenth Century Theatre*, 15: 9–33.

Fogerty, Elsie (1903). *The Antigone of Sophocles. Adapted and Arranged for Amateur Performance in Girls' Schools* (London).

Foley, Helene (1999–2000). 'Twentieth-Century Performance and Adaptation of Greek Tragedy', in Martin Cropp, Kevin Lee, and David Sansone (eds.), *Euripides and the Tragic Theatre in the Late Fifth Century* (= *ICS* Special Issues 24–5; Champaign, IL), 1–13.

Foot, Jesse (1811). *The Life of Arthur Murphy* (London).

Foot, Paul (1980). *Red Shelley* (London).

Foote, Samuel (1747). *A Treatise on the Passions so Far as they Regard the Stage* (London).

Foskett, Daphne (1972). *A Dictionary of British Miniature Painters* (London).

Foulkes, Richard (1997). *Church and Stage in Victorian England* (Cambridge).

Fowell, Frank, and Palmer, Frank (1913). *Censorship in England* (London).

France, Peter (1966, ed.). *Racine, Athalie* (Oxford).

Francillon, R. E. (1914). *Mid-Victorian Memories* (London, New York, and Toronto).

Francklin, Thomas (1754). *Translation: A Poem*, 2nd edn. (London).

——(1758). *The Tragedies of Sophocles, from the Greek*, 2 vols. (London).

——(1762). *Orestes a Tragedy*, in *The Works of M. de Voltaire. Translated from the French by Dr. Smollett and Others*, 36 vols. (London, 1761–5), xiv, 22–119.

——(1780). *The Works of Lucian, from the Greek* (London).

——(1806). *The Oedipus Tyrannus of Sophocles. Acted at the Triennial Visitation of Reading School. Translated by Dr. Franklin* (Reading).

Franke, Olga (1939). *Euripides bei den deutschen Dramatikern des achtzehnten Jahrhunderts* (Leipzig).

Franklin, Michael J. (1995, ed.). *Sir William Jones: Selected Poetical and Political Prose Works* (Cardiff).

Fraser, Flora (1996). *The Unruly Queen: The Life of Queen Caroline* (London and Basingstoke).

Frenzel, Elizabeth (1962). *Stoffe der Weltliteratur* (Stuttgart).

Fuseli, Henry (1975). *Henry Fuseli 1741–1825. Tate Gallery Exhibition Catalogue* (London).

Gagen, Jean E. (1954). *The New Woman: Her Emergence in English Drama 1600–1730* (New York).

Garafala, Lynn (1993). 'The Travesty Dancer in Nineteenth-Century Ballet', in Ferris (ed.), 93–106.

Garber, Marjorie (1993). *Vested Interests: Cross-Dressing and Cultural Anxiety* (Harmondsworth).

Gardner, Vivien (1992). 'Introduction', in Gardner and Rutherford (eds.), 1–16.

—— and Rutherford, Susan (1992, eds.). *The New Woman and Her Sisters: Feminism and Theatre 1850–1914* (Hemel Hempstead).

Garrick, David, and Colman, George (1766). *The Clandestine Marriage, A Comedy* (London).

Gascoigne, George, and Kinwelmershe, Francis (1566). *Jocasta: A Tragedie writen in Greke by Eurepedes, translated and digested into acte* (London).

Gaster, Theodor H. (1969). *Myth, Legend, and Custom in the Old Testament: A Comparative Study with Chapters from Sir James G. Frazer's Folklore in the Old Testament* (New York), i.

Gaunt, William (1952). *Victorian Olympus* (London).

Geanakopoulos, Deno J. (1976). 'The Diaspora Greeks: The Genesis of Modern Greek National Consciousness', in N. P. Diamandouros, J. P. Anton, John A. Petropoulos, and Peter Topping (eds.), *Hellenism and the First Greek War of Liberation (1821–1830): Continuity and Change* (Thessaloniki), 59–77.

Genest, John (1832). *Some Account of the English Stage, from the Restoration in 1660 to 1830*, 10 vols. (Bath).

George, M. Dorothy (1952). *Catalogue of Political and Personal Satires preserved in the Department of Prints and Drawings in the British Museum, Vol. X: 1820–1827* (London).

—— (1959). *English Political Caricature to 1792* (Oxford).

Gay, John (1967 [1711]). *Excerpts from the English Theophrastus, or, The Manners of the Age (1702)*, with an introduction by W. Earl Britton (New York).

Gerrard, Christine (1994). *The Patriot Opposition to Walpole: Politics, Poetry and National Myth 1725–1742 (Oxford)*.

Gibbon, Edward (1776–88). *The History of the Decline and Fall of the Roman Empire*, 6 vols. (London).

Gilder, Rosamond (1931). *Enter the Actress: The First Women in the Theatre* (London, Bombay, and Sydney).

Gildon, Charles (1698). *Phaeton, or, The Fatal Divorce. A Tragedy. As it is Acted at the Theatre Royal. In Imitation of the Antients* (London).

——(1701). *Love's Victim; or, the Queen of Wales* (London).

——(1702). *A Comparison between the Two Stages* (London).

——(1718). *The Complete Art of Poetry*, 2 vols. (London).

Gillespie, Stuart (1988). *The Poets on the Classics: An Anthology* (London and New York).

——(1992). 'A Checklist of Restoration English Translations and Adaptations of Classical Greek and Latin Poetry, 1660–1700', *Translation and Literature*, 1: 52–67.

Glasse, George Henry (1781). *ΚΑΡΑΚΤΑΚΟΣ ΕΠΙ ΜΩΝΗ sive Cl. Masoni Caractacus Græco carmine redditus cum versione Latino a Georgio Henrico Glasse* (Oxford).

Gleckner, Robert F. (1997). *Gray Agonistes: Thomas Gray and Masculine Friendship* (Baltimore and London).

Gliksohn, Jean-Michel (1985). *Iphigénie de la Grèce antique à l'Europe des Lumières* (Paris).

Glover, Richard (1734). *Leonidas: A Poem* (London).

——(1753). *Boadicia* [sic] (London).

——(1777). *Medea: A Tragedy* (in The New English Theatre vol. 12) (London).

——(1790). *Medea: A Tragedy in Five Acts*, by Mr. Glover (London).

——(1799). *Jason: A Tragedy in Five Acts* (London).

Godwin, William (1793). *An Enquiry Concerning Political Justice* (London).

——(1801). *Thoughts Occasioned by the Perusal of Dr Parr's Spital Sermon, Preached At Christ Church, April 15, 1800: Being A Reply to the Attacks of Dr Parr, Mr Mackintosh, the Author of an Essay On Population, and Others* (London).

——(1988). *Things as They Are or the Adventures of Caleb Williams*, ed. M. Hindle (Harmondsworth).

Goffe, Thomas (1633). *The Tragedy of Orestes, written by Thomas Goffe, Master of Arts, and Student of Christs Church in Oxford, and Acted by the Students of the Same House* (London).

——(1656). *Three Excellent Tragedies. Viz The Raging Turk, or Bajazet the Second. The Courageous Turk, or, Amurath the First. And the Tragœdie of Orestes*, 2nd edn. (London).

Goldhill, Simon (2002). *Who Needs Greek? Contests in the Cultural History of Hellenism* (Cambridge).

Goldie, Mark (1999, ed.). *The Reception of Locke's Politics from the 1690s to the 1830s* (London), i.

Golding, William (1995). *The Double Tongue* (London).

Goodwin, Albert (1979). *The Friends of Liberty: The English Democratic Movement in the Age of the French Revolution* (London).

Gosse, Edmund (1884, ed.). *The Works of Thomas Gray*, 4 vols. (London).

Grant, Douglas (1951). *James Thomson: Poet of 'The Seasons'* (London).

Gray, Charles Harold (1931). *Theatrical Criticism in London to 1795* (New York).

Gray, Thomas (1757). *Odes: The Progress of Poesy and The Bard* (Strawberry Hill).

Green, Clarence C. (1934). *The Neo-Classic Theory of Tragedy in England during the Eighteenth Century* (Cambridge, MA).

Greene, Donald (1984, ed.). *Samuel Johnson: The Major Works* (Oxford).

Gregory, John (1774). *A Father's Legacy to his Daughters*, 2nd edn. (London).

Grene, Nicholas (1984). *Bernard Shaw: A Critical View* (London and Basingstoke).

Grewal, Inderpal (1990). 'The Guidebook and the Museum: Imperialism, Education and Nationalism in the British Museum', in Patrick Scott and Pauline Fletcher (eds.), *Culture and Education in Victorian England* (Lewisburg, PA), 195–217.

Griffin, Ernest (1959). 'The Dramatic Chorus in English Literary Theory and Practice' (diss. Columbia).

Griffin, Jasper (ed.) (1999), *Sophocles Revisited: Essays Presented to Sir Hugh Lloyd-Jones* (Oxford).

Grote, George (1846–56). *A History of Greece*, 12 vols. (London).

Grove 7 = *The New Grove Dictionary of Music and Musicians*, 2nd edn., ed. Stanley Sadie, 29 vols. (London, 2001) [7th edn. counting from the original *Dictionary*].

Guest, Ivor (1972). *The Romantic Ballet in England*, 2nd edn. (London and Nairobi).

Guest, L. Haden ([1911]). 'An Appreciation', in Anon. ([1911], ed.).

Gustafson, Zadel Barnes (1881). *Genevieve Ward: A Biographical Sketch* (London).

Gwynn, Robin (2001). *Huguenot Heritage: The History and Contribution of the Huguenots in Britain*, 2nd edn. (Brighton).

Hall, Edith (1966, ed.). *Aeschylus' Persians* (Warminster).

—— (1997*a*). 'Greek Plays in Georgian Reading' *Greece & Rome*, 44: 54–76.

—— (1997*b*). 'Talfourd's Ancient Greeks in the Theatre of Reform', *International Journal of the Classical Tradition*, 3: 283–307.

—— (1997*c*) 'Literature and Performance', in P. Cartledge (ed.), *The Cambridge Illustrated History of Ancient Greece* (Cambridge), 219–49.

Hall, Edith (1999*a*). 'Sophocles' Electra in Britain', in J. Griffin (ed.), 261–306.

—— (1999*b*). 'Classical Mythology in the Victorian Popular Theatre', *International Journal of the Classical Tradition*, 5: 336–66.

—— (1999*c*). '1845 and All That: Singing Greek Tragedy on the London Stage', in Michael Biddiss and Maria Wyke (eds.), *The Uses and Abuses of Antiquity* (Bern), 37–53.

—— (1999*d*). 'Medea and British Legislation before the First World War', *Greece & Rome*, 46: 42–77.

—— (1999*e*). 'Actor's Song in Tragedy', in Simon Goldhill and Robin Osborne (eds.), *Performance Culture and Athenian Democracy* (Cambridge), 96–122.

—— (2002*a*). 'Tony Harrison's *Prometheus: A View from the Left*', *Arion*, 10: 129–40.

—— (2002*b*). 'The Ancient Actor's Presence since the Renaissance', in Easterling and Hall, 419–34.

—— (2002*c*). 'The Singing Actors of Antiquity', in Easterling and Hall, 3–38.

—— Macintosh, Fiona, and Taplin, Oliver (2000, eds.). *Medea in Performance 1500–2000* (Oxford).

—— (2004*a*). 'Towards a Theory of Performance Reception', *Arion*, 12, 111–48.

—— (2004*b*). 'Introduction: Why Greek Tragedy in the Late Twentieth Century', in Hall, Macintosh, and Wrigley (eds.), 1–46.

—— (forthcoming *a*), 'Aeschylus' Clytemnestra versus her Senecan tradition', in F. Macintosh, P. Michelakis, E. Hall, and O. Taplin (eds.) *Agamemnon in Performance*.

—— (forthcoming *b*), 'The Mother of All Sea-Battles: Cultural Responses to Aeschylus' *Persians* from Xerxes to Saddam Hussein', in Bridges, Hall, and Rhodes (eds.), *Cultural Responses to the Persian Wars*.

—— Macintosh, Fiona, and Wrigley, Amanda (2004, eds.). *Dionysus since 69: Greek Tragedy at the Dawn of the Third Millennium* (Oxford).

Haller, William (1917). *The Early Life of Robert Southey 1774–1803* (New York).

Hamilton, Cicely (1909). *Marriage as Trade* (London).

Hammond, Brean S. (2000). ' "O Sophonisba! Sophonisba O!"': Thomson the Tragedian', in Terry (ed.), 15–33.

Harbage, Alfred (1935). *Sir William Davenant: Poet Venturer 1606–1668* (Philadelphia, London, and Oxford).

Harding, James (1979). *Artistes Pompiers: French Academic Art in the 19th Century* (London).

Hardwick, Lorna (1997). 'Women and Classical Scholarship in the 19th Century', *CA News*, no. 17 (December), 2–4.

—— (2000*a*). 'Theatres of the Mind: Greek Tragedy in Women's Writing in England in the Nineteenth Century', in Lorna Hardwick, P. E.

Easterling, Stanley Ireland, Nicholas Lowe, and Fiona Macintosh (eds.), *Theatre: Ancient and Modern* (Milton Keynes), 68–71.

—— (2000*b*). *Translating Words, Translating Cultures* (London).

Hare, Arnold (1977). *Theatre Royal, Bath: A Calendar of Performances at the Orchard Street Theatre 1750–1805* (Bath).

Harrison, Tony (2002). *Plays 4* (London).

Hartigan, Karelisa V. (1995). *Greek Tragedy on the American Stage: Ancient Drama in the Commercial Theater, 1882–1994* (Westport, CT).

Hartman, Mary S. (1985). *Victorian Murderesses* (London).

Haydon, Colin (1993). *Anti-Catholicism in Eighteenth-Century England* (Manchester and New York).

Hazlitt, William (1917). 'My First Acquaintance with Poets', in George Sampson (ed.), *Hazlitt: Selected Essays* (Cambridge), 1–20; first published in *The Liberal* (1823).

Hearnshaw, F. J. C. (1929). *The Centenary History of King's College, London 1828–1929* (London).

Heilbroner, Robert L. (1986, ed.). *The Essential Adam Smith* (Oxford).

Heitner, Robert B. (1964). 'The Iphigenia in Tauris Theme in Drama of the Eighteenth Century', *Comparative Literature*, 16: 289–309.

Henkle, Roger (1980). *Comedy and Culture: England 1820–1900* (Princeton).

Heraud, Edith (1898). *Memoirs of John A. Heraud* (London).

Heraud, John (1857). *Medea in Corinth* (British Library Add. MS 52967 X).

Herford, C. H., Simpson, Percy, and Simpson, Evelyn (1941, eds.). *Ben Jonson* (Oxford).

Heron, Matilda (1861). *Medea. A Tragedy in Three Acts, Translated from the French of 'Ernest Legouvé'* (London).

Heywood, Thomas (1874). *The Dramatic Works of Thomas Heywood*, iii (London).

Hicks, Anthony (2000). 'Handel's Oreste', essay in programme to Covent Garden production, 9–10 (London).

Hiffernan, Paul (1770). *Dramatic Genius in Five Books* (London).

Highet, Gilbert (1949). *The Classical Tradition: Greek and Roman Influences on Western Literature* (Oxford and London).

Highfill, Philip A., Burnim, Kalman A., and Langham, Edward A. (1973–93). *A Bibliographical Dictionary of Actors, Actresses, Musicians, Dancers, Managers and Other Stage Personnel in London, 1660–1800* (Carbondale, IL, and Edwardsville, IL).

Hill, Aaron (1709). *A Full and Just Account of the Present State of the Ottoman Empire in All its Branches* (London).

—— (1731). *Advice to the Poets. A Poem* (London).

Hill, Aaron (1754). *The Works of the Late Aaron Hill, Esq.*, 2nd edn., 4 vols. (London).

Hinchcliffe, Arnold P. (1985, ed.). *T. S. Eliot, Plays: A Casebook* (Basingstoke and London).

Hindle, Maurice (1988). 'Introduction' to Godwin (1988).

Hines, Samuel Philip (1966). 'English Translations of Aristophanes' Comedies 1655–1742' (Ph.D. diss., University of North Carolina at Chapel Hill).

Hiscock, W. G. (1946). *A Christ Church Miscellany* (Oxford).

Hobhouse, John Cam (1855). *Travels in Albania and Other Provinces of Turkey in 1809 & 1810*, 2nd edn. (London).

Hoffer, Peter C., and Hull, N. E. H. (1984). *Murdering Mothers: Infanticide in England and New England 1558–1803* (New York and London).

Hogan, John (1873, ed.). *The Medea of Euripides* (London).

Hogan, Robert (1994, ed.). *The Poems of Thomas Sheridan* (Newark, London, and Toronto).

Hogg, James (1977). *Robert Browning and the Victorian Theatre* (London).

Hogg, Thomas Jefferson (1906). *The Life of Percy Bysshe Shelley*, ed. Edward Dowden (London).

Holford-Strevens, Leofranc (1999). 'Sophocles in Rome', in J. Griffin (ed.), 219–59.

Holledge, Julie (1981). *Innocent Flowers: Women in the Edwardian Theatre* (London).

Holroyd, Michael (1988–1992). *Bernard Shaw*, 5 vols. (London).

Holmström, K. G. (1967). *Monodrama, Attitudes, Tableaux Vivants* (Stockholm).

Hope, Thomas (1809). *Costumes of the Ancients* (London; new edn. 1841).

Horne, Richard Hengist (1844, ed.). *A New Spirit of the Age*, 2 vols. (London).

House, Humphry (1955). *All in Due Time: The Collected Essays and Broadcast Talks* (London).

Howarth, David (1976). *The Greek Adventure: Lord Byron and Other Eccentrics in the Greek War of Independence* (London).

Howe, Elizabeth (1992). *The First English Actresses: Women and Drama 1660–1700* (Cambridge).

Hughes, Derek (1996). *English Drama 1660–1700* (Oxford).

Hume, David (1739). *A Treatise of Human Nature* (London).

Hume, Robert D. (1976). *The Development of English Drama in the Late Seventeenth Century* (Oxford).

Hurd, Richard (1749). *Q. Horatii Flacci Ars Poetica: Epistola ad Pisones* (London).

——(1751). *Q. Horatii Flacci Epistola ad Augustum* (London).

Hurdis, James (*c*.1800). *A Word or Two in Vindication of the University of Oxford and of Magdalen College in Particular, from the Posthumous Aspersions of Mr. Gibbon* (Bishopstone).

Hurst, Isobel (2003). ' "The Feminine of Homer": Classical Influences on Women Writers from Mary Shelley to Vera Brittain' (D. Phil. thesis, Oxford).

Hutcheson, Francis (1728). *An Essay on the Nature and Conduct of the Passions and Affections* (London).

Huys, Marc (1995). *The Tale of the Hero who was Exposed at Birth in Euripidean Tragedy: A Study of Motifs* (Leuven).

Hynes, Samuel (1968). *The Edwardian Turn of Mind* (London).

Ibsen, Henrik (1972). *The Oxford Ibsen*, ed. James Walter McFarlane, vol. iii (Oxford, London, New York, and Toronto).

ILN = *Illustrated London News*.

Ingram, William Henry (1965). 'Theobald, Rowe, Jackson: Whose Ajax?', *Library Chronicle*, 31/2: 91–6.

——(1966). 'Greek Drama and the Augustan Stage: Dennis, Theobald, Thomson' (Ph.D. diss., University of Pennsylvania).

Ittershagen, Ulrike (1999). *Lady Hamiltons Attitüden* (Mainz).

Jackson, Allan Stuart (1993). *The Standard Theatre of Victorian London* (London and Toronto).

Jackson, Mark (1996). *New-Born Child Murder: Women, Illegitimacy and the Courts in Eighteenth-Century England* (Manchester).

Jacobus de Voragine (1993). *Readings on the Saints*, trans. William Granger Ryan, 2 vols. (Princeton).

——(1998). *Iacopo da Varazze: Legenda aurea*, ed. Giovanni Paolo Maggioni, 2 vols. (Florence).

Jacobs, Eva (1989). 'An Unidentified Illustration of an English Actress in a Voltairean Tragic Role: Mary Ann Yates as Electra', *Studies on Voltaire and the Eighteenth Century*, 260: 245–56.

Jadwin, Lisa (1993). 'Clytemnestra Rewarded: The Double Conclusion of *Vanity Fair*', in Alison Booth (ed.), *Famous Last Words: Changes in Gender and Narrative Closure*, 35–61 (Charlottesville, VA, and London).

Jebb, R. C. (1890, ed.). *Sophocles, Antigone*, 3rd edn. (Cambridge).

Jenkin, Fleeming (1878). 'Browning's "Agamemnon" and Campbell's "Trachiniae" ', *Edinburgh Review*, 147: 406–36; repr. in Jenkin (1887), i. 3–43.

——(1887). *Papers Literary, Scientific, &c. By the Late Fleeming Jenkin, Professor of Engineering in the University of Edinburgh. Edited by Sidney Colvin and J. A. Ewing, with a Memoir by Robert Louis Stevenson*, 2 vols. (London and New York).

Jenkyns, Richard (1980). *The Victorians and Ancient Greece* (Oxford).

Jenkyns, Richard (1991). *Dignity and Decadence* (London).

Jensen, Gerard E. (1915, ed.). *The Covent-Garden Journal by Sir Alexander Drawcansir, Knt., Censor of Great Britain*, 2 vols. (New Haven, London, and Oxford).

Jerrold, Walter (1914). *Douglas Jerrold: Dramatist and Wit*, 2 vols. (London).

Jodrell, Richard Paul (1781). *Illustrations of Euripides on the Ion and the Bacchae*, 2 vols. (London).

—— (1789). *Illustrations of Euripides, on the Alcestis* (London).

Johnson, Charles (1710). *The Force of Friendship* (London).

—— (1731). *The Tragedy of Medæa* (London).

Johnson, James (1972). 'The Classics and John Bull, 1660–1714', in H. T. Swedenberg (ed.), *England in the Restoration and the Early Eighteenth Century* (Berkeley, Los Angeles, and London), 1–26.

Johnson, Samuel (1749). *Irene: a Tragedy* (London).

—— (1794). *The Lives of the Most Eminent English Poets*, 4 vols. (London).

Johnson, Thomas (1705, ed.). *Sophocles Tragoediæ, Ajax et Electra* (Oxford).

—— (1708, ed.). *Sophoclis Tragoediæ, Antigone et Trachiniae* (Oxford).

—— (1746, ed.) *Sophocles Tragoediæ, Oedipus Tyrannus, Philoctetes et Oedipus Coloneus* (Oxford).

Johnston, John (1990). *The Lord Chamberlain's Blue Pencil* (London).

Johnstone, John (1828, ed.). *The Works of Samuel Parr*, 8 vols. (London).

Jones, Edward (1784). *Musical and Poetical Relicks of the Welsh Bards: Preserved by Tradition, and Authentic Manuscripts from Remote Antiquity* (London).

Jones, Ernest (1953). *Sigmund Freud: Life and Work*, i: *The Young Freud 1856–1900* (London).

Jones, Richard Foster (1919). *Lewis Theobald: His Contribution to English Scholarship with Some Unpublished Letters* (New York).

Jones, Thora Burnley, and Nicol, Bernard De Bear (1976). *Neo-Classical Dramatic Criticism 1560–1770* (Cambridge).

Jones, Vivien (1990, ed.). *Women in the Eighteenth Century: Constructions of Femininity* (London).

Jongh, Nicholas de (2000). *Politics, Prudery and Perversions: The Censoring of the English Stage 1901–1968* (London).

Jopling, Louise (1925). *Twenty Years of My Life 1867–1887* (London).

Joyner, William (1671). *The Roman Empress* (London).

Jump, John D. (1972). *Burlesque* (London).

Kaarsholm, Preben (1989). 'Pro-Boers: Pro-Boerism and Romantic Anti-Capitalism on the European Continent during the South African War', in Samuel (ed.), 110–26.

Kames, Henry Home, Lord (1763). *The Elements of Criticism*, 2nd edn., 3 vols. (Edinburgh).

Keates, Jonathan (1992). *Handel: The Man and his Music* (London).

Kelly, John A. (1936). *German Visitors to English Theaters in the Eighteenth Century* (Princeton).

Kennedy, Dennis (1985). *Granville Barker and the Dream of Theatre* (Cambridge).

Kenrick, W[illiam] (1774, ed.). *The Poetical Works of Robert Lloyd*, 2 vols. (London).

Kern, Jean B. (1966) 'James Thomson's Revisions of *Agamemnon*', *Philological Quarterly*, 45: 289–303.

Kerrigan, John (1996). *Revenge Tragedy* (Oxford).

Kestner, Joseph (1989). *Mythology and Misogyny: The Social Discourse of Nineteenth-Century British Classical-Subject Painting* (Madison, WI).

Kettle, Michael (1977). *Salome's Last Veil: The Libel Case of the Century* (London).

Ketton-Cremer, R. G. (1940). *Horace Walpole: A Biography* (London).

Kewes, Paulina (1998). *Authorship and Appropriation: Writing for the Stage in England, 1660–1710* (Oxford).

Kidson, Alex (2002). *George Romney 1734–1802* (London and San Marino, CA).

Kierkegaard, Søren (1987). *Either/Or*, Part I, ed. and trans. Howard V. Hong and Edna H. Hong [= *Kierkegaard's Writings*, iii] (Princeton); first published as *Enten/Eller: Et Livs-Fragment udgivet af Victor Eremita* (Copenhagen, 1843).

Kingsley, Charles (1855). *The Heroes* (London).

Knapp, Mary E. (1961). *Prologues and Epilogues of the Eighteenth Century* (New Haven).

Knight, R. C. (1950). *Racine et la Grèce* (Paris).

Knös, Börje (1962). *L'Histoire de la littérature néo-grecque* (Stockholm and Uppsala).

Kucich, Greg (1996). 'Eternity and the Ruins of Time: Shelley and the Construction of Cultural History', in Betty T. Bennet and Stuart Curran (eds.), *Shelley: Poet and Legislator of the World* (Baltimore and London), 14–29.

Kurth, Peter (2001). *Isadora: A Sensational Life* (Boston, New York, London).

Kurtz, Donna (2000). *The Reception of Classical Art in Britain* (Oxford).

Lacoste, Louis (1712). *Creüse l'Athénienne, Tragédie mise en musique par Mr de la Coste* (Paris).

Lagrange-Chancel, François Joseph de (1697). *Oreste et Pilade, ou Iphigénie en Tauride* (Paris).

La Mesnardière, Hippolyte-Jules Pilet de (1640). *La Poëtique* (Paris).

Landor, Walter Savage (1859). *The Hellenics*, rev. edn. (Edinburgh).

Langbaine, Gerard (1691). *An Account of the English Dramatick Poets* (Oxford).

Larrabee, Stephen A. (1943). *English Bards and Grecian Marbles* (New York).

Legouvé, Ernest (1893). *Sixty Years of Recollections, translated with notes by Albert D. Vandam*, 2 vols. (London and Sydney).

Leighton, Angela (1992). *Victorian Women Poets* (Hemel Hempstead).

Lemercier, Louis (1797). *Agamemnon, Tragédie en Cinq Actes* (Paris).

Lemon, Mark (1856). *Medea: a Tragedy in One Act*, British Library Add. MS 52960 L.).

Lemprière, John (1788). *Bibliotheca Classica: A Classical Dictionary* (Reading).

Lemprière, Raoul (1981). 'The Theatre in Jersey 1778–1801', *Bulletin of the Société Jersiaise* no. 106, vol. xxiii/1, 115–23.

Lennox, Charlotte (1759). *The Greek Theatre of Father Brumoy*, 3 vols. (London).

Leppmann, Wolfgang (1968). *Pompeii in Fact and Fiction*, English translation (London and Toronto).

Lessing, Gotthold Ephraim (1968). *Gesammelte Werke*, ed. Paul Rilla, 10 vols. (Berlin and Weimar).

Levacher de Charnois, Jean Charles (1790–2). *Recherches sur les costumes et sur les théâtres de toutes les Nations tant anciennes que modernes* (Paris).

Levey, Michael (1963). *From Giotto to Cezanne* (London).

Levin, Harry (1931). *The Broken Column: A Study in Romantic Hellenism* (Cambridge, MA).

Levine, Joseph M. (1991). *The Battle of the Books: History and Literature in the Augustan Age* (Ithaca, NY, and London).

——(1999). *Between the Ancients and the Moderns: Baroque Culture in Restoration England* (New Haven and London).

Lewes, George Henry (1875). *On Actors and the Art of Acting* (London).

Lewis, Brian (1980). *The Sargon Legend* (Cambridge, MA).

Lillo, George (1731). *The London Merchant, or The History of George Barnwell* (London).

Lipsey, Roger (2001). *Have You Been to Delphi? Tales of the Ancient Oracle for Modern Minds* (Albany, NY).

Little, Arthur M. (1893). *Mendelssohn's Music to the Antigone of Sophocles* (diss. Leipzig, published Washington, DC).

Llewellyn, Alexander (1972). *The Decade of Reform: The 1830s* (Newton Abbot).

Lloyd-Jones, Hugh (1982). *Blood for the Ghosts: Classical Influences in the Nineteenth and Twentieth Centuries* (London).

Locke, John ('1690'). *Two Treatises of Government* (London).

—— (1993). *Two Treatises of Government*, ed. Mark Goldie (Everyman edn.; London).

Loftis, John (1963). *The Politics of Drama in Augustan England* (Oxford).

Lolière, Frédéric (1907). *La Comédie-Française: Histoire de la maison de Molière de 1658 à 1907* (Paris).

Lowe, Solomon (1719). Κοινὰ καινῶς: *An Appendix to Grammar, containing Rhetoric and Prosody with directions for composing . . . elegantly. . . . To which are added . . . Rudiments of the French and Greek Tongues* (London).

LS = Emmet L. Avery, C. B. Hogan, A. H. Scouten, G. W. Stone, and W. Van Lennep, *The London Stage, 1660–1800: A Calendar of Plays, Entertainments and Afterpieces*, 5 parts in 11 vols. (Carbondale, IL, and Edwardsville, IL: Southern Illinois University Press, 1965–8).

Lucas, Hippolyte (1847). *Alceste* (Paris).

Luttrell, Narcissus (1857). *A Brief Historical Relation of State Affairs from September, 1678 to April, 1714*, 6 vols. (Oxford; repr. Farnborough, 1969).

Lynch, James (1953). *Box, Pit and Gallery: Stage and Society in Johnson's London* (Berkeley and Los Angeles).

Lyndsay, David (1822). *The Nereid's Love*, in *Dramas of the Ancient World* (Edinburgh).

McCabe, Richard A. (1993). *Incest, Drama and Nature's Law 1550–1700* (Cambridge).

McCarthy, Lillah (1933). *Myself and Friends* (London).

McClure, Ruth (1981). *Coram's Children: The London Foundling Hospital in the Eighteenth Century* (New Haven and London).

McDonagh, Josephine (2003). *Child Murder and British Culture 1720–1900* (Cambridge).

McDonald, Marianne, and Walton, J. Michael (2002, eds.). *Amid Our Troubles: Irish Versions of Greek Tragedy* (London).

Macintosh, Fiona (1994). *Dying Acts: Death in Ancient Greek and Irish Tragic Drama* (Cork).

—— (1995). 'Under the Blue Pencil: Greek Tragedy and the British Censor', *Dialogos*, 2: 54–70.

—— (1997). 'Tragedy in Performance: Nineteenth- and Twentieth-Century Productions', in Easterling (ed.), 284–323.

—— (1998) 'The Shavian Murray and the Euripidean Shaw: Major Barbara and the Bacchae', *Classics Ireland*, 5: 64–84.

—— (2000*a*). 'Introduction: The Performer in Performance', in Hall, Macintosh, and Taplin (2000, eds.), 1–31.

—— (2000*b*). 'Medea Transposed: Burlesque and Gender on the Mid-Victorian Stage', in Hall, Macintosh, and Taplin (2000, eds.), 74–99.

—— (2001). 'Alcestis in Britain', *Cahiers du GITA* 14: 281–308.

Macintosh, Fiona (2002). 'King's First Libation Bearers: London's Greek Plays in the 1880s', *Dialogos*, 8.

—— (forthcoming). 'Viewing Agamemnon in Nineteenth-Century Britain', in Macintosh, Michelakis, Hall, and Taplin (forthcoming, eds.).

—— Michelakis, Pantelis, Hall, Edith, and Taplin, Oliver (forthcoming, eds.). *Agamemnon in Performance 458 BC–2004 AD* (Oxford).

McKillop, Alan D. (1957, ed.). *James Thomson (1700–1748): Letters and Documents* (Lawrence, KS).

—— (1958). 'Thomson and the Licensers of the Stage', *Philological Quarterly*, 37: 448–53.

Mackinlay, Sterling (1927). *Origin and Development of Light Opera* (London).

Mackinnon, Alan (1910). *The Oxford Amateurs: A Short History of the Theatricals at the University* (London).

MacMillan, Duncan (1994). 'Woman as Hero: Gavin Hamilton's Radical Alternative', in Perry and Rossington (eds.), 78–98.

Macpherson, James (1765). *The Works of Ossian, Son of Fingal*, 2 vols. (London).

Macready, William Charles (1912). *The Diaries of William Charles Macready, 1833–1851*, ed. William Toynbee, 2 vols. (London).

McSweeney, Kerry (1993, ed.). *Elizabeth Barrett Browning: Aurora Leigh* (Oxford).

Maffei, Francesco Scipione (1723–5). *Teatro italiano*, 3 vols. (Verona).

Maguire, Nancy Klein (1992). *Regicide and Restoration: English Tragicomedy, 1660–1671* (Cambridge).

—— (2000). 'Tragicomedy', in Fisk (ed.), 86–106.

Manners, Lady Victoria, and Williamson, Dr G. C. (1924). *Angelica Kauffmann, R.A.: Her Life and Work* (London; repr. New York, 1976).

Mansel, Henry Longueville (1873). *The Phrontisterion*, in *Letters, Lectures, and Reviews*, ed. Henry W. Chandler (London).

Mansfield, Sue (1980, ed.). *The Subjection of Women, by John Stuart Mill* (Arlington Heights, IL).

Marsden, Jean I. (2000). 'Spectacle, Horror and Pathos', in Fisk (ed.), 174–90.

Marshall, Gail (1998). *Actresses on the Victorian Stage: Feminine Performance and the Galatea Myth* (Cambridge).

Marston, Westland (1888). *Our Recent Actors*, 2 vols. (London).

Martin, Robert Bernard (1974). *The Triumph of Wit: A Study of Victorian Comic Theory* (Oxford).

Martin, Sir Theodore (1900). *Helena Faucit: Lady Martin* (Edinburgh and London).

Martin-Harvey, John (1933). *The Autobiography of Sir John Martin-Harvey* (London).

Marx, Karl and Engels, F. (1979). *Collected Works*, xi. London.

Mason, William (1752). *Elfrida, A Dramatic Poem* (London).

—— (1759). *Caractacus: A Dramatic Poem. Written on the Model of the Antient Greek Tragedy by the Author of Elfrida* (London).

—— (1772). *Animadversions on the Present Government of the York Lunatic Asylum* (York).

—— (1788*a*). *Memoirs of the Life and Writings of Mr William Whitehead* (London).

—— (1788*b*). *An Occasional Discourse, Preached in the Cathedral of St. Peter in York, January 27, 1788, on the Subject of the African Slave-Trade* (York).

—— (1796). *Caractacus* (London).

—— (1811). *The Works of William Mason, M.A.*, 4 vols. (London).

Massie, Joseph (1759). *Farther Observations Concerning the Foundling-Hospital* (London).

Mathias, T. J. (1823). *Carattaco, poema drammatico scritto sul modello della tragedia greca antica da Guglielmo Mason* (Naples).

Maude, Cyril (1903). *The Haymarket Theatre* (London).

Maurice, Thomas (1779). *Poems and Miscellaneous Pieces with a Free Translation of the Oedipus Tyrannus of Sophocles* (London).

—— (1806). *The Fall of the Mogul: A Tragedy, Founded on an Interesting Portion of Indian History, and Attempted Partly on the Greek Model* (London).

—— (1822). *A Free Translation of the Oedipus Tyrannus* (London).

Maxwell, Margaret (1963). 'Olympus at Billingsgate: The Burlettas of Kane O'Hara', *Educational Theatre Journal*, 15: 130–5.

Mayer, David (1971). 'Billy Purvis: Travelling Showman', *Theatre Quarterly*, 1: 27–34.

Meakin, Annette (1911). *Hannah More* (London).

Meehan, Michael (1986). *Liberty and Poetics in Eighteenth-Century England* (London, Sydney, and Dover, NH).

Mercer, Thomas (1774). *Poems* (Edinburgh).

Metcalfe, Cranstoun (1893). *Hecuba à la Mode; or, The Wily Greek and the Modest Maid* (London).

Michelini, Ann (1987). *Euripides and the Tragic Tradition* (Madison, WI).

Mikoniatis, I. G. (1979). 'The Greek War of Independence on the London Stage 1821–1833', *'Επιστημονικὴ 'Επετηρίδα τῆς Φιλοσοφικῆς Σχολῆς τοῦ Πανεπιστημίου Θεσσαλονίκης*, 18: 331–43.

Miller, Betty (1953). ' "This Happy Evening": The Story of Ion', *The Twentieth Century*, 154, no. 917 (July), 53–9.

Milsand, Joseph-Antoine (1849), 'Le drame contemporain en Angleterre', *Revue des deux mondes*, n.s. 19/4: 832–60.

Milton, John (1738). *Areopagitica: A Speech for the Liberty of Unlicens'd Printing, to the Parliament of England. First published in the year 1644. With a Preface, by Another Hand* (London).

—— (1952–5). *The Poetical Works*, ed. H. Darbishire, 2 vols. (Oxford).

—— (1962). *The Complete Prose Works of John Milton*, iii: *1648–9*, ed. Merrit Y. Hughes (New Haven).

—— (1963) *Areopagitica, and Of Education*, ed. Michael Davies (London and New York).

—— (1997). *John Milton: Complete Shorter Poems*, ed. John Carey (London and New York).

Mimoso-Ruiz, Duarte (1982). *Médée antique et moderne: Aspects rituels et socio-politiques d'un mythe* (Paris).

Mitford, John (1851, ed.). *The Correspondence of Horace Walpole, Earl of Orford, and the Rev. William Mason*, 2 vols. (London).

—— (1853, ed.). *The Correspondence of Thomas Gray and William Mason* (London).

Mitford, Mary Russell (1818). 'Reading School Play', *Reading Mercury and Oxford Gazette*, vol. 96, no. 4505 (Monday, 26 October), 3, col. 3.

—— (1821), 'Representation of the *Orestes* of Euripides at Reading School', *Reading Mercury and Oxford Gazette*, 99, no. 5163 (Monday, 5 November), 5, col. 3.

—— (1824), 'Reading, Sat. Oct. 16th', *Reading Mercury and Oxford Gazette*, 102 no. 5367 (Monday, 18 October), 3, col. 2.

—— (1827). Review of *Hecuba* at Reading School, *Reading Mercury and Oxford Gazette*, no. 5563, p. 3. col 2 (Monday, 22 October).

—— (1835). *Belford Regis; or Sketches of a Country Town*, 3 vols. (London).

—— (1854*a*). *The Dramatic Works of Mary Russell Mitford*, 2 vols. (London).

—— (1854*b*). *Atherton, and Other Tales*, i (London).

—— (1872). *Letters of Mary Russell Mitford*, ed. Henry Chorley (2nd ser.), 2 vols. (London).

Miyoshi, Masao (1969). *The Divided Self: A Perspective on the Literature of the Victorians* (New York).

Momigliano, Arnaldo (1969). *Studies in Historiography* (London).

Monk, Ray (1996). *Bertrand Russell: The Spirit of Solitude* (London).

Montagu(e), Lady Mary Pierrepont Wortley (1763). *Letters of the Right Honourable Lady M–y W—y M——e*, 3rd edn. (London).

Moore, Edward (1748). *The Foundling* (London).

Moore Smith, G. C. (1923). *College Plays Performed in the University of Cambridge* (Cambridge).

Morell, Thomas (1749). *Hecuba, Translated from the Greek of Euripides* (London).

—— (1773). Αἰσχύλου Προμηθεὺς Δεσμώτης: *Cum Stanleiana versione . . . quibus suas adjecit . . . ac Anglicanam interpretationem T. Morell, S.T.P.* (London).

Morgan, David (1975). *Suffragists and Liberals* (Oxford).

Morgan, Fidelis (1981). *The Female Wits: Women Playwrights on the London Stage 1600–1720* (London).

Morley, Henry (1866). *Journal of a London Playgoer from 1851 to 1866* (London).

Morris, William (1856). *The Defence of Guenevere, The Life and Death of Jason, and Other Poems* (London and Oxford).

—— (1868). *The Earthly Paradise*, 3 vols. (London).

Mounet-Sully, Jean (1917). *Souvenirs d'un tragédien* (Paris).

Motter, T. H. Vail (1929). *The School Drama in England* (London, New York, and Toronto).

—— (1944). 'Garrick and the Private Theatres: With a List of Amateur Performances in the Eighteenth Century', *ELH* 11: 63–75.

Mueller, Martin (1980). *Children of Oedipus and Other Essays on the Imitation of Greek Tragedy 1550–1800* (Toronto, Buffalo, and London).

Mullan, John (1988). *Sentiment and Sociability: The Language of Feeling in the Eighteenth Century* (Oxford).

Munich, Adrienne (1989). *Andromeda's Chains: Gender and Interpretation in Victorian Literature and Art* (New York).

Murphy, Arthur (1772). *The Grecian Daughter* (London).

—— (1773). *Alzuma* (London).

Murray, Gilbert (1897). *A History of Ancient Greek Literature* (London).

—— (1900). *Andromache* (London).

—— (1901). 'National Ideas, Conscious and Unconscious', *International Journal of Ethics*, February [= repr. in id., *Essays and Addresses* (Oxford, 1921)].

—— (1902). 'Introductory Essay: *The Bacchae* in relation to Certain Currents of Thought in the Fifth Century', in G. C. Warr (ed.), *The Athenian Drama: A Series of Verse Translations from the Greek Dramatic Poets*, iii: *Euripides Translated into Rhyming Verse* (London), xix–lxviii.

—— (1905). *The Trojan Women of Euripides* (London).

—— (1906). *The Medea of Euripides* (London).

—— (1911). *Oedipus, King of Thebes* (Oxford).

—— (1913). *Euripides and his Age* (London).

—— (1915). *The Alcestis of Euripides* (London).

—— (1933). *Aristophanes: A Study* (Oxford).

Nalbach, Daniel (1972). *The King's Theatre 1704–1867: London's First Opera House* (London).

Naxton, Michael (1986). *The History of Reading School* (Reading).

'Neil, Ross' [Augusta Webster] (1883). 'Orestes', in *Andrea the Painter* (London), 181–238.

Neville, Alexander (1563). *The Lamentable Tragedie of Oedipus the Sonne of Laius Kyng of Thebes out of Seneca* (London).

Newdick, Robert S. (n.d. *a*). *Talfourd as a Dramatist* (unpublished typescript, pre-1939; Reading Public Library).

——(n.d. *b*). *Sir Thomas Noon Talfourd* (unpublished typescript, pre-1939; Reading Public Library).

Newton, Stella Mary (1974). *Health, Art and Reason: Dress Reformers of the 19th Century* (London).

Newton, Thomas (1581, ed.). *The Tenne Tragedies of Seneca* (London).

Nichols, John (1817–18). *Illustrations of the Literary History of the Eighteenth Century*, 3 vols. (London).

Nichols, R. H., and Wray, F. A. (1935). *The History of the Foundling Hospital* (London).

Nicoll, Allardyce B. (1925). *British Drama*, 4th edn. (London, Toronto, Bombay, and Sydney).

——(1952–9). *A History of English Drama 1660–1900* (Cambridge).

Nolan, Edward (1866). *Iphigenia; or, The Sail!! The Seer!! And the Sacrifice!!* (London).

——(1867). *Agamemnon at Home; or, The Latest Particulars of that Little Affair at Mycenae. A Burlesque Sketch* (Oxford).

Nordau, Max (1895). *Degeneration* (London).

Norwood, Gilbert (1921). *Euripides and Shaw* (London).

Noverre, Jean Georges (1804). *Médée, ballet tragi-pantomime* (Paris).

ODNB = *Oxford Dictionary of National Biography*, 60 vols. (Oxford, 2004).

O'Hara, Kane (1764). *Midas: an English Burletta* (Dublin).

——(1773). *The Golden Pippin: an English Burletta* (London).

Oldfather, C. H. (1935). *Diodorus of Sicily*, 6 vols. to 15. 19 (Cambridge, MA, and London).

Ormond, Leonee (1968). 'Female Costume in the Aesthetic Movement of the 1870s and 1880s', *Costume*, 2: 33–8.

Osmaston, Francis P. B. (1928). *Original Transcripts with Text from Hellenic Drama* (London).

Oulton, Walley Chamberlain (1796). *The History of the Theatres of London*, 2 vols. (London).

Owen, A. L. (1962). *The Famous Druids: A Survey of Three Centuries of English Literature on the Druids* (Oxford).

Owen, Robert (1703). *Hypermnestra; or, Love in Tears. A Tragedy* (London).

Owen, Susan J. (2000). 'Drama and Political Crisis', in Fisk (ed.), 158–73.

Owenson, Sydney [later Lady Morgan] (1809). *Woman: or, Ida of Athens*, 4 vols. (London).

Padel, Ruth (1996). 'Ion: Lost and Found', *Arion*, 4: 216–24.

Palaeologus, Gregorios (1824). *The Death of Demosthenes. A Tragedy in Four Acts. In Prose. Translated from the Modern Greek* (Cambridge).

Palgrave, Francis Turner (1871). *Lyrical Poems* (London).

Palmer, Henrietta R. (1911). *List of English Editions and Translations of Greek and Latin Classics Printed before 1641* (London).

Pankhurst, E. Sylvia (1931). *The Suffragette Movement* (London, New York, and Toronto).

Parker, Christopher (1995, ed.). *Gender Roles and Sexuality in Victorian Literature* (Aldershot).

Parker, L. P. E. (2003). 'Alcestis: Euripides to Ted Hughes', *Greece & Rome*, 50.

Pattison, George (1992). *Kierkegaard: The Aesthetic and the Religious. From the Magic Theatre to the Crucifixion of the Image* (Basingstoke and London).

Payne, Deborah C. (1995). 'Reified Object or Emergent Professional? Retheorizing the Restoration Actress', in J. Douglas Canfield and Deborah C. Payne (eds.), *Cultural Readings of Restoration and Eighteenth-Century Theatre* (Athens, GA, and London), 13–38.

Peacock, John (1995). *The Stage Designs of Inigo Jones* (Cambridge).

Pearsall, Ronald (1973). *Victorian Popular Music* (Newton Abbot).

Pemble, John (1988). *The Mediterranean Passion: Victorians and Edwardians in the South* (Oxford and New York).

Pennant, Thomas (1781). *Tours in Wales*, ii: *The Journey to Snowdon* (London).

Pentzell, Raymond (1967). 'New Dress'd in the Ancient Manner: The Rise of Historical Realism in Costuming the Serious Drama of England and France in the Eighteenth Century' (Ph.D. diss., Yale).

Perry, Gill (1994). 'Women in Disguise: Likeness, the Grand Style, and the Conventions of "Feminine" Portraiture in the Work of Sir Joshua Reynolds', in Perry and Rossington (1994, eds.), 18–40.

—— and Rossington, Michael (1994, eds.). *Femininity and Masculinity in Eighteenth-Century Art and Culture* (Manchester and New York).

Peters, Catherine (1987). *Thackeray's Universe: Shifting Worlds of Imagination and Reality* (London).

Peters, Julie Stone (2000). *Theatre of the Book 1480–1880* (Oxford).

'Philogamus' (1739). *The Present State of Matrimony: or, The Real Causes of Conjugal Infidelity and Unhappy Marriages* (London).

Pichat, Michel (1825). *Léonidas, tragédie en cinq actes* (Paris).

Pikeryng, John (1567). *A Newe Enterlude of Vice conteyning the History of Horestes with the cruell revengment of his Fathers death upon his one naturall Mother* (London).

Pinney, Thomas (1963, ed.). *Essays of George Eliot* (London).

Planché, James Robinson (1845). *The Golden Fleece, or, Jason in Colchis and Medea in Corinth: A Classical Extravaganza in Two Parts* (Lacy's Acting Edition) (London).

——(1846). *The Birds of Aristophanes* (London).

——(1872). *The Recollections and Reflections of J. R. Planché*, 2 vols. (London).

——(1879). *The Extravaganzas 1825–1871*, ed. T. F. Dillon Croker and Stephen Tucker, 5 vols. (London).

——(1986). *Plays*, ed. Donald Roy (Cambridge).

——(1901). *Recollections and Reflections: A Professional Autobiography*, rev. edn. (London).

——and Dance, Charles (1834). *Olympic Revels* (London).

Poe, Edgar Allan (1845). 'The Antigone at Palmo's', *Broadway Journal*, 12 April, repr. in Poe (1965), xii. 130–5.

——(1965). *The Complete Works of Edgar Allan Poe*, ed. James A Harrison (New York).

Pompignan, J. J. le Franc de (1770). *Tragédies d'Eschyle* (Paris).

Pope, Alexander (1738). *One Thousand Seven Hundred and Thirty Eight, a Dialogue, Something Like Horace* (Edinburgh and London).

——(1797). *The Works of Alexander Pope*, ed. J. Warton, 9 vols. (London).

Potter, Robert (1775). *Observations on the Poor Laws, On the Present State of the Poor, and on Houses of Industry* (London).

——(1777). *The Tragedies of Æschylus Translated* (Norwich).

——(1788). *The Tragedies of Sophocles* (London).

——(1827). *The Hecuba of Euripides, Represented at the Triennial Visitation of Reading School, October 15, 16, 17, 1827. Translated by Mr Potter* (Reading).

Pressly, Nancy (1979). *The Fuseli Circle in Rome: Early Romantic Art of the 1770's* (New Haven).

Prest, John (2000). 'Balliol, for Example', in Michael Brock and M. C. Curthoys (eds.), *The History of the University of Oxford*, vii: *Nineteenth-Century Oxford* (Oxford), 159–69.

Price, Cecil (1975). *Theatre in the Age of Garrick* (Oxford).

Prins, Yopie (1999). *Victorian Sappho* (Princeton).

Protopapa-Mpoumpoulidou, Glykeria (1958). *Τὸ θέατρον ἐν Ζακύνθῳ* (Athens).

Puchner, Walter (1996). 'Die griechische Revolution von 1821 auf dem europäischen Theater', *Südostforschungen*, 55: 85–127.

Pullan, Brian (1989). *Orphans and Foundlings in Early Modern Europe* (Reading).

Purdom, C. B. (1955). *Harley Granville Barker: Man of the Theatre, Dramatist and Scholar* (London).

Purkiss, Diane (1996). *The Witch in History* (London and New York).

——(1998, ed.). *Three Tragedies by Renaissance Women* (London).

Pye, James Henry (1792). *A Commentary Illustrating the Poetic of Aristotle* (London).

Quincey, Thomas de (1863). 'The *Antigone* of Sophocles as Represented on the Edinburgh Stage', in *The Art of Conversation and Other Papers* (Edinburgh), xiii. 199–233.

Racine, Jean (1674). *Iphigénie* (Paris).

——(1691). *Athalie* (Paris).

Ralph, James [alias A. Primcock] (1731). *The Taste of the Town: or, a Guide to All Publick Diversions* (London).

——(1743). *The Case of our Present Theatrical Disputes, Fairly Stated, in which is Contained a Succinct Account of The Rise, Progress and Declension of the Ancient Stage* (London).

Rapin, René (1674). *Les Réflexions sur la poétique de ce temps et sur les ouvrages des poètes anciens et modernes* (Paris); ed. E. T. Dubois (Geneva, 1970).

Rasbotham, Dorning (1774). *Codrus: A Tragedy* (London).

Rauzzini, Venanzio (1783). *Creusa in Delfo; a New Serious Opera* (London).

Rawson, Elizabeth (1969). *The Spartan Tradition in European Thought* (Oxford).

Raysor, Thomas Middleton (1936, ed.). *Coleridge's Miscellaneous Criticism* (London).

Redford, Donald B. (1967). 'The Literary Motif of the Exposed Child', *Numen*, 14: 209–28.

Reece, Robert (1865). *Prometheus; or, the Man on the Rock! A New Original Extravaganza* (London).

——(1868a). *Agamemnon and Cassandra; or, The Prophet and Loss of Troy! A Classical Burlesque, Founded on the 'Agamemnon' of Æschylus* (Liverpool).

——(1868b). *Agamemnon and Cassandra, or The Prophet and Loss of Troy* (British Library Add. MS 53067).

Reed, Isaac (1812, ed.). *Biographica Dramatica*, 3 vols. (London).

Rees, Terence (1964). *Thespis: A Gilbert and Sullivan Enigma* (London).

——(1978). *Theatre Lighting in the Age of Gas* (London).

Reid, Jane Davidson (1993). *Oxford Guide to Classical Mythology in the Arts*, 2 vols. (New York and Oxford).

Renaud, Ralph E. ([1911]). 'Most Wonderful Dancer', in Anon. ([1911], ed.).

Reynolds, Ernest (1936). *Early Victorian Drama* (Cambridge).

Reynolds, Margaret (2000). 'Performing Medea; or, Why is Medea a Woman?', in Hall, Macintosh, and Taplin (2000, eds.), 119–43.

Reynolds, Matthew (2003). 'Browning and Translationese', *Essays in Criticism*, 53: 97–128.

Ribeiro, Aileen (1984). *The Dress Worn at Masquerades in England 1730 to 1790* (New York).

Riley, Kathleen (2005). 'Reasoning Madness: The Reception and Performance of Euripides' *Herakles*' (D.Phil. thesis, Oxford).

Ristori, A. (1907). *Memoirs and Artistic Studies of Madame Ristori* (London).

Ritchie, J. Ewing (1857). *The Night Side of London* (London).

Robe, Jane (1723). *The Fatal Legacy: A Tragedy* (London).

Roberdeau, John Peter (1804). *Fugitive Prose and Verse*, 2nd edn. (London).

—— (1814) *Thermopylae; or the Repulsed Invasion*, in *The New British Theatre*, ed. John Galt, ii (London), 251–310.

Roberts, David (1989). *The Ladies: Female Patronage of Restoration Drama 1660–1700* (Oxford).

Roberts, Jennifer Tolbert (1994). *Athens on Trial: The Antidemocratic Tradition in Western Thought* (Princeton).

Robinson, Henry Crabb (1872). *Diary, Reminiscences, and Correspondence*, ed. Thomas Sadler, 3rd edn., 2 vols. (London and New York).

Robortello, Francesco (1552). Αἰσχύλου τραγῳδίαι ἑπτά: *Aeschyli tragoediae septem. A Francisco Robortello . . . nunc primum ex manuscriptis libris ab infinitis erratis expurgatae, ac suis metris restitutae* (Venice).

Rogers, Priscilla Sue Marquardt (1986). 'Greek Tragedy in the New York Theatre: A History and Interpretation' (Ph.D. diss., Michigan).

Rose, Lionel (1986). *The Massacre of the Innocents: Infanticide in Britain 1800–1939.* (London, Boston, and Henley).

Rosenfeld, Sybil (1960). *The Theatre of the London Fairs in the Eighteenth Century* (London).

—— (1972–3). 'Neo-Classical Scenery in England: A Footnote', *Theatre Notebook,* 27: 67–71.

—— (1978). *Temples of Thespis: Some Private Theatres and Theatricals in England and Wales, 1700–1820* (London).

—— (1981). *Georgian Scene Painters and Scene Painting* (Cambridge).

Rotaller, Georgius (1550). *Sophoclis Ajax Flagellifer, et Antigone, ejusdem Electra* (Lyon).

Rothstein, Eric (1967). *Restoration Tragedy* (Westport, CT).

Rowe, Nicholas (1709, ed.). *The Works of Mr William Shakespear*, 6 vols. (London).

Rowlands, Henry (1723). *Mona Antiqua Restaurata: An Archaeological Discourse on the Antiquities of the Isle of Anglesey, the Ancient Seat of the British Druids* (Dublin).

Roworth, Wendy Wassyng (1992, ed.). *Angelica Kauffman: A Continental Artist in Georgian England* (Brighton and London).

Rucellai, Giovanni (1726). *L'Oreste* (Rome).

Ruskin, John (1851–3). *The Stones of Venice*, 3 vols. (London).

Russell, Gillian (1995). *The Theatres of War: Performance, Politics and Society 1793–1815* (Oxford).

Rutherford, Susan (1992). 'The Voice of Freedom: Images of the Prima Donna', in Gardner and Rutherford (eds.), 95–113.

Rymer, Thomas (1674). *Reflections on Aristotle's Treatise of Poesie with Reflections on the Whole of the Ancient and Modern Poets and the Faults Noted* (London).

—— (1678). *The Tragedies of the Last Age Consider'd and Examin'd by the Practice of the Ancients and by the Common Sense of all Ages* (London).

—— (1693). *A Short View of Tragedy, its Original, Excellency, and Corruption* (London).

Sadie, Stanley (1992, ed.). *The New Grove Dictionary of Opera* (London: Macmillan).

St. Clair, William (1998). *Lord Elgin and The Marbles* (Oxford and New York).

Sala, George Augustus (1864). *Robson: A Sketch* (London).

Salmon, Eric (1986, ed.). *Granville Barker and his Correspondents: A Selection of Letters by him and to him* (Detroit).

Salter, W. H. (1911). *Essays on Two Moderns* (London).

Sambrook, James (1991). *James Thomson, 1700–1748: A Life* (Oxford).

—— (1993). *The Eighteenth Century: The Intellectual and Cultural Context of English Literature 1700–1789*, 2nd edn. (London and New York).

Samuel, Raphael (1989, ed.). *Patriotism: The Making and Unmaking of British National Identity*, i: *History and Politics* (London and New York).

Sands, Mollie (1979). *Robson of the Olympic* (London).

Saschek, Ernst (1911). *Thomas Noon Talfourd als Dramatiker* (diss. Leipzig).

Sauer, Elizabeth (2002). 'Milton and Dryden on the Restoration stage', in Claude J. Summers and Ted-Larry Pebworth (eds.), *Fault Lines and Controversies in the Study of Seventeenth-Century Literature*, 88–110.

Saxon, A. H. (1978). *The Life and Art of Andew Ducrow* (Hamden, CT).

Sayer, Robert (1772). *Les Métamorphoses de Melpomène* (London).

Sayers, Frank (1830). *Poetical Works* (London).

Schiff, Gert (1973). *Johann Heinrich Füssli 1741–1825*, 2 vols. (Zurich and Munich).

Schlegel, A. W. von (1840). *Lectures on the Drama*, English translation by John Black, 2nd edn. (London).

Schleiner, Louise (1990). 'Latinized Greek Drama in Shakespeare's Writing of Hamlet', *Shakespeare Quarterly*, 41: 29–48.

Schoch, R. W. (2002). *Not Shakespeare: Bardolatory and Burlesque in the Nineteenth Century* (Cambridge).

Scott, Clement (1892). *Thirty Years at the Play* (London).

Scott, Mary Jane W. (1988). *James Thomson, Anglo-Scot* (Athens, GA, and London).

Scott, Walter (1808, ed.). *The Works of John Dryden,* vi (London).

——(1870). 'An Essay on the Drama', in *The Miscellaneous Works of Sir Walter Scott* (Edinburgh), vi. 217–395.

——(1883, ed.). *The Works of John Dryden,* vi, rev. and corr. George Saintsbury (Edinburgh).

Senelick, Laurence (1993). 'Boys and Girls Together: Subcultural Origins of Glamour Drag and Male Impersonation on the Nineteenth-Century Stage', in Ferris (ed.), 82–5.

——(1997, ed.). *Tavern Singing in Early Victorian London: The Diaries of Charles Rice for 1840 and 1850* (London).

Settle, Elkanah (1708). *The Siege of Troy. A Tragi-Comedy, as it Has Been Often Acted with Great Applause* (London).

Seward, Anna (1811). *Letters of Anna Seward, Written between the Years 1784 and 1807* (Edinburgh and London).

Shaftesbury, Anthony Ashley Cooper, 3rd Earl of (1711). *Characteristicks of Men, Manners, Opinions, Times* (London).

Shanley, Mary Lyndon (1981–2). ' "One Must Ride Behind": Married Women's Rights and the Divorce Act of 1857', *Victorian Studies,* 25: 355–76.

——(1989). *Feminism, Marriage and the Law in Victorian England 1850–1895* (London).

Sharma, Virendra (1979). *Studies in Victorian Verse Drama* (Salzburg).

Shattock, Charles H. (1958, ed.). *Bulwer and Macready: A Chronicle of the Early Victorian Theatre* (Urbana).

Shaw, George Bernard (1960). *Major Barbara,* ed. Dan H. Laurence (Harmondsworth).

——(1986). *Major Critical Essays* (Harmondsworth).

Shebbeare, John (1754). *The Marriage Act. Containing a Series of Interesting Adventures,* 2 vols. (London).

Shelley, Percy Bysshe (1820*a*). *Prometheus Unbound: A Lyrical Drama in Four Acts with Other Poems* (London).

——(1820*b*). *Œdipus Tyrannus; or, Swellfoot the Tyrant. A Tragedy* (London).

——(1822). *Hellas: A Lyrical Drama* (London).

——(1882). *The Cyclops of Euripides. A Satyric Drama, Translated into English by P. B. Shelley. Performed in the Original Greek at Magdalen College School, Oxford* (Oxford).

——(1886). *The Cenci: A Tragedy in Five Acts,* introd. Alfred Forman and H. Buxton Forman, prologue John Todhunter (Shelley Society Publications, 4th ser., Miscellaneous, 3; London).

——(1920). *A Philosophical View of Reform (Now Printed for the First Time) together with an Introduction and Appendix by R. W. Rolleston* (London).

——(1965). *The Complete Works of Percy Bysshe Shelley*, ed. Roger Ingpen and Walter E. Peck, 10 vols. (London and New York).

——(1970). *The Complete Poetical Works of Percy Bysshe Shelley*, ed. Thomas Hutchinson, 2nd edn. corr. G. M. Matthews (Oxford).

——(2003). *The Major Works*, ed. Zachary Leader and Michael O'Neill (Oxford).

Shepley, N. (1988). *Women of Independent Mind: St. George's School, Edinburgh and the Campaign for Women's Education 1888–1988* (Edinburgh).

Sheppard, J. T. (1920). *The Oedipus Tyrannus of Sophocles* (Cambridge).

——(1927). *Aeschylus & Sophocles: Their Work and Influence* (New York).

Sherbo, Arthur (1957). *English Sentimental Drama* (East Lansing, MI).

Sheridan, Thomas (1725). *The Philoctetes of Sophocles: Translated from the Greek* (Dublin).

Sherwood, Mary Martha (1910). *The Life and Times of Mrs. Sherwood (1775–1851), from the Diaries of Captain and Mrs Sherwood*, ed. F. J. Harvey Darton (London).

Shiels, Robert (1753). *Lives of the Poets of Great-Britain and Ireland, 'by Theophilus Cibber'*, 5 vols. (London).

Shirley, William (1750). *Edward the Black Prince* (London).

——(1759). *Observations on a Pamphlet lately Published, entitled, The Genuine and Legal Sentence Pronounced by the High Court of Judicature of Portugal upon the Conspirators against the Life of his Most Faithful Majesty* (London).

——(1762). *The Rosciad of C-v-nt G-rd-n* (London).

——(1765). *Electra, a Tragedy; and the Birth of Hercules, a Masque* (London).

Showalter, Elaine (1977). *A Literature of their Own: British Women Novelists from Brontë to Lessing* (Princeton).

Sideris, Giannis (1976). Τὸ 'Αρχαῖο Θέατρο στὴ Νέα 'Ελληνικῆ Σκηνή 1817–1932 [*Ancient Greek Theatre on the Modern Greek Stage 1817–1932*] (Athens).

Sikes, Frank (1869). *Hypermnestra; or, the Danaides. A Sensational Burlesque* (British Library Add. MS 53075 L).

Silk, M. S. (2001). 'Aristotle, Rapin, Brecht' in Øivind Andersen and Jon Haarberg (eds.), *Making Sense of Aristotle* (London), 173–95.

——and Stern, J. P. (1981). *Nietzsche on Tragedy* (Cambridge).

Simon, Erika (1990). 'Ion', *Lexicon Iconographicum Mythologiae Classicae* (Zurich), v/1: 702–5.

Simpson, Eve Blantyre (1898). *Robert Louis Stevenson's Edinburgh Days* (London).

Simpson, Michael (1998). *Closet Performances: Political Exhibitions and Prohibition in the Dramas of Byron and Shelley* (Stanford, CA).

Smith, Bruce R. (1988). *Ancient Scripts and Modern Experience on the English Stage 1500–1700* (Princeton).

Smith, Edmund (1719). *The Works of Mr Edmund Smith ... To Which is prefix'd, A Character of Mr. Smith, by Mr. Oldisworth*, 3rd edn. (London).

—— (1777). *Phædra and Hippolitus* (Bell's British Theatre, 10; London).

—— (1796). *Phædra and Hippolitus* (British Theatre, 26; London).

[Smith, J.] (1827). 'Creon the Patriot: A Tragedy by ...' (name erased, Norwich; British Library Add. MS 42890, fos. 273–314).

Smith, Jean, and Toynbee, Arnold (1960, eds.), *Gilbert Murray: An Unfinished Autobiography* (London).

Smith, John (1771). *Choir Gaur; The Grand Orrery of the Ancient Druids, Commonly Called Stonehenge, on Salisbury Plain, Astronomically Explained, and Mathematically Proved to be a Temple Erected in the Earliest Ages for Observing the Movements of the Heavenly Bodies* (Salisbury).

Snyder, Edward D. (1923). *The Celtic Revival in English Literature* (Cambridge, Mass).

Soldene, Emily (1897). *My Theatrical and Musical Recollections* (London).

Sotheby, William (1799). *The Battle of the Nile* (London).

—— (1800). *Cambrian Hero, or Llewelyn the Great* (Egham).

Spathes, Dimitris (1986). 'Sophocles' *Philoctetes* in N. Pikkolo's Adaptation: The First Performance of an Ancient Greek Tragedy in Modern Greek Theatre History' (in Greek). reprinted in *Ο Διαφωτισμός και το Νεοελληνικό θέατρο* (*The Enlightenment and the Modern Greek Theatre* (Thessaloniki), 145–98.

Speaight, Robert (1954). *William Poel and the Elizabethan Revival* (London).

Speck, W. A. (1983). *Society and Literature in England 1700–60* (Dublin).

Spedding, B. J. (1869). *Ino; or, the Theban Twins. A Classical Burlesque* (London).

Spencer, Terence (1954). *Fair Greece, Sad Relic: Literary Philhellenism from Shakespeare to Byron* (London).

Spicer, Henry (1855). *Alcestis: A Lyric Play* (London).

Springarn, J. E. (1909, ed.). *Critical Essays of the Seventeenth Century* (Oxford).

Srebrny, Stefan (1984). *Teatr Grecki i Polski* (Warsaw).

Stafford, Fiona J. (1988). *The Sublime Savage: A Study of James Macpherson and The Poems of Ossian* (Edinburgh).

—— (1994). *The Last of the Race: the Growth of a Myth from Milton to Darwin* (Oxford).

Stanley, Thomas (1655). *The Clouds of Aristophanes, added not as a comicall divertisement for the reader . . . but as a necessary supplement to the Life of Socrates*, in *The History of Philosophy* (London).

—— (1663). *Αἰσχύλου τραγῳδίαι ἑπτά: cum . . . versione & commentario* (London).

Starr, H. W., and Hendrickson, J. R. (1966, eds.). *The Complete Poems of Thomas Gray* (Oxford).

Stedman, Jane W. (1969). *Gilbert before Sullivan* (London).

Stein, Richard L. (1987). *Victoria's Year: English Literature and Culture, 1837–38* (New York and Oxford).

Steinberg, M. P. (1991). 'The Incidental Politics to Mendelssohn's Antigone', in R. L. Todd (ed.), *Mendelssohn and his World* (Princeton), 137–57.

Steiner, George (1961). *The Death of Tragedy* (London).

—— (1984). *Antigones* (Oxford).

Stern, Bernard Herbert (1940). *The Rise of Romantic Hellenism in English Literature 1732–1786* (Menasha, WI).

Stirling, Edward (1881). *Old Drury Lane*, 2 vols. (London).

Stockdale, Percival (1778). *An Inquiry into the Nature and Genuine Laws of Poetry* (London).

Stoker, David (1993). 'Greek Tragedy with a Happy Ending: The Publication of Robert Potter's Translations of Aeschylus, Euripides, and Sophocles', *Studies in Bibliography*, 46: 282–303.

Stokes, John (1972). *Resistible Theatres: Enterprise and Experiment in the Late Nineteenth Century* (London).

Stone, Lawrence (1992). *Uncertain Unions: Marriage in England, 1660–1753* (Oxford).

—— (1993). *Broken Lives: Separation and Divorce in England, 1660–1857* (Oxford).

—— (1995). *Road to Divorce: A History of the Making and Breaking of Marriage in England* (Oxford and New York).

Stowell, Sheila (1992). *A Stage of their Own: Feminist Playwrights of the Suffrage Era* (Manchester).

Strachan, John (2000). ' "That is True Fame": A Few Words about Thomson's Romantic Period Popularity', in Terry (ed.), 247–70.

Stray, Christopher (1998). *Classics Transformed: Schools, Universities, and Society in England, 1830–1960* (Oxford).

Stromberg, Roland N. (1954). *Religious Liberalism in Eighteenth-Century England* (Oxford).

Stuart, Charles Douglas, and Park, A. J. (1895). *The Variety Stage* (London).

Stuart, James, and Revett, Nicholas (1762). *The Antiquities of Athens Measured and Delineated* (London), i.

Stukeley, William (1740). *Stonehenge: A Temple Restor'd to the British Druids* (London).

—— (1743). *Abury, a Temple of the British Druids* (London).

—— (1763*a*). *A Letter from Dr Stukeley to Mr Macpherson* (London).

—— (1763*b*). *Palaeographia Sacra* (London).

Sturmy, J. (1722). *Love and Duty; or, The Distress'd Bride*, 2nd edn. (London).

Styrke, I. (1816). *Euripides's Alcestis Burlesqued* (London).

Summers, Montague (1932). *Dryden: The Dramatic Works*, iv (London).

—— (1934). *The Restoration Theatre* (London).

Summerson, John (1966). *Inigo Jones* (Harmondsworth).

Swinburne, Algernon Charles (1865). *Atalanta in Calydon: A Tragedy* (London).

—— (1876). *Erechtheus: A Tragedy* (London).

—— (1901). *Atalanta in Calydon; and, Lyrical Poems*, with an introduction by William Sharp (Leipzig).

Talfourd, Francis (1850). *Alcestis, the Original Strong-Minded Woman: A Classical Burlesque in One Act* (Lacy's Acting Edition) (London).

—— (1857). *Atalanta, or the Three Golden Apples, an Original Classical Extravaganza* (London).

—— (1858). *Pluto and Proserpine; or, the Belle and the Pomegranate. An Entirely New and original Mythological Extravaganza of the 0th Century* (London).

—— (1859). *Electra in a New Electric Light* (London).

—— (n.d.). *Alcestis, the Original Strong-Minded Woman: a Classical Burlesque in One Act*, 3rd edn. (London).

Talfourd, Thomas Noon (1821). 'West London Theatre. Revival of the Œdipus Tyrannus', *New Monthly Magazine and Literary Journal*, vol. 3 (1 December), 613–15.

—— (1827). 'The Drama', *New Monthly Magazine*, vol. 21 (1 November), 462–5.

—— (1827–52). 'Transcripts of 19 Original Letters by Thomas Noon Talfourd, deposited in collections in the U.S.A. Collected by W. S. Ward' (Reading Public Library).

—— (1841). *Speech for the Defendant, in the Prosecution of the Queen v. Moxon, for the Publication of Shelley's Works* (London).

—— (1841–54). Unpublished diary, in 'Private Personal Memoranda' (Talfourd Collection, Reading Public Library).

—— (1844). *Tragedies; to Which are Added a Few Sonnets and Verses*, 4th edn. (London).

—— (1850*a*). 'Rymer on Tragedy', in *The Modern British Essayists*, second USA series (Philadelphia), vii. 21–8; first published in *The Retrospective Review*.

——(1850*b*). 'Hazlitt's Lectures on the Drama', in *The Modern British Essayists*, second USA series (Philadelphia), vii. 68–73; first published in *The Edinburgh Review*.

——(n.d.). 'Newspaper Cuttings of Sir Thomas Noon Talfourd' (scrapbook collection, Reading Public Library).

——(1854). 'Mr. Justice Talfourd', obituary in *The Literary Gazette and Journal of Belles Lettres, Science, and Arts*, no. 1939 (18 March), 254–5 (London).

Taplin, Oliver (1997). 'The Chorus of Mams', in Sandie Byrne (ed.), *Tony Harrison, Loiner* (Oxford), 171–84.

Tate Gallery (1975). *Henry Fuseli 1741–1825* (London).

Taylor, D. J. (1999). *Thackeray* (London).

Taylor, George (1972). ' "The Just Delineation of the Passions'': Theories of Acting in the Age of Garrick', in Kenneth Richards and Peter Thomson (eds.), *Essays on the Eighteenth-Century English Stage* (London), 51–72.

——(1989). *Players and Performances in the Victorian Theatre* (Manchester and New York).

——(2000). *The French Revolution and the London Stage 1789–1895* (Cambridge).

Teignmouth, John Shore, 1st Baron (1804). *Memoirs of the Life, Writings and Correspondence of Sir William Jones* (London).

Terry, Richard (2000, ed.). *James Thomson: Essays for the Tercentenary* (Liverpool).

Thackeray, William Makepeace (1846). *Notes of a Journey from Cornhill to Grand Cairo* (London).

——(1903). *Burlesques, From Cornhill to Grand Cairo and Juvenilia* (London and New York).

——(1968). *Vanity Fair*, edited with an introduction by J. I. M. Stewart (Harmondsworth).

The Drama (1821–5) = *The Drama; or, Theatrical Pocket Magazine*, 7 vols.

Theobald, Lewis (1714). *Electra: A Tragedy. Translated from Sophocles, with Notes* (London).

——(1715*a*). *The Persian Princess: or, the Royal Villain. A Tragedy* (London).

——(1715*b*). *The Clouds. A Comedy. Translated from the Greek of Aristophanes* (London).

——(1715*c*). *Plutus: or, The World's Idol. A Comedy. Translated from the Greek of Aristophanes* (London).

——(1715*d*). *Oedipus, King of Thebes. A Tragedy. Translated from Sophocles* (London).

——(1731). *Orestes. A Dramatic Opera* (London).

Theobald, Lewis (1733). *The Works of Shakespeare in Seven Volumes, Collated with the Oldest Copies, and Corrected; with Notes, Explanatory and Critical* (London).

Thompson, Robert (1995). *The Glory of the Temple and the Stage: Henry Purcell (1659–1695)* (London).

Thomson, James (1735–6). *Liberty* (London).

——(1738). *Agamemnon. A Tragedy* (London).

——(1750). *Agamemnon, ein Trauerspiel*, translated by Johann David Michaëlis (Göttingen).

——(1756). *Des Herrn Jacob Thomson sämtliche Trauerspiele aus dem Englischen übersetzt, mit einer Vorrede von Gotthold Ephraim Lessing* (Leipzig).

——(1771). *Agamemnon, ein Trauerspiel in fünf Aufzügen* (Frankfurt and Leipzig).

——(1773). *The Works of James Thomson*, vol. iii (London).

——(1775). *Edward and Eleonora* (London).

——(1780). *Agamemnon, tragédie en 5 actes et en vers, traduite de l'anglais de feu M. Thompson [sic], représentée pour la première fois à Paris le 18 janvier 1780* (Paris).

——(1795). *Edward and Eleonora* (British Theatre, 26; London).

Thorndike, Sibyl (1936). 'Gilbert Murray and Some Actors', in J. A. K. Thomson and A. J. Toynbee (eds.), *Essays in Honour of Gilbert Murray* (London).

——(with Lewis Casson) (1960). 'The Theatre and Gilbert Murray', in Smith and Toynbee (eds.), 149–75.

Tickner, Lisa (1987). *The Spectacle of Women: Imagery of the Suffrage Campaign 1907–14* (London).

Tillyard, Stella (1995). *Aristocrats: Caroline, Emily, Louis and Sarah Lennox 1740–1832* (London).

Todhunter, John (1879). *Alcestis* (London).

——(1880). *A Study of Shelley* (London).

——(1886). *Helena in Troas* (London).

Topouzes, Kostas (1992, ed.) Σοφοκλέους Φιλοκτήτης (Athens).

Trapp, Joseph (1742). *Lectures on Poetry Read in the Schools of Natural Philosophy at Oxford: Translated from the Latin, With Additional Notes* (London; facsimile reprint by the Scolar Press with Introductory Note by Malcolm Kensall, Menston, 1973).

Travers, Seymour (1941). *Catalogue of French Theatrical Parodies (1789–1914)* (New York).

Trevelyan, G. O. (1858). *The Cambridge Dionysia: A Classic Dream* (Cambridge).

Trevor-Roper, Hugh (1988). *Archbishop Laud*, 3rd edn. (Basingstoke and London).

Trewin, J. C. (1960). *Benson and the Bensonians* (London).

Trussler, Simon (1994). *The Cambridge Illustrated History of British Theatre* (Cambridge and New York).

Tsigakou, Fani-Maria (1981). *The Rediscovery of Greece: Travellers and Painters of the Romantic Era* (London).

Turner, Frank (1981). *The Greek Heritage in Victorian Britain* (New Haven and London).

—— (1989). 'Why the Greeks and not the Romans in Victorian Britain?', in G. W. Clarke, *Rediscovering Hellenism: The Hellenic Inheritance and the English Imagination* (Cambridge, 1989), 61–81.

Tydeman, William, and Price, Steven (1996). *Wilde: Salome* (Cambridge).

Uglione, Renato (1997, ed.). *Atti delle giornate di studio su Medea, Torino 23–24 ottobre 1995* (Turin).

Uglow, Jenny (1997). *Hogarth: A Life and a World* (London).

Valpy, Richard (1804). *Poems, Odes, Prologues, and Epilogues, Spoken on Public Occasions at Reading School* (London).

—— (1814). 'A Short Sketch of a Trip to Paris in 1788', *The Pamphleteer*, 3: 189–552.

—— (1821). *The Orestes of Euripides, as Performed at the Triennial Visitation of Reading School, October 1821: Chiefly from Mr. Potter's Translation* (Reading).

—— (1826). *Poems, Odes, Prologues, and Epilogues, Spoken on Public Occasions at Reading School* (London).

—— (1827). *The Hecuba of Euripides, Represented at the Triennial Visitation of Reading School. Translated by Mr. Potter* (Reading).

Valsa, M. (1960). *Le Théâtre grec moderne, de 1453 à 1900* (Berlin).

Vance, Norman (1997). *The Victorians and Ancient Rome* (Oxford).

Vandenhoff, George (1860). *Leaves from an Actor's Notebook* (New York and London).

Vaughan, Anthony (1979). *Born to Please: Hannah Pritchard, Actress* (London).

Veevers, Erica (1989). *Images of Love and Religion: Queen Henrietta Maria and Court Entertainments* (Cambridge).

Venn, J. A. (1954). *Alumni Cantabrigienses, Part II: 1752–1900*, vi (Cambridge).

Vernant, Jean-Pierre (1988). ' The Tragic Subject: Historicity and Trans-historicity', in Vernant and Vidal-Naquet (1988), 237–47.

—— and Vidal-Naquet, Pierre (1988). *Myth and Tragedy in Ancient Greece*, English translation by Janet Lloyd (New York).

Verrall, A. W. (1890*a*, ed.). Εὐριπίδου ῎Ιων: *The Ion of Euripides* (Cambridge).

Verrall, A. W. (1890b). 'Preface' to *The Ion of Euripides: As Arranged for Performance* (Cambridge).

——(1895). *Euripides the Rationalist* (Cambridge).

Victor, Benjamin (1761). *The History of the Theatres of London and Dublin from 1730 to the Present Time*, 2 vols. (London).

——(1776). *Original Letters, Dramatic Pieces, and Poems*, 3 vols. (London).

Vidal-Naquet, Pierre (1988). 'Oedipus in Vicenza and in Paris: Two Turning Points in the History of Oedipus', in Vernant and Vidal-Naquet (1988), 361–80.

——(1995). *Politics Ancient and Modern*, English translation by Janet Lloyd (Cambridge).

Vince, Ronald W. (1988). *Neoclassical Theatre: A Historiographical Handbook* (New York, Westport, CT, and London).

Vincent-Buffault, Anne (1991). *The History of Tears: Sensibility and Sentimentality in France*, English translation (Basingstoke).

Visser, Colin (1980). 'Scenery and Technical Design', in Robert D. Hume (ed.), *The London Theatre World 1660–1800* (Carbondale, IL, and Edwardsville, IL), 66–118.

Voltaire, François Marie Arouet *dit* (1719). *Œdipe, Tragédie (avec Lettres écrites par l'auteur)* (Paris; repr. Amsterdam, The Hague, and London).

Vondel, Joost van den (1666). *Vondels Ifigenie in Tauren uit Euripides, Treurspel* (Amsterdam).

Waith, Eugene M. (1971). *Ideas of Greatness: Heroic Drama in England* (London).

Wakefield, Gilbert (1794, ed.). *Tragoediarum Delectus*, 2 vols. (London).

Walkley, W. B ([1911]). 'The New Dancer', in Anon. ([1911], ed.).

Walkowitz, Judith R. (2003). 'The "Vision of Salome": Cosmopolitanism and Erotic Dancing in Central London, 1908–1918', *American Historical Review*, 108: 337–76.

Wallace, Jennifer (1997). *Shelley and Greece: Rethinking Romantic Hellenism* (London and Basingstoke).

Walpole, Horace (1768). *The Mysterious Mother* (Strawberry Hill).

——(1937). *Correspondence* (Yale edn.), i–ii (New Haven and London).

Walton, J. Michael (1987). *Living Greek Theatre: A Handbook of Classical Performance and Modern Production* (New York and London).

Ward, A. W. (1875). *A History of English Dramatic Literature to the Death of Queen Anne*, ii (London).

Ward, Geneviève (1881). 'Medea's Big Boy', *The Era Almanack*, 127–8.

——and Whiting, Richard (1918). *Both Sides of the Curtain* (London, New York, Toronto, and Melbourne).

Warner, W. (1595). *Menaecmi. A Pleasant and Fine Conceited Comoedie, taken out of the most excellent wittie poet Plautus: Chosen purposely from out the rest, as least harmefull, and yet most delightfull. Written in English* (London).

Warr, G. C. W. (1886). *The Tale of Troy, and The Story of Orestes* (London).

——(1900). *The Oresteia of Aeschylus, Translated and Explained* (London).

——and Crane, Walter (1887). *Echoes of Hellas: The Tale of Troy and the Story of Orestes from Homer and Æschylus . . . Presented in 82 Designs by Walter Crane* (London).

Wartelle, André (1978). *Bibliographie historique et critique d'Eschyle et de la tragédie grecque* (Paris).

Wase, Christopher (1649). *The Electra of Sophocles: Presented to Her Highnesse the Lady Elizabeth; With an Epilogue Shewing the Parallel in two Poems, The Return, and The Restauration. By C.W.* (The Hague).

Watson, George (1973). *The English Ideology: Studies in the Language of Victorian Politics* (London).

Watts, Diana (1914). *The Renaissance of the Greek Ideal* (London).

Webb, Timothy (1977). *Shelley: A Voice Not Understood* (Manchester).

——(1982). *English Romantic Hellenism 1700–1824* (Manchester and New York).

Webster, Augusta (1868). *The Medea of Euripides, Literally Translated into English Verse* (London and Cambridge).

——(1870). *Portraits*, 2nd edn. (London).

——(1879). *A Housewife's Opinions* (London).

Weimann, Robert (1976). *Structure and Society in Literary History* (Charlottesville, VA).

Wesley, John (1906). *The Journal of the Rev. John Wesley*, ed. F. W. Macdonald, 4 vols. (London).

West, Francis (1984). *Gilbert Murray: A Life* (London, Canberra, and New York).

West, Gilbert (1749). *Odes of Pindar, with several other Pieces in Prose and Verse* (London).

West, Richard (1726). *Hecuba: A Tragedy* (London).

Wetmore, Kevin J. (2002). *The Athenian Sun in an African Sky: Modern African Adaptations of Classical Greek Tragedy* (London).

Wheatley, K. E. (1956). *Racine and English Classicism* (Austin, TX).

Whitehead, William (1754). *Creüsa, Queen of Athens: A Tragedy* (London).

——(1777). *The Roman Father* (London).

——(1778). *Creusa, Queen of Athens* (Bell's British Theatre, 20; London).

——(1788). *Plays and Poems*, iii: *Poems, to which are Prefixed Memoirs of his Life and Writings by W. Mason* (London).

Whitman, Alfred (1902). *Valentine Green* (London).

Whitworth, Charles (1771, ed.). *The Political and Commercial Works of that Celebrated Writer Charles D'Avenant LL.D.*, 5 vols. (London).

Williams, E. E. (1937). 'Athalie: The Tragic Cycle and the Tragedy of Joas', *Romanic Review*, 36–45.

Williams, Ioan (1970, ed.). *The Criticism of Henry Fielding* (London).

Williams, Thomas (1856). *Medea: A Tragedy in Three Acts* (London).

Wills, Freeman (1898). *W. G. Wills, Dramatist and Painter* (London, New York, and Bombay).

Wills, W. G. (1872). *Medea: A Tragedy in 3 Acts* (British Library Add. MS 53110 N).

Wilson, Duncan (1987). *Gilbert Murray OM, 1866–1957* (Oxford).

Wilson, John (1973). *CB: A Life of Sir Henry Campbell-Bannerman* (New York).

Wilson, John Harold (1958). *All the King's Ladies: Actresses of the Restoration* (Chicago).

Wilson, Patrick (1971). *Murderess* (London).

Winterer, Caroline (2001). *The Culture of Classicism: Ancient Greece and Rome in American Intellectual Life, 1780–1910* (Baltimore and London).

Winton, Calhoun (1974). 'Sentimentalism and Theater Reform in the Early Eighteenth Century', in Larry S. Champion (ed.), *Quick Springs of Sense: Studies in the Eighteenth Century* (Athens, GA), 97–110.

Wolfram, Sybil (1987). *In-Laws and Outlaws: Kinship and Marriage in England* (London and Sydney).

Wood, Christopher (1983). *Olympian Dreamers* (London).

Wood, Ellen (Mrs Henry) (1861). *East Lynne* (London).

Woodberry, G. E. (1909, ed.). *The Cenci by Percy Bysshe Shelley* (Boston & London).

Woodcock, George (1989). 'The Meaning of Revolution in Britain, 1770–1800', in Crossley and Small (eds.), 1–30.

Woodhouse, C. M. (1969). *The Philhellenes* (London).

Woods, Charles (1949). 'Fielding's Epilogue for Theobald', *Philological Quarterly*, 28: 419–24.

Wooler, Jack [= Frank Sikes] (1851). *Jason and Medea: A Comic. Heroic. Operatic. Burlesque-Spectacular Extravaganza* (British Library Add. MS 43036, fos. 276–307).

Woolf, Virginia (1925). 'On Not Knowing Greek', in *The Common Reader* (London), cited from the 12th impression (London, 1975).

Wordsworth, Jonathan (1997). *The Bright Work Grows: Women Writers of the Romantic Age* (Poole).

Wyndham, Henry Saxe (1906). *The Annals of Covent Garden Theatre from 1732 to 1897*, 2 vols. (London).

Yeats, W. B. (1962). *Selected Poetry*, ed. A. Norman Jeffares (London).

——(1989). *Letters to the New Island,* ed. G. Bornstein and H. Witemeyer (New York).

Young, Sir George (1862). *On the History of Greek Literature in England From the Earliest Times to the End of the Reign of James the First* (London and Cambridge).

Zeitlin, Froma (1996). *Playing the Other: Gender and Society in Classical Greek Literature* (Chicago).

Zimbardo, Rose A. (1986). *A Mirror to Nature: Transformation in Drama and Aesthetics 1660–1772* (Lexington, KY).

Index

The index contains references to all plays and authors, ancient and post-Renaissance, which occur substantially in the text and footnotes, and to all topics which are the subject of comment. Dates of important individuals are given in the index as a useful guide to their period of activity. In the many cases where a figure appears in several works, e.g. Medea, Oedipus, the references are grouped as follows:

(i)   under the name of the mythical figure in general
(ii) the Greek original or originals which provided later authors with inspiration
(iii) later plays, adaptations or translations in alphabetical order of play title and then of author.

Page references in italic type are to illustrations or captions.

à Beckett, Gilbert Abott,
    burlesques 383 and n. 147
A King and No King, Francis
    Beaumont and John
    Fletcher 25, 215
A New Spirit of the Age, Richard
    Hengist Horne 285
A Philosophical View of Reform,
    Shelley 239
*A Plot and No Plot, or Jacobite
    Cruelty*, John Dennis 44
Abbey Theatre, Dublin, proposed
    Oedipus Tyrannus at 535–6
Abrahams, Ethel 513 and n. 106
Accius, version of *Ion* 130–2
Acharnians, Aristophanes xi
Achilles, Abel Boyer 32, 34, 36,
    78–9, 79–80, 87–8
Achilles, John Gay 105
Act of Settlement, 1701: 42, 43 n.
    41, 51
Act of Union, 1707 51
acting

development of emotional
    range 80
styles
    of Adelaide Ristori 412
    French, German
        compared 526–8
    naturalism 432, 539
    symbolism 432
    see also actors, actresses
actors, actresses
    American, Australian ixx–xx
    first blind 2–3
    increasing importance of female
        roles 79–82, 83 n. 44
    relevance of social origins 484–5
    sculptural metaphor, simile 328,
        335, 484
    social standing 395–7, 484–5
    women in 'breeches' roles 129
        and n. 8, 273, 311, *312*, 342,
        353, 367–1, 385, 396; *see also*
        cross-dressed roles *and
        individual performers*

Actresses' Franchise League 514, 515, *517*

Adam & Eve (tavern), 'classical' entertainments at 389

Adam Bede, George Eliot 421

Adams, George 147, 172, 219

Adams, William Davenport 354 and n. 24

Addison, Joseph, see *Cato*

Adelphi (Adelphoe), Terence 244, 245

Adelphi Theatre
    antiquarian design 269
    burlesques in 352–3, 380, 406

Admeto, rè di Tessaglia, Handel 118 and n. 44, 439 n. 116

Admetus (mythical figure)
    portrayals of 456–7
    representations of 434–5, 441–2, 443–6, 460–1

'Admetus and Alcestis', Lewis Campbell 446–7

Adrastus, representations of 293–300

Adrastus; a Tragedy, R. C. Dallas 273 n. 30

adultery
    aggravated, as ground for divorce 419
    fascination with, reflected in adaptations of Greek tragedy xvi

Aegeus, representation of 392 and n. 5

Aegisthus (Ægisthus)
    compared with Francis Charteris 115
    parallel with Cromwell 165
    representations of 125, 153, 155, 157–9, 163, 168–72, 180, 374

Aegisthus, raising the veil, discovers the body of Clytemnestra,

Benjamin West's lost painting 177 and n. 62, *178*

Aeneid, as source of inspiration 67, 110, 359, 377, 385

Aeschylus
    attempts to introduce to British theatre 99–101
    impact of first English translation xx, 111, 209–10 and n. 104, 221
    indictment for impiety 199
    influence on
        Henry Fielding xvii
        James Thomson 110–11
    interest in, stimulated by Browning 431, 433, 454
    perceptions of barbarians in xxi–xxii
    Potter's perception of 221
    problem of accessibility 111 and n. 26, 209
    publicized by King's College *The Story of Orestes* 465
    reputation in Britain 475
    source for burlesques 359–60, *360*
    Stanley's editions 40, 100–1 and n. 4, 154
    suitability of plays for performance 316–18
    Theobald's lost translations 55, 111 and n. 26
    see also individual plays

Aesthetic movement, mockery by Gilbert and Sullivan 387

aesthetics, modern, significance of Lessing's *Laocoon* 127

Africa, Greek tragedy in vii n. 2

Against Celsus, Origen 149

Agamemnon (mythical figure)
    interest in archaeology's 'Death Mask' 449
    portrayals of 107, 334, 453

representations of 108, 112–15, 169

Agamemnon, Aeschylus
Browning's 'transcript' of 433, 449, 451, 454, 456
productions
at Balliol College 451–4, *454*, 456, 476, 532
at Bradfield College 457 n. 71
by Campbell and Jenkin 451–2
in English-speaking world 455
at Oxford 387, 455
quoted by Hazlitt xvii
Richard Cumberland's admiration for 210 and n. 104
as source of inspiration *349*, 383

Agamemnon and Cassandra; or, The Prophet and Loss of Troy, Robert Reece, burlesque 359

Agamemnon at Home; or, The Latest Particulars of that Little Affair at Mycenae, Edward Nolan 373, 383–4 and n. 150

Agamemnon, James Thomson
actresses in 80, 98
alterations to original 106 and n. 19, 112–15
attempt to domesticate Aeschylus 99–101
and censorship 105–6 and n. 18, 106–7, 542
chorus confined to staged rituals 197
concept of socially responsible drama 103
influence on Continent 124–7
links with other plays 105
manifesto of Whig ideals 50, 102, 104–8
popularity 106 and n. 20

as She-Tragedy 78 n. 22, 112–15
sources 109–12
translation into German verse 126

Agamemnon, Seneca 163
Agamemnon, Lemercier 125
Agamemnone, Alfieri 124

Ajax, Sophocles
Cambridge University production 476
translations, editions
anonymous 75 and n. 19, *76*
Latin, by Rotaller 163
by Thomas Johnson 154

Alabaster, William, *Roxana* 117 n. 39

Alan's Wife, Florence Bell and Elizabeth Robins 518

Albert, Prince Consort 318, 319

Albert Memorial, Homeric portions of frieze 475

Albion's Triumph, masque 204

Alcestis (mythical figure)
identified with Elizabeth Barrett Browning 444
operatic tradition 441 n. 19
poems about
Browning's *Balaustion's Adventures* 442–6
various 443 n. 25
portrayals of 436, 439, 467, 485–6
representations of 63, 362, 434–8, 441–2, 443–6, 519–20
type of 'distressed mother' 63

Alcestis, Euripides
adaptation by Gildon 66, 117–18
Campbell's reworking of 446–7
continuing influence 72
expurgation at Reading School 255
link with *The Winter's Tale* 519–20

Alcestis, Euripides (*cont.*):
  productions
    in aid of Building Fund 506 n.
      106, 519 and n. 128
    at Bradfield College 456–7
      and n. 71
    in 1855 334, 438
    music for 456–7 n. 70
    by OUDS 458–9, 485–6
    in Queen's College, 1886 457,
      458
    in Reading School 253, 255,
      261
    school 455, 456 n. 70
    in University of London
      445 n. 35
    at Westminster School 117
  Robert Browning's reworking
    of 433, 446–7, 456–7 and n.
    70
  source for
    burlesque 360, 362, 384
    Charles Gildon's *Phaeton* 71
    Edward and Eleonora xiii, 66,
      116–17, 118–20
    Milton 116–17, 253, 446
  suitability for performance by
    women 460–1
  translations, editions
    by Francis Hubback 445 n. 35
    by Gerald Warre Cornish
      445 n. 45, 513 n. 106,
      519 n. 128
    by Murray 519–20
Alceste, Alfieri 435, 442
Alceste, ou le triomphe d'Alcide,
  (opera) Lully 117–18,
  439 n. 16
Alcestis, Henry Spicer
  acting of Charlotte Vandenhoff
    439
  Gluck's music 439
  'improvement' of Euripides 443

    production at St James's
      Theatre, 1856 439–42 and
      n. 19, *440*
  spectacle 459
Alcestis (opera), Gluck 439 and
  n. 16, 440–1
Alcestis, James Thomson 103, 118,
  445
Alcestis, John Todhunter 445–6
  and n. 35
Alcestis, Lucas 439–41, 442, 443
Alcestis; the Original Strong-
  Minded Woman: A Classical
  Burlesque in One Act, Frank
  Talfourd
  burlesque 362, 373–4, 379, 381,
    433–8 and n. 12, *437*, 443
  paratragic response to operatic
    tradition 438
  popularity, revivals 436 and
    n. 12, 459
Aletes, representations of 139,
  140, 144, 150
Alexander the Great, model for
  Oedipus 25–6 and n. 73
Alexandros Mavrokordatos,
  Prince xi, 266, 267 n. 8
Alexandros Morousis, Prince 265
Alfieri, Vittorio 124–5, 272–3, 277,
  435
Alfred, James Thomson 99
Ali Pacha; or, The Signet Ring 272
Allan, Maud (1873–1956)
  allegations of sexual deviancy
    548
  background 548, 553 n. 90
  controversial *Salome* 538, 548,
    551–3
  reception as dancer 528, 548–54,
    550, *552*
Allan, Theodore 553 n. 90
Allen, Woody, *Mighty*
  Aphrodite 197–8

alliteration, favoured in burlesque 365

Alma-Tadema, Lawrence, and mockery of Aesthetic movement 387, 476, 479

Almeira
actresses portraying 162
representations of 157–62

Alphonso/Osmyn, representations of 157–62, 170

Althea, actresses portraying 79–80

Alzire, Voltaire 170

Alzuma, Arthur Murphy 169–72

Amcott, Vincent, classical burlesques 376, 381, 383–4

America
Greek tragedy in vii n. 2; *see also individual plays*
productions in
Antigone 317, 321, 336–7
IT, *Trojan Women* 543–4 and n. 58
Ristori's Medea 404
repercussions of War of Independence 183–4, 186
support for independence
in 'Celtic' Britain 184
from William Mason 190, 214
use of Mendelssohn's music 336
vogue for Mason's poetry 213

Amherst, J. 240–1

Ammianus Marcellinus 203

Amphitryo, performance at Reading School 247

An Inquiry into the Nature and Genuine Laws of Poetry, Richard Stockdale 208

Anderson, Mary 287

Andria, Terence 134

Andromache (mythical figure)
portrayals of 79, 515
type of 'distressed mother' 63

Andromache, Euripides
influence 67
source for Charles Gildon 71
translation by Gilbert Murray 515

Andromache, John Crowne 34

Andromache Mourning the Death of Hector, Gavin Hamilton 89

Andromaque, Racine 67

Anglesey (Mona)
Caractacus in 184, 187–92, 214
Rowlands' view of ancient culture 204–5
scenery in Mason's *Caractacus* 188–9
setting for balletic version of *Caractacus* 213–14
Tacitus' references to, as source for Mason 203

Anglicanism, attitudes to Greek tragic metaphysics 147–50

Ango-Saxon culture, *see* Britain, ancient

Anthony and Cleopatra, Burnand 386

Anthony and Cleopatra, Shakespeare 452

anthropology, comparative, and understanding of Greek tragedy 202

anticlericalism
and responses to Whitehead's *Creusa* 147–50
shared by Francklin and Voltaire 220

Antigona (*opera*), Francesco Bianchi 317 and n. 4

Antigone (mythical figure)
costuming of 281, 348
Dennis's view of erotic passion 91
model for Evelina 187–8

Antigone (mythical figure) (*cont.*):
portrayals of 82, 281, 316, 322,
325–8, *329*, 330–1, 335–6,
348
relevance to Clytemnestra
engraving in *Vanity Fair*
347 n. 82
replaced by Medea in public
taste 392–3
representations of 218–20, 223,
274, 294, 296, 302, 303–7,
321, 322, 331–2, 340–1
Antigone, Edward Fitzball 267,
274–5
Antigone, George Meredith 330
Antigone, Margaret Sandbach 330
Antigone, Sophocles
ballet included in Covent
Garden production 322–3
at Bradfield College 457 n. 71
burlesques of 56, 339–45, 360
in Dublin 325–7
exploitation of comic potential
323, 337–45
German interest in xiv–xv, xix
317–21
impact 330–2
important adaptations 317,
319–20
inspiration for neo-classical
painting 275 n. 38
intellectual reception of
327–32
neglect prior to nineteenth
century 317
overwhelming popularity
317–18, 320
performance in Athens, 1867 336
planned, at Bradfield College
478
possibly performed in Greek at
St John's, Cambridge
244 n. 2
'Potsdam' 319–21
recitations from, at Reading
School 253 and n. 41
revival at Drury Lane 331–2 and
n. 41
role of chorus 197, 200, 453
Romantic fascination with incest
theme 240
royal command performances
318–19
as source 173, 274, 294–5
translations, editions
by Alexander Rangavis 336
by Hölderlin 318
by Johann Jakob Christian
Donner 320, 321
Latin, by Rotaller 163
by Thomas Johnson 154
by William Bartholomew
319 n. 8, 321
travesties 336–41
versions with Mendelssohn's
music
archaeological accuracy 343
German interest xix,
317–21
influence 198, 300, 317,
318–19, 320, 322–25, *323*,
325, 331–2, 335–6, 340–1,
343, 344, 351 n. 5, 378,
430, 439, 441
Antigone in Berlin, Adolf
Glassbrenner 339
Antigone Travestie, Edward Leman
Blanchard 338–41, 381
anti-semitism, in reaction to Maud
Allan 551–3
Apollo, portrayals of 456–7
Apollo and Daphne, Lewis
Theobald 54
Apollonius Rhodius, *Argonautica*,
as source of inspiration 344,
359, 399, 424

Appius and Virginia, John Dennis 48

Archaeologia Britannica, Edward Lhuyd 192 n. 26

archaeology, classical
increasing interest in 268–9, 432, 449, 455, 477–8
influence on Covent Garden *Antigone* 324–5

Archer, William 495, 518

architecture
classical, theatrical recreation of 268–9, 269–72, 273, 277–81; *see also* stage design
ugly urban, targeted in burlesque of *The Birds* 346–7

Archive of Performances of Greek and Roman Drama, Oxford University x

Areopagitica, Milton, Thomson's preface 105–6

Argentile and Curan, William Mason 191 n. 18

Argentina, Ristori's performance as Medea in 404

Argive royal family, Thomson's concept of 112–15

Argonautica, Apollinarius Rhodius 344, 359, 399, 424

Argos, setting for Talfourd's *Ion* 302–3

Ariadne; or, The Bull!! The Bully!! And the Bullion!!, Vincent Amcott 376, 381, 383–4

Arion; or, the Story of a Lyre, Burnand 366, 370, 380

Aristophanes
Gilbert Murray's study on, dedicated to Shaw 491–2
reception of performances xi–xii, xxi, 244
reflection of taste for parody 55
translation by Theobald 55
use of father–son conflicts 363
see also individual plays

Aristophanes' Apology, Robert Browning 449–51 and n. 53

Aristotle
adaptors' choice of Greek texts praised by 130
attitudes to 'Rules' 51–2, 52–3
definition of tragedy 14–15
Poetics
attention paid to Iphigenia plays 33
Dacier's translation, commentary 18, 28, 132, 153–4, 155–7, 198, 217–18
influence 14–15, 43 n. 41

army, standing, maintenance, a political concern 297–8

Arne, Thomas (1710–78)
lost score for *Caractacus* 195–6 and n. 41
music for
Elfrida commissioned from 194
Oedipus, King of Thebes, 28 n. 81
The Sacrifice of Iphigenia 32

Arnold, Matthew (1822–88)
attitude to translation 451
call for national theatre 432
on infanticide 422–3
inspired by
Helen Faucit's Antigone 330
Sophocles viii, 330–1 and n. 36
Merope, formative influences viii, 331

Arnold, Thomas, edition of Thucydides 302

art, artists, *see* visual arts *and individual artists, works*

Ashcroft, Peggy 152

Asquith, Margot, response to
    Maud Allan 548–9 and n. 76,
    553
Astley's Theatre
  Ducrow's 'hippodramatic'
      entertainments 388–9
  productions
    pro-Greek 271
    spectacular 284
Atalanta in Calydon, Swinburne,
    sources of inspiration 331
Atalanta, George Hawtrey 387
*Atalanta, or the Three Golden
    Apples, an Original Classical
    Extravaganza* 359
Athalie, Racine, influence on
    Whitehead 132–3 and n. 21
Athena, Athene
  portrayals of 486
  representations of 486
Athens
  ancient
    conceptual link with early
        Britain 184–7
    democracy
      conflicting approaches
          to 301–3 and nn. 64–5
      model 50–1 and n. 53, 58
    idealized in *The Athenian
        Captive* 304–7
    reminder of slavery in 306–7
    Theseion, inspiration for
        Penshaw monument 306,
        307
  modern, performance of
      Antigone in 1867 336
  see also British School of
      Archaeology, Athens
Atherton, Mary Russell Mitford
    257
Augusta, Princess of Wales, later
    Queen Dowager 120, 121, 168
'Augustan' principles 51–2

Aulularia, Plautus 249
Aulus Didius, representation
    of 187, 188, 189–90
Aureng-Zebe, Dryden 38
Aurora Leigh, Elizabeth Barrett
    Browning 330
Australia
  actresses from xix–xx
  Frank Benson's tour with
      Oresteia 455
  success of *Antigone* in 335
Austria, popularity of declamatory
    style of acting 424
authenticity, search for, in plays,
    performances
  demands of 198–9
  in first British 18, 336, 457
  in Reading School 261–3
  in stage design 268–9, 277–80,
      326–7, 439, 463 and n. 8,
      477–8
  in various productions 347, 361,
      431–2, 438, 447–9 and n. 47,
      450, 451–2, 477

Bacchae, Euripides
  as source of inspiration 91, 360,
      381, 383–4
  impact on Nietzsche xv
  link with *Major Barbara* 505–8
      and n. 68
  recoil from 'pagan theology' 147
  translation by Gilbert Murray
      472, 494, 497–9, 551
Bachofen, J. J. 474
Baillie, Joanna, *Constantine
    Palaiologos* 272
Baily, Edward Hodges 441 n. 18
Bainbridge, Beryl, *According to
    Queeney* 64
Bajazet, Racine 162
Baker, Sir Richard, *Chronicle of the
    Kings of England* 116

Balaustion's Adventure, Robert
Browning 442–6, 449,
456–7 n. 70
ballet, popularization 367
Balliol College, Oxford
classical burlesques at 383–4
production of *Agamemnon*
451–4, *454*, 476
Bankes (Banks), John
as forerunner of 'she-tragedy'
67 n. 8
The Destruction of Troy 66–7,
78
Bannister, John, music for *Circe*
38
Barker, *see* Granville Barker
Barnes, Joshua, *Euripidis quae
extant omnia* 71
Barrett, Elizabeth, *see* Browning,
Elizabeth Barrett
Barry, Ann, *see* Crawford
Barry, Elizabeth 72, 79, 180
Barry, Spranger 121–2
Barry, W. Francis 332
Bartholomew, William 319 n. 8,
333–4
Bateman, Isabel 425, *426*
Bayley, Peter (?1778–1823) *Orestes
in Argos* 267, 275–7, *278, 279*
Baynes, Mrs 448
Beattie, James 198
Beaumont and Fletcher, *A King
and No King* 25, 215; *Knight
of the Burning Pestle* 355–6
Bébé et Jargon, P. A. Capelle and
P. Villiers 404 n. 48
Bedford College, London
co-production of *Medea* 513
Greek plays, supported by
Murray and Barker 514
productions
in aid of building funds 513
and n. 106, 519 and n. 128

of *Alcestis* 445 n. 35
Beerbohm, Max, review of
Hippolytus, 1904 495, 549
Beethoven, Ludwig von, music for
*The Ruins of Athens; A
Dramatic Masque* 333
Belford Regis, Mary Russell
Mitford 251, 256, 257
Bell, Florence, collaboration with
Elizabeth Robins 518
Bell, William Boscawen, *The Queen
of Argos; a Tragedy in Five
Acts* 273 n. 30
Bennett, Langton 225
Benson, Frank (1858–1939)
in Bradfield *Alcestis* 456–7
as Clytemnestra 432, 453
London venue for *Oresteia* 492
and n. 13
at Lyceum Theatre under Irving
and Terry 454
proponent of Balliol
Agamemnon 452, 453
tour with *Oresteia* 455, *455*, 476
touring company 476 n. 45
Bentley, Richard 201–2 and n. 69,
207
Betterton, Mary 79 and n 30
Betterton, Thomas 3, 71 n. 15, 72,
162
Bianchi, Francesco, *Antigona* 317
and n. 4
bible, the, conceptual links with
Greek drama xxi, 132 and
n. 18
bigamy, adultery aggravated by, as
woman's ground for divorce
419
Billing, Noel Pemberton 553
Birds, Aristophanes 345–7, *346*
birth control, effect of increase in
information about 484–5
Bishop, Henry 334

Bizet, Citizen and H. Chaussie
  *Médée ou l'Hôpital des
  fous* 404 n. 48
Black-Eyed Susan, Douglas
  Jerrold 314
Blake, William, engraving of
  Edward and Eleonora 123, *123*
Blanchard, Edward Leman
  (1820–89)
  Antigone Travestie 338 and n. 58
  Hugenot connections 34 n. 19
  not impressed by Matilda
    Heron's Medea 423
  socio-educational background
    372
  use made of Greek tragedy xv
blank verse, preference for 52
Blessington, Lady 282
blindness, of Oedipus,
  metaphorical paradigm 11, 13
Blunt, Wilfrid Scawen 495–6
Boaden, James 213
*Boadicea the Beautiful; or,
  Harlequin Julius Caesar and
  the Delightful Druid*, Burnand
  383
Boadicea, Richard Glover 94, 129
Bockett, B. B. 259–60, *260*
Boeckh, A., classical scholar 320,
  431
Bodmer, Johann Jakob, *Kreusa*
  289 n. 27
Boer War
  general reactions to 509–11
  Murray's revulsion against 508
    and nn. 85–6
Boheme, Mrs 82, 83
Bond, William 105
Bonduca, Beaumont and Fletcher
  203–4
Boscawen, William Bell, *The Queen
  of Argos: A Tragedy in Five
  Acts* 273 n. 30

Bourchier, Arthur 494, 495
Bourke, Annie *368*
Bournemouth Girls High School,
  production of *Alcestis*
  456–7 n. 70
Boyer, Abel (1667–1729)
  Achilles 32, 34, 36, 78–9
  Compleat French Master 35
  Huguenot background 35 and
    n. 21
  Royal Dictionary 35
  version of *Iphigenia* 32, 35 and
    n. 23, 61, 62, 85
  views on
    emotional impact of
      Iphigenia 85
    'improvement' of Euripides
      97
    'player that makes the poet' 79
boys, representation of females
  258
Bracegirdle, Anne 71 n. 15, 79,
  152, 162
Braddon, Mary Elizabeth, *Lady
  Audley's Secret* 422
Bradfield College, Berks
  Barker's *IT* at 543, 544 n. 58
  Greek plays 253, 456–7 and
    n. 71, 495
  Greek theatre 456–7 and n. 71
  planned *Antigone* 478
Brahm, Otto, 'father of
  naturalism' 539
Brailsford, H. N. 504
Brand, Ibsen ix
Bransby, Mr 95
Brasenose College, Oxford,
  production of *Ion* 286
Brazil, Ristori's Medea in 404
breeches roles 129 and n. 8, 273,
  311, *312*, 342, 353, 367–71,
  385, 396
Bristed, Charles 348–9, 427 n. 125

Britain, ancient, fusion of classical and British revivalism 183–93, 202–7, 208
Britannia, equation with Minerva 333–4
British Archaeological Association 477
British Empire
  expansion
    radical objections to 297–8
    reflected in theatre 38–9, 48–9, 92
  Murray's equation of Athens with 511
  relevance of *Antigone* to victims of 332
British Museum, classical acquisitions 290 and n. 35
British School of Archaeology, Athens 462 and n. 2, 478
British theatre
  adaptation to expansionism 38–9, 48–9, 92
  advocates of national 102–3, 432
  attendance at burlesques 351–4
  basic movements in presentation of Greek tragedy xviii
  campaign for repeal of Theatrical Patents Act 416
  censorship in, *see* censorship
  cult of tears 81
  dominance of Whig ideals 40, 41–9, 50–4, 58–9, 282–4
  and emergence of journalism 61
  emphasis moved from passion to compassion 83–8
  experiments
    with form, aesthetics 61–2
    with unadapted performance 427
  'fairground' 339, 371, 388–9, 390

fascination with opera 52–3
feminization 78–88
genres
  burlesque, 56, 338, 350–5, 427; *see also* burlesque *and individual plays*
  drama of sensibility 86
  historical tragedies 285–6
  she-tragedy invented 70–8; *see also* she-tragedy
  'Pageant Tragedy' 37–8
  revenge tragedy 163
  satyr plays 236
  sentimental tragedies 88–92
  growing dislike of neoclassicism 51, 52–3, 208–9, 319, 427
Huguenot associations 34 and n. 19
link of aesthetic, political preferences 14
manifestations of Romantic Hellenism 282–4
as medium for moral education 84
mid-nineteenth-century absence of serious, classical drama 351
patriotism 266
as political propaganda 42, 239
Puritan Ordinance banning stage plays, 1642 163 164–5, 244
recoil from Restoration excesses 70
reflections of colonial destiny 38–9, 48–9
reopened after Restoration 165
response to
  anxieties about succession, Jacobitism xvi, 43–4, 44–5, 139, 148; *see also* monarchy

British theatre (*cont.*):
  Greek War of Independence 270–2
  retreat from continental culture 551–4
  romantic engagement with British history 124
  technological advances 277–80
  types of tragic heroines 62–3
  unpopularity of declamatory style of acting 424
  use of chorus, *see* chorus
  widespread adaptations of plots 53–4
  see also spectacle; stage design; theatres (buildings)
Britons at Navarino, H. M. Milner 271
Brooke, Henry, *Gustavus Vasa* 106
Brookfield, Charles E., Examiner of Plays 531–2 n. 22
Brough, Robert (1828–60)
  instructions to actors 438
  Medea; The Best of Mothers, with a Brute of a Husband 408–15, 436
  radicalism 372
  The Siege of Troy 351–2, *352*, 358–9
Brough, William, burlesques 372, 383
Brougham, Lord, 229–30, 395, 468 and n. 18
Brown, John 202
Browning, Elizabeth Barrett (1806–61)
  association with Mary Russell Mitford 256
  Aurora Leigh 330
  on Electra 182
  Field Talfourd's portrait 287
  identification with Alcestis 444
    inspired by Covent Garden *Antigone* 330
  Wine of Cyprus 85
Browning, Robert (1812–89)
  Aristophanes' Apology 440–51 and n. 53
  attitude to translation 451
  Balaustion's Adventure 442–6, 449, 456–7 n. 70
  at Balliol College *Agamemnon* 454
  classical scholarship 446–7 and n. 39
  early career in the theatre 443 n. 27
  Euripides a source of inspiration 330, 442–3
  at first night of *Ion* 282, 286
  influence of *Ion* 286
  reworking of classics 433, 446–7, 456 and n. 70
  source for Todhunter's *Alcestis* 445
  style of Talfourd and, compared 308 n. 7
  The Ring and the Book 330
Bruce, W. N., as Agamemnon 452, 453
Brumoy, Pierre (1688–1742)
  Le Théâtre des Grecs 172, 200, 219, 247
  perception of Oedipus 219, 220
  perturbed by sentiments in *Electra* 179
Brutus, projected, by Alexander Pope 190 and n. 15
Buchanan, George, works 111–12, 117
Buckley, Theodore Alois 432, 433
Buckstone, John 361, 370
Bulley, Frederick 255
Bullock, Mrs 82

Bulwer (Bulwer-Lytton), Edward
(1831–91)
   association with Talfourd 291,
      308 n. 79
   classical Athens seen as model
      for national theatre 102
   criticism of censorship 314
   history of Athens 301
   proponent of heroic tragedy 436
   proposal for *Oedipus Tyrannus*
      332–3
   reaction against elite control of
      classics 291
   on suitability of Greek tragedy
      for performance 316–17
   The Last Days of Pompeii 296
      and n. 50, 314
Bunbury, Lady Sarah (née
      Lennox) 89, 130 and n. 11
Burdett, Sir Francis 229–30
Burke, Edmund 231
burlesque
   adverse views of 385–6
   ambivalent position on women
      374
   contemporary detail in ancient
      setting 379–82
   costume for 357–8
   creation of genre 55
   as cultural appreciation 377–9
   developed for political ends
      491–2
   distancing from social
      implications 383
   elements, in *Vanity Fair* 348
   and extravaganza 343, 355 and
      n. 28
   implicit politics 105, 348–9
   importance xviii, 390, 410, 413,
      430–1, 436, 438
   important dance routines 367
   inaccessibility 354–5

   inspiration from Greek tragedy
      358–3
   long tradition, influences on
      355–7
   medium of doggerel rhyming
      verse 365
   mingling of Shakespearean,
      Greek elements 56
   mock-erudite tone 377–8
   musical components 345–7, 356,
      366–71 and n. 76
   neglected by scholars 354–5
   on other than classical themes
      383 n. 148
   Planché's concept of 343, 347,
      355 and n. 28, 477
   popularity in elitist contexts
      383–5
   productions of Sophocles'
      Electra 152
   proliferation 351–4
   radicalism criticized in 373
   replication of ancient stage
      conventions 378
   routines borrowed from circus,
      sport, fairgrounds 339, 371,
      388–9, 390
   search for authenticity 477
   as self-definition 379–82
   self-mockery 365–6
   semi-serious instruction in
      mythology 378
   seriousness attached to 410,
      436
   socio-educational background of
      authors 371–7
   spectacle in 366, 370–1
   transcendence of class barriers
      350–5, 390, 436, 438
   travesty a sub-category of 339–40
   and Victorian taste for comedy
      382–8

burlettas
  defined 355 and n. 27
  of Kane O'Hara 56–8
  see also burlesque
Burn, Robert 469
Burnand, Francis C. (1836–1917)
  admiration for Robson 412
  burlesques 357, 358, 359, 364,
    366, 371, 377, 383
  reviews for Punch 459
  socio-educational background
    372, 410, 431
Burne-Jones, Edward 441 n. 18,
    443 n. 25, 453
Burnell, Henry 40
Burton, Frederick 327, *329*
Busiris, Edward Young 42
Bute, John Stuart, third Earl of
    167–72
Butler, Samuel 286 and n. 17
Byron, Henry xv, 363, 372
Byron, Lord (1788–1824)
  concept of 'fascination' shared
    with Talfourd 295 and n. 47
  impact of classical antiquities
    on 290 n. 35
  influence of Mason 211
  influence on Victorian
    burlesque 356–7
  Orpheus, Latin puns 364–5
  parodic verse on *Medea* 356
  philhellenism 267, 292
  'Translation of The Nurse's
    Dole in the *Medea* of
    Euripides' 400 n. 35

Ça ira, echoes of 238
Caesar, Julius 202 n. 75, 203
Caius Gracchus, James Knowles
    284
Calcraft, John 326–7, 334–5
Caleb Williams, William Godwin
    227

Calkin, Miss E. 513 n. 106
Calvert, Louis 503
*Cambrian Hero, or Llewelyn the
    Great*, William Sotheby
    213–14
Cambridge Ritualists 497, 507
Cambridge University
  Amateur Dramatic Club 410
  Burnand's attempt to stage
    burlesques at 375–6
  early productions in 8
  Greek plays, 7–8, 32 n. 6, 151,
    262–3, 391, 438, 457, 476,
    478, 486, 529, 534, 538
Cambro-Britons, James Boaden
    213
Campbell, Frances Pitt 431–2, 448
Campbell, Lewis (1830–1908)
  association with Jowett 451–2
  influential translations 448, 456,
    473 and n. 37, 513 n. 106
  on links between Euripides and
    Ibsen 490
  performance as Anthony 452
  productions of authentic Greek
    tragedy 431–2, 447–9,
    451–2
  reworking of Euripides'
    Alcestis 446–7
Campbell-Bannerman, Henry,
  'Methods of Barbarism'
    speech 509–10 and n. 90
Capelle, P. A. and P. Villiers, *Bébé
    et Jargon* 404 n. 48
Caractacan Society 213
Caractacus
  equation with American rebels
    184
  representation of 187–9
Caractacus, William Mason
  ancient Greek tragedy the model
    for xiii, xv, 184, *186*
  appeal in America 214

artworks inspired by 184, *185*
balletic version, 1808 213–14
conjunction of political, aesthetic
    aspects 184–6
consequences, impact 209–14
depth, ethical complexity
    189–90, 208–9, 214
druidical lore 206–7
music for 194–6
significance in debate over
    chorus 184, 196–8, 201, 225
sources 184
success 209 n. 101, 211, 216
theme 184
title-page *186*
translation into other languages
    213, 225
Caractacus, Elgar 195–6
*Caractacus being Paraded Before the
    Emperor Claudius*, Thomas
    Davidson *185*
Carlise, Earl of 504
Carlisle, Countess of 504
Carloni, 'The Public Entry of the
    Queen into Jerusalem' 231
Caroline, Queen (wife of
    George II) 104, 107
Caroline, Queen (wife of
    George IV) 229–33, *229*, 238,
    284; see also *Oedipus Tyrannus,
    or Swellfoot the Tyrant*
Carter, Hubert 514
Carter, Huntly 553–4
Casaubon, Isaac 35
Case, Janet, acclaimed Electra 182,
    457, 486
Cassius Dio, writings searched for
    druidical lore 203, 207
Cassandra (mythical figure)
    compared with Mother Shipton
    115
    portrayals of 98, 110–11, 463,
    467, 482–3, 515

representations of 474
Casson, Lewis 262 n. 5, 514
Catholic Emancipation Act,
    1829 284
Catiline, Ben Jonson 196
Cato, Joseph Addison
    actors in 308
    dependence on Roman history
    41, 134, 184
    manifesto of Whiggism 308
    performed at Reading
    School 249
    regular revivals 308
    Talfourd's debt to 308
Caulfield, Thomas *186*
Celsus 149
Celtic revival, Mason's influence
    on, 213; *see also* Britain,
    ancient; druids
censorship
    Advisory Board on, members
    537–8 and n. 43
    in British theatre
    challenges to 105–6 and nn.
    18–19, 112–15, 167,
    314–15, 528–34, 541–2,
    554
    consequences 355 and n. 26
    periods of xiii, 6, 99, 102–4
    and n. 13, 314–15, 528–34
    significance of precedent 532
    in Ireland 535, 536
    see also individual plays
Channel Islands, link with Reading
    School 247
Channel Tunnel, dream of 347,
    381–2
Characteristicks, Earl of
    Shaftesbury 52
Charles I 9–10, 163–4, 165
Charles II
    response of dramatists to 25–9,
    44, 48

Charles II (*cont.*):
  reward of Stanley 101
  support for Greek visitors 38
  Wase's celebration of
    Restoration 165
Chartists 299
Chaussier, H. with Citizen Bizet,
    Médée ou l'Hôpital des fous
    404 n. 48
Chénier, Marie-Joseph,
    representation of Oedipus
    226, 239
Cherubini
  Médée 404
  parodies of *Médée*, 404 and n. 48
  representation of Iphigenia 62
Chesterfield, Lord 172–3
children
  custody of
    conditions for award to
      mother 416, 420, 435
    severity of English law 290,
      394–5, 409
  emotive use of, in 'she-tragedy'
    71, 72, 85
  see also infanticide
China, tragic traditions compared
    with Sophocles 202
chorus
  abandonment
    in Stanmore School 197,
      225–6, 262
    substitution in *The Mourning
      Bride* 161
    supported by Dryden 16, 26
    until modern times 197–8 and
      nn. 47–8
  absent from Whitehead's
    Oedipus 191 n. 18
  Aeschylean, acceptability 209
  class profile 199–200
  condemnations of 209 and
    n. 100, 210

debate over 184, 196–8,
    198–202, 225–6
druidical, popularity 213
druids in Mason's *Caractacus*
    conflated with 188–9
hostility to 197
interrogatory, subversive,
    dissenting potential 217,
    233–9
laughable
  in New York *Antigone* 337
  Punch's depiction of 377–8
Mason's contribution to
  appreciation of 188–9,
  207–9, 217, 225, 233
Potter's representation of 221
as purveyor of morality 199
rehearsals for *The Story of
    Orestes* 465 and n. 11
replaced by heckling crowd 26
repudiation by Dennis 155
revival, politicized 207–9, 239
selection for physical attributes
    485
separation from actors 453
study of role xix
survival in oratorio 197
theories about origins 205–6
use
  advocated by Rymer 16
  in *Antigone* 322, *323*, 343,
    378, 439 and n. 15
  in *Antigone Travestie* 340,
    341, 344–5
  in Barker's productions 526,
    543
  in Balliol *Agamemnon* 453
  in British theatre, early
    examples 196–7 and n. 42
  in burlesque 341–2, 378–9,
    398
  by Clark 240
  in *Elfrida* 194

in French revolutionary
  Oedipus 217
by Maurice 234, 266
in 'Mendelssohn' *Antigone*
  439
by Milton 12–13, 197
in Murray's *Hippolytus* 496
  and n. 29
in Poel/Murray *Bacchae* 551
in Racine's *Athalie* 133
in Reading School
  productions 250, 262
in Reinhardt's *Oedipus Rex*
  524, 526, 539–40
retreat from, revival 554
by Shelley 233–4, 236–9, 267
in Spicer's *Alcestis* 439
in Todhunter's *Helena in
  Troas* 458
Christ Church, Oxford,
  performance of *Tragedie of
  Orestes* 163
Christianity, and Greek religion
  147–50, 310–11, 329–30
Christopherson, John, *Jephtha*
  32 n. 8
Chudleigh, Elizabeth 30, *31*
Cibber, Susannah Maria 94,
  110–11
Cibber, Theophilus 108, 111
Cicero, *On Divination* 149
Circe, Charles Davenant
  absence of jingoism, Whig
    ideals 39 40
  adaptation of *IT* 36
  appeal to women 78
  characteristics, significance
    37–41, 49
  Dryden's prologue 37
  exotic setting 38–9
  influence of Greek tragedy xv,
    xvi, 55 n. 72
  influence on Theobald 58–9

love interest 38, 39
music for 38, 41
tragic ending 54
circus
  routines borrowed from, in
    burlesque 371
  working-class access to classical
    myth, history
    through 388–9, 390
civil war
  conceptual link with incest,
    intra-familian conflicts 9,
    12
  regicide and, fear of 26
Clairon, Claire 152, 173–4, 175
  and n. 57
Clancy, Michael 2–3
clandestine marriage, *see* marriage
Clark, George Somers 240
Clark, John Willis 438
class, social
  divisions
    augmented by education in
      classics 350, 374–7
    explored in Whitehead's
      Creusa 142–3
    transcended by classical
      burlesque 350–5
  relevance
    to access to classical myth,
      history 350–1, 363–4,
      388–90
    to attitudes to
      infancticide 518–19
    to marriage of George
      Warr 472 and n. 32
    to reception of Dorothy
      Dene 484
  see also social status
classical archaeology, *see*
  archaeology
Classical Journal, edited by
  Abraham John Valpy 248

classics, culture
  accessibility 350–1, 363–4, 388–90
  appropriation through
    burlesque 377–89
  changing pattern of
    patronage 290
  link with performance history xx
  new fashion for academic
    productions of Greek
    plays 387–8, 431–3
  relative interest in Roman,
    Greek models 66 and n. 7
classics, education and scholarship
  class divisions augmented by
    350, 374–7
  effect of changes in curriculum
    431–2
  gulf between universities and
    theatre 375–6
  in background of burlesque
    authors 371–7
  in eighteenth-century Scotland
    111–12
  in nineteenth century 354
  past and future x, xxi–xxii
  reaction against elite control of
    291
  significance of performance
    history of *Trojan Women*
    510–11
  targeted by burlesques 383–5
    and n. 153
  translation out of ancient
    languages xiv
Clement of Alexandria,
    Exhortation to the Greeks 149
Cleon 302
clergy, classical influences on xvii
Clouds, Aristophanes
  burlesque of 55, 384–5
  Stanley's translation 40, 101 and
    n. 4
Clytemnestra (mythical figure)

comparison with Catherine
    Hayes 115
  engravings, paintings of
    347 n. 82, *349*, 453 and n. 64,
    465
  exculpation of murderer of
    92 n. 82
  exculpation of 108, 109–10
  figure representing, in *Alzuma*
    171–2
  identification with Queen
    Caroline 107
  perceptions of xxi–xxii, 55 n. 72,
    111
  portrayals of 79–80, 125, 334,
    369, 432, 453, 515
  representations of 109, 112–15,
    125, 153, 155, 157–9, 163,
    168, 176, 179, 363
Clytemnestre, Alexandre Soumet
    275
Cobbett, William 298, 302
Cobden Club 469
Coburg Theatre, pro-Greek
    dramas 270–2, 273 n. 31
Codrus, Dorning Rasbotham 50–2
    and n. 59
Cogniard, Grange and Bourdois,
    La Médée en Nanterre 405–6
Colchester School 228
Coleman, John 327
Coleridge, Mary 489, 499–500
Coleridge, Samuel Taylor 179
Collier, Jeremy
  *A Short View of the Immorality
    and Profaneness of the
    English Stage* 70
  opposed by Dennis 79
Collier, John 453 and n. 64
Collins, Wilkie, *The Woman in
    White* 422
Collins, William 193
Colman, George (1732–94)

co-author of *The Clandestine Marriage* 141–2
staging of Mason's plays at Covent Garden 194–6
The Sun Poker, inspiration for *Olympic Revels* 357
colonialism, colonial rule, response of British theatre 38–9, 48–9, 183–4; see also *Caractacus*
Comédie-Française
  regular appearances of Oedipus 5, 218
  productions in Roman theatre at Orange 125, 477
  see also Mounet-Sully *and individual plays*
compassion, arousal in spectactors 83–8
confidants, in *The Mourning Bride*, choral substitutes 161
Congreve, William (1670–1720)
  accused of plagiarism 162
  influence of Sophocles' *Electra* 153, 157–62
  response to Dacier 157–62
conservatism, aesthetic, in Victorian age 373, 377
Constantine I 11, 12
Constantine Palaiologos, Joanna Baillie 272
Constantinople, fall of 272
Constantius Chlorus 1, 12
Continent
  educational performances of classical drama 243–4
  genre of adapted Greek tragedies 272–3
  many nineteenth-century productions of *Antigone* 317–18
  responses to Greek War of Independence 267

see also individual nations, authors, and plays
Cooper, Frederick Fox, *Ion Travestie* 286 and n. 14, 302, 338, 339
Cooper, James Fenimore, *The Last of the Mohicans* 296
Cooper, John 211
Copyright Act ('Talfourd's Act'), 1842 290
Coram, Thomas 135, *136*, 137
Coriolanus, portrayal of 282
Coriolanus, Shakespeare
  conceptual link with Thebes xxi
  significance of 1811 set design 269
Coriolanus, The Invader of his Country, John Dennis 44
Cork and Orrery, Earl of 172
Corn Laws, opposition meetings in Covent Garden Theatre 300
Corneille, Pierre (1606–84)
  English response to 15, 33
  English translations 83
  James Thomson compared with 126
  perception of Oedipus 217, 218
  view of chorus in *Medea* 199–200
  see also individual plays
Cornish, Gerald Warre 513 n. 106, 519 n. 128
corsetry, liberation from 549
costume
  acclaimed, in *Helena in Troas* 477–8
  ancient
    in *Arion* 380
    for Balliol College *Agamemnon* 453
    carefully researched by Jenkin 449, *450*
    in Covent Garden *Antigone* 324

costume (*cont.*):
  ancient (*cont.*):
    David Garrick's interest in
      128 n. 3, 174 and n. 55,
      195, 225
    for *Electric in a New Electric
      Light*, authenticity 361
    for 'Mendelssohn' *Antigone*,
      praise for 478–9
    in Oxford Greek plays *460*
    for productions of *Electra*
      174–5
    in Reading School's
      performances 259, 261–2
    for Stanmore School
      productions 225
  impact of Les Ballets Russes 546
  influence of Charles Kemble 280
  liberating 549–51
  notable, in OUDS *Alcestis*
    458–9
  in Planché's burlesque of *The
    Birds* 345–7
  revealing, responses to 30–2,
    31, 280–1 and n. 48, 367
  Ristori's, as *Medea 403*, 404
  study of xix, 280, 3 n. 106
Costumes of the Ancients, Thomas
  Hope 280
Cotes, Samuel 176 and n. 61
Court Theatre (also Royal Court
  Theatre)
  partnership of Barker and
    Vedrenne at 496
  productions at
    of Gilbert Murray's
      translations 431, 492,
      494–5, 496
    of Shaw's plays 494–5
    see also individual plays
Courtney, W. L. (1850–1928)
  emendations of Murray's
    Oedipus 539

funding of *Helena in Troas* 459
response to Maud Allan 549
roles 453, 456–7, 532
versions of *Oedipus Tyrannus*
  532, 536
Covent Garden Theatre
  capacity 417
  contribution of Macready
    299–300
  daring productions at 30–2
  meetings to oppose Corn Laws
    in 300
  new (1809)
    architecture 268–9 and n. 13,
      277
    Kemble's inaugural address
      269
    opening, 1809 269–70
    pantomimes 351–2
    patriotic pageant, 1798 xiii,
      166 n. 27
    productions, *see under individual
      plays*
    survival in eighteenth century
      104
Craig, Edward Henry Gordon 487,
  544, 545 n. 62
Crane, Mary 484
Crane, Walter (1845–1915)
  association with
    Dorothy Dene 484
    George Warr 463–4, 469–70
      and n. 25, 471, 482, 486
Crawford, Ann (Ann Barry) 65,
  74, 81, 122, 152
Creon (mythical figure)
  portrayals of 295, 337, 340
  representations of 218–20, 223,
    274, 294, 296, 303–7, 321,
    322, 340–41, 406, 425–6
Creusa
  brother–sister bond with
    Hyllus 304

emotional range demanded of
actress 80
identification with mothers of
foundling children 137
moral dimension 88, 95
need for exculpation of 96–7
portrayals of 129 and n. 7, *131*
representations of 87, 88, 95,
140–7, 400–1, 406, 414, 424
type of 'distressed mother' 63
see also *Kreusa*
Creusa in Delfo, Venazio Rauzzini
151
Creusa, Queen of Athens, William
Whitehead
actresses in 80, 89, 129
anti-Catholicism 148
departure from original *Ion* 132
emotional tenor 129
fear of Jacobites echoed in 139,
144
implications of social status
explored 142–3
and interest in clandestine
marriage 140–7
perhaps known to Talfourd
289 n. 26
popularity 129–30 and n. 6
Racine's *Athalie* compared 133
reflection of concerns about fate
of foundlings 138–9
religious (irreligious)
dimension 147–50
'she-tragedy' 66, 95
significance xv, 128, 129 n. 7,
130, 132–4
Creüse l'Athénienne, Lacoste's
opera 132, 133–4, 151
Cromwell, Oliver, Aegisthus
paralleled with 165
cross-dressed roles
association of Maud Allan
with 553

contribution to spectacle in
burlesques 370
exploited in 'Adelphi
Screamers' 352–3
females played by boys,
men 268, 369 and n. 86,
374, 385, 388
London scandal of 1869–70 70,
452
popularity in burlesques 362,
367–9, 385
prohibited in Oxford
University 452, 458, 485–6
relative to status of actresses
396–7
study of xix
success of 'breeches' roles 129 n.
8, 273, 311, *312*, 342, 353,
367–71, 385, 396
Crowne, John
influence of Aeschylus on 101
works 34, 67, 101
cruelty, adultery aggravated by, as
woman's ground for divorce
419
Cumberland, Richard 135, 210
and n. 104
Curse of Minerva, Lord Byron 292
Cushman, Charlotte 311, *312,* 326
Cusins, Adolphus 503, 504, 505–8
custody, *see* children
Cyclops, Euripides, translations, by
Shelley 234

Dacier, André (1651–1722)
commentary on *Poetics* 18, 28,
132, 153–4, 155–7, 198,
217–18
Congreve's response to 157–62
defence of chorus 198, 199–200
influence 217–19
misgivings concerning
matricide 159 n. 13, 178

Dacier, André (1651–1722) (*cont.*):
  perception of Oedipus 217, 218
  Protestant background 35
  translations of Sophocles 28, 75,
    153–4, 155–7
Dacier, Anne 35
Dall, Nicholas 188–9
Dallas, R. C., *A Tragedy* 273 n. 30
Dalton, Richard 134–5
Dalzel, Andrew xvi
dance
  craze in England 548–9 and n. 77
  devaluation 528
  impact of Les Ballets Russes 546
  importance
    in burlesque 367, 370
    Gordon Craig's concept of
      544
    stressed by Reinhardt 528
  influence of
    Isadora Duncan 544–8
    Maud Allan 548–54
  in travesties, fashion for 367
Daniel, Samuel, *The Tragedie of
  Cleopatra* 196
D'Annuncio, Gabriele, *La città
  morta* 532 n. 22
danseuse en travesti, fashion for 367
Darius, King of Persia, John
  Crowne 101
Darley, George 310 and n. 84
Darter, William 250–1
Das Goldene Vließ, see Grillparzer
D'Aubignac, Abbé de 15 and n. 42
Davenant, Charles (1656–1714)
    xvi, 36–7, 37–8, 39, 40, 48, 60,
    61; see also *Circe*
Davenant, William 36–7, 38
David, Jacques-Louis 275 and
    n. 38, 301
Davidson, Thomas, *Caractacus
  being Paraded Before the
  Emperor Claudius* 185

Davies, Revd Syned 190
Davies, Very Revd Rowland 38 n. 29
Davison, Emily 513 and n. 106
Dawson, Douglas 533
Dear Old Charlie, Charles E.
    Brookfield 531–2 n. 22
Death, Euripidean figure of,
    influence 117 and n. 39
Declaration of Independence,
    1776 184–5
Defoe, Daniel 110
Deianira, type of distressed
    mother 65–6
Delap, John (1725–1812) 64–6 and
    n. 3, 90, 188 and n. 7
Delectus sententiarum Graecorum,
    Richard Valpy 247
Delphi, Delphic oracles
  alleged fraudulent nature
    149–50 and n. 51, 150–1
  as prototype of Foundling
    Hospital 135, 138, 149
democracy
  Athenian, conflicting approaches
    to 301–3 and nn. 64–5,
    306–7
  dominant theme in Talfourd's
    works 314
  municipal, introduction in
    Britain 298
  parallels between ancient,
    modern 50 and n. 53, 59
Demofoonte, Metastasio 273
Dene, Dorothy (1859–99) 463 and
    n. 5, 467, 482–4 and n. 70
Denman, Lord Chief Justice 282
Dennis, John (1657–1734)
  adaptation of *IT* 36
  anti-Catholicism 51
  anti-Jacobitism 44–5
  concept of compassion 83–4
  and contiguity of political, poetic
    freedom 52–3

debt to Racine 48
dislike of Continental opera 53
on erotic love in Greek tragedy
91
Francophobia 33–4, 51, 52–3
on nature and function of drama
62, 155
projected interpretation of
Phaedra myth 88 n. 65
radical Whiggism 45–9, 61
rejection of supernatural
causation 48
repudiation of chorus 155
Talfourd's essay on 287 n. 24
*The Grounds of Criticism in
Poetry* 52
use made of Greek tragedy xv,
60, 61, 72
on women in the theatre 79
Description of Greece, Pausanias 65
deviant behaviour, in Greek
tragedy, censored in
burlesque, 385; *see also* incest;
infanticide; sexual deviancy
Devrient, Edward 430, 433
Diaghilev 546
*Diana Preparing for the Chase,
Tableau Vivant* 390
Dickens, Charles (1812–70)
admiration for Robson's Medea
412–13
antipathy to Greek, Roman
classics 351, 375
association with Talfourd 287,
290
at first night of *Ion* 282
social concerns 351, 354
Dickinson, Willoughby 512
Dido, Burnand 359, 377, 385
Die Braut von Messina, Schiller
196 n. 42
Die Hermannschlacht,
Klopstock 213

Die Jahreszeiten, Haydn 99
Diodorus 204–5
Diogenes Laertius 203
Dionysus
cult of, echoes of, in Salvation
Army 499–505
representations of 497–9, 502,
505–8
Dirce; or, The Fatal Urn 273–4,
281
distressed mother, *see* she-tragedy
divorce
inauguration of Royal
Commission, 1850 399
law regulating
assault added to grounds for
427
attempts to reform 395
based on canon law 394
debate over 398, 401–2, 408–9
and n. 57, 415–16,
417–18, 425, 435–6
unequal rights of women 418,
419–20
see also Divorce and
Matrimonial Causes Act;
marriage
Divorce and Matrimonial Causes
Act, 1857 140, 381, 401–2,
415–16 and n. 78, 419–20,
425–6
Dobbs, J., *Petraki Germano; or,
Almanzar the Traitor* 271
Dobree, Peter Paul, Euripidean
scholar 251, 262
Dolce, Ludovico x
Dominique and Biancolelli,
La Méchante Femme
404 n. 48
Don Carlos, Otway 38
Don Juan, Lord Byron 356–7
Donner, Johann Jakob
Christian 320

Dorset Garden Theatre
  Davenant associations 37
  forestage 17–18
  performance spaces 17
  scenic innovations 7, 14
Douglas, Lord Alfred 553
Douglass, John 417
Dover Beach, Matthew Arnold
  330 n. 36
Dramatic Literature, Schlegel 326
druids
  admiration for resistance to
    Rome 190 and n. 15
  astronomical lore 206
  combination with Greek
    interests 192–3 and nn.
    25–6
  eighteenth-century craze for
    192–3 and nn. 25–6, 202–7
  Grand Lodge of the Order of
    Druids 213
  revivalism, and Mason's
    Caractacus 184–6, 188–9,
    198–202
  theories on ritual of choral
    singing 205
Drury Lane Theatre
  capacity 417
  enlargement by Kemble 268–9
  pantomimes 338, 351–2, 375
  pro-Greek dramas 271–2
  productions, *see under individual
    plays*
  scenic innovations 7, 17, 269,
    277–80
  survival in eighteenth century
    104
Dryden, John (1631–1700)
  ancient and modern sources
    acknowledged 21–2
  collaboration with
    Lee, 17 and n. 47
    William Davenant 37

  debt to Sophocles 21–4
  Dennis's admiration for 45
  Essay on Dramatic Poesie 15,
    22, 27
  fascination with deviant
    sexuality xvi
  importance xv
  influences on 14–17, 20, 22,
    66–7
  introduction of love interest 38
  pro-classical stance 22
  reworking of Shakespeare 17,
    20–1
  source for *The Mourning Bride*
    162
  writings on nature and function
    of drama 62
Du Roullet, Marie-François-Louis
  Gand Leblanc 439
Dublin
  burlesques performed in 359
  pro-Greek dramas 272
  see also Abbey Theatre *and
    individual plays*
Ducrow, Andrew 284, 388–9
Duke's theatrical company 14, 37
Duncan, Augustin 546
Duncan, Isadora 544–8 and nn. 62,
  65, 67
Duncan, Raymond 545 n. 66
Duncan, William 203 n. 72
Duncombe, William, *Junius
  Brutus* 105
Durham, John Lambton, first Earl
  of 306, *307*
Dutch, translations into 41 and
  n. 37

Earthly Paradise, William
  Morris 443 n. 25
East Lynne, Ellen Wood 422
Echoes of Hellas, George Warr 470
  and n. 28

Edinburgh
  government's response to
    Porteous Riots 105
  Helen Faucit's *Antigone* in 326,
    327–8
  new theatre, 1773 193
Edinburgh University,
  performances of authentic
    Greek tragedy 431,
    448
Edward I 116
Edward VII 548
Edward and Eleonora, James
  Thomson
  actresses in 82
  censorship of xiii, 99, 103,
    106–7, 120–1
  deviation from Euripides'
    Alcestis 120–1
  emotive, sentimental
    drama 116–20
  frontispiece *119*
  political ideals, parallels in 102,
    120–1, 122
  popularity, revivals 121–4 and
    n. 52
  'she-tragedy' 66
  sources 66, 116–17, 118–20
Edward the Black Prince, William
  Shirley xiii, 166–7 and n. 27
Egisthus, *see* Aegisthus
Egypt, ancient, fashion for settings
  based on 61
Electra (mythical figure)
  brother-sister bond with
    Pylades 304
  costuming of 280, 361
  identified with the sun, in
    Johnson's masque
    361 n. 49
  portrayals of, 152, 174–5 and
    n. 54, *176*, 182, 361, 457,
    513 n. 106

recoil from Sophocles' depiction
    of 178–9
  representations of 157, 163,
    178–82, 361 and n. 49
Electra, Christopher Wase 40,
  163–5, *164*
Electra, Euripides
  scant attention paid to 61, 152
  source for Talfourd's *The
    Athenian Captive* 305
  translation by Gilbert Murray
    511
Electra, Sophocles
  aesthetic exemplar 152–62
  appreciation by women writers
    182
  conceptual link with *Hamlet* xxi
    155, 159
  first attempt to stage 166
  Frank Talfourd's burlesque of
    374
  herald of feminism 182
  influence on Congreve 153, 161–2
  link with *Oedipus Tyrannus*
    153–4, 162
  morality of matricide
    questioned, justified 155,
    159 and n. 13
  paintings of Benjamin West 46
  as political manifesto 162–72
  productions
    costumes 174–5
    first British, 1883 182
    at Girton College, 1883 18,
      336, 457
    in aid of Building Fund
      506 n. 106
    scenery 174
  prominence, influence xviii,
    152–3, 318
  prototype of tragic heroine 75
  published in Bell's British
    Theatre series 175

recitation from, permitted 244

reworking in *The Mourning Bride* 170

significance of 'recognition' scene 157–62, 173

as source 78 n. 22, 152, 163, 267, 275, 304, 316–17, 531 and n. 19

tragic traditions of Chinese theatre compared 202

translations, editions
anonymous, 1714 154 and n. 6, 199
by Dacier 28, 153–7, 217–18
by Crébillon 154
by Francklin 173–8
by Longpierre 154
by Rotaller into Latin 163
by Theobald 154, *156*, 175
by Thomas Johnson 154
flurry of vernacular 28
into French, English, importance xx, 163

visualized 172–8

Electra, William Shirley xiii, 103, 167–72, 529

Electra in a New Electric Light, Frank Talfourd 360–2, 374, 379, 385

Electra, The Lost Pleiade, ballet 360–1

Électre
Crébillon's production 154
Longpierre's production 154

Elektra, Richard Strauss, reaction to 551

electric light, introduction 360–1

Elements of Greek Grammar, The, Richard Valpy 247

Elements of the Latin Language, The, Richard Valpy 247

Eleonora, portrayals of 122, 123–4

Elfrida, portrayals of 211

Elfrida, William Mason
influence of Greek tragedy xv
music commissioned for 194
reflection of radicalism 190–1 and n. 18
role of chorus 200–1
success 194–5, 209 n. 101, 211
translation into other languages 213

Elgin marbles 261, 290 n. 35

Eliot, George, (1810–50) 182, 331–2 and n. 41, 421, 454

Eliot, T. S. 151, 493

Elizabeth, Princess, daughter of Charles I 164–5, *164*

elopement, teenage, prevention of 141

Elrington, Thomas 2–3

Elwart, Antoine 439

Elysium, Thomas Mercer 193

England and the English, Edward Bulwer 314–15

English literature, departments of, approach to performance history of Greek drama xiv

Enlightenment, the
adoption of Oedipus as figure of 217
and attitudes to religion in Greek tragedy 147–50

Enquiry Concerning Political Justice, William Godwin 228

erotic love, passion
and women in Greek tragedy 91
threat to absolute power 39

Essay on Dramatic Poesie, An, John Dryden 15, 22, 27

Essay on the Nature and Conduct of the Passions and Affections, An, Francis Hutcheson 84

Essays in Church Music, William Mason 191 n. 18

Eton College, *Agamemnon*
  at 453–4
Eumenides, Aeschylus
  Cambridge production,
    1885 457, 475, 476, 486
  in Frank Benson's touring
    production of *Oresteia*
    455
  influence on Theobald's
    Orestes 55 n. 72, 111 n. 26
  Stanford's music 475, 478
  in Wakefield's school
    selection 289
Eunuchus, Terence, Westminster
  School production 34 n. 17
Euphrasia
  portrayals of 180, *181*
  representations of 179–82
Euripides
  accessibility 71, 78 and n. 22,
    496
  adaptations
    domination by suffering
      herioine 66–70
    to evoke sympathy 85–8
    to support different
      ideologies 60
  Browning's championship of
    433, 449–51
  Buckley's translations 433
  denounced by classical scholars
    443 and n. 26
  educational study encouraged
    253–4
  foundling tales 128
  ghost of, in burlesque 366
  importance of performance
    history 510–11
  'improv'd' by eighteenth century
    dramatists 97–8
  links with
    George Bernard Shaw 490–1
    Ibsen 490–1

  performances, directed by
    Valpy 251–2
  Potter's perception of 221
  problems presented by women in
    plays of 96–7
  rewriting for performance in
    English x
  'she-tragedies' derived from
    66–70, 71–8, 86 and n. 59
  size of women's roles 258
  source for
    burlesque 360
    Goffe's *Tragedie of Orestes* 163
  see also individual plays
Euripides and his Age, Gilbert
  Murray 510–11, 514
'Euripides and Mr. Murray',
  T. S. Eliot 493
Euripides and Shaw, Gilbert
  Norwood 490
Euripidis quae extant omnia, Joshua
  Barnes 71
Euripides the Rationalist, Arthur
  Verrall 498 n. 40
European theatre, emphasis on
  physicality 546 and n. 70
Eurydice Hiss'd, Henry Fielding
  104
eurythmics 546 n. 70
Evans, Thomas, see *Oedipus*
Evelina, representation of 187
Exclusion crisis 24–5
Exhortation to the Greeks, Clement
  of Alexandria 149
extravaganza, and burlesque 343,
  355 and n. 28, 477

Facta et Dicta Memorabilia,
  Valerius Maximus 180 and
  n. 71
Factory Act, 1833 296
Faerie Queen, Edmund Spenser
  229

Fair Helen, Amcott 383–4

fairground theatre 339, 356, 371, 388–9, 390

Farr, Florence 496 and n. 29

Farren, Elizabeth 65

Farren, William *69*

fascination, Romantic concept of 295 and n. 47

fate, implacable, inexorable, concept of 22, 24

father–son conflicts
    in Talfourd family 360, 363, 374 n. 108
    use by Aristophanes 363

fathers, rights of custody 394–5, 409, 416, 420, 435

Faucit, Harriet 326, 416 n. 78

Faucit, Helen (1817–98)
    combination of fame with domestic stability 396
    impact 327–8
    practice of sculptural effects 335
    tragic roles 281, 311, *313*, 316, 326–7, *329*, 330–1, 334–5, 348, 539

Faucit, John Savill 240–2, 267, 274, 326

Felton, Cornelius C. 286–7

females, *see* cross-dressed roles; women

femininity
    adaptation of Greek women to fit notions of 91–2, 178–82
    Victorial ideal 327–8
    see also actors, actresses; she-tragedy; women

feminism
    George Warr's sympathies 474–5
    prefigured in perception of Medea 393
    see also New Woman; suffragettes

fiction, and Greek tragedy xx–xxi

Fielding, Henry (1707–54)
    burlesque of high tragedy 355–6
    classical influences on xvii
    foundling novels 135
    response to *Oedipus* (Dryden and Lee) 1–2
    satires on Walpole 104 and n. 14
    sources 111 and n. 26
    The Tragedy of Tragedies 58, 60
    views on role of chorus 201

filial piety, representation of 180 and n. 71

filicide, unintentional, in *The Roman Empress*, Joyner 11

Fire of London, 1666 25

Fisher, John 213

Fitzball, Edward (1792–1873) 267, 274–5, 280

Fitzgerald, Percy, on burlesque 316, 327, 379

Flashar, Helmut vii

Flaxman, John 211–13 and n. 111

Fletcher, Constance Emily, *see* Warr

Fletcher, John (with Francis Beaumont), *A King and No King* 25

Fogerty, Elsie 336

Forster, John (with Francis Beaumont), association with Talfourd 282, 287

foundling heroes
    expansion of literature 134–5
    perennial fascination 128 and n. 2, 133, 134
    search for archetypes 137–8
    in Shelley's *Oedipus Tyrannus* 231
    see also foundlings; Ion

Foundling Hospitals, British

boys destined for military, naval
service 139
children viewed as objects of
social experiment 138
Delphi as prototype of 135, 138,
149 and n. 51
establishment, aims 135, 137–8
and n. 32
opposition arguments 137 and
n. 29
foundlings
Continental approach to care
of 135, 149
debate about nature or
nurture 138–9
social problem in eighteenth
century 135, 140, 151
Fragment of an Antigone, Matthew
Arnold 331
France
impact of Dacier's translations of
Sophocles 154
performances of *Persians* for
patriotic purposes 265–6
and n. 6
popularity of Talfourd's *Ion*
in 286 and n. 18
response to authority of
monarchy 15
staging of burlesques in
359 n. 46
see also Francophobia; French
Revolution; French theatre
Francklin, Thomas (1721–84)
adaptations to eighteenth-
century concept of
femininity 179
anticlericalism 220
attacks on Theobald's
translations 175
background, career 172–3, 220
recoil from Greek tragic
metaphysics 147–8

translations
of *Electra* 175–8
of Lucian 177
of Sophocles 147, 172–8,
219–21, 250
respect for 173, 175–8
version of Voltaire's *Oreste*
278 n. 22
Francophobia, 33–6 and n. 15, 51,
52–3
Freake, Lord and Lady 464 and
n. 12, 481
Frederick, Prince of Wales 104,
105, 107, 120
freedom, *see* liberty
French Archaeological Society in
Athens 521
French language, translations
into xx, 163, 265, 522
French Revolution
admiration for Athenian
democracy among British
supporters 300–1
classical models invoked in
support of 216, 217
importance of Greek history
in 265 n. 2
interest in James
Thomson 124–5
republican symbols from ancient
Rome invoked during 216
French theatre
acting styles in Germany and,
compared 526–8
apolitical Hellenism in 49
and debate over chorus 199
Greek tragedy in
English responses 33–6, 87,
154
extension of emotional
range 319
importance of Seneca 67
influence xix, 5–16

French theatre (*cont.*):
  link of aesthetic, political
    preferences 14, 15
  models for women dramatists 83
  neglect of *Antigone* 317
  perception of Oedipus 5, 7, 219,
    221, 521–6, 539
  see also neoclassicism *and*
    individual authors,
    dramatists
Freud, Sigmund, impact of
  Oedipus viii, 494, 524–6 and n.
  9
Friedrich Wilhelm IV, King of
  Prussia 319, 320
friendship, male 46
Frode, Philip, *The Fall of*
  Saguntum 42
Frogs, Aristophanes
  influence 104, 506–7
  Jenkin's production of 448 n. 47
  Shaw's version 505
  translation by Gilbert
    Murray 472, 494
Fuseli, Henry, depiction of
  Clytemnestra and
  Aegisthus 129 and n. 5, 177

Gadsby, Henry 456–7 n. 70
Gaelic culture, conceptual link
  between ancient Greece
  and 186–7 and n. 4
Gager, William 8
Gaiety Theatre, visit of Comédie
  Française, 1879 432
Gandy, Joseph Michael 289 n. 26
Garrick, David (1717–79)
  ambition to stage Euripides'
    Hecuba 195
  co-author of *The Clandestine*
    Marriage 141–2
  envious of Covent Garden's
    Elfrida 194

expansion of acting skills 80
Huguenot antecedents 34
interest in ancient costume
  128 n. 3, 174 n. 55, 195,
  225
partnership with Hannah
  Pritchard 129, 144, *145*
Prologue and Epilogue for
  Electra 174
refusal to stage Sophocles
  unadapted 173
rejection of
  A King and No King 215
  Alzuma 171
  Shirley's *Electra* 166
roles 128–9, 140, 143 n. 42
urged to attempt *Oedipus*
  Tyrannus 195
Garrick Theatre, production of
  travesty of *Ion* 286
Garrison Theatre, Woolwich,
  burlesque at 395
Gascoigne, George, and Francis
  Kinwelmershe, *Jocasta*,
  1566–7 x, 8
Gay, John, *Achilles* 104, 105, 356
Geffroy, E., actor, as Oedipus
  522
Gell, William 230
Genod, Michel Philibert, *The Oath*
  of the Young Warrior 301
George I 43, 50
George II 43, 104, 105, 107, 130 n.
  12, 169
George III 130 n. 2, 168–72, 220,
  241, 242
George IV (previously Prince of
  Wales) 130 n. 12, 168, 169,
  176–7, 229–32, 242, 284, 294
Germany
  civilian hysteria against 553
  experiments with *Ion* 289 and
    n. 27

impact of James
Thomson 125–7
interest in *Antigone* xix, 317–18
popularity of declamatory style
of acting 424
post-Kantian philosolphy,
influence of *Antigone* 320–1
reccption of Greek tragedy 430,
431, 433
repudiation of French
neoclassicism 319
Teutonic revival, influence of
Mason 213
Gerrald, Joseph 182, 224, 226–8
and n. 46
Getting Married, George Bernard
Shaw 492
Giardini, Felice de 191 n. 18
Gibbon, Edward, *The Decline and
Fall of the Roman
Empire* 183–4
Gilbert, W. S. 354, 391; see also
Gilbert and Sullivan operas
Gilbert and Sullivan operas 353,
354, 386–7, 482
Gildon, Charles (1665–1724)
adaptations of Greek tragedy
xv, 66
association with Quinault 118
on erotic love in Greek
tragedy 91
exculpation of Medea 92
ideology 71 n. 13
praise of *Ion* 132
sources, influences on 71,
117–19
stress on tragic passions 83
view of *Iphigenia*, Dennis 53–4
see also *Love's Victim, Phaeton*
Gioas, Rèdi Giuda, Metastasio 132
and n. 18
Girton College, Cambridge
Electra, 1883

first authentic British
production 18, 336, 457
use of Mendelssohn's *Antigone*
music 336
Gladstone, William Ewart 359,
365, 469, 475–6
Glasse, George Henry 225
Glorious Revolution, 1688
attitudes to Greek tragedy
after 41–9, 54, 149
dramatic defences of ideals of
105, 108
Glover, Richard (1712–85)
classical models for free nation-
states 50
Medea, as 'she-tragedy' 66
in 'Patriot' opposition 104
pro-feminine alteration of Greek
plots 86–7
see also *individual plays*
Gluck
Alcestis 439 and n. 16, 440–1
Iphigenia in Tauride 62
music used by Isadora
Duncan 546 n. 67
Godwin, E. W. 459, 463, 466–7,
477, 480, 485–6, 487, 544
Godwin, William 223–4, 227, 228
Goethe, Johann Wolfgang von
impact of Greek tragedy on xv,
318, 319–20
staging of *The Birds* 345
theatrical experiments 319
Goffe, Thomas, *The Tragedie of
Orestes* 163
Golding, William 150–1
Gorsedd, first 192 n. 26
Granville Barker, Harley
(1877–1946)
associations
with Murray, Shaw 492,
494–5, 511, 520 n. 129
with William Poel 495

Granville Barker, Harley
  (1877–1946) (*cont.*):
 influence of Reinhardt 538,
   542–3, 553
 model for Cusins 504
 protest at censorship 529, 542
 staging of plays about women's
   suffrage 512–13
 supporter of Bedford College
   Greek plays 514
 Waste refused licence 529
Gray, Herbert Branston 456–7 and
   n. 71
Gray, Thomas 124 and n. 53, 130,
   192 and n. 25, 211
Great Commoner, The (William
   Pitt the elder, Earl of
   Chatham) 167
Great Exhibition, 1851 438
Grecian Saloon, The 353, 399–401
Greece
 ancient
   appeal to nineteenth-century
     Britons 308–9
   compared, contrasted with
     modern 270
   conceptual link between
     Gaelic culture and 186–7
     and n. 4
   fascination with ruins 267–70,
     271
   fusion of classical and ancient
     British revivalism 89 and
     n. 71, 183–93, 202–7, 208,
     217
   growing interest in 38
   history recalled in War of
     Independence 264–7
   inspiration of, under Valpy 262
   music of, conceptual link with
     Celtic culture 192–3
   nineteenth-century play
     inspired by 284

 perceptions of xix
 reconciliation of religion with
   Christianity 149–50, 310,
   311, 329–30
 relationship between history
   and Greek drama xxi
 Whig ideals derived from 50
 modern
   link with Italian centres of
     scholarship 265 and n. 3
   performance of *Antigone* in
     1867 336
   performances of Aeschylus'
     Persians for patriotic
     purposes 265–6 and n. 6
   relationship with Ottoman
     Empire xi, xix 38–9
   support for uprising 267 and
     n. 10
   under domination of Ottoman
     Empire 333
   response to War of
     Independence, 1821–9
     xi, 264, 270–2, 300–1
Greek drama
 censorship of 103; *see also*
   individual plays
 combination with interest in
   druids 192–3 and nn. 25–6
 educational performances in
   Britain 243–6
 erotic responses to 484–6
 music for, *see* music *and*
   individual composers and
   plays
 new fashion for academic
   productions 387–8
 numerous foundling tales 128
 performance history
   approach of academic world
     xiv
   in Edwardian period xi
   as performance texts x–xi

prominence of Sophocles'
Electra 152; *see also*
Cambridge University,
Greek plays
revival of interest, reasons for viii
rewriting for performance in
English ix
socio-political
influences xvii–xviii
stage conventions replicated in
burlesque 378
taste for parody 55
vivifying influence of
performance 262–3
vogue for, in 1880s 455–6, 484–6
widespread influence on cultural
life ix
see also Greek tragedy
Greek language
accessibility 256–7
in burlesques 364–5
quest for authenticity in Reading
School productions 262
Greek myth, exemplar for
problems of succession 43
Greek Orthodox Church, first
established in London xi
Greek style, promotion in social
hellenism 479–82, *481*
Greek tragedy
adaptations
emergence of genre in
nineteenth century 272
inspired by Continental
versions 130
to justify Whiggism xviii
44–9, 50–4
appeal of 'she-tragedy' 78 and
n. 22
approach of academic world xiv,
430–3
basic movements on British
stage xviii

brief revival in 1830s 436
conceptual links with biblical
narratives xxi, 132 and
n. 18
demands of authentic
revival 198–9
developing vogue, 1880s 430–3
Dryden's debt to 21–4
eighteenth-century attitudes to
religion in 147–50
examples in Africa vii n. 2
exploitation of comic
potential 338–41, 341–9
exposure of middle, lower
classes to 290 and n. 35,
309, 350, 362, 371–7,
389–90, 470
German reception of 430, 431
impact on canonical
thinkers xiv–xv
importance of Schlegel's
lectures 318, 320, 443, 475,
478
increasing interest in domestic
aspects 291
interrelation of aesthetic, social,
legislative, and political
change xv–xvi
in Ireland vii n. 2, 3
manifestation of English
classicism 66 and n. 7
in North America vii n. 2
obsession with destructive
effects of war xi and n. 10
parallel with art of sculpture 328
perceptions of, hero-centred
524
in Poland vii n. 2
politicization after 1688, 41–9
possibility of successful
performance debated
316–18
potential future influence xxii

Greek tragedy (*cont.*):
  rediscovery in British theatre xi,
    267–8
  reflection of Whig concept of
    liberty 331
  susceptibility to different
    interpretations xxii
  translations into vernacular x,
    xx
  understanding enlarged by
    comparative
    anthropology 202
  various authors making use of xv
  and Victorian perception of
    destiny 331
  see also British theatre *and*
    individual plays
Grein, J. T. 490, 548
Grey, Lord 229–30, 282
Grignion, Charles, engraving of
  The Mourning Bride 160
Grillparzer, Franz (1791–1872)
  Das Goldene Vließ, source for
    The Golden Fleece 343, 395,
    402
  version of Medea 399, 400, 402,
    424, 443, 489
Grote, George 50 and n. 58
Gucht, Gravelot van der 1 n. 2, 1.3
Guernier, Louis du 34, *47, 76,*
  155, 156
Gustavus Adolphus, King of
  Sweden 504
Gustavus Vasa, Henry Brooke 106,
  120

Haemon, representations
  of 340–1; *see also* Hermon
Hamilton, Cecily 518
Hamilton, Emma 30 and n. 3
Hamilton, Gavin 89
Hamlet, Shakespeare xxi, 155, 159,
  177, 249

Handel, George Friederic
  (1685–1759)
  Admeto, rè di Tessaglio 118 and
    n. 44, 439 n. 16
  ballet divertissements 31–2
  concerts, donations in aid of
    foundlings 137
  incidental music xix, 346
  Oreste (1734) 31–2, 34, 36, 49,
    62 and n. 81
  survival of Greek chorus in
    oratorios 197
  Water Music used for *The Deep,*
    Deep Sea 366–7
Hanoverian monarchy,
  acceptance 42, 43, 51
Harcourt, Robert 537
Hardy, Thomas 224, 332
Harrison, Jane 458, 463 n. 4, 467–8
  and n. 20, 472 and n. 32,
  477–9, 485–6, 497
Harrow School 228, 453–4
Hartley, Elizabeth 194, 195
Harwicke, Philip Yorke, first Earl
  of 140–2, 144
Hastings, Captain 267 and n. 10
Haughton, Miss 150
Hawthorne, Nigel 141 n. 40
Hawtrey, George 387
Hayman, Francis, *The Finding of*
  the Infant Moses in the
  Bulrushes 137–8
Haymarket Theatre, famed for
  lavish spectacle 370–1; *see also*
  individual plays
Hazlitt, William xvi, xxx, 291, 315
  and n. 95
Healthy and Artistic Dress Union
  482
Heath, James, frontispiece to
  Edward and Eleonora 119
Hecuba (mythical figure)
  need for exculpation of 96–7

portrayals of 80, 98, 113, 258, 543–4, *545*

representations of 63, 85, 87

Hecuba, Alexander Neville 8

Hecuba, Euripides

burlesque of 386

expurgation at Reading School 255

Garrick's ambition to stage 195

performances

directed by Valpy 252–3

at Reading School 255, 262

social resonance 510

Hecuba, John Delap 64, 80, 85–6, 87

Hecuba, Richard West 66, 84, 97–8 and n. 98

Hecuba à la Mode; or, The Wily Greek and the Modest Maid, Cranstoun Metcalfe 366

Hegel, G. W. F. 320–1

Helen, Euripides

influence on Delap 65 n. 3, 188 n. 7

scant attention to, in eighteenth century 61

source for Charles Gildon 71, 117–18

Helena in Troas, John Todhunter 458–9

acclaimed set, costumes 477–8

actors, actresses in 462–3, 484

C. H. Lloyd's music for 459

comments of W. B. Yeats 486

E. J. Godwin a designer of 459, 463, 477, 485–6

fund-raising performance 462 and n. 2, *464*

inspired by Homer 476

Hellas, Shelley xi, 234, 239, 266–7, 304

Hellenism

apolitical, in French drama 49

appeal to nineteenth-century Britons 308–9

and British revivalism 183–93, 202–7, 208, 217

influence on Talfourd 292–3, 310–11

Romantic, compatibility with Nonconformist spirituality 310–11

second wave in Britain 217

Hemans, Felicia 435

Hengler's Circus, Argyle Street 459, 462–8 and n. 2, 544

Her (later His) Majesty's Theatre

Barker's *IT* at 544 n. 58

innovation of electric light 360–1

Heracles (Hercules) (mythical figure)

portrayals of 456–7

Heracles, Euripides

Browning's version 449–51

Byron's reference to 254 n. 42

educational study encouraged 253–4

performances

at Reading School *244,* 253–4, 261–2

reviews 254, 256

source for Glover's Medea 90

Heraclidae, Euripides

adaptation by John Delap 64–5

source for Mason's *Caractacus* 188

Hercules, *see* Heracles (Hercules) *and individual works*

Hercules, Handel 197

'Hercules, Pluto, Alcestis, Admetus', Walter Savage Landor 443 n. 25

'Hercules restores Alcestis to Admetus', sculpture by Edward Hodges Baily 441 n. 18

'Hercules Wrestling with Death for the Body of Alcestis', painting by Lord Leighton 441

Heraud, Edith 335 and n. 48, 416–17

Heraud, John (1799–1887)
dramatic critic 416, 423, 425
Huguenot associations 34 n. 19, 416
Medea in Corinth 352, 419
review of Legouvé's *Medea* 402 n. 40
Videna; or, the Mother's Tragedy 416
Wife or no Wife 416

Hermon, representations of 340–1

Hero and Leander, fairground entertainment 356

Heron, Matilda 423

Hibernia Freed, William Young 42

Hiffernan, Paul 179

Hill, Aaron 102–3, 107 n. 22

Hindus, oppressed by Islam, identification with Greek chorus 234

hippodrama, access to classical myth, history through 388–9, 390

Hippolytus, Euripides
adaptation by Edmund Smith 43, 71–2
chorus of washerwomen 194
continuing influence 72
performance by pupils of Thomas Sheridan 246
production at Lyric Theatre 495–6, 549
representation of 88
role of chorus 199
as source 11, 190–1, 293–4

translation by Gilbert Murray 472, 494, 495–6, 549

Hippolytus-Phaedra myth 11, 71–4, 8; see also *Phaedra and Hippolitus*

His Majesty's Theatre, *see* Her Majesty's Theatre

Historical Register for the Year 1736, Henry Fielding 104

History of Greece, Connop Thirlwall 302

HMS Iphigenia 32

Hobhouse, Emily 509, 510 n. 90

Hobhouse, John, *Travels in Albania and Other Provinces of Turkey in 1809 & 1810* 269 and n. 17

Hobhouse, Leonard 509

Hofmannstahl, Hugo von, translation of *Oedipus Rex* 523–4, 539

Hoftheater, Weimar 319–21

Hogarth, William 1–2 and n. 2, 141–2

Hogg, Thomas Jefferson, *Life of Shelley* 228

Hölderlin, F., translation of *Antigone* 318

Holiday, Henry 482

Homer
inspiration for Warr's *The Story of Troy* 462, 475–6
parallel influences of Ossian and 193
recitations from, at Reading School 253
Victorian privileging of 475–6

homosexuality 79, 484–5; *see also* sexual deviancy

Hope, Thomas, *Costumes of the Ancients* 280

Hopkins, Gerald Manley 451 and
n. 53
Horace, Corneille, source for
Whitehead 129 and n. 6
Horace, Katherine Philips 83
Horestes, John Pikering 163 and
n. 18; *see also* Orestes
Horn, Charles 273–4
Horne, Richard Hengist 282, 285,
308, 311
hornpipes 250–1, 270 and n. 20
Horton, Priscilla 342, 345–6,
367–8, 396, 397
Hubback, Francis 445 n. 35,
519 n. 128
Hull, Thomas xv, 122
Humboldt, Wilhelm von 127 and
n. 63
Hume, David, *A Treatise of Human
Nature* 84
Hunt, Leigh 285
Hunter, Mrs 77
Hurd, Richard 200, 202
Hutcheson, Francis, *An Essay on
the Nature and Conduct of
the Passions and Affections*
84
Huxley, Leonard 448
Hyllus
brother–sister bond with Creusa,
inspiration for 304
representations of 303–7
Hypermnestra, Frank Sikes 380,
381
Hypermnestra, or Love in Tears,
Robert Owen 43

Ibsen, Henrik
Brand ix
concept of New Woman 393,
488–9
George Warr's approach, in
context of 474

influence on Wilamowitz,
491 n. 10
links with Euripides 490–1
Iliad 352, *352*, 358–9
*Illustrations of Euripides on the Ion
and the Bacchae*, Paul
Jodrell 132
Imaginary Conversations, Walter
Savage Landor 305
Imperial Institute, South
Kensington 445 n. 35
incest
in adaptations of Greek tragedy
fascination with xvi, 6, 24
recoil from 6, 242
adultery aggravated by, as
woman's ground for
divorce 419
conceptual links
with *ancien régime* 240
with civil war 9–10
with monarchy 7, 9–10, 240
with regicide, parricide 22, 24
criminalization 24, 532–3
dramatic use as expression of
social defiance 239–40
ground for censorship 530–4
and nn. 19, 24, 27
metaphor for political
corruption 9, 240
Oedipus and Jocasta driven to, in
Dryden and Lee 23–4
shifting attitudes to 534
theme taken up by Godwin 227
Indian Civil Service, education of
candidates for 468–9 n. 21,
473 and n. 35
Indian Emperor, John Dryden 162
Indian Queen, John Dryden 162
Infant Custody Acts 290, 394–5,
416, 420, 435
Infant Life Protection Act,
1872 423

infanticide
  concern for tragic cases of
      518–19
  by Medea
    and exculpation of Medea
        92–5, 96–7, 385, 392, 393,
        397–8
    explanations of 396–7, 419
    in Lemon's version 407–8
    in Murray's *Medea* 515
    relevance to child mortality in
        Victoran age 422–3, 424
    recoil from, in British
        theatre 391, 392, 424–5,
        518
Ino, representations of 374
Ino; or, The Theban Twins,
    B. J. Spedding 365, 370, 381
Ion (mythical figure)
  depiction of concern over
      ignominious birth 142–3
      and n. 42
  German experiments with 289
      and n. 27
  portrayals of 282, *283*, 286, 287,
      299–300, 311, *312,* 321, 322
  representations of 128, 138–9,
      282, 293–5, 302–3
  use as Christian name 286 and
      n. 17
Ion, Arthur Verrall's version 151
Ion, Euripides
  educational study
      encouraged 253–4
  inspiration for various
      productions 151
  recoil from 'pagan theology' 147
  rediscovery of 61, 130–4, 138
  Schlegel's adaptation 289 n. 27,
      319–20
  setting in Athens 303
  as source 66, 128, 129 n. 7, 130,
      293, 294, 304

  in Wakefield's school selection
      289
  watercolour sketches for
      production of, 1820
      289 n. 26
Ion, Thomas Talfourd
  concept of utopian freedom in
      293
  criticisms of 309–10
  distinguished audience at
      premiere 282
  domestic ambience 291–2
  echoes of Whig concept of
      liberty 331
  ecstatic review of first
      performance 310 n. 84
  influence of Addison's *Cato* 308
  playbill *313*
  political thrust 284, 293–300,
      363, 436
  popularity
    frequent editions 285 and n. 9
    frequent productions,
        revivals 286, 333, 351 n. 5
  positive republicanism 303, 304
  presented in New York 321
  productions
    at Covent Garden, 1836 260,
        282, *292*
    with all-female cast 286
  religious commitment 310–11
  significance of setting in Argos
      302–3
  sources 233 n. 63, 289 n. 26,
      293–5
  stage design 290–1
  translation into Greek Iambics
      286 and n. 17
Ion Travestie, Frederick Fox
    Cooper 286 and n. 14, 302,
    338, 339, 367
Iona Taurina, representation of
    231–3

Iphigenia (mythical figure)
  after the Glorious Revolution
    41–9, 54
  comic dimension 54–60
  eighteenth-century productions
    featuring 32
  happy endings 54
  Huguenot associations 33–6
  influence of John Locke 44–9
  link with Jephtha's
    daughter xxi, 32 and n. 8
  popularity 30–3
  portrayals of 79, 543–4
  prototype of virtue in distress
    72–5
  Royalist interpretations 36–41
  and the Whigs 50–4
Iphigenia, Abel Boyer 32, 35 and
  n. 23, 62
Iphigenia, John Dennis
  actresses in 79
  adaptation of *IT* 36
  British colonial overtones 38–9
  cheerful tone 53–4
  chorus confined to staged
    rituals 197
  influence xiv–xv, 44–9, 60, 61, 72
  jingoistic tenor 39
  radical Whiggism in 45–6, 50–4
Iphigenia, devised by Isadora
  Duncan 546 n. 67
Iphigenia, Johnson, actresses
  in 70–80
Iphigenia in Aulis, Euripides
  Aristotle's attention to 33
  as source 32 n. 8, 109, 360,
    546 n. 67
  Dryden's debt to 21, 33
  Erasmus' translation into Latin
    33
  fame in England 33, 62
  first translation into English 33
  human sacrifice averted in 54

  influence of Racine 33–6
  productions
    in Dublin 334
    nineteenth-century 32 n. 6
Iphigenia in Tauride, Gluck 62
Iphigenia in Tauride, Thomas
  Traetta 62
Iphigenia in Tauris, Euripides
  adaptation to different
    ideologies 60–1
  Aristotle's attention to 33
  characterization of Thoas 49
  conceptual link with *The*
    Tempest xxi, 37
  English language adaptations 36
  influence on aesthetics of
    tragedy 72
  international interest 36
  place in history of British
    theatre 61–4, 71
  productions
    by Barker 543–4 and n. 58
    in Cambridge, 1894 32 n. 6
    in Greek, in 1887 513 n. 106
  significance of 'recognition'
    scene 157
  as source 31–2, 36, 62, 546 n. 67
  translations, editions
    by Gilbert West 46
    by Murphy 526
  see also Iphigenia (mythical figure)
Iphigenia; or, The Sail!! The Seer!!
  And the Sacrifice, Edward
  Nolan, alliteration 365
Iphigénie, Michel Le Clerc and
  Jacques de Coras 41 n. 37
Iphigenie auf Tauris, Goethe xv
Iphigénie en Aulide, Racine
  nineteenth-century
    productions 32 n. 6
  performances in England
    34 n. 17
  success 33

Ireland
　censorship in 535, 536
　Dr Thomas Sheridan, pioneer of
　　Greek tragedy in 3
　Greek tragedy in vii n. 2, 3
　literary revival, and the Greek
　　classics 186–7 and n. 4
Irene, Samuel Johnson 129 n. 7
Iroquois, parallels between Greek
　tragedy and indigenous
　culture 202
Irving, Henry 454
Ismene, representations
　of 218–20, 223, 274, 294, 296,
　302, 303–7, 321, 322, 331–2,
　340–1
Italy, Renaissance, cultural links
　with Greece 265
Ixion; or, the Man at the Wheel,
　Francis Burnand 364, 369,
　370, 373, 376

Jacobitism
　fear of, and opposition to
　　Bute 171
　response of theatre to xvi, 44,
　　44–5, 139, 148, 165–7, 191
Jacques-Dalcroze, Émile, system
　of eurythmics 546 n. 70
James II (formerly Duke of
　York) 25–6, 43, 44, 166–7
Janauschek, Fanny 424
Jane Shore, Nicholas Rowe 75
Janet's Repentance, George Eliot
　182
Janin, Jean-Marie, *Oreste* 275
Jason
　portrayals of 514
　representations of 90–1, 342–5,
　　344, 385, 397–9, 400–1,
　　406–8, 418–19, 425–6
Jason and Medea
　themes for

burlesque, contemporary
　detail 381
　masque 93
*Jason and Medea: A Comic. Heroic.
　Tragic. Operatic. Burlesque-
　Spectacular Extravaganza*,
　Jack Wooler 380, 399–401,
　414
*Jason and Medea: A Ramble after a
　Colchian*, burlesque 395
Jebb, Richard 336, 473 and
　n. 37
Jenkin, Fleeming (1833–85)
　association with production of
　　Agamemnon 451–2
　productions of authentic Greek
　　tragedy 431, 448–9 and n. 47,
　　450
　review of Browning's
　　Agamemnon 451
Jenkin, Mrs Fleeming 431, 448–9,
　452
Jephtha, John
　Christopherson 32 n. 8
Jephtha's daughter, conceptual
　link with Iphigenia xxi, 32
　and n. 8
Jerrold, Douglas 287, 314
Jersey, Island of, theatrical
　traditions 247
Joas, biblical story as source for
　French drama 132–3 and
　n. 19
Jocasta
　portrayals of 79, 81, 82, 83, 524,
　　525, 543
　representations of 22–4, 67, *525*,
　　533, 534
　suicide *19*
Jocasta, Gascoigne and
　Kinwelmershe x, 8
Jodrell, Paul 117–18 nn. 39–42,
　132, 146–7

Johnson, Charles (1649–1748)
  on arousal of compassion in
    spectators 84
  concept of virtue 86–7
  exculpation of Medea 92–3
  plagiarizing of Boyer's *Iphigenia*,
    35 and n. 23
  The Tragedy of Medea, as 'she-
    tragedy' 66
  use made of Greek tragedy 61
Johnson, James 233
Johnson, Samuel, (1709–89) 64,
  120
  admiration for Congreve's *The
    Mourning Bride* 159 and
    n. 14
  Irene 129 n. 7
  on purpose of tragedy 222–3
Johnson, Thomas 154
Jones, Avonia 423
Jones, Henry Arthur 531 and n.
  22, 533–4
Jones, Inigo 204 and n. 81
Jones, William 214, 225, 234, 245,
  262 n. 2, 302 n. 66
Jonson, Ben 196, 351 n. 49
Jopling, Louise 462–3, 479, 482
Joseph Andrews, Henry
  Fielding xvii, 222 and n. 26,
  135
journalism, emergence, and the
  British theatre 61
Jowett, Benjamin 451–2
Joyner, William xvi, 10–12 and
  n. 31
Judas Iscariot, conceptual link with
  Oedipus xxi, 8 and n. 19
judiciary, appointments to,
  concern with 297
Julian, Mary Russell Mitford 256
Julius Caesar, Shakespeare 245
Junius Brutus, William
  Duncombe 105

Kauffman, Angelica (1741–1807)
  Death of Alcestis, 123 and n. 51
  inspired by Francklin's
    Sophocles 177–8
  painting of Eleonora 123 and
    n. 51
  scene from *Elfrida* 211,
    213 n. 111
Keats, John 292
Kemble, Charles 268, 275, 277,
  278, 280–1
Kemble, John Philip 3, 123–4,
  268, 269, 280, 308
Kemble, Sarah, *see* Siddons, Sarah
Kierkegaard, Søren viii
Killigrew, Thomas 37
King John, Shakespeare 247–8,
  249, 280
King Lear, Shakespeare 249, 250
King's College, London
  first attempt to publicize
    Aeschylus *Oresteia* 465
  Ladies' Department 465 and
    n. 11, 466 and n. 12, 470,
    484
  share of University Endowment
    Fund 462
  tradition of producing Greek
    plays 465 n. 11, 466
King's Theatre (formerly Queen's
    Theatre)
  first performance of Smith's
    Phaedra and Hippolitus 72
  spectacle at 392
kingship, *see* monarchy
Kingsley, Charles, *The Heroes* 424
Kingsway Theatre, adaptation for
    Barker's *IT* 543–4; *see also*
    individual plays
Kinwelmershe, Francis, *see*
    Gascoigne, George, and
    Francis Kinwelmershe
knickerbockers, *fin de siècle* 397

Knight, Mrs 79–80
Knight of the Burning Pestle,
  Beaumont and Fletcher
  355–6
Knowles, James 284, 300
Kotzebue, August von, *The Ruins
  of Athens; A Dramatic
  Masque* 333–4
Koun, Karolos 197–8
Kreusa, Johan Jakob
  Bodmer 289 n. 27
Krupp, Friedrich Alfred, model for
  Undershaft 502

La Belle Hélène, Offenbach, comic
  adaptation of 383–4
La città morta, Gabriele
  D'Annunzio 532 n. 24
La Clairière, Coqueteau de, *Pylade
  et Oreste* 41 and n. 37
La Méchante Femme, Dominique
  and Biancolelli 404 n. 48
La Médée en Nanterre, Coignard,
  Grange, and Bourdois 405–6
La Mesnardière, Hippolyte Jules
  Pilet de 152–3
La Sorcière, C. Sewrin 404 n. 48
La Thébaïde, Racine 44, 82
Lachmann, Hedwig, translation of
  Salome for opera 538
Lacoste, Louis 132, 133, 151
Lacroix, Jules, translation of
  Oedipus Tyrannus into
  French 522, 524, 539
Lacy, Miss 280
Lacy's Acting Edition 355
Lady Audley's Secret, Mary
  Elizabeth Braddon 422
*Lady Sarah Bunbury Sacrificing to
  the Graces*, Joshua
  Reynolds 89, 130 n. 11
Lagrange-Chancel, *Oreste et
  Pilade* 48, 49

Landor, Walter Savage 282, 305,
  446 n. 25
Lang, Mrs Andrew 466, 476
Langtry, Lily 484 and n. 72
Laocoon, Gotthold Ephraim
  Lessing 125, 126
'L'Après Midi d'un faune',
  Nijinksy ballet 546–7 n. 72
Latin, quotations from, in
  burlesques 365
Latin drama
  comedy traditionally performed
    at Westminster School 34 n.
    17, 248 and n. 19, 261
  educational performances in
    Britain 243–6
Latin language
  Renaissance, adaptors' choice of
    Greek texts in 130
  use in 'Judge and Jury
    Society' 388
Laud, Archbishop 248–9
laughing songs 361
Lawrence, Ann 425
*Lazaria the Greek; or the Archon's
  Daughter* 270–1
Le Cid, Pierre Corneille 15
Le Marseillaise, sources of
  inspiration 264–5 and n. 2
Le Serment des Horaces, Jacques-
  Louis David 301
Le Siège de Corinthe, Rossini 275
Le Théâtre des Grecs, Pierre
  Brumoy 172, 200, 219, 247
League of Nations 508
Lee, Nathaniel (1655–92) 17 and
  n. 47, 27; see also *Oedipus*
Leech, John 383
Legouvé, Ernest, production of
  Euripides' *Medea* 402–4, *403*,
  404–5, *405*, 406, 423, 430, 441,
  443, 489
Leighton, Frederick

association with
Dorothy Dene 463 and n. 5,
482, 483–4 and n. 70
George Warr 463–4, 471
feminist sympathies 482
painting of classical
subjects 441 n. 18
standing in art world 480 and
n. 59
Lemercier, Louis Jean
Népomucène 125
Lemon, Mark
burlesque on *Medea* 352–3, 371,
378, 382, 406–8
editor of *Punch*, on comic
potential of *Antigone* 338
Lemprière, Dr, classical
dictionary 358, 378
Lennox, Charlotte 90, 172, 219
Leonidas, King of Sparta, striking
scenery 277 and n. 45
Leonidas, Richard Glover 50, 94,
266 n. 7
Lepanto, Battle of 265
Les Ballets Russes 547, 553
Les Héraclides, Jean-François
Marmontel 188 n. 7
Les Huguenots, Myerbeer, music
adapted for burlesque 366
Les Perses, French version inspired
by Aeschylus 265
Lessing, Gotthold Ephraim
125–7
Levey, Richard, musical director
of Theatre Royal, Dublin 334
Lewes, George Henry 302 and n. 6,
353, 404, 410
Liberty, James Thomson 50, 102,
105–6, 109, 125
liberty, ideal of
association with
ancient Greece 50, 52, 272,
300–1

Whiggism 50, 102, 105–6,
109, 125, 331
concern for, in Aeschylean
choruses 221
contiguity of political, poetic
52
in opposition to tyranny,
asserted by Dennis 46–8,
51–4
post 1688 50–4
precondition for flourishing
art 52
symbolized by spoken tragedy in
contrast to opera 53
Liberty Asserted, John
Dennis 46–8
Liberty & Co., social
hellenism 480, 481
Licensing Act, 1737 103–4 and
n. 13, 105, 106, 121
Life of Shelley, Thomas Jefferson
Hogg 228
lighting, introduction of
electric 360–1
Lillo, George 104, 126
Lindsay, David, *The Nereid's
Love* 273 n. 30
Little Red Riding Hood,
pantomime 351–2
Liverpool
burlesques performed in 359
Parthenon Rooms, *Tableau
vivant* at 390
Lloyd, C. H., music for *Helena in
Troas* 459
Lloyd, Robert 208–9
Locke, John 42, 45, 46–9
London Corresponding
Society 224
London Greek Committee 271
and n. 21
London Society for the Extension
of University Teaching 470

London University, Endowment
Fund 462
Longinus, *On the Sublime* 52
Longpierre, *Médée* 404 n. 48
Lord, Daisy 518–19
*Lord Byron in Athens; or, The
Corsair's Isle* 272 n. 24
Lord Chamberlain, *see* censorship
L'Oreste, see *Oreste, L'*
lost civilization theme, in
Talfourd's works 314
Louis XVI 227
Loutherburg, Philippe de 174,
268
love
clandestine, compatibility with
virtue 139
erotic
in Greek tragedy 91
as threat to absolute power 39
interest, introduction,
development 38, 39
heterosexual, homosexual 79,
484–5
marriage for
encouragement 141
importance affirmed 142,
144–6
prevention open to moral
criticism 142
in Spicer's *Alcestis* 442
*Love and Duty or the Distres't
Bride*, Sturmy 43 and n. 41
'Love Leading Alcestis', Burne-
Jones 441 n. 18
Love's Victim, Charles Gildon 66,
71 and n. 15, 79, 117–18
Lowe, Solomon 246 and n. 10
lower classes, access to higher
education 470
Lucan 75, 203
Lucas, Hippolyte, version of
Alcestis 439–41, 442, 443

Lucian, translation by Thomas
Francklin 177
Lucifera's Procession, Fairy Queen,
G. Humphrey 229, 229–31
Lufkeen, Mr, delineation of *The
Grecian Statues* 389
Lully, *Alceste* 117–18, 439 n. 16
Lyceum Theatre
Benson's association with 454,
456
burlesques performed in 365
under Irving and Terry 454
see also individual plays
Lyndsay, David, *The Nereid's
Love* 273 n. 30
Lyric Theatre, Murray's
Hippolytus at 495–6
Lysistrata, Aristophanes 530 and
n. 16

Macaria, representation of 65–6,
90
Macaulay, Thomas Babington,
Lord 35, 306–7, 309–10
Macbeth, Davenant's musical
version 38
Macbeth, Shakespeare 59–60,
129
McCarthy, Lillah (1875–1960)
roles played by 498, 524, 540,
545, 543–4
suffragette 515
Macfarren, John 324
Mackie, Charles 112
Mackinnon, Alan 456
Macklin, Charles 129 and n. 9
Macklin, Maria 129 and n. 9
Maclise, Daniel 287, *288*
Macpherson, James (1736–96)
193
Macready, William (1793–1873)
adverse criticism of Covent
Garden *Antigone* 324

association with Talfourd 287
Browning's *Strafford* composed
  for 286
influence 299–300 and n. 54,
  311, 315, 326
refusal to produce *The Murder
  Room* 316–17
rejection of proposed *Oedipus
  Tyrannus* 332–3
republicanism 284, 300
roles played by 282, *283*, 286,
  299–300, 303, 306 n. 71
'sent up' in *Ion Travestie*
  286 n. 14
Madden, Samuel, *Themistocles, the
  Lover of his Country* 42, 105
Mafei, Marchese Francesco
  Scipione, advocate of national
  theatre 102 n. 6
Maid of Athens, Lord Byron 357
Major Barbara, George Bernard
  Shaw
  Court Theatre production *501*
  debt to Murray 502–3
  sources 491, 492–3, 499–500,
    505–8 and n. 68
Mallet, David 106
Mansell, Henry
  Longueville 384–5
Maria Stuart, Schiller 404
Marie-Antoinette 240
Markland, Jeremiah 172
Marmontel, Jean-François, *Les
  Héraclides* 188 n. 7
marriage
  and impossibility of
    remarriage 401
  clandestine
    interest in, reflected in
      Creusa 140–7
    legitimacy a concern in
      British theatre 141–2 and
      n. 40

minimum age for legal 141
  procedures 140
  and protection of vulnerable
    young women 141
  control of extreme parental
    authority 141
  early Victorian concept of 420
  emerging debate over marital
    violence 427
  entering into, prior to Marriage
    Act 140–1, 146
  Ibsen's concept of 488–9
  impecunious, disastrous for
    woman in mid-Victorian
    Britain 434–5
  institution scrutinized in
    Talfourd's *Alcestis* 435–6
  laws regulating
    Divorce and Matrimonial
      Causes Act, 1857 140,
      381, 401–2, 415–16 and
      n. 78
    Marriage Act 1753 140–2,
      144
    Married Women's Property
      Acts, 1870, 1882 420
    reconsideration 419–20
    significance of Medea 393–4,
      418–19, 419–22
  for love
    encouragement of 141
    importance affirmed in
      Whitehead's
      Creusa 144–6
    prevention open to moral
      criticism 142
    in Spicer's *Alcestis* 442
  progressive Whig attitude to 49
  Shaw's comments on 488–9
  state of, to be favoured over
    desertion 401
  with deceased wife's sister,
    controversy over 408 n. 57

Marriage à-la-Mode,
  Hogarth 141–2
Marriage as Trade, Cecily
  Hamilton 518
Marston, Westland 244
Martin, Theodore 326
Martin-Harvey, John
  (1863–1944) *523*, 524, 536,
  540, 541
masks, absence from Balliol
  Agamemnon 453
Mason, William (1725–97)
  admiration for Alexander
    Pope 190
  anti-slavery view 189 n. 10
  appeal to both conservatives and
    radicals 208–9
  association with John Delap 188
    and n. 7
  background, education 194–5
  belief in women druids 203
  classicism attacked 208
  completion of Whitehead's
    translation of *Oedipus
    Tyrannus* 134 and n. 25,
    191 n. 18, 215, 216
  freemason 213
  impact in the visual arts 211–13
    and n. 111
  influence of Greek tragedy
    on xiii, xv
  interest in church music 191 and
    n. 18
  monument in Westminster
    Abbey 211, *212*
  passed over for poet
    laureateship 130
  political stance 181
  pro-American views 184, 189
  radicalism, philanthropy 190–2
  tragedies in Grecian model xiii,
    xv, 190–1
  use of chorus 198, 200–2, 225

see also *Elfrida; Caractacus*
Masque of the Druids, John
  Fisher 213
masques, court, tradition of 37–8
Mathews, Charles (1776–1835)
  xv, 342–5, 353, 378, 396
Matilda, Thomas Francklin 173
matricide, concerns about morality
  of, on stage 155, 159 and n. 13,
  179–82
Matrimonial Causes Act, 1878 427
matrimony, *see* divorce; marriage
Matrimony, John
  Shebbeare 142 n. 41
Mattocks, Isabella 194
Maurice, F. D. 457
Maurice, Thomas (1754–1824)
  influence of Parr 225 and n. 37
  influence on Shelley's
    philhellenism 228–9
  *Poems and Miscellaneous Pieces
    with a free translation of the
    Oedipus Tyrannus of
    Sophocles* 222, 240 and n. 97
  source for Faucit 240
  sources 266
  use of politicized chorus 234,
    239
Mavrokordatos, *see* Alexandros
Maynooth controversy 341–2, *342*
Mayr, Simon 391–2
Medea (mythical figure)
  as abandoned wife 435
  as anti-heroine 404–8 and n. 48
  attractive to painters 81, 424
  in burlesque 393, 397, 409–10,
    491
  depicted to evoke
    sympathy 85–6, 398–9,
    400–1, 402–4, 413, 423,
    514
  different approaches of male,
    female authors 420–1

ethnicity 424
exotic sorceress 424
focus for debate on divorce 416,
435
infanticide by
attributed to madness 93–4,
95
exculpation 92–5, 96–7, 385,
392, 393, 397–8
explanations of 396–7, 419
recoil from, in British
theatre 391, 392
as model of maternal devotion
425
patriarchal perception of
xxi–xxii
portrayals of 79–80, *81*, 82, 93,
94 and n. 91, 113, 114, 125,
174, 334, 342–5, 352–3, 369
and n. 86, 396, 402–4, *403*,
405, 408, 410–15, *411*, 423,
424–9, *426*, *428*, 436, 514
prototype of
'distressed mother' 63, 71,
393, 422–3, 424
the New Woman 429, 488–90,
511
representations of 90–1, 385,
397–9, 406–8, 408–15,
418–19, 423–9, 488–9
singers portraying 391–2 and
n. 6
stream of dramas on theme
of 392–3, 402; *see also*
individual plays
Victorian women identified with
predicament 395, 398,
422–3
Medea, Euripides
adaptations
by Gildon 66, 71, 118
by Grillparzer 399, 400, 402,
424, 443, 489

by Legouvé 402–4, *403*,
404–5, *405*, 406, 423, 430,
441, 443, 489
burlesque on theme of 342–5,
344
Byron's parodic lines from 356
continuing influence 72, 82,
423
discovery coincident with
discovery of New
Woman 511
musical burlesques of 56
performances
directed by Valpy 252–3
first in English translation
391
at Rugby School 225 n. 39
by University and Bedford
Colleges 513
permanent place in British
repertoire vii–viii, 351 n. 5
recitations from, at Reading
School 253
role of chorus 199–200
source for
burlesque 360
John Heraud 415–19
Joyner 11 n. 28
Planché's *The Golden*
Fleece 359
Talfourd's *The Athenian*
Captive 304
Wills's *Medea in Corinth* 425
translations, editions
into German 512
by Gilbert Murray 511–16
by Joseph
Montanelli 404 n. 45
'Women of Corinth'
speech 11 n. 28, 398, 409,
488–9, 511
Medæa, Charles Johnson, see *The*
Tragedy of Medæa

Medea, Richard Glover
    classical model for free nation-
        state 50
    emotional range demanded of
        actors 80, 90–1
    exculpation of Medea 93–5,
        392
    Mary Ann Yates's acclaimed
        performance 174
    pro-feminine alteration of Greek
        plots 86–7
    revivals 94 n. 91
    as 'she-tragedy' 66, 90–1
    sources 91
Medea, Seneca 391 and n. 3
Medea in Athens, Augusta
    Webster 421, 489
Medea in Corinth, John
    Heraud 352, 395, 416–19,
    430
Medea in Corinth, William Gordon
    Wills 425–6
Medea in Corinto (opera), Simon
    Mayr, reaction to 391–2
*Medea; or, a Libel on the Lady of
    Colchis*, Mark Lemon 352–3,
    371, 378, 382, 406–8, 414,
    424
*Medea; The Best of Mothers, With a
    Brute of a Husband*, Robert
    Brough 408–15, *411*, 436
Medea's Kettle 55
Médée, Cherubini 404 and n. 48
Médée, Corneille 92–3
Médée, Longpierre 404 n. 48
Médée, Noverre, spectacular
    ballet 393
Médée ou l'Hôpital des fous, Citizen
    Bizet and H. Chaussier
    404 n. 48
Melbourne, Lord 282, 290 and
    n. 33

Melpomene, tragic Muse, on
    Mason's monument 211, *212*
men
    increasing anxieties about
        effeminacy 484–5
    playing women's parts, *see* cross-
        dressed roles
Menaechmi, Plautus 244
Mendelssohn, Felix Bartholdy
    (1809–47)
    music for *Antigone* 197, 300,
        317, 318–19, 320, 322–5,
        331–2, 335–6, 378
    music for *Oedipus at
        Colonnus* 318–19, 335
    search for librettist 343
    use of *Antigone* music for other
        productions 336
Mercadente, Saverio 332–3
Mercer, Thomas 193
Meredith, George, *Antigone* 330
Merope, Matthew Arnold viii, 331
Metamorphoses, Ovid 359, 363,
    366–7
Metastasio 132 and n. 18, 273
Metcalfe, Cranstoun 366, 386
Metropolitan Police, depicted in
    classical burlesque 381
Michalis, Johann David, verse
    translation of Thomson's
    Agamemnon 126
Midas, Kane O'Hara 56–8, 356
middle classes
    access of lower, to higher
        education 470
    access to classical culture 350,
        362, 389–90
    appeal to, of ancient Greece 309
    authors of burlesque frequently
        drawn from 371–7
    creation of cultured 290 and
        n. 35

liberal, hopes reposed in Queen
Victoria 303
Talfourd's concept of
potential 299
taste for private theatricals 383
see also classics
Mighty Aphrodite, Woody
Allen 197
Mile End Green, performance af
Oedipus Tyrannus, 1714 218,
246
Mill, Helen Taylor 396
Mill, John Stuart 396, 420
Milner, H. M., *Britons at
Navarino* 271
Milton, John (1608–74)
commendation of recitation of
classics 245
influence on Dryden 14–15,
15–16, 20, 24
inspired by Euripides'
Alcestis 116–17, 253, 446
interest in Greece 38
link of monarchy with tyranny,
incest 10
republicanism 12–13, 20
used by Parr in teaching of
Greek 226
see also *Samson Agonistes*
Minerva, equation with
Britannia 333–4
Minotaur, in Shelley's *Oedipus
Tyrannus* 231–3, 238–9
Mitford, Mary Russell
(1787–1855)
association with Talfourd 287
Belford Regis 251
at first night of *Ion* 282
literary career,
associations 256–7 and n. 52
response to Reading School
performances
personal 256–8

reviews 243, 250 n. 33, 251–2,
254, 255, 256, 261, 263
see also *Rienzi*
Mitford, William, *The History of
Greece* 301 and n. 64
Momigliano, A. 301 n. 64
Mona, *see* Anglesey
Mona Antiqua Restaurata, Henry
Rowlands 204
monarchy
concepts of
in Davenant's *Circe* 39–40
'king and no king' 25–9
link with incest xvi, 7, 9–10,
240
'the lazy' 39–40
contrast between tyrannical
ageing, and idealistic
youth 309
Exclusion crisis 24–5
French responses to authority
of 15
Hanoverian, acceptance 42, 43
Joyner's attitude to 10–12
Milton's rejection of 12–13, 20
as mirror of family, Faucit's
representation of 242
and republicanism, in Talfourd's
Ion 298–300, 303
responses of theatre
to autocracy of Louis XIV 15
to succession problems xvi, 7,
12, 43–4
Sophoclean concept
relevance to English 7, 157–8,
159
Restoration interest in 9–10
see also regicide
Moncrieff, William, *Zoroaster*
277–80
Monmouth, Earl of 27
Montanelli, Joseph, translator of
Medea 404 n. 45

Moore, Albert Joseph 335
Moore, Edward, *The
    Foundling* 135
morality, public, censorship to
    protect 528–9
More, Hannah 310 n. 85
Morell, The Revd T., translation
    of *Hecuba* 97 n. 98
Morgan, Lady (Sydney Owenson),
    Woman: or, Ida of Athens 270
Morganwg, *see* Williams, Edward
Morley, Henry 353, 369–70, 412,
    439
Morris, William, *The Life and
    Death of Jason* 424
motherhood
    ideological associations 92
    issues of, relevance of *Medea*
        515
    see also infanticide *and individual
        plays*
Mounet-Sully, Jean (1841–1916)
    impact, influence viii, 432–3,
        494, 521–6, 527, 534,
        540
    Isadora Duncan's response to
        545 and n. 65
Movement for the Abolition of
    University Tests 468
Mr Buckstone's Ascent of Parnassus,
    James Robinson Planché 370
Municipal Corporations
    Commission 298
murder, Victorian age's fascination
    with 415, 421–3, 425
Murphy, Arthur 153, 159–62 and
    n. 40
Murphy, Margaret 518–19
Murray, Gilbert (1866–1957)
    admiration for Reinhardt's
        Oedipus 540–1
    approach to translation 472–3
    attitude to censorship 529, 536

background, career xvii, 494–5,
    497 and n. 31, 511
comparison with George
    Warr 471–3
concepts of religion,
    politics 497–9
influence of translations xii, 472,
    492–5
on links between Euripides and
    Ibsen 490
related to W. S. Gilbert 491
relationship with George Bernard
    Shaw 491–4, 502–3
resistance to Poel's attempt to
    alter *Bacchae* 498 and
    n. 40
revulsion against Boer War 508
    and nn. 85–6
support of suffragettes 511–12
supporter of Bedford College
    Greek plays 514
view of
    incest 533–4, 535
    Sophocles 535
    see also individual plays
Murray, Lady Mary 504
music
    of ancient Greece, conceptual
        link with Celtic
        culture 192–3 and n. 26
    in burlesque 345–7, 356, 366–71
        and n. 76
    concept of liberating powers 549
    in productions of Greek
        tragedy xi, xix, 28 and n. 81
    *see also individual composers and
        plays*
music hall, rise 377
Mycenae, interest in excavations
    at 449
myth, ancient
    exemplar for problems of
        succession 43

light entertainment derived
from 54–5, 338–9, 378

Nadir Shah, William Jones 234
nakedness, semi-nakedness,
innovative feature in
productions 30–2, *31*, 280 and
n. 48
Napoleon, equation with Xerxes
266 n. 7
national theatre, call for 102–3,
432
nationalism, German, and interest
in Greek tragedy 318–21
naturalism
in Reinhardt's *Oedipus* 539
rise, in theatre 432
Nazi rallies, models for 526
Neander, approach to neo-
classicism 16
neoclassicism
association with backward-
looking regimes 208
in debate over chorus 198–9
linking of Oedipus and Electra
themes 153–4
repudiation of 51, 52–3, 208–9,
319, 427
Neville, Alexander, *Oedipus* 8 and
n. 18
New British Theatre, The, edited by
Abraham John Valpy 248
New Royalty Theatre, burlesques
performed in 360
New Woman
appearance on British stage 429
Barker's plays on 495
concept of 393, 395–6, 396–7,
414
food for thought in Euripides'
Alcestis 460–1
impact of Balliol College
Agamemnon 456

links between Medea and 429,
488–90, 511
opponents of 489–90
see also suffragettes
New York
productions of *Antigone* in 317,
321, 336–7
Talfourd's *Ion* presented in 321
Newcastle, Duke of 167, 169
Newdick, Robert S. 285 n. 7
Newton, Charles 471, 479, 484
Newton, Thomas 8 n. 18
Nicander, representation of 142–3,
143–6, 147
Nicholas Nickleby, Dickens'
readings from 375
Nicholson, Renton 375, 388,
390
Nicoll, Allardyce, importance of
theatre history xiv–xv
Nietzsche, Friedrich (1844–1900)
concept of liberating power of
music 549
impact of *Bacchae* on xv
influence on Reinhardt's *Oedipus
Rex* 523–4, 540
ostracism 498
relationship with Wagner 493
and n. 18
Nijinsky 546 and n. 72
Nikolaïdis, John xi, 225
Nile, Battle of the, and literary
echoes of Salamis 266 and
n. 7
Nobel, Alfred, model for
Undershaft 502
Nolan, Edward 365, 373
Nonconformists, influence of 287,
310–11
Nordau, Max 489–90
North of England Council for the
Higher Education of
Women 470

Norton, Caroline 394–5
Norwich Grammar School, Parr's
    period at 228
Norwich Theatre Royal,
    production of Fitzball's
    Antigone 274
Norwood, Gilbert, *Euripides and
    Shaw* 490
novels, apocalyptic, 'last of the
    race' 296
Noverre, Jean-Georges
    Iphiginia in Aulide 62 and n. 83
    spectacular ballet *Médée* 392

oath themes, popularity in 1820s
    301
'Ode on the Music of the Grecian
    Theatre' (lost), William
    Collins 193
Ode to Adversity, Thomas Gray
    124
Ode to Liberty, Collins 185
Odeion of Herodes Atticus,
    Athens, performance of
    Antigone in, 1867 336
Odyssey, as source 109, 358–9, 364
Oedipe, Pierre Corneille
    as source 22, 23, 24, 241
    Dryden and Lee's version
        compared 5, 217
    English response to 9
    influence 9
    Joyner's Oedipus contrasted
        with 10
Oedipe, Voltaire 5, 227
Œdipe-Roi, Marie-Joseph Chénier,
    representation of Oedipus
    226, 239
Œdipe Roi, Sophocles, Mounet-
    Sully's interpretation 521–6,
    527
Oedipus (mythical figure)
    circumstances of death 9

compatibility of character with
    revolutionary
    principles 226–7
concept of 'English' 1–29
conceptual link with Judas
    Iscariot xxi, 8 and n. 19
eighteenth-century reception
    of 217–22
figure of the Enlightenment 217
French reception of 7, 219, 221,
    521–6
impact on Freud viii, 494, 525–6
link with radicalism 240
model for Caractacus 187–8
and nature of kingship 26, 220
persistent moral reservations
    about 215–16
portrayals of 522–6, *527*, 540, 546
representations of 10, 22–4,
    217–22, 222–8, 240, 241–2,
    282, 294, 368, 534, 539–42
symbolism in final exits 20
as tragic foundling 128
see also under individual plays
Oedipus, Seneca
    influence on Dryden and Lee
        22, 24
    sixteenth-century versions 7–8
Oedipus at Colonus, Sophocles
    actors, actresses in 335
    Dryden and Lee's version
        compared 5–6
    Mason's work compared
        favourably with 211
    Mendelssohn's music for 318–19
    model for William Mason's
        Caractacus xiii, xv, 184,
        186, 187–8
    performance in 1859 446
    royal command performances
        318–19
    as source 12–13, 184, 295, 360
    symbolism of Oedipus' exit 20

unlikely reading from, at
    Reading School 253 n. 41
Oedipus Tyrannus, (*Oedipus Rex*),
    Sophocles
attempts to stage 534–8
censorship
    imposed 6, 103, 529–34
    lifted 534–8
as domestic rather than heroic
    tragedy 220, 221
Dryden's debt to 21
far-reaching implications 318
Faucit's musical version 240–2,
    267, 274, 326
'hubris' chorus published to
    illustrate career of Kaiser
    xi n. 10
inspiration for neo-classical
    painting 275 n. 38
Isadora Duncan's production
    (*OR*) 546
Lacroix's version (*OR*) 521–8,
    539
lifting of ban 538
link with *Electra* 153–4, 162
much favoured in France 153,
    216, 220
paradigmatic tragedy 28
performances
    at Cambridge, 1887 529, 534,
        539
    in Mile End Green, 1714 218,
        246
    by pupils of Thomas
        Sheridan 246
    at Reading School 348, 350–1
    at Stanmore School, 1776 xi,
        174 n. 55 195, 225
permanent place in British
    repertoire vii
reasons for British engagement
    with 216–17

Reinhardt's production 522–6
    and n. 5, *523*, 538–42, 546,
    547, 548, 553, 554
as source 12, 293–4, 360
translations, editions, versions
    by Dacier 28, 153–4,
        217–18
    by Francklin 220–1, 250
    by Gilbert Murray 533–4,
        537–8, 539
    by John Sheppard 522
    by Jules Lacroix (into
        French) 522
    by Maurice 222–4, 266
    by W. B. Yeats 536
    by W. L. Courtney 531, 533
    by Whitehead (unfinished)
        134 and n. 25
Oedipus, Alexander Neville 8 and
    n. 18
Oedipus, anonymous, early
    translation 8 and n. 18
Oedipus, Dryden and Lee
    actresses in 81
    and censorship 6, 531 n. 19, 532,
        539
    chorus confined to staged
        rituals 197
    death of Oedipus in 9
    debts to Shakespeare 17
    direct influence 5–6, 62
    far-reaching implications 318
    fascination with deviant
        sexuality xvi
    feminine perspective 67
    first performance 1
    French versions compared 5
    influence of Beaumont and
        Fletcher 26
    misgivings about incest in xvi,
        22, 23–4, 215–16, 239–40,
        531 n. 19, 532

Oedipus, Dryden and Lee (*cont.*):
  parallels with Evans's version
    9 n. 22
  political resonances 24–9
  Purcell's incidental music 28
  rise and fall in popularity 217, 218
  significance 1–7
  source for Faucit 241–2
  sources 3–5, 21–4
  star performers 3
  tragedy of spectacle 17–18
Oedipus, Thomas Evans,
    publication, 1615 9 and n. 22
Oedipus, William Gager 8
Oedipus, Whitehead, completed by
    Mason 134 and n. 25,
    191 n. 18, 215, 216
*Oedipus, A Musical Drama in 3
    Acts*, John Savill Faucit 240–2
    and n. 99, 267, 274
Oedipus and Antigone (lost), John
    Flaxman 211–13
Oedipus in the Haymarket,
    Planché 378
Oedipus, King of Thebes, George
    Somers Clark (prose
    translation) 240
Oedipus, King of Thebes, Gilbert
    Murray's version 537–8
Oedipus, King of Thebes, Lewis
    Theobald, illustrated *47*
Oedipus, King of Thebes, Robert
    Potter, metaphysical
    orientation 221
Oedipus, King of Thebes, Thomas
    Arne 28 n. 81
Oedipus Masque,
    J. E. Galliard 28 n. 81
Oedipus Oetaeus, pseudo-
    Seneca 197
*Oedipus Tyrannus, or Swellfoot the
    Tyrant*, Shelley
  awareness of Greek original 233

  comic dimensions 235–6
  considered a failure 235 n. 70
  importance of chorus 233, 236–9
  parallel with satyr plays 236
  plot, themes 235–9
  political objectives 239
  relation to crisis over Queen
    Caroline 231–3
  suppression 233, 240
  title page 235
Of Education, John Milton,
    influence 117, 245, 253
Ogygia, island of 205
O'Hara, Kane (?1714–82) 56–8, 356
Oldfield, Mrs 79 and n. 30
Olive, Edyth 514, *515*, 516
Olympic Devils, James Robinson
    Planché 358
Olympic Revels, James Robinson
    Planché 338–9, 357–9
Olympic Theatre, burlesques
    in 338–9, 357, 366–7
On Divination, Cicero 149
'On Not Knowing Greek', Virginia
    Woolf 182
On the Sublime, Longinus 52
*One Thousand Seven Hundred and
    Thirty Eight, a Dialogue,
    Something Like Horace*,
    Alexander Pope 115
opera
  impact of Continental 52–3
  introduction of term 36
  IT a source for 62
  light, taste for 353
  significance of *Dirce* 273–4
  Sophocles' *Electra* rendered as
    psychosexual 152
  source of music for parodies in
    burlesque 366
  toleration of unnatural violence
    in 392
  see also individual works

Opium Wars 266, 384
Oracle of Delphi, authentic
    representations of scenery
    268
oracles, Oedipus' consciousness of
    ordinances 23
Oreste, Alfieri 124
Oreste, Giovanni Rucellai 41 and
    n. 37, 48
Oreste, Handel 34, 36, 49, 62 and
    n. 81
Oreste, Jean-Marie Janin, source
    for Bayley 275
Oreste, L', Benedetto Michaeli 62
Oreste, L', Giangualberto
    Barlocci 62
Oreste, Voltaire
  and Sophocles' *Electra* 152,
    173–4, 175
  source for Murphy's
    Alzuma 170
  Thomas Francklin's
    version 78 n. 22, 220
Oreste et Électre, 'Grand Tragic
    Ballet' 175–6
Oreste et Pilade, Lagrange-
    Chancel 48, 49
Oresteia, Aeschylus
  Frank Benson's tour with 432
  London venue for Benson's 492
    and n. 13
  reasons for Warr's choice of
    474–6
  translations, by Warr 472–3
  see also individual plays
Orestes (mythical figure)
  as analogue for son of George
    III 168
  as analogue for Young
    Pretender 166
  conceptual link with Hamlet xxi,
    155
  costuming of 280

figure representing, in
    Alzuma 171–2
  portrayals of 275, 277, *278*, 371
  representations of 90–1, 104,
    157–2, 163, 180, 334, 385
Orestes, Euripides
  educational study
    encouraged 253–4
  English translation published at
    Reading School 254
  murder of Clytemnestra 92 n. 83
  performances
    at Reading School 243–4,
      251–2, 254, 259, 262, 304
    reviewed by London *Star*
      256
    reviewed by Mitford 243,
      254, 261, 263
Orestes, Lewis Theobald
  adaptation of *IT* 36
  and comic dimension of
    Iphigenia 54–60, 356
  influence of Aeschylyus'
    Eumenides 55 n. 72, 11 n. 26
  scenic, musical elements 59–60
Orestes, Pikering's ('*Horestes*') 163
    and n. 18
Orestes, Thomas Francklin 174
Orestes in Argos, Peter Bayley
  costuming of 280–1
  frontispiece *278*
  playbill *276*
  sources 267, 275–7
  visual impact 277, *279*
Origen, *Against Celsus* 149
Orpheus, transvestite portrayal
    of 367
Orpheus; or, the Magic Lyre,
    Burnand 383
Orpheus and Eurydice, Henry Byron,
    burlesque 363, 370, *371*
Osmyn (Alphonso), representations
    of 157–62, 170

Ossian 193–4
Ottoman Empire
  conceptual link with
    Achaemenid Persia 265
  equation with barbaric
    opponents of Greece
    38–9
  Greece under domination of
    333
  importance of relationship with
    Greece xi, xix
  see also Greece, modern
Our Greek Play, anon., 1892
  387–8
*Our School, or, Scraps and Scrapes
  in Schoolboy Life*, B. B. Bockett
  (Oliver Oldfellow) 259–60
Ovid 130, 359, 363, 366–7
Owen, Robert, *Hypermnestra, or
  Love in Tears* 43
Owenson, Sydney, *see* Morgan
Oxford Classical Texts, Murray's
  contribution to 494
Oxford University
  anxieties about cross-dressed
    theatricals 452
  ban on theatrical
    performances 286, 384, 431
  defied 286
  cross-dressed roles
    prohibited 452, 458,
    485–6
  early productions in 8
  Greek plays
    fashionable events 459
    importance 457
    privileging of Homer 476
  political, religious controversies
    satirized 384–5
  Triennial Visitation of Reading
    School 248–50
  undergraduate theatricals 383–5
    and n. 152

see also Oxford University
  Dramatic Society *and
  individual colleges*
Oxford University Dramatic
  Society
  Alan Mackinnon the founder
    of 456
  Alcestis, 1887 458–9, 485–6

Paine, Tom 301–2
Palace Theatre 548–9, 551
Palaeologus, Gregorios, *The
  Death of Demosthenes*
  273 n. 30
Palairet brothers, in Reading
  School's *Orestes* 254
Palgrave, Francis Turner,
  'Alcestis: A Poem' 443 n. 25
*Pan, or, the Loves of Echo and
  Narcissus*, Henry
  Byron 379–80, *380*
Pandora 357
Pankhurst, Emmeline 512
Pankhurst, Sylvia 518
pantomime
  annual, at Drury Lane 338
  danseuse en travesti tradition
    367
  mid-nineteenth-century
    development 351–2
Paradise Lost, John Milton,
  adaptation for stage 15–16
parody, taste for, in ancient
  Greece 55
'Parr rebellion' 227–8
Parr, Samuel (1747–1825)
  association with Richard
    Valpy 248
  early member of London Greek
    Committee 271 n. 21
  Greek plays staged at Stanmore
    School 174 n. 55 192, 225,
    244, 431

influence 224–8, 228–2, 234
influence of Milton 253
radicalism 224, 227–8
satirical illustrations *229*,
229–31
Spital Sermon 228
support for Queen Caroline 230
Parratt, Walter 453
parricide
execution of Charles I perceived
as 9–10
ground for censorship 530–4
link with incest, regicide 22, 24
recoil from, in adaptations of
Greek tragedy 6
rejection by Joyner 11
Parry, John Welsh 192
Parson Adams, sources for 111 and
n. 26
Parthenon, influence on stage
design 290
passion, relation between reasons,
sympathy and 84
Pasta, Giuditta 391–2 and n. 6
Patience, Gilbert and Sullivan 387
*Patient Penelope; or, The Return
of Ulysses*, Francis Burnand
364
Patriot King, Whig concept
of 114–15
Patriot opposition, membership,
aims 104–8
patriotism, dominant theme in
Talfourd's works 314
Pausanias, *Description of Greece* 65
Peace and Wealth,
Aristophanes 244
Peacock, Thomas Love 531 n. 19
Peel, Robert 342, *342*
Penelope
actresses portraying 77
as prototype of distressed
mother 75–8

Penshaw Monument, 306, *307*
Pentheus, representations of
497–9, 505–8
Pentheus, Amcott 381, 383–4
'people's theatre', Reinhardt's
concept of 521–6
Pepys, Samuel 79
performance genres,
importance xviii
performance history, effect on
scholarly opinion of ancient
texts xxii
performance styles, *see* acting *and
under individual artists*
Pergami, Bartolomeo 231, *232*
Persia, ancient, fashion for
theatrical settings, revivals
61
Persian Princess, Lewis
Theobald 55 n. 72
Persians, Aeschylus
actors, actresses in 514
burlesque of 384
cultural, historical impact 264–7
and nn. 2–7
French version (*Les Perses*)
inspired by Aeschylus
265
influence xi, 55 n. 72, 101
Karolos Koun's use of chorus,
1960s 197–8
performances
in Britain, 1907 265–6
for patriotic purposes, in
France, Greece
265–6
publication of speech by Darius
to illustrate effects of
war xi n. 10
Renaissance enactment 265
as source 234
translation by B. J. Ryan
262 n. 5, 514

Peru
    setting for *Alzuma* 169–72
    theatrical traditions of Rome
       and, compared 202
Peterloo massacre 237, 289
*Petraki Germano; or, Almanzar the
    Traitor*, J. Dobbs, pro-Greek
    stance 271
Phaedra
    need for exculpation of 96–7
    portrayals of *73, 74*, 79, 515
    pro-feminine figure 87
    representations of 86 and n. 59,
       87, 199
    type of 'distressed mother' 63
    inspiration for Thomas
       Rymer 70
    Madame Rachel's acclaimed
       performance in 402
    nineteenth-century
       productions 32 n. 6
    source for John Dennis 48
    success, influence 71
Phaedra and Hippolitus, Edmund
    Smith
    actresses in 79
    importance 88 n. 65
    popularity 72 and n. 16
    revivals 88, 129, 133
    'she-tragedy' 66, 71–2 and n. 16,
       86 and n. 59
Phaeton, Charles Gildon 36, 66,
    71, 118
Phèdre, Racine
*Phaeton; or, Pride Must Have a
    Fall*, William Brough 383
Phanariot community, Odessa,
    production of Sophocles'
    Philoctetes 272
Pharsalia, Lucan 75
Phaeton, Quinault, influence 49,
    71, 118
Phèdre, see Phaedra

Phenomenology, Hegel 320–1
Phidias 318
Philip, Ambrose 42, 67, *68, 69*
Philips, Katherine 83
Phillips, William, *Hibernia
    Freed* 42
Philoctetes, Sophocles
    inspiration for neo-classical
       painting 275 n. 38
    Mason's work compared
       favourably with 211
    performance by pupils of
       Thomas Sheridan 246
    as source 110, 190–1, 272
    translation by Thomas
       Sheridan 110, 246
    in Wakefield's school
       selection 289
Phocion 310–11
Phoenician Women (*Phoenissae*),
    Euripides
    archetypal civil war tragedy 9,
       43–4
    as source 43–4, 66, 82, 190–1,
       274, 293–4
    unlikely reading from, at
       Reading School 253 n. 41
Phorbas, representation of 143–4,
    148–9
photography, impact on accuracy
    of theatrical
    productions 324–5
physicality, of performer, emphasis
    on 546 and n. 70
Pichat, Michel, *Léonidas* 277 n. 45
Pikering, John, *Horestes* 163 and
    n. 18
Pirithoüs, the Son of Ixion,
    Burnand 371
plagiarism
    Congreve accused of 162
    widespread in eighteenth
       century 3

Plague, 1665, response of
dramatists to 25, 27
Planché, James Robinson
(1794–1880)
archaeological interests 343,
477
burlesque of *The Birds* 345–7,
346
concepts of burlesque and
extravaganza 343, 355 and
n. 28, 477
Huguenot associations 34 n. 19
Olympic Devils 358
Olympic Revels, burlesque of
classical mythology
338–9
search for authenticity 347, 432,
477
socio-educational background
372
stated objectives 347
see also *The Golden Fleece*
Plautus
performance of plays by pupils of
Thomas Sheridan 245
plays performed at Reading
School 249
popularity of plays on
Continent 244
Pliny the Elder, writings searched
for druidical lore 203
*Pluto and Proserpine; or the Belle
and the Pomegranate, An
Entirely New and Original
Mythological Extravaganza of
the 0th Century*, classical
burlesque, H. J. Byron, 359,
381 n. 139
Plutus, Aristophanes
translations
by Henry Burnell 40
by Theobald 55, *56*
by Young and Fielding xvii

Poe, Edgar Allan 336–7
Poel, William (1852–1934)
association with Granville
Barker 495
interest in Murray's
Hippolytus 494, 495
productions of *Alcestis* 445 n. 35,
519 and n. 128
staging of Murray's *Bacchae* 498
and n. 40, 551
*Poems and Miscellaneous Pieces with
a free translation of the Oedipus
Tyrannus of Sophocles*,
Thomas Maurice 222
Poems on Various Subjects, Thomas
Talfourd 289
poetic justice, concept of, and death
of Oedipus 9
Poetics, see Aristotle
Poiret, Paul 549
Poland, Greek tragedy in vii n. 2
politics
butt of humour in Theobald's
IT 59
place at centre of culture, in age
of reform 314–15; *see also*
Reform Act *and individual
authors, plays*
and religion, concepts of
Murray, Shaw 497–9
see also Tories; Whigs
Polynices, Sophoclean, model for
Arviragus 188
Pomponius Mela 203
Poor Law Amendment
Act, 1834 296
Pope, Alexander (1688–1744)
admired by William Mason 190
commendation of *The Fatal
Legacy* 82 and n. 42
at opening of Thomson's
Agamemnon 106
in 'Patriot' opposition 104

Pope, Alexander (1688–1744)
  (*cont*.):
  projected *Brutus* 190 and n. 15
  satire on Walpole as
    'Egisthus' 115
Pope, Elizabeth (Elizabeth
  Younge) *68*, 94 n. 91, *131*, *158*
pornography, *poses plastiques*
  verging on 389–90
Porson, Richard (1759–1808) 155,
  251–2, 252–3, 256–7
Porteous Riots, Edinburgh 105
Porter, Mary Ann 80, 93, 113–14
Portsmouth, burlesques performed
  in 359
Portugal, Ristori's performance as
  Medea in 404
poses plastiques 30 and n. 3, 389–90
Potsdam, staging of *Antigone* in
  Neues Palace 320
Potter, Robert
  in praise of Mason 210–11
  translations 111 and n. 26,
    209–10 and n. 104, 220–2
power, absolute, threatened by
  erotic passion 39
Poynter, E. J. 463–4, 471
Pre-Raphaelites, fascination with
  Alcestis 443 n. 25
Pretenders, Old and Young,
  ancient models for 43–4
Prince of Wales, *see* Frederick,
  Prince of Wales
Prince's Hall, Piccadilly 462–8,
  474–5
Princess's Theatre, Oxford Street,
  production of *The Ruins of
  Athens; A Dramatic
  Masque* 333–4
Pritchard, Hannah (1711–68) 80,
  129 and n. 7, 144, *145*
private theatricals, popularity of
  Whitehead's *Creusa* 130

Prometheus, anonymous
  pantomime 111 n. 26
Prometheus, costume in *Olympic
  Revels* 358
*Prometheus; or, the Man on the
  Rock!*, Robert Reece 359–60,
  360, 367, *368*
Prometheus and Pandora, see
  Olympic Revels
Prometheus Bound, Aeschylus
  parallels in *Samson Agonistes* 13
  translations
    by Augusta Webster 473
    by Potter 111 and n. 26,
      209–10 and n. 104
Prometheus Unbound, Shelley 234,
  237, 239
property, invidious laws 401–2,
  416, 420
Protestant succession, *see*
  monarchy
Protestantism, and classical
  scholarship 35
public good, Whig principle
  of 114–15
public houses, access to classical
  culture through 389–90
Pullen, Alice, *see* Dene, Dorothy
Punch
  Antigone cartoons *323*, 337–8,
    342
  appeal of 354
  on Maynooth controversy 342,
    342
  reviews
    of *Helena in Troas* 463 and
      nn. 7–8, 467–8
    of Oxford Greek plays 459, *460*
Punishment of Incest Act,
  1908 532–3
puns, essential to burlesque
  364–5
Purcell, Henry xix, 28, 38

Puritans
  association of theatricals with
    Roman Catholicism 163
  Ordinance banning stage plays,
    1642 163, 164–5, 244
  royalist dramatists' attacks
    on 163–5
Purvis, Billy, fairground
  theatre 388–9
Pygmalion, George Bernard Shaw,
  source of inspiration 483 and
  n. 70
Pygmalion and Galatea, myth
  reflected in association of
  Leighton and Dene 483–4
Pylade et Oreste, Coqueteau de La
  Clairière 41 and n. 37
Pylades
  brother–sister bond with
    Electra 304
  figure representing, in
    Alzuma 171–2
Pythia, representation of 150

Qualification of Women
  Act, 1907 512
*Queen Dido, or the Trojan
  Ramblers* 55
Queen Mab, Shelley 293
Queen's College, Harley Street
  Alcestis
    music for 456–7 n. 70
    performance, 1886 457, *458*
Queen's Theatre (later King's
  Theatre)
  Antigone painted on proscenium
    arch 335
  burlesques performed at 367
  first performance of Smith's
    Phaedra and Hippolitus 72
  see also King's Theatre *and
    individual plays*
Quin, James, actor 107

Quinault, Philippe 49, 71, 118
Quincey, Thomas de 327–8,
  329–30

Rachel, Madame 402–3
Racine
  influence 33–6, 44, 67, 70
  influence of Euripides'
    Ion 132–3
  portrayal of Hippolytus–Phaedra
    myth 11
  source for *The Mourning
    Bride* 162
  see also individual plays
racism
  echoes of 351, 373
  in Nolan's *Agamemnon at
    Home* 383 n. 150
radicalism
  explicit, alien to burlesque 373
  link with Sophoclean
    Oedipus 240
  Parr's connections with 227–8
  and rereading of *Oedipus
    Tyrannus* 216–17
  and support for Queen
    Caroline 229–31
  *see also under individual
    protagonists*
railways, obsession with, in
  burlesque 346–7,
  381–2
Raleigh, Walter 538
Ralph, James 51, 200
Rangavis, Alexander, translation of
  Antigone 336
Rape of Proserpine, Lewis
  Theobald 54
Rapin de Thoyras, *History of
  England* 116
Rapin, Père, *Les Réflexions sur la
  poëtique*, Rymer's
  translation 16–17

Rasbotham, Dorning 50–1 and
n. 59
Rauzzini, Venazio, *Creusa in
Delfo* 151
Reading Abbey, girls school at 249
Reading, Berks.
Amateur Musical Society 251
social, cultural life 249–50, 257,
259–60
Talfourd the first elected MP
for 290
Reading School
impact on Thomas
Talfourd 287–9
link with Channel Islands 247
performances
of Greek tragedy 243–4, 248,
250–1, 251–2, 253–4, 255,
257, 259, 261–3, 304, 431
quest for authenticity 261–3
Triennial Visitation 248–50
venue for Greek plays 251
see also Mitford; Valpy
reason, relation between passion,
sympathy and 84
recognition scenes
in Bayley's *Orestes in Argos* 277
in Dryden and Lee's *Oedipus* 22
in Talfourd's *Ion* 293–4
significance 157–62, *160*, 172, 173
Redford, George Alexander,
Examiner of Plays 530 and
n. 16, 532–3, 534, 535, 536,
537, 541–2
Reece, Robert 359–60, *360*, 367
Reflections on the French Revolution,
Edmund Burke 231
Reform Act, 1832 281, 284, 285,
298–9, 306
reform movement 284–5, 363,
372–3 and n. 102
regicide
and civil war 26

echoes of Greek drama, in *The
Athenian Captive* 303–4
link with fear of incest,
parricide 22
relevance of Sophoclean theme
to English monarchy 7,
157–8, 159
Sophocles' treatment of 22
Reinhardt, Max (1873–1943)
concept of 'people's theatre' 526
'cosmopolitan corporeality' 528,
546, 547
influence 542–3 and n. 56, 548
productions
Medea 512
Oedipus Rex 522–6 and n. 5,
523, 538–2, 546, 547, 548,
553, 554
Wilde's *Salomé* 538, 548
religion
concept of features shared by
Greek, druidical 204
concern for, in Aeschylean
choruses 221
eighteenth-century attitudes
to 147–50
link between radical, and love of
classics xvii
and politics, concepts of Murray,
Shaw 497–9
reconciliation of Greek with
Christianity 149–50,
310–11, 329–30
Religious Dramatic Society,
University of London 35
republicanism
and association of monarchy with
incest 9–10
attractions of Aeschylus'
Persians 265 n. 2
inspired by Greek, Roman
models 50
in John Milton 12–13, 20

Thomas Talfourd's sympathy
with 298–300, 373 and
n. 102
and Whig adaptations of Greek
tragedy 50
Restoration, The
experiments with Greek
tragedy xviii
strength of French influence
xix, 7
vogue for heroic drama 13–14
Wase's celebration of 165
see also monarchy
resurrection motif, difficulties for
British theatre-goers
117–18 n. 42
revenge tragedy, first English 163
Reynolds, Joshua 89 and n. 71,
180
Rhigas, revolutionary
balladeer 264–5 and n. 2
rhyme, and blank verse, attitudes
to 52
Rice, Charles 389
Rich, John 58
Richardson, John 339
Richardson, Samuel 90
Richmond, W. B. 453
Rienzi, Mary Russell Mitford 308
Rigg, Diana 429
Ristori, Adelaide
(1822–1906) 402–4 and n. 45,
403, *405*, 412, 438
Ritualists, Cambridge 497, 507
Robe, Jane (*floruit* 1723), *The Fatal
Legacy* 44 and n. 45, 66, 82–3
and n. 42
Roberdeau, John Peter 248,
266 n. 7
Robin Hood, pantomime
theme 351–2
Robin Hood, William Brough 383

Robins, Elizabeth 518
Robinson Crusoe, source for
Thomson's *Agamemnon* 110
Robinson, Henry Crabb 290 and
n. 33, 392
Robson, Eleanor 504
Robson, Frederick 369 n. 86,
410–15, *411*, 436, 436–8
Rochlitz, Johann Friedrich,
adaptation of *Antigone* 319–20
Rodd, Rennell 453
Roman Empress, The, Joyner xvi
Romanticism
as focus for rebels, social
critics 239–40
German, influence of
Sophocles 318
impact of acquisition of classical
antiquities 290 n. 35
influence of Mason 211
Thomson recognized as a
forerunner of 126
Rome, ancient
admiration for druids' resistance
to 190 and n. 15, 202–4
conceptual link between early
Britain and 184–7, 190,
191–2
conceptual links between history
and drama xxi. 184–6
nineteenth-century play inspired
by 284
parallel with growth of British
empire 183, 184
plays deriving from comedies x
and n. 8
republican symbols invoked by
French revolutionaries
216
revivalism 61, 89 and n. 71
theatrical traditions of Peru and,
compared 202

Rome, ancient (*cont*.):
  tragedies, as manifestation of
    English classicism 66 and
    n. 7
  Whig ideals derived from 50,
    105
Romeo and Juliet, Shakespeare 335
Romney, George
  cartoons of Aeschylus 209, *210*
  *Medea Contemplating the Murder
    of her Children* 95 and n. 95,
    96
Romola, George Eliot 332
Ross, Lady Katherine 78
Rossini, *Le Siege de Corinthe* 275
Rotaller, Georgius 163
Rousseau, Jean Jacques 86
Rowe, Nicholas (1674–1718)
  concept of tragedy 75–8
  Electra compared with
    Hamlet 155, 179
  Jane Shore 75
  scholarship, influence 75–8 and
    n. 19
  she-tragedies revived 88
  Tamerlane 42
  use of term 'she-tragedy' 75
Rowlands, Henry 204
Roxana, William
  Alabaster 117 n. 39
Royal Academy 173, 176–7, 479,
  480
Royal Commission on
  Divorce 399, 417–18
Royal Court Theatre, *see* Court
  Theatre
Royal Institution, educational
  policy 470, 471
Royal Navy, Valpy's interest
  in 246–7
Royal West London Theatre,
  significant *Oedipus* at 240–2,
  274

Royalists, responses to Greek
  drama xvii
Royalty Theatre 364
Rubens, 'Simon and Pero (Roman
  Charity)' 180 n. 71
Rucellai, Giovanni, *Oreste* 41 and
  n. 37, 48
Rugby School, *Medea* performed
  at 225 n. 39
ruins, classical, theatrical
  recreation of 268–9, 269, 273,
  277–81
Rule Britannia, origins,
  context 99, 104–5
Ruskin, John 475
Russell, Bertrand 494
Russell, Lord John 285
Ryan, B. J., translation of
  Persians 262 n. 5, 514
Rymer, Thomas (1641–1713)
  A Short View of Tragedy 266
  concept of Greek tragic
    heroines 69–70
  influence on Dryden 16–17
  proposed relocation of
    Aeschylus' *Persians* to
    Spain 101
  Talfourd's essay on 287 n. 24
  use made of Greek tragedy xv

sacrifice
  of maiden, popularity of
    theme 32, 62, 64–5
  for the public good, in Whig
    ideology 114–15
Sadayakko 545 and n. 63
Sadler's Wells Theatre 419
St Andrews University,
  performances of authentic
  Greek tragedy 431, 448
St Bartholomew's Fair 356
St George's Hall, London 453–4
St James's Hall 335 n. 48

St James's Theatre, classical
burlesques 359; *see also*
individual plays
St John's College,
Cambridge 244 n. 2
St John's College, Oxford 383
St Leonard's School, St Andrews
456
Salamis, Battle of 264, 265 n. 2,
266
Sallé, Marie 30–1, 62
Salome, Oscar Wilde 538, 551–3
Salomé, Richard Strauss 538, 551
Salvation Army
links between Dionysiac cult
and 499–500
Shaw's response to 500–2; see
also *Major Barbara*
Samson Agonistes, John Milton
and Aristotelian definition of
tragedy 14–15
influence on Dryden 14–15,
15–16, 20
not designed for performance 13
sources in Greek tragedy 12–14
translation into Greek 225
use of chorus 196
Sandbach, Margaret, *Antigone* 330
Sandford, Samuel 17
Sappho, burlesques, variants 385
Sappho, William Mason 191 n. 18
Sappho; or, Look Beford You Leap,
Burnand 383
Sargon, myth of 128 and n. 1
satire, rejection in favour of
romantic approach 124
satyr plays, *Oedipus Tyrannus, or
Swellfoot the Tyrant* as 236
savage, educable, concepts of 49
Savoy Theatre 431, 511
Saxe-Meiningen Company 432
and n. 5
Sayers, Frank 211

Scaliger, Joseph 35
Scandinavia, contribution of
authors from xix–xx
Scarron, Paul, *Virgile travesti* 339
scenery, *see* spectacle; stage design
Schiller, *Die Braut von Messina*,
experimental use of
chorus 196 n. 42
Schlegel, August Wilhelm von
(1767–1845)
adaptation of *Ion* 289 n. 27,
319–20
denunciation of Euripides 443
Dramatic Literature 326
lectures on Greek tragedy 318,
320, 443, 475, 478
Schliemann, archaeological
excavations 449, 455, 475–6
Schweitzer, Anton 441 n. 19
Scotland
criminalization of incest 532
English fear of domination of
government by Scots
168
Scott, Walter
recoil from depiction of
incest 530
response to *Oedipus*, Dryden
and Lee 1, 5–6, 9, 215 and
n.2
Scott, William, Professor of
Greek 112
sculptural metaphor, simile 328,
335, 484
sculpture, Greek 125–6, 280,
545–6
Sellers, Eugénie, *see* Strong
Seneca
adaptors' choice of Greek texts
dramatized by 130
compared unfavourably with
Mason 211
influence 22, 66–7, 125

Seneca (*cont.*):
  performance of plays on
    Continent 244
  portrayal of Hippolytus–Phaedra
    myth 11, 86 n. 59
  as source 109, 112, 163
sensibility, eighteenth-century
  concept of 90–1, 124
Septem, Aeschylus 253 n. 41
Settle, Elkanah, *The Siege of
  Troy* 54
Seven Years War 170, 172, 183–4
Seward, Anna 211
Sewrin, C., *La Sorcière* 404 n. 48
sexual deviancy
  fascination with xvi
  Maud Allan accused of 548, 553
  see also homosexuality; incest
Shaftesbury, Earl of 27, 52
Shakespeare, William
  conceptual links with Greek
    drama xxi
  inspiration for Todhunter's
    Alcestis 445
  productions of, fashion for
    classical sets 268
  source of inspiration for
    burlesque 358–9
  use of chorus 196
Shaw, Fiona 152, 429
Shaw, George Bernard
  (1856–1950)
  attitude to incest 534 n. 27
  championship of Euripides 490
  concepts of religion,
    politics 497–9, 499–5
  criticisms of Edith Olive 515
  fascination with Nietzsche,
    Schopenhauer 493
  inspiration for *Pygmalion* 483
    and n. 70
  links with Euripides 490–1
  on marriage 488–9

  protest at censorship 529
  reaction to Murray's *Bacchae*
    499
  relationshp with Gilbert
    Murray 472, 491–4
  testimony to importance of
    theatre xvii
  see also individual plays
'she-author', origin of term 82 n. 42
she-tragedy
  classical sources 66–70
  coining of term 75
  echoed in visual arts 89 and n. 71
  focus on 'sensibility' 90–2
  impact of actresses, women
    authors, dramatists 78–8
    and n. 44, 90, 114
  importance xviii
  invention in British theatre 70–8
  move from passion to
    compassion 83–8
  transformation of original
    Agamemnon to 112–15
Shebbeare, John, *The Marriage
  Act* 141–2 and n. 41
Shelley, Percy Bysshe (1792–1822)
  appeal of Greek tragedy to
    radicalism of xiii, 208,
    231–3, 242
  engagement with Oedipus myth
    217, 318
  impact of acquisitions of classical
    antiquities 290 n. 35
  influence 228–9, 292–3
  inspiration for Beatrice 180
  regenerative view of history
    293 n. 42
  romantic Hellenism 186–7,
    266–7, 292–3
  Todhunter's study of 531 n. 20
  see also *Hellas; Oedipus Tyrannus,
    or Swellfoot the Tyrant*
Shelley Society 530–1

Sheppard, John 521, 522–3
Sheridan, Richard Brinsley
    (1751–1816) 245, 394
Sheridan, Dr Thomas
    (1687–1738) 3, 110, 244–5
Sheridan, Thomas (actor)
    (1719–88) 3, *4*, 245
Sherwood, Mary 249
Shiels, Robert, *Life of*
    Thomson 127
Shirley, William xiii, 103, 166–7,
    179, 277, 529
Short View of the Immorality and
    Profaneness of the English
    Stage, A, Jeremy Collier 70
Short View of Tragedy, A, Thomas
    Rymer 266
Shrewsbury School, *Ion* translated
    into Greek iambics at 286 and
    n. 17
Siddons, Sarah (1755–1831)
    née Kemble 268
    roles 94 and n. 91, 123–4, 152,
        180, 181, 211
    Talfourd impressed by 307–8
    techniques modelled on Greek
        statuary 280
'Simon and Pero (Roman
    Charity)', Rubens 180 n. 71
Sitwell family, in *The Tale of*
    Troy 476
Slangweazy tendency, and
    censorship 531 and
    n. 22
slavery
    abolition 284–5, 306–7
    opposition to 189 n. 10, 191
    unendurable in Talfourd's
        Athens 311
Smirke, Robert 268–9 and n. 13,
    270
Smith, Adam, *Theory of Moral*
    Sentiments 89

Smith, Araminta, translation of
    Heracles 254 n. 42
Smith, Edmund
    adaptation of Euripides'
        Hippolytus 43, 71–2
    Phaedra and Hippolitus, 'she-
        tragedy' 66, 71–2 and n. 16,
        86 and n. 59
    use made of Greek tragedy 61
Smith, J., *Creon the Patriot* 272
Smith, John 206
Smith, Madeleine 415
Smith, Rebecca 425 n. 18
Smith, William 194
Smollett, Tobias, lost masque on
    Alcestis 118 and n. 44
social hellenism
    in fashion *481*
    manifestations of 479–82
social status
    disparities in, challenged by
        burlesque 348–9, 350; *see*
        also individual plays
    implications explored in
        Whitehead's *Creusa* 142–3
        and n. 42
    relevance to
        attitudes to infanticide
            518–19
        life of Dorothy Dene 484
        marriage of George Warr 472
            and n. 32
Society of the Friends of the
    People 224
Sohrab, William Jones 265 n. 2
Soldene, Emily 353
song
    central to burlesque 366–71 and
        n. 76
    see also music
Songs of the Governing Classes,
    Robert Brough 372, 415
Sophianos, Michael 265

Sophocles
  concept of monarchy, tyranny
      relevance in England 7,
          157–8, 159
    Restoration interest in 9–10
    topicality in 1820s 273
  Dryden's debt to 21–4
  English engagement with 318
  influence on James
      Thomson 110
  Potter's perception of 221
  proliferation of nineteenth-
      century productions 316–18
  psychoanalytical readings of
      Theban royal family
      xxi–xxii
  rewriting for performance in
      English x
  Robert Louis Stevenson's
      reaction to 447–8
  source for burlesque 360
  translations, editions
    by Adams 147, 172
    by Dacier 198
    by Francklin 147, 172–8, 220
    by Jebb 473 n. 37
    by Potter 220–2
    by Stanley 154
    by Theobald 55, 172
    by William Bartholomew
        319 n. 8
  see also individual plays
Sophonisba, Alfieri 124
Sophonisba, James Thomson 103,
    109, 124
Sotheby, William 213–14, 266 n. 7
Soumet, Alexandre,
    Clytemnestre 275
South Africa, *see* Boer War
South Kensington
  building for ladies' college 464
      and n. 12, 470
  'Hellenism' 481

South Villa, Regents' Park,
    performances in 445 n. 35,
        513 n. 106
Southey, Robert 211
Spain
  imperialism attacked by
      Murphy 170–2
  Ristori's Medea in 404
Spanish Armada 266
spectacle
  in burlesque 366, 370–1 and
      n. 90
  development in British theatre
      7, 14, 35
  in Dryden and Lee's *Oedipus*
      17–18
  in *Helena in Troas* 459
  increasing taste for 267–8,
      277–81, 284, 392, 441, 478–9
  in Lewis Theobald's *Orestes*
      59–60
  in productions of *Alcestis* 334,
      459
  in Wooler's *Jason and Medea*
      399–400
  see also stage design
Spedding, B. J., stage directions
    365
Sphinx, Brough brothers, actresses
    in 368–9, *369*
Spicer, Henry, *Alcestis* 439–2 and
    n. 19, *440*, 443
sporting competitions, routines
    borrowed from, in burlesque
    371
stage design
  attempts at authenticity 268–9,
      277–80, 439, 463 and n. 8,
      477–8
  decor based on classical
      figures 389
  elaborate, in Hoftheater,
      Weimar 320

for
  Bayley's *Orestes in Argos*,
    visual impact 277
  burlesque 364
  Covent Garden *Antigone* 324,
    439
  Dirce, importance of 273
  *Electra in a New Electric
    Light* 361
  Fitzball's *Antigone* 274–5
  Helena in Troas 459, 463 and
    n. 8, 477–8
  Mason's *Caractactus* 188–9
  Mendelssohn *Antigone*, praise
    for 478–9
  Planché's burlesque of *The
    Birds* 345–7
  Reading School's Greek
    plays 251–2
  Spicer's *Alcestis* 439–41
  increased attention to 174
  influence of
    Gordon Craig 544
    Reinhardt 539–40, 543
  notable, in OUDS *Alcestis*
    458–9
  see also spectacle
stage directions, for burlesque
  361–2, 365
staging, separation of chorus from
  actors 453
Standard Theatre, Shoreditch
  352, 417, 419, 430 and n. 2
Stanford, Charles Villiers 475, 478
Stanislavsky, *Antigone* 336
Stanley, Thomas 40, 100–2 and
  n. 4, 154
Stanmore School
  abandonment of chorus 197
  association of William Jones
    with 302 n. 66
  Greek plays staged at 174 n. 55,
    192, 225, 245, 248, 431

Parr's period at 228
state, the
  concept of, in Talfourd's *Ion*
    299
  Utilitarian concept of
    functions 297
statuary, statues
  experiments with sculptural
    effects 280, 335
  taste for 125–6, 280, 328, 484,
    545–6
Steele, Richard
  admiration for Greek tragedy
    88
  The Conscious Lovers 135
Stevenson, Robert Louis
  447–8
Stockdale, Percival 208
Stoker, Mrs Bram 476
stone circles, druidic, association
  with ancient Greeks 204,
  205
Stonehenge 204 and n. 81, 205,
  206
Stowe gardens, classical models 50
  and n. 56
Strafford, Robert Browning 286
Strand Theatre, burlesques
  performed at 362, 363,
  364, 365, 366, 374, 387,
  433–4
Strauss, Richard
  censored *Salome* 538, 551
  reaction to *Elektra* 551
Strong, Eugénie 463 and n. 4
Stuart, James, *The Antiquities of
  Athens* 268
Stukeley, William 203, 205
Sturmy, *Love and Duty or The
  Distres't Bride* 43 and n. 41
Styrke, Issachar 434
Suetonius Paulinus, last stand of
  druids against 184

suffrage
  George Warr's approach, in
    context of 474
  universal male 298–9; *see also*
    Reform Act
  women's
    campaign for 414–15, 420,
      429, 512–13
    Dickinson's Private Members'
      Bill 512
    importance of *Medea*
      in 511–19
    irrelevance of *Alcestis* 519–20
    series of plays about 512–13
    supported by Murray 511–12
suicide
  committed in the common good
    in Addison's *Cato* 308 see also
      Ion
  by Talfourd's classical
    heroes 308
Sullivan, Arthur 354; *see also*
  individual operas
supernatural, the, rejection by
  Dennis 48
Suppliants, Aeschylus, Isadora
  Duncan's dances for 546
Swift, Jonathan 104
Swinburne, Algernon xv, 31
sympathy
  concept of, as pivotal element in
    good society 85
  evocation of, in visual arts,
    drama 89
  relation between passion,
    reason 84
Synge, J. M., protest at censorship
  529

tableaux vivants
  erotic, pornographic
    aspects 389–90
  Victorian taste for 30 and n. 3, 479

Tacitus 184, 203
Taglioni, Paul, ballet
  Electra 360–1
Talbot, William Fox 324
Talfourd, Field 287
Talfourd, Francis (Frank)
  (1828–62)
  as actor 286, 436 and n. 12, *437*
  inspired by Ovid 359
  obituary 385–6
  socio-educational
    background 360, 372,
    373–4 and n. 108, 431
  see also *Alcestis: the Original*
    Strong-minded Woman;
    Electra in a New Electric
    Light
Talfourd, Rachel 287, 310
Talfourd, Thomas Noon
  (1795–1854)
  anti-slavery views 306–7, 311
  association with Bulwer-
    Lytton 291
  concept of 'fascination' shared
    with Byron 295 and n. 47
  debt to Valpy 260, 287–9
  editor of works of Charles
    Lamb 287 n. 24
  essays on Dennis and
    Rymer 287 n. 24
  impressed by Sarah
    Siddons 307–8
  influence of Hannah More's
    'sacred dramas' 310 n. 85
  introduction of Infant Custody
    Act, 1839 290, 394–5, 435
  philanthropy 290
  pivotal position in British
    theatre 308 and nn. 77, 79
  proponent of heroic tragedy 436
  radical, republican stance 151,
    284 and n. 5, 285, 299,
    303–7, 312, 314–15

reception of
  initial triumphant
    success 285–7
  later neglect 285 and n. 7,
    311–12
  reviews
    of *Dirce* 273–4
    of Reading School's
      Hecuba 255
  socio-political background xvii,
    255, 281, 287–91, *288*,
    318–21, 372
  sources of inspiration 233 n. 63,
    262, 292–3, 301, 307–9, 318
  style of Browning and,
    compared 308 n. 78
  support for repeal of Theatrical
    Patents Act 416
  view of classical Athens as model
    for national theatre 102
  see also *Ion*; *The Athenian
    Captive*
Talfourd, W. 436 n. 13
Talma, Citizen 125, 277 n. 45,
  280 n. 48
Tamerlane, Nicholas Rowe 42
Tarquin's Overthrow, William
  Bond 105
Taylor, Helen 396
Temple, Richard 50
Tennyson, Lionel, in *The Tale of
  Troy* 466
Terence 34 n. 17, 244, 245
Ternan, Mrs 334
Terry, Ellen 454, 544
Test and Corporation Act, repeal,
  1828 284; *see also* University
  Test Acts
Thackeray, William
  Makepeace 287, 375
The Acting National Drama 355
The Ambitious Stepmother,
  Nicholas Rowe, themes 75

'The *Antigone* and its Moral',
  George Eliot 331–2 and n. 41
The Antiquities of Athens, James
  Stuart 268
The Athenian Captive, Thomas
  Talfourd
  concept of utopian freedom
    in 293
  death of Thoas 306 and n. 71
  democratic ideals 300
  denunciation of slavery 306–7
  editions of 285 n. 9
  political trajectory 284, 303–7
  religious commitment 310–11
  sources 304
  stage design 290
The Auditor, started in opposition
  to *The North Briton* 170
The Bard, Thomas Gray 192 and
  n. 25, 213
The Battle of Argoed Llwfain,
  William Whitehead 192 and
  n. 26
*The Battle of the Nile: A Dramatic
  Poem on the Model of the Greek
  Tragedy*, anon. 266 and n. 7
The Beggar's Opera, John Gay
  356
*The Birds of Aristophanes:
  A Dramatic Experiment in One
  Act*, James Robinson
  Planché 345–7, *346*, 359,
  367–8, 381–2
The Birth of Hercules, masque 166
The Briton, Ambrose Philip 42
The Captives, John Delap 65 n. 3,
  188 n. 7
The Careless Shepherdess, Thomas
  Goffe 163–4
The Cenci, Shelley
  association with Dryden and
    Lee's *Oedipus* 6
  banned, finally licensed 6, 530–1

The Cenci, Shelley (*cont.*):
  sources 180, 531
  themes of incest, parricide 6,
    530
The Chinaid, anon., burlesque
  of Aeschylus' *Persians* 266,
    530
The Citizen, William Shirley 166
The Clandestine Marriage,
  Garrick and Colman 141–2
  and n. 40
The Comic History of Rome, Gilbert
  Abott à Beckett 383
The Como-cal Hobby,
  G. Humphrey *232*
The Confidential Clerk, T. S. Eliot
  151
The Conquest of Granada, John
  Dryden 25–6, 66–7
The Conscious Lovers, Richard
  Steele 135
The Continence of Scipio, Benjamin
  West 46
The Death of Agamemnon, see
  Agamemnon, James Thomson
The Death of Alexander the Great,
  fairground drama 388
The Death of Demosthenes,
  Gregorios Palaeologus
  273 n. 30
The Death of Lucretia, Gavin
  Hamilton 89
*The Decline and Fall of the Roman
  Empire*, Edward Gibbon
  183–4
*The Deep Deep Sea; or, Perseus and
  Andromeda; an Original
  Mythological, Aquatic,
  Equestrian Burletta*, Planché
  366–7
*The Destruction of Jerusalem by
  Titus Vespasian*, John
  Crowne 101

The Destruction of Troy, John
  Bankes 66, 67 n. 8, 78
The Distres't Mother, Ambrose
  Philips 67, *68, 69*, 79, 98
The Doll's House, Ibsen 488
The Double Tongue, William
  Golding 150–1
The Duchess of Malfi 417
The Earl of Warwick, Thomas
  Francklin 173
The Examiner, attacks on Shirley
  in 170
The Factory Girl, politicized
  melodrama 314
The Fair Penitent, Nicholas
  Rowe 75–6
The Fall of Saguntum, Philip
  Frode 42
*The Fall of the Mogul, A Tragedy,
  Founded on an Interesting
  Portion of Indian History, and
  Attempted Partly on the Greek
  Model* 234, 236, 266
The Fatal Friendship, Catherine
  Trotter 83
The Fatal Legacy, Jane Robe 44
  and n. 45, 66, 82–3
*The Finding of the Infant Moses in
  the Bulrushes*, Francis
  Hayman 137–8
'The Fine Young English
  Gentleman', sung in *The
  Golden Fleece* 344–5, 398
The Foundling, Edward Moore 135
The Golden Calf, politicized
  melodrama 314
*The Golden Fleece; or, Jason in
  Colchis and Medea in Corinth*,
  James Robinson Planché
  actors, actresses in 368, 396, 410
  burlesque 342–5, *344*, 477
  Greek tag phrases 364
  influence, popularity 356–7

paratragic response to operatic
tradition 438
relevance to debate on divorce
395
role of chorus 378
significance of cross-dressed
roles 397
sources 342–5, 359, 378, 402
spectacle in 344, *344*
The Golden Pippin, Kane O'Hara
58
The Grand Duke, Gilbert and
Sullivan 482
The Grecian Daughter, Arthur
Murphy 153, 171–2, 180
*The Greeks and the Turks; or, the
Intrepidity of Jemmy, Jerry,
and a British Tar*,
C. E. Walker 270
The Grounds of Criticism in Poetry,
John Dennis 52
The Gypsey King, used in *Antigone
Travestie* 341
The Herald, or Patriot Proclaimer,
William Shirley 166
The Heroes, Charles Kingsley
424
The History of Greece, William
Mitford 301 and n. 64
*The History of Tom Jones, A
Foundling*, Henry Fielding 135
The Importance of Being Earnest,
Oscar Wilde 151
The Indian Queen, Dryden 38
The Lady of Lyons, Edward
Bulwer 308 n. 79
The Last Days of Pompeii, Edward
Bulwer-Lytton 296 and n. 50,
314
The Last of the Mohicans, James
Fenimore Cooper 296
The Life and Death of Jason,
William Morris 424

*The London Merchant, or The
History of George Barnwell*,
Lillo 126
'The Love of Alcestis', William
Morris 443 n. 25
The Marriage of Bacchus, James
Robinson Planché 365, 378
The Merchant of Venice,
Shakespeare 249
The Mill on the Floss, George
Eliot 332
*The Monument: A Poem Sacred to
the Immortal Memory of the
Best and Greatest of Kings*,
John Dennis 44–5, 52
The Mourning Bride, William
Congreve
influence of Sophocles'
Electra 153, 161–2
Miss Younge as Zara in *158*
popularity 157, 162
'recognition' scene 157–62, *160*
sources 162, 170, 180
*The Mufti's Tomb; or, The Turkish
Misers* 271
The Murder Room 316–17
The Mysterious Mother, Horace
Walpole 227
The Nereid's Love, David
Lyndsay 273 n. 30
The New Antigone, W. Francis
Barry 332
The New Spirit in Drama and Art,
Huntly Carter 553–4
The North Briton
attacks on Bute 167–8
The Auditor started in opposition
to 170
The Oath of the Young Warrior,
Michel Philibert Genod 301
*The Paphian Bower; or, Venus and
Adonis*, James Robinson
Planché 367

'The Passions, An Ode for Music',
William Collins 193
The Persian Princess, Lewis
Theobald 58
The Pickwick Papers, Charles
Dickens 290
The Press Gang, politicized
melodrama 314
*The Queen of Argos: A Tragedy in
Five Acts*, William Bell
Boscawen 273 n. 30
The Quintessence of Ibsenism,
George Bernard Shaw 488
*The Revolt of the Greeks; or, the
Maid of Athens* 271
The Ring and the Book, Robert
Browning 330
*The Rival Queens; or, the Death of
Alexander the Great*,
Nathaniel Lee 388
The Roman Empress, William
Joyner 10–12 and n. 28
The Roman Father, William
Whitehead 141, 301
The Royal Suppliants, John
Delap 64–6, 90, 188
*The Ruins of Athens; A Dramatic
Masque*, August von
Kotzebue 333
*The Ruins of Athens; A Dramatic
Masque*, translation by
William Bartholomew
333–4
The Seasons, James Thomson 99,
125–6
The Shewing up of Blanco Posnet,
George Bernard Shaw 535
The Siege of Memphis, Durfey
38
*The Siege of Missolonghi; or, the
Massacre of the Greeks* 271
The Siege of Troy, Elkanah
Settle 54

The Siege of Troy, Robert
Brough 351–2, *352*,
358–9, 365–6, 381, 385
The Sphinx, brothers Brough 380
The Story of Orestes, George
Warr 462–4 and n. 9, *464*,
467–8, 471, 478, 482
The Story of Troy, appearance of
Rennell Rodd in 453
The Subjection of Women, John
Stuart Mill 420
*The Suliote; or, The Greek
Family* 271–2
The Tale of Troy, George Warr
actors, actresses in 464, 476
performances for King's
College 465–6 and n. 12,
470
supported by Frederic
Leighton 482
tableaux from Homer 462, 464
and n. 9, 465, 466
*The Taming of Bucephalus, the Wild
Horse of Scythia; or the
Youthful Days of Alexander the
Great*, Andrew Ducrow 284
The Tempest, Shakespeare xxi, 37,
60
The Tragedie of Cleopatra, Samuel
Daniel 196
The Tragedie of Orestes, Thomas
Goffe 163
The Tragedies of Sophocles,
translated by Robert
Potter 220–2
The Tragedy of Medæa, Charles
Johnson 66, 86, 86–7, 88,
92–3
*The Tragedy of Tragedies; or, The
Life and Death of Tom Thumb*,
Henry Fielding 58, 60, 355–6
The Tuscan Treaty, William
Bond 105

The Unnatural Mother, anonymous
woman dramatist 82
The Victim, Charles Johnson 35
and n. 23
The West Indian, Richard
Cumberland 135
The Winter's Tale,
Shakespeare 117, 335, 445–6,
519–20
*The Wishes; or Harlequin's Mouth
Opened*, Richard Bentley
201–2 and n. 69, 207
The Woman in White, Wilkie
Collins 422
The Works of Ossian, Son of Fingal,
James Macpherson 193
Theatre Act, 1968 103
Théâtre de la République,
formation 125
Théâtre des Grecs, Le, Pierre
Brumoy 172, 179, 200, 219,
220
Theatre of Dionysus, Athens,
performance of *Oedipe Roi*,
1899, 521
Theatre Regulation Act, 1843 397,
528–9, 529–4
Theatre Royal, Dublin
search for authenticity 326–7
structure 326–7
see also individual plays
theatres (buildings)
decor based on classical
figures 389
ekkyklēma 17
exploitation of scenic
innovations 7, 14, 17–18,
277–80
forestage 17–18
Greek, at Bradfield
College 456–7 and n. 71
influence of Reinhardt 539–40,
543

largest in Britain 352
Restoration 18–20
restored Roman, at Orange
477
scenic stage 18
skēnē 18
theologeion/roof space 18–19
vista stage 18–20
see also stage design *and
individual theatres*
Theatrical Patents Act, repealed,
1843 290, 416
Thebes, conceptual link with plot
of *Coriolanus* xxi
Themistocles (ship), captained by
Hastings 267
*Themistocles, the Lover of his
Country*, Samuel Madden 42,
105
Theobald, Lewis (1699–1744)
apolitical stance 41–2, 61
Apollo and Daphne 54
characterization of
Electra 179–80
debt to Dacier 218
dramatic criticism 55 and n. 73
Greek scholarship 55
influence of *Circe* 58–9
mingling of Shakespearean, Greek
elements 56 and n. 76
possibly co-translator of
Sophocles' *Ajax* 75 and
n. 19
translations attacked by
Francklin 175
translations by 55, 75 and n. 19,
111 n. 26, 154–5, *156*
writings on nature and function
of drama 62
see also individual works
Theodectes, lost *Lynceus* 43 n. 41
Theory of Moral Sentiments, Adam
Smith 89

Thermopylae; or, the Repulsed Invasion, John Peter Roberdeau 248, 266 n. 7

Theseus, Sophoclean, model for Arviragus 188

Thespis, or the Gods Grown Old, Gilbert and Sullivan 354, 386–7 and n. 167

Thirlwall, Connop, *History of Greece* 302

Thoas
  death of, in Talfourd's *The Athenian Captive* 306 and n. 71
  portrayals of 303
  representations of 39–40, 49, 62, 303–7, 311

Thomas, Neville 201

Thomson, James (1700–48)
  advocate of national theatre 102–3 and n. 6
  ardent Whig 99, 102
  classical scholarship 111–12
  compared with Pierre Corneille 126
  forerunner of Romanticism 126
  importance xv, xviii, 124–7
  influence of Euripides on xiii, 66
  memorial 99, *100*
  opposition to Robert Walpole 99, 102, 103, 104–8
  relationship with Aaron Hill 107 n. 22
  view of classical models for free nation-states 50
  see also individual works

Thorndike, Sybil *xii,* 512

Thrale, Hester 65

Thucydides, on Athenian hair accessories 261–2

Thyestes, John Crowne 67

Thyestes, Seneca 163

Tieck, Ludwig 320

Timon of Athens, Shakespeare 269

Tiresias, representations of 218–20, 222–4, 223, 274, 294, 296, 302, 303–7, 304–5, 321, 322, 331–2, 340–1

To a Friend, Matthew Arnold 330

Todhunter, John (1839–1916)
  debt to Browning 445
  Helena in Troas 458–9
  preface for production of *The Cenci* 531 and n. 20
  rivalry with Warr 467
  study of Shelley 531 n. 20
  version of *Alcestis* 445 and n. 35, 467

Tom Thumb, Henry Fielding 1–2, 355–6

Tomkins, Charles 274–5

Tories
  associated with oppression of labouring classes 295–6
  defeat, 1830 284–5
  response to Dryden and Lee's *Oedipus* 29
  unpopularity under George IV 284

Toynbee Hall, extension lectures 472 and n. 33

Trachiniae, Sophocles
  actors, actresses in 513
  as source 110, 197, 293–4
  Lewis Campbell's productions 447–8
  performances in aid of Building Fund 506 n. 106
  Robert Louis Stevenson's reaction to 447–8
  staged at Stanmore School 174 n. 55, 225
  translations, editions

by Campbell 448–9
by Parr, 253
by Thomas Johnson 154
Traetta, Thomas, *Iphigenia in Tauride* 62
tragedy
  acceptance of Aristotelian definition 14–15
  concept of, and death of Oedipus 9
  Dryden on 'grounds of criticism in' 21
  revival in England 308 and n. 79
  see also Greek tragedy
tragi-comedy, legitimacy discussed 53–4
tragic heroines, *see* Greek tragedy; she-tragedy *and individual characters*
Tragoediarum Delectus, Gilbert Wakefield 253–4
Trail, F. T. 364
translation
  conflicting approaches to 451 and n. 54
  growing awareness of performative context 473 and n. 37
  into modern languages xiv–xv, xx, 46
  recognition of need for 494
  see also under individual works
transvestism, *see* cross-dressed roles
Trapp, Joseph 53 and n. 64
travesty, sub-category of burlesque 339–40
treason trials, reflected in drama of period 221–8
Treatise of Human Nature, A, David Hume 84
Tree, Ellen 291, 292, 311, 321

Tree, Herbert Beerbohm (1853–1917) 462, 466, 534, 537
Tree, Maud (Mrs Beerbohm) 462, 466 and n. 13, 479
Trench, Herbert 537, 538–9
Trial by Jury, Gilbert and Sullivan 387
Trinity College, Cambridge 8
Troades, Seneca 66, 244
Troilus and Cressida, Shakespeare 20–1, 33, 358
Trojan Women, Euripides
  Barker's production 509, 543–4, *545*
  parallels in Boer War ix, xxi–xxii, 510
  permanent place in British repertoire vii
  translation by Gilbert Murray xvii, 508, 510–11
  Sybil Thorndike in *xii*
Trotter, Catherine, *The Fatal Friendship* 83
Turkey, fashion for theatrical settings, revivals 61; *see also* Ottoman Empire
Turner, William Dawson 468–9 n. 21, 470
tyrannicides, liberty song in praise of 302 and n. 66
tyranny
  contrast between idealistic youth and 309
  liberty in opposition to, asserted by Dennis 46–8
  link with monarchy, incest 7, 10
  Sophoclean theme
    relevance to English monarchy 7
    topicality in 1820s 273
  Talfourd's concept of fight against 284, 293, 300

Tyrtaeus, source for *Le Marseillaise* 265 n. 2

Ulysses, Nicholas Rowe 76–8, *77*
Undershaft, Andrew 502–5 and n. 49
United States
 contribution of actresses from xix–xx
 popularity of Talfourd's *Ion* in 286–7
 see also America
universities, British
 absence of performances of authentic Greek drama 431
 effect of
  arrival of women 432
  changes in classical curriculum 431–2
 see also individual institutions
University College, London
 co-production of *Medea* 513
 production of *Alcestis* 445 n. 35
 share of University Endowment Fund 462
University Endowment Fund 462
University Test Acts, movement for abolition 469
Utilitarianism, on function of the law 297

Valentius, in Joyner's *The Roman Empress* 10–12
Valerius Maximus' *Facta et Dicta Memorabilia* 180 and n. 71
Vallouis, Simonin 175–6 and n. 60
Valpy, Abraham John 248 and n. 18
Valpy, Richard (1754–1836)
 admired by Mary Russell Mitford 256
 association with Samuel Parr 248

attraction to plays with strong female roles 258
career, characteristics 244–5, 246–50
influence of Richard Porson 251–2
methods 259–60, *260*
performances directed by 250–6, 270 n. 20, 431; *see also* Reading School
Talfourd's debt to 260, 287–9
textbooks by 247
Vandenhoff, Charlotte 322, 326, 334, 348
Vandenhoff, George 321, 337
Vandenhoff, John 295, 322, 332 n. 41
Vanity Fair, Thackeray 347–8 and n. 82
Vaughan, Felix 224–5
Vedrenne, Paul 496, 498
Venus and Adonis; or, the Two Rivals & the Small Boar, Francis Burnand
 antipathy to classical education 376–7
 burlesque 357, 358
 contemporary detail 381 n. 139
 semi-serious instruction in mythology 378
 use of
  Greek language 364
  Latin puns 365
Verrall, Arthur 151, 498 and n. 40, 519
Verses to the People of England, William Whitehead, link of singing in ancient Britain, ancient Greece 193
Vestris, Eliza (1797–1856)
 association with Planché, influence of 477

collaboration with Robinson in
Olympic Devils 358
manager of Olympic
Theatre 338–9, 357
marriage to Charles
Mathews 342, 396
roles 273, 342–5, 357, 366–7,
396, 397
Vestris, Françoise 125
Vezin, Hermann, in *Helena in
Troas* 462
Victoria, Queen 300, 303
Victorian age
aesthetic conservatism 373, 377
comic expression in 382–7
fad genre 422
fascination with murder
trials 415, 421–3, 425
position of women
abandoned, without
future 401, 407–8
identified with Medea's
predicament 395, 398,
422–3
in marriage 420, 434–5
see also custody; marriage;
New Woman
perception of Greek
tragedy xviii, 331
privileging of Homer 475–6
rise of music hall 377
taste for
comedy, burlesque 379–82,
383–8
spectacle 441, 478–9
tableaux vivants 30 and n. 3,
479
Videna; or, the Mother's Tragedy,
John Heraud 416
Villiers, P., with P. A. Capelle,
Bébé et Jargon 404 n. 48
Violante, Madame, troupe of
Dublin child actors 246 n. 8

Virginius, James Knowles 284,
300, 308
virtue
compatibility with clandestine
love 139
concern for, in Aeschylean
choruses 221
eighteenth-century
understanding of 83–8
in distress, taste for, in eighteenth
century 72–3, 98
female, ideological associations
92
pro-feminine representations
of 85–8
Rousseau's conceptualization
of 86
visual arts
classical subjects favoured 27,
38, 46, 89 and n. 71,
275 n. 38, 441 and n. 18, 453
and n. 64, 476
importance of George Warr's
associations with 479
inspiration from Greek
tragedy xx–xxi, 89 and
n. 71, 123 and n. 51,
130 n. 11, 177 and n. 62,
178, 211, 213 n. 111, 275 and
n. 38, 301
Voltaire 33, 217, 220, 272–3, 277;
see also individual plays
Vondel, Joost van den 41 and n. 37
Votes for Women, Elizabeth
Robins 512–13, 514

Wagner, Richard 127 and n. 63,
493 and n. 18
Wakefield, Gilbert 253–4 and
n. 42, 289
Waldstein, Charles 479
Wales, *see* Welsh language; Welsh
music

Walker, C. E., *The Greeks and the Turks; or, the Intrepidity of Jemmy, Jerry, and a British Tar* 270

Walpole, Horace 42, 113, 190–2, 209–10, 227

Walpole, Robert
  conflict with 'Patriot' opposition 99, 102, 103, 104–8
  dramatists' covert assaults on 50
  introduction of censorship 104, 106–7
  satirized as 'Egisthus' 115
  unpopularity 58–9

Wannamaker, Zoe 152

Ward, Geneviève 335, 427 and n. 125, *428*

Warr, Constance Emily (wife of George) 472 and n. 32

Warr, George Charles Winter (1845–1901)
  approach to translation 472–3
  background, career xvii, 464–1 and nn. 10, 19, 21, 23–4, 29
  breadth of learning 468 and n. 19, 471 and n. 29
  engagement with visual arts 471
  Gilbert Murray compared 471–3
  importance xviii, 486–7
  links with art world 479
  marriage 472 and n. 32
  radicalism 469–70, 486
  translation of *Oresteia* 472
  see also individual plays

Warr, Henry 468–9 n. 21

Warre-Cornish, Dr 445 n. 45

Warton, Joseph 85

Wase, Christopher 40, 163–5, *164*

Wasps, Aristophanes, comic update 384

Waste, Granville Barker 529

Watts, G. F. 463–4, 471, 482, 483

Wayte, William 472 n. 32

Webb, Beatrice 504–5

Webb, John 204 n. 81

Webster, Augusta
  campaigner for women's rights 421
  criticism of Browning's translations 451
  translations 421, 473, 489

Weekes, Eliza 361, 363

Welsh language 204

Welsh music, song 192–3 and n. 26; *see also* druids

Wesley, John 121

West, Benjamin 46, 177 and n. 62, *178*

West, Richard 61, 66, 124 n. 53

Westminster School
  performances of Latin plays 34 n. 17, 248 and n. 19, 261
  production of *Alcestis* 117

Whelan, Frederic 539

Whigs
  attitudes to religion 147–50 and n. 49
  butt of humour in Theobald's *IT* 59
  ideal of sacrifice for the public good 11, 114–15
  internecine conflicts 167–72
  perception of link between Graeco-Roman and early British cultures 190, 191–2
  pervasiveness of ideals in British theatre 40, 41–9, 50–4, 58–9, 282–4
  presentation of Greek tragedy to appeal to xviii, 44–9, 50–4
  response to Dryden and Lee's *Oedipus* 29

sources for adaptations of Greek
tragedy 50
support for Queen
Caroline 229–30
see also *Iphigenia*, John Dennis
White, Henry *279*
Whitehead, William (1715–85)
background, education 134, 143
combination of Greek and
druidical interests 192, 193
friendship with William
Mason 130, 134 and n. 25
near-agnosticism 134, 139
poet laureate 130 and n. 12
use made of Greek tragedy xv,
61
Whig outlook 133, 301
see also individual plays
Wieland, C. M. 441 n. 19
Wife or no Wife, John Heraud 416
Wilamowitz-Möhlendorff,
U. von 491 n.10, 498, 512
Wilberforce, William, anti-slavery
stance 189 n. 10
Wilde, Constance 462–3
Wilde, Oscar (1856–1900)
association with
Balliol *Agamemnon* 452–3
Lily Langtry 484
editor of *Women's World* 460–1
friendship with Rennell
Rodd 453
inspiration for 'handbag'
scene 151
interest in revivals of
classics 453
see also *Salome*
Wilkes, John 167–8, 208, 227–8
William III and Mary 41, 43,
44–5
William IV 284
Williams, Edward (Iolo
Morganwg) 192 n. 26

Wills, William Gordon, *Medea in
Corinth* 425–6
Winchester School, performance of
Agamemnon at 453–4
Winckelmann, J. 475
Wine of Cyprus, Elizabeth Barrett
(Browning) 85
Wingfield, Lewis 370
Woffington, Peg 246 n. 8
Wollstonecraft, Mary 182
Woman: or, Ida of Athens, Sydney
Owenson 270
women
access to higher education
buildings for 464 and n. 12,
470, 484, 511 and n. 106,
513 and n. 106; *see also*
rights *below and* suffrage
effects 432, 456–7
Warr's ambitions 470
actresses, *see* actors, actresses *and
individual players*
ambivalent position in
burlesque 374
in audiences at burlesques 374
and n. 111
authors, dramatists 78–88 and
n. 44, 90
centrality of suffering female
in sentimental tragedy
89–92
concepts of
in Ibsen, Shaw 488
sexuality 89–90, 419
dedication of plays to 78
enabled to sit on local
councils 512
equation of beautiful with
statues 328
Francklin's *Sophocles* aimed
at 173
in Greek drama
and erotic love 91

women (*cont.*):
in Greek drama (*cont.*):
value of different
interpretations,
reassessments xxii
health, exercise movements,
'hellenizing' of 549 and
n. 77
ideals of womanhood enshrined
in Antigone 328
jokes at expense of 383 n. 150
playing male parts, *see* actors,
actresses; breeches roles;
cross-dressed roles
poor, awakening of social
conscience about 518–19
position in Victorian age
abandoned, without
future 401, 407–8
concept of ideal 327–8
identified with Medea's
predicament 395, 398,
422–3, 488–90
in marriage 420, 434–5
recoil from Sophocles' depiction
of 178–9
rights, emancipation
contribution of John Stuart
Mill 420
debate on marital violence
427
increasing debate over 393,
395, 396–7, 414, 417–18
invidious property
laws 401–2, 416, 420
significance of increased
theatre-going 78
size of Euripidean roles 258
social realities reflected in
Lemon's *Medea* 407–8
suffragettes, *see* suffrage
suitability of *Alcestis* for
performance by 460–1

traumatized, Charlotte Lennox's
novels about 90
treatment of, Bristed's horror
at 427 n. 125
Valpy's attraction to plays with
strong 258
victims of male
oppression 11 n. 28
see also custody; divorce;
marriage; New Woman
Women at the Thesmophoria,
Aristophanes 75
Women Beware Women, Thomas
Middleton 391 n. 3
Women's Liberation
Movement 429
Women's Social and Political
Union 512
Women's World 460–1
Wood, Ellen, *East Lynne* 422
Wooler, John (Jack) 353, 399–401
Woolf, Virginia 182
Woolnoth, Thomas *278*
Wordsworth, William 211, 282,
290
working classes
access to classical myth,
history 388–90
exposure to Greek tragedy 350,
362
see also classics
Wright, Edward 352–3, 408

Xuthus, representation of 142–3,
146, 148–9

Yates, Mary Ann (1728–87) 80, *81*,
82, 94–5, 129, 152, 174–5 and
n. 54, *176*, 180
Yeats, W. B., (1865–1939) 186–7,
486–7, 496, 528, 529,
535–6
Yorkshire Petition, 1780 191

Young, Edward, *Busiris* 42
Young Pretender, Orestes as
    analogue for 166
Young, Revd William xvii,
    111 n. 27
youth, perceived, in ancient
    Greeks 309
Ypsilantis, Alexandrus 264

Zante, island of 265 and n. 3
Zeno, Apostolo 132
Zoroaster, William
    Moncrieff 277–80
Zoroastrians, oppressed by Islam,
    identification with Greek
    chorus 234